Aisha Franz

SHIT IS REAL

Originally published in German by Reprodukt.

The translation of this work was supported by a grant form the Goethe-Institut.

drawnandquarterly.com

First edition: April 2018 | Printed in China | 10 9 8 7 6 5 4 3 2 1

Cataloging data available from Library and Archives Canada.

Published in the USA by Drawn & Quarterly, a client publisher of Farrar, Straus and Giroux. Orders: 888.330.8477. Published in Canada by Drawn & Quarterly, a client publisher of Raincoast Books. Orders: 800.663.5714. Published in the United Kingdom by Drawn & Quarterly, a client publisher of Publishers Group UK. Orders: info@pguk.co.uk.

AISHA FRANZ

SHiT iS REAL

TRANSLATiON BY NiCHOLAS HOUDE
DRAWN & QUARTERLY

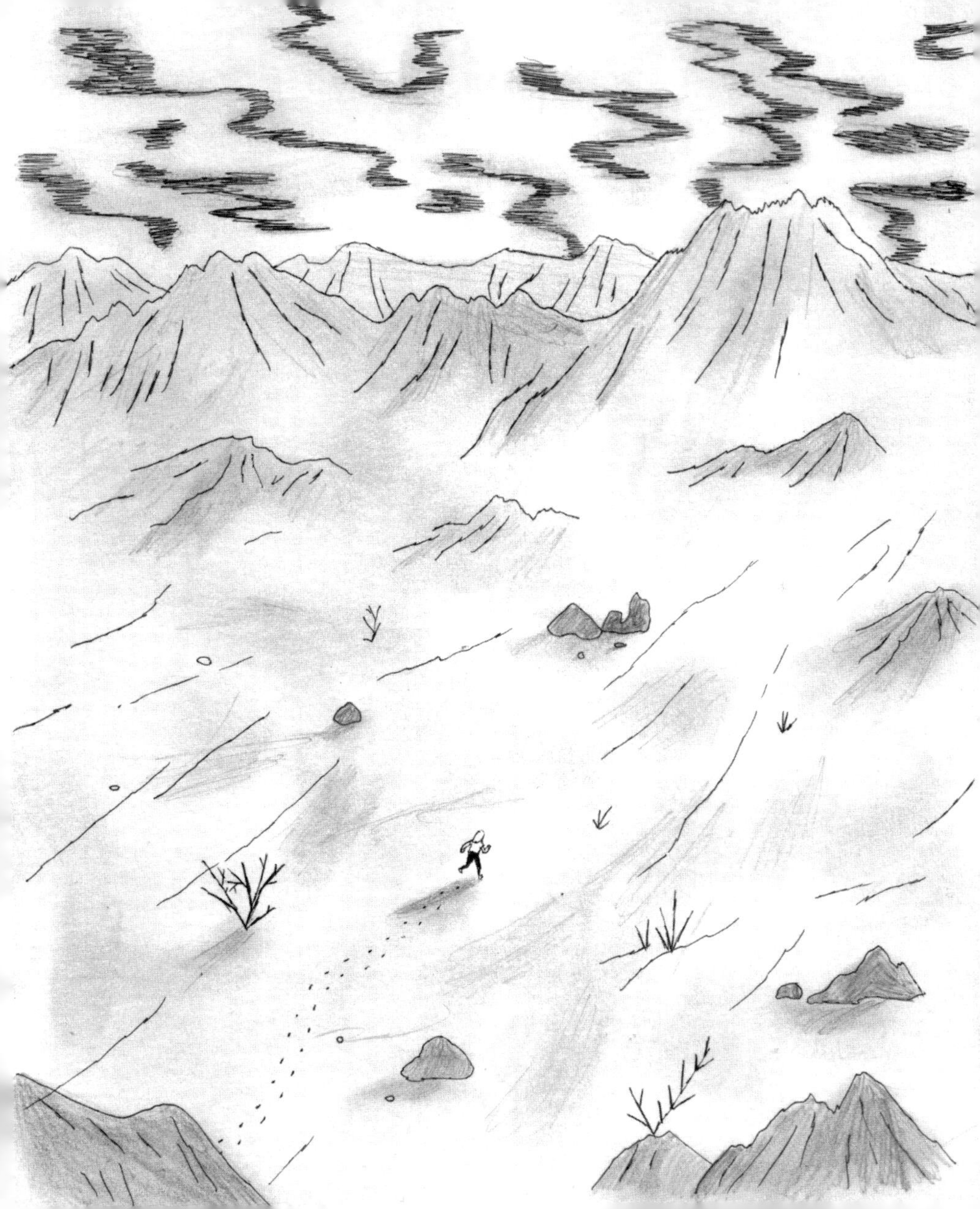

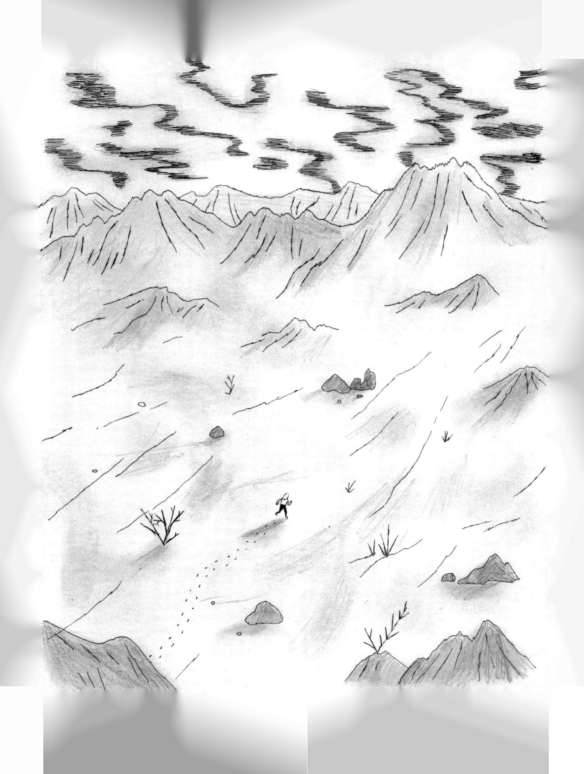

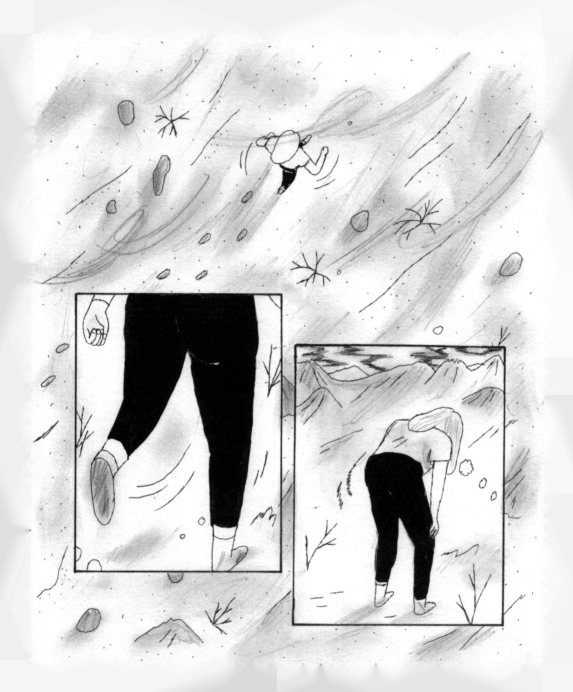

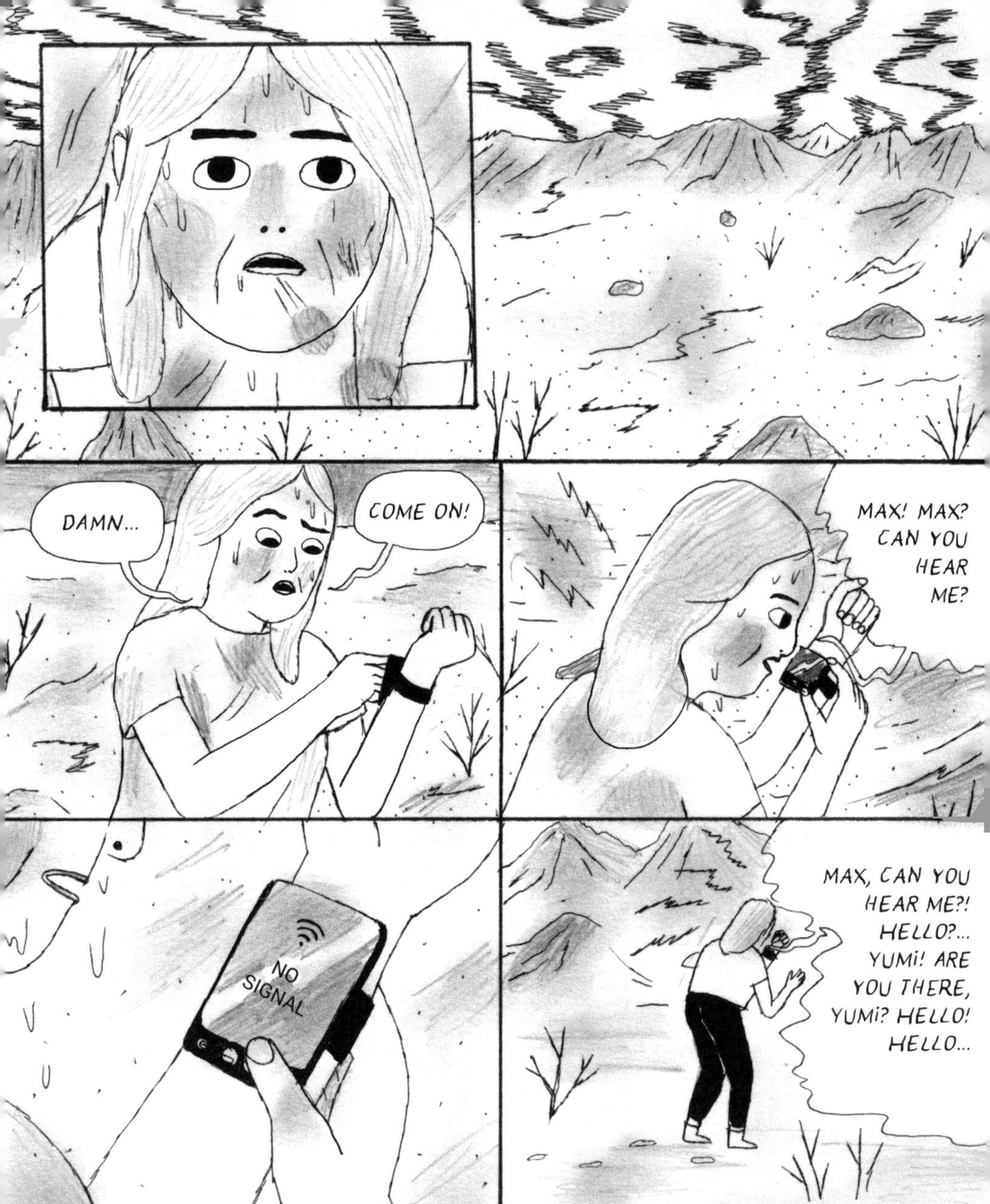
DAMN...
COME ON!
MAX! MAX? CAN YOU HEAR ME?
NO SIGNAL
MAX, CAN YOU HEAR ME?! HELLO?... YUMI! ARE YOU THERE, YUMI? HELLO! HELLO...

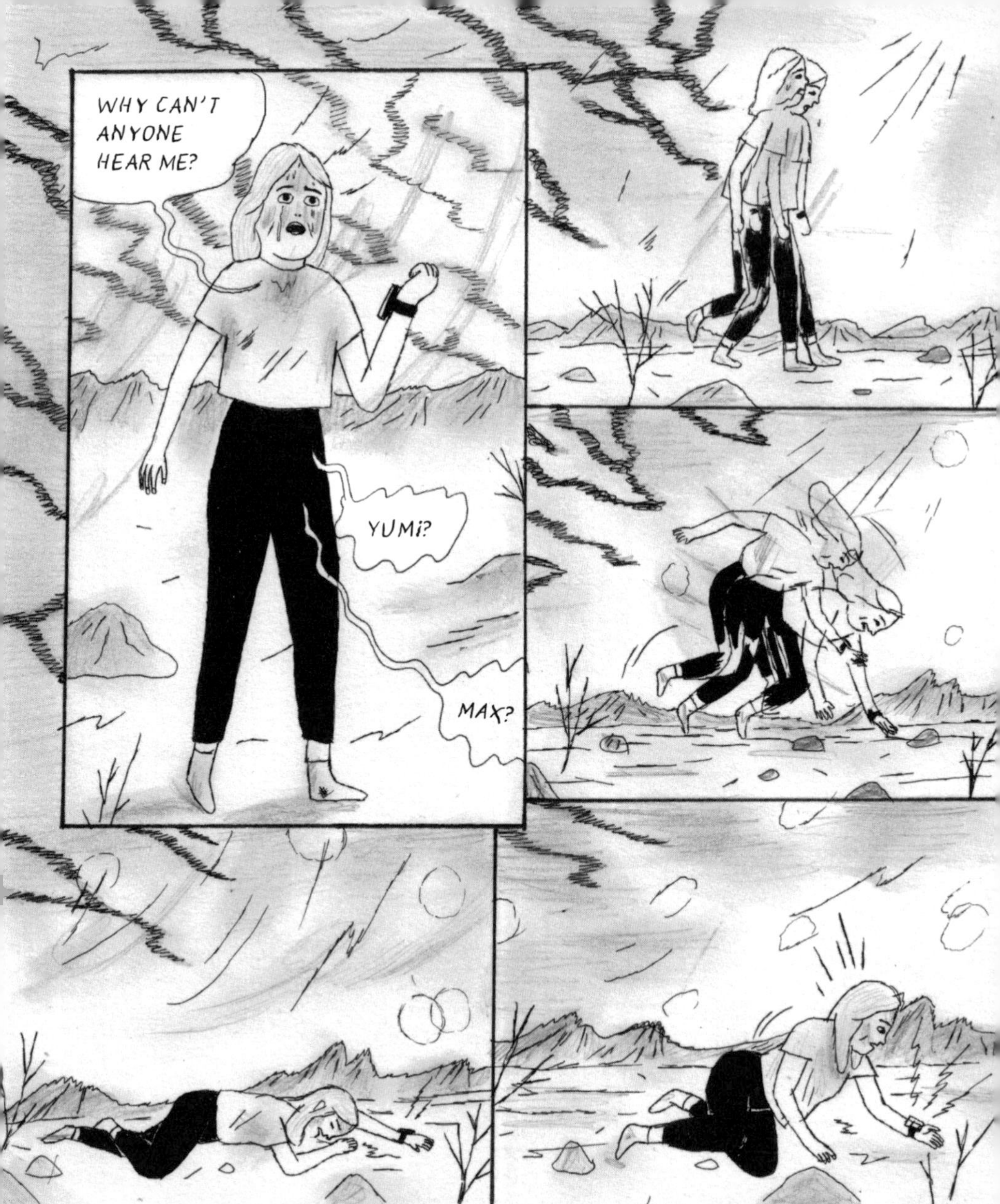
WHY CAN'T ANYONE HEAR ME?
YUMI?
MAX?

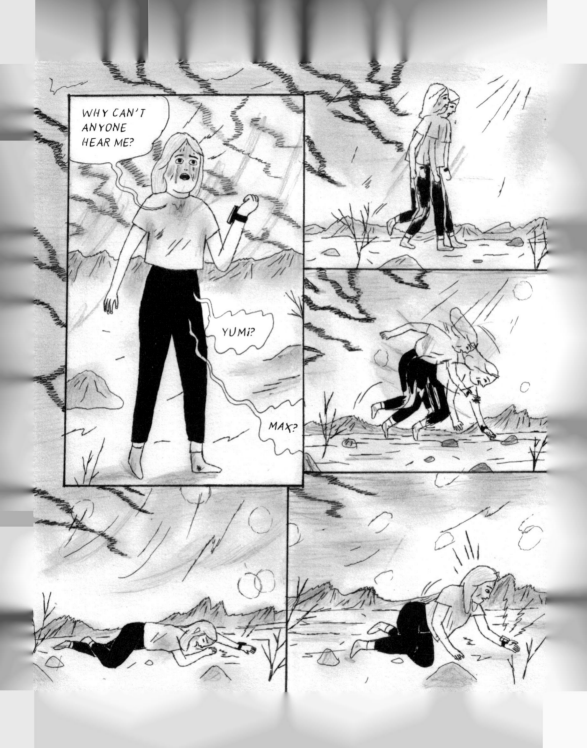

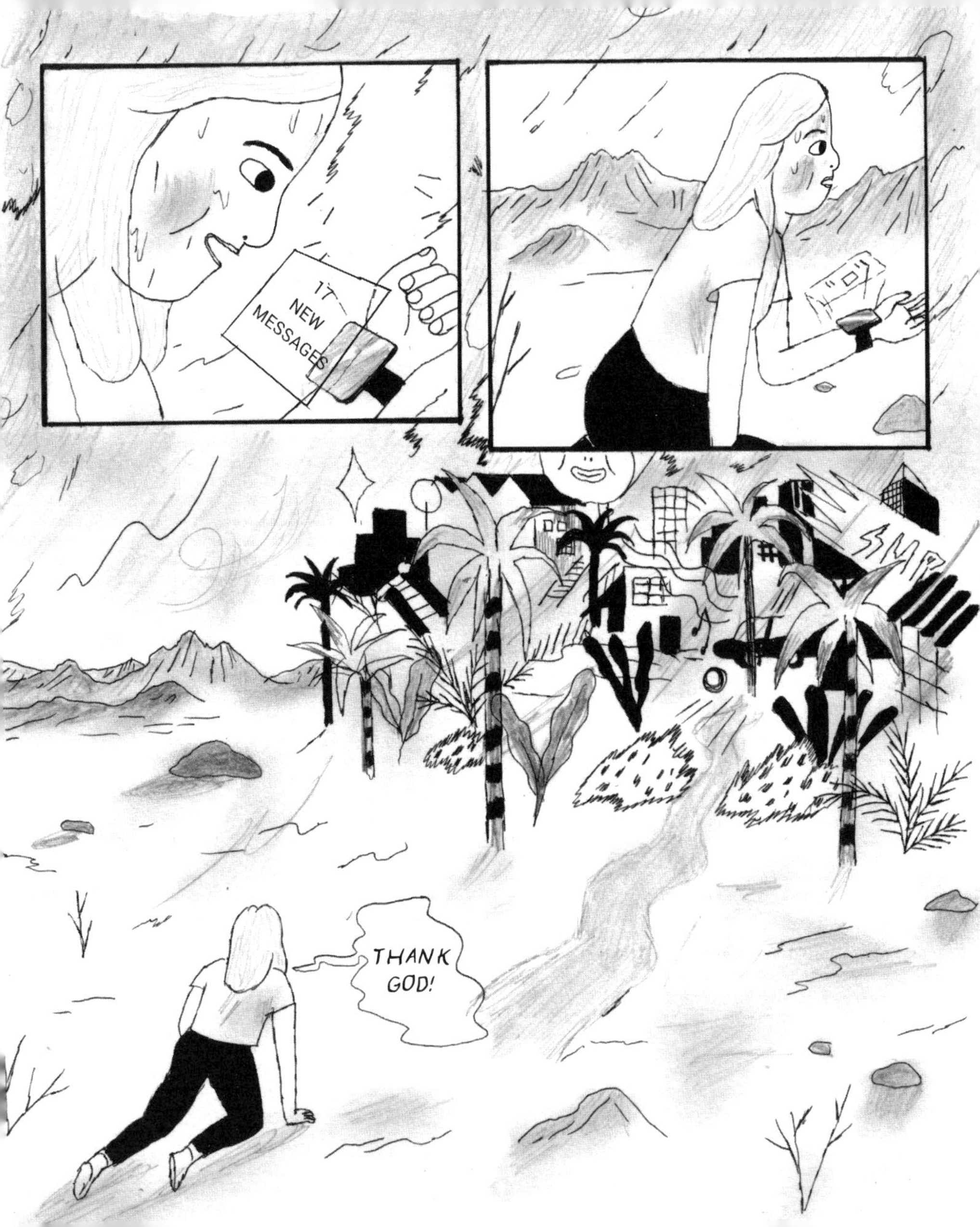
17 NEW MESSAGES
THANK GOD!

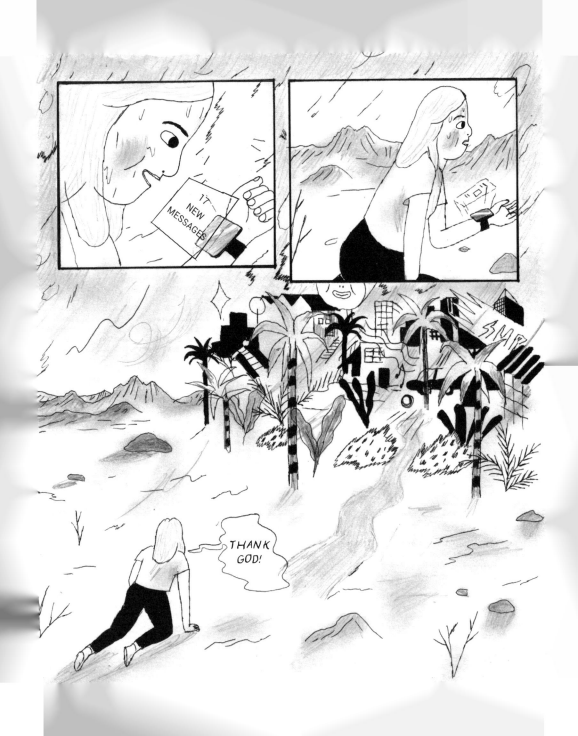

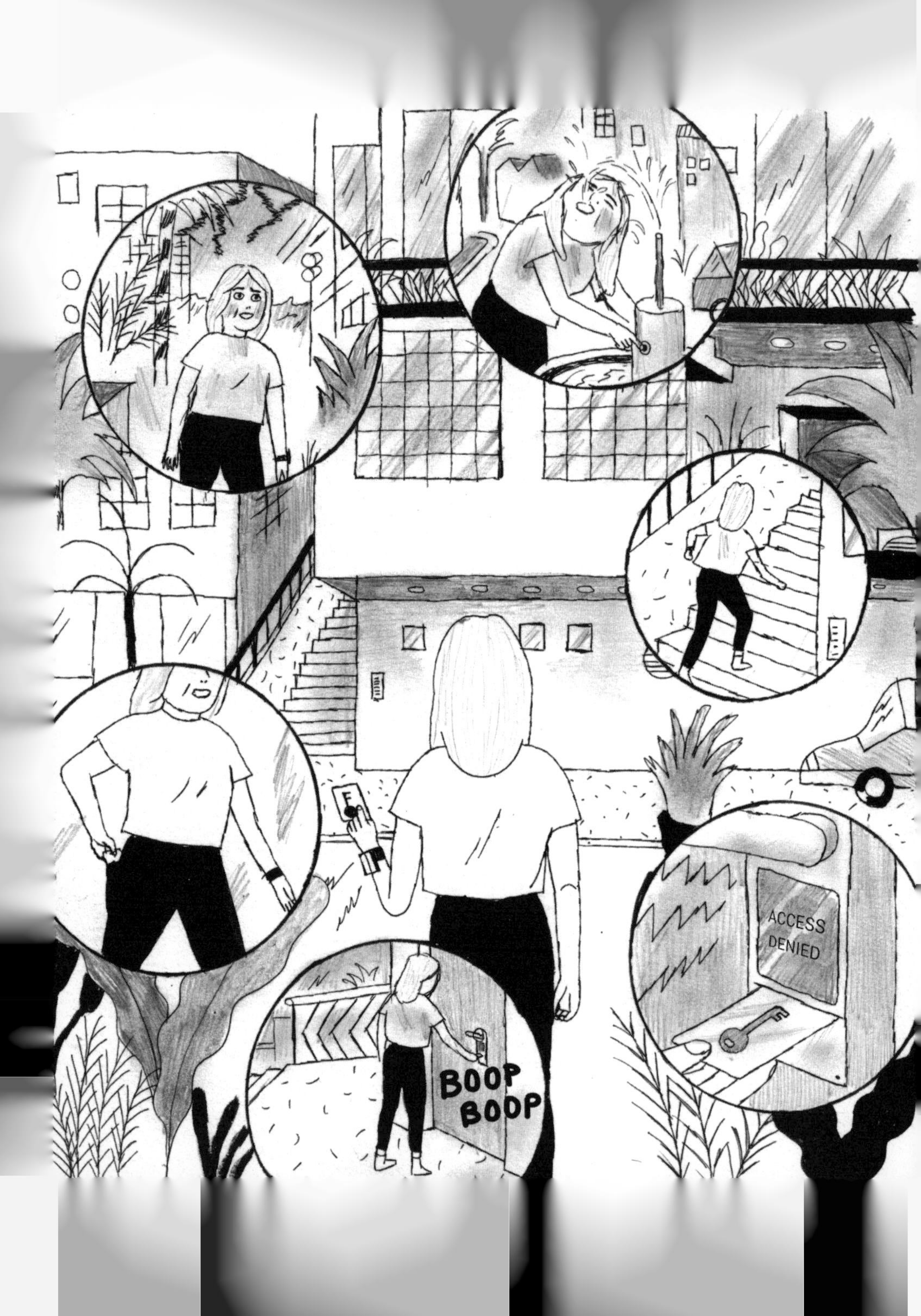
ACCESS DENIED
BOOP BOOP

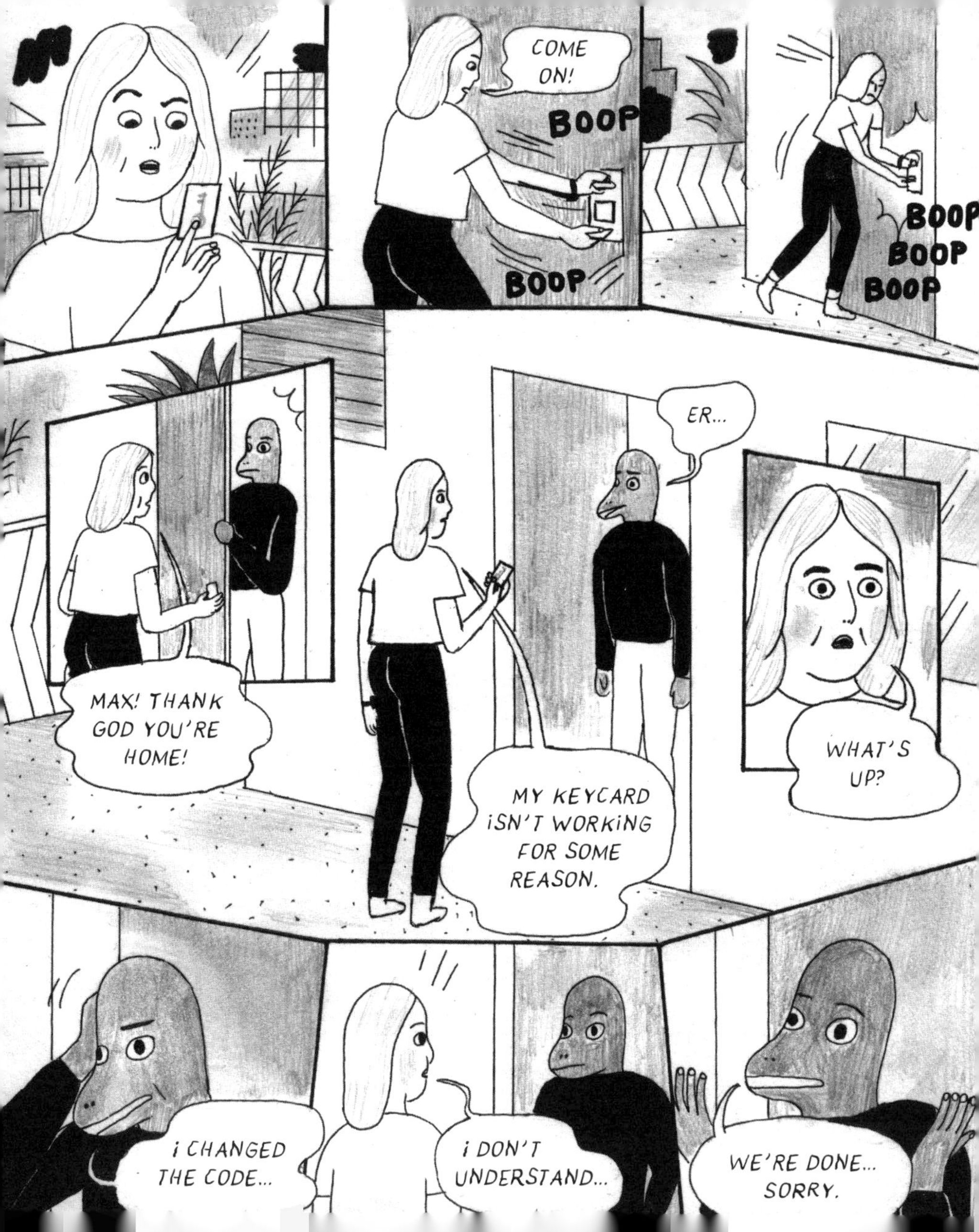
COME ON!
BOOP
BOOP
BOOP
BOOP
BOOP
MAX! THANK GOD YOU'RE HOME!
ER...
MY KEYCARD iSN'T WORKiNG FOR SOME REASON.
WHAT'S UP?
i CHANGED THE CODE...
i DON'T UNDERSTAND...
WE'RE DONE... SORRY.

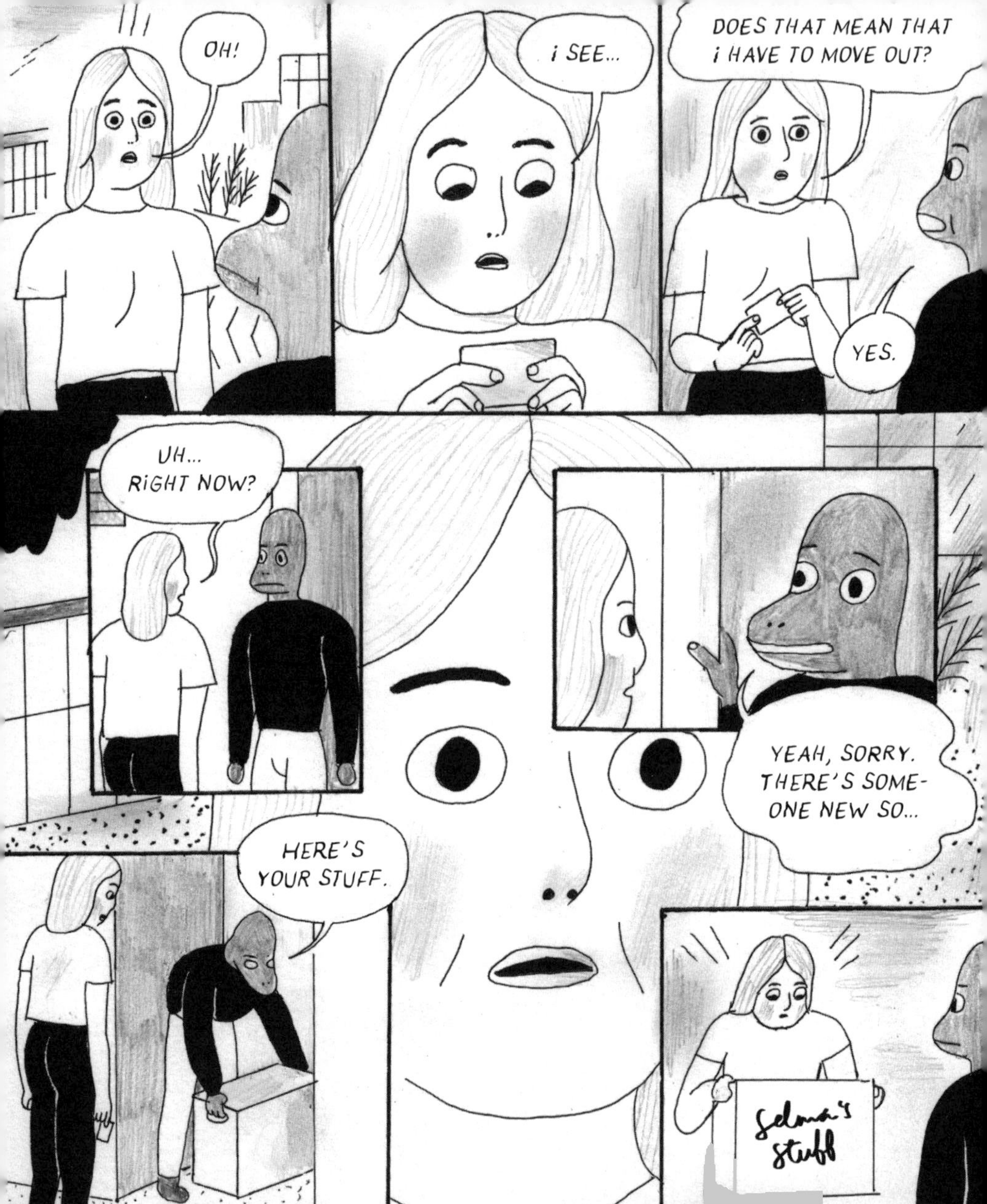
OH!
i SEE...
DOES THAT MEAN THAT i HAVE TO MOVE OUT?
YES.
UH... RiGHT NOW?
YEAH, SORRY. THERE'S SOME-ONE NEW SO...
HERE'S YOUR STUFF.
Selma's stuff

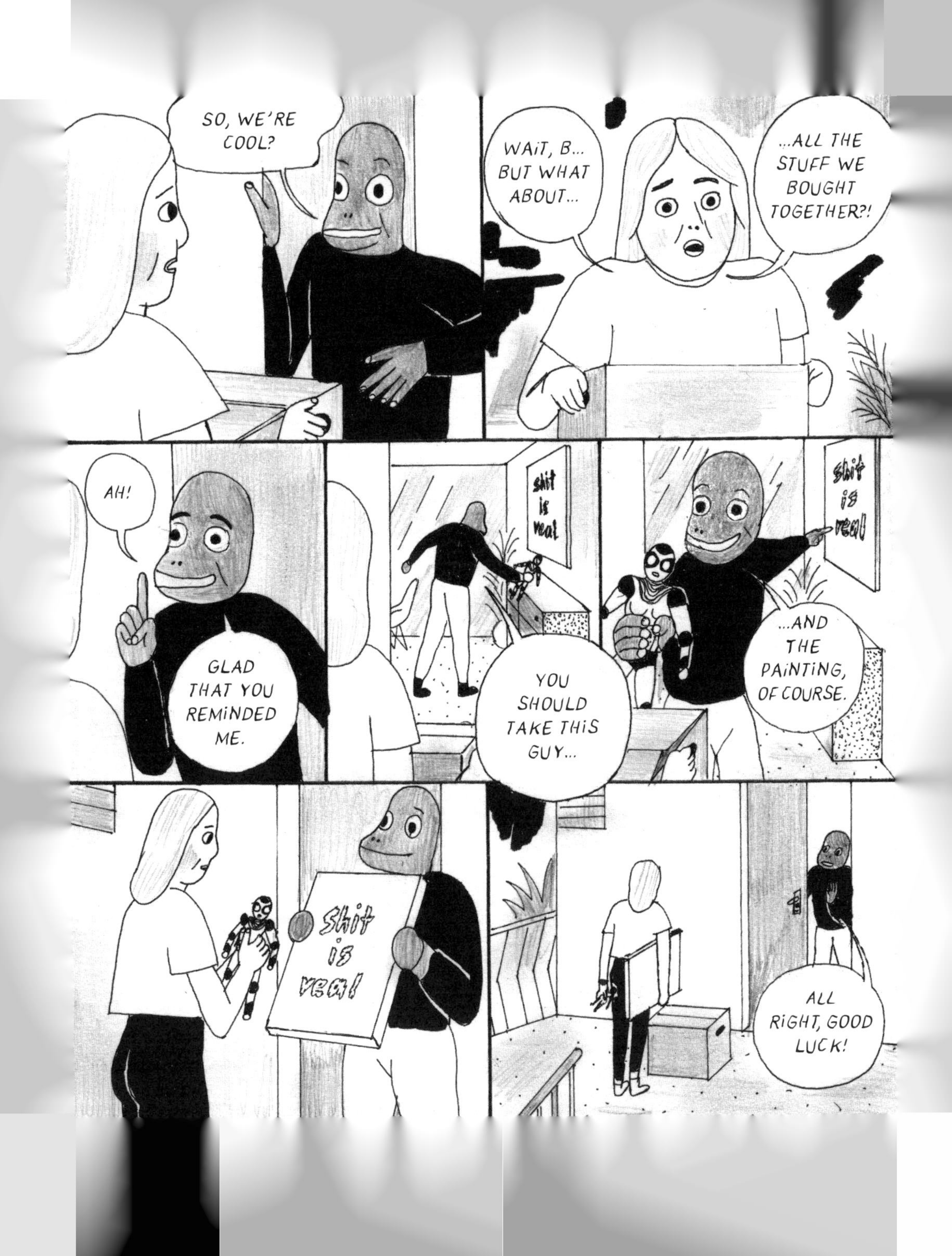
SO, WE'RE COOL?
WAIT, B... BUT WHAT ABOUT...
...ALL THE STUFF WE BOUGHT TOGETHER?!
AH!
GLAD THAT YOU REMINDED ME.
Shit is real
YOU SHOULD TAKE THIS GUY...
...AND THE PAINTING, OF COURSE.
Shit is real
ALL RIGHT, GOOD LUCK!

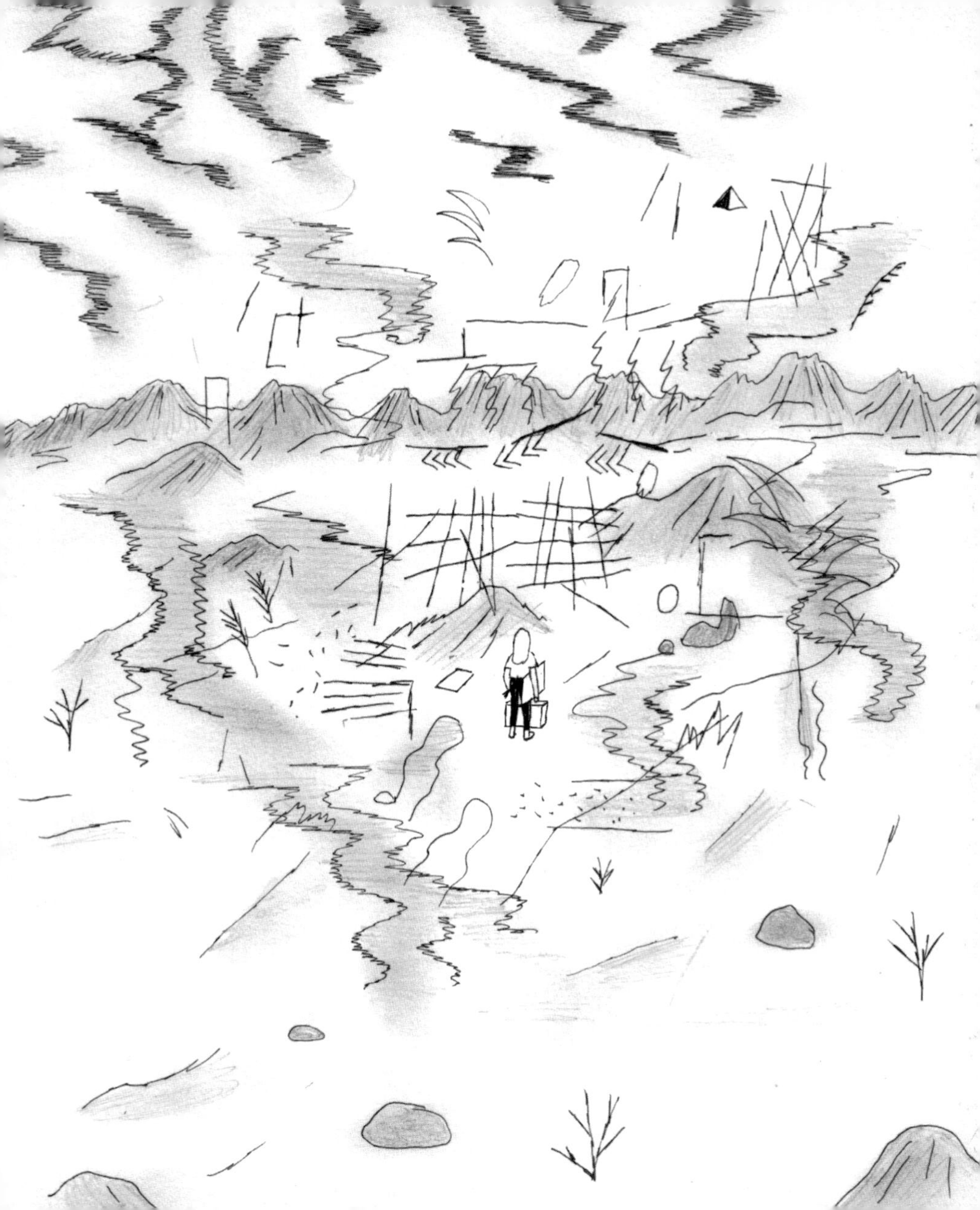

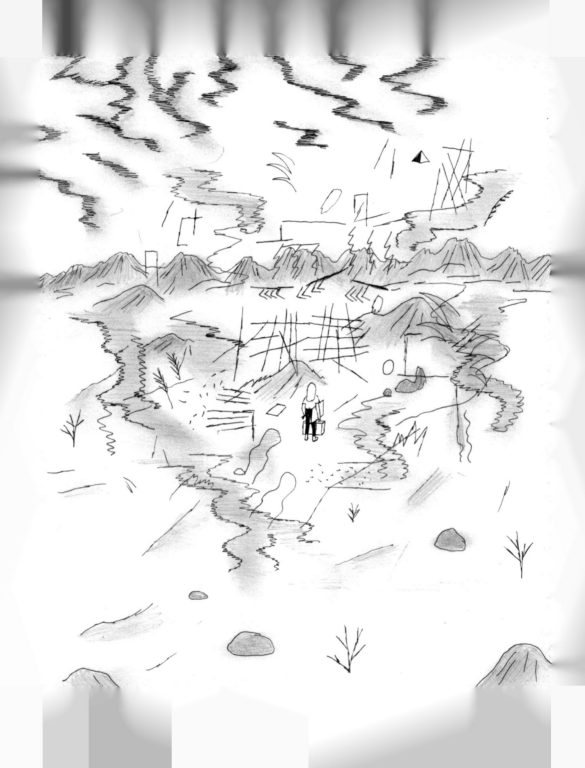

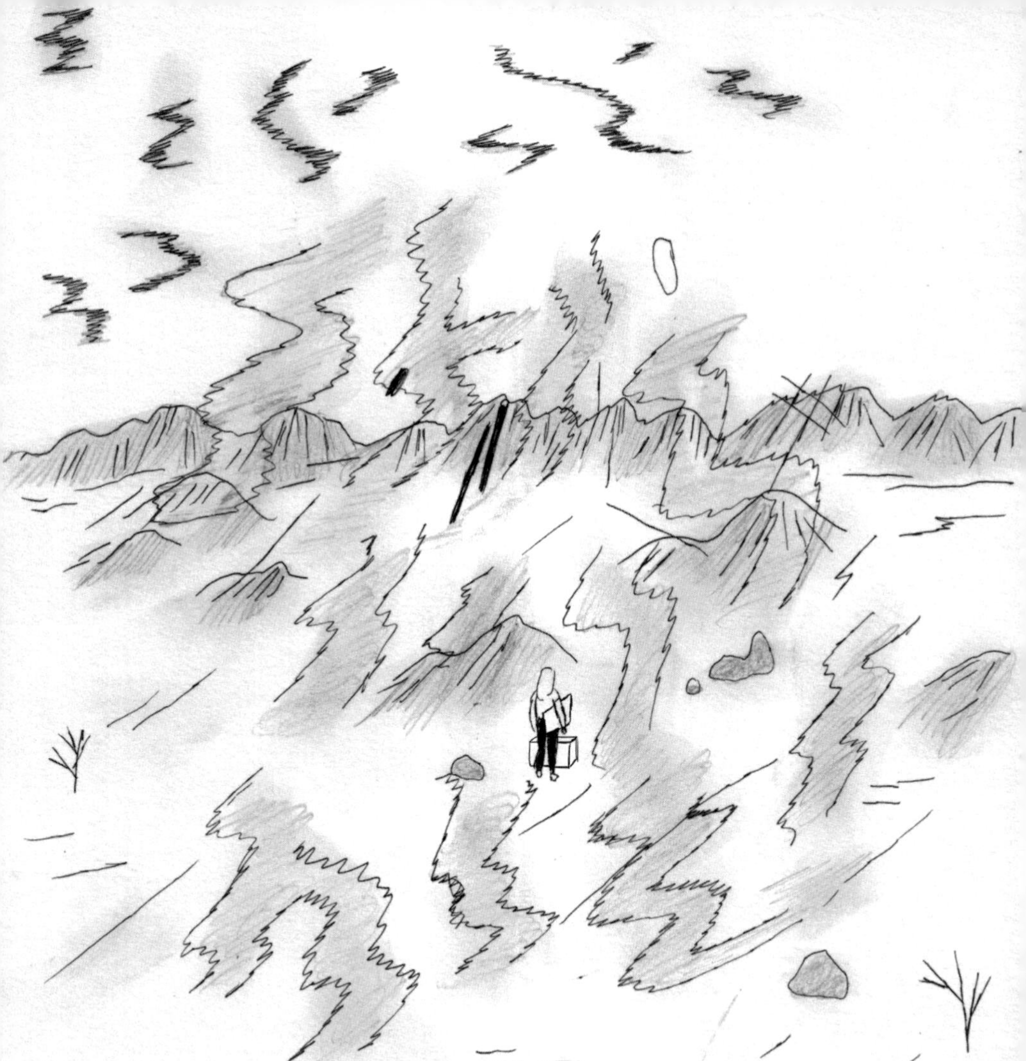

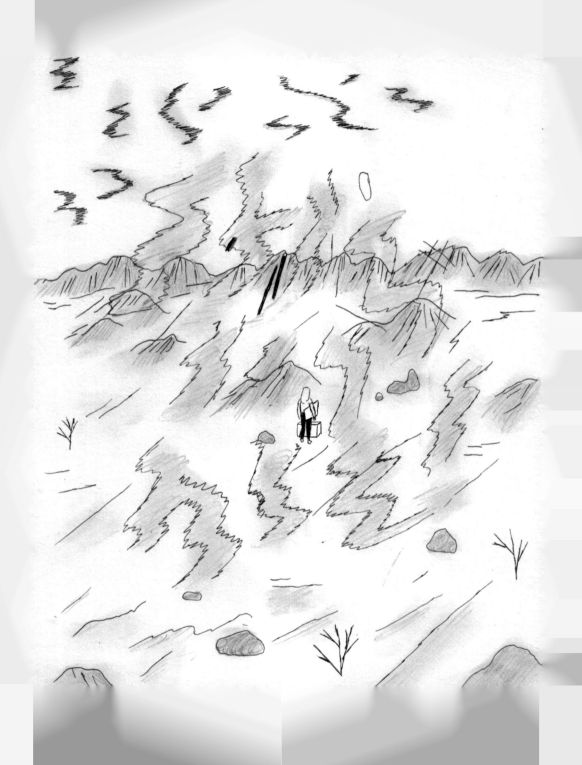

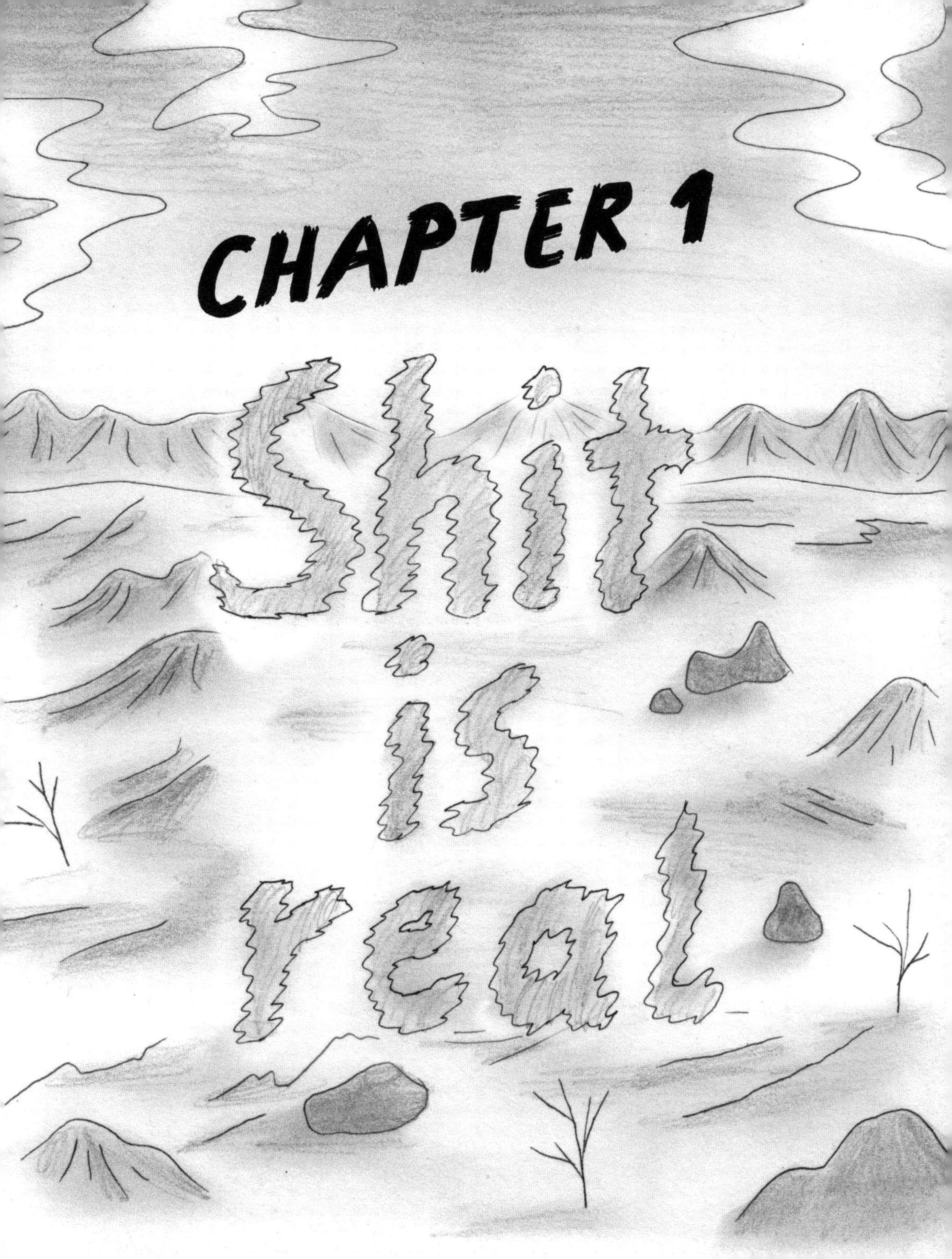
CHAPTER 1
Shit is real

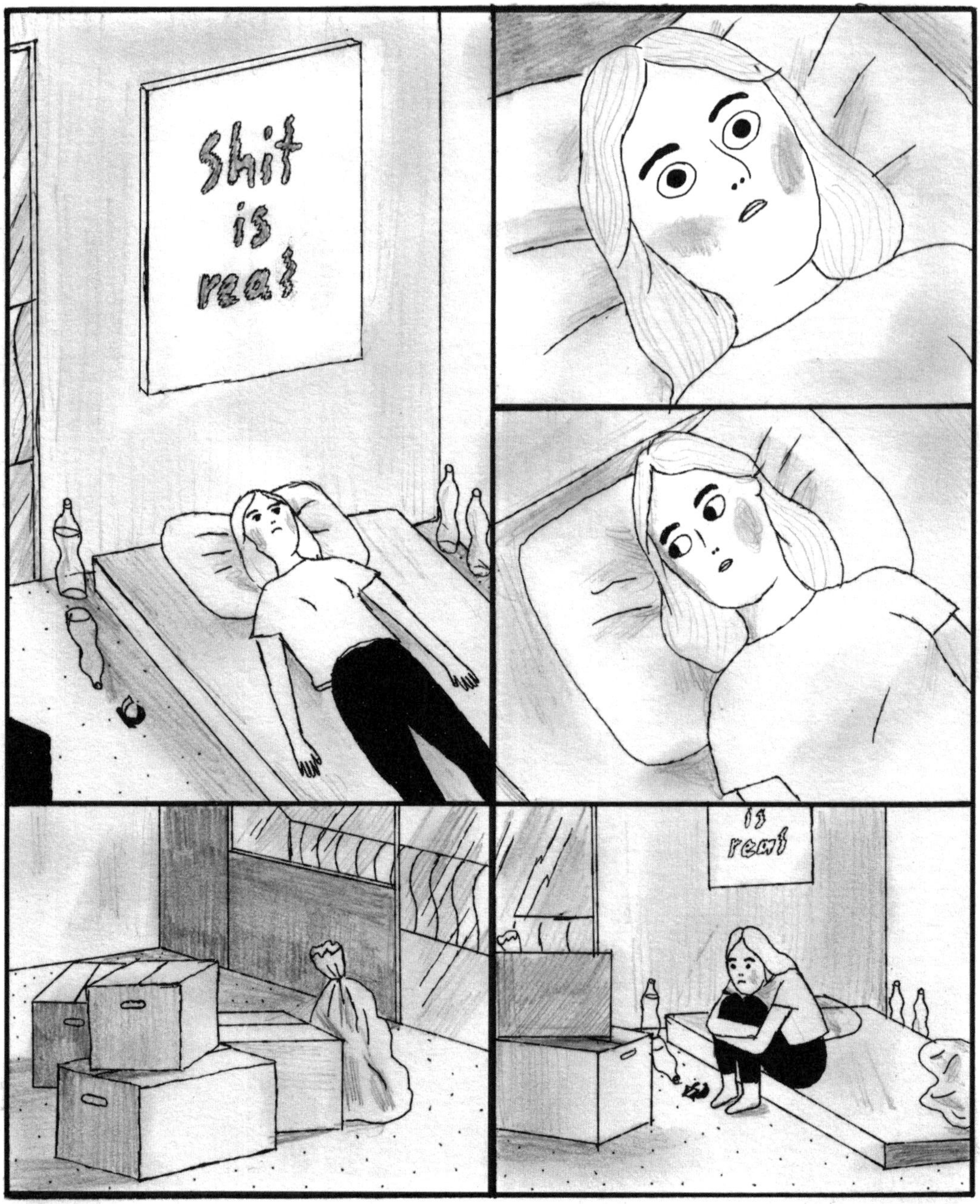
shit is real
is real

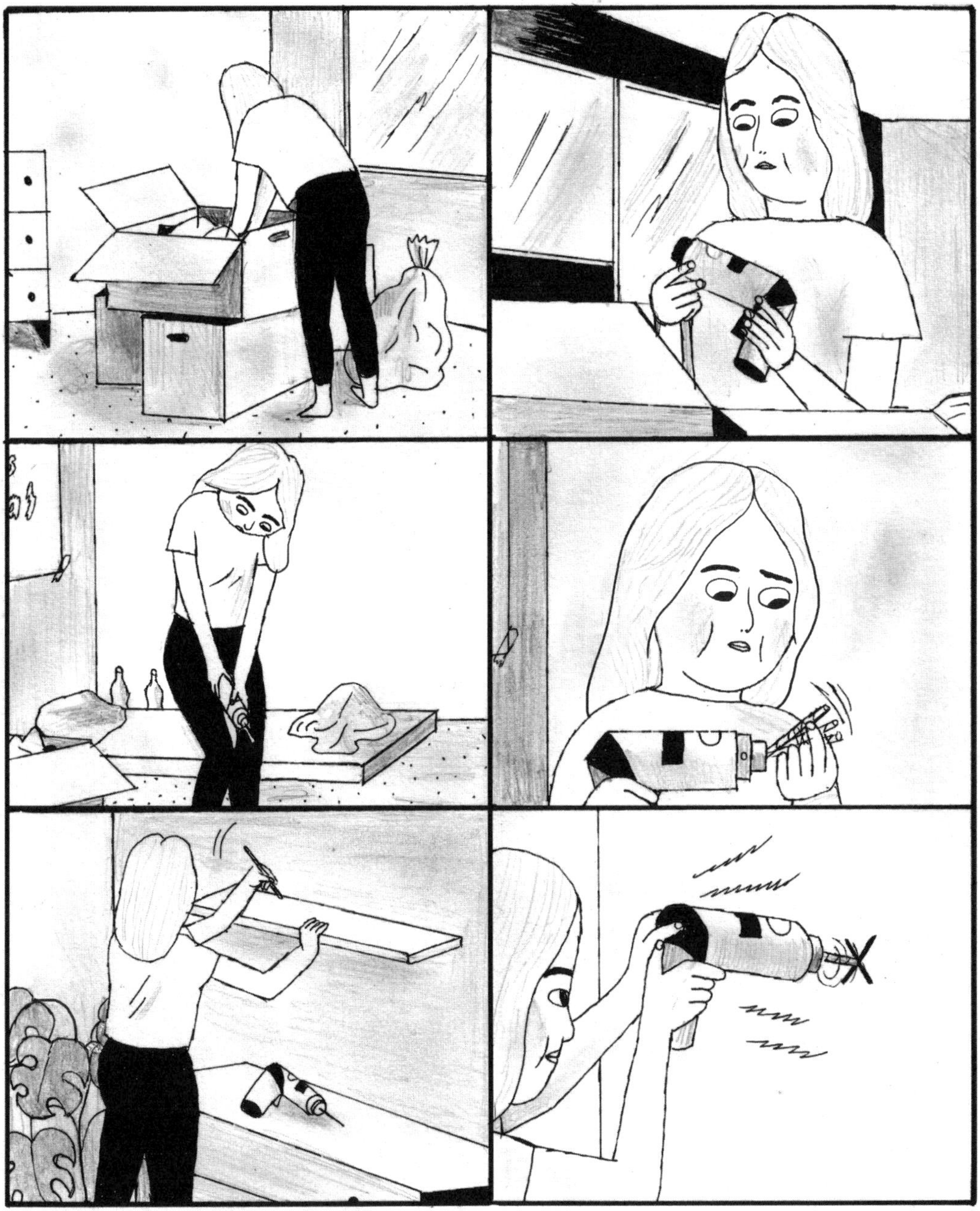

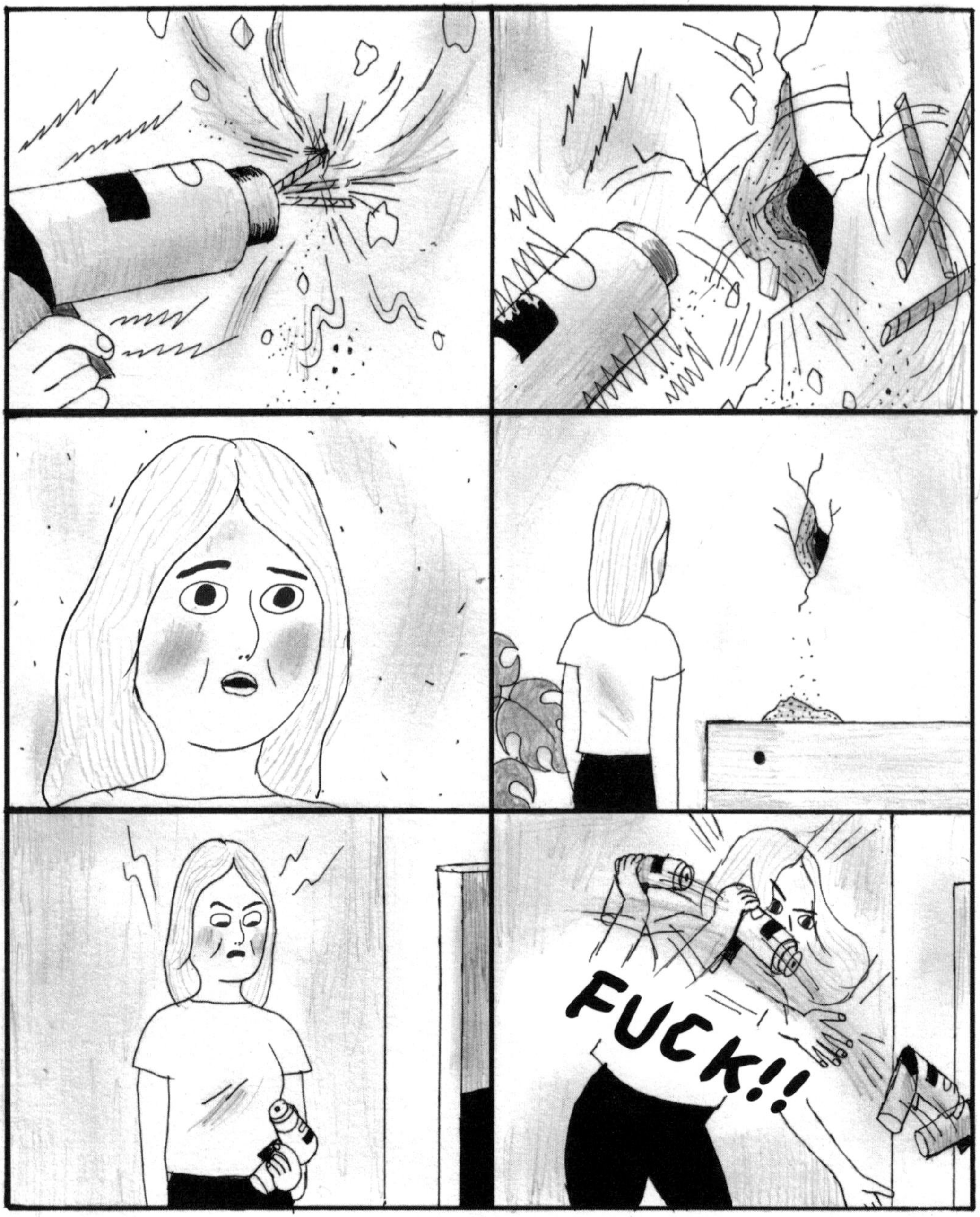
FUCK!!

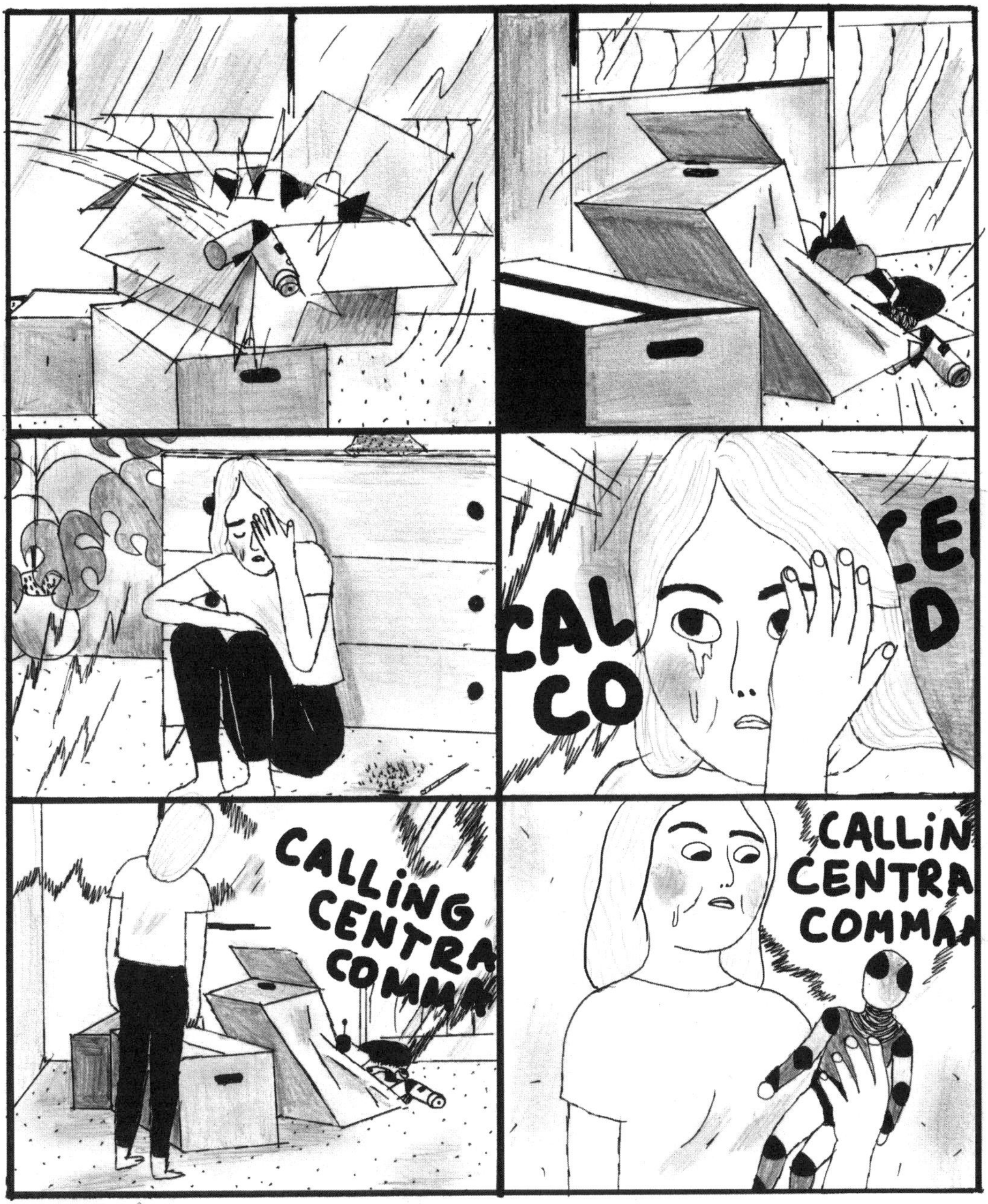
CAL
CO
CE
D
CALLING
CENTRA
COMMA
CALLIN
CENTRA
COMMA

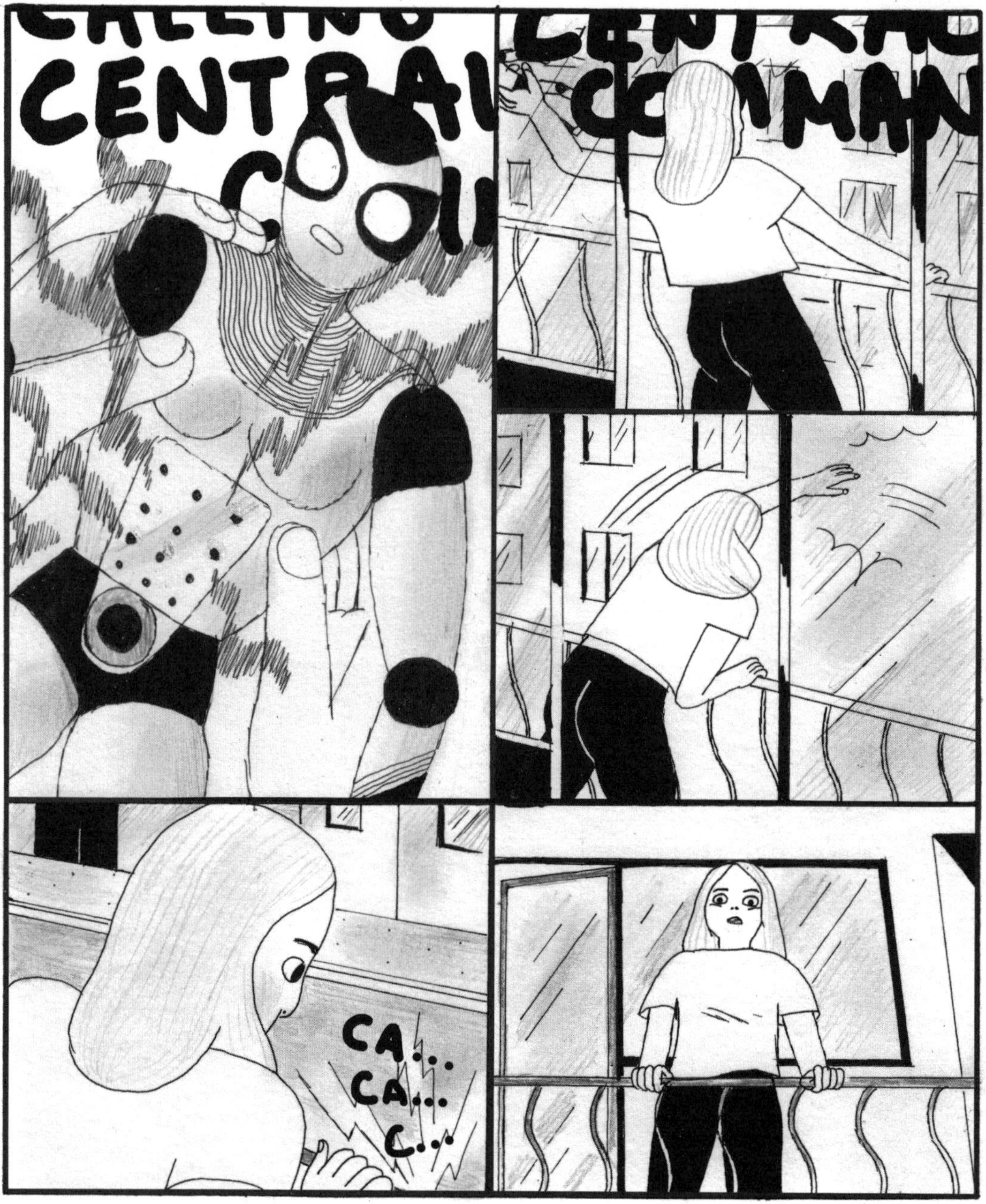
CENTRAL
CO
COMMAN
CA...
CA...
C...

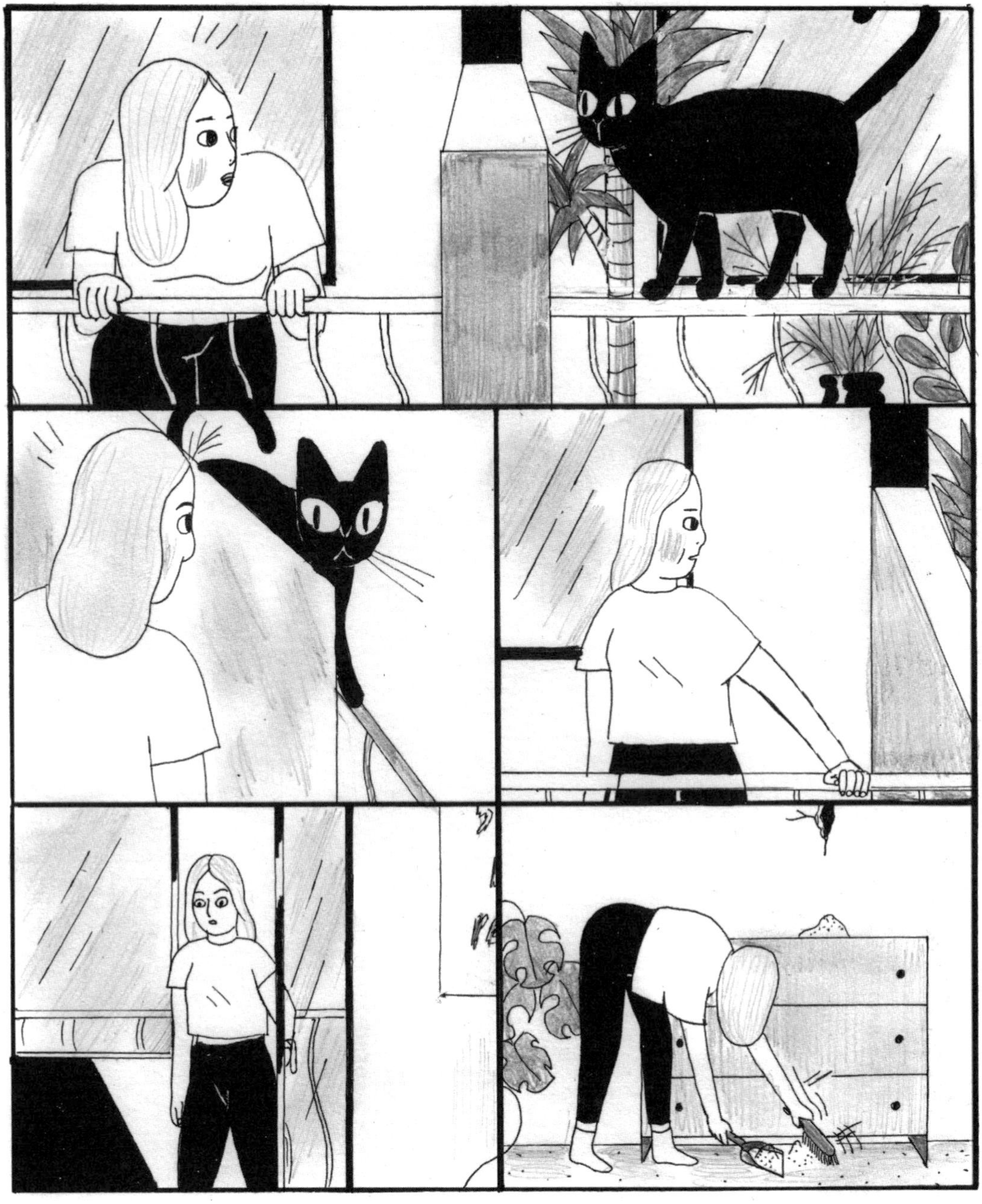

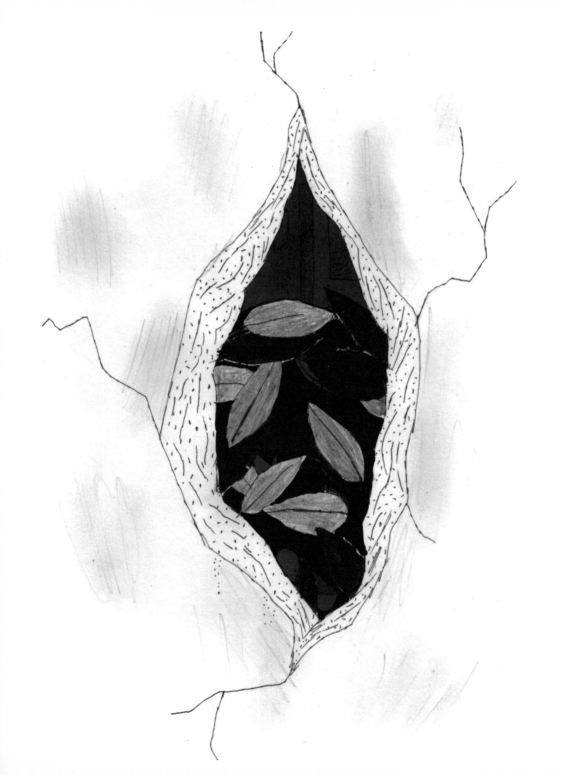

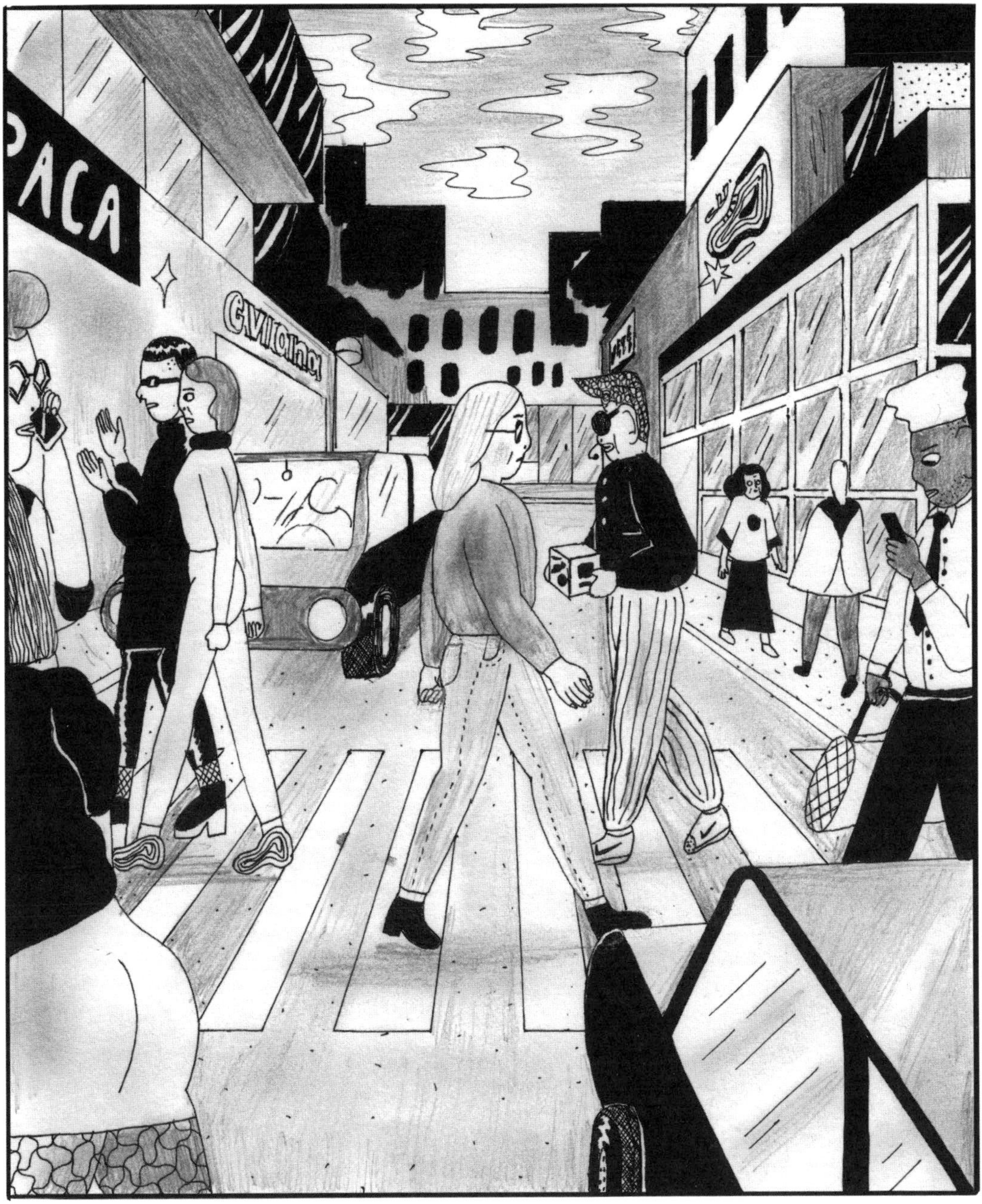
PACA

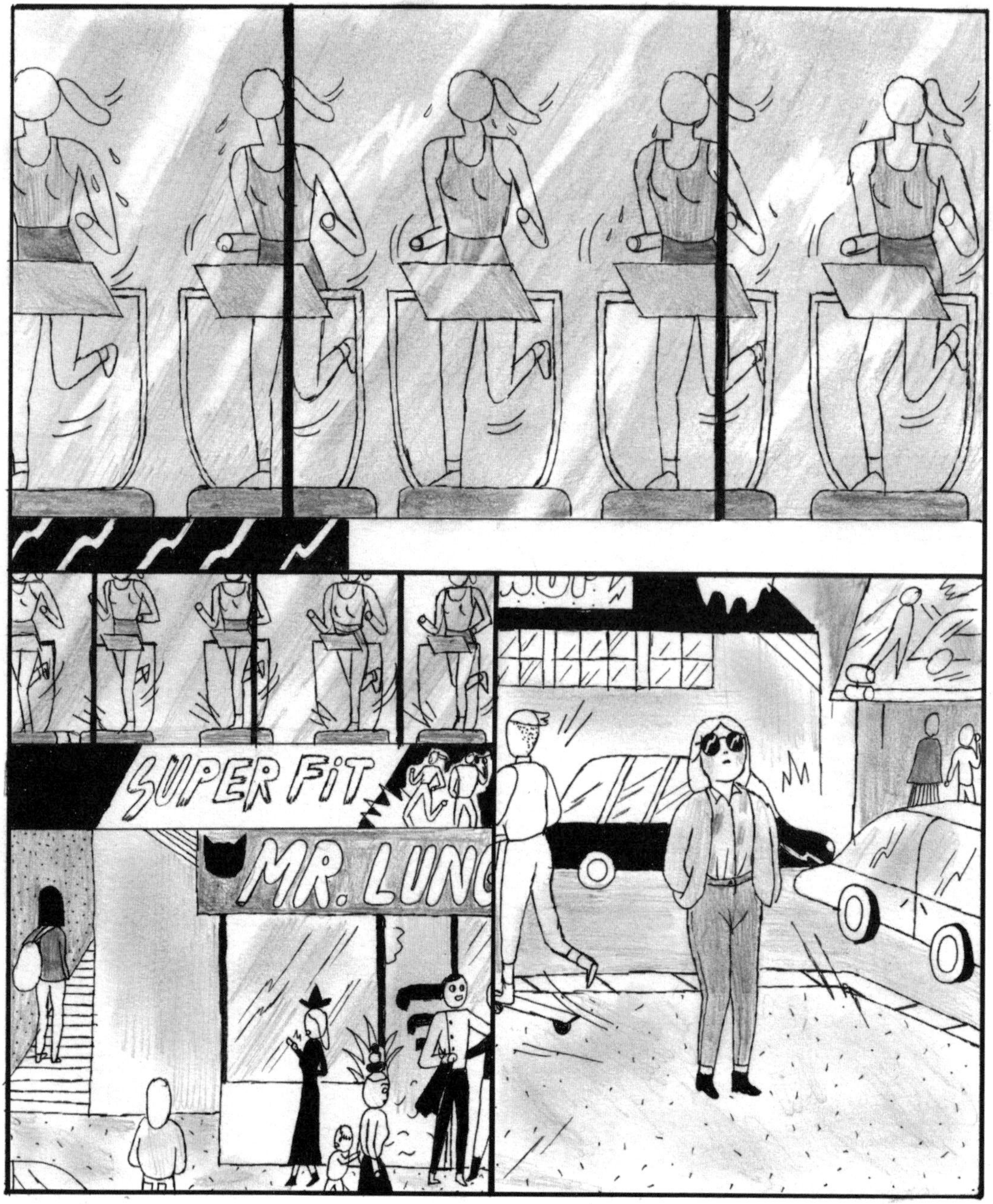
SUPER FIT
MR. LUNC

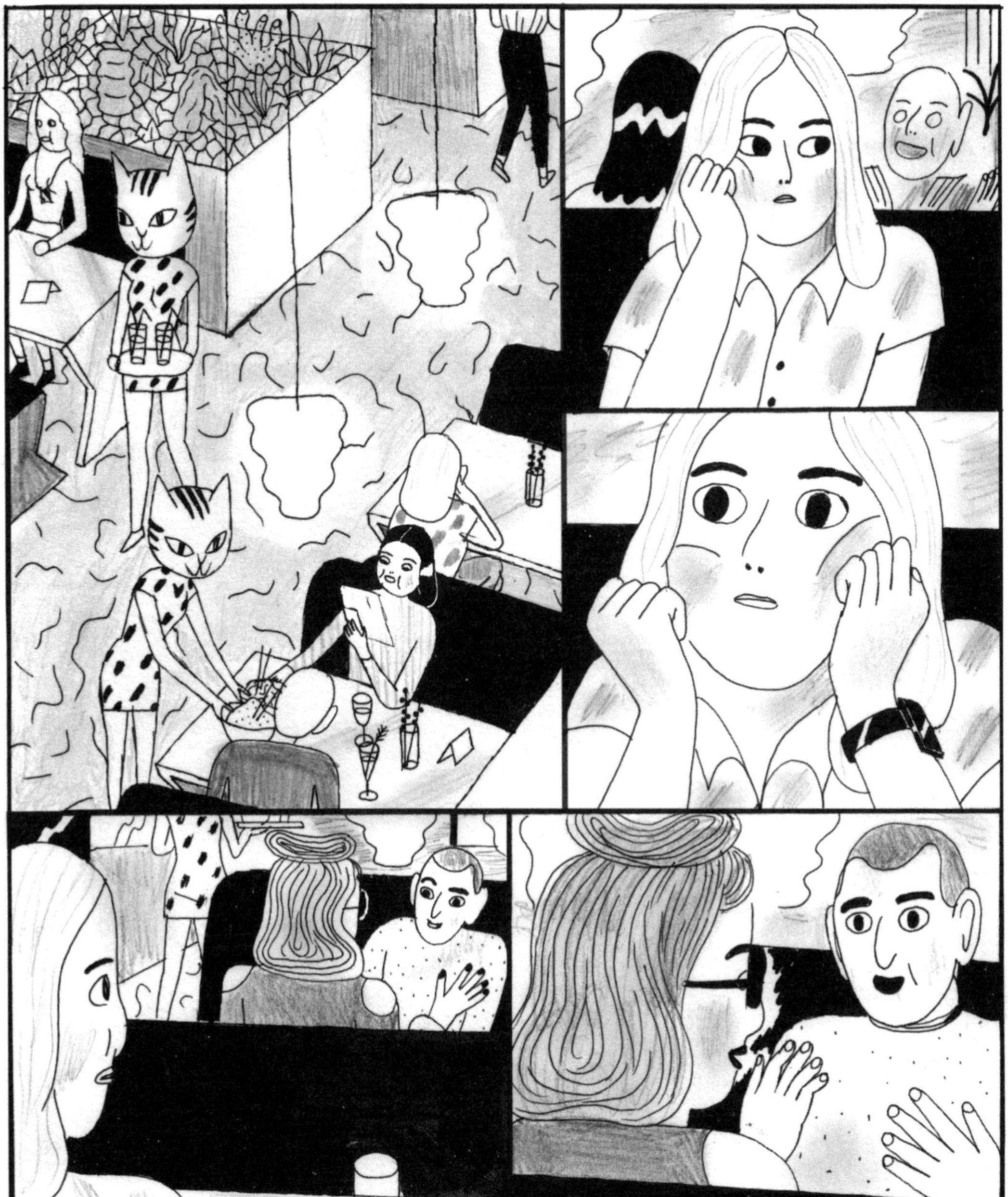

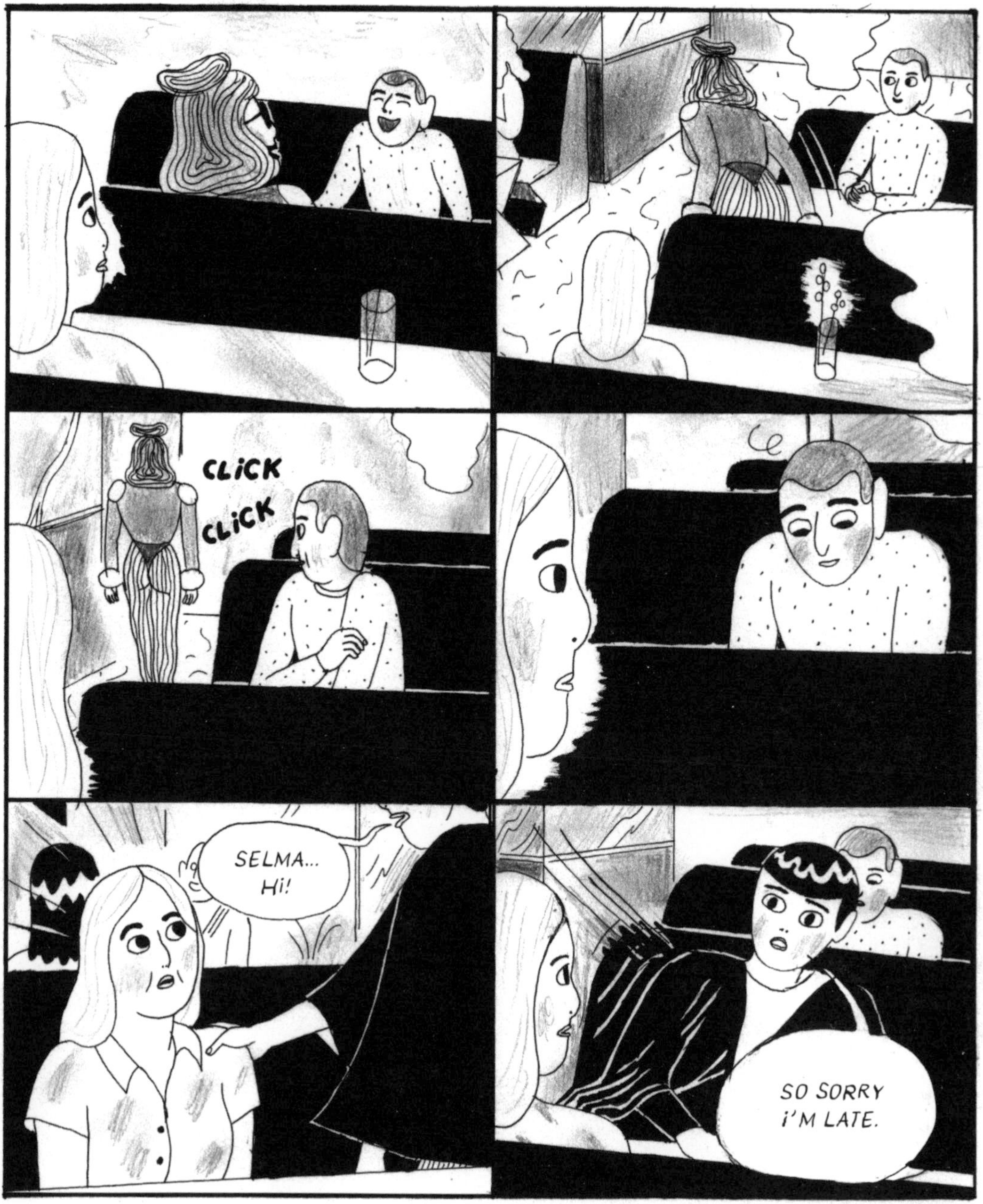
CLICK
CLICK
SELMA... Hi!
SO SORRY i'M LATE.

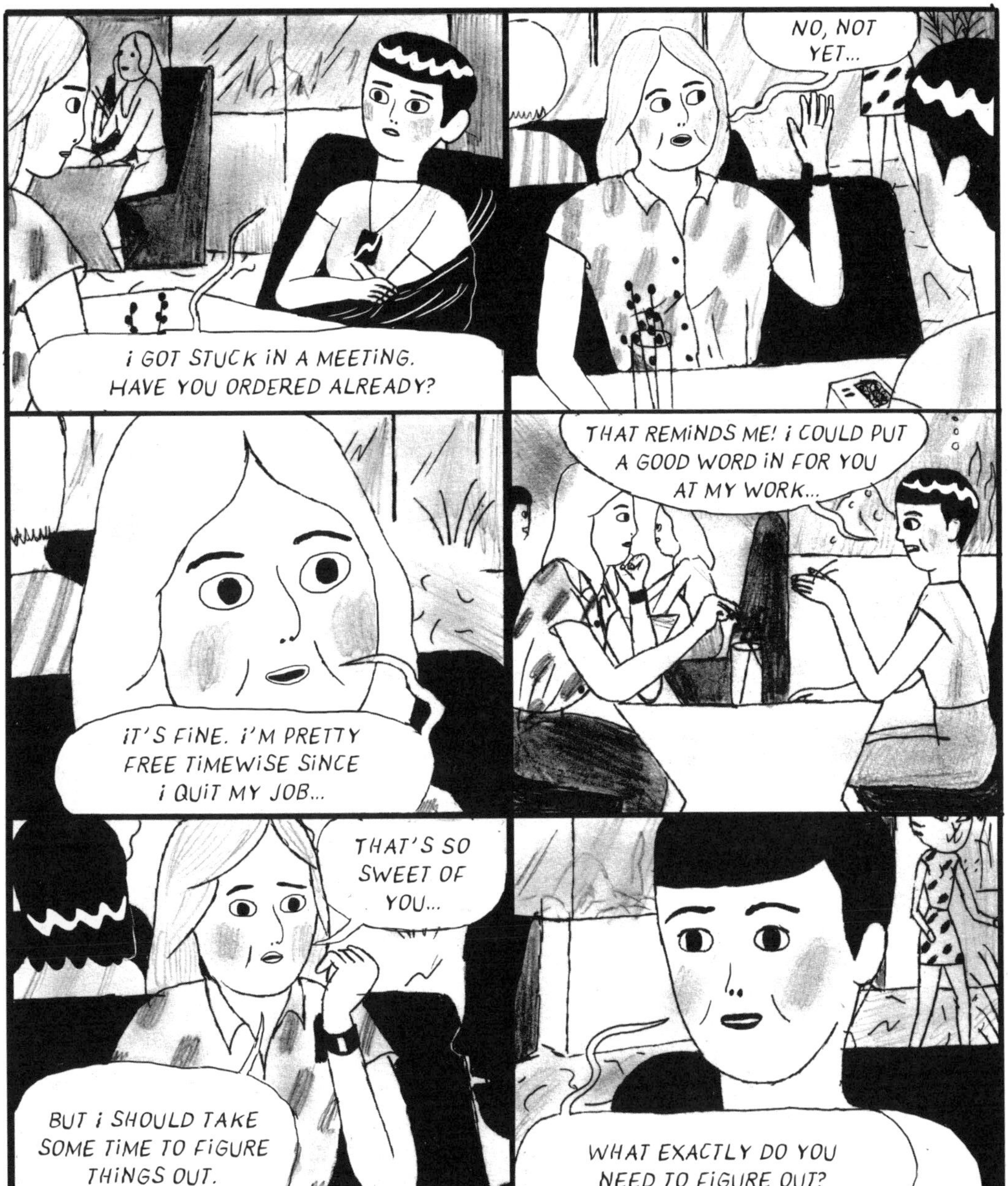
I GOT STUCK IN A MEETING. HAVE YOU ORDERED ALREADY?
NO, NOT YET...
IT'S FINE. I'M PRETTY FREE TIMEWISE SINCE I QUIT MY JOB...
THAT REMINDS ME! I COULD PUT A GOOD WORD IN FOR YOU AT MY WORK...
THAT'S SO SWEET OF YOU...
BUT I SHOULD TAKE SOME TIME TO FIGURE THINGS OUT.
WHAT EXACTLY DO YOU NEED TO FIGURE OUT?

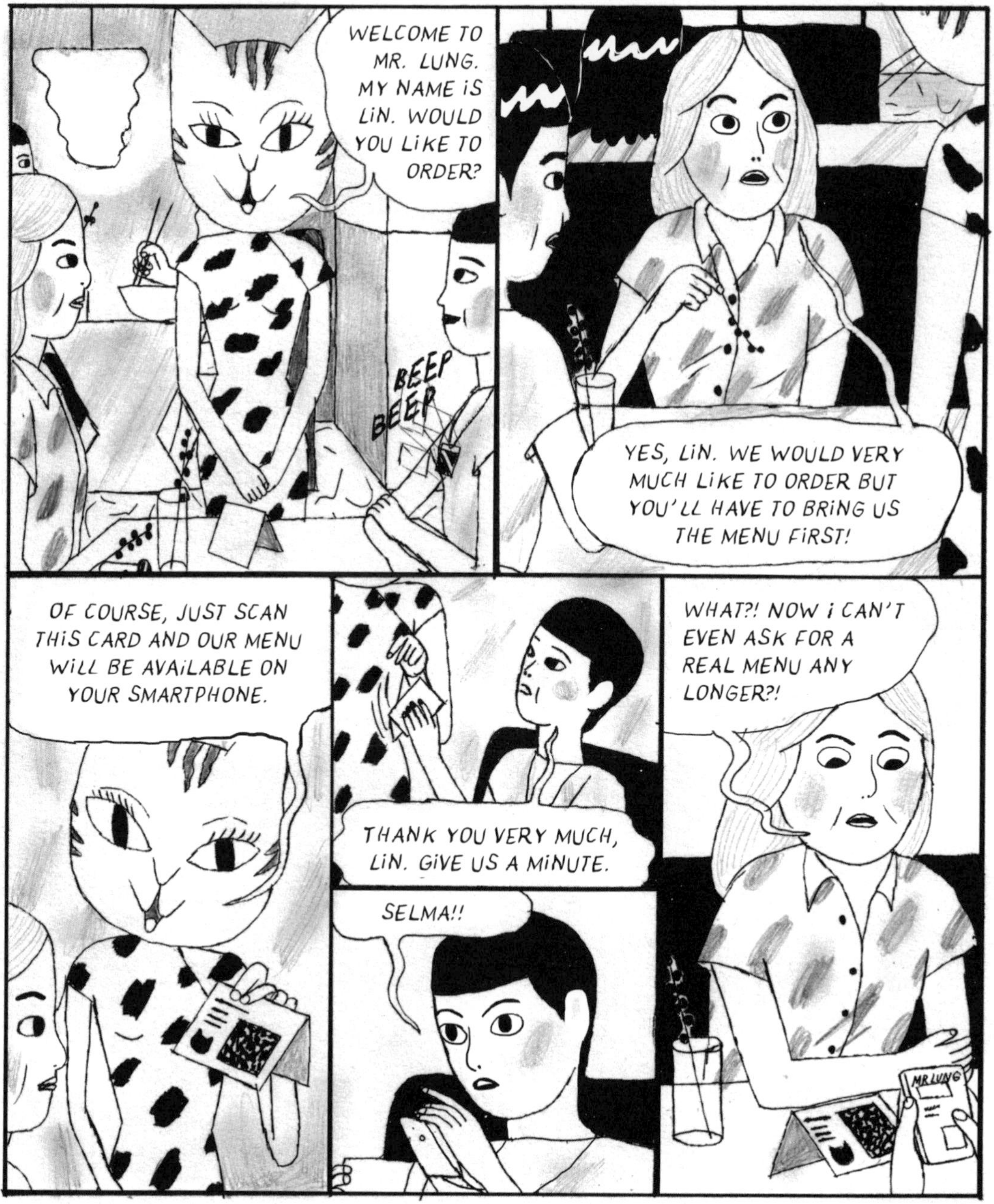
WELCOME TO MR. LUNG. MY NAME iS LiN. WOULD YOU LiKE TO ORDER?
BEEP BEEP
YES, LiN. WE WOULD VERY MUCH LiKE TO ORDER BUT YOU'LL HAVE TO BRiNG US THE MENU FiRST!
OF COURSE, JUST SCAN THiS CARD AND OUR MENU WiLL BE AVAiLABLE ON YOUR SMARTPHONE.
THANK YOU VERY MUCH, LiN. GiVE US A MiNUTE.
SELMA!!
WHAT?! NOW i CAN'T EVEN ASK FOR A REAL MENU ANY LONGER?!
MR LUNG

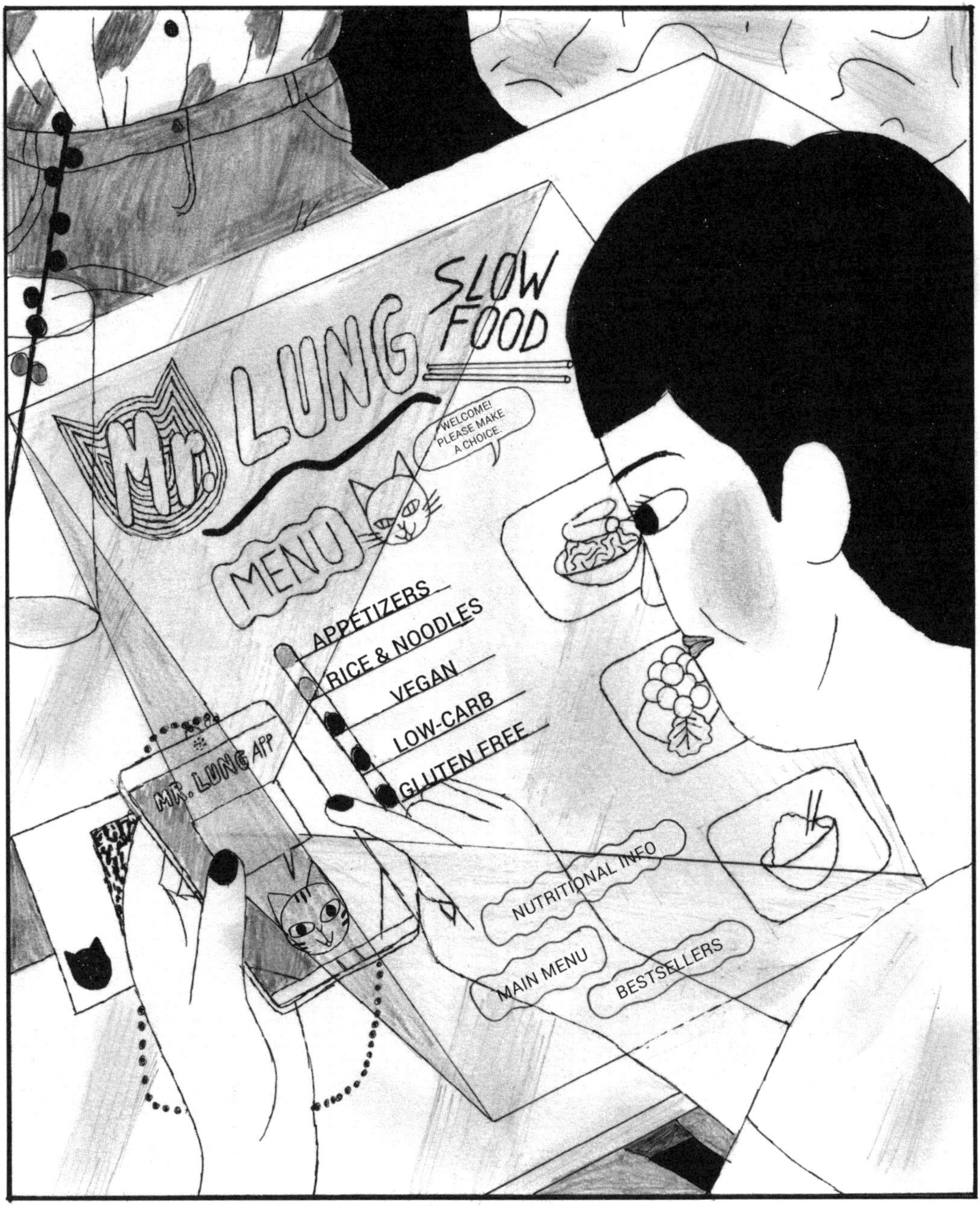
Mr. LUNG
SLOW FOOD
WELCOME! PLEASE MAKE A CHOICE.
MENU
APPETIZERS
RICE & NOODLES
VEGAN
LOW-CARB
GLUTEN FREE
MR. LUNG APP
NUTRITIONAL INFO
MAIN MENU
BESTSELLERS

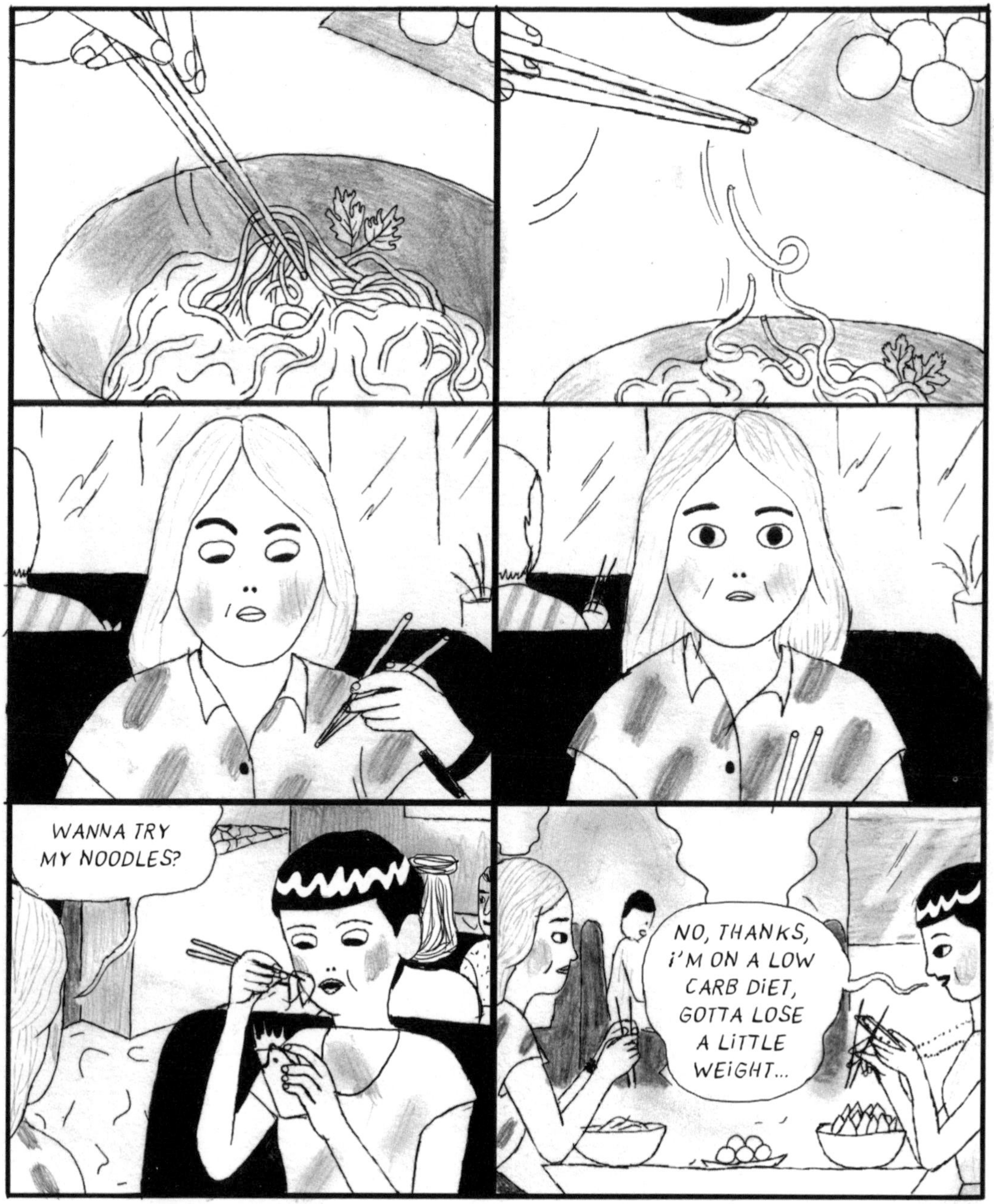
WANNA TRY MY NOODLES?
NO, THANKS, I'M ON A LOW CARB DIET, GOTTA LOSE A LITTLE WEIGHT...

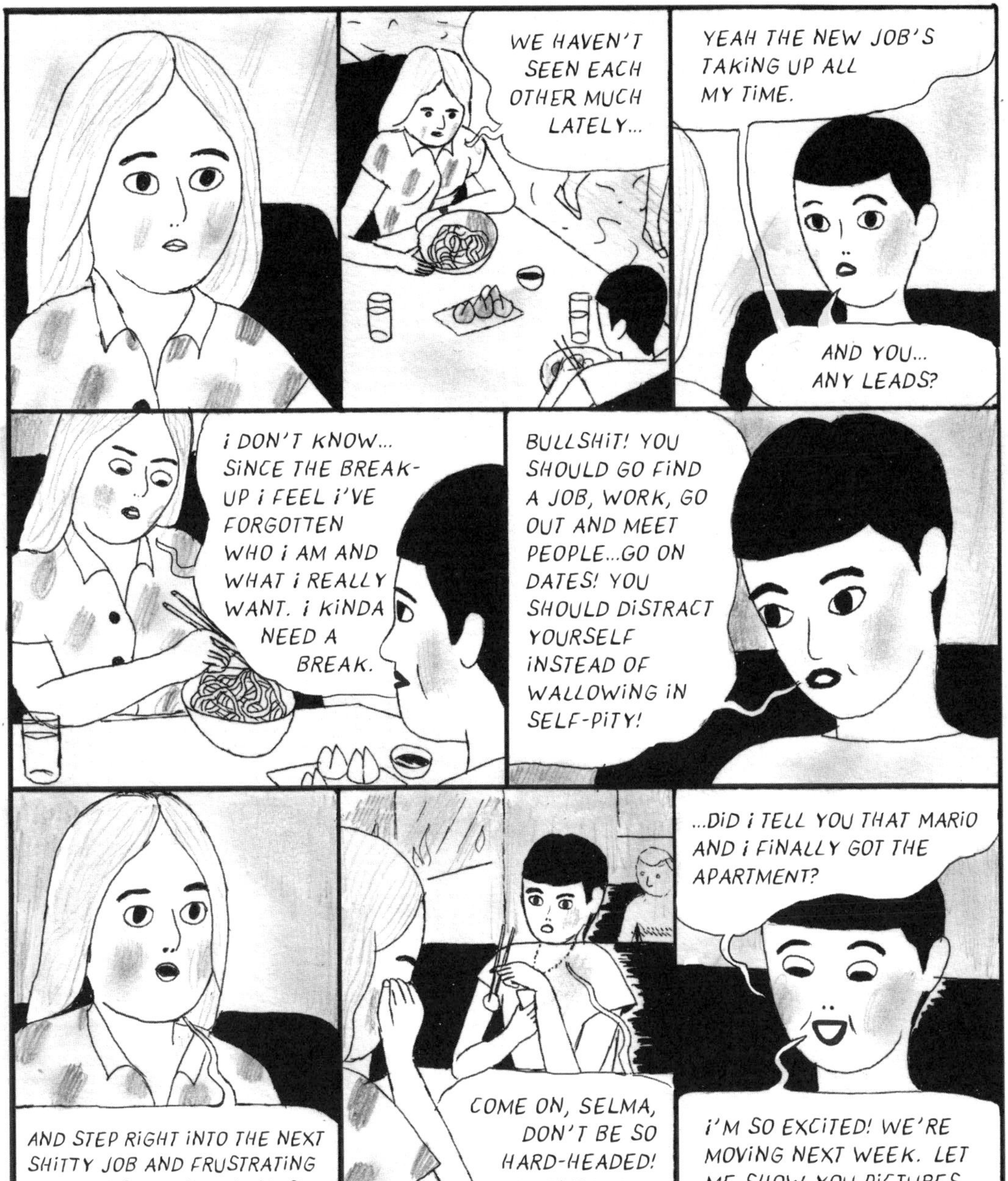

WE HAVEN'T SEEN EACH OTHER MUCH LATELY...
YEAH THE NEW JOB'S TAKING UP ALL MY TIME.
AND YOU... ANY LEADS?
i DON'T KNOW... SiNCE THE BREAK-UP i FEEL i'VE FORGOTTEN WHO i AM AND WHAT i REALLY WANT. i KiNDA NEED A BREAK.
BULLSHiT! YOU SHOULD GO FiND A JOB, WORK, GO OUT AND MEET PEOPLE...GO ON DATES! YOU SHOULD DiSTRACT YOURSELF iNSTEAD OF WALLOWiNG iN SELF-PiTY!
AND STEP RiGHT iNTO THE NEXT SHiTTY JOB AND FRUSTRATiNG RELATiONSHiP?! NO, THANKS!
COME ON, SELMA, DON'T BE SO HARD-HEADED! BY THE WAY...
...DiD i TELL YOU THAT MARiO AND i FiNALLY GOT THE APARTMENT?
i'M SO EXCiTED! WE'RE MOVING NEXT WEEK. LET ME SHOW YOU PiCTURES...

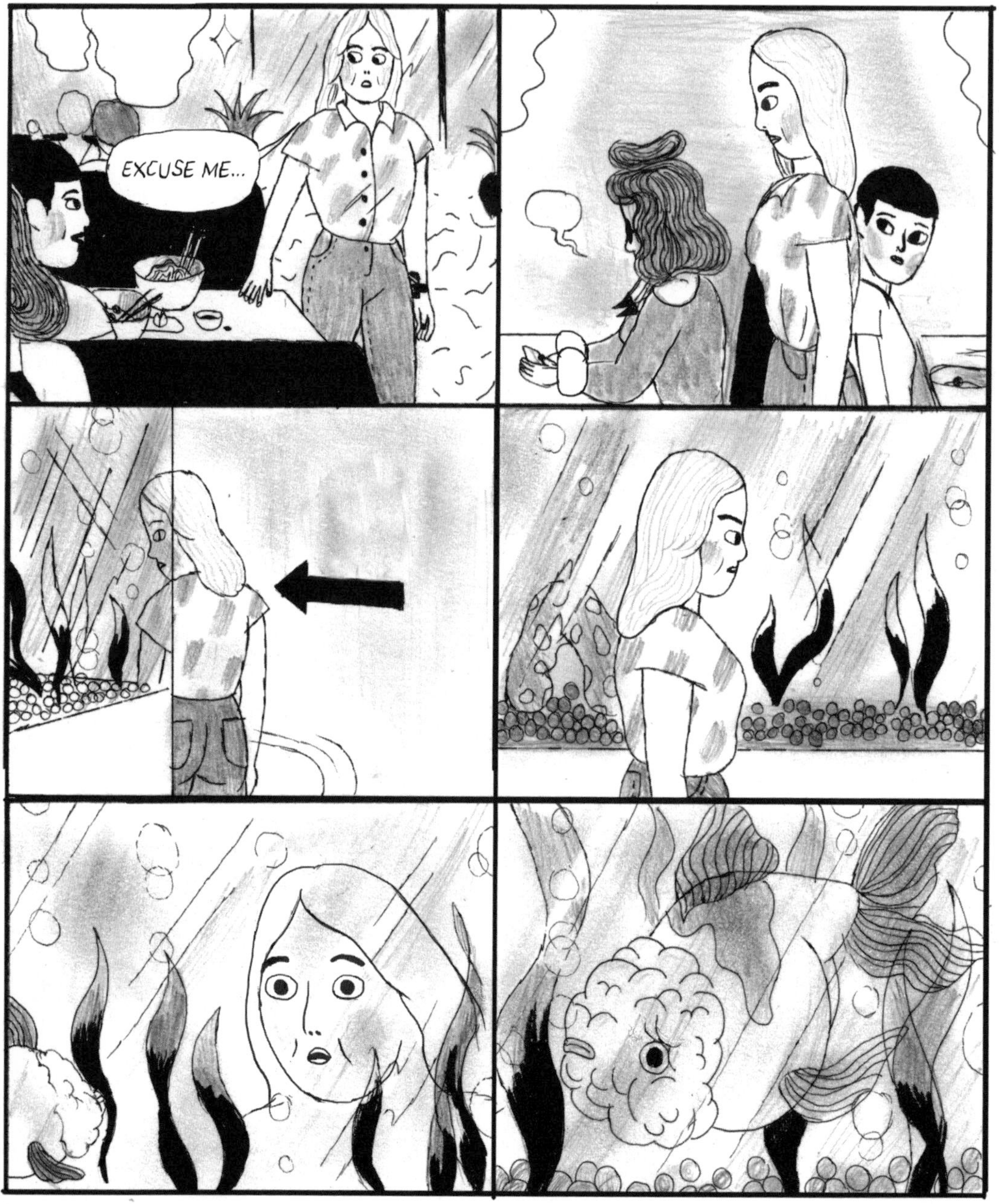
EXCUSE ME...

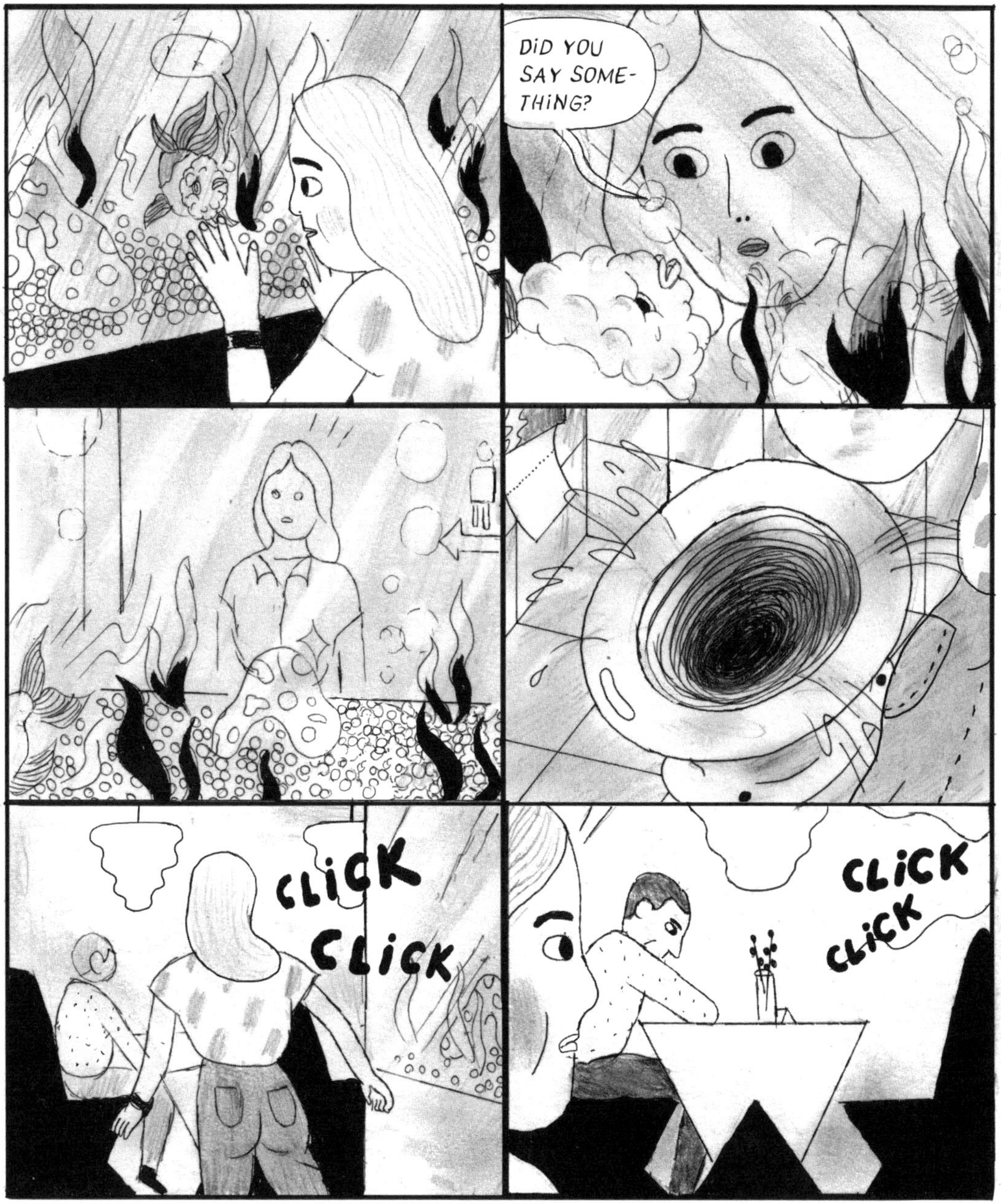
DID YOU SAY SOME-THING?
CLICK CLICK
CLICK CLICK

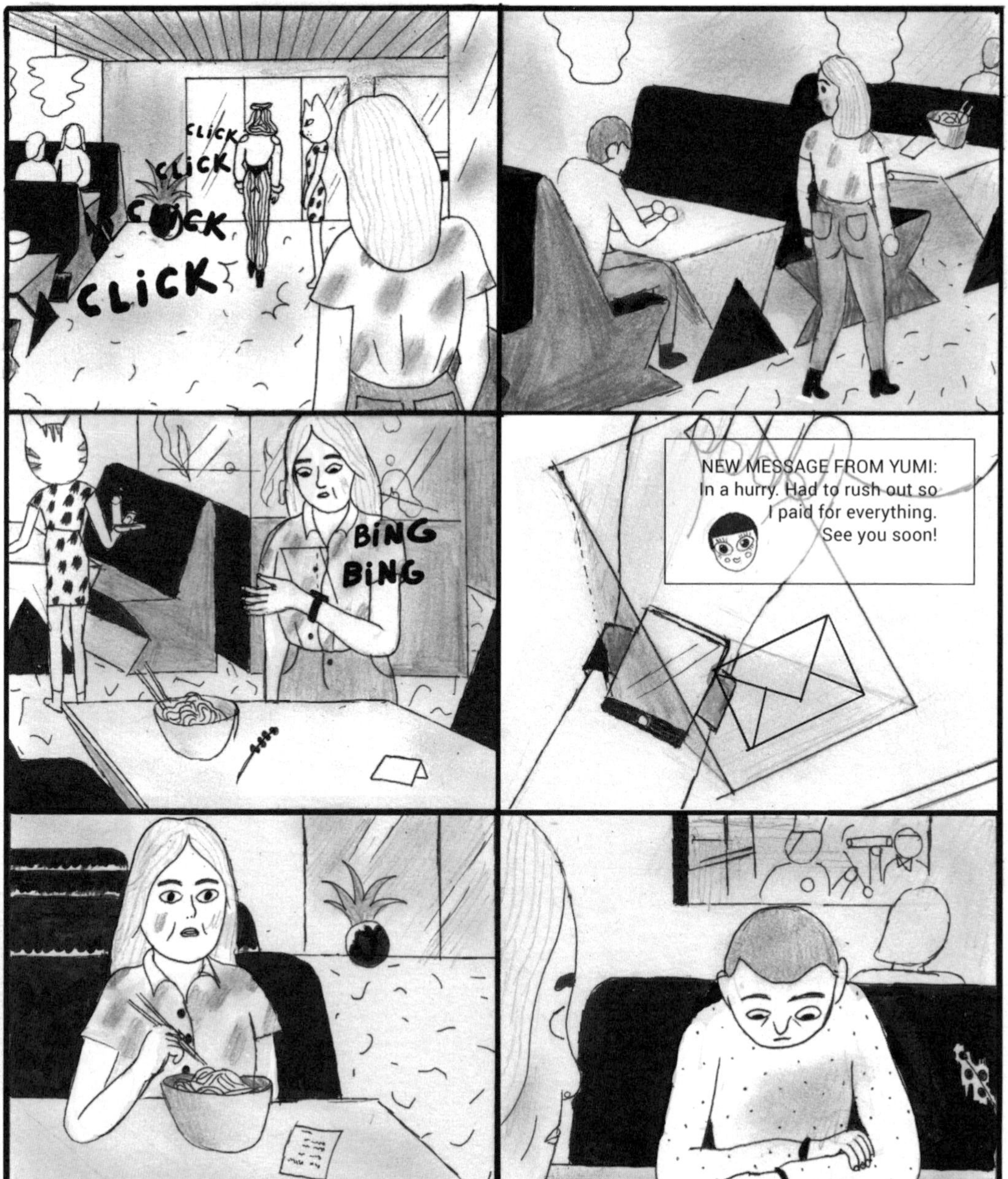
CLICK
CLICK
CLICK
CLICK
BING
BING
NEW MESSAGE FROM YUMI:
In a hurry. Had to rush out so
I paid for everything.
See you soon!

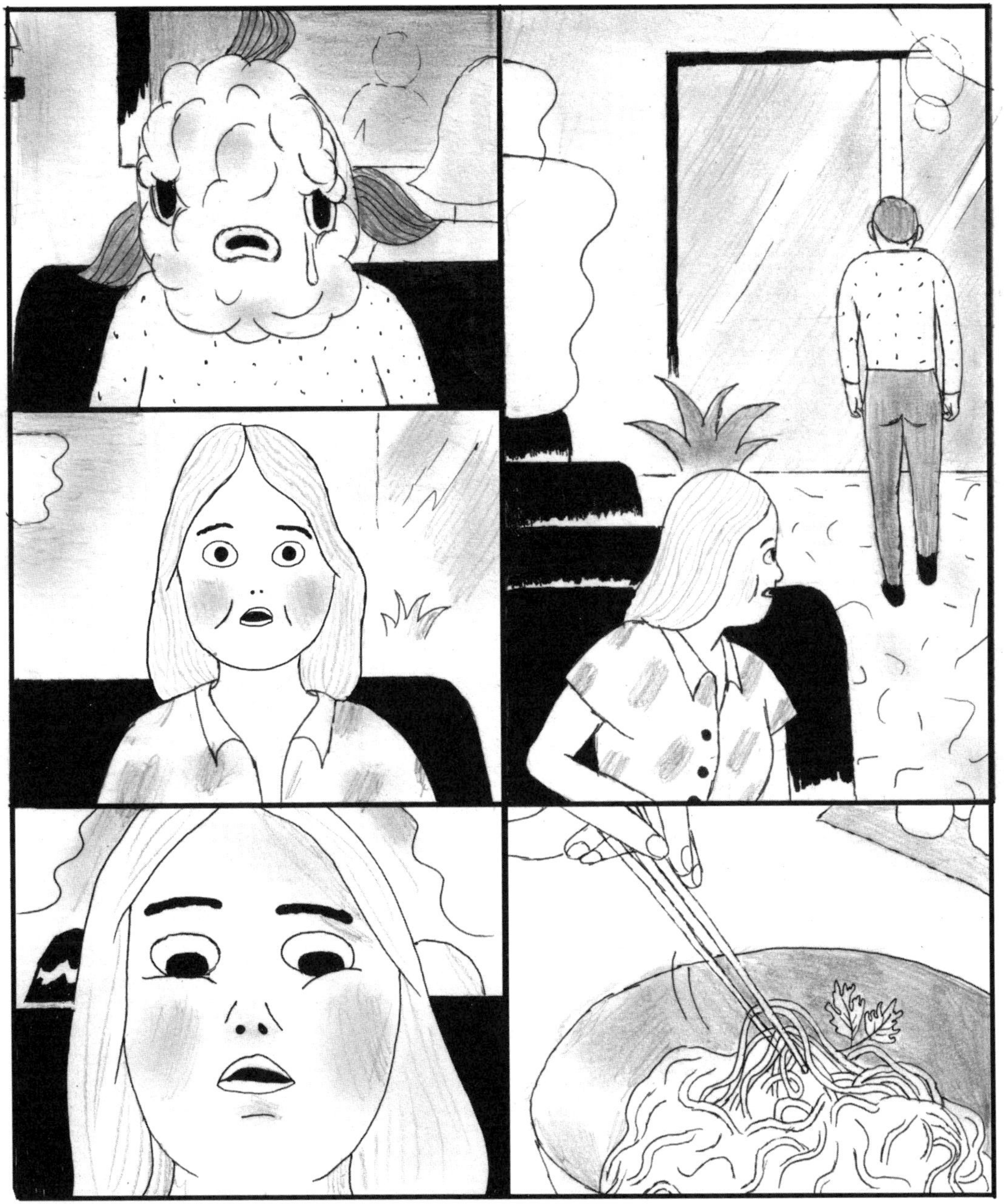

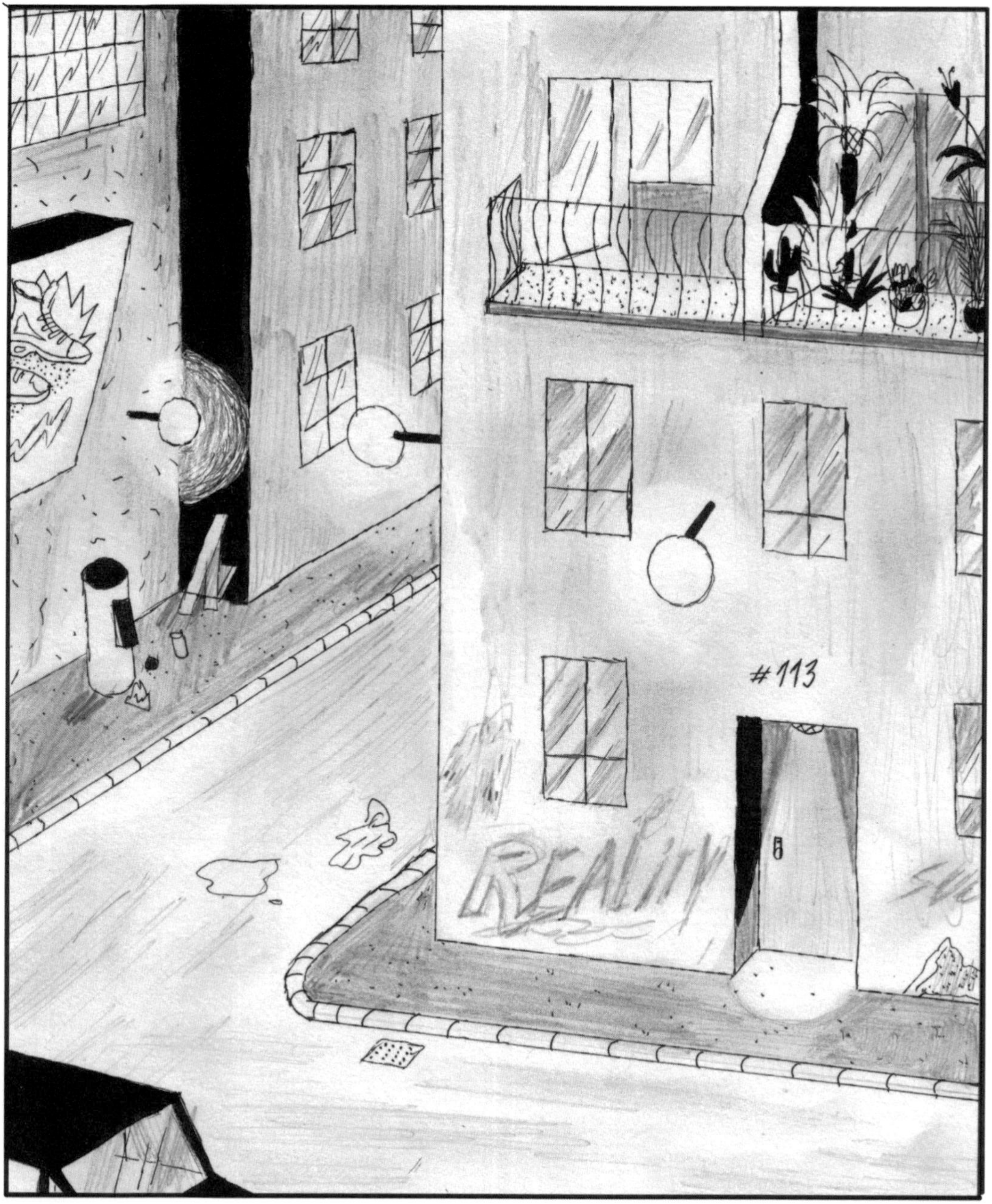

#113
REALITY

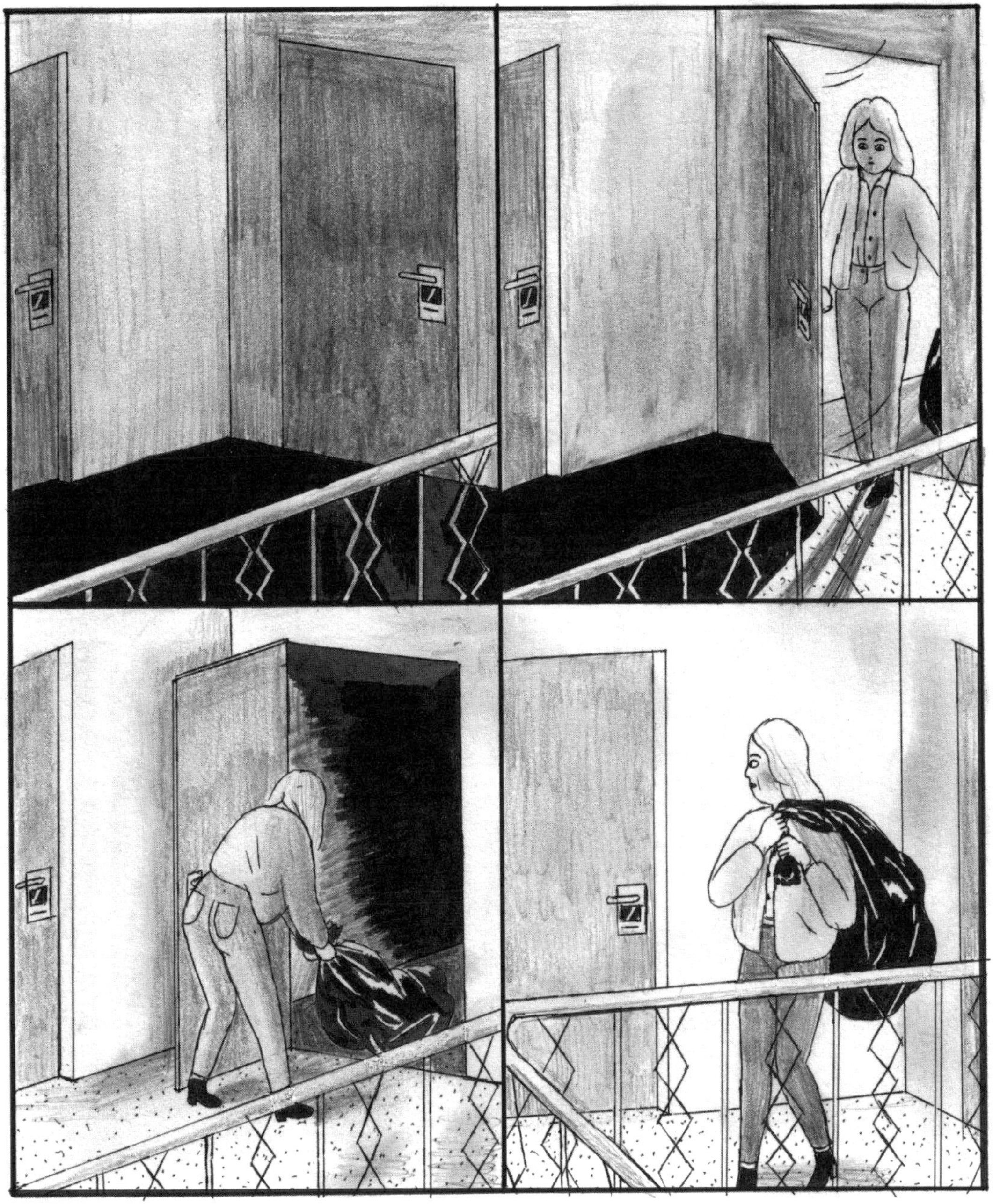

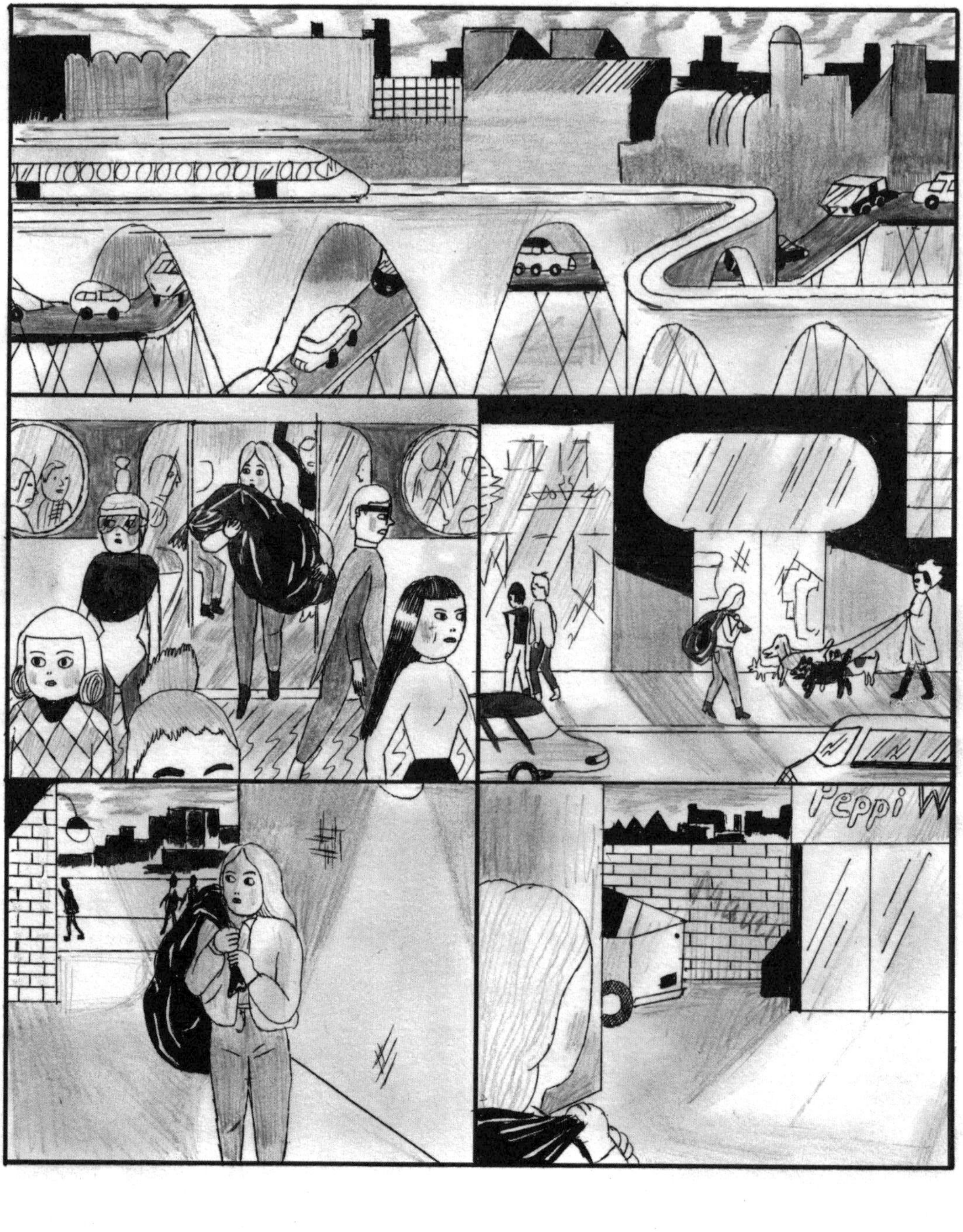
Peppi W

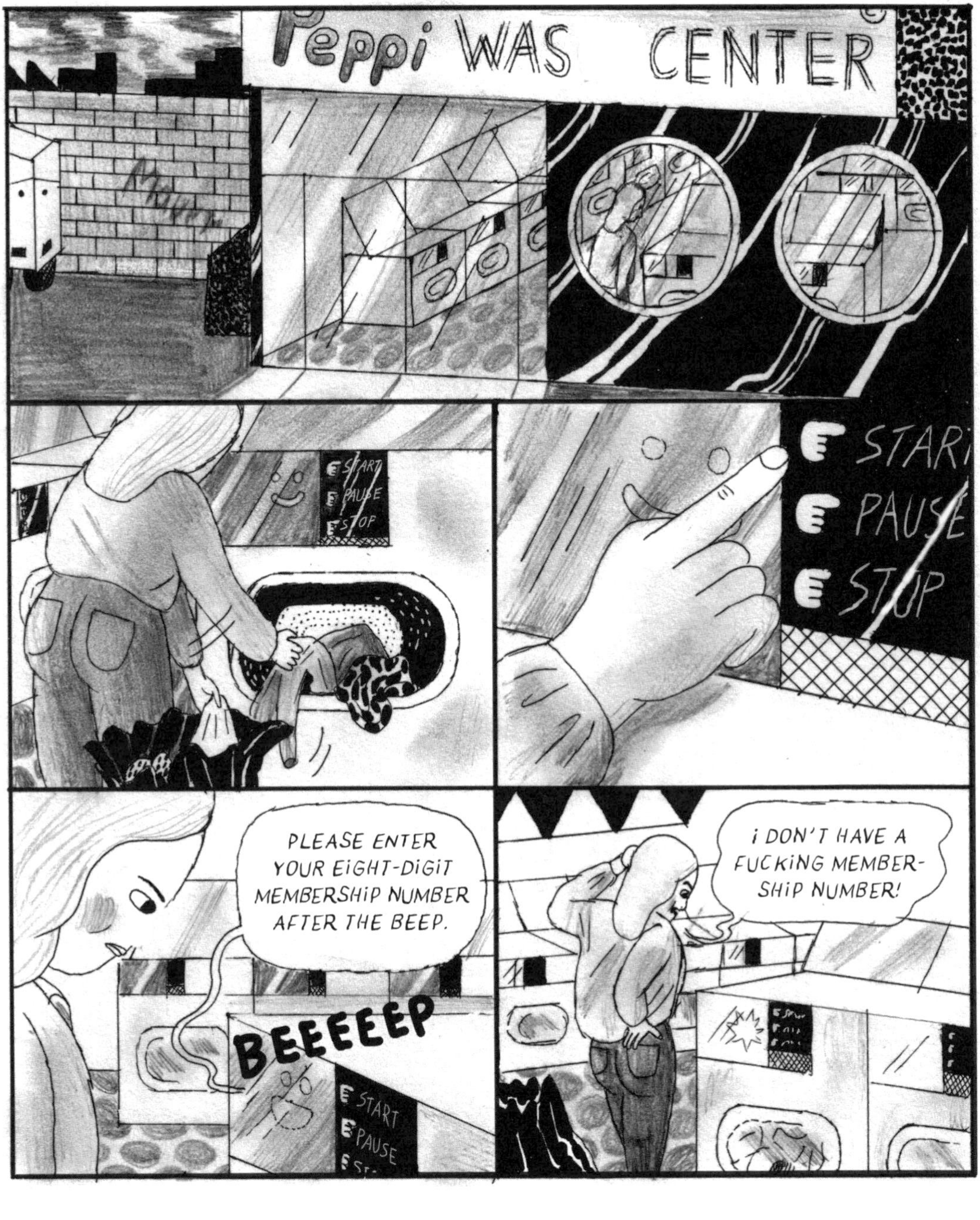
Peppi WAS CENTER
START
PAUSE
STOP
START
PAUSE
STOP
PLEASE ENTER YOUR EIGHT-DIGIT MEMBERSHIP NUMBER AFTER THE BEEP.
BEEEEEP
START
PAUSE
I DON'T HAVE A FUCKING MEMBERSHIP NUMBER!

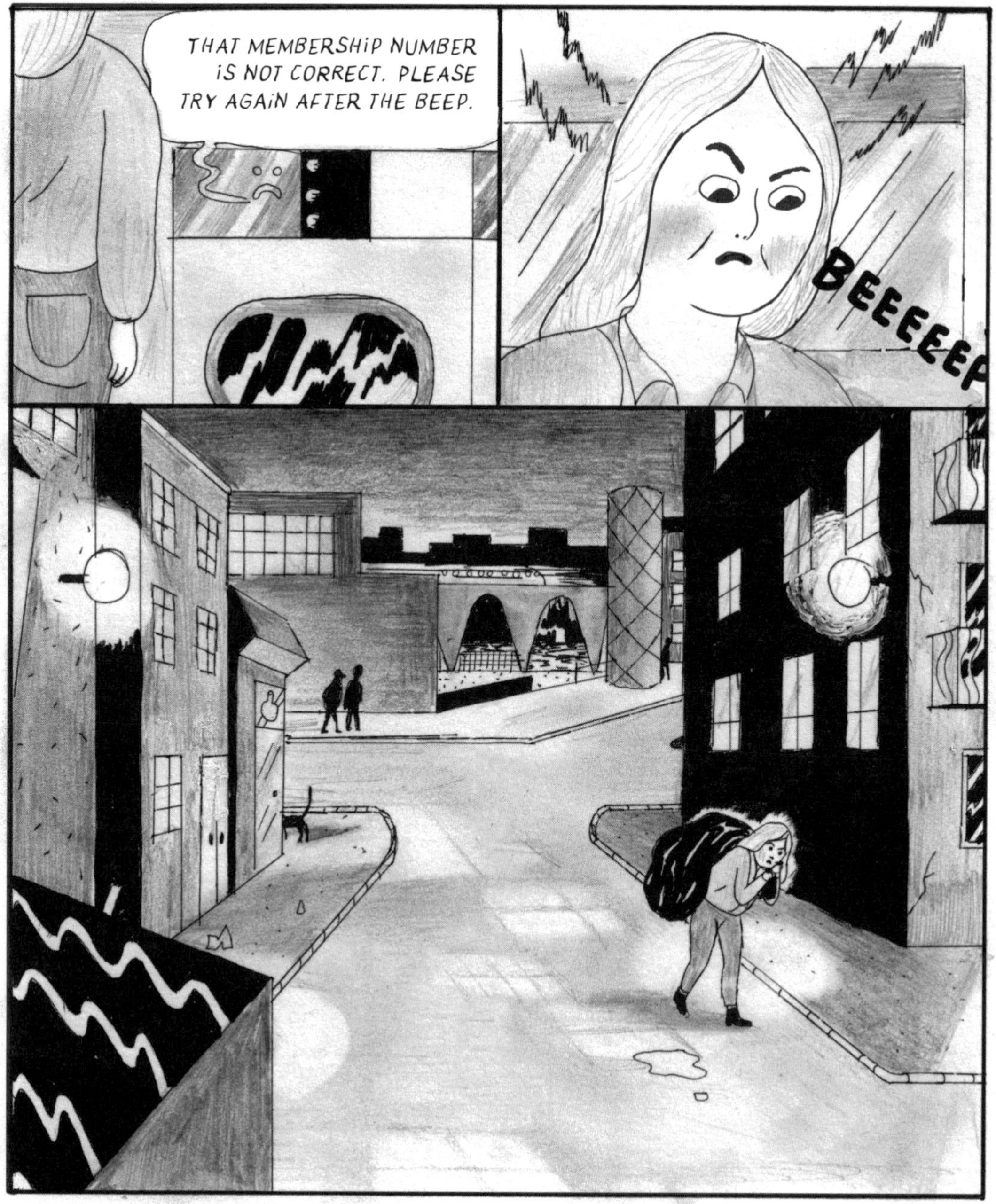
THAT MEMBERSHIP NUMBER IS NOT CORRECT. PLEASE TRY AGAIN AFTER THE BEEP.
BEEEEEEP

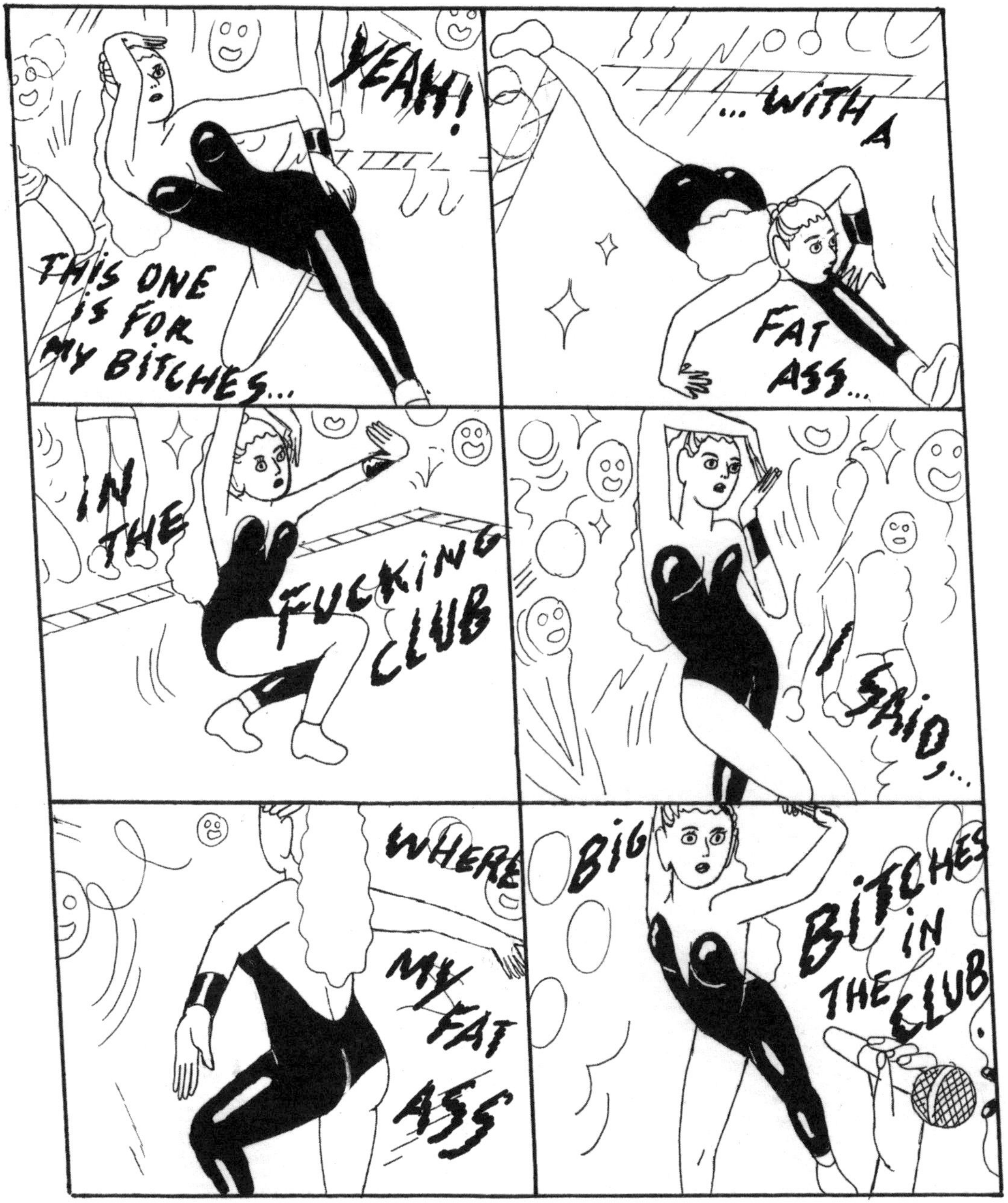
YEAH!
THIS ONE IS FOR MY BITCHES...
...WITH A
FAT ASS...
IN THE
FUCKING CLUB
I SAID,...
WHERE
MY FAT ASS
BIG
BITCHES IN THE CLUB

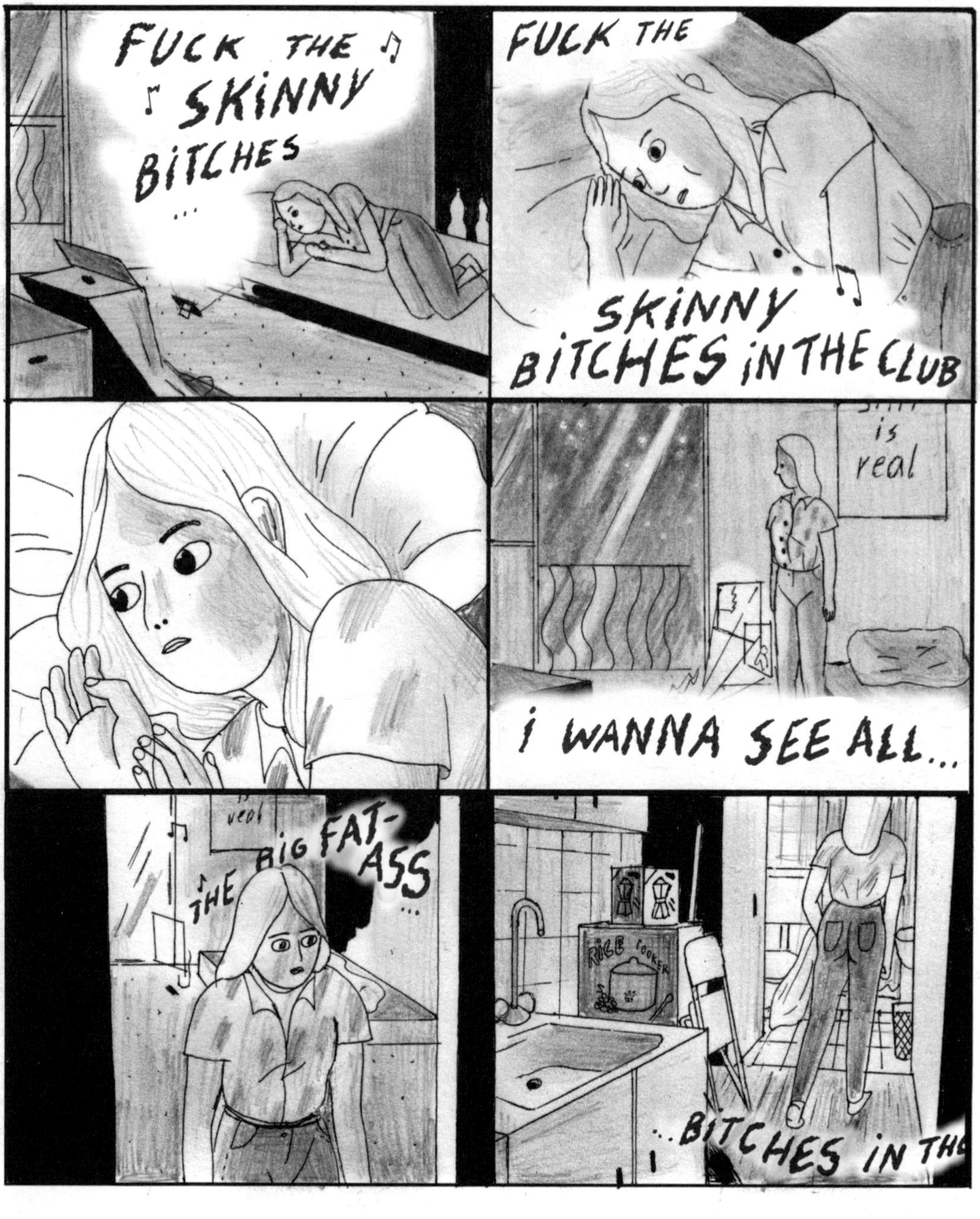
FUCK THE SKINNY BITCHES ...
FUCK THE
SKINNY BITCHES IN THE CLUB
is real
I WANNA SEE ALL...
THE BIG FAT-ASS ...
...BITCHES IN THE

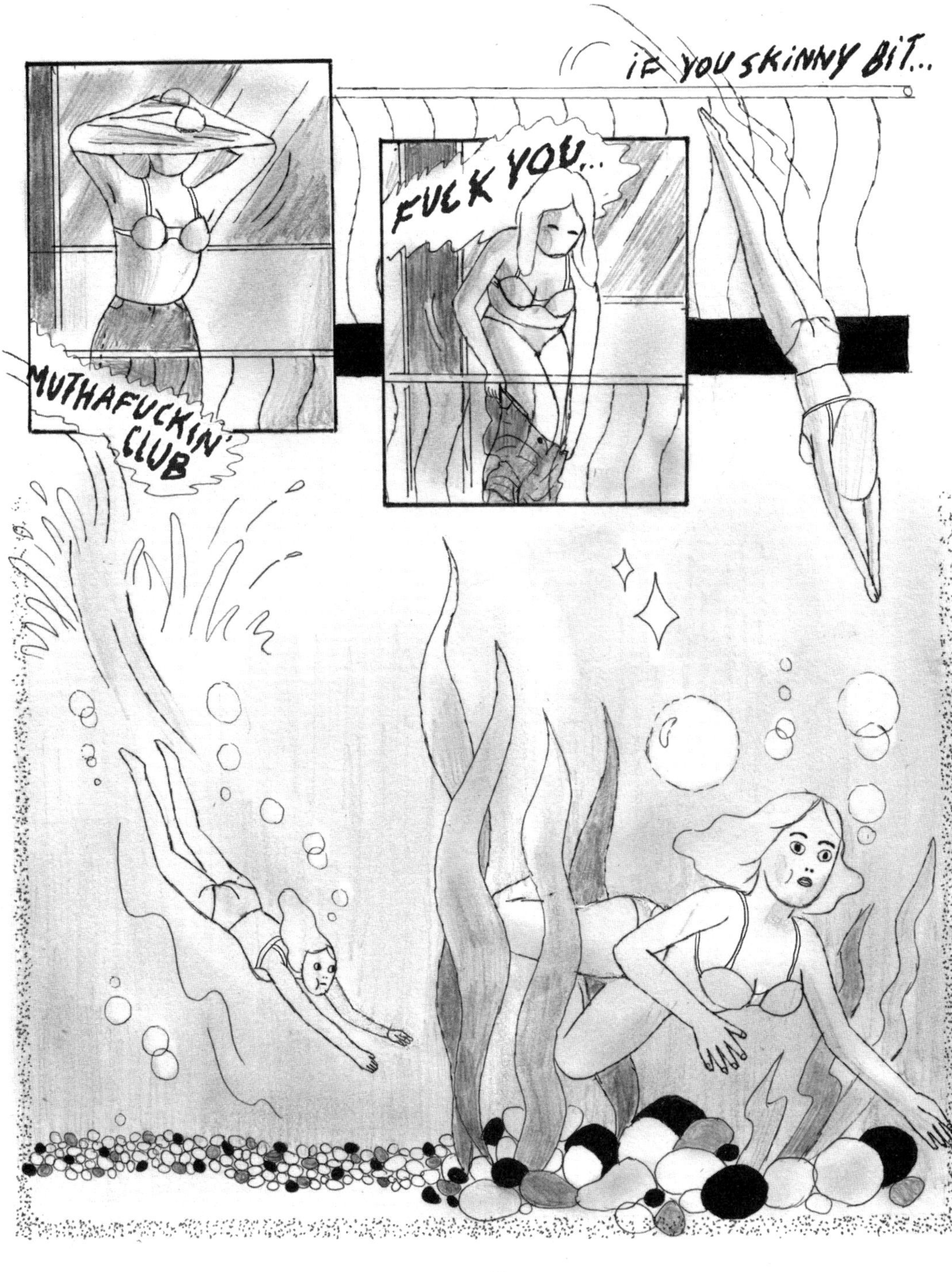
MUTHAFUCKIN' CLUB
FUCK YOU...
IF YOU SKINNY BIT...

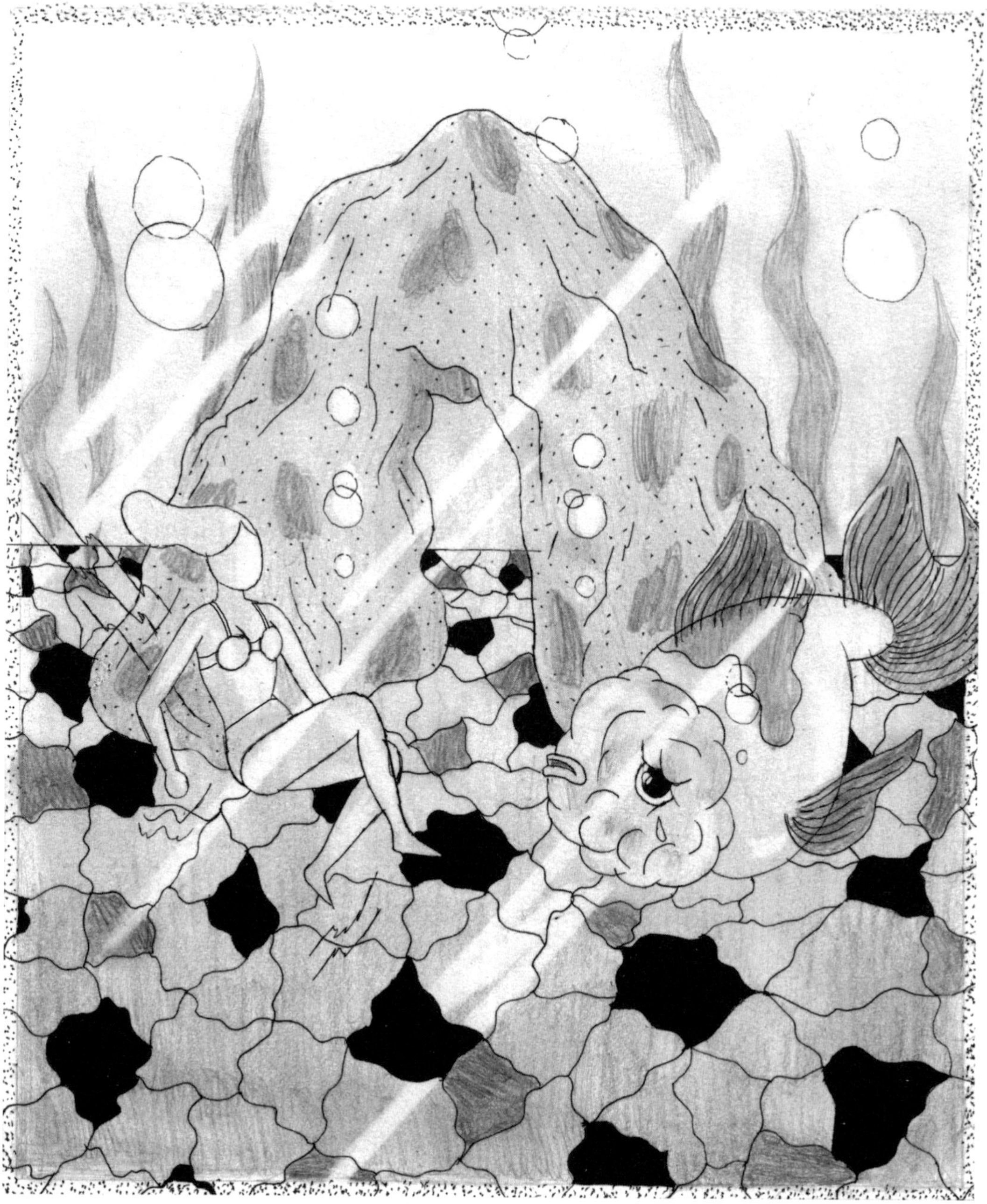

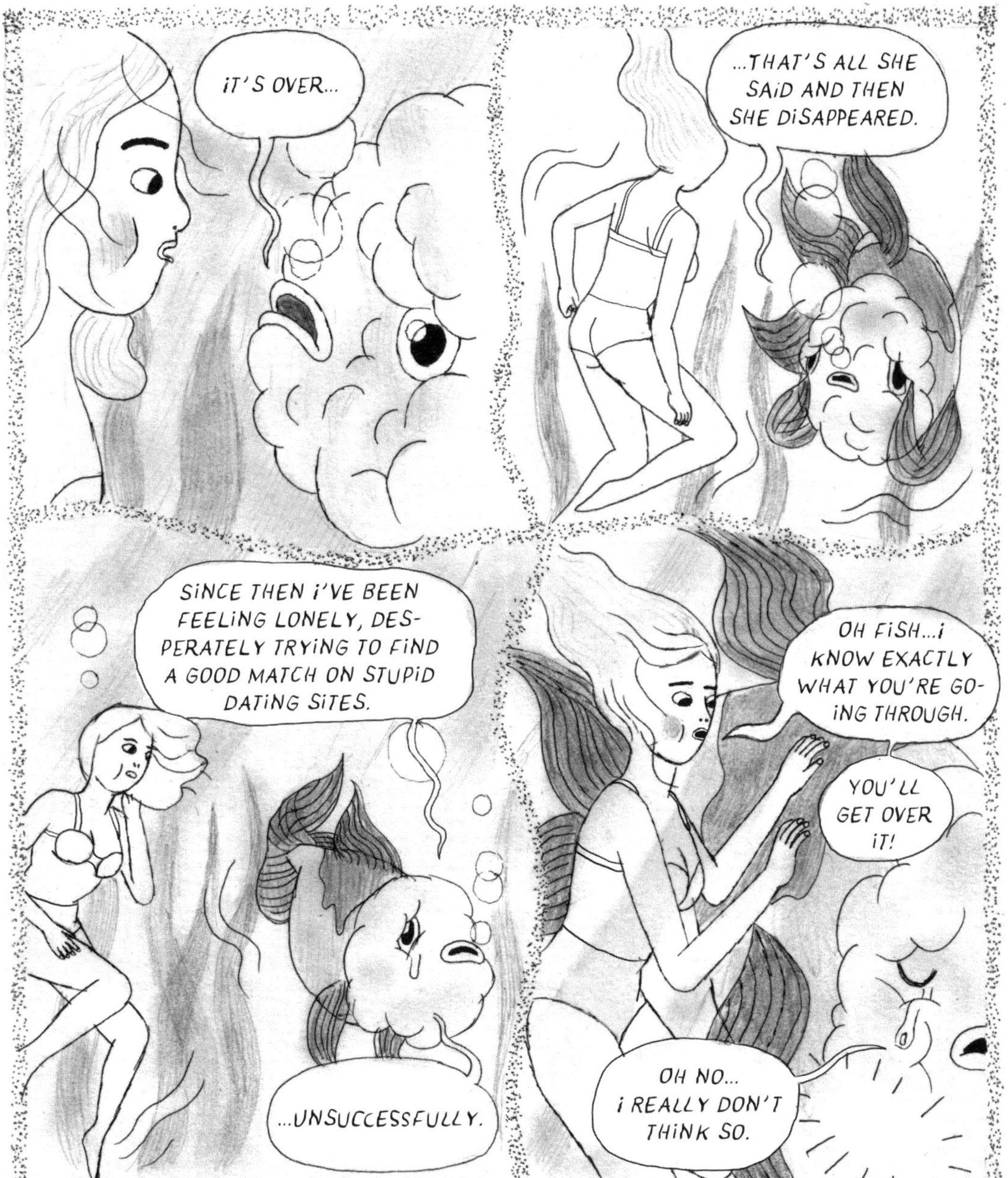
IT'S OVER...
...THAT'S ALL SHE SAID AND THEN SHE DISAPPEARED.
SINCE THEN I'VE BEEN FEELING LONELY, DESPERATELY TRYING TO FIND A GOOD MATCH ON STUPID DATING SITES.
...UNSUCCESSFULLY.
OH FISH...I KNOW EXACTLY WHAT YOU'RE GOING THROUGH.
YOU'LL GET OVER IT!
OH NO... I REALLY DON'T THINK SO.

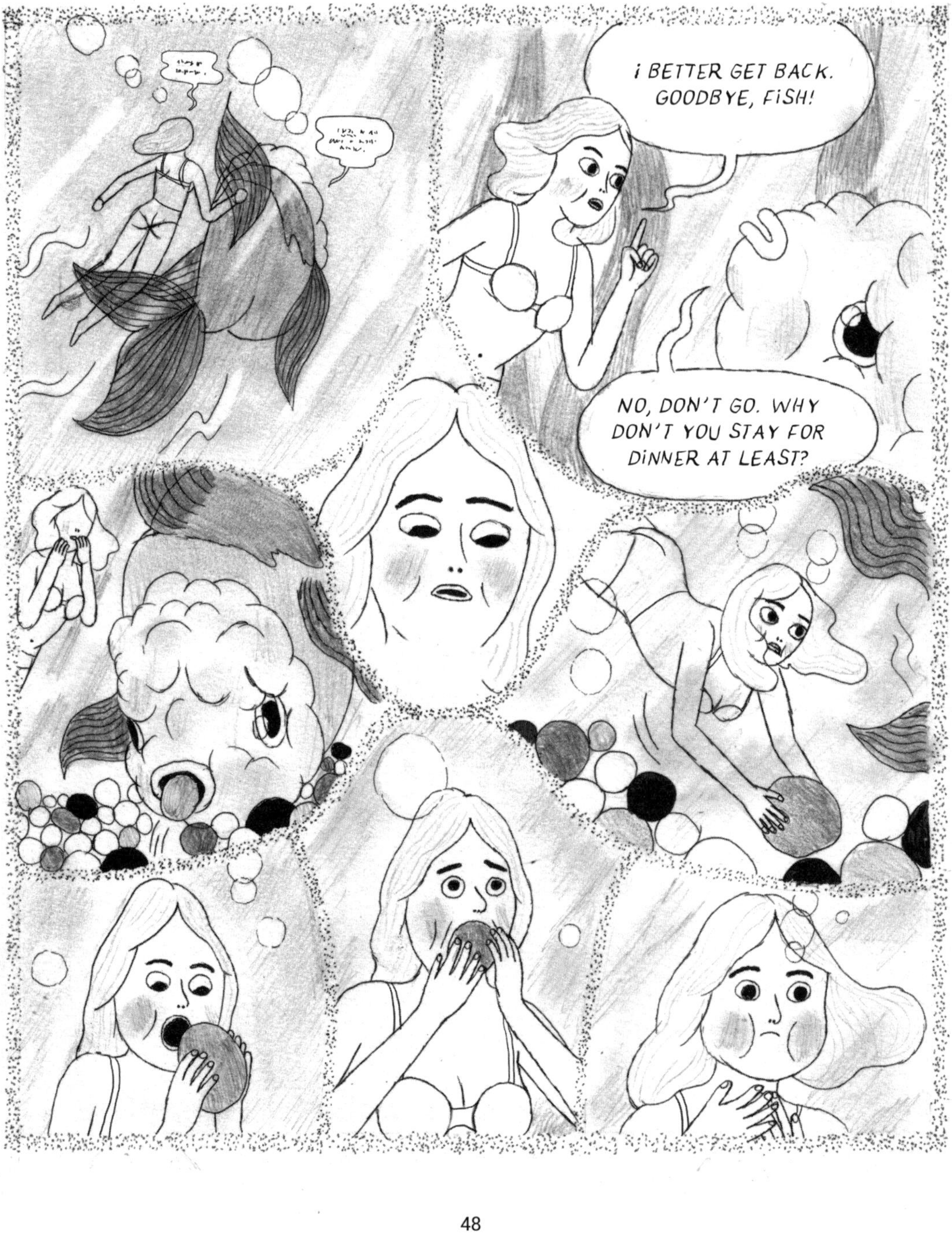
i BETTER GET BACK. GOODBYE, FiSH!
NO, DON'T GO. WHY DON'T YOU STAY FOR DiNNER AT LEAST?

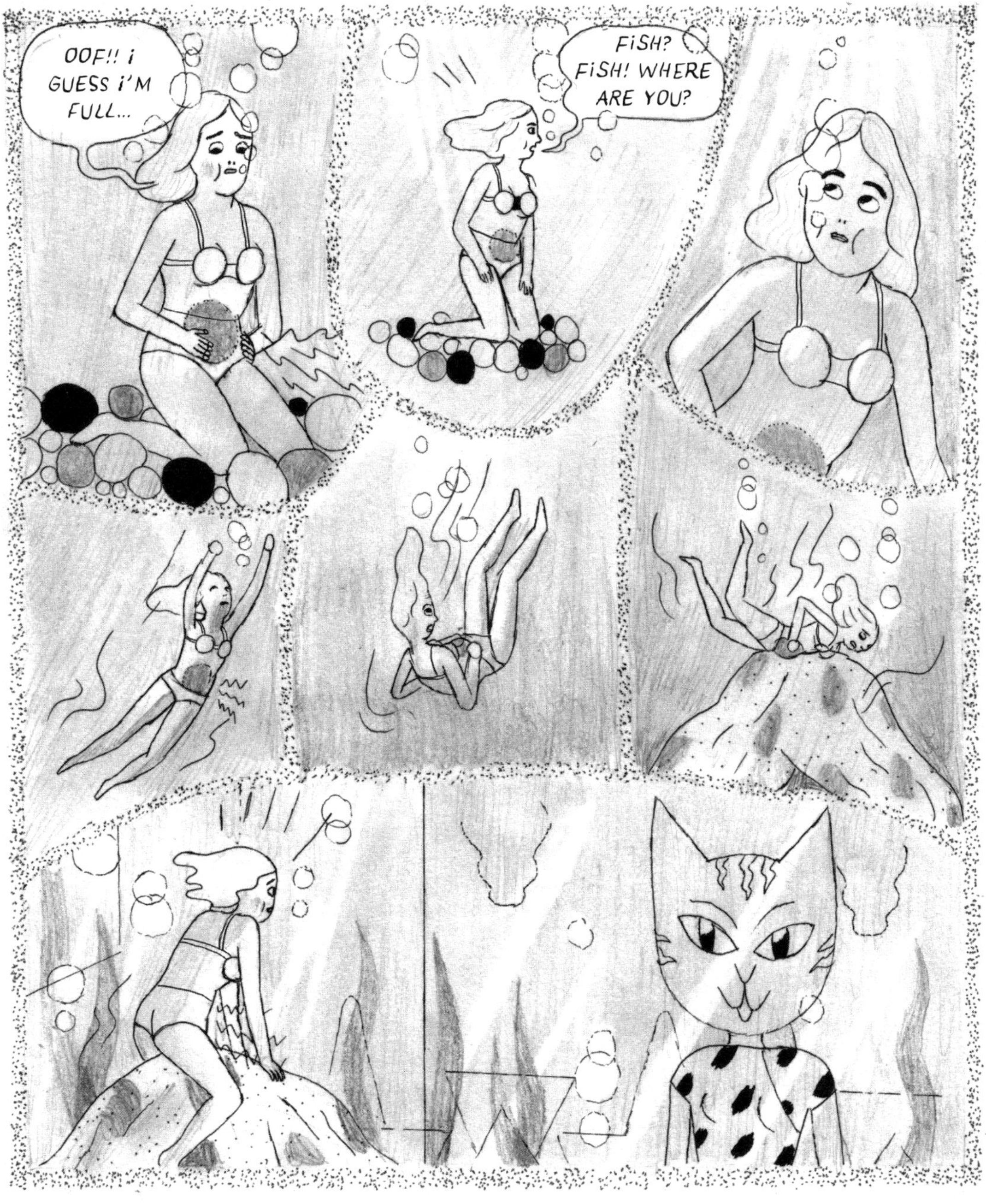
OOF!! i GUESS i'M FULL...
FiSH? FiSH! WHERE ARE YOU?

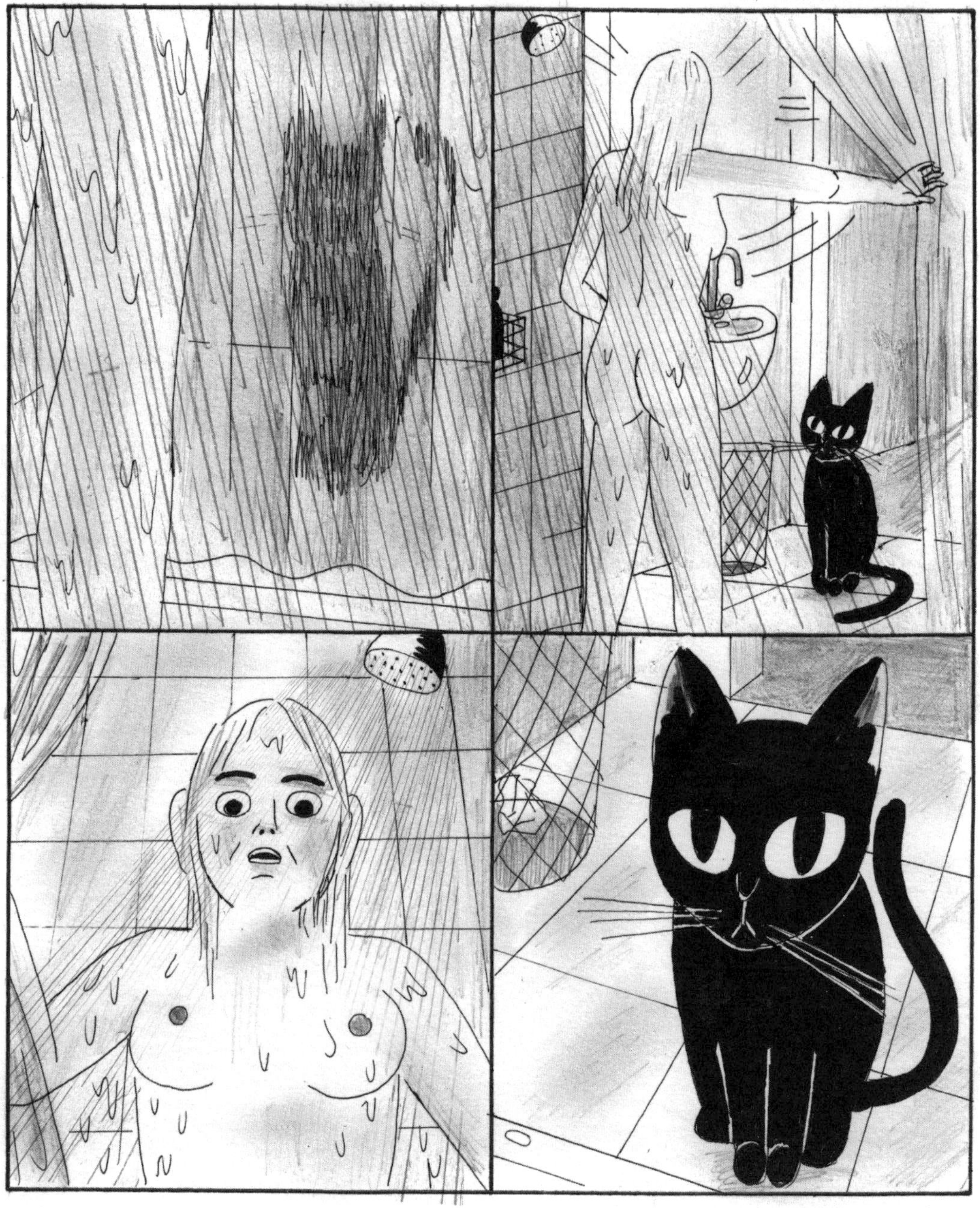

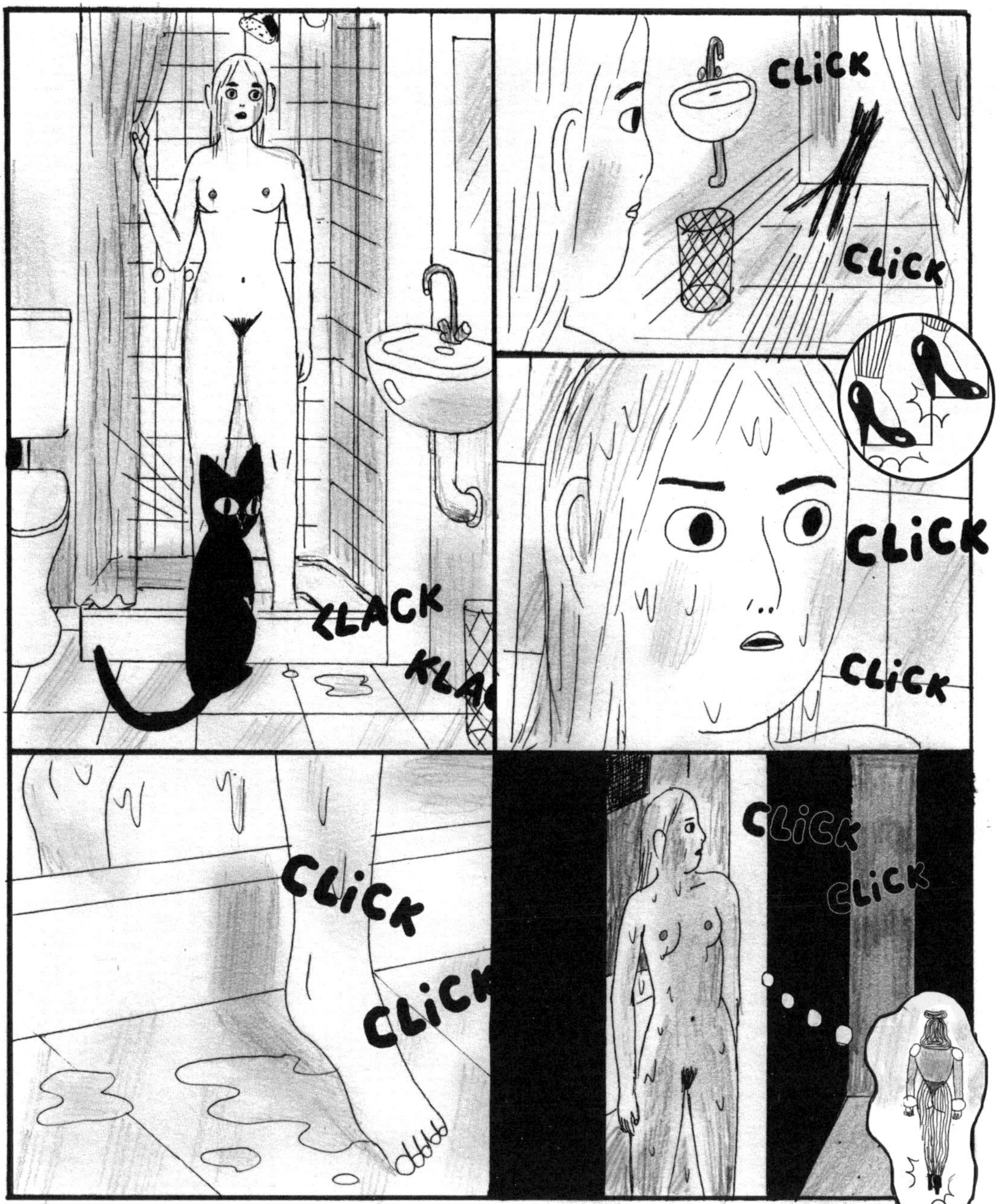
KLACK
KLAC
CLICK
CLICK
CLICK
CLICK
CLICK
CLICK
CLICK
CLICK

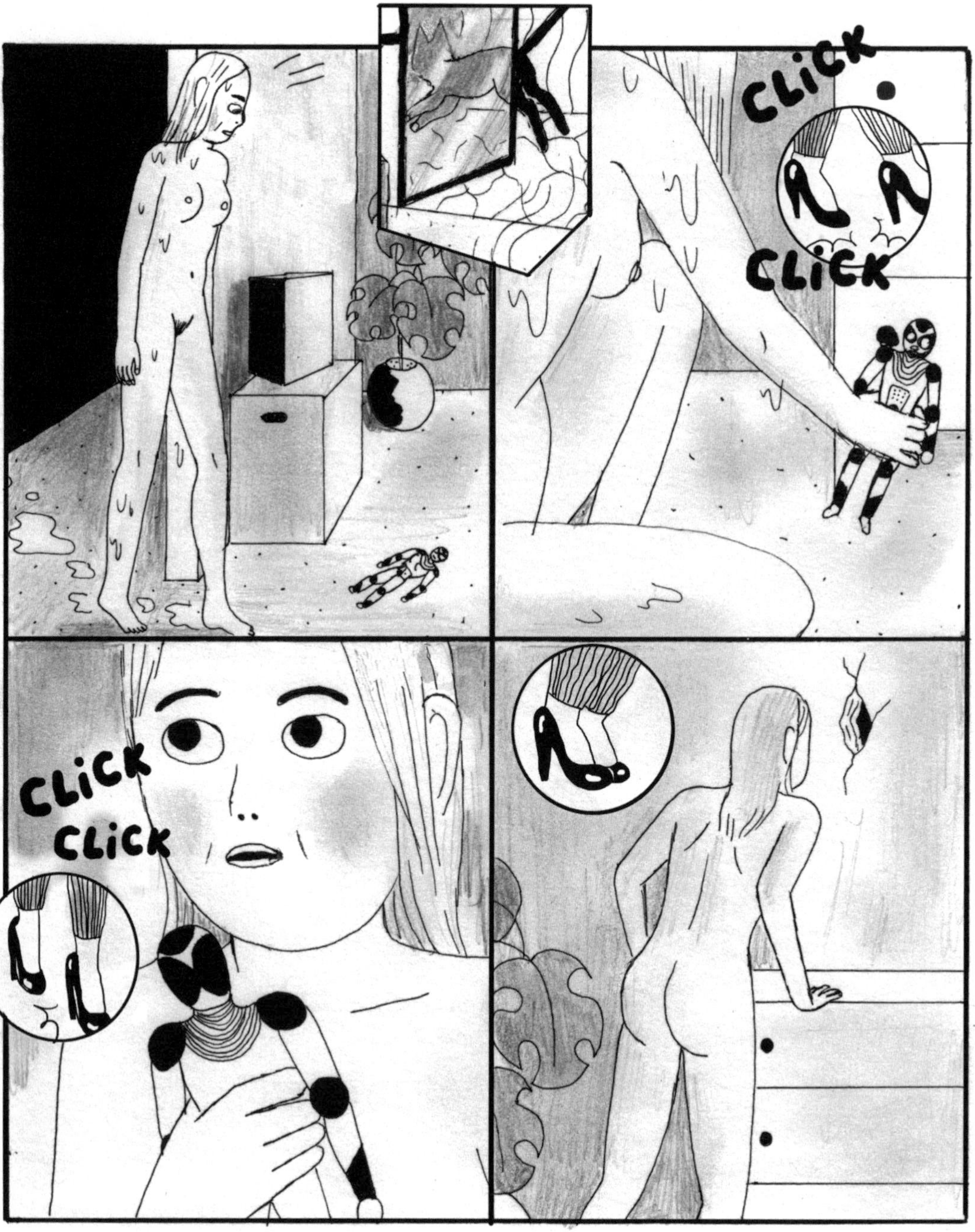
CLICK
CLICK
CLICK
CLICK

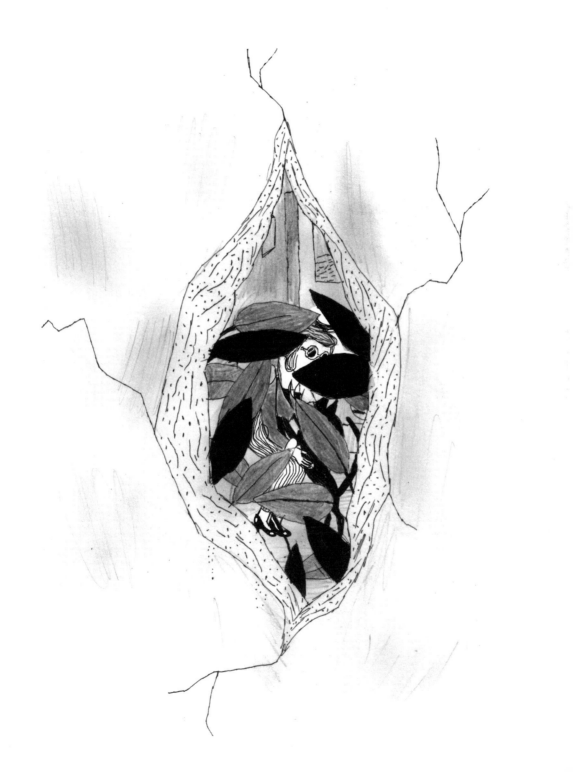

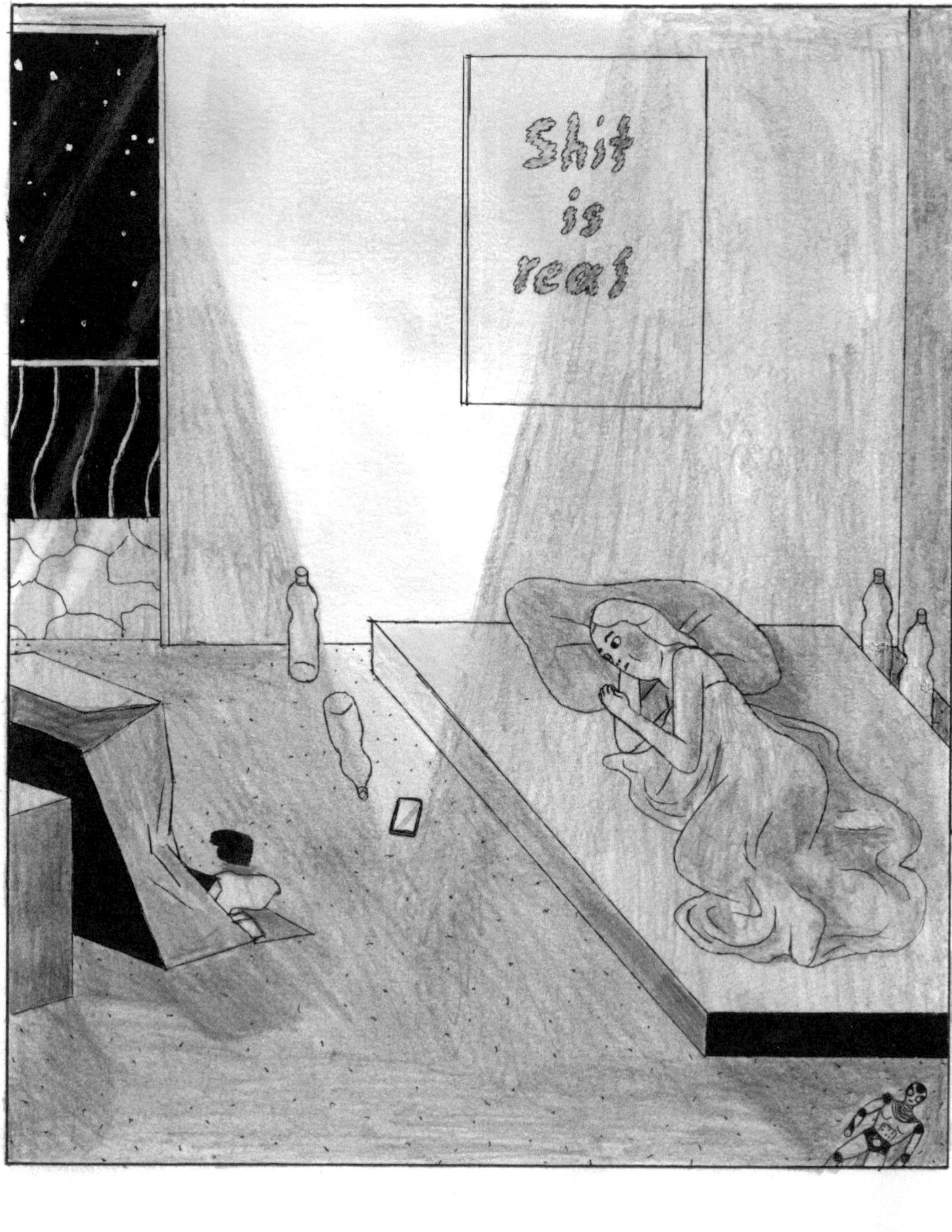
Shit
is
real

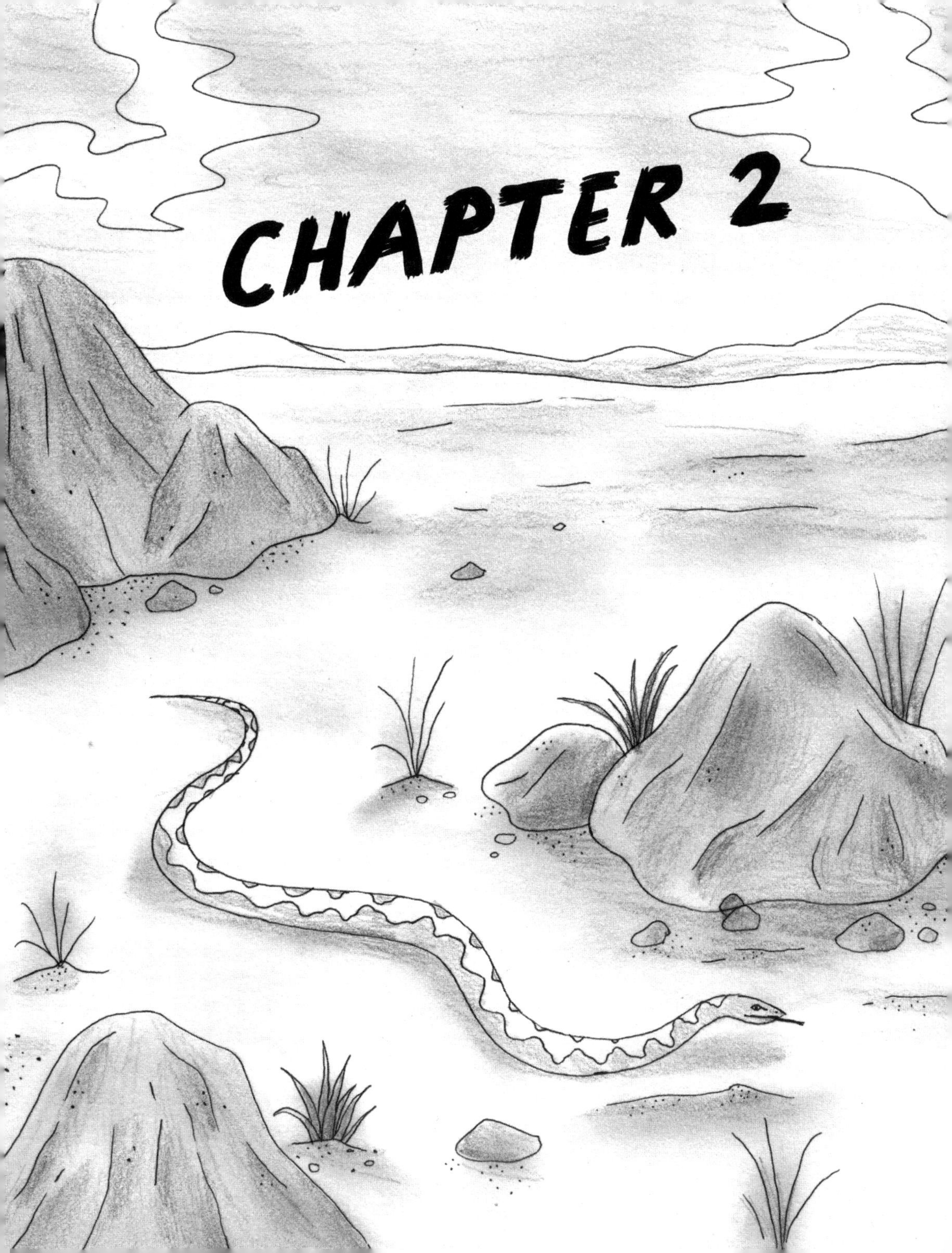
CHAPTER 2

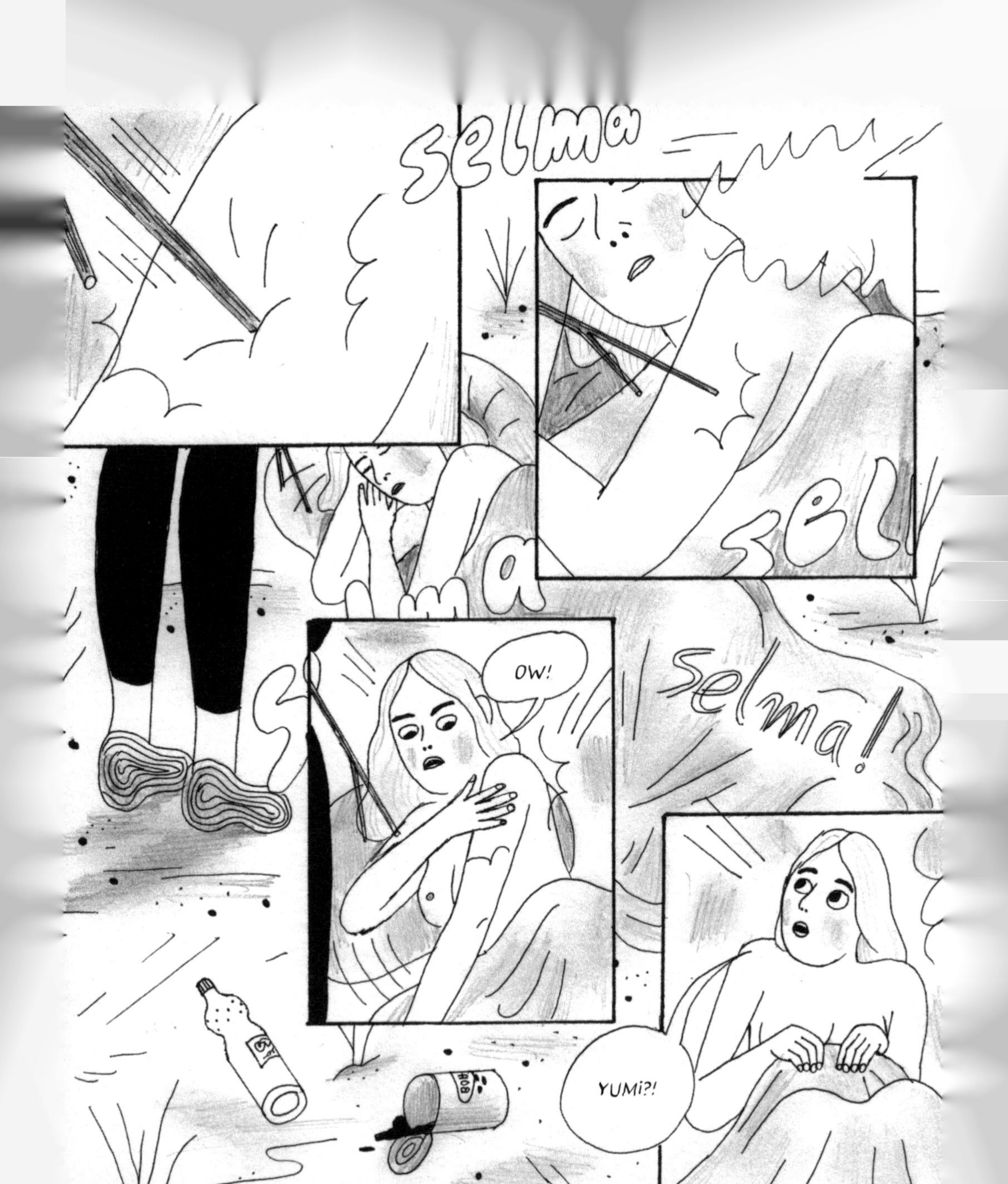
selma
sel
OW!
selma!
YUMI?!

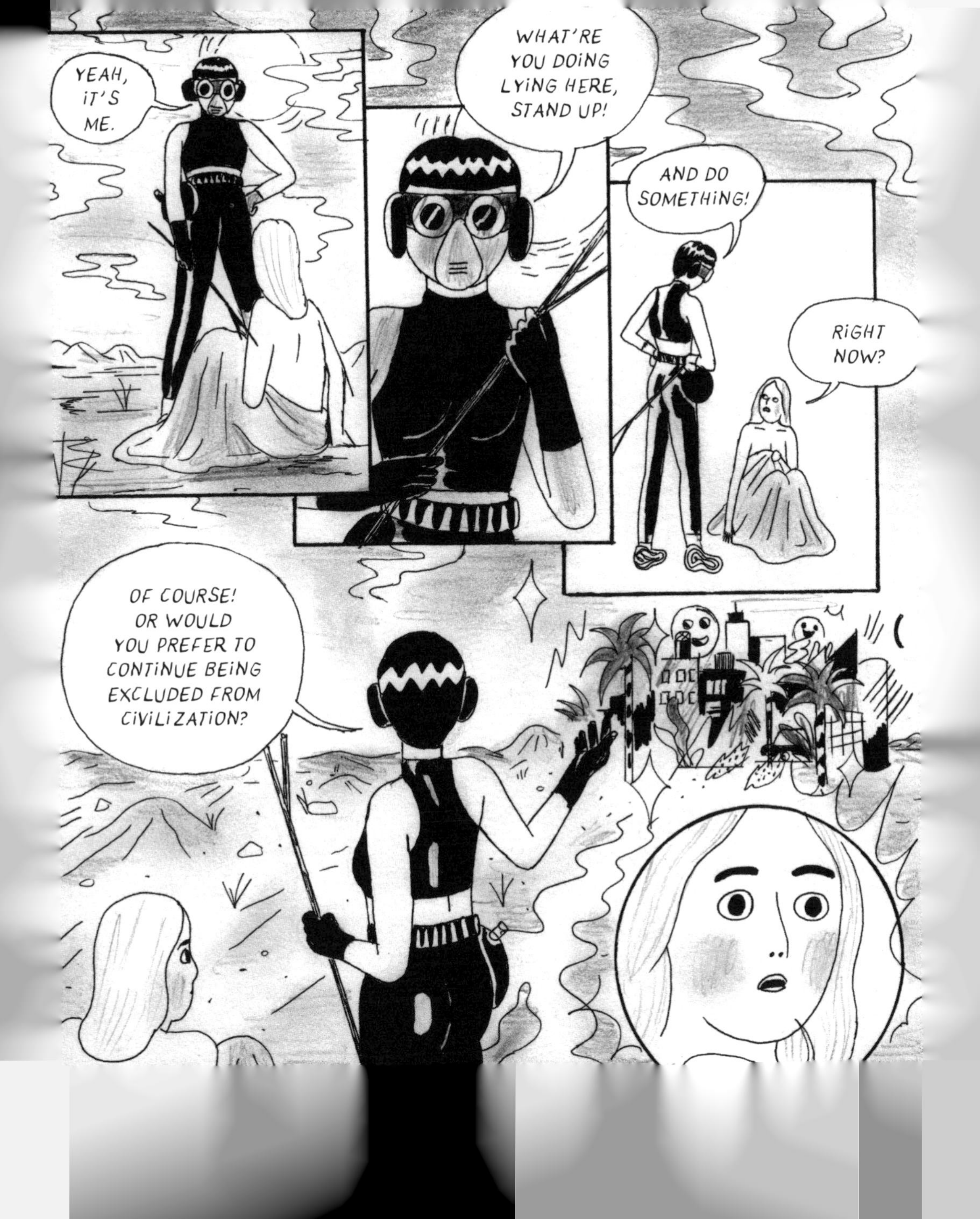
YEAH, IT'S ME.
WHAT'RE YOU DOING LYING HERE, STAND UP!
AND DO SOMETHING!
RIGHT NOW?
OF COURSE! OR WOULD YOU PREFER TO CONTINUE BEING EXCLUDED FROM CIVILIZATION?

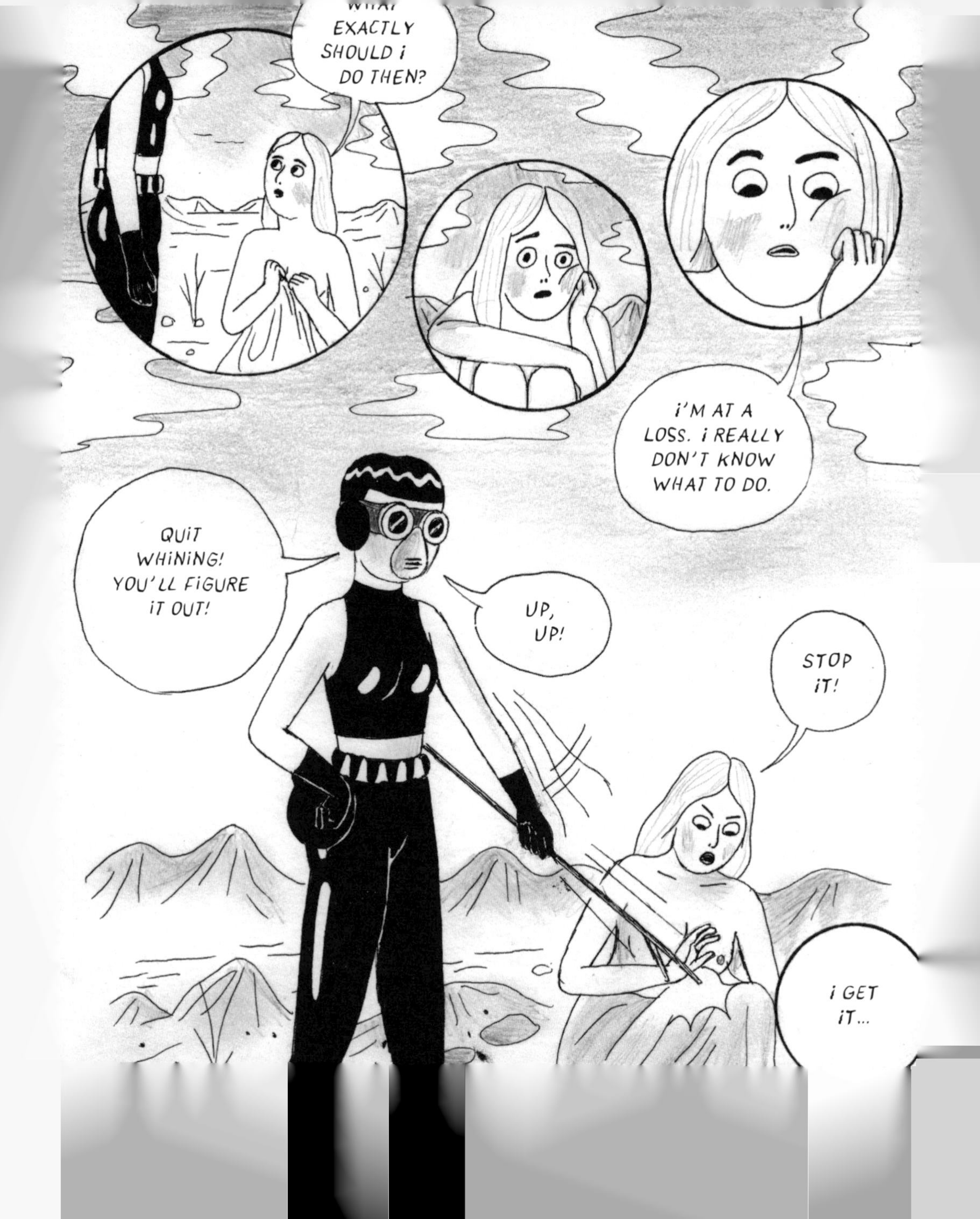
EXACTLY SHOULD i DO THEN?
i'M AT A LOSS. i REALLY DON'T KNOW WHAT TO DO.
QUIT WHiNiNG! YOU'LL FiGURE iT OUT!
UP, UP!
STOP iT!
i GET iT...

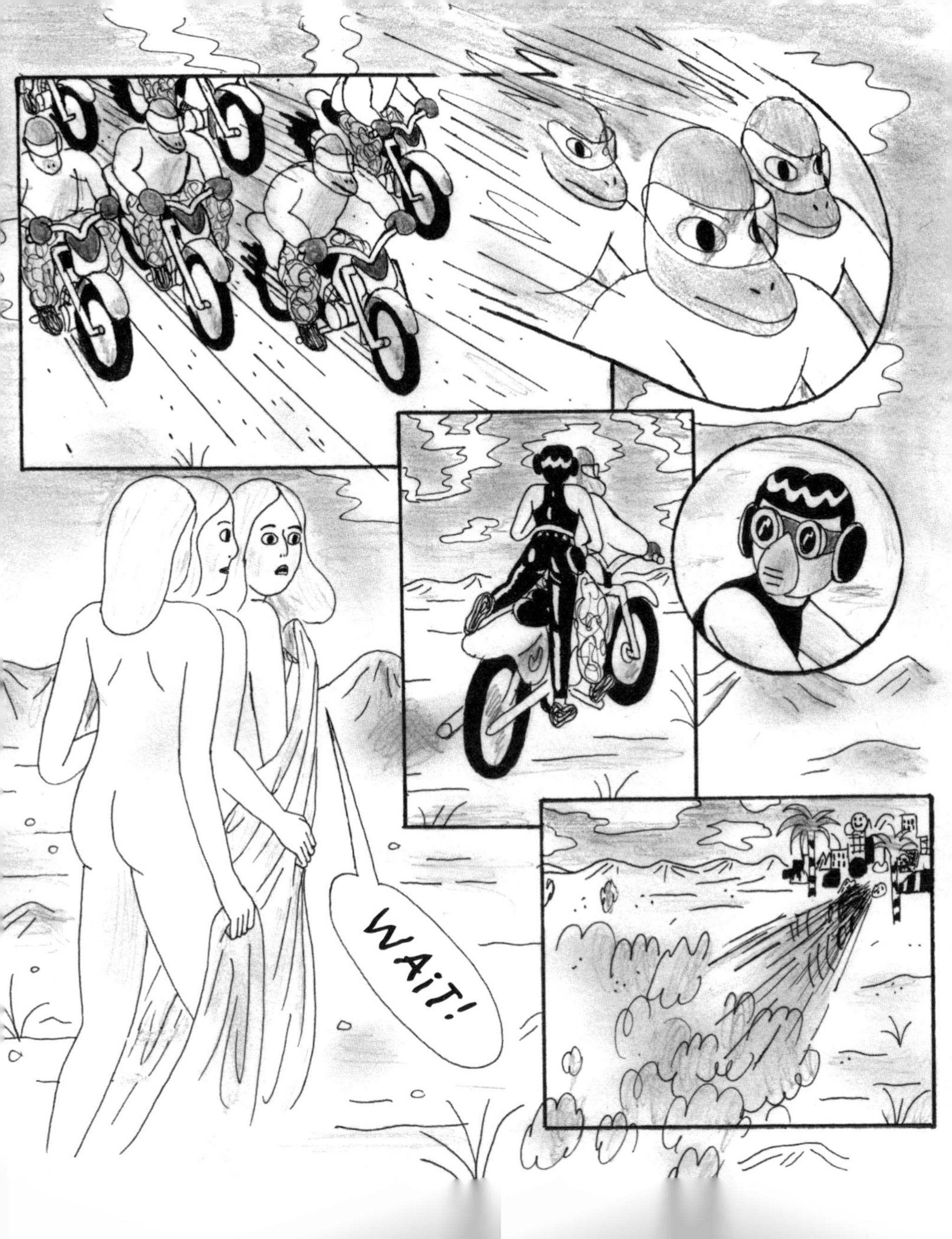
WAIT!

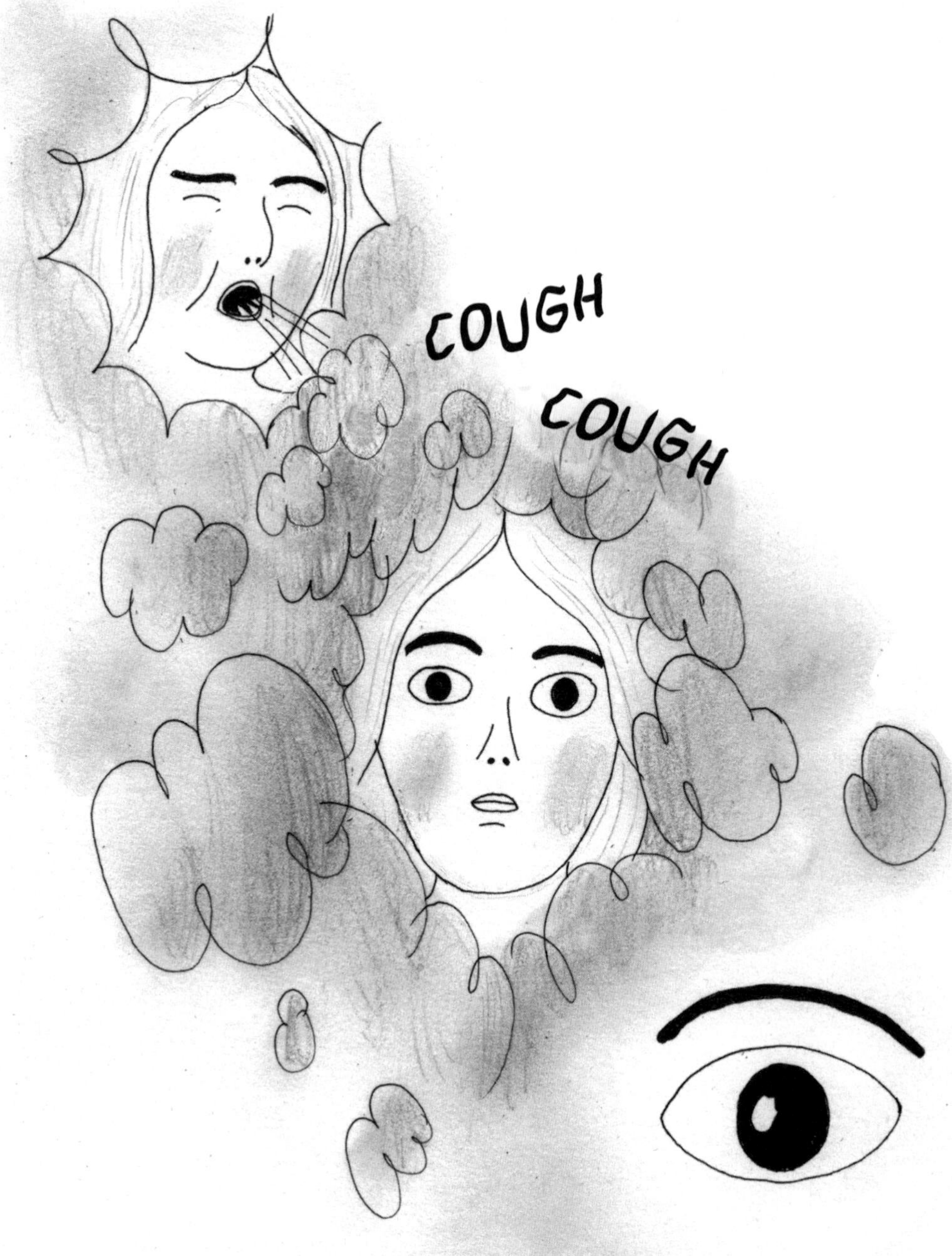
COUGH
COUGH

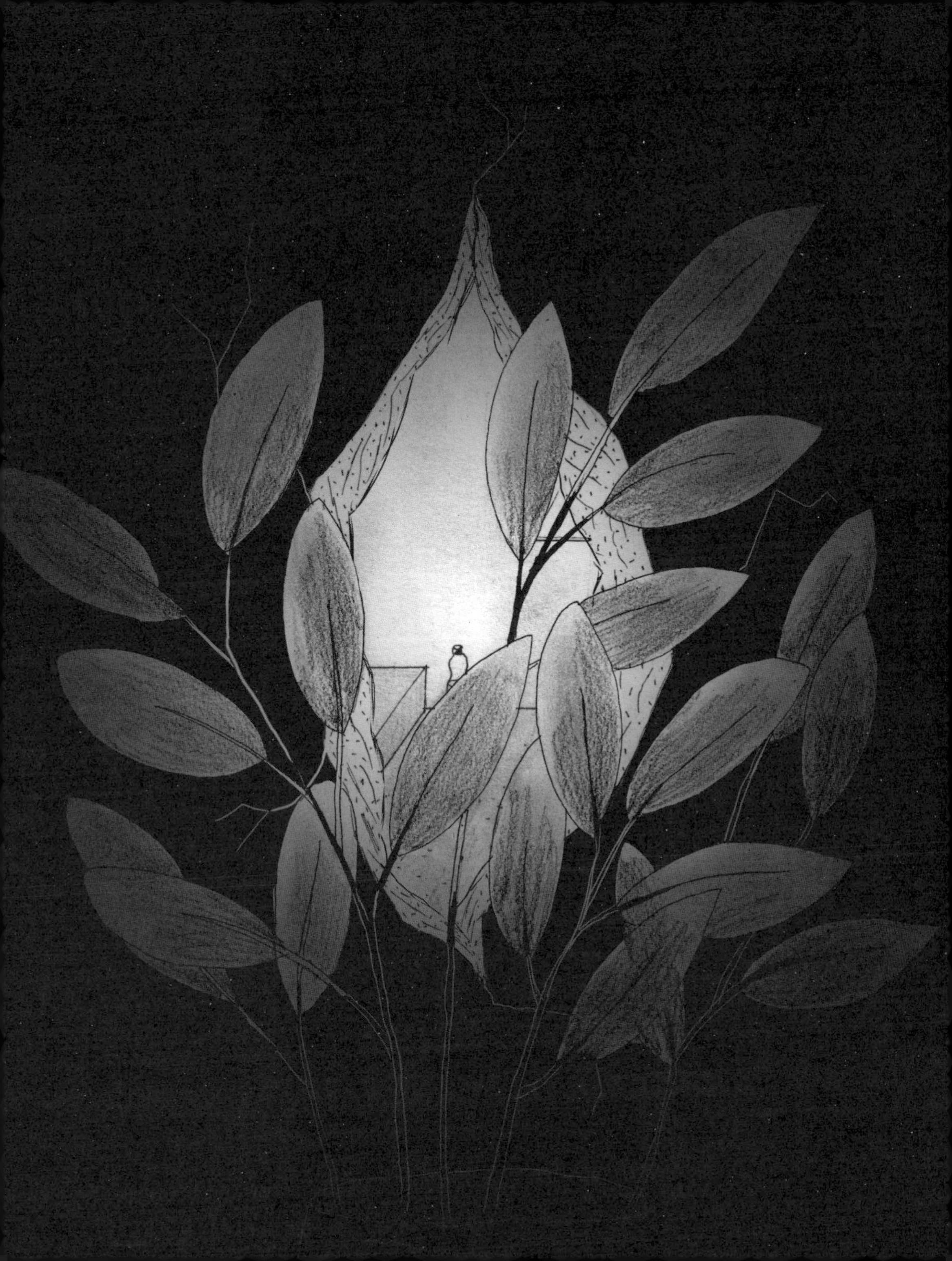

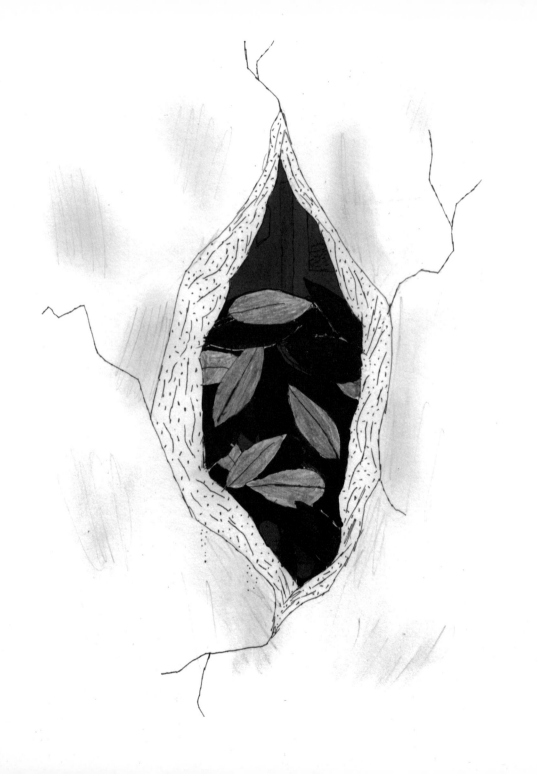

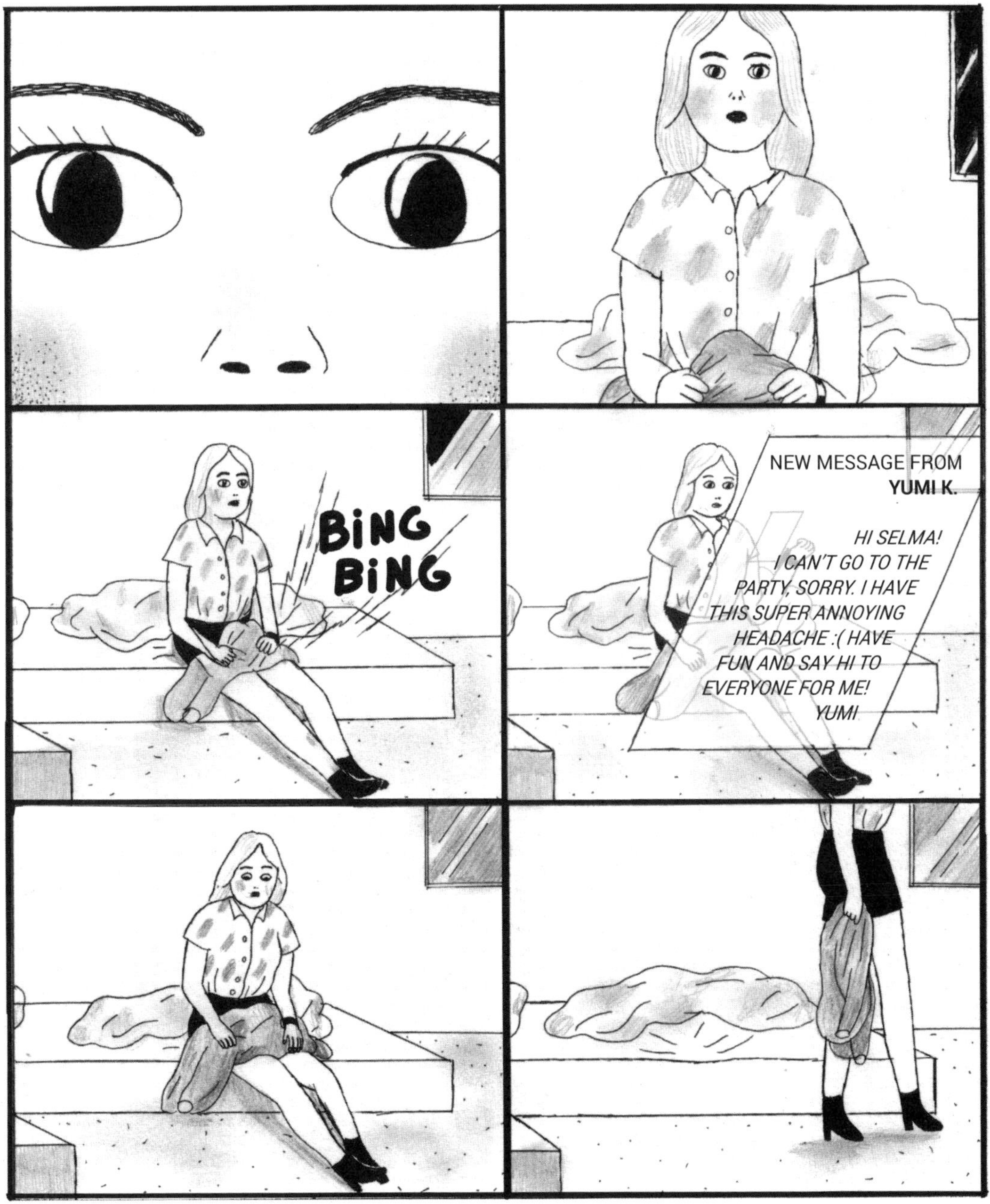
BING
BING
NEW MESSAGE FROM
YUMI K.
HI SELMA! I CAN'T GO TO THE PARTY, SORRY. I HAVE THIS SUPER ANNOYING HEADACHE :(HAVE FUN AND SAY HI TO EVERYONE FOR ME! YUMI

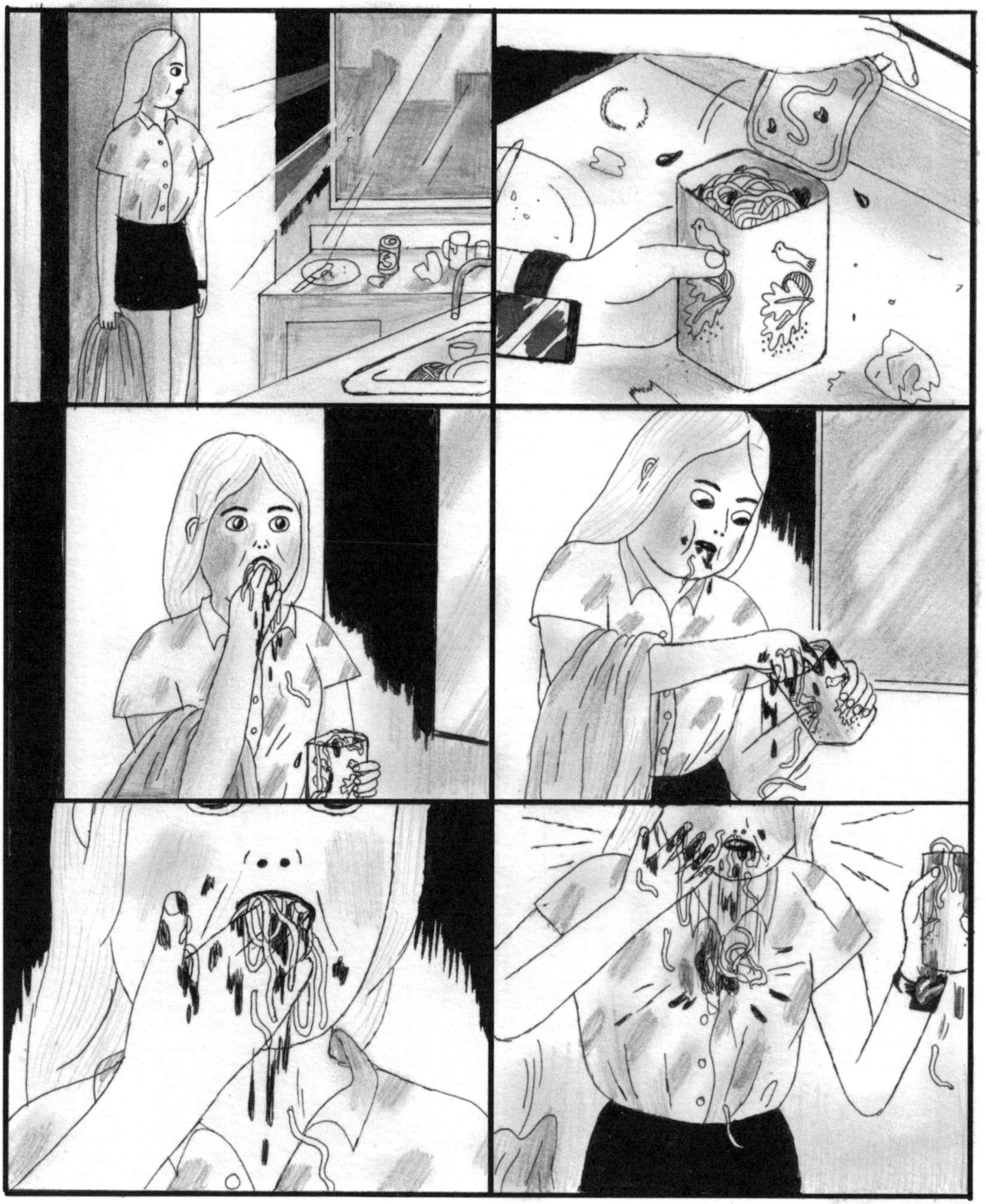

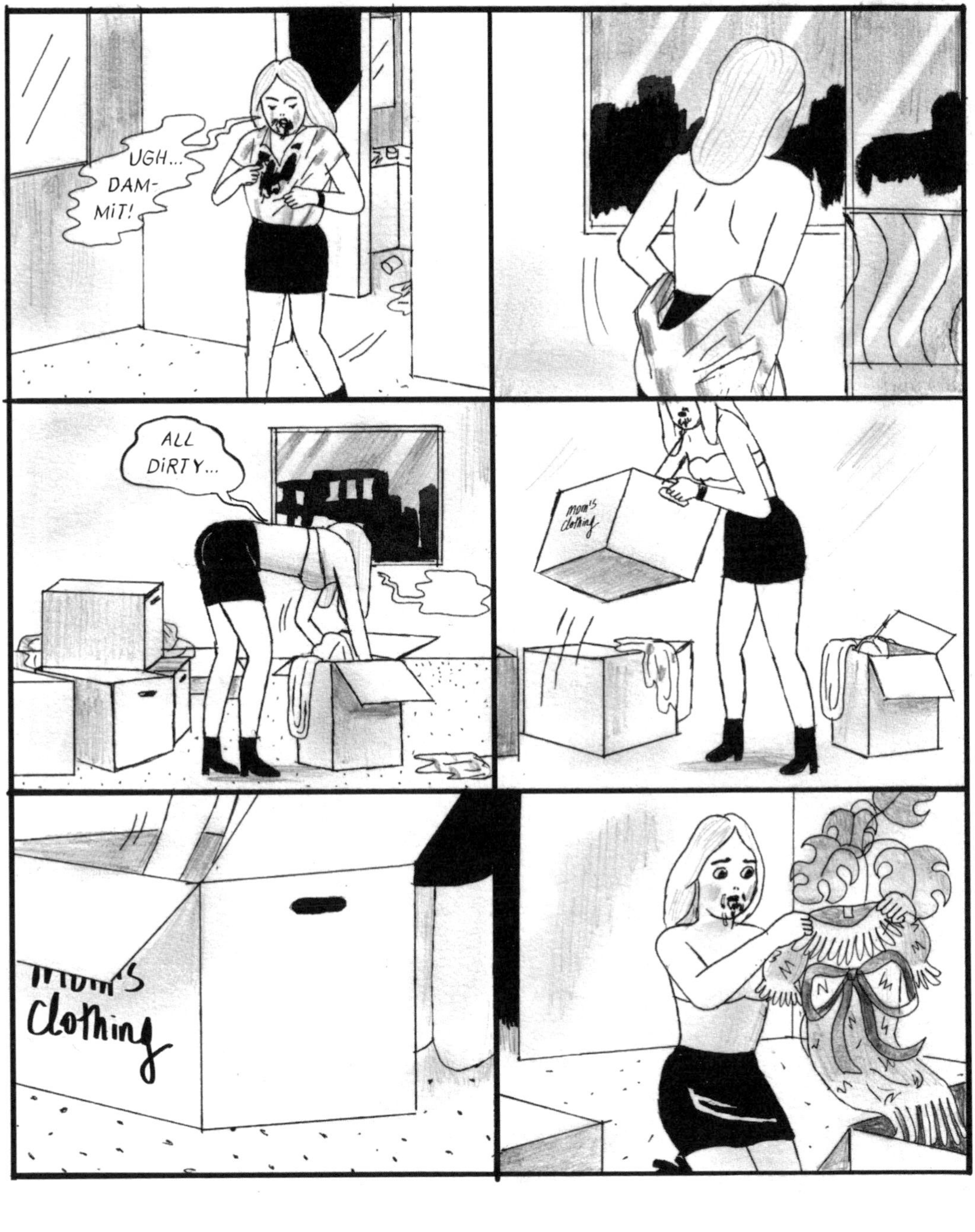
UGH... DAM-MIT!
ALL DIRTY...
Mom's Clothing
Mom's Clothing

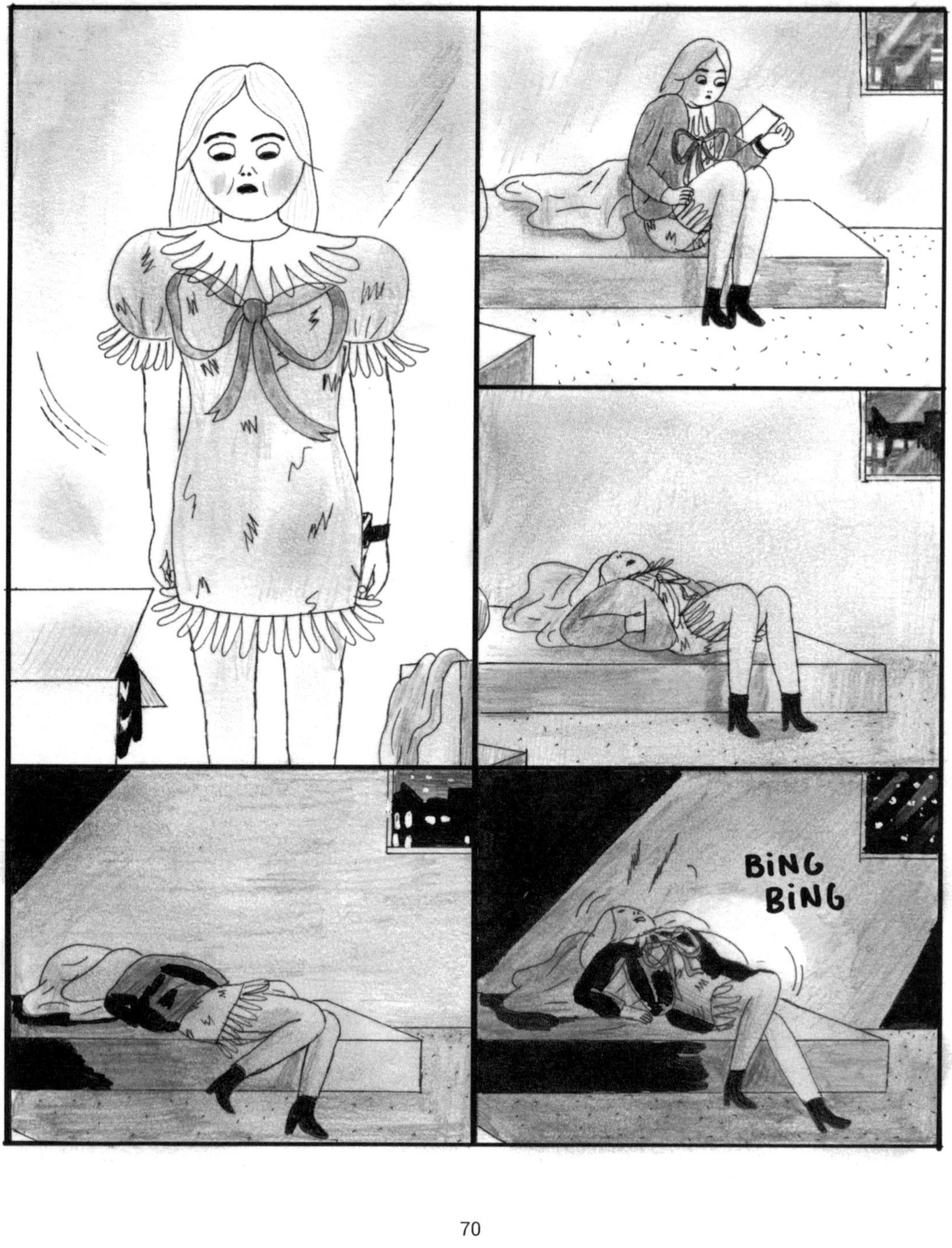
BiNG
BiNG

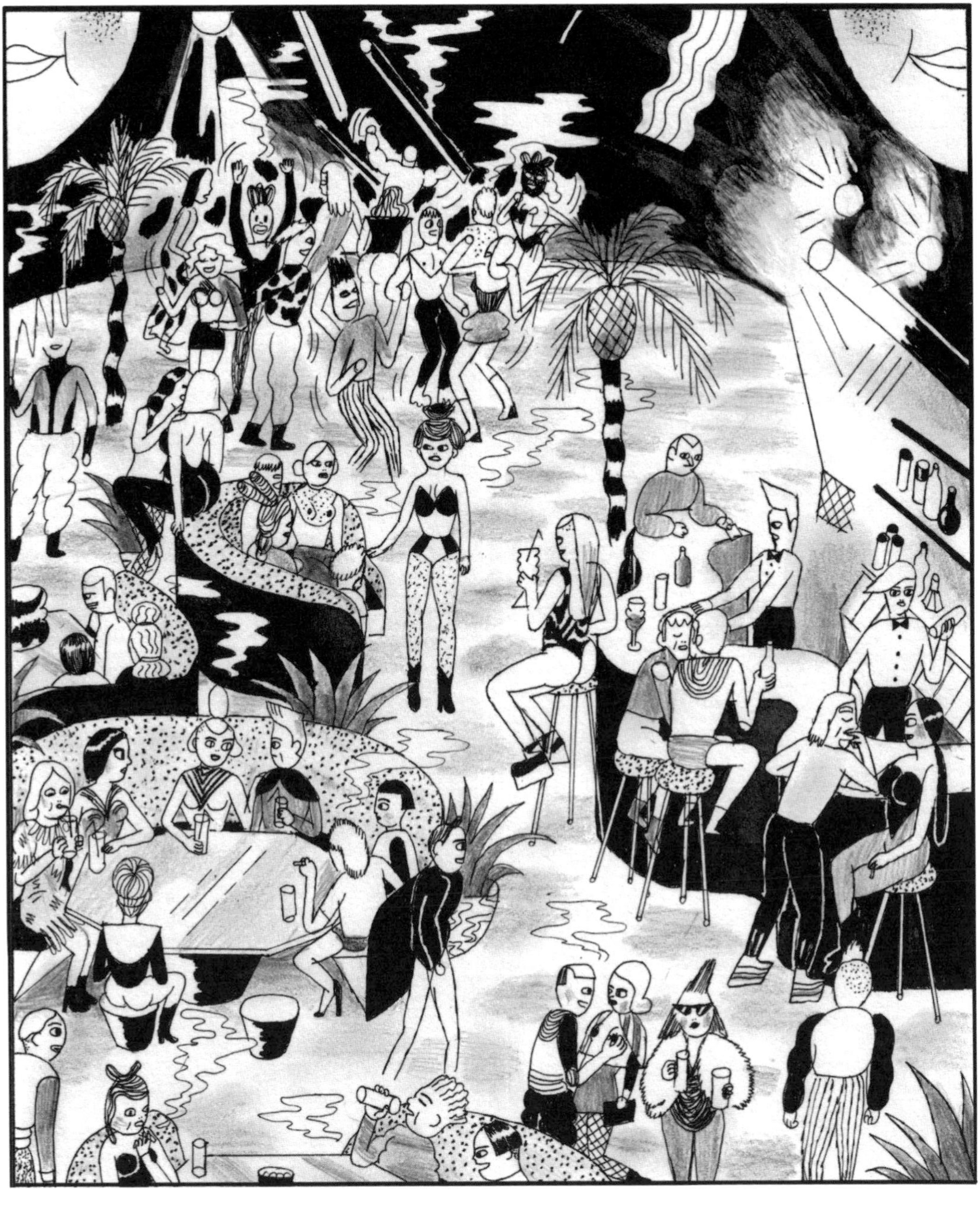

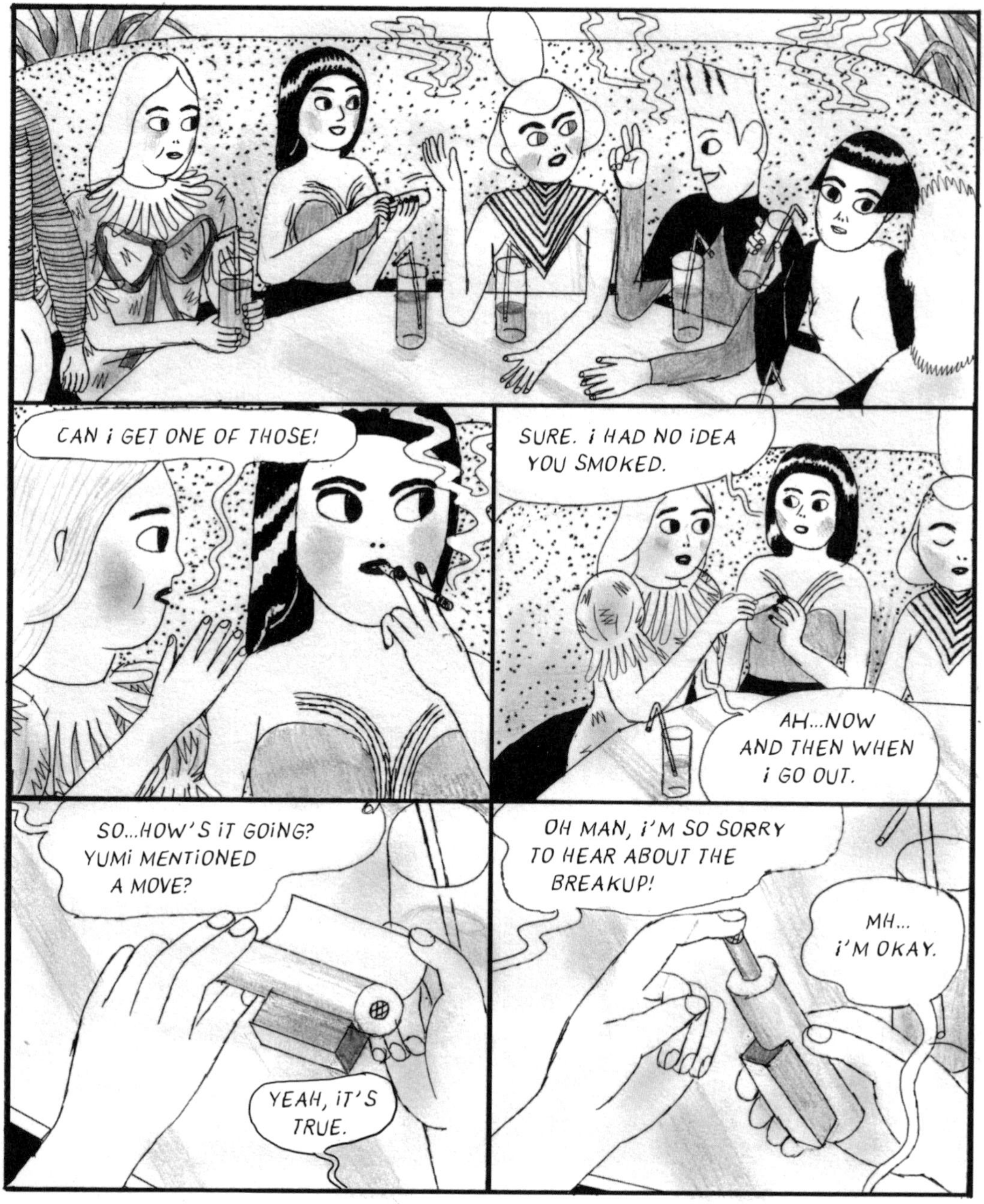

CAN i GET ONE OF THOSE!
SURE. i HAD NO iDEA YOU SMOKED.
AH...NOW AND THEN WHEN i GO OUT.
SO...HOW'S iT GOiNG? YUMi MENTiONED A MOVE?
YEAH, iT'S TRUE.
OH MAN, i'M SO SORRY TO HEAR ABOUT THE BREAKUP!
MH... i'M OKAY.

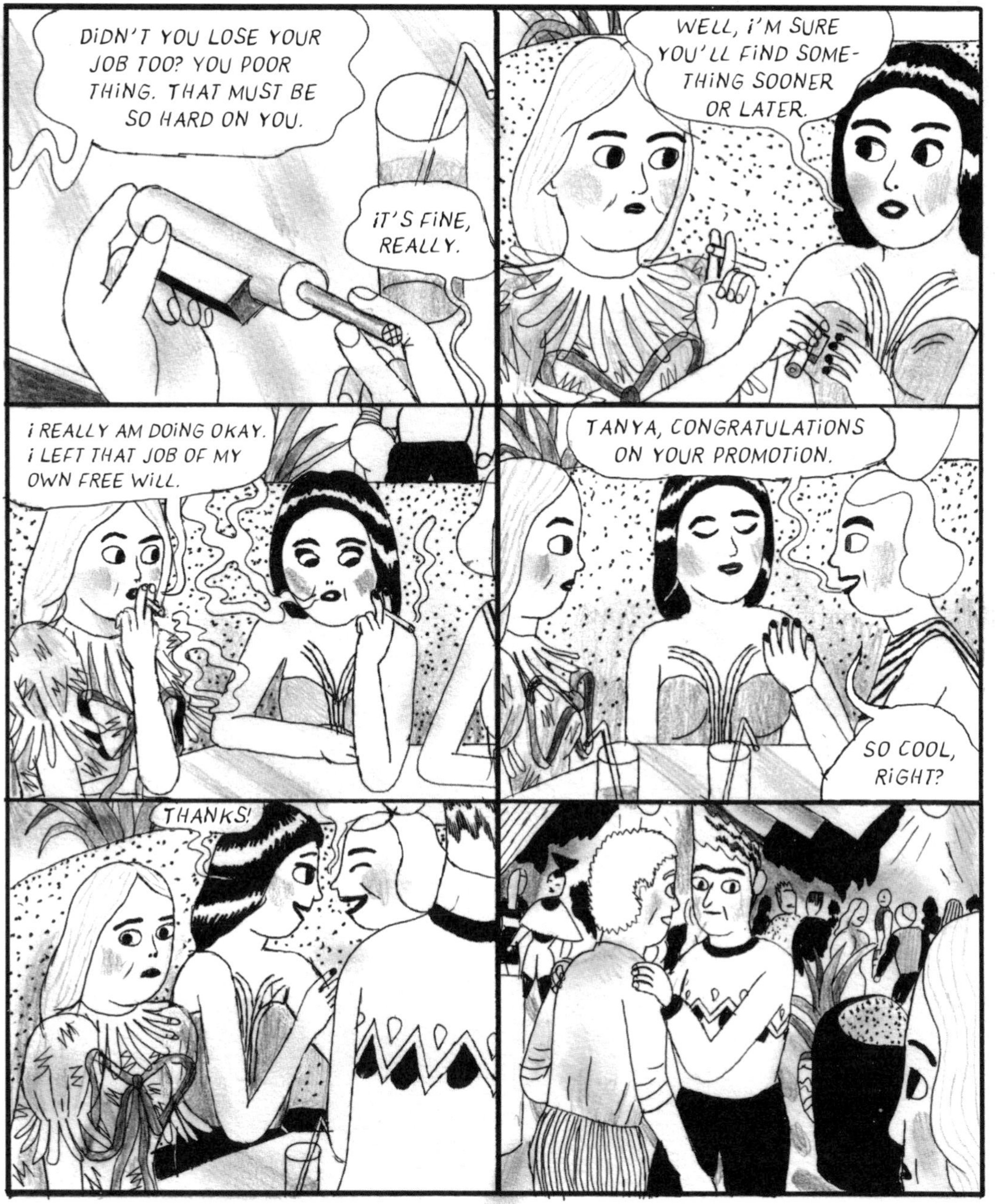
DIDN'T YOU LOSE YOUR JOB TOO? YOU POOR THING. THAT MUST BE SO HARD ON YOU.
IT'S FINE, REALLY.
WELL, I'M SURE YOU'LL FIND SOME-THING SOONER OR LATER.
I REALLY AM DOING OKAY. I LEFT THAT JOB OF MY OWN FREE WILL.
TANYA, CONGRATULATIONS ON YOUR PROMOTION.
SO COOL, RIGHT?
THANKS!

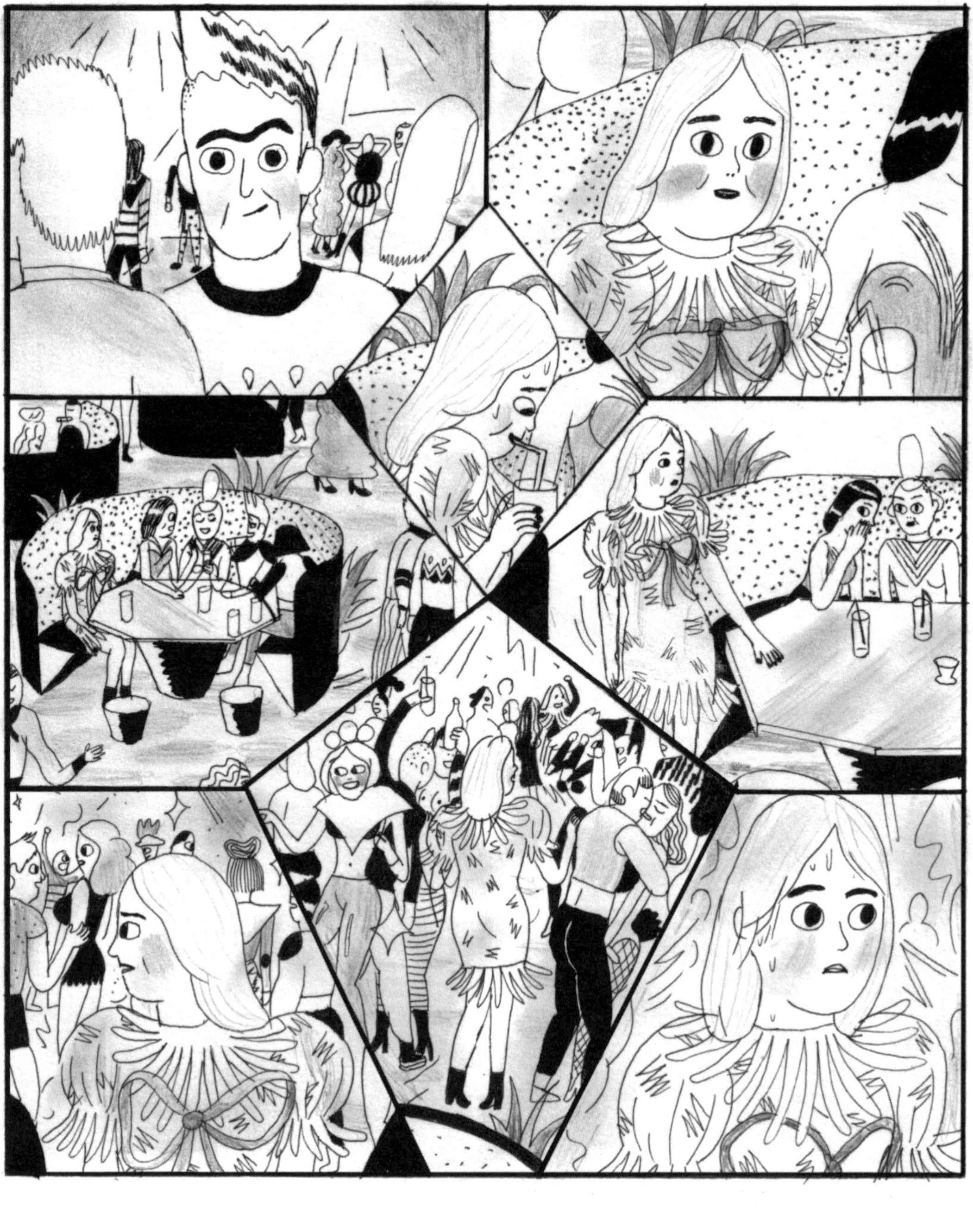

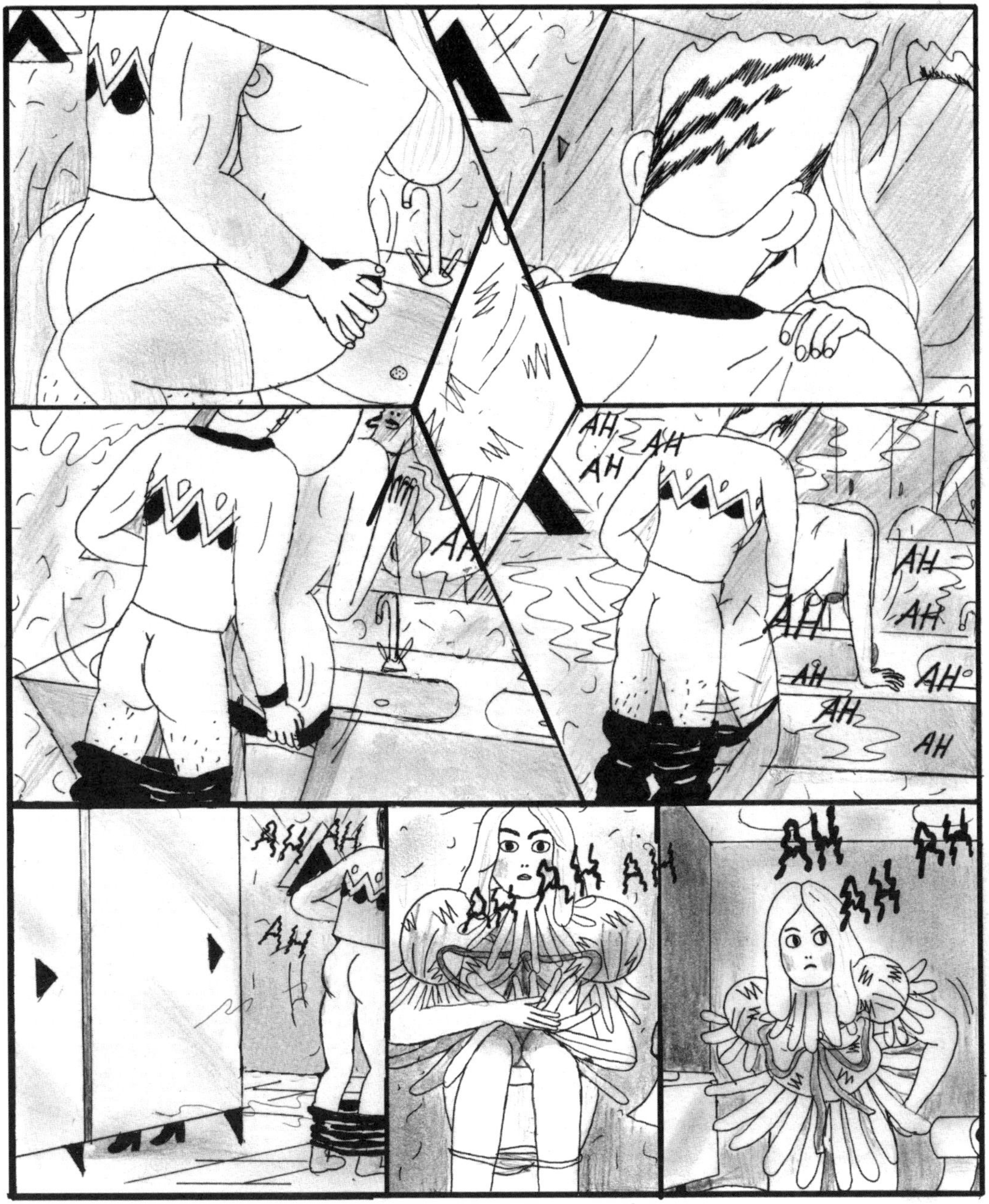
AH
AH
AH
AH
AH
AH
AH
AH
AH
AH
AH
AH
AH
AH
AH
AH
AH
AH
AH
AH

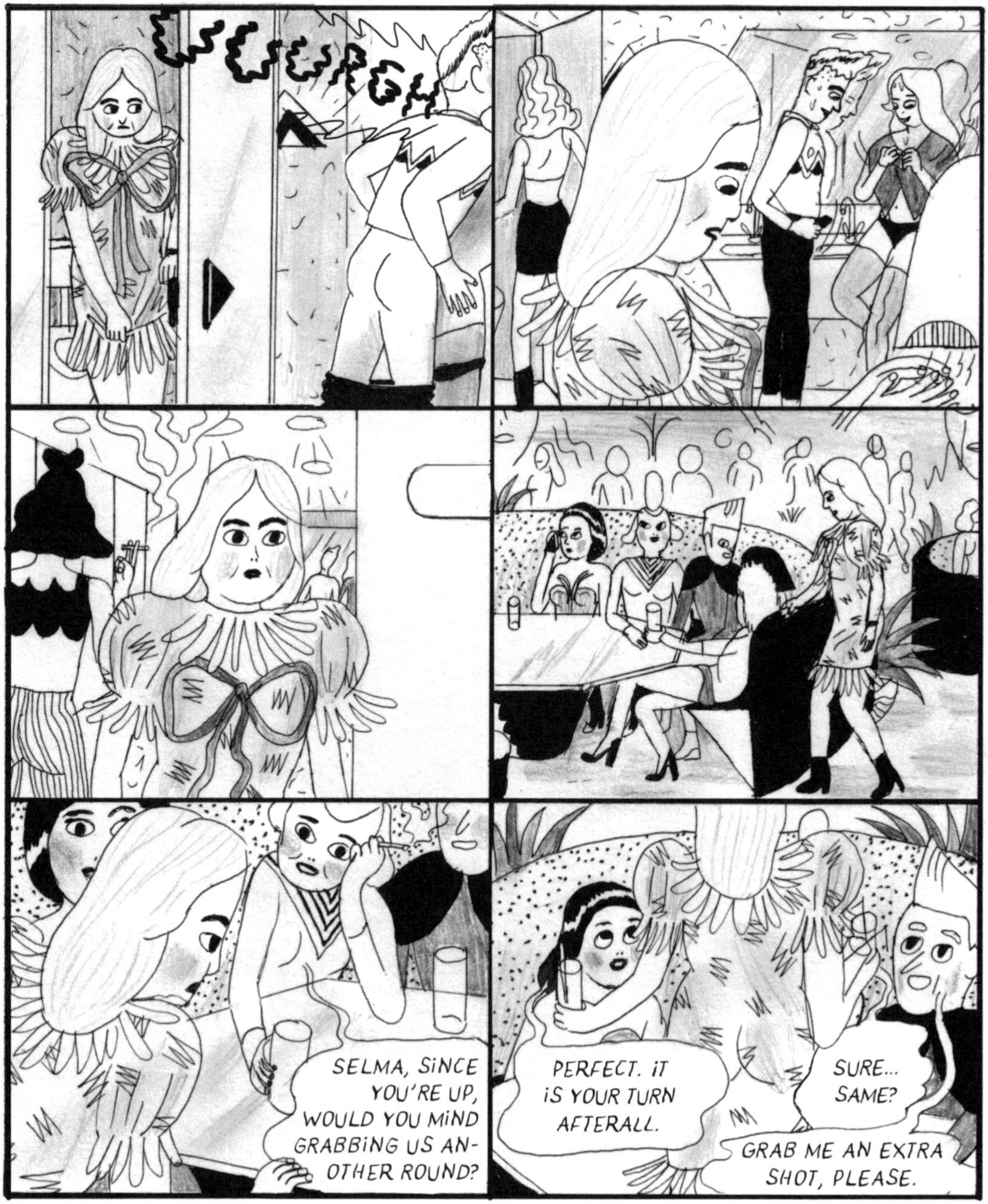
UGGRGH
SELMA, SINCE YOU'RE UP, WOULD YOU MIND GRABBING US AN-OTHER ROUND?
PERFECT. IT IS YOUR TURN AFTERALL.
SURE... SAME?
GRAB ME AN EXTRA SHOT, PLEASE.

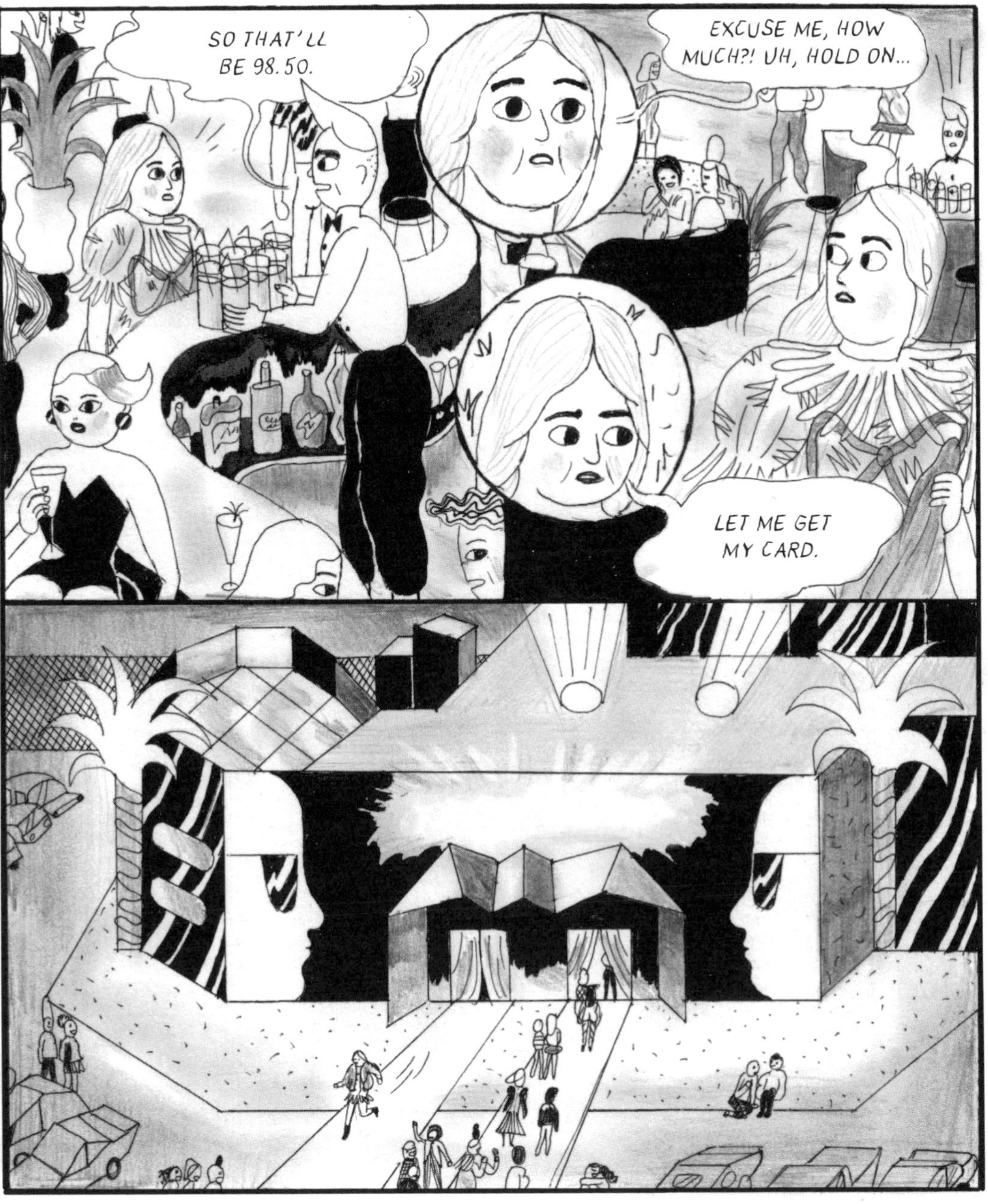
SO THAT'LL BE 98.50.
EXCUSE ME, HOW MUCH?! UH, HOLD ON...
LET ME GET MY CARD.

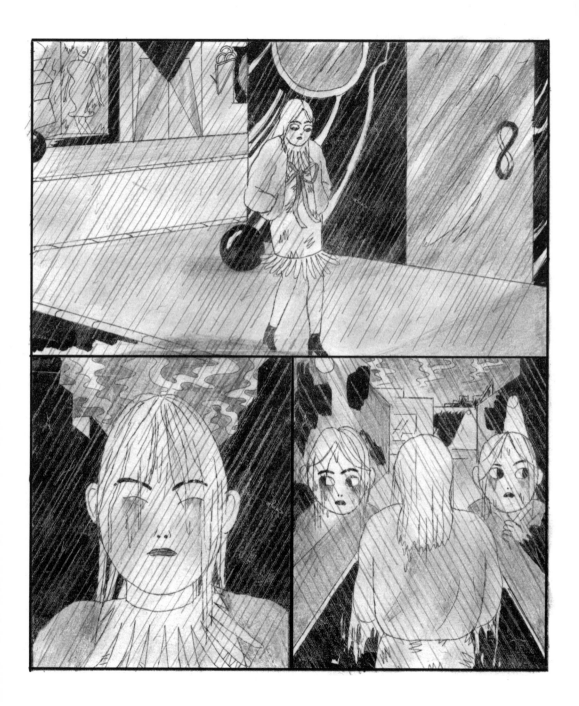

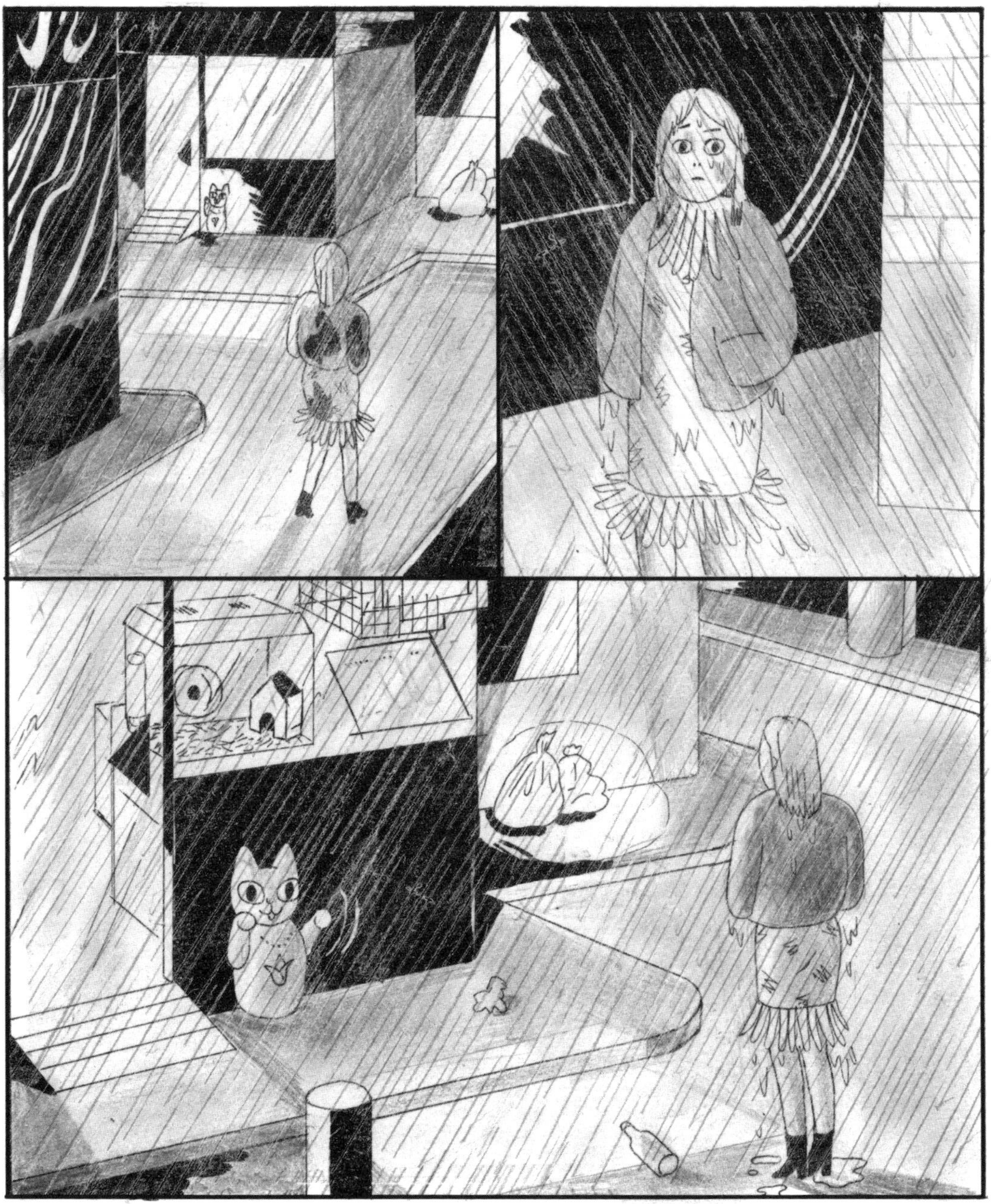

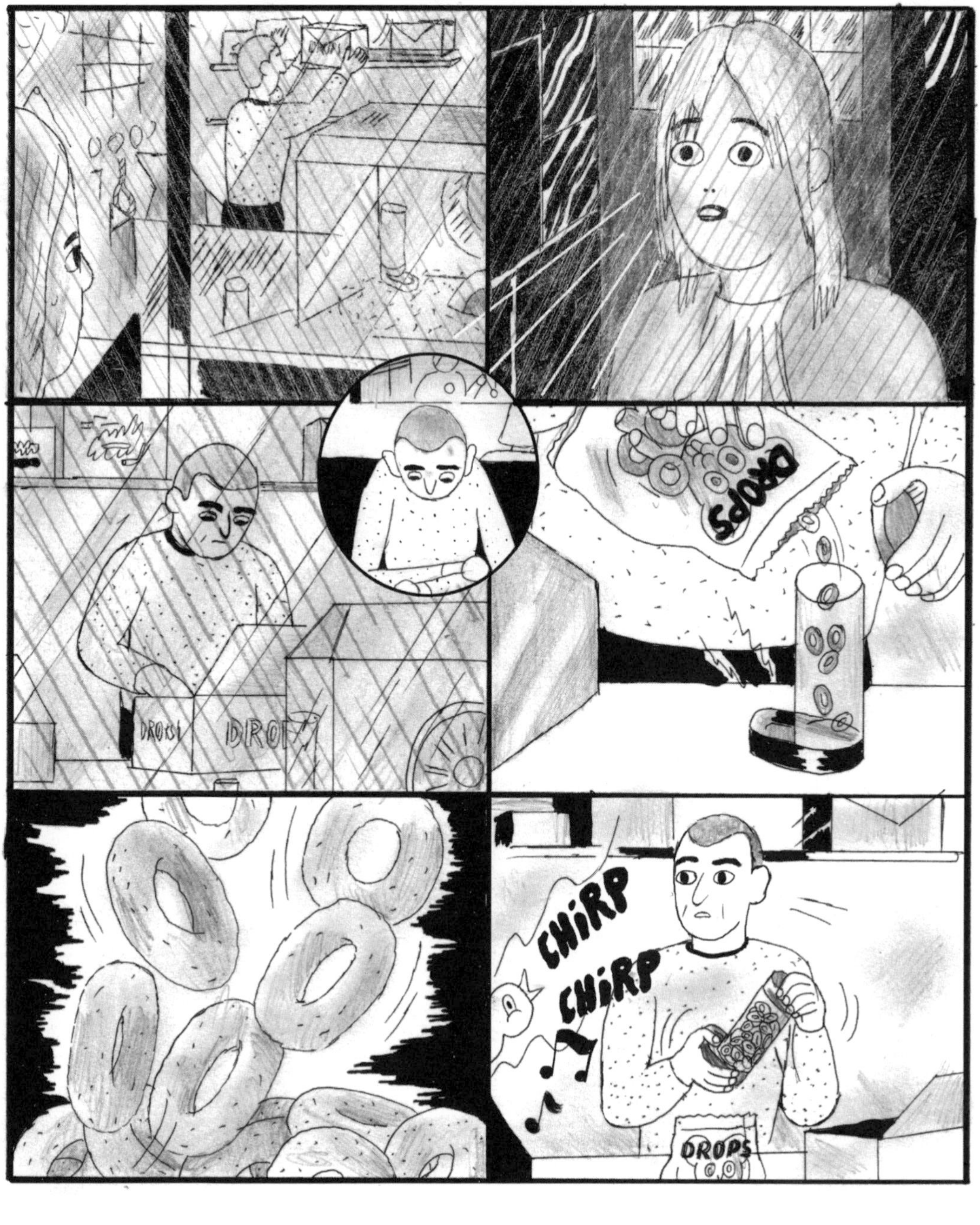
DROPS
DROPS
CHIRP
CHIRP
DROPS

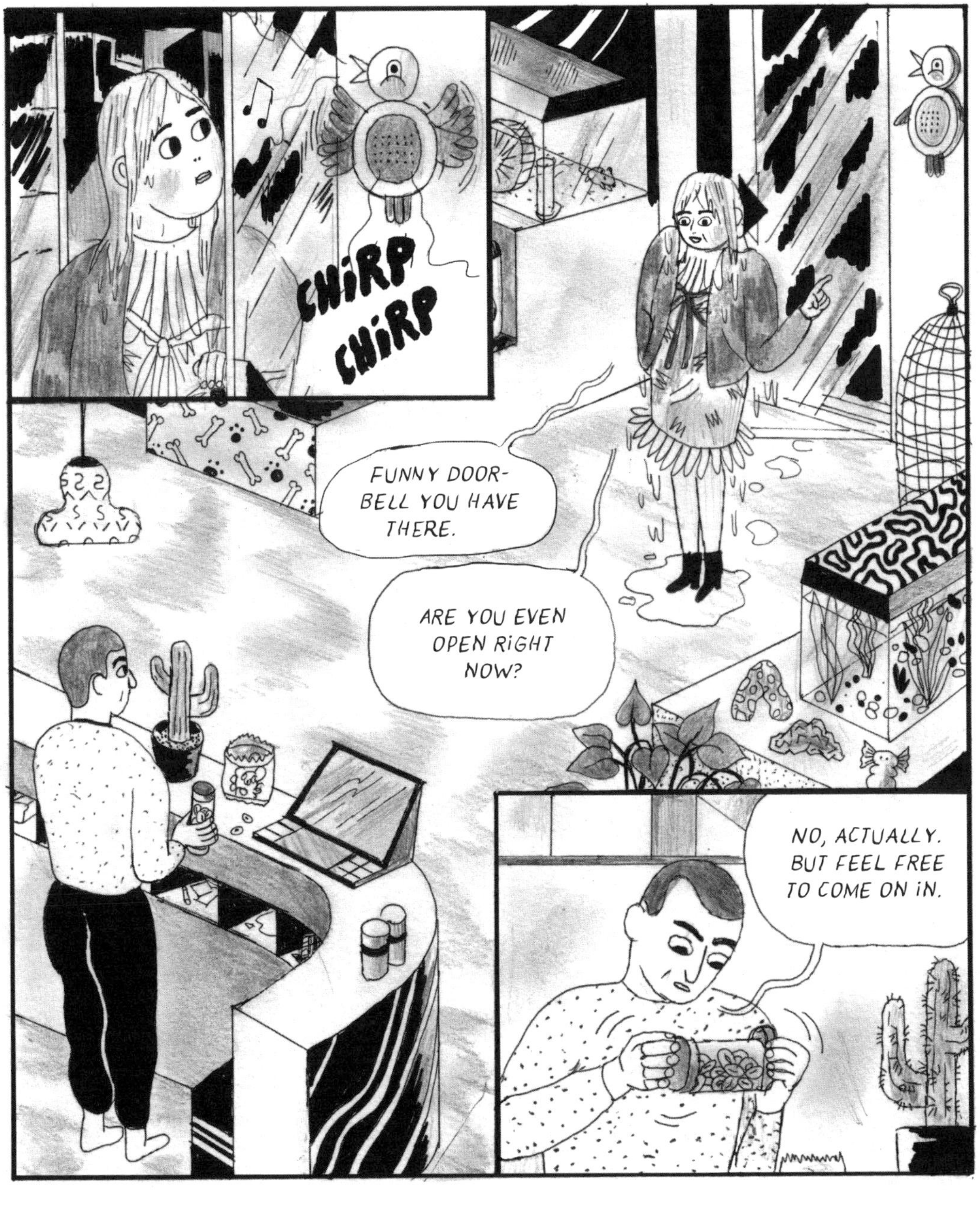
CHIRP CHIRP
FUNNY DOORBELL YOU HAVE THERE.
ARE YOU EVEN OPEN RIGHT NOW?
NO, ACTUALLY. BUT FEEL FREE TO COME ON IN.

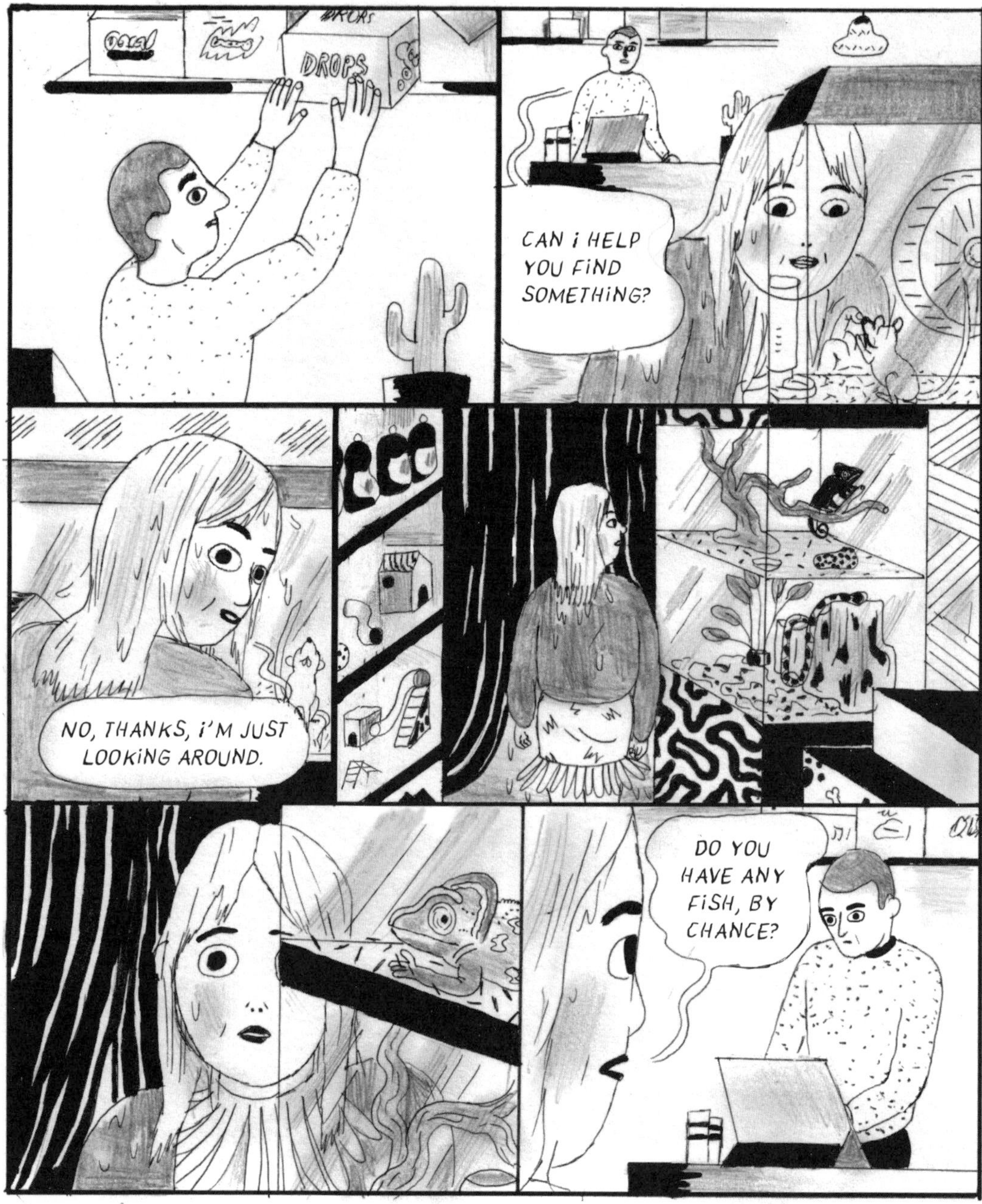
CAN I HELP YOU FIND SOMETHING?
NO, THANKS, I'M JUST LOOKING AROUND.
DO YOU HAVE ANY FISH, BY CHANCE?

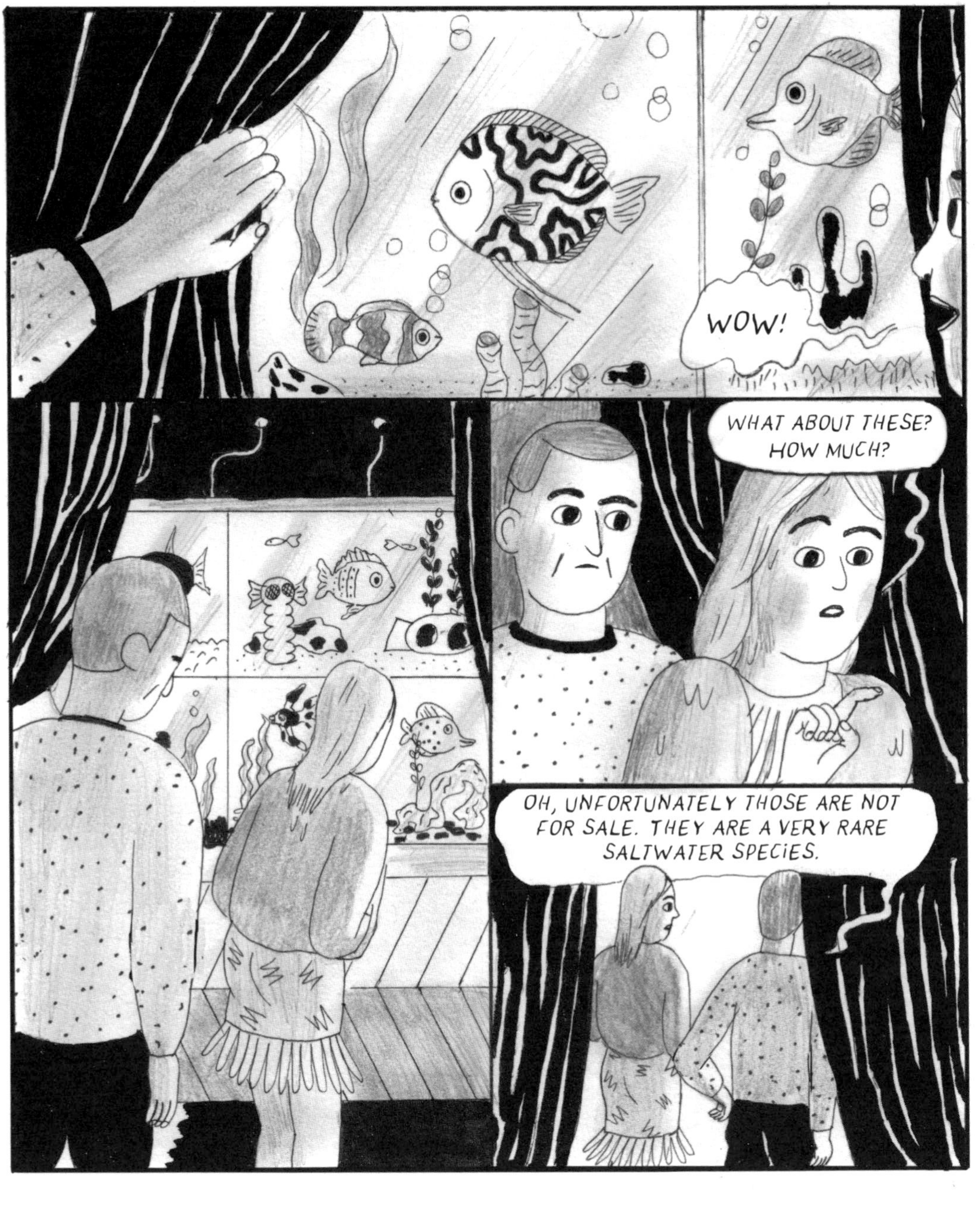
WOW!
WHAT ABOUT THESE? HOW MUCH?
OH, UNFORTUNATELY THOSE ARE NOT FOR SALE. THEY ARE A VERY RARE SALTWATER SPECIES.

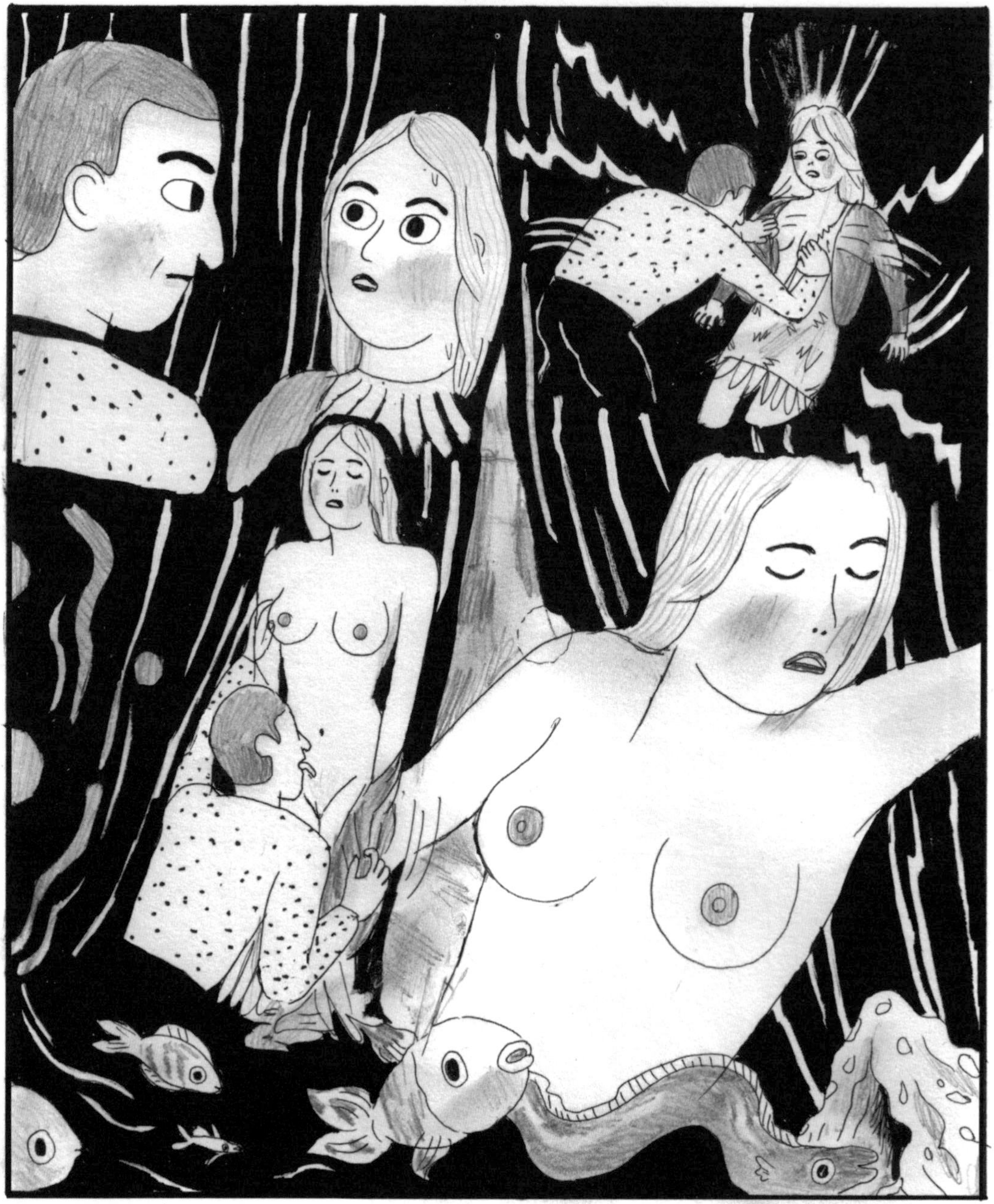

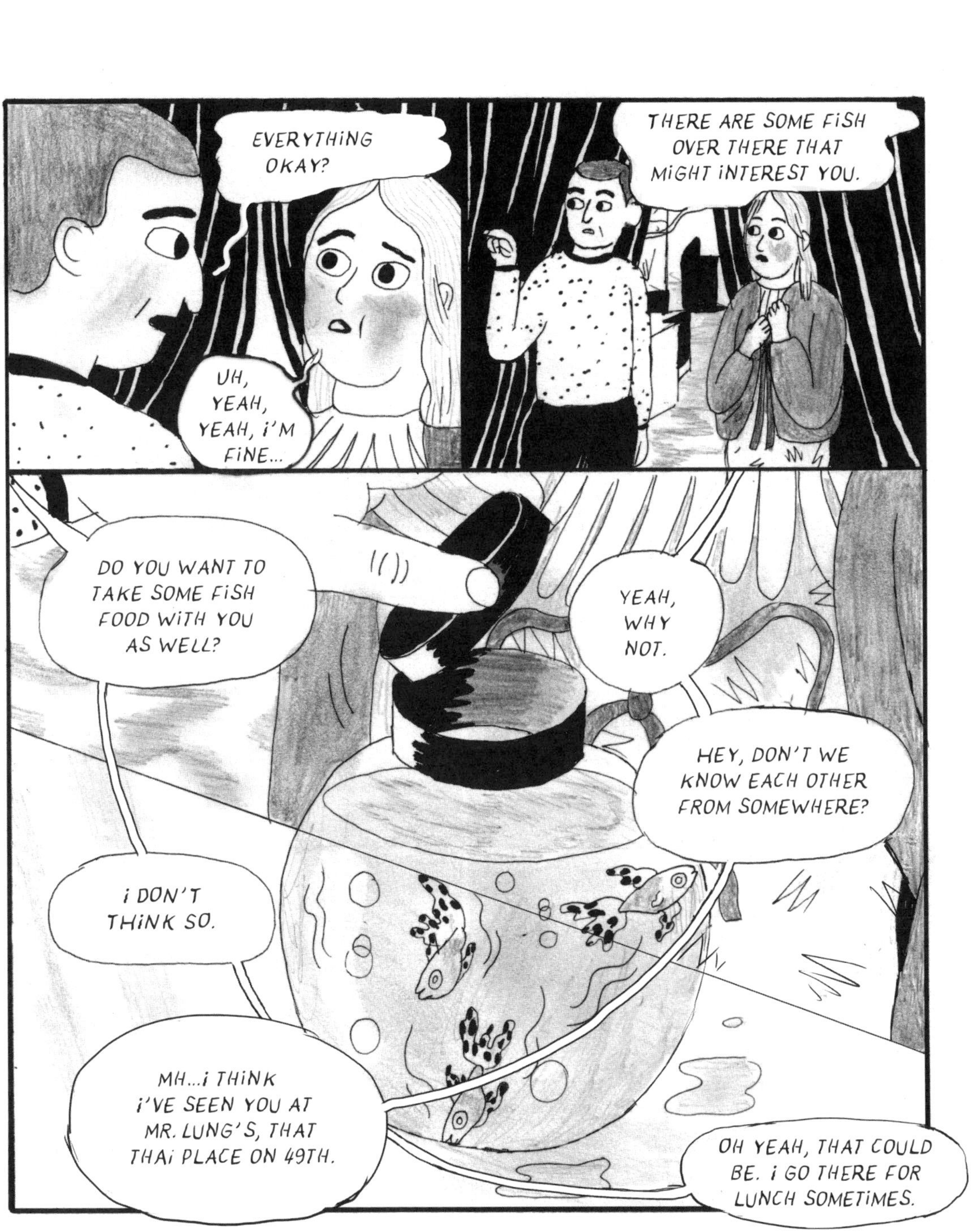
EVERYTHING OKAY?
UH, YEAH, YEAH, i'M FiNE...
THERE ARE SOME FiSH OVER THERE THAT MiGHT iNTEREST YOU.
DO YOU WANT TO TAKE SOME FiSH FOOD WiTH YOU AS WELL?
YEAH, WHY NOT.
HEY, DON'T WE KNOW EACH OTHER FROM SOMEWHERE?
i DON'T THiNK SO.
MH...i THiNK i'VE SEEN YOU AT MR. LUNG'S, THAT THAi PLACE ON 49TH.
OH YEAH, THAT COULD BE. i GO THERE FOR LUNCH SOMETiMES.

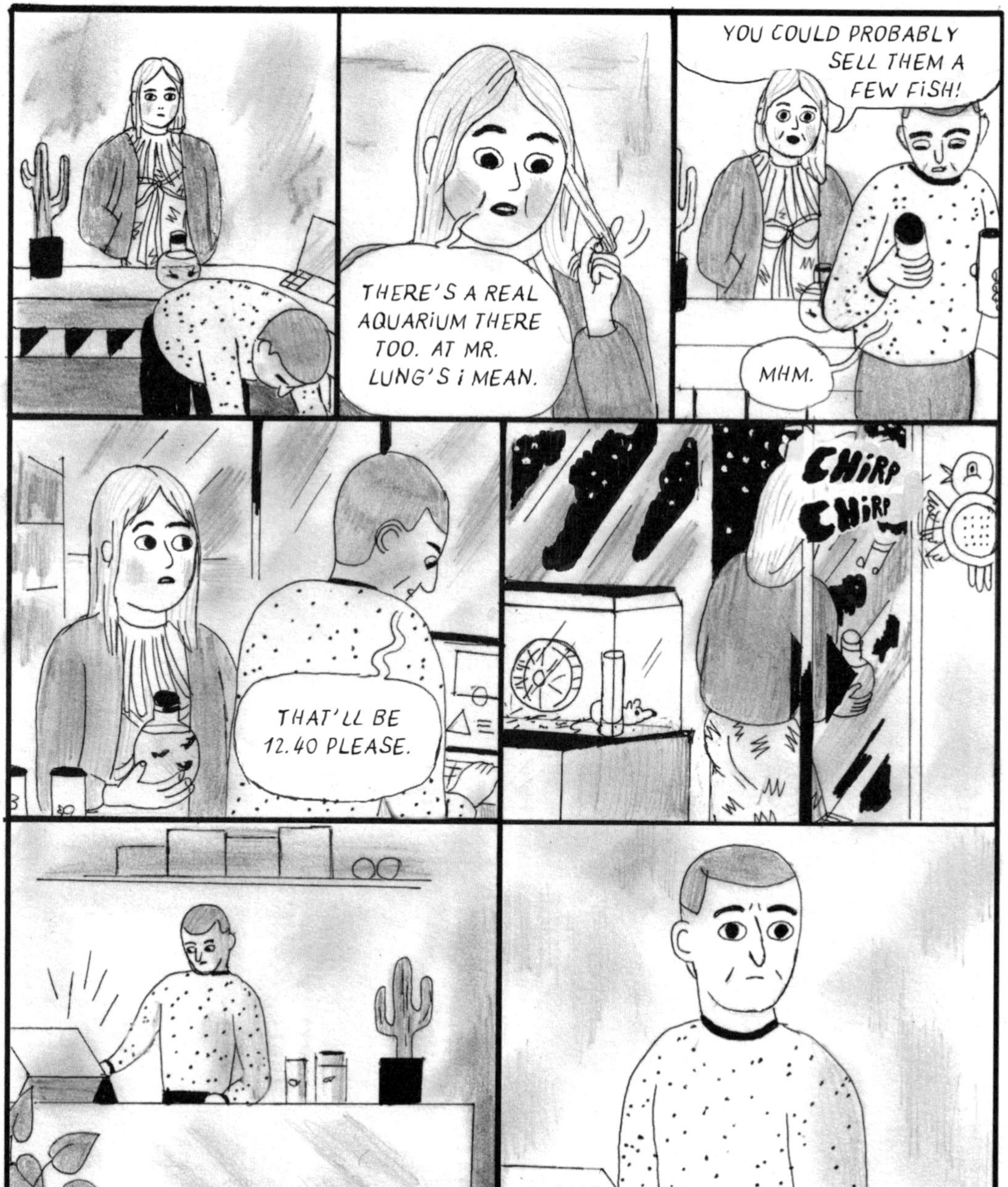
THERE'S A REAL AQUARIUM THERE TOO. AT MR. LUNG'S I MEAN.
YOU COULD PROBABLY SELL THEM A FEW FISH!
MHM.
THAT'LL BE 12.40 PLEASE.
CHIRP
CHIRP

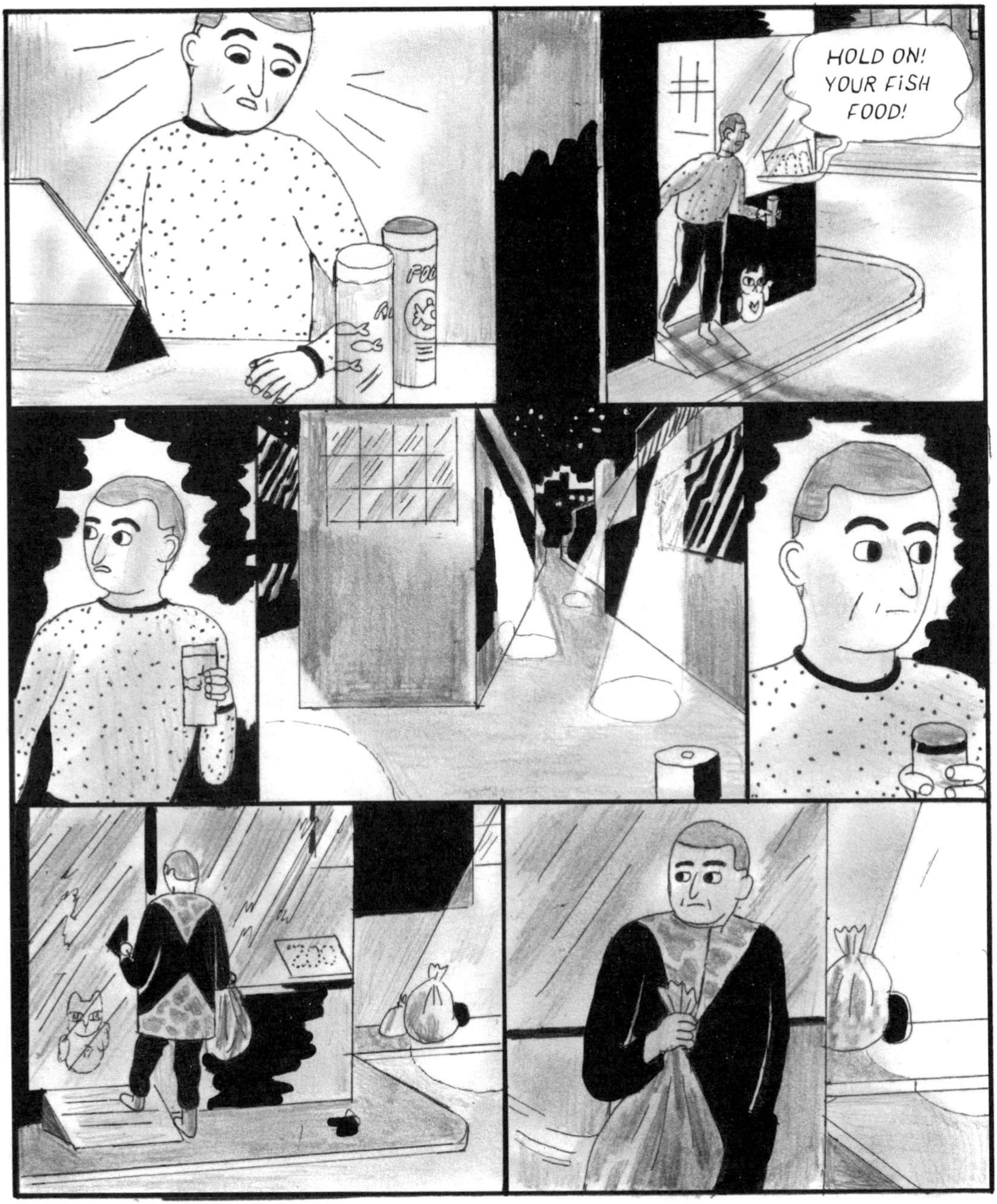
HOLD ON! YOUR FISH FOOD!

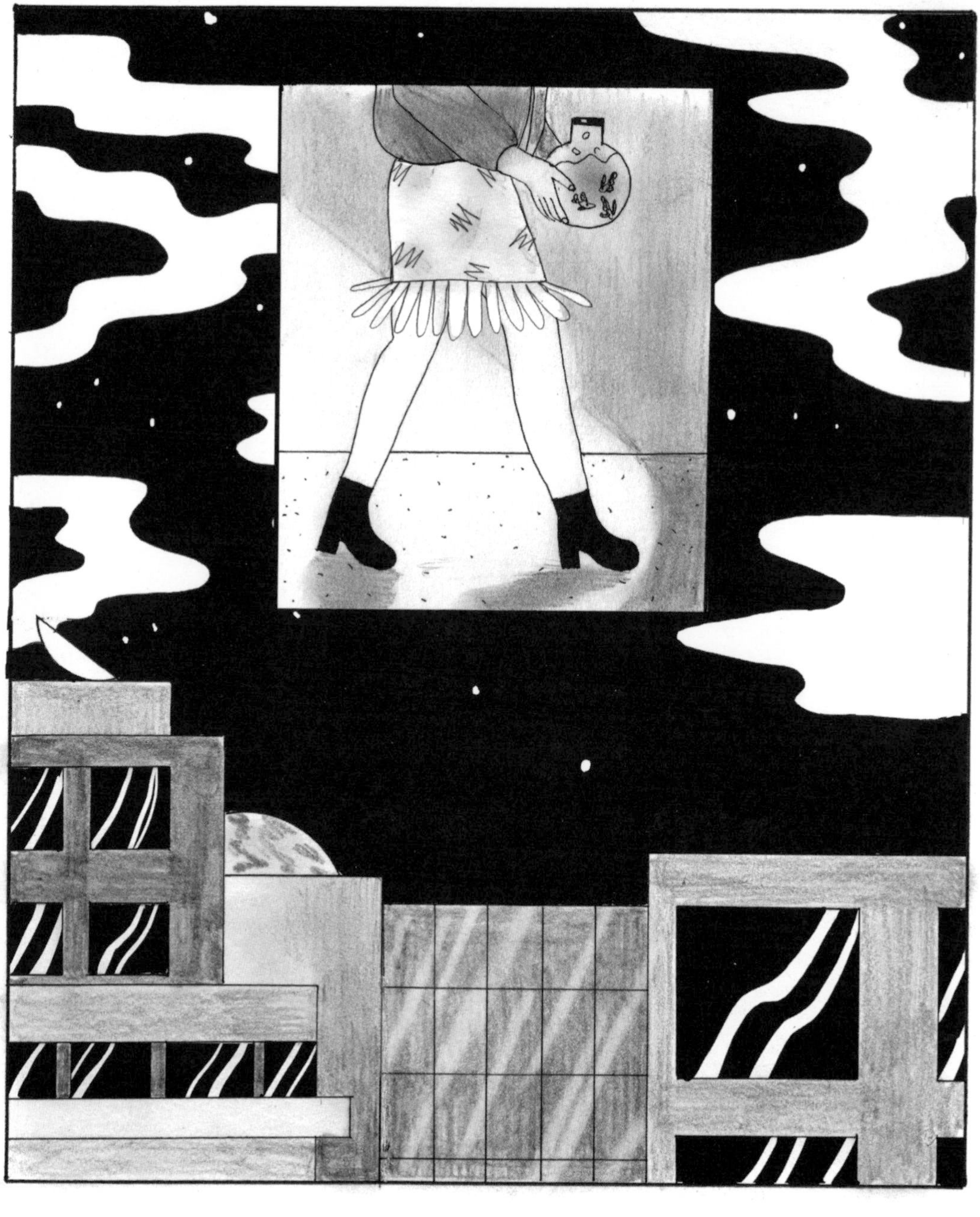

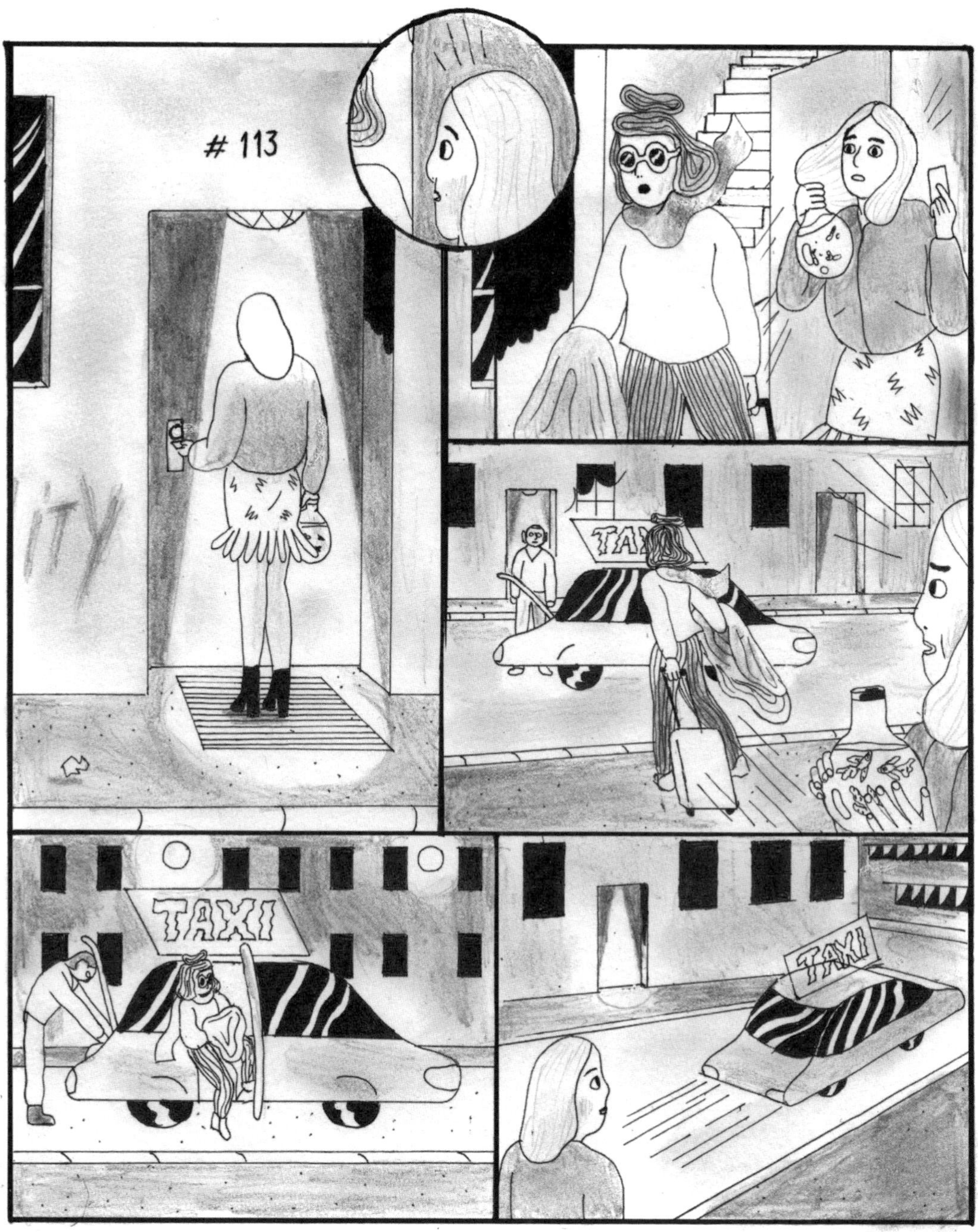

113
TAXI
TAXI
TAXI

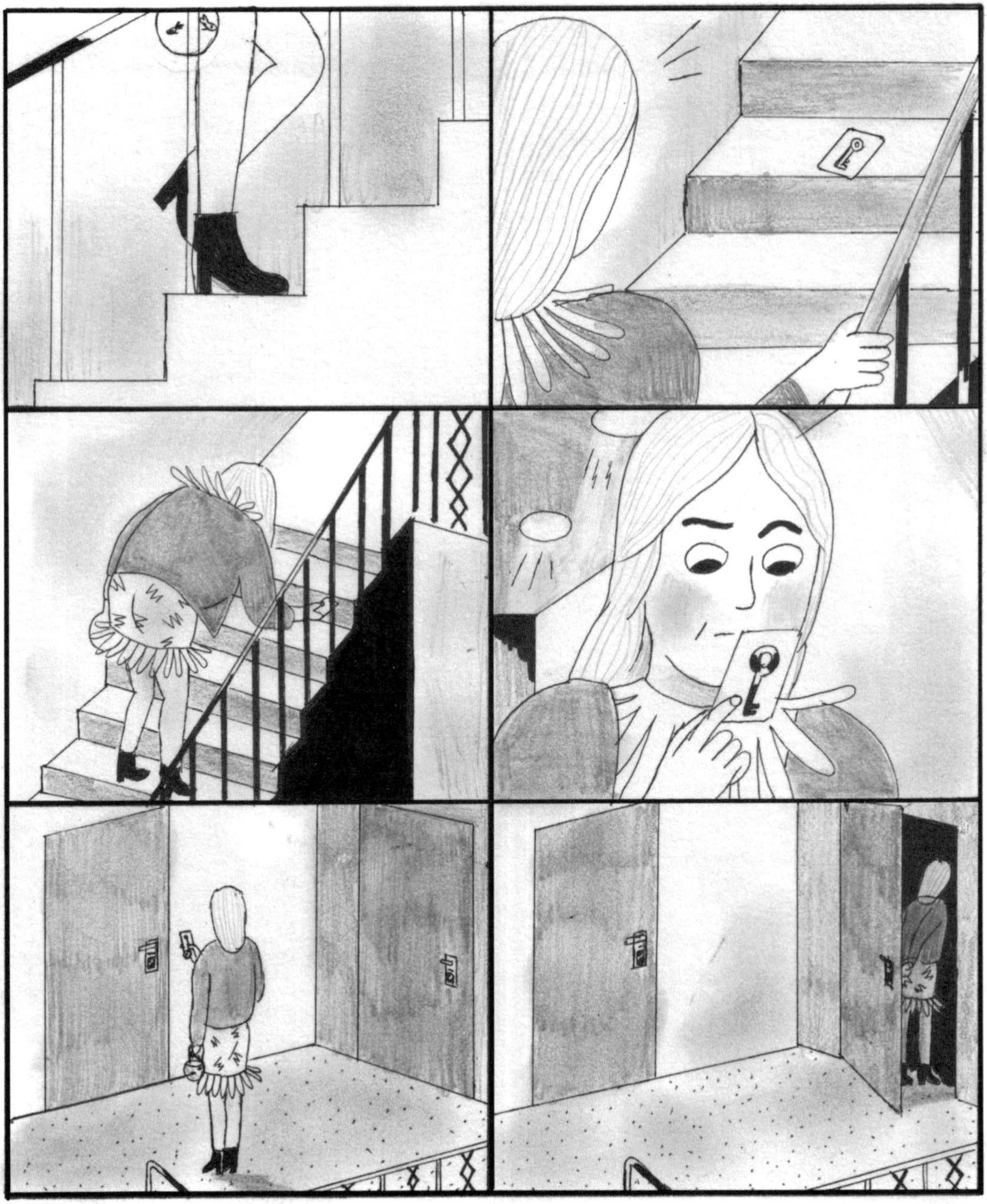

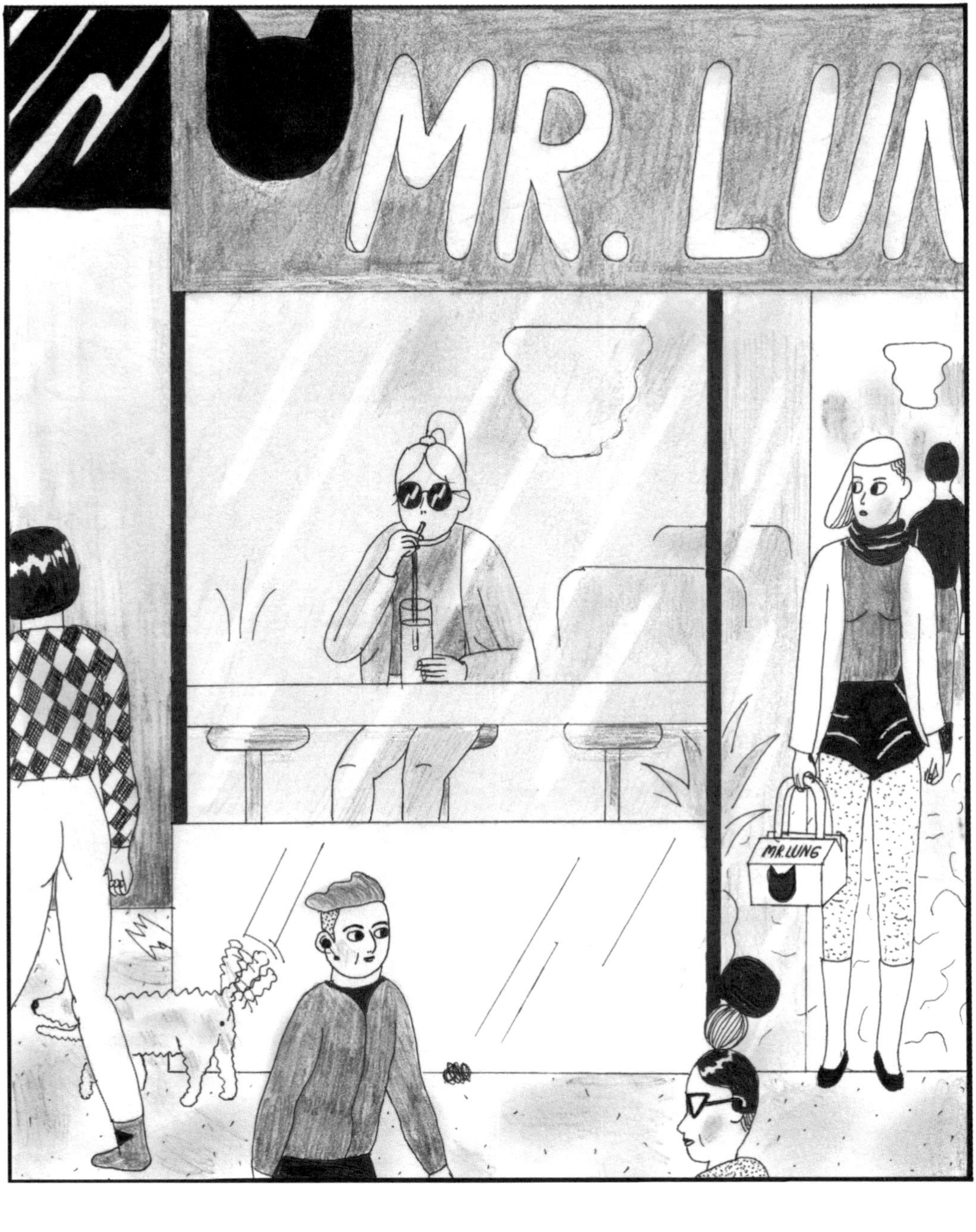
MR. LUN
MR.LUNG

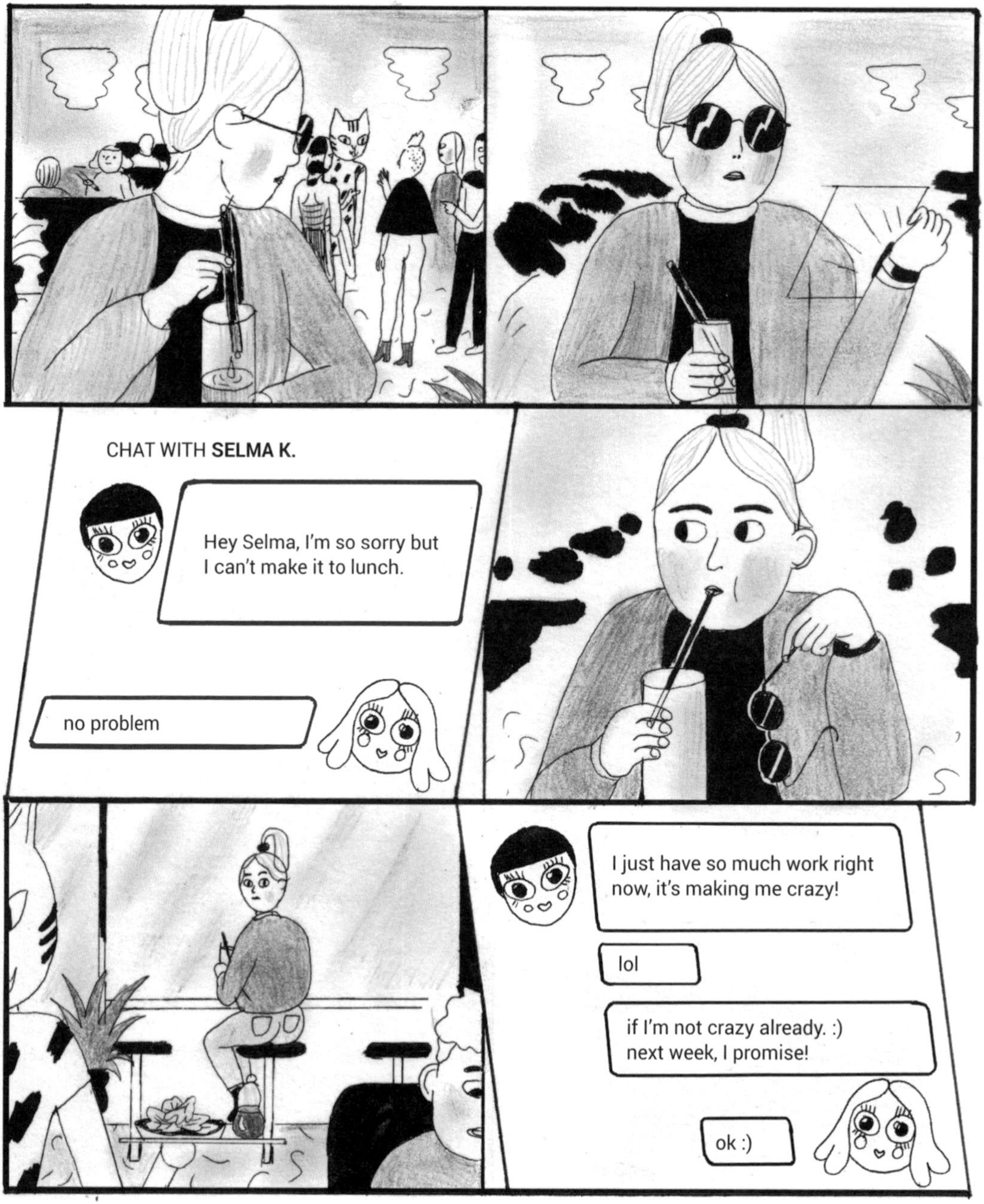
CHAT WITH SELMA K.
Hey Selma, I'm so sorry but I can't make it to lunch.
no problem
I just have so much work right now, it's making me crazy!
lol
if I'm not crazy already. :) next week, I promise!
ok :)

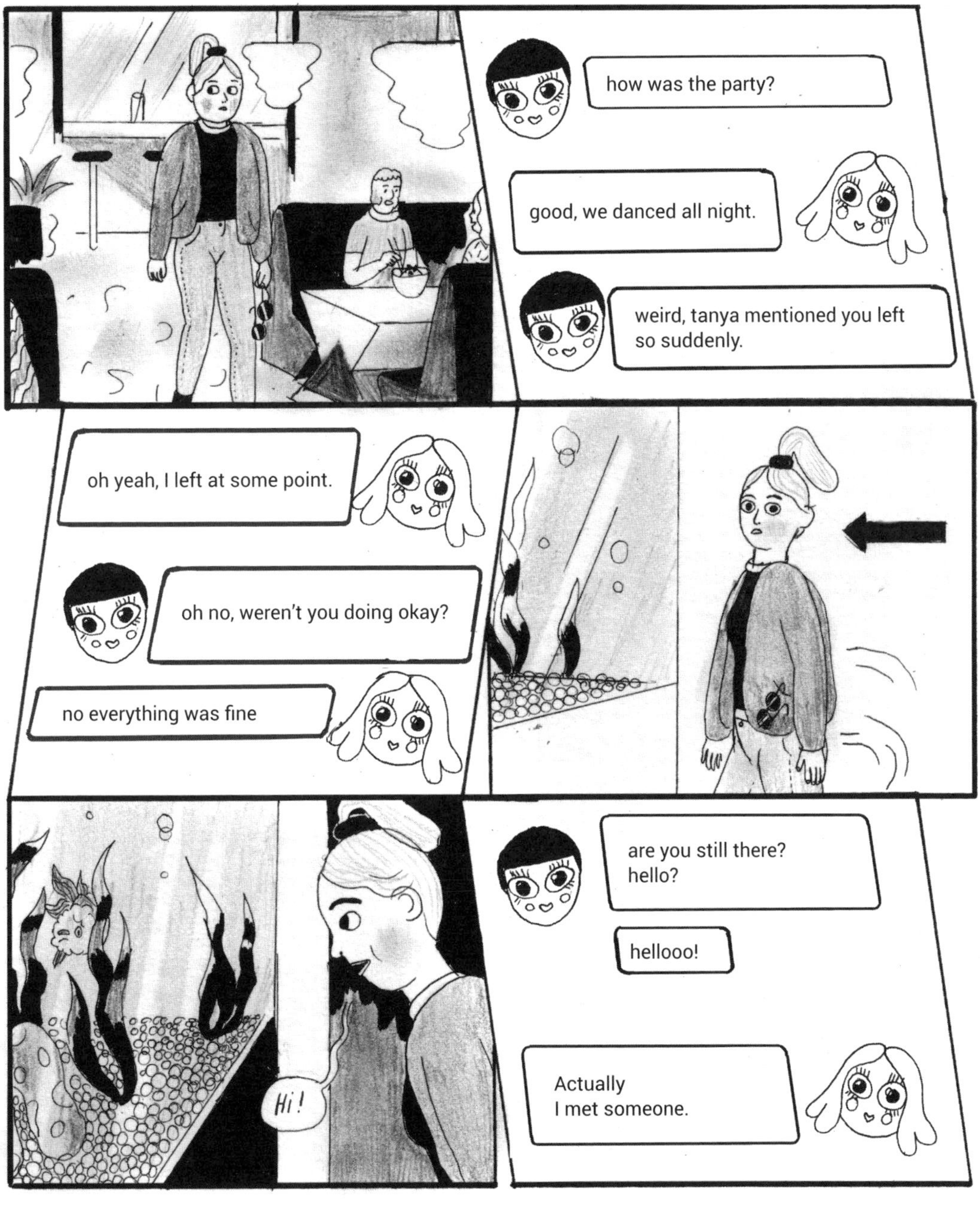
how was the party?
good, we danced all night.
weird, tanya mentioned you left so suddenly.
oh yeah, I left at some point.
oh no, weren't you doing okay?
no everything was fine
Hi!
are you still there? hello?
hellooo!
Actually I met someone.

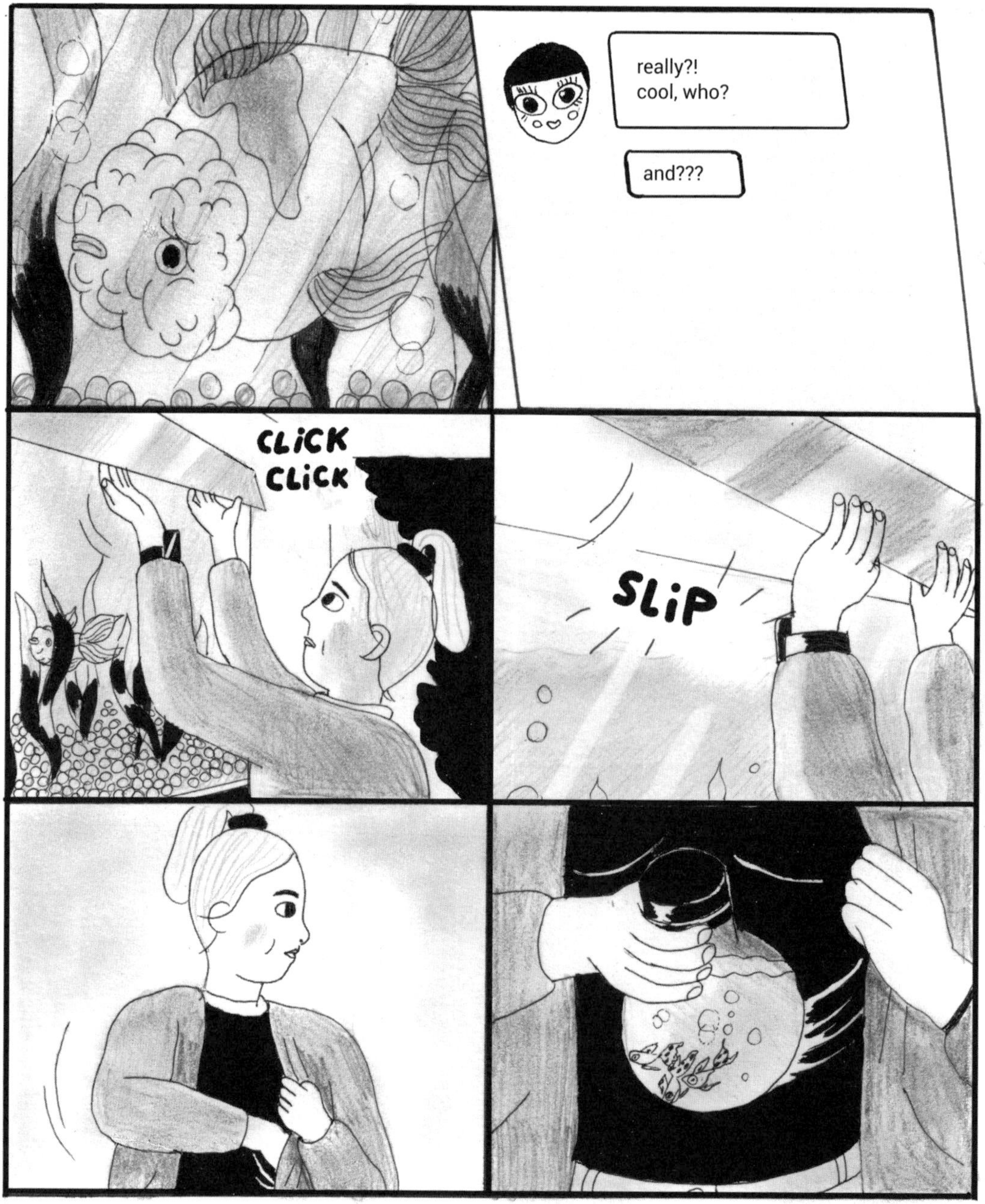
really?!
cool, who?
and???
CLICK
CLICK
SLIP

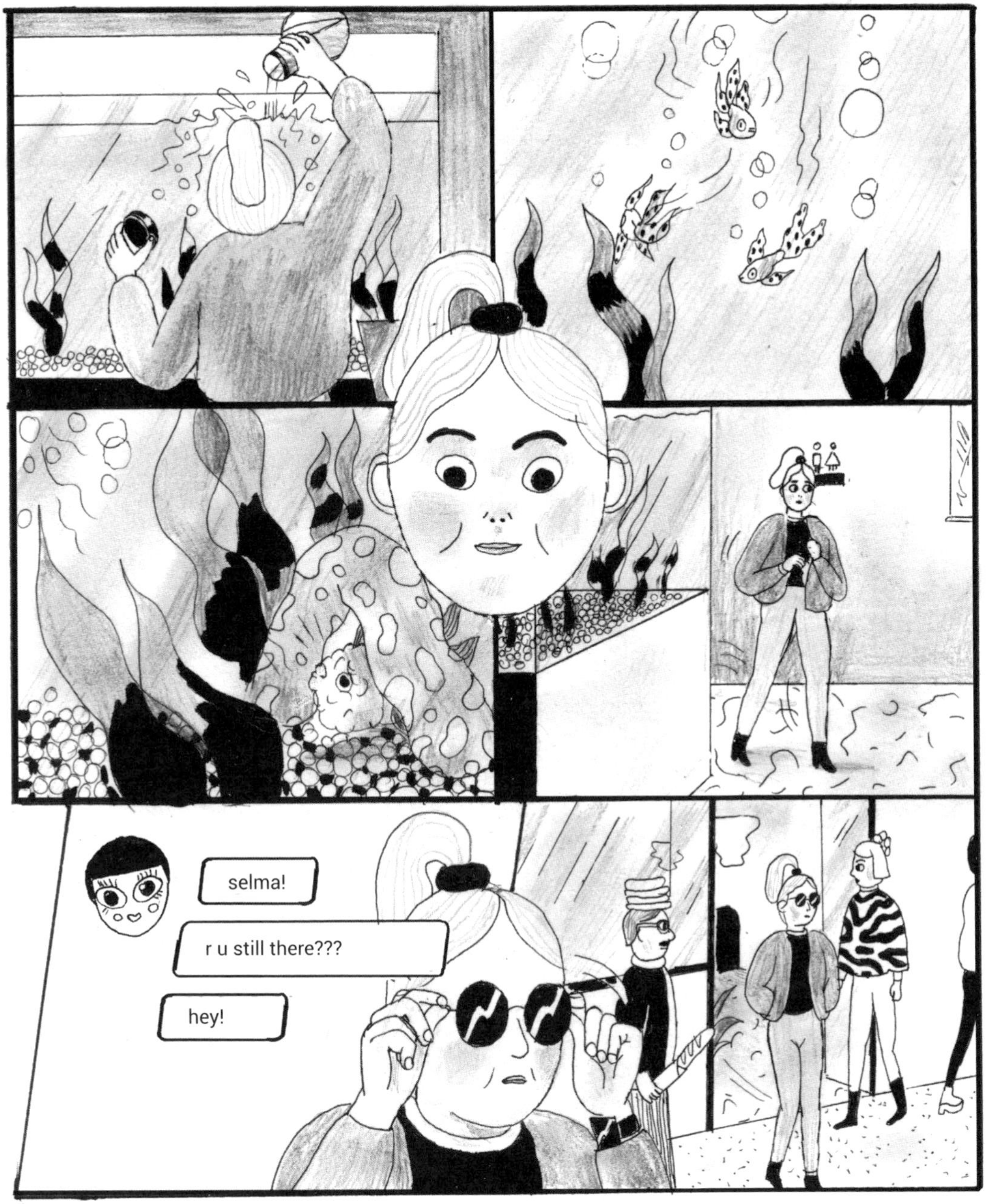
selma!
r u still there???
hey!

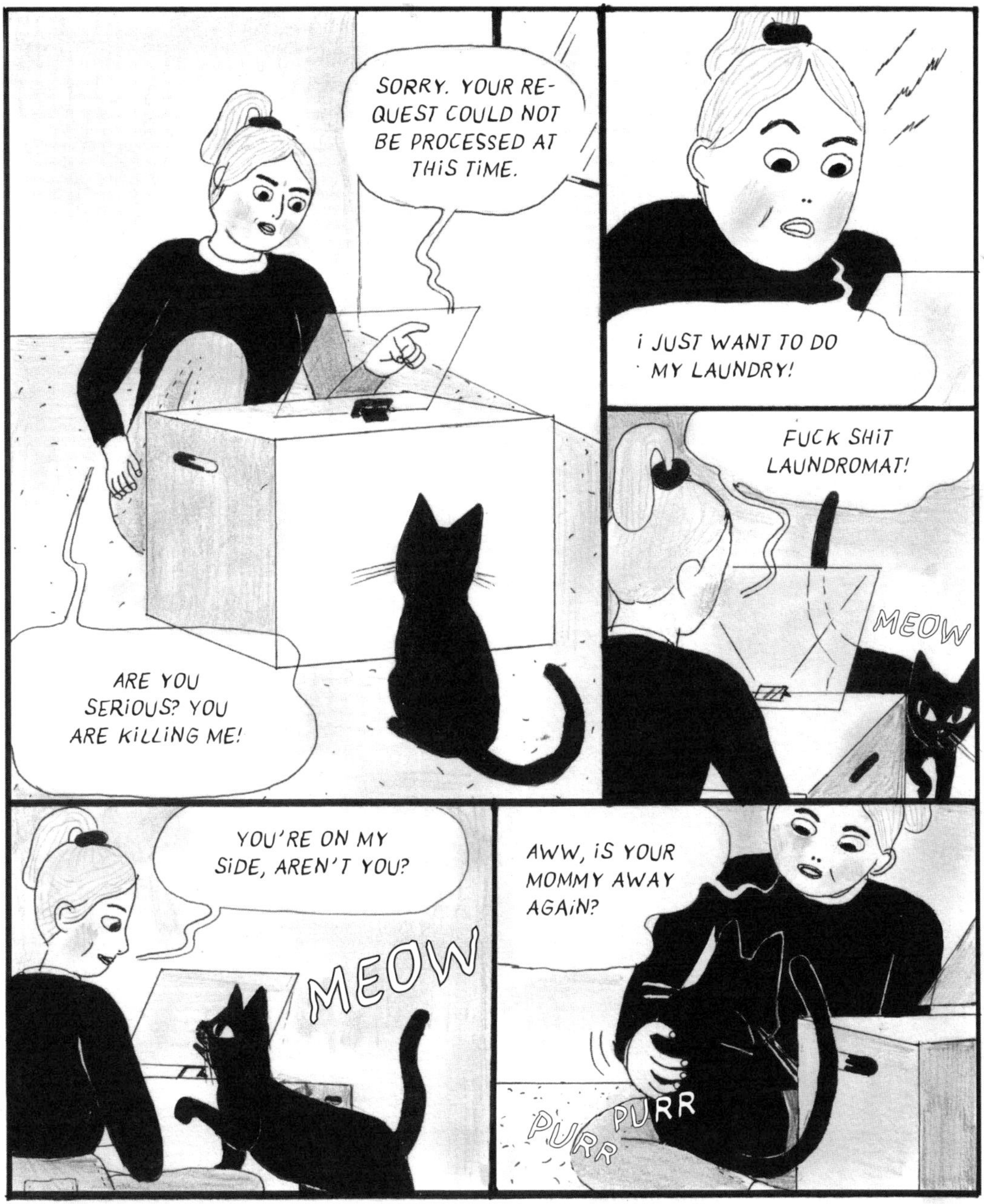
SORRY. YOUR RE-QUEST COULD NOT BE PROCESSED AT THIS TIME.
ARE YOU SERIOUS? YOU ARE KILLING ME!
I JUST WANT TO DO MY LAUNDRY!
FUCK SHIT LAUNDROMAT!
MEOW
YOU'RE ON MY SIDE, AREN'T YOU?
MEOW
AWW, IS YOUR MOMMY AWAY AGAIN?
PURR
PURR

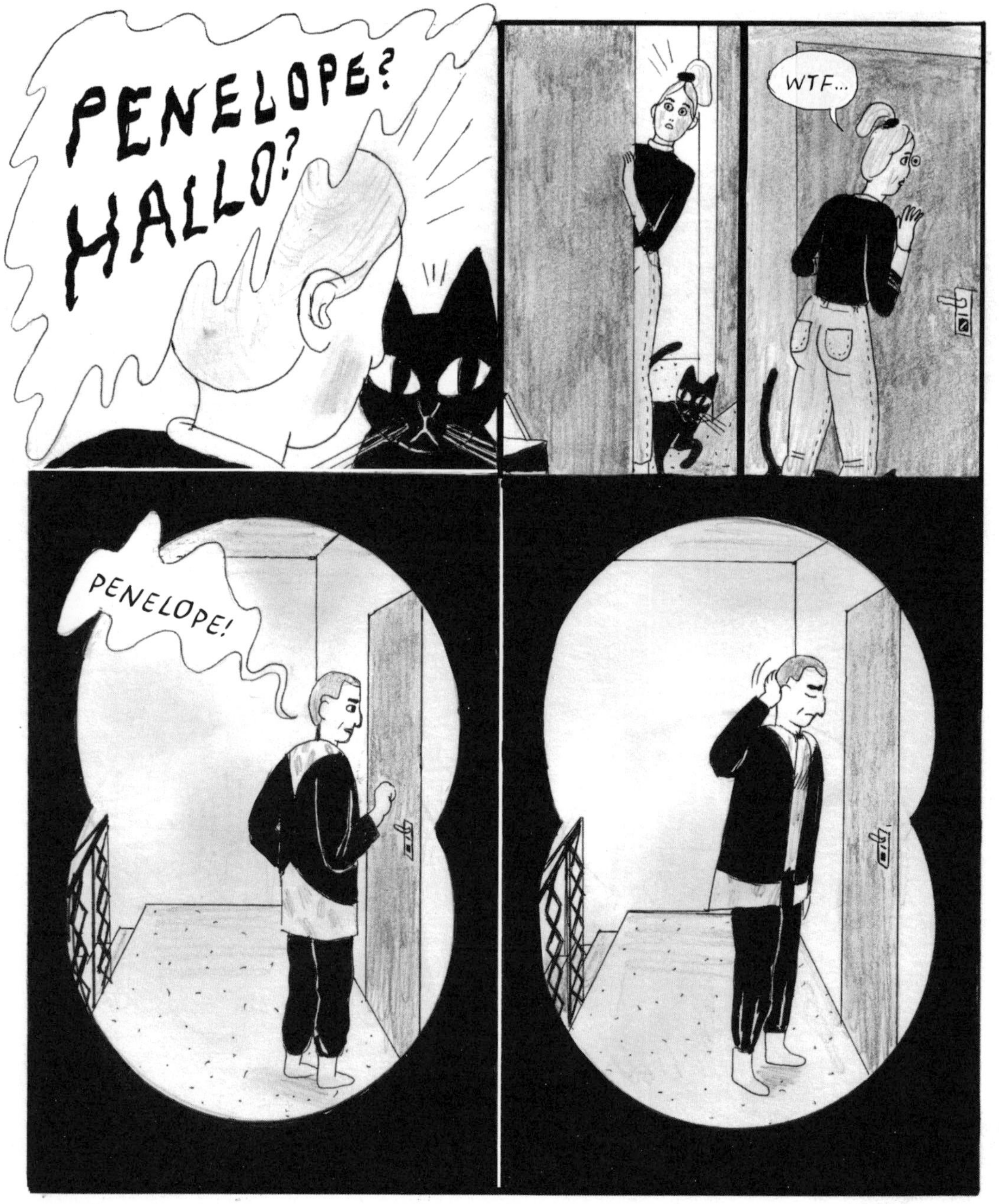
PENELOPE? HALLO?
WTF...
PENELOPE!

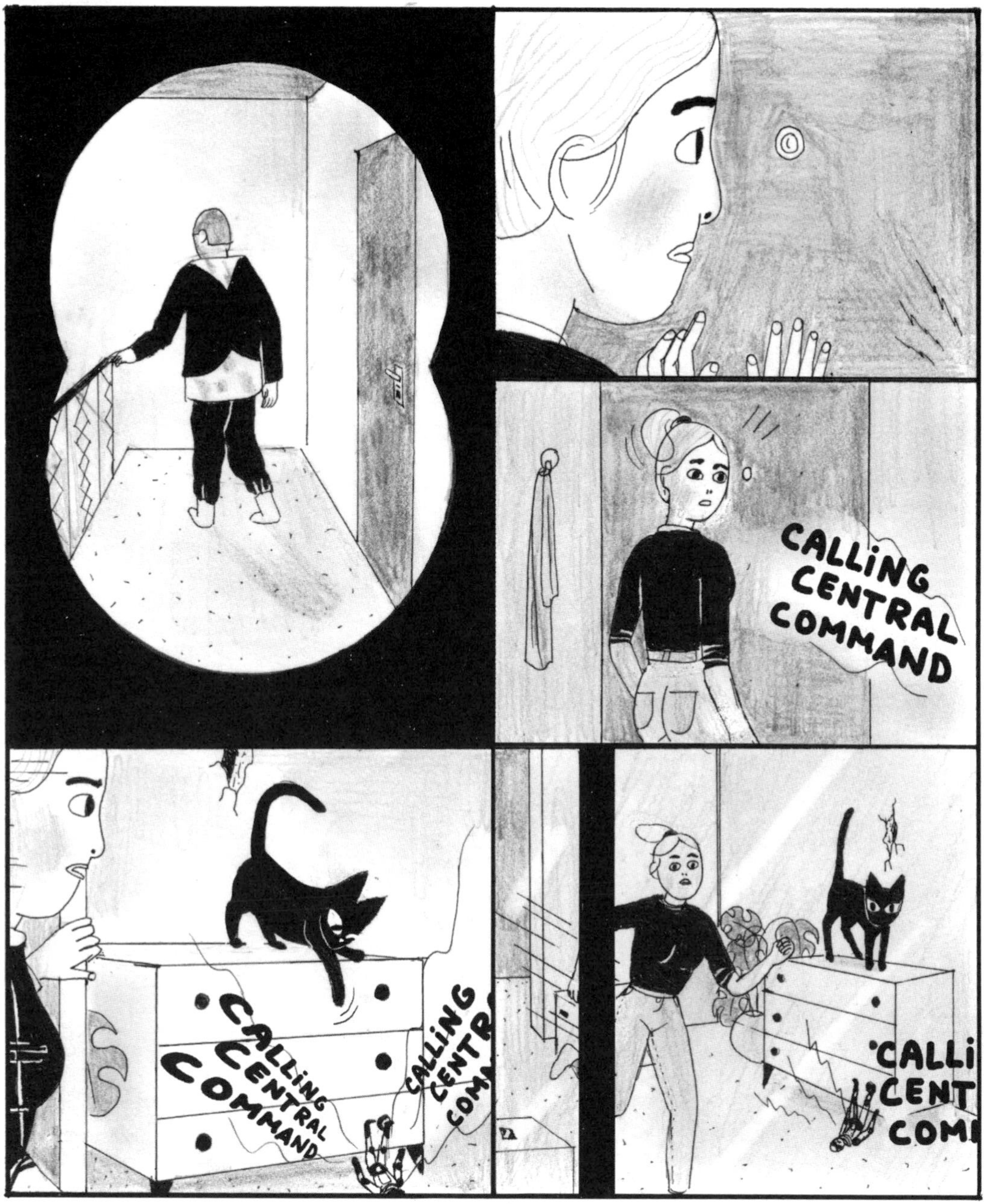
CALLING CENTRAL COMMAND
CALLING CENTRAL COMMAND
CALLING CENTR
COM
CALLI
CENT
COM

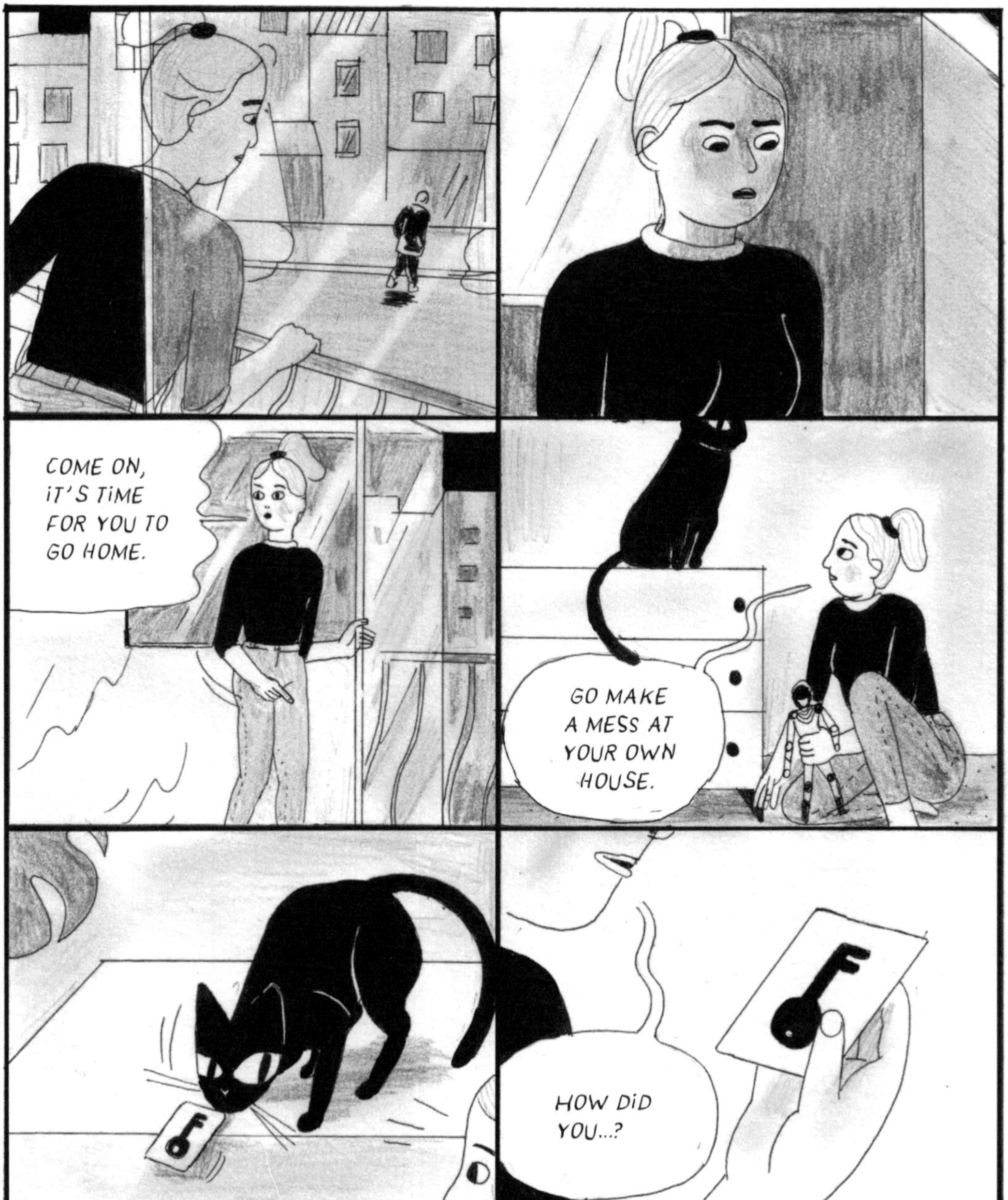
COME ON, IT'S TIME FOR YOU TO GO HOME.
GO MAKE A MESS AT YOUR OWN HOUSE.
HOW DID YOU...?

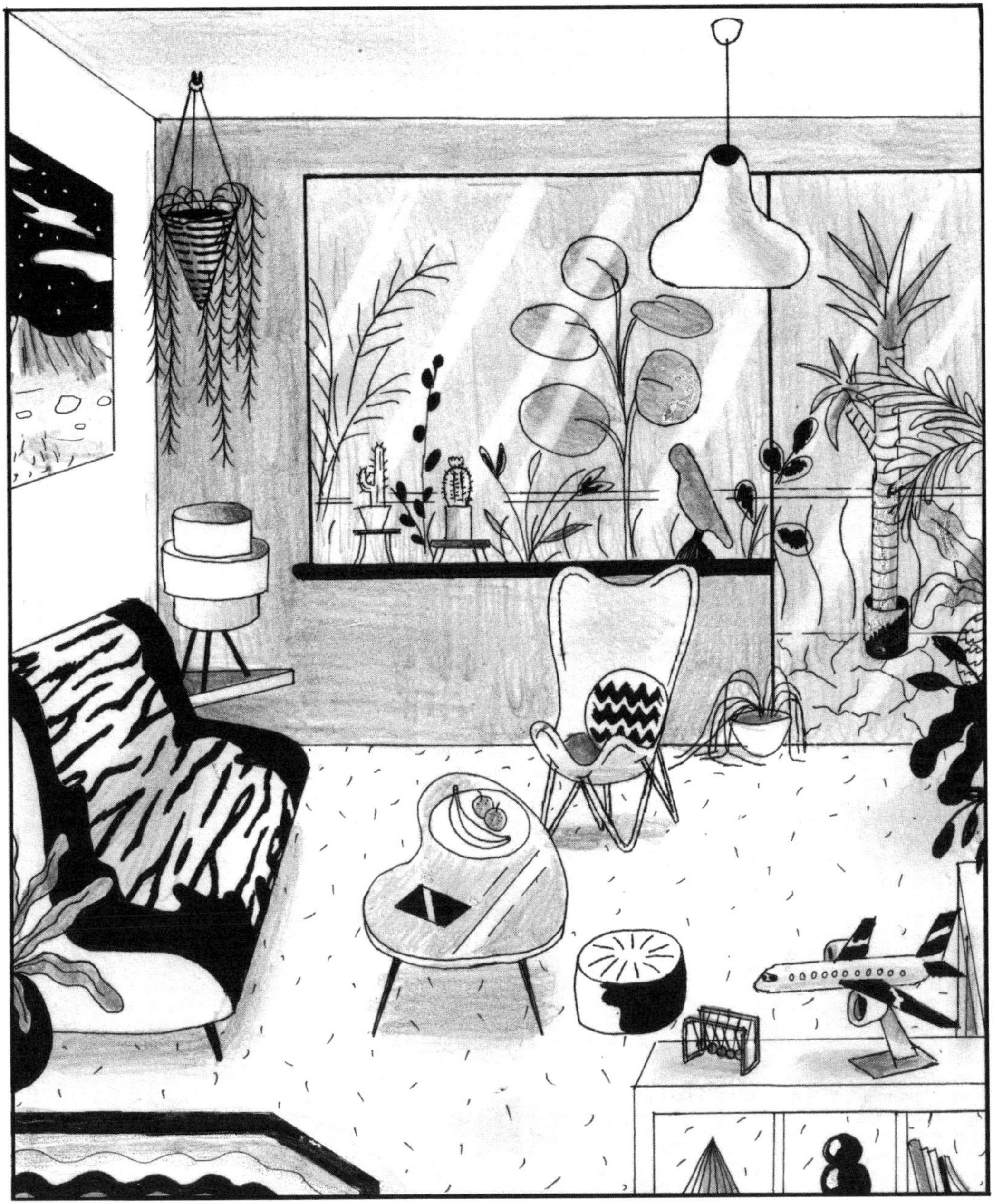

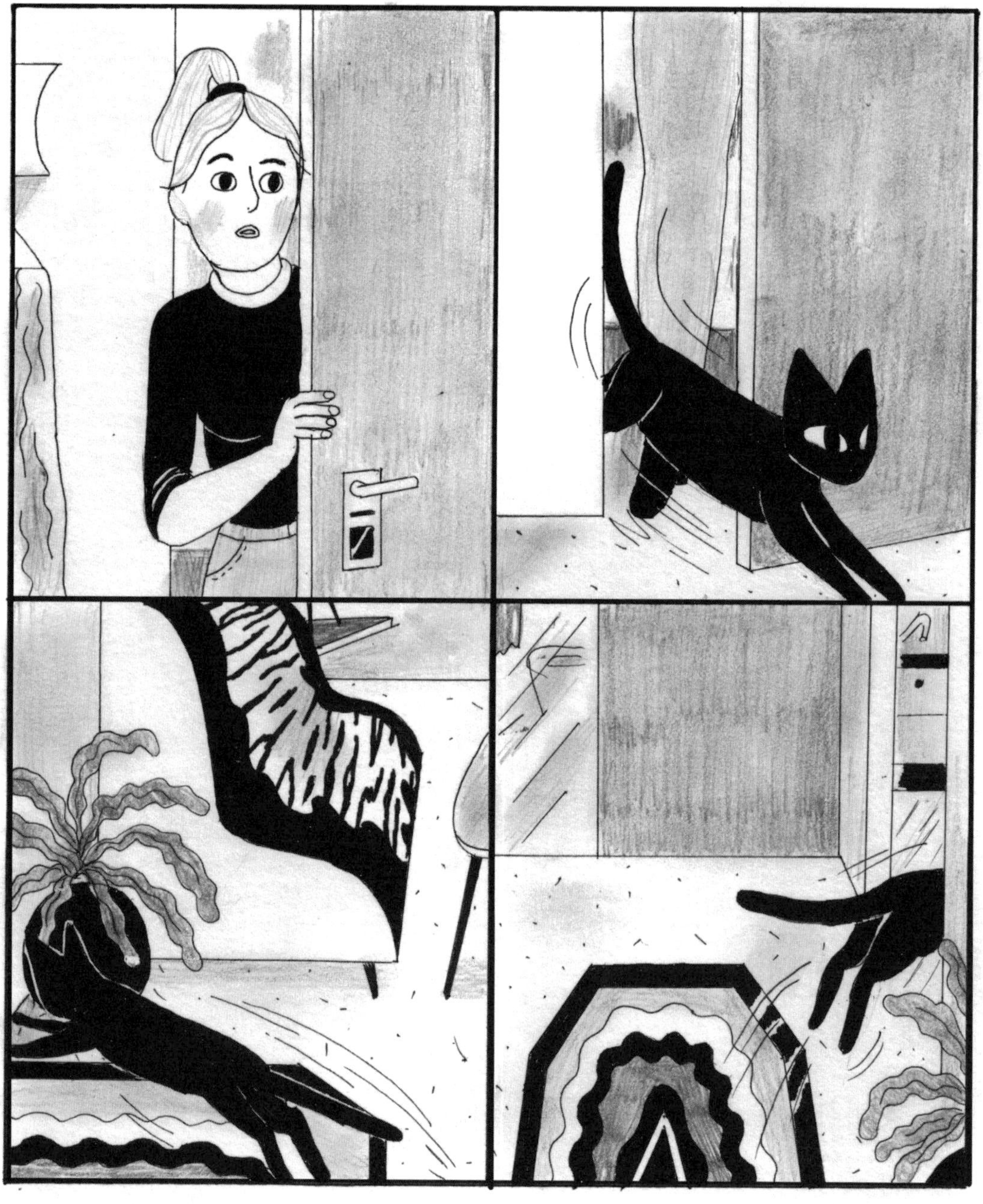

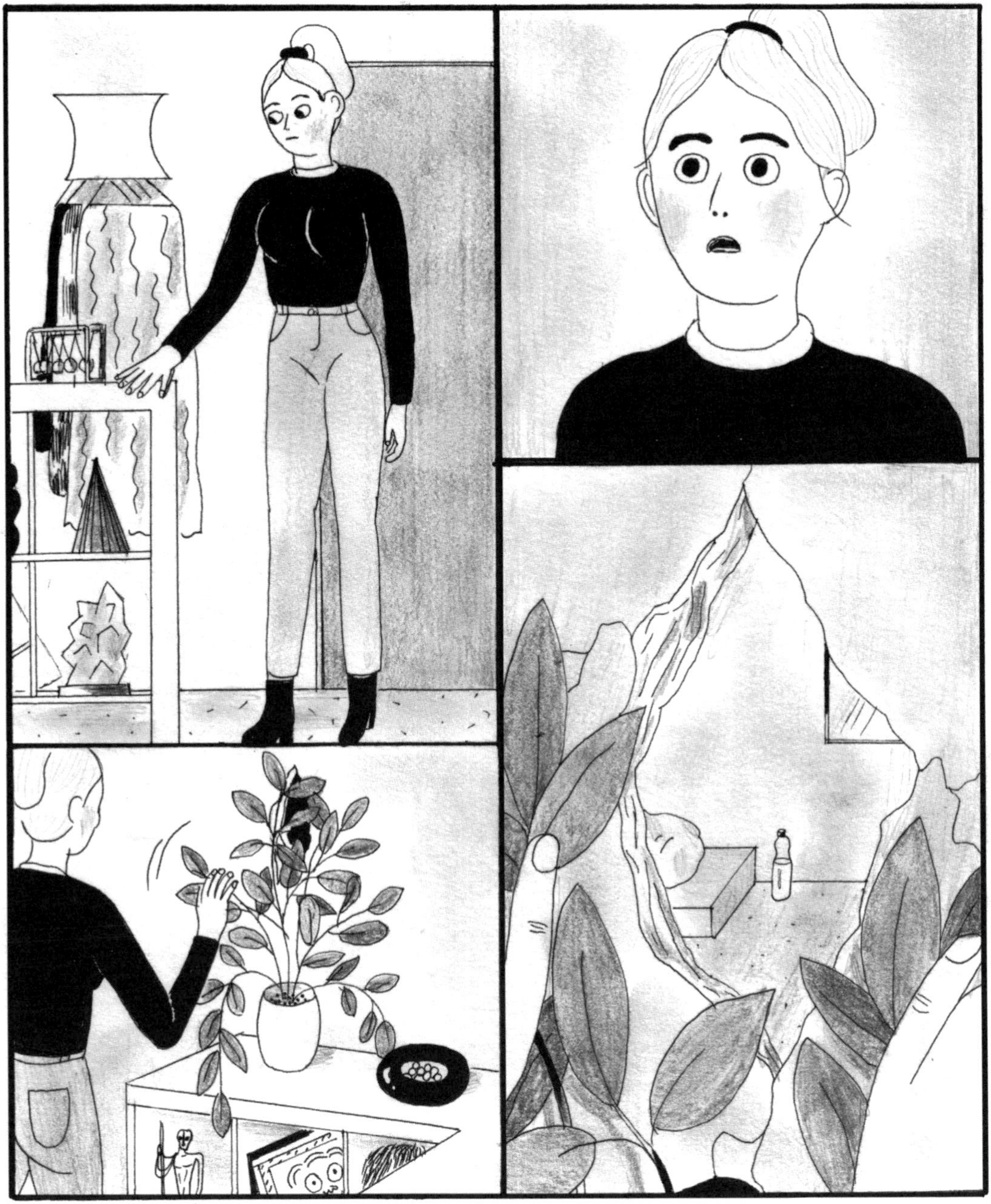

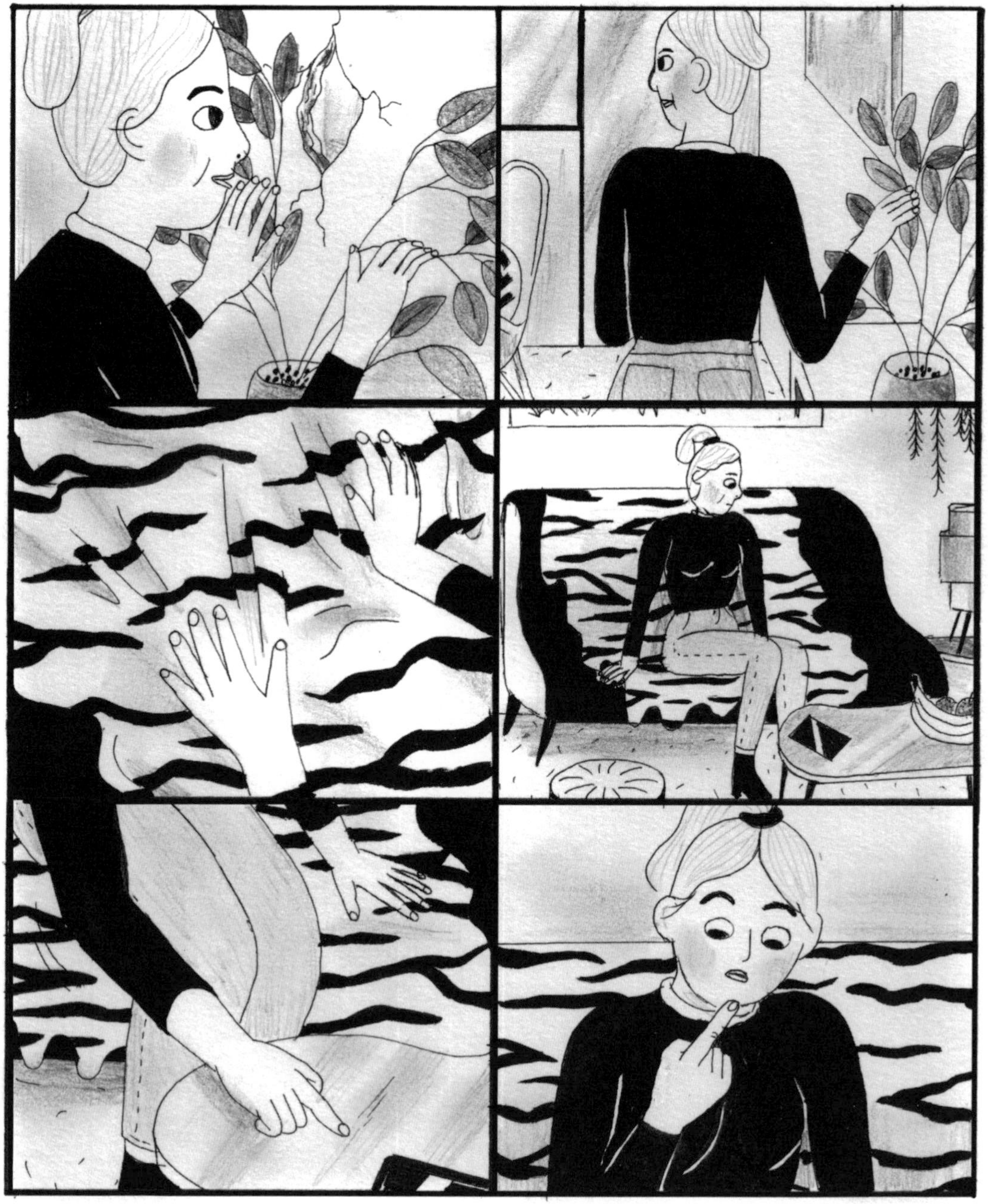

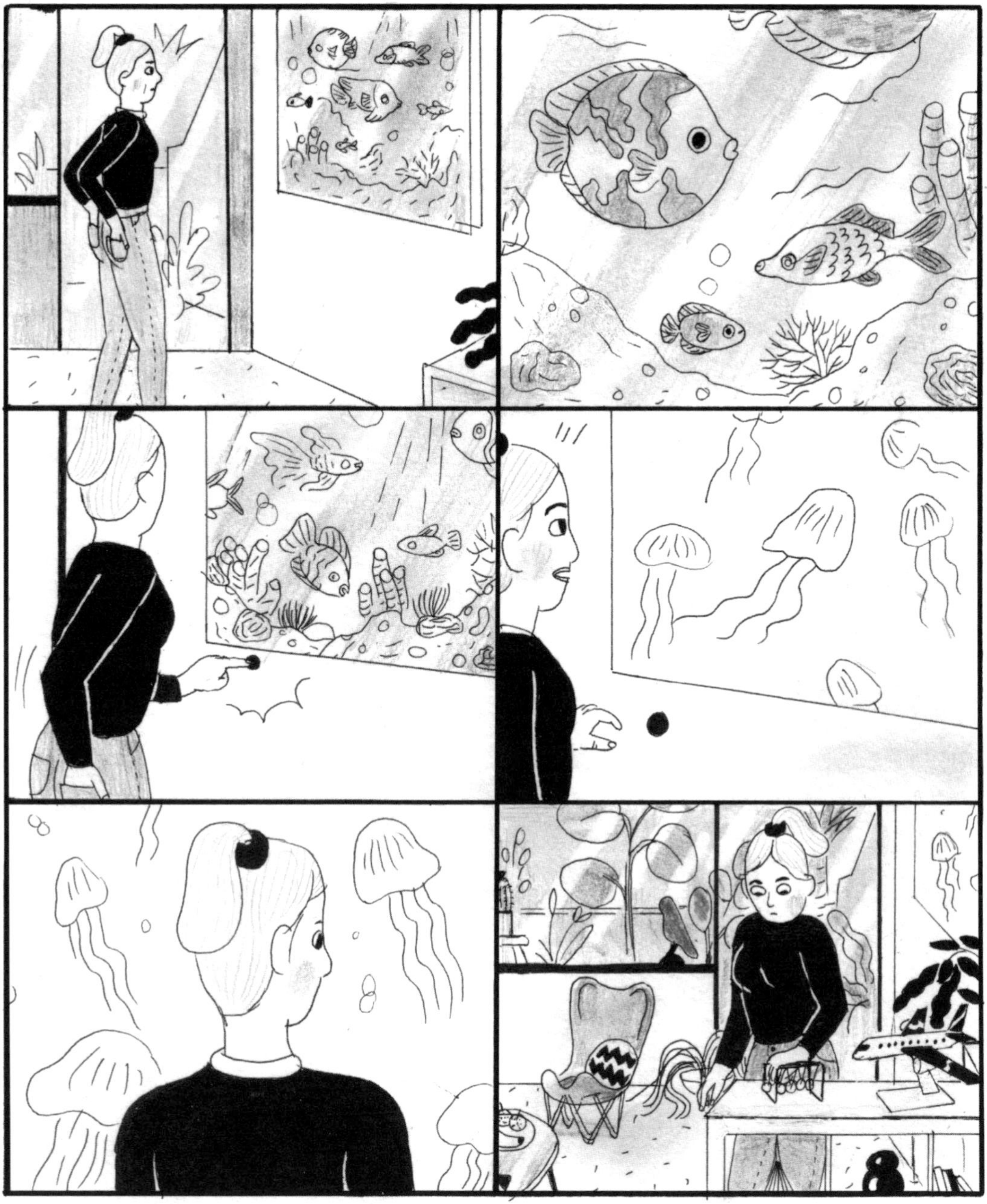

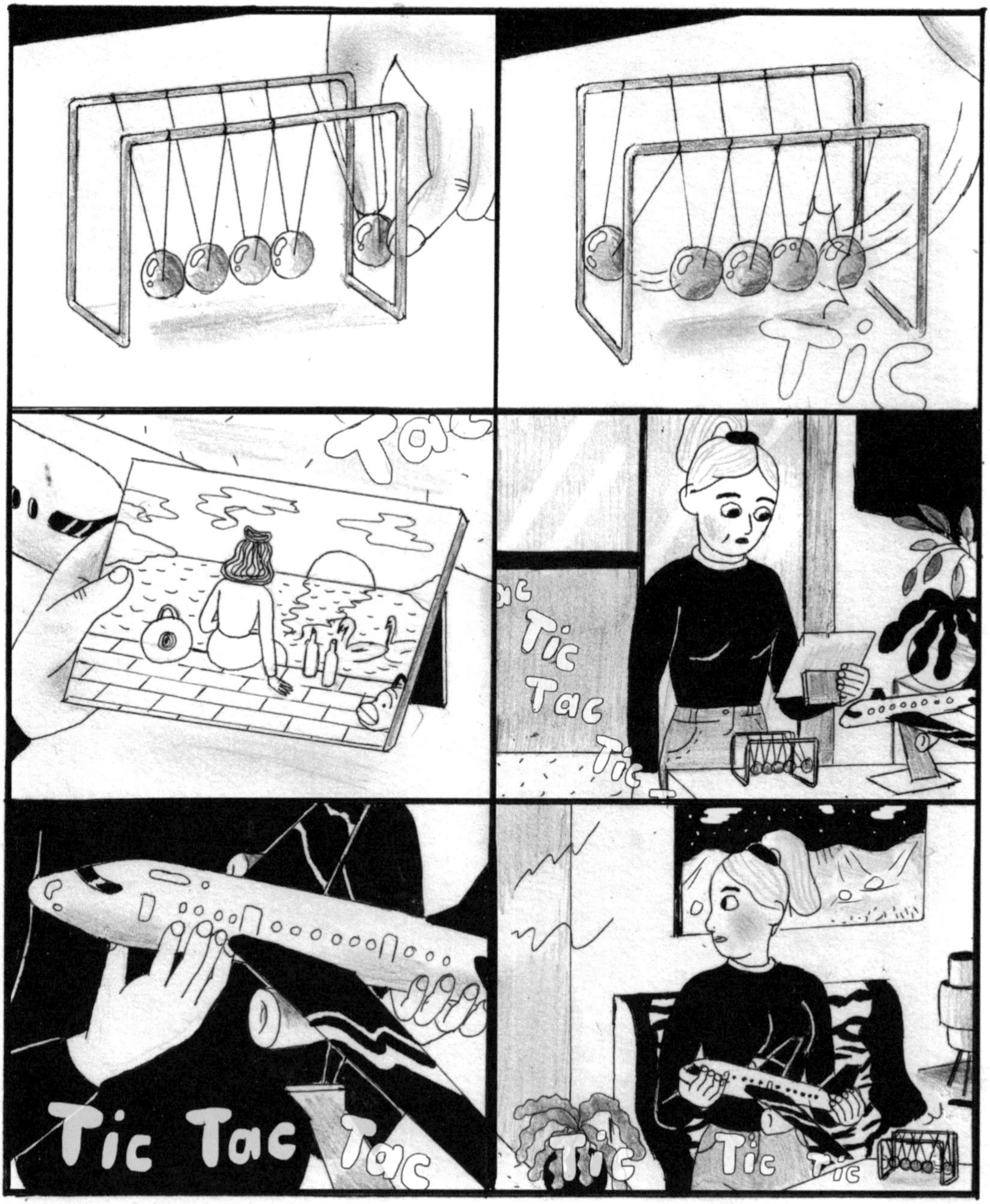
Tic
Tac
Tic
Tac
Tic
Tic Tac
Tac
Tic
Tic
Tic

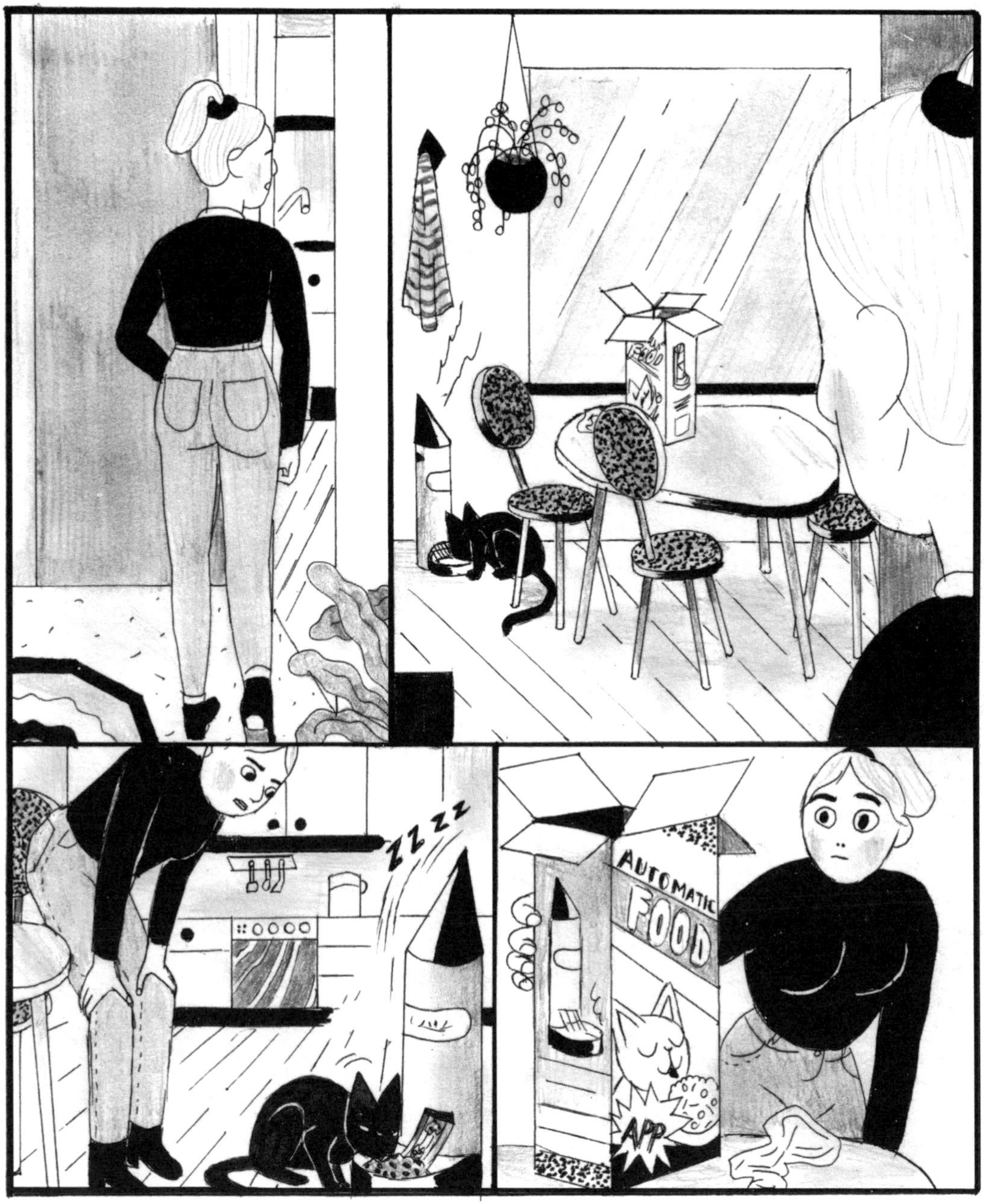
ZZZZ
AUTOMATIC FOOD
APP

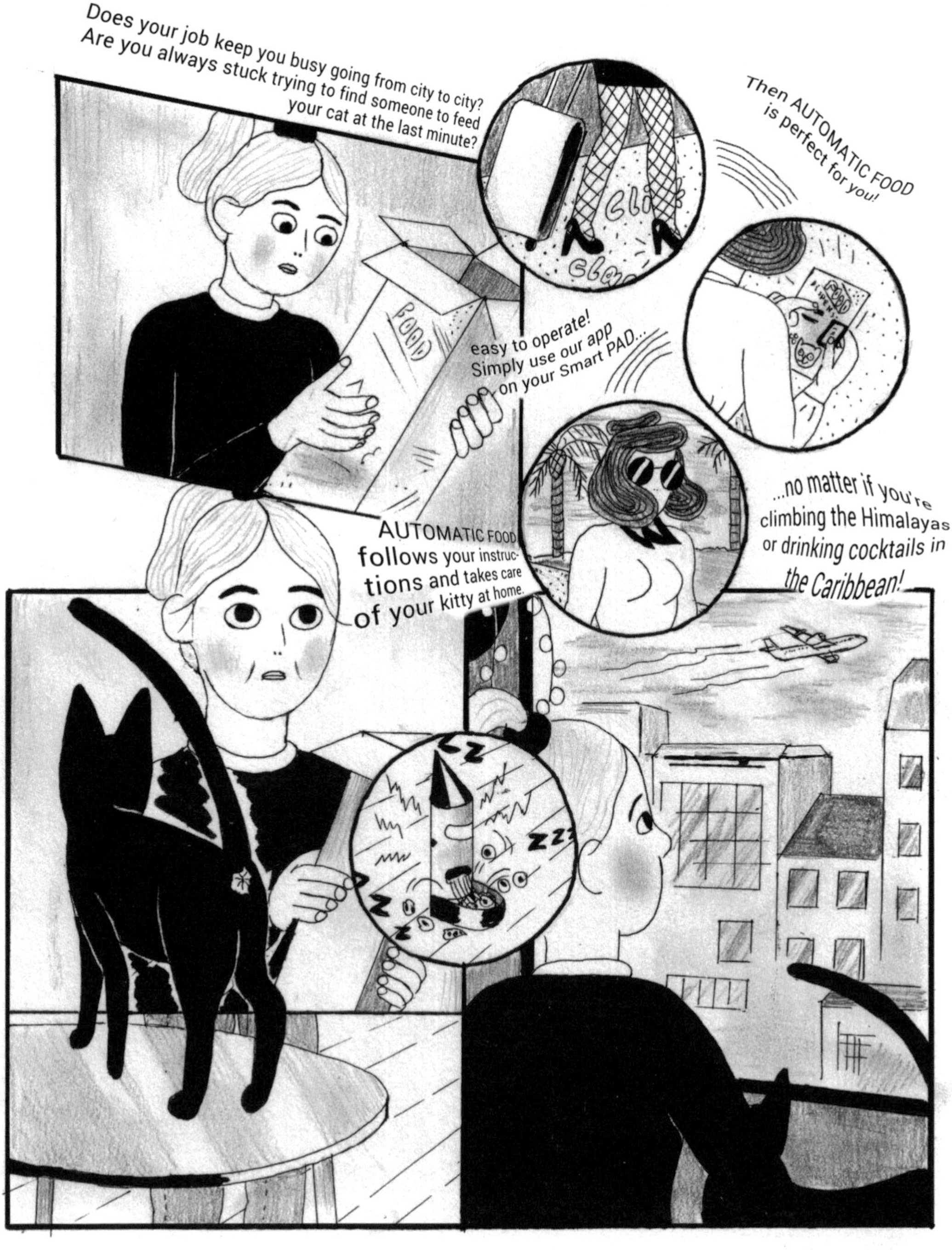
Does your job keep you busy going from city to city? Are you always stuck trying to find someone to feed your cat at the last minute?
Then AUTOMATIC FOOD is perfect for you!
easy to operate! Simply use our app on your Smart PAD...
...no matter if you're climbing the Himalayas or drinking cocktails in the Caribbean!
AUTOMATIC FOOD follows your instructions and takes care of your kitty at home.

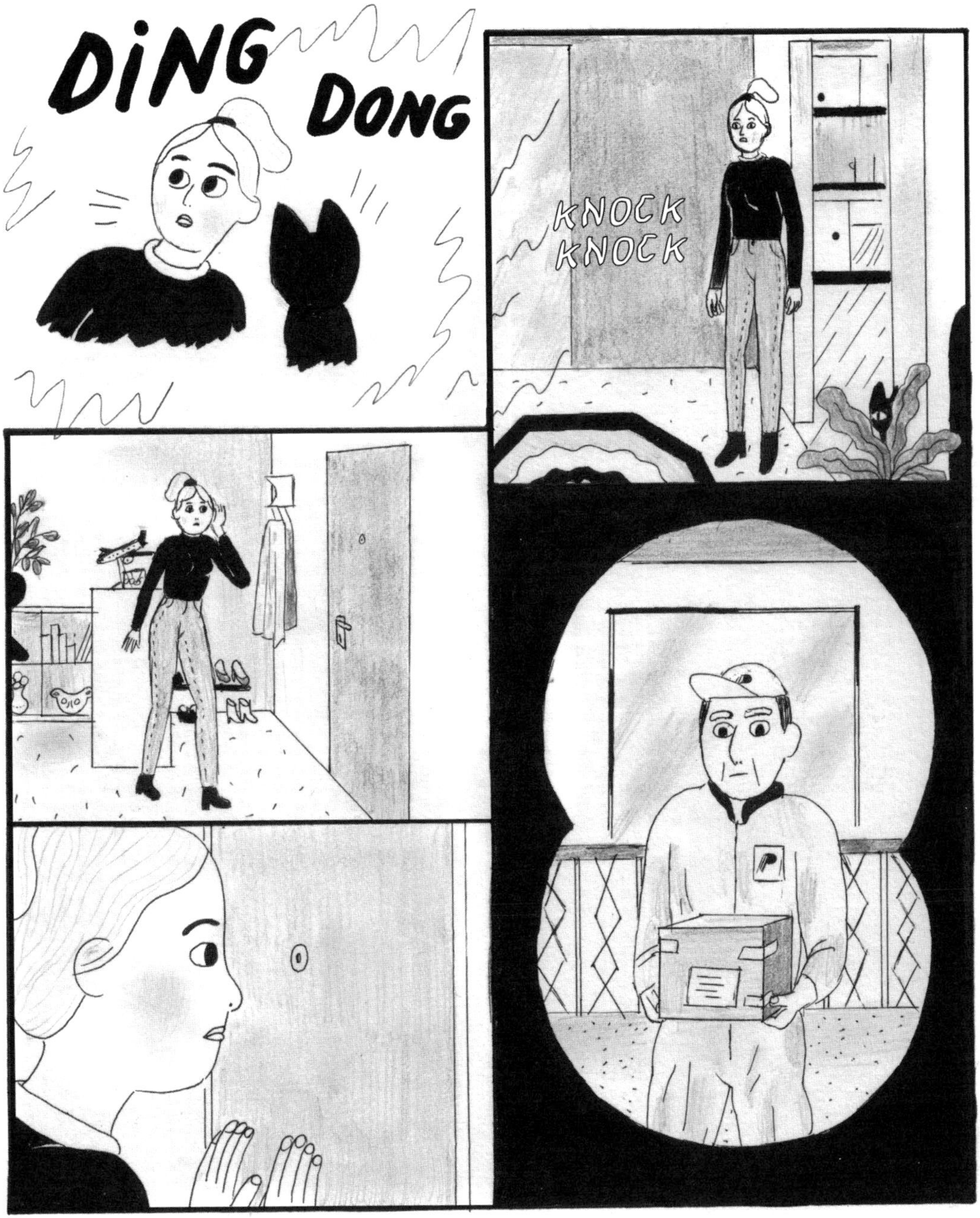
DING
DONG
KNOCK
KNOCK

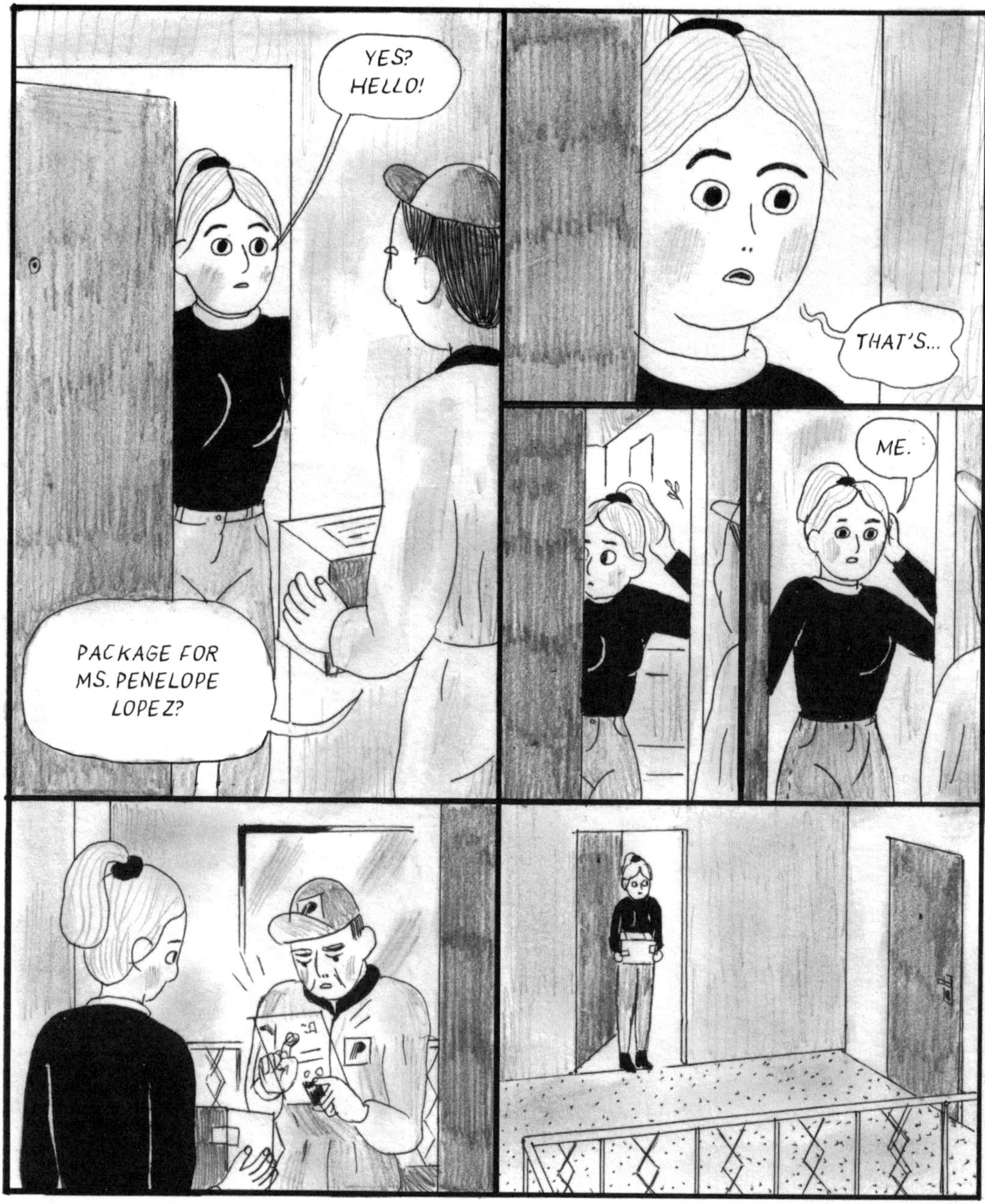
YES? HELLO!
PACKAGE FOR MS. PENELOPE LOPEZ?
THAT'S...
ME.

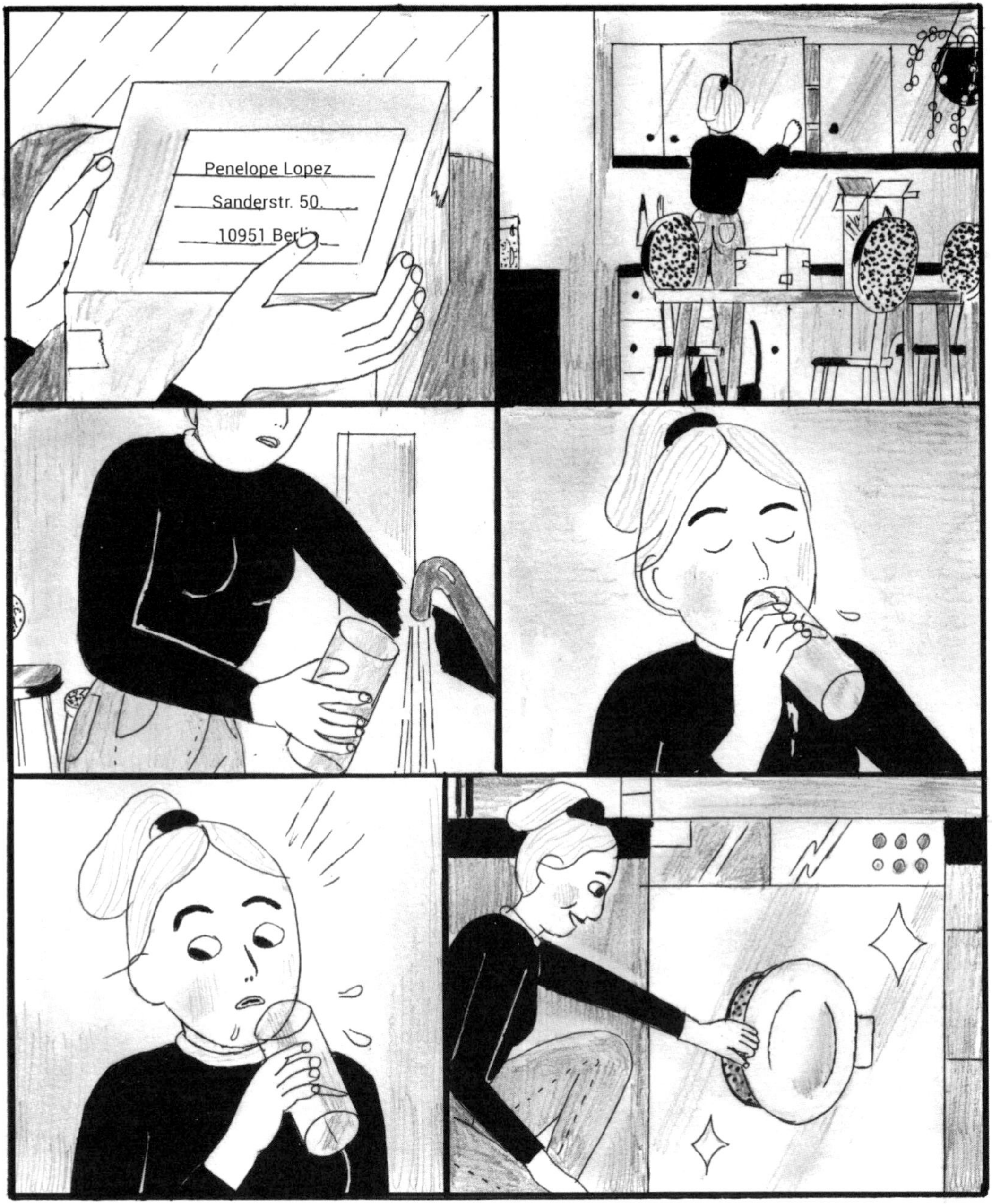
Penelope Lopez
Sanderstr. 50.
10951 Ber

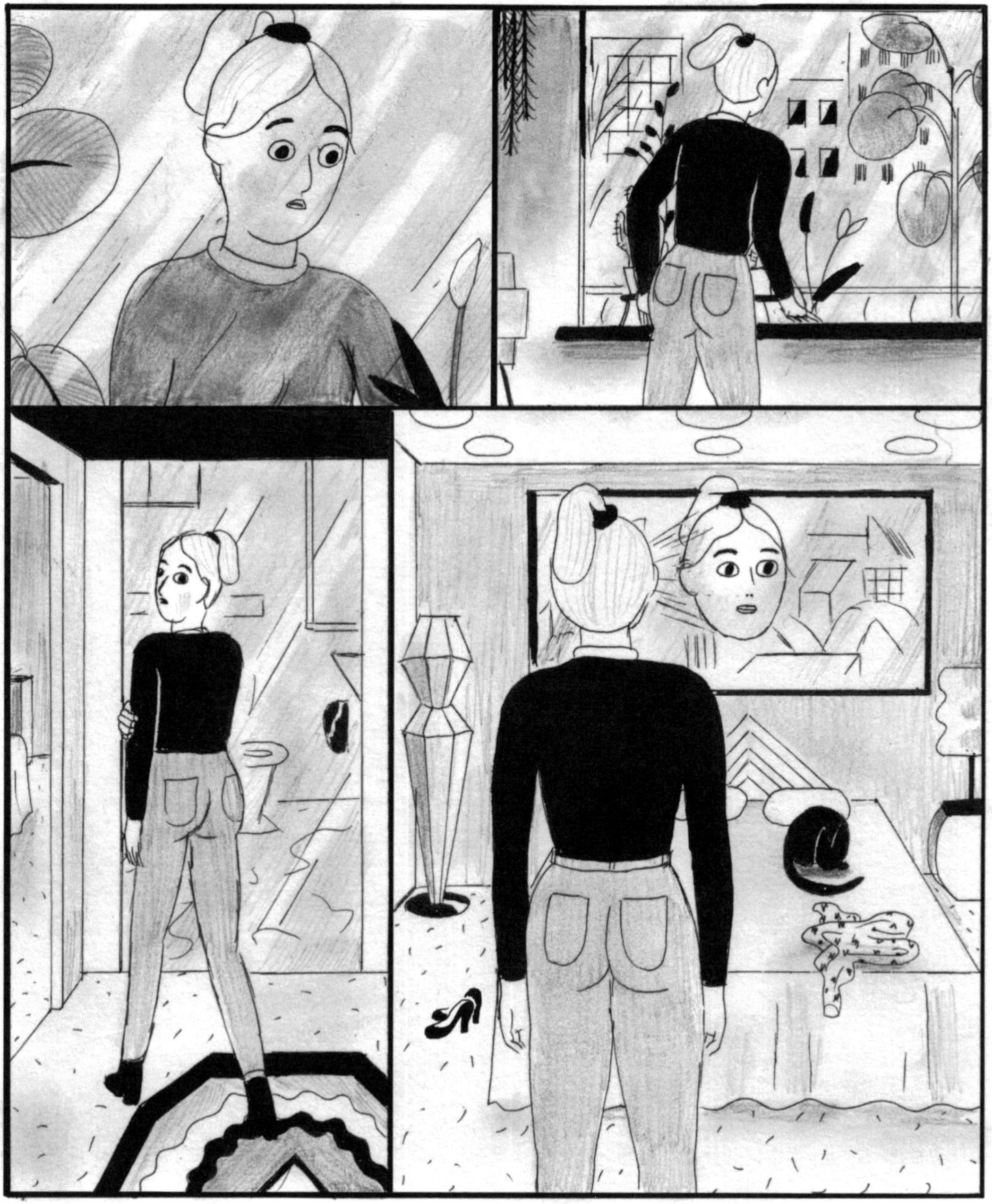

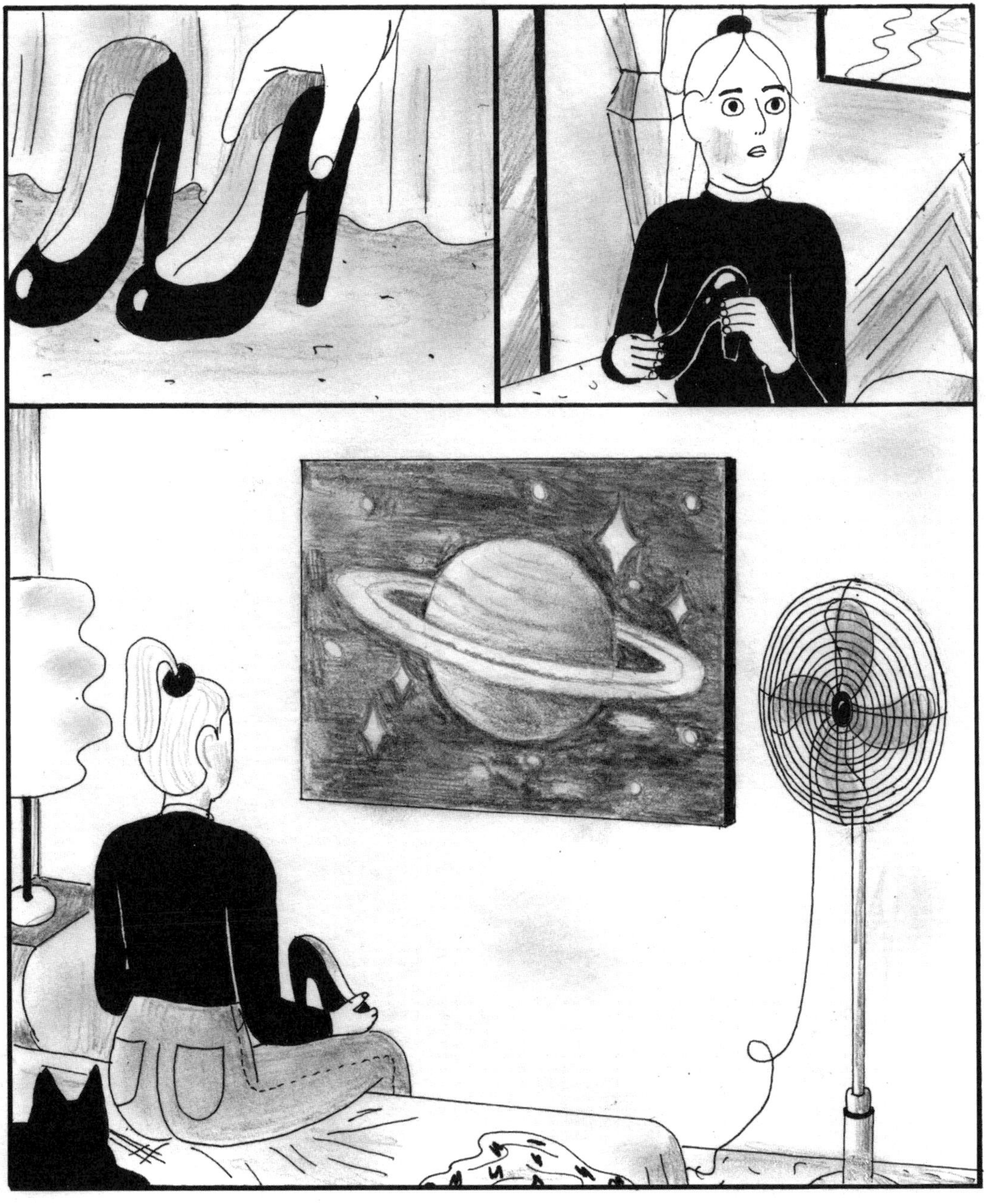

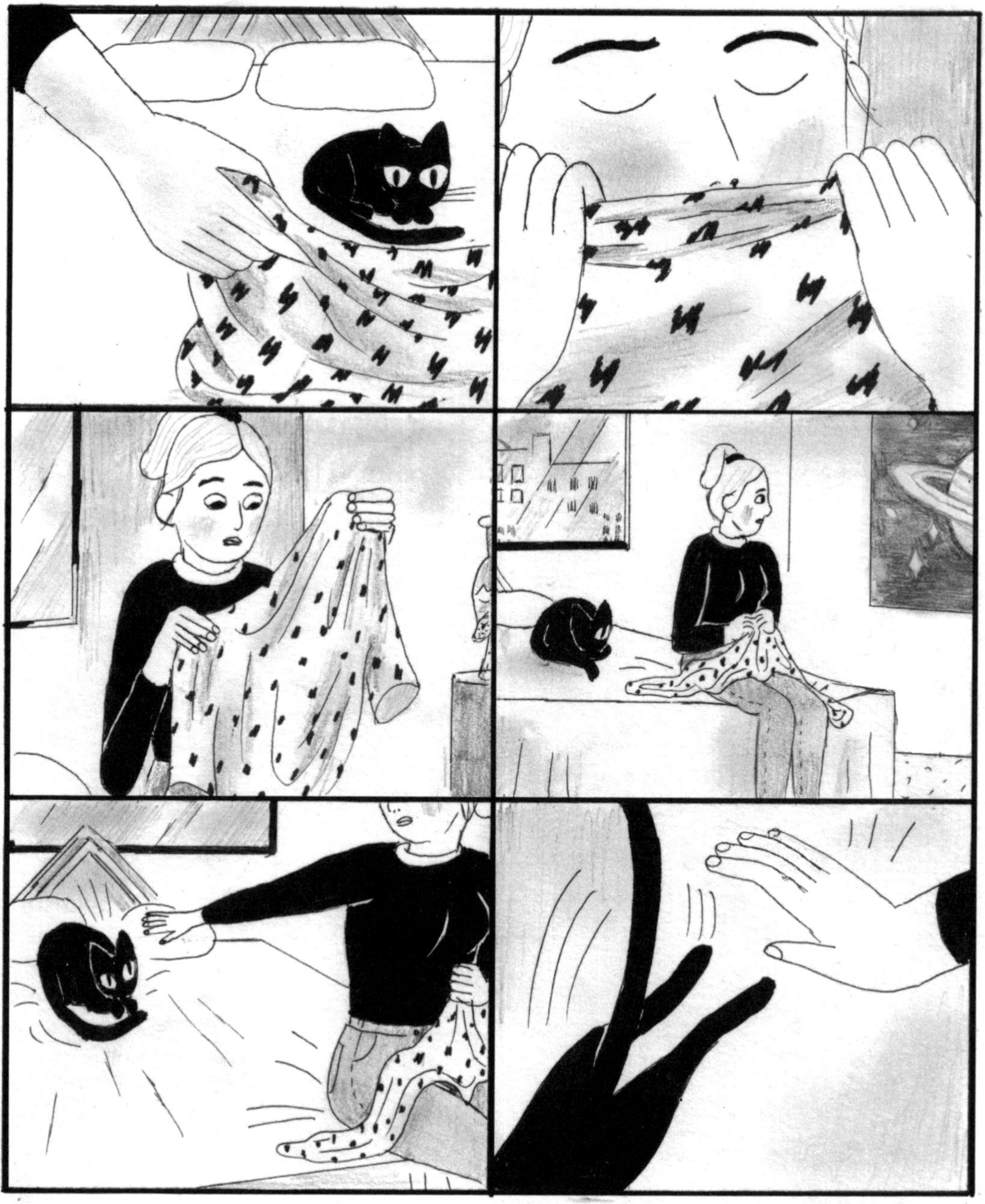

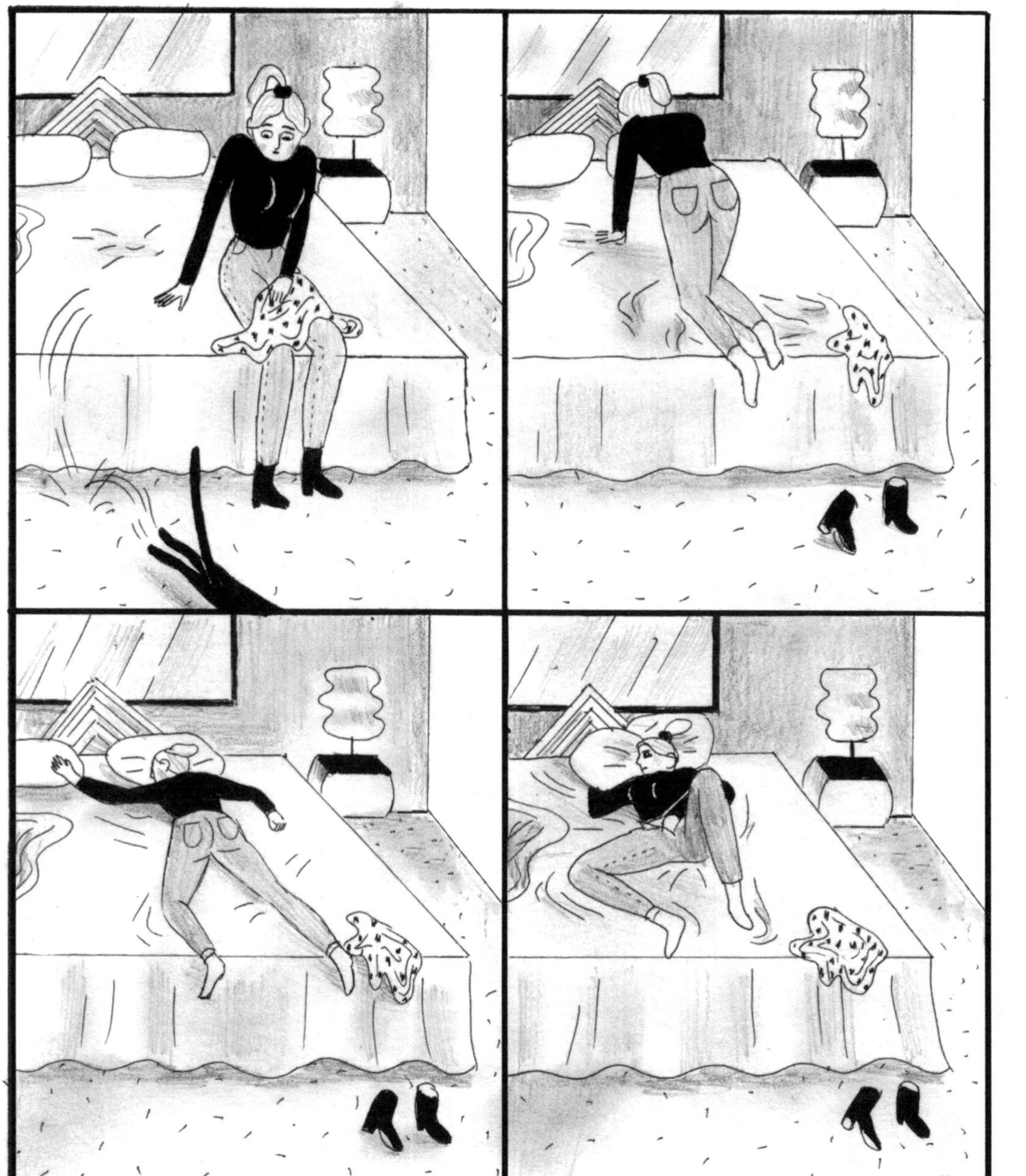

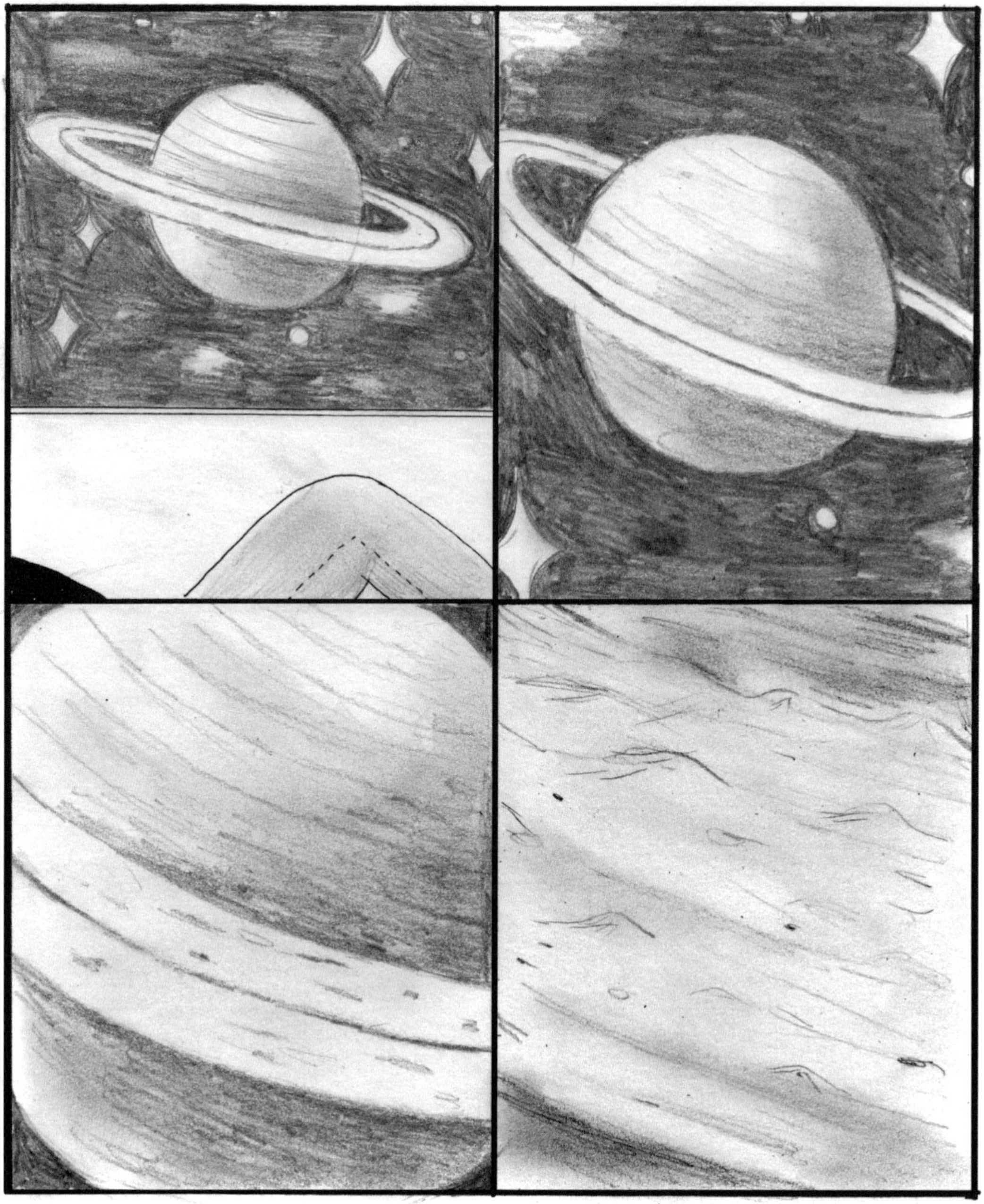

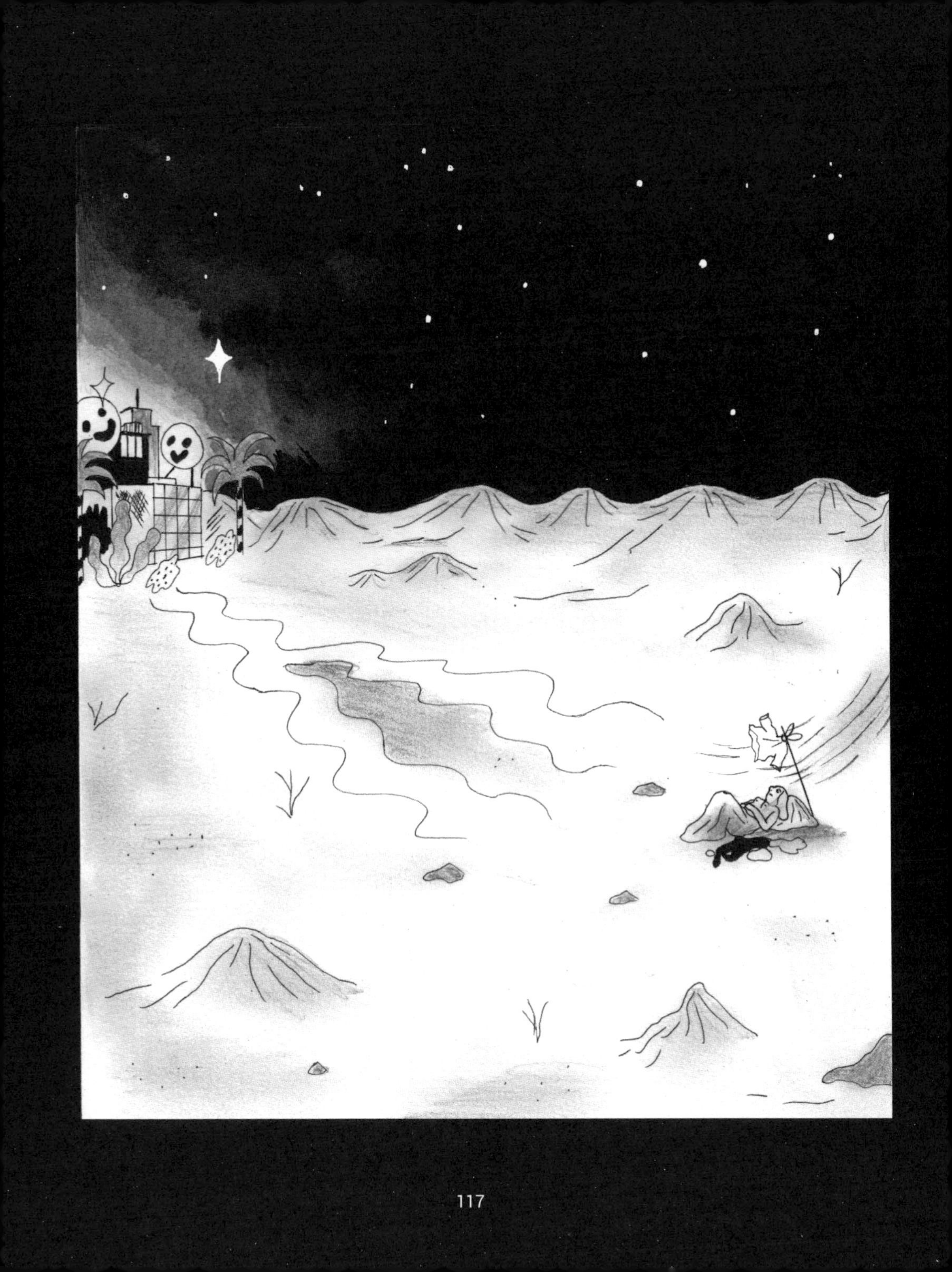

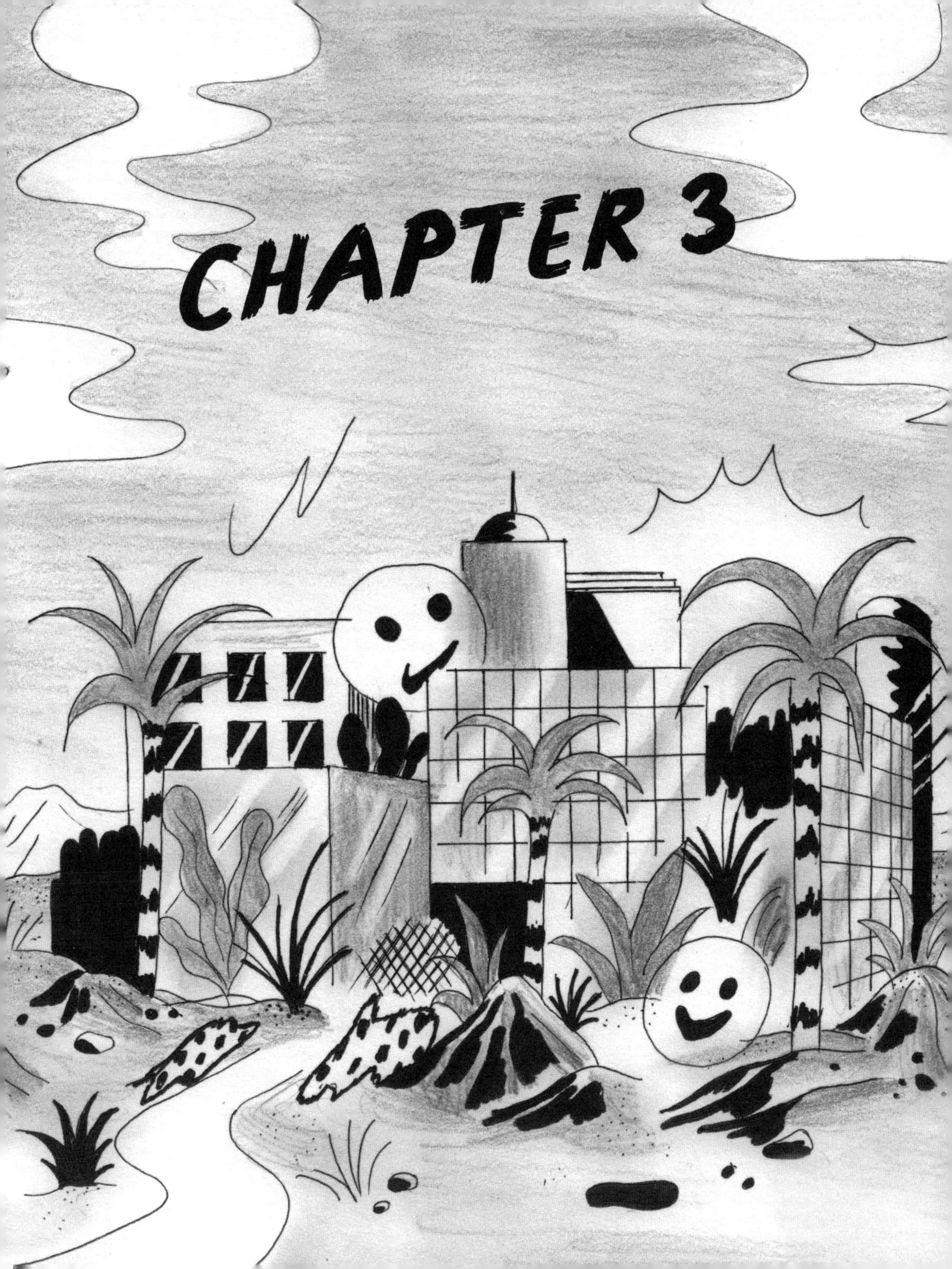
CHAPTER 3

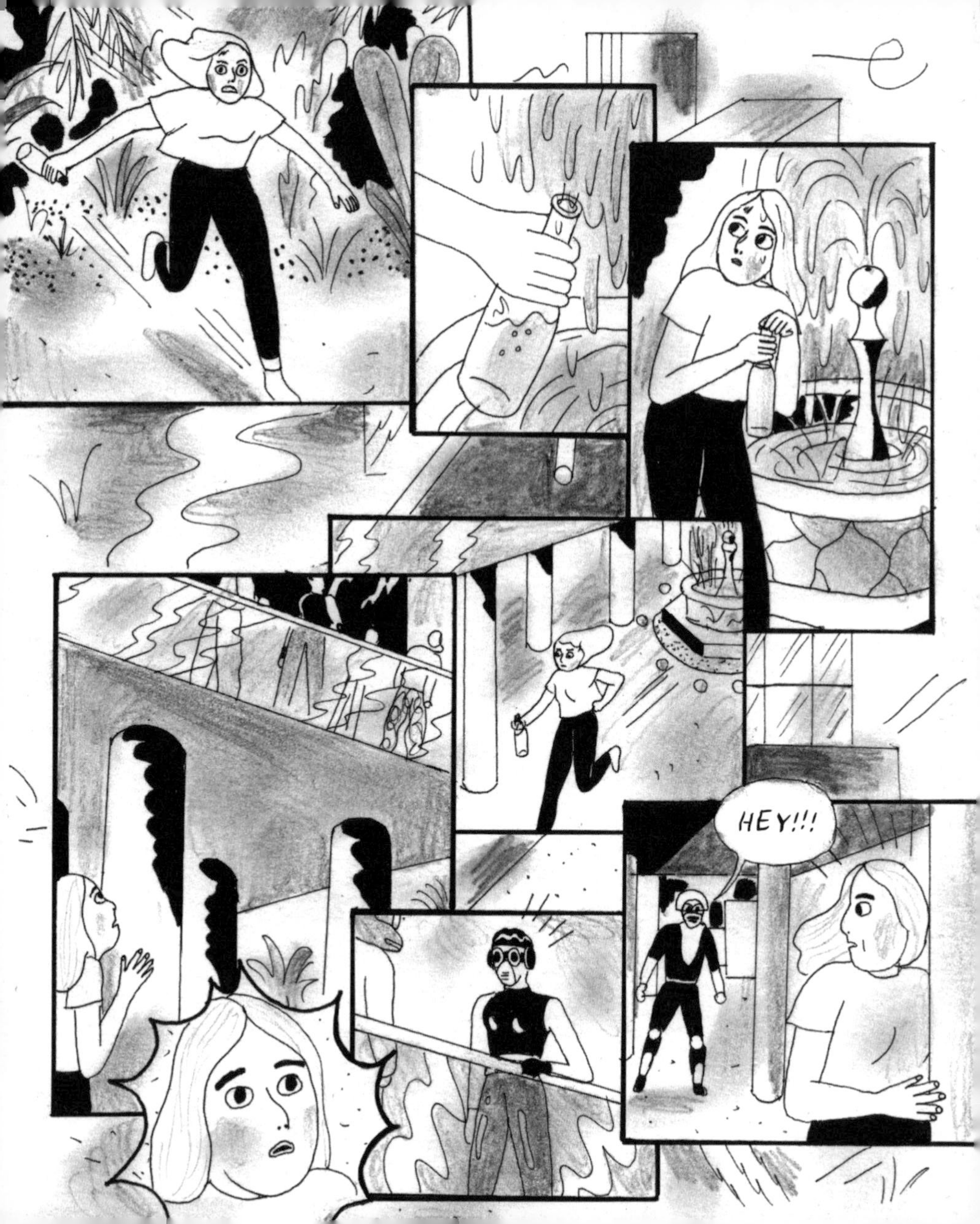
HEY!!!

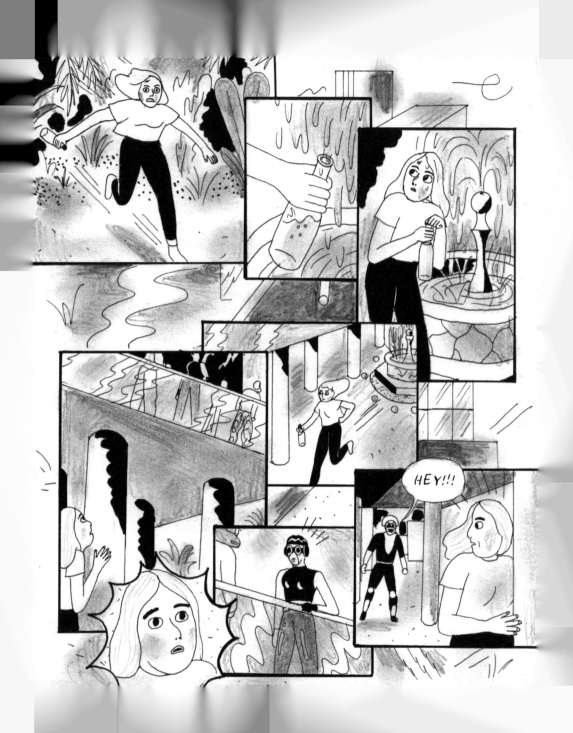

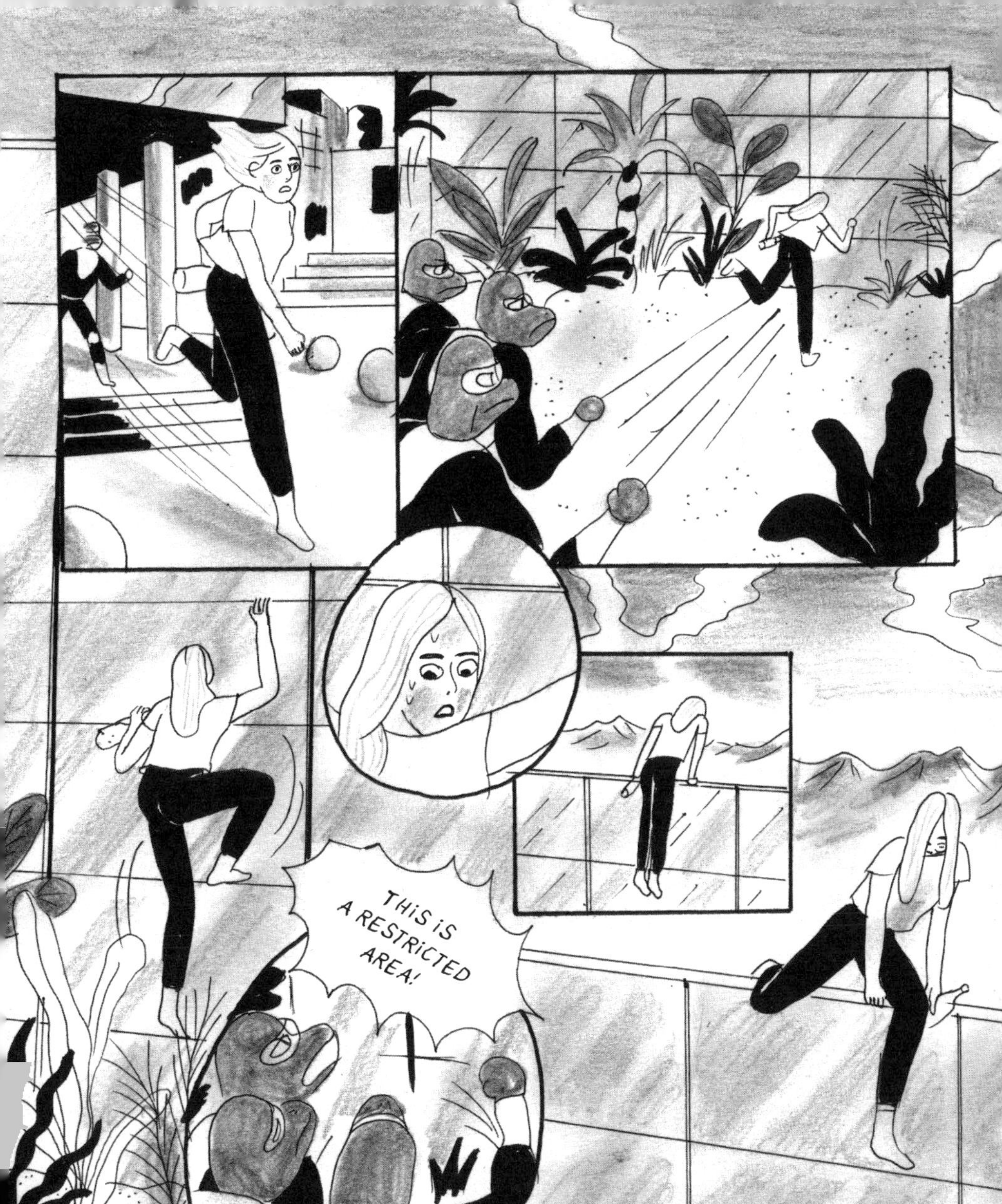
THIS IS A RESTRICTED AREA!

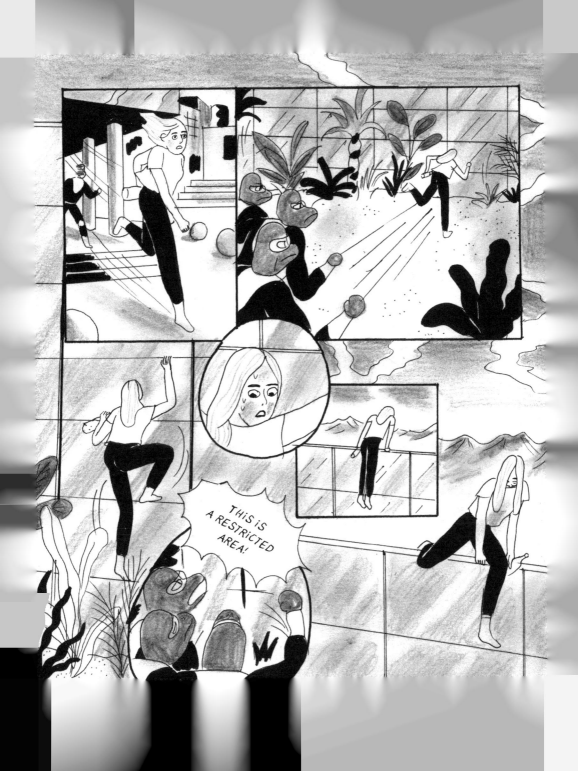

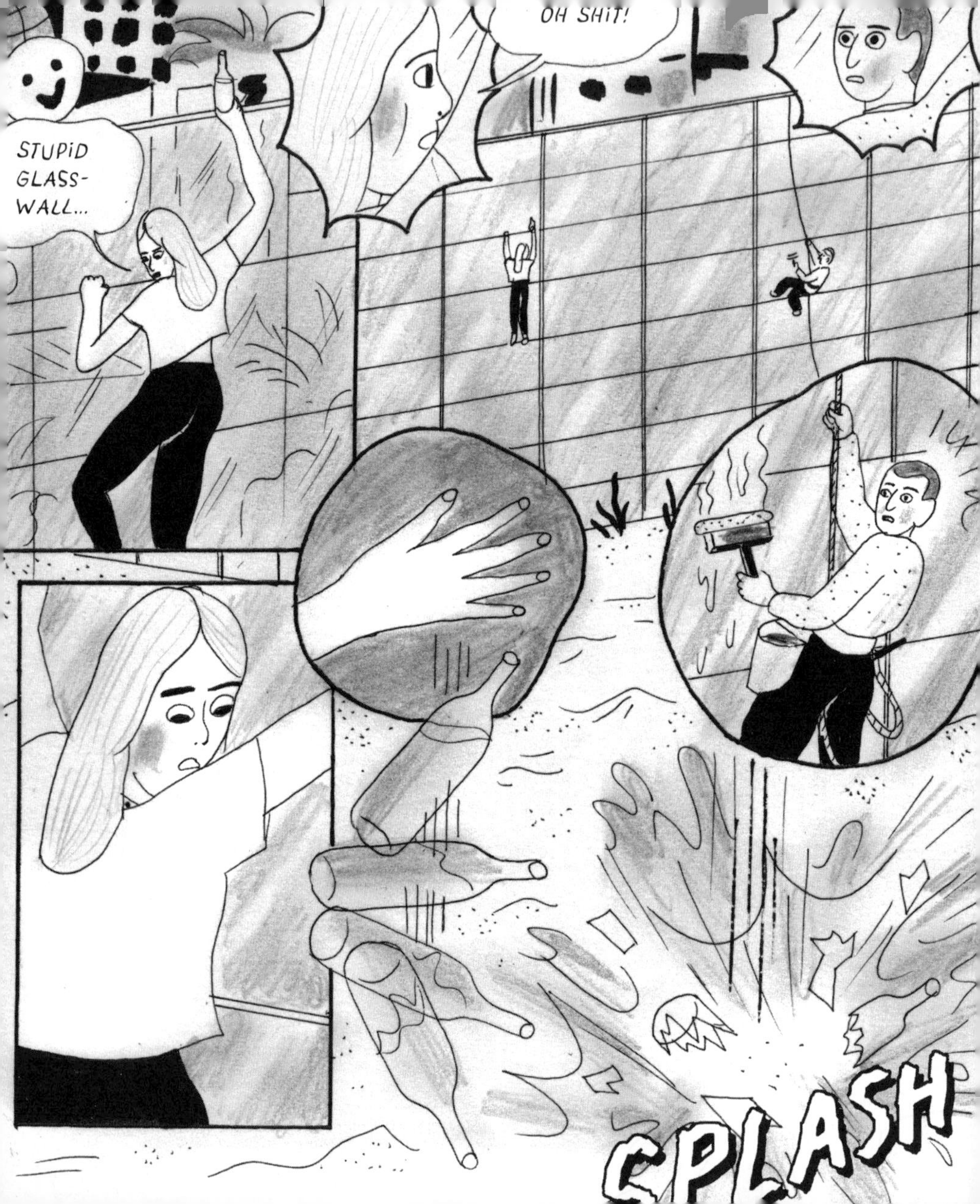
STUPID GLASS-WALL...
OH SHIT!
CPLASH

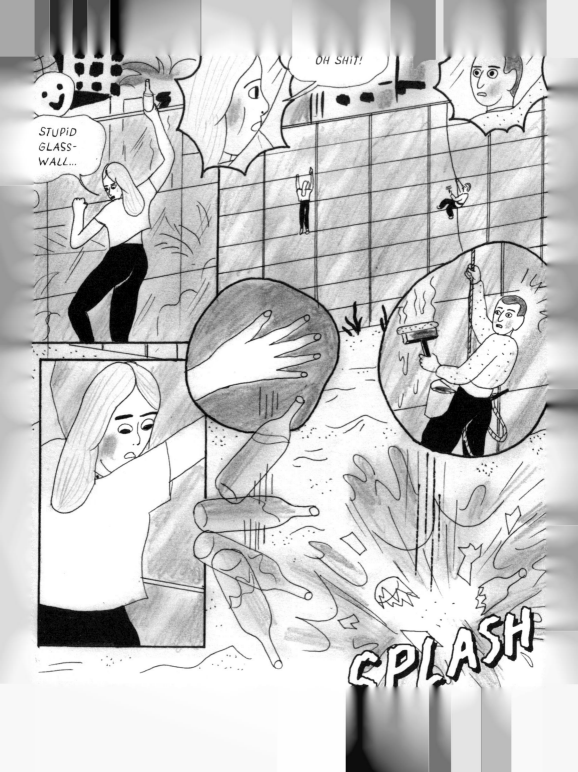

CLOSED

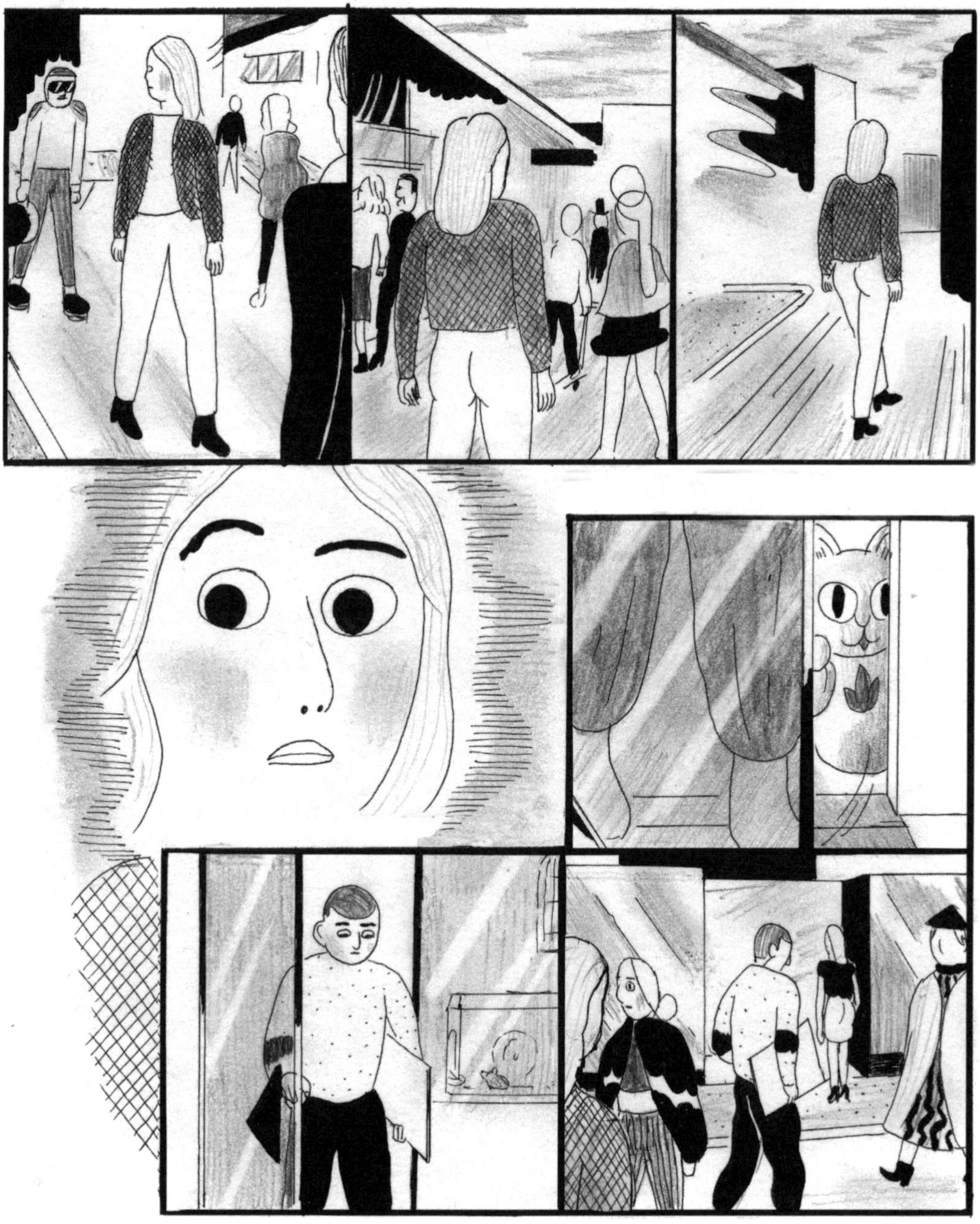

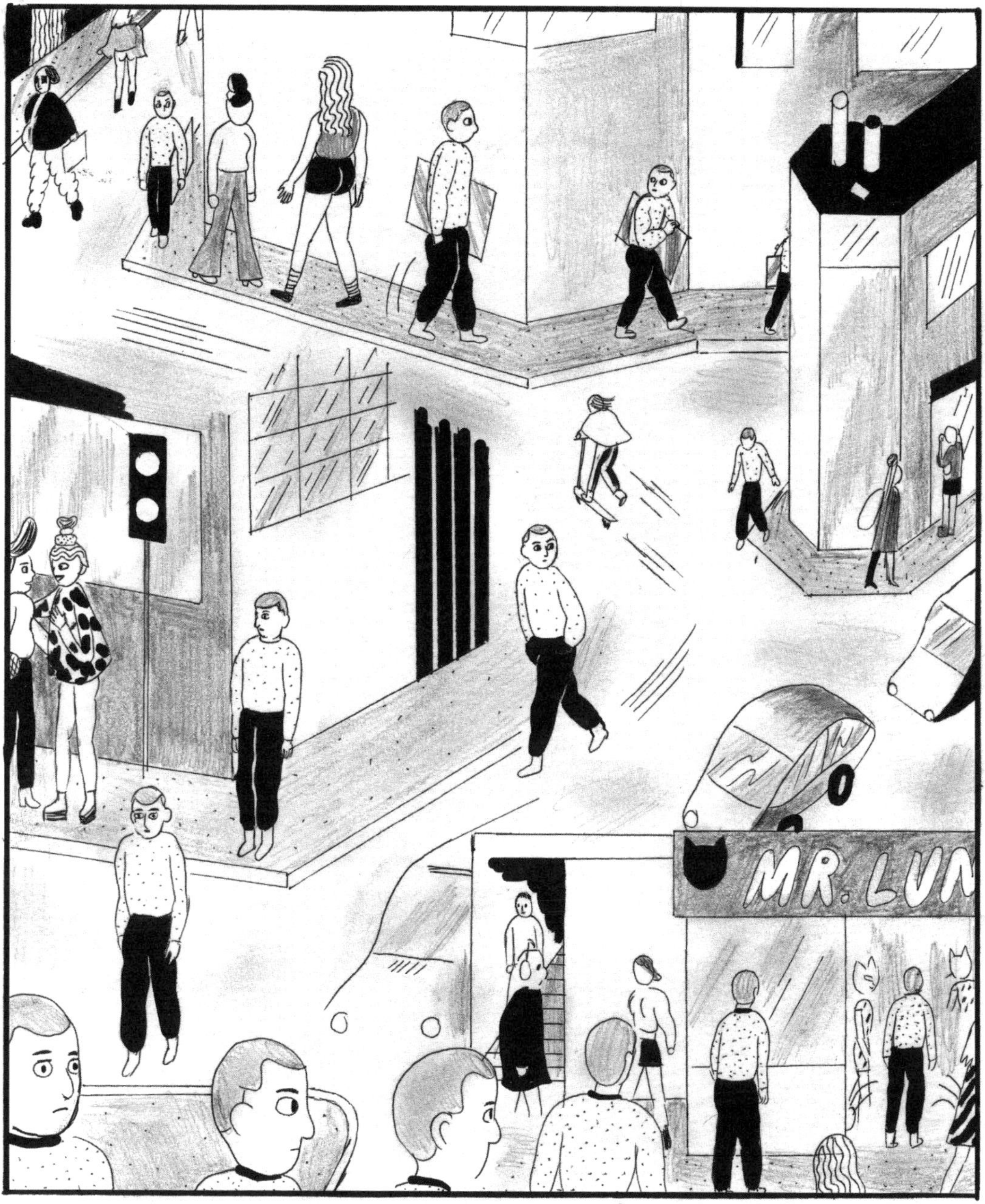
MR. LUN

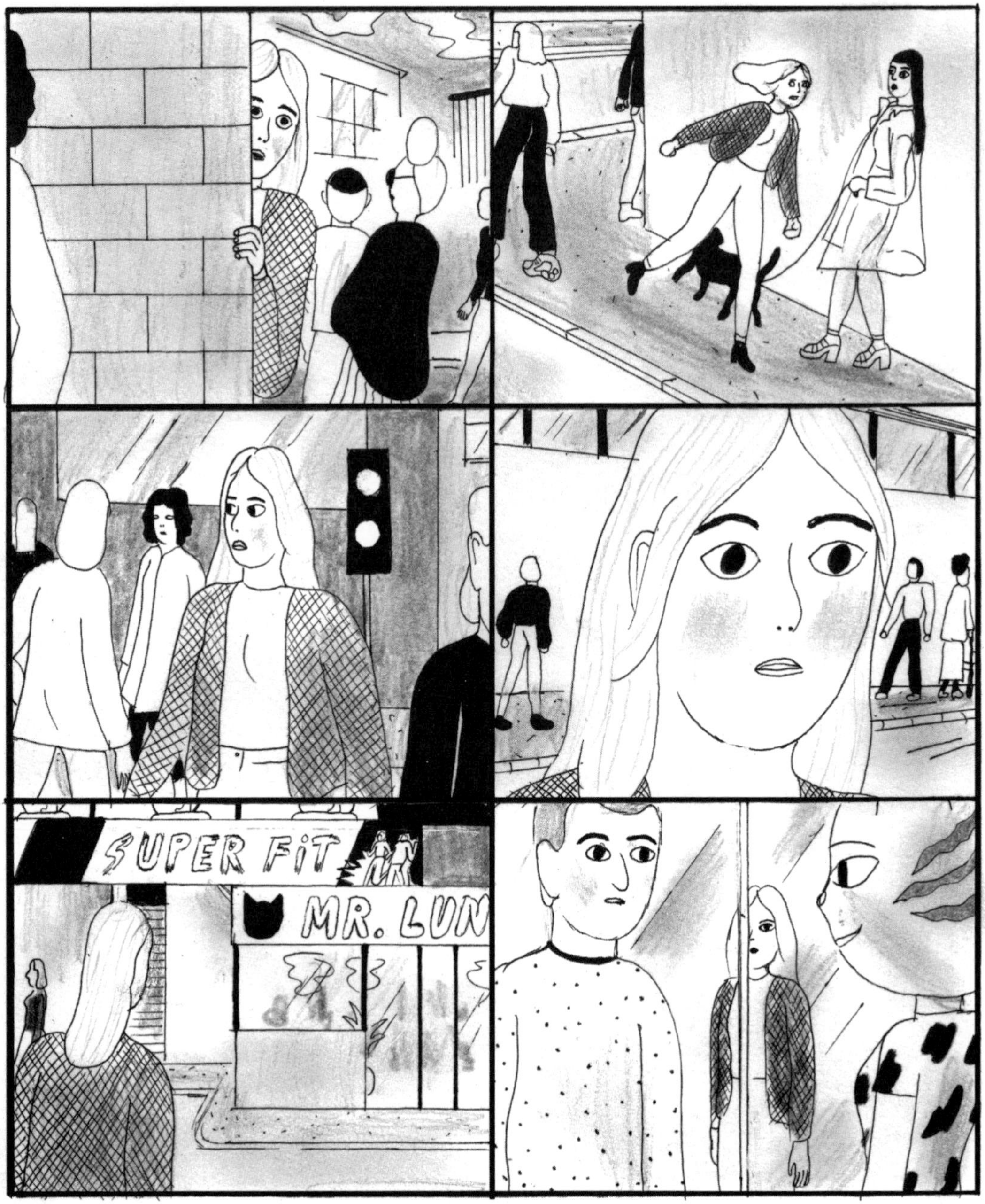
SUPER FIT
MR. LUN

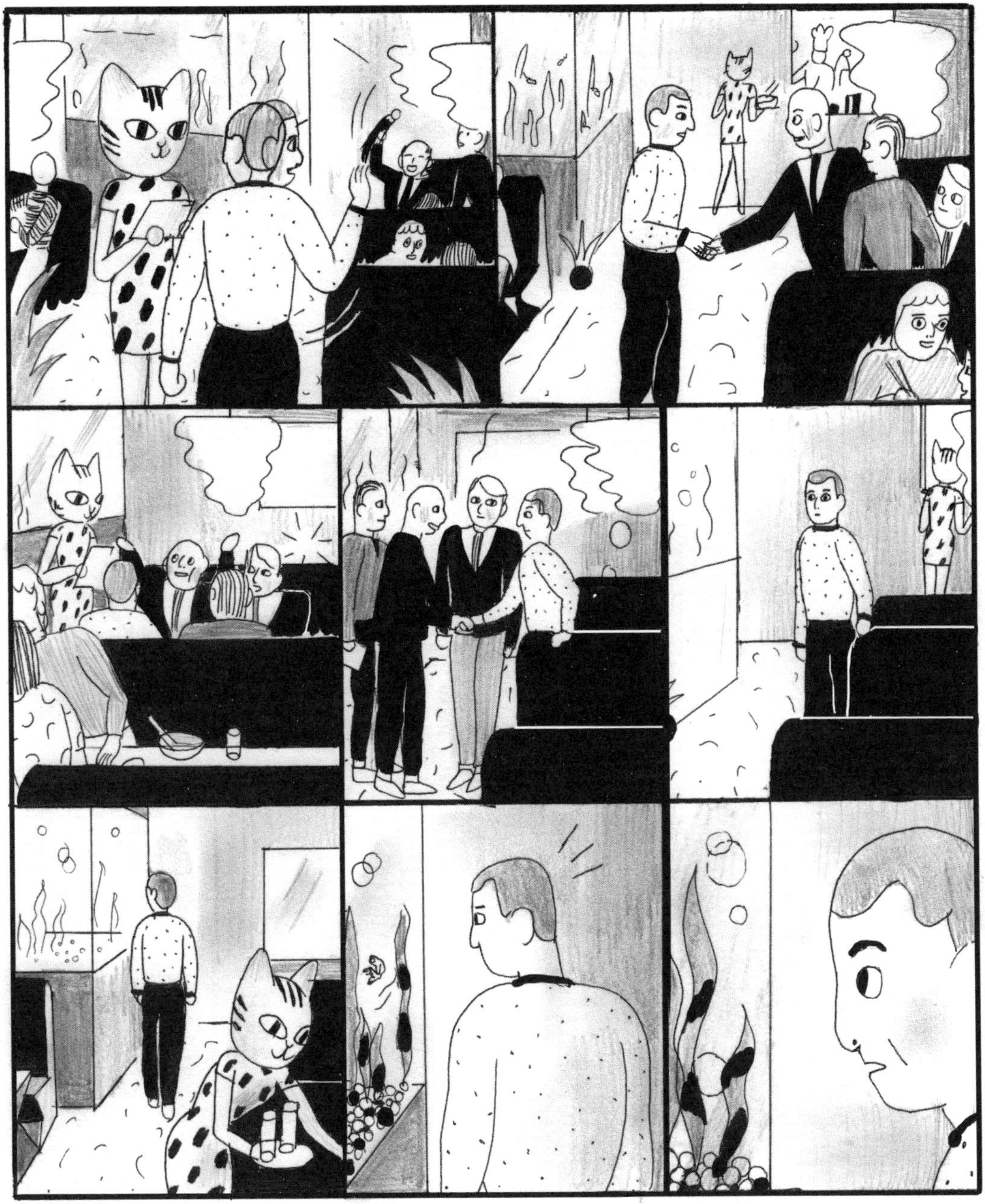

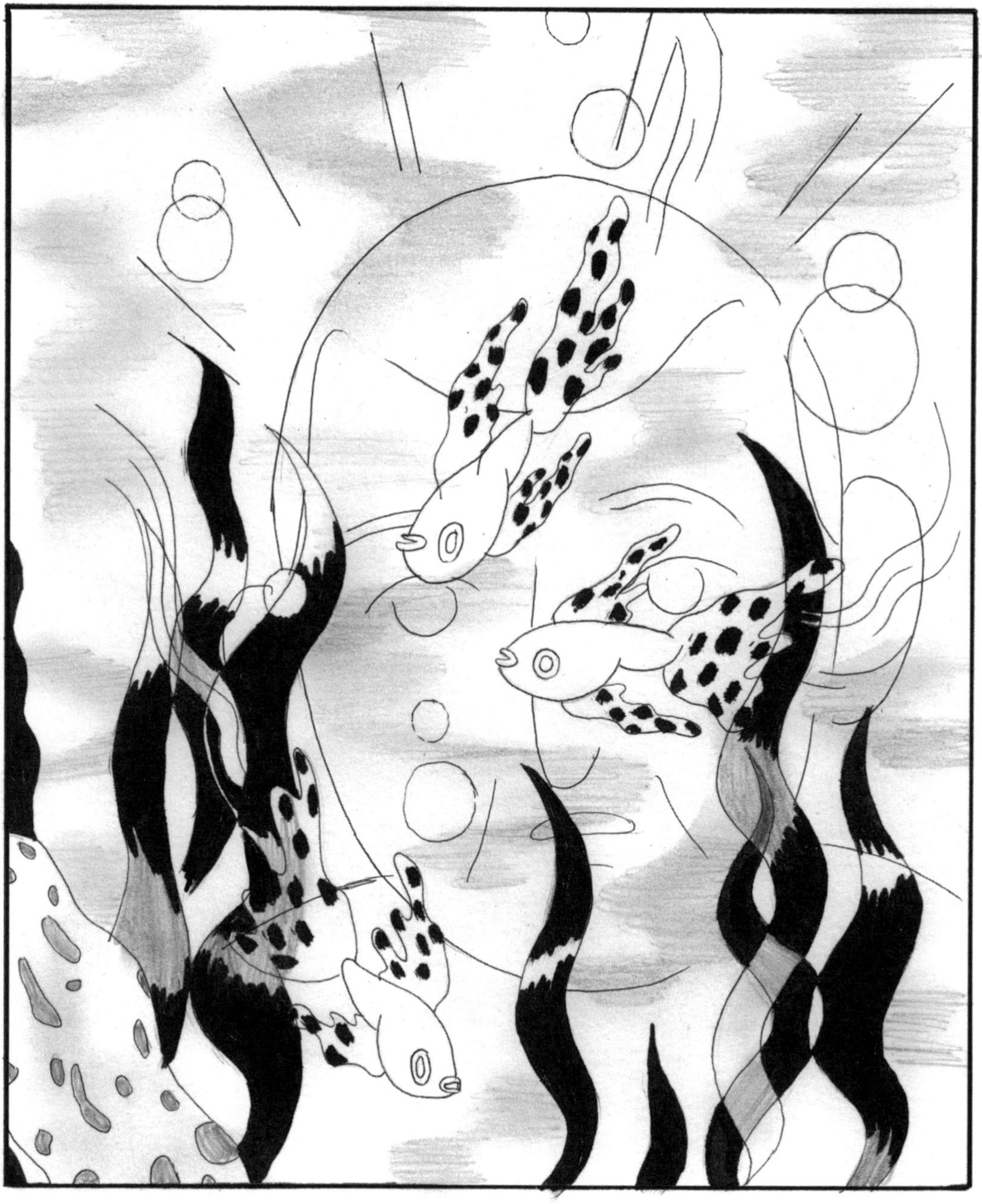

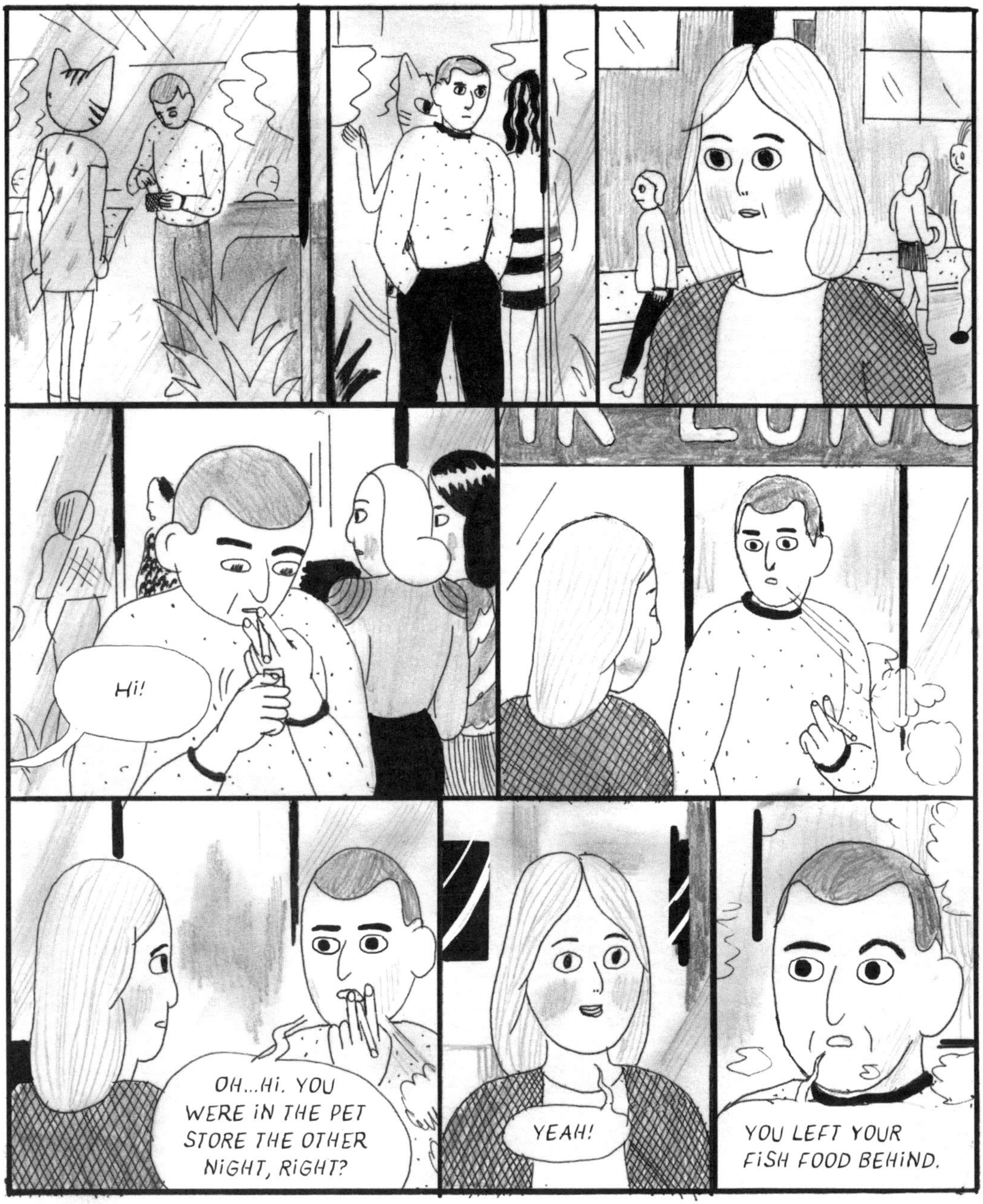
HI!
OH...HI. YOU WERE IN THE PET STORE THE OTHER NIGHT, RIGHT?
YEAH!
YOU LEFT YOUR FISH FOOD BEHIND.

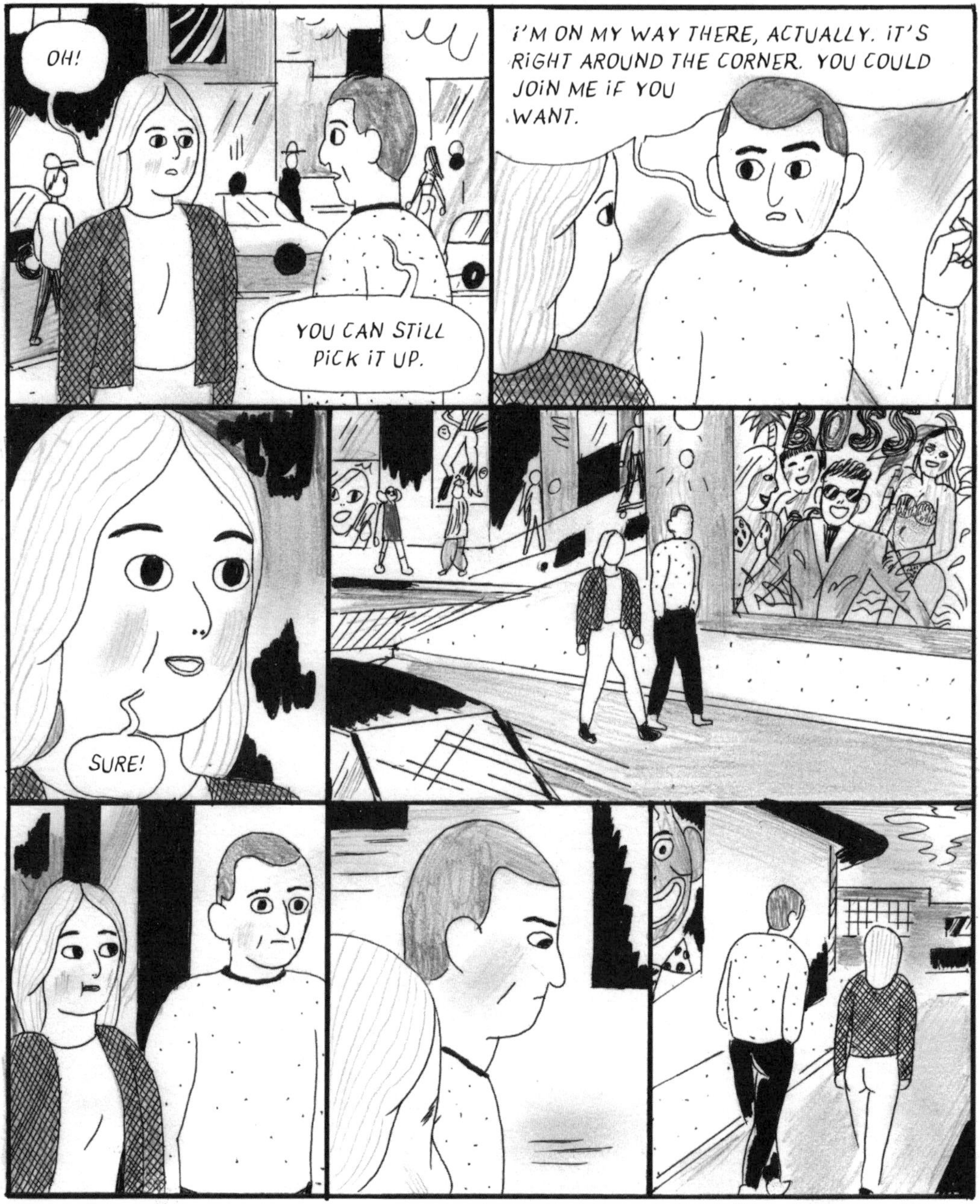
OH!
YOU CAN STILL PICK IT UP.
I'M ON MY WAY THERE, ACTUALLY. IT'S RIGHT AROUND THE CORNER. YOU COULD JOIN ME IF YOU WANT.
SURE!
BOSS

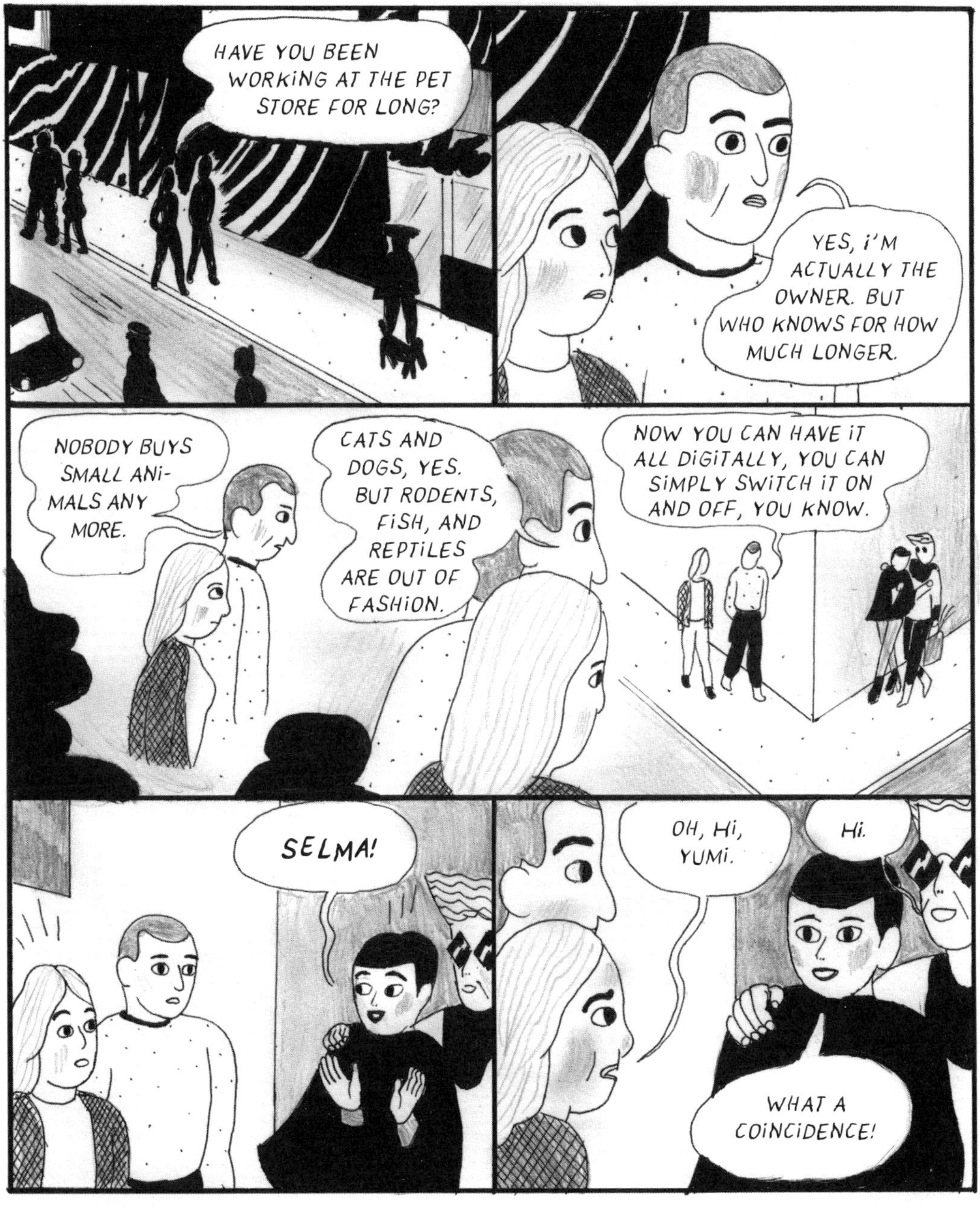
HAVE YOU BEEN WORKING AT THE PET STORE FOR LONG?
YES, I'M ACTUALLY THE OWNER. BUT WHO KNOWS FOR HOW MUCH LONGER.
NOBODY BUYS SMALL ANI-MALS ANY MORE.
CATS AND DOGS, YES. BUT RODENTS, FISH, AND REPTILES ARE OUT OF FASHION.
NOW YOU CAN HAVE IT ALL DIGITALLY, YOU CAN SIMPLY SWITCH IT ON AND OFF, YOU KNOW.
SELMA!
OH, HI, YUMI.
HI.
WHAT A COINCIDENCE!

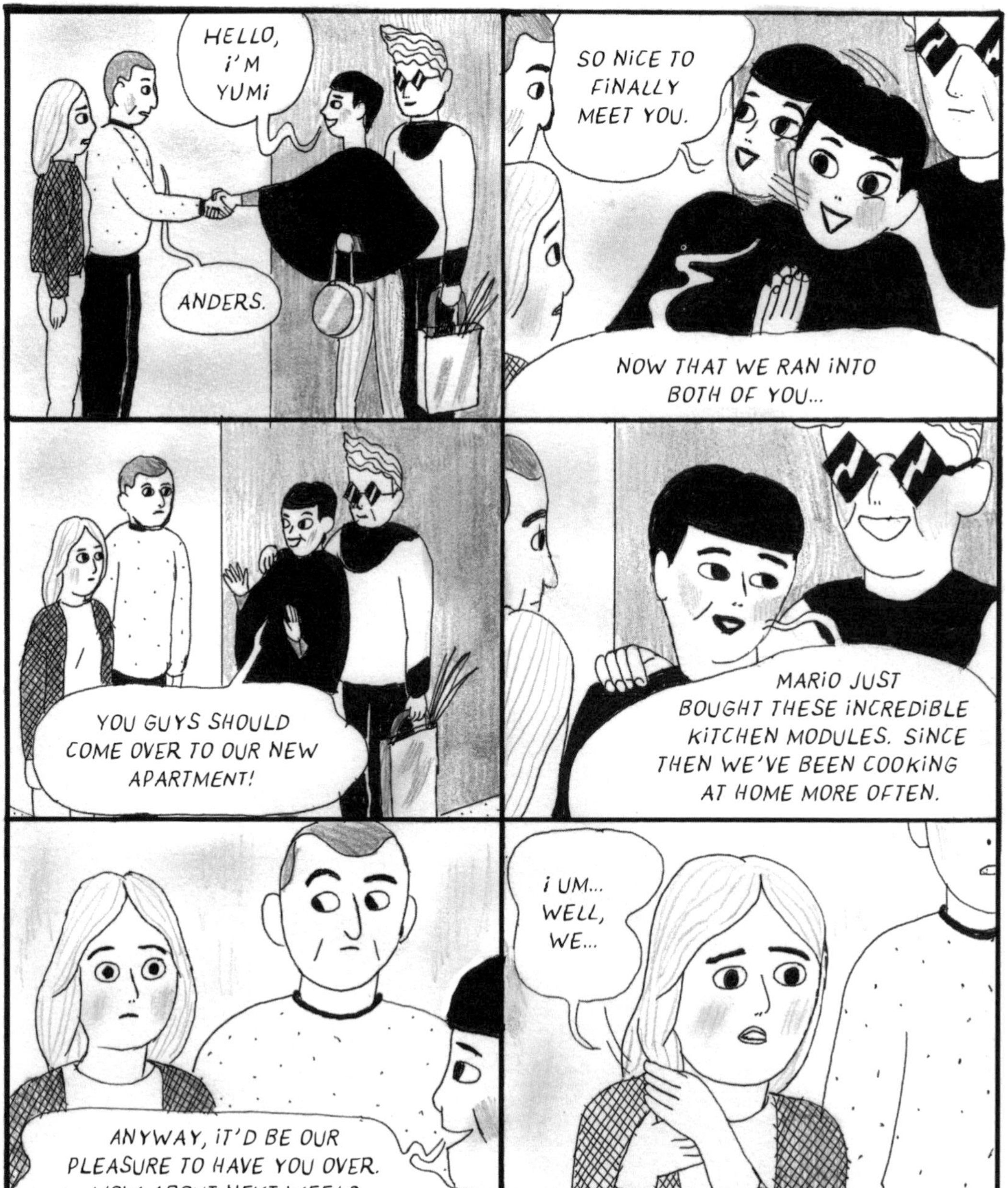
HELLO, I'M YUMI
ANDERS.
SO NICE TO FINALLY MEET YOU.
NOW THAT WE RAN INTO BOTH OF YOU...
YOU GUYS SHOULD COME OVER TO OUR NEW APARTMENT!
MARIO JUST BOUGHT THESE INCREDIBLE KITCHEN MODULES. SINCE THEN WE'VE BEEN COOKING AT HOME MORE OFTEN.
ANYWAY, IT'D BE OUR PLEASURE TO HAVE YOU OVER. HOW ABOUT NEXT WEEK?
I UM... WELL, WE...

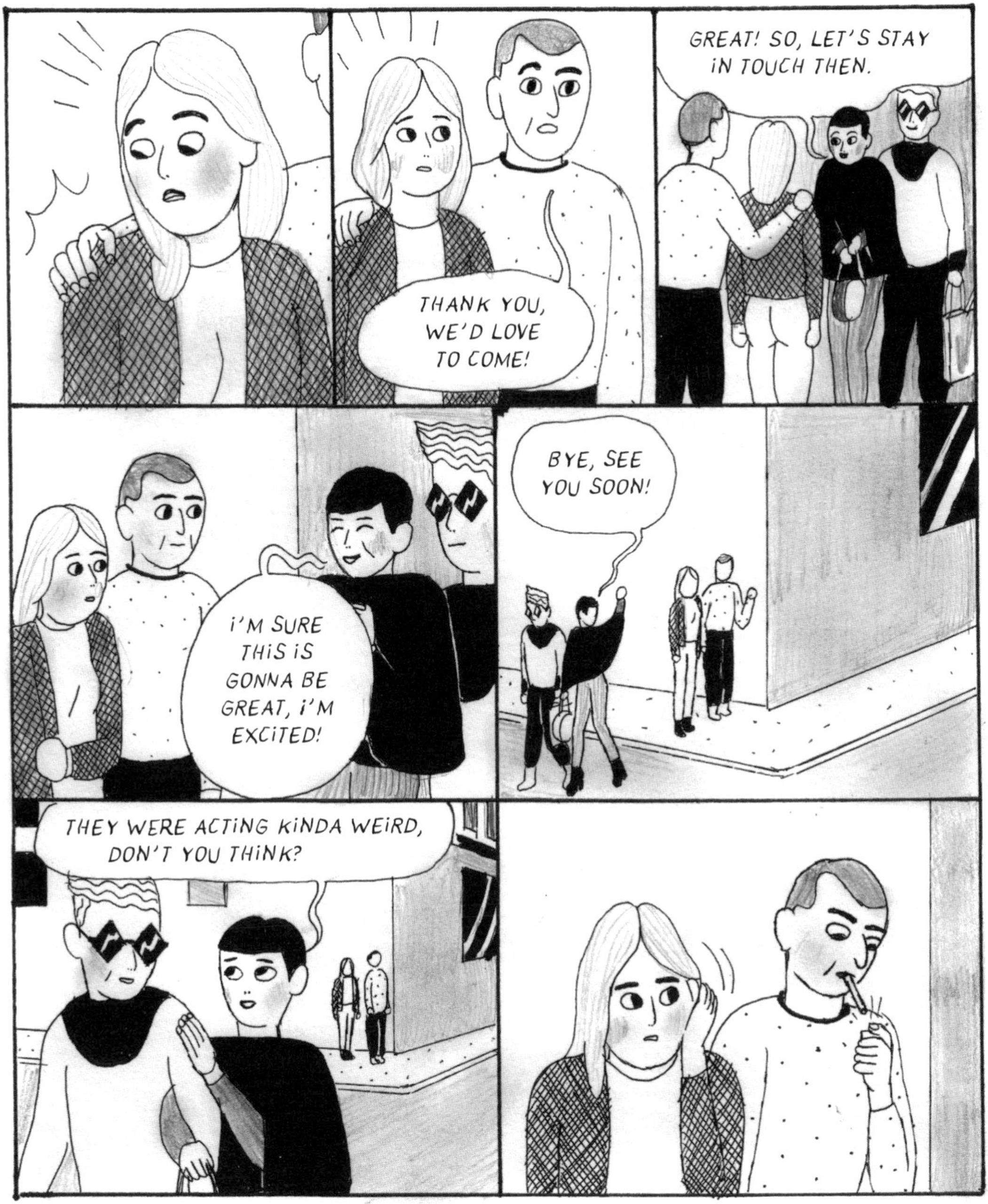
THANK YOU, WE'D LOVE TO COME!
GREAT! SO, LET'S STAY IN TOUCH THEN.
I'M SURE THIS IS GONNA BE GREAT, I'M EXCITED!
BYE, SEE YOU SOON!
THEY WERE ACTING KINDA WEIRD, DON'T YOU THINK?

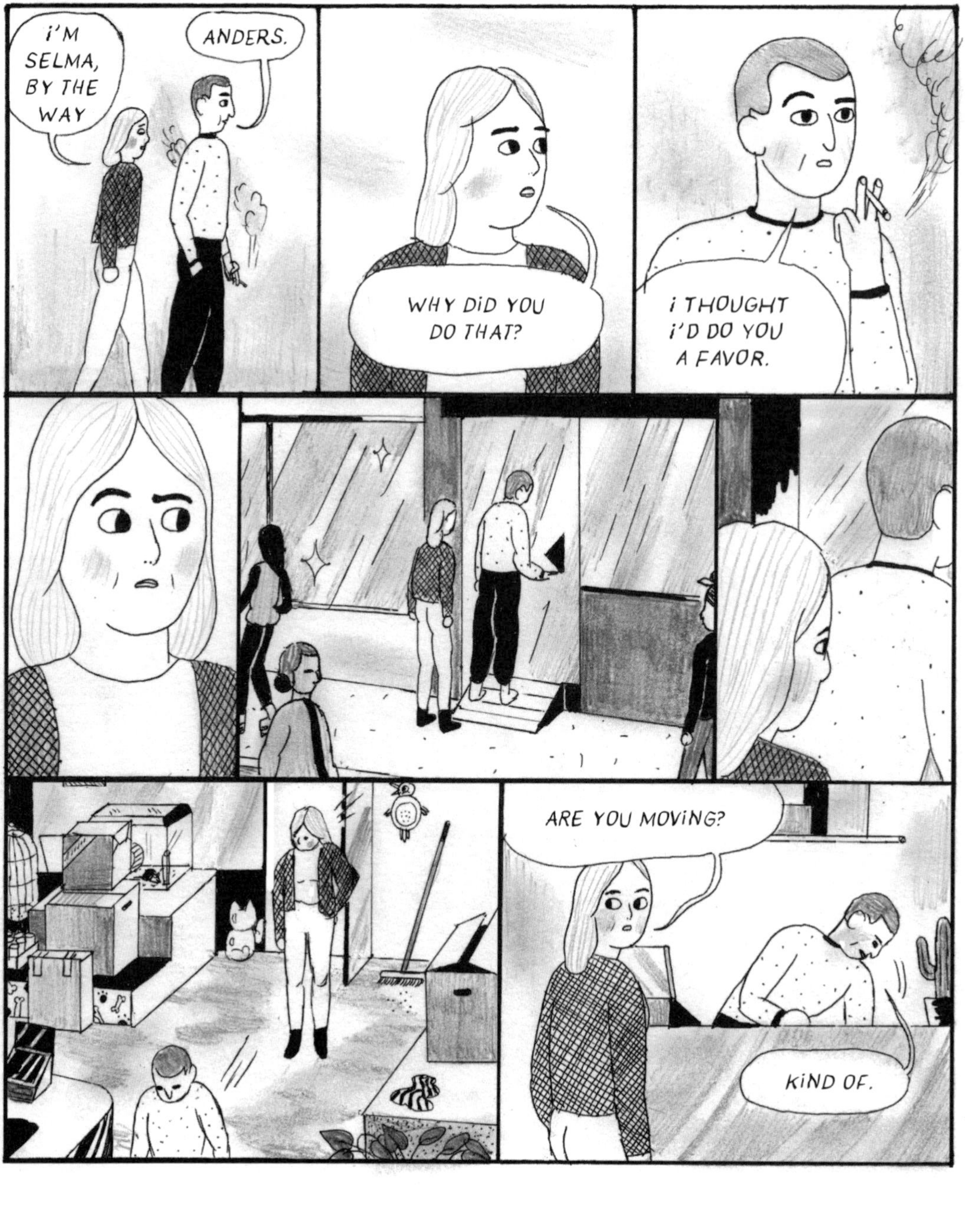
I'M SELMA, BY THE WAY
ANDERS.
WHY DID YOU DO THAT?
I THOUGHT I'D DO YOU A FAVOR.
ARE YOU MOVING?
KIND OF.

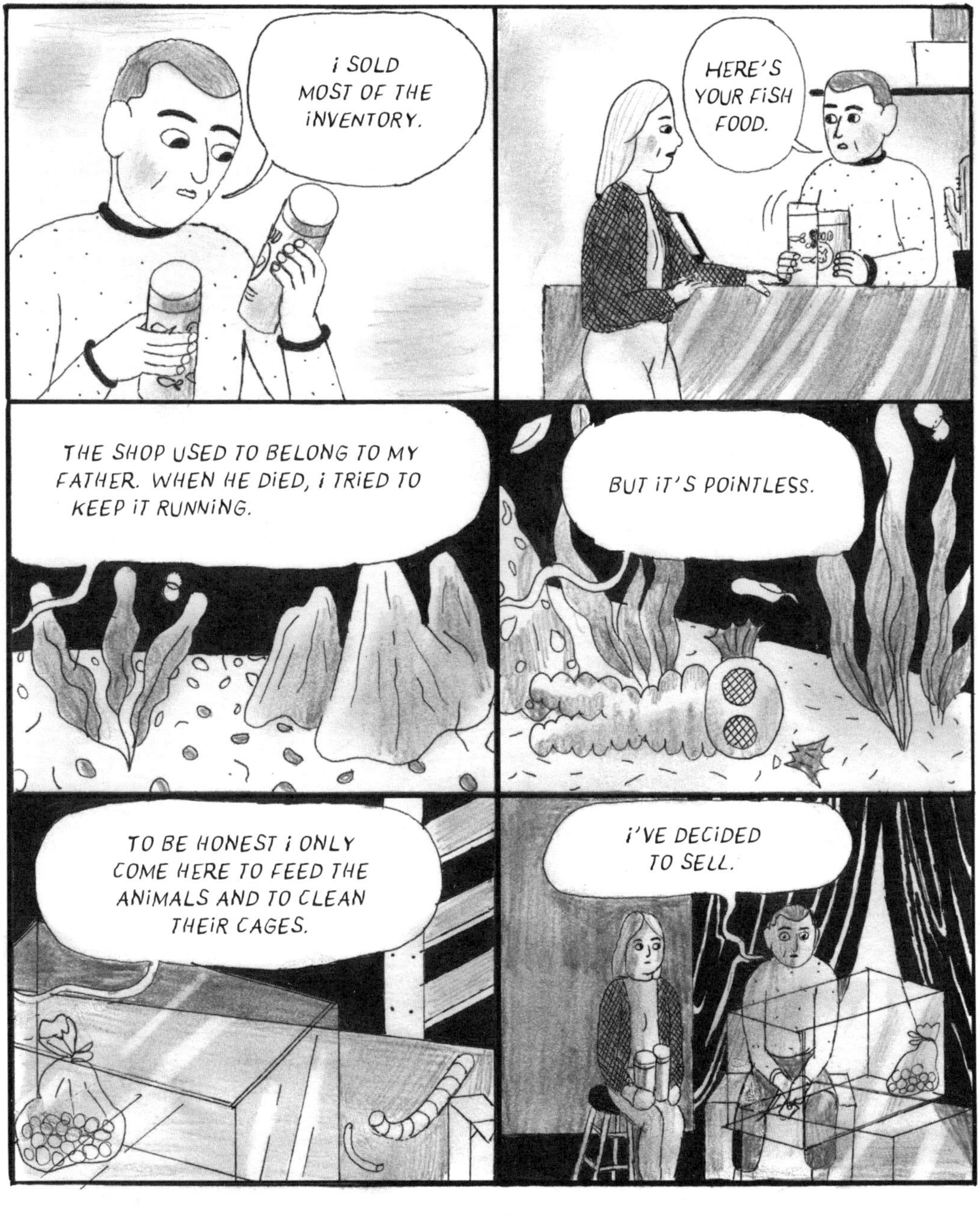
I SOLD MOST OF THE INVENTORY.
HERE'S YOUR FISH FOOD.
THE SHOP USED TO BELONG TO MY FATHER. WHEN HE DIED, I TRIED TO KEEP IT RUNNING.
BUT IT'S POINTLESS.
TO BE HONEST I ONLY COME HERE TO FEED THE ANIMALS AND TO CLEAN THEIR CAGES.
I'VE DECIDED TO SELL.

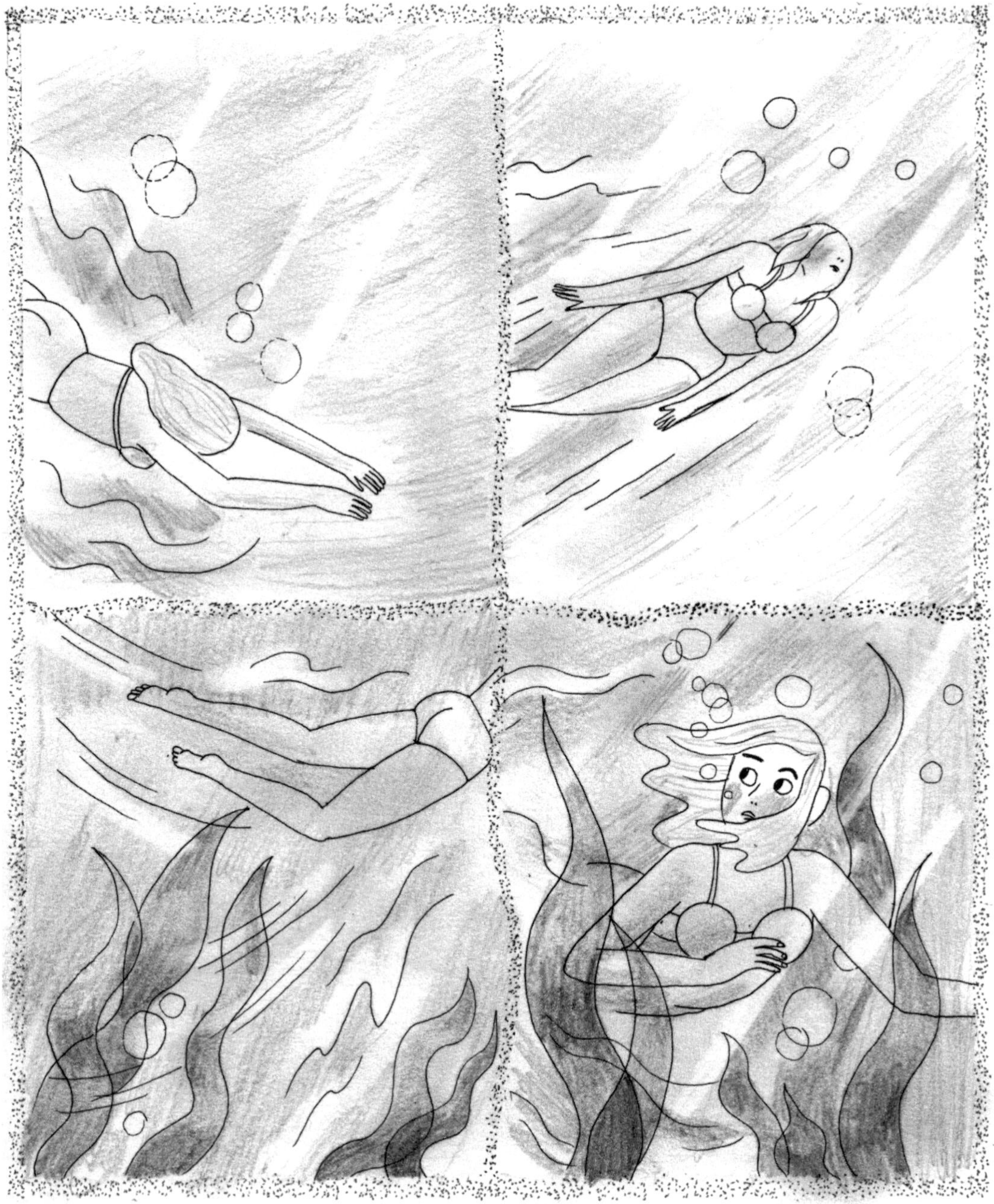

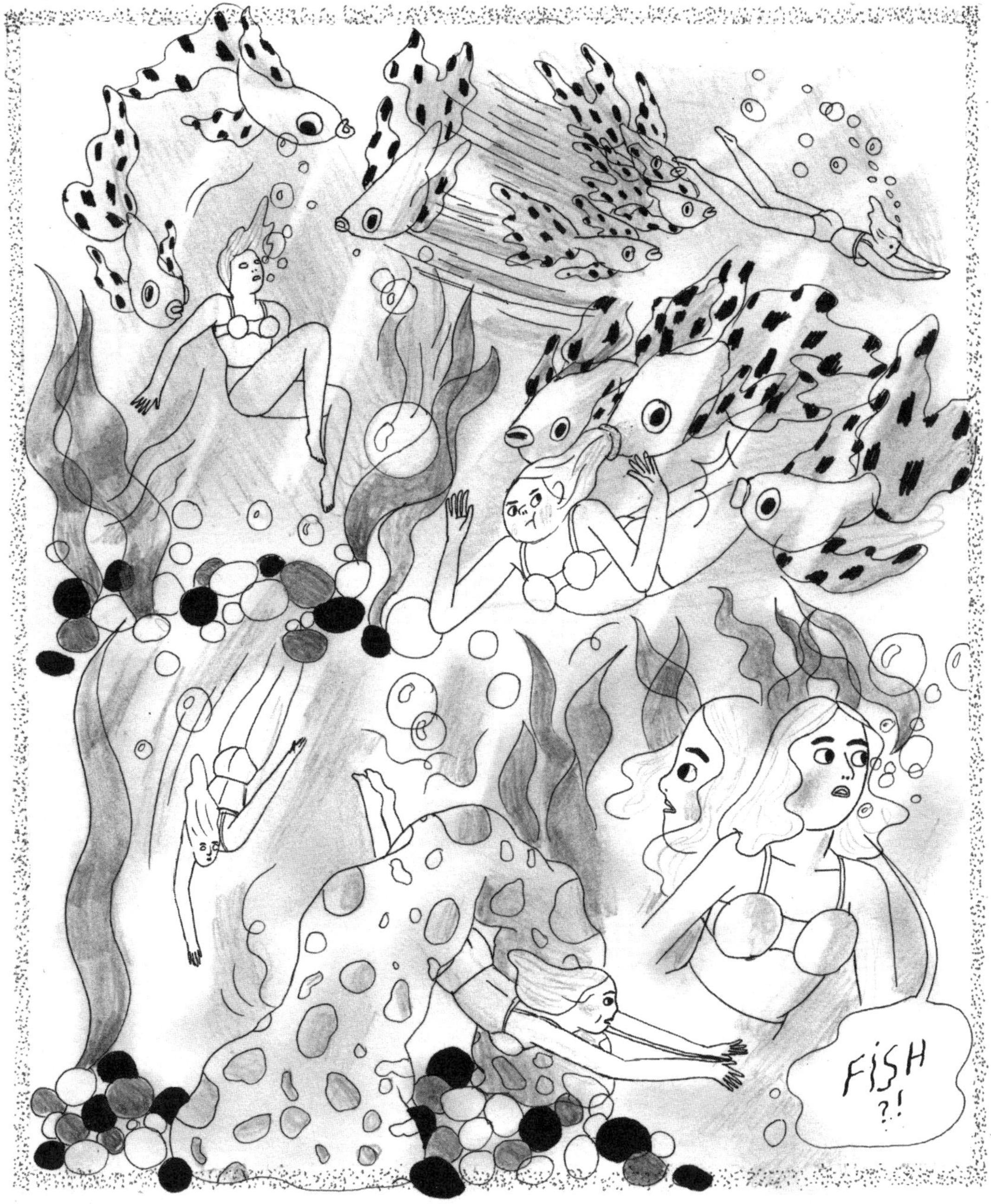
FISH ?!

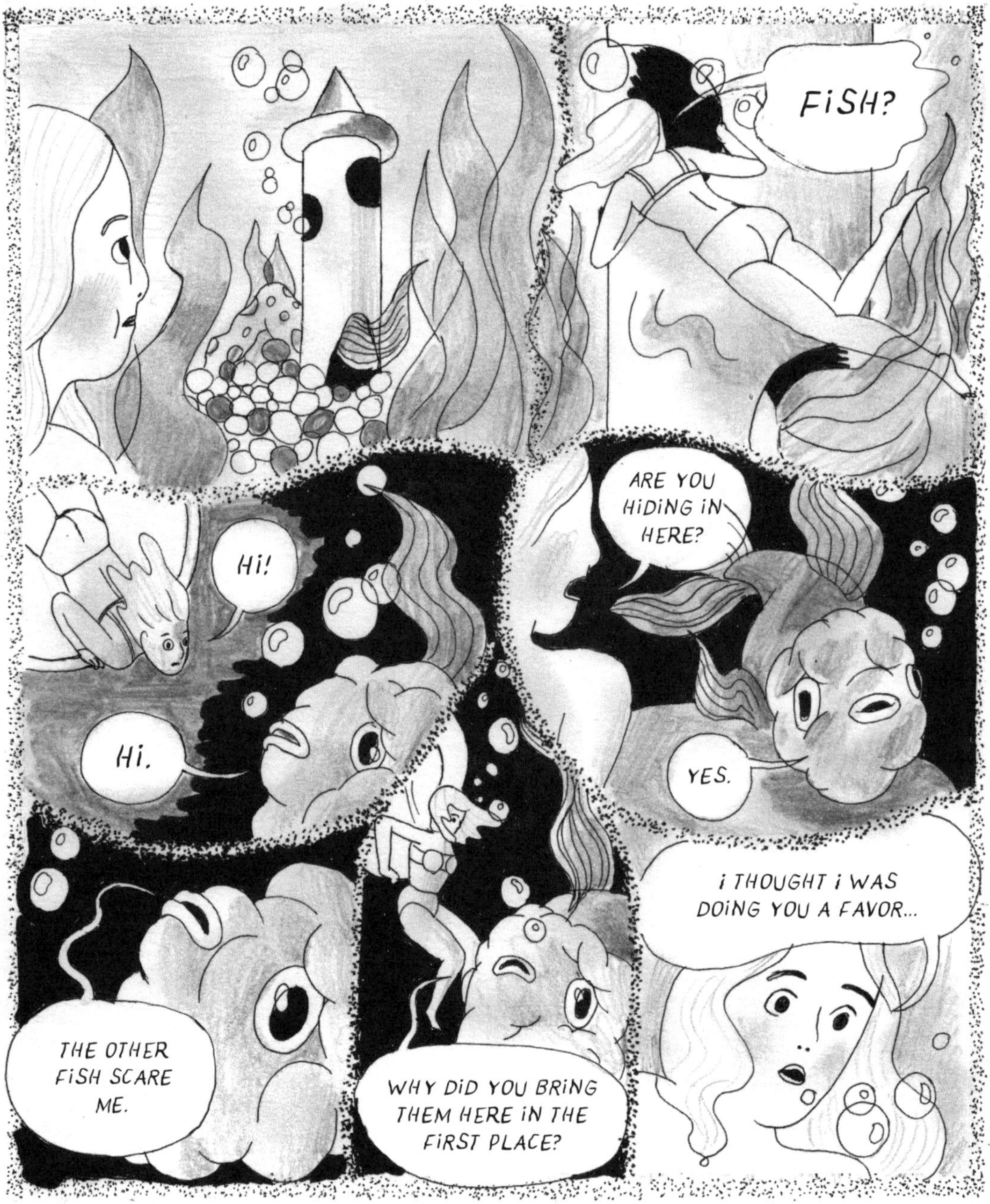
FiSH?
Hi!
Hi.
ARE YOU HiDiNG iN HERE?
YES.
THE OTHER FiSH SCARE ME.
WHY DiD YOU BRiNG THEM HERE iN THE FiRST PLACE?
i THOUGHT i WAS DOiNG YOU A FAVOR...

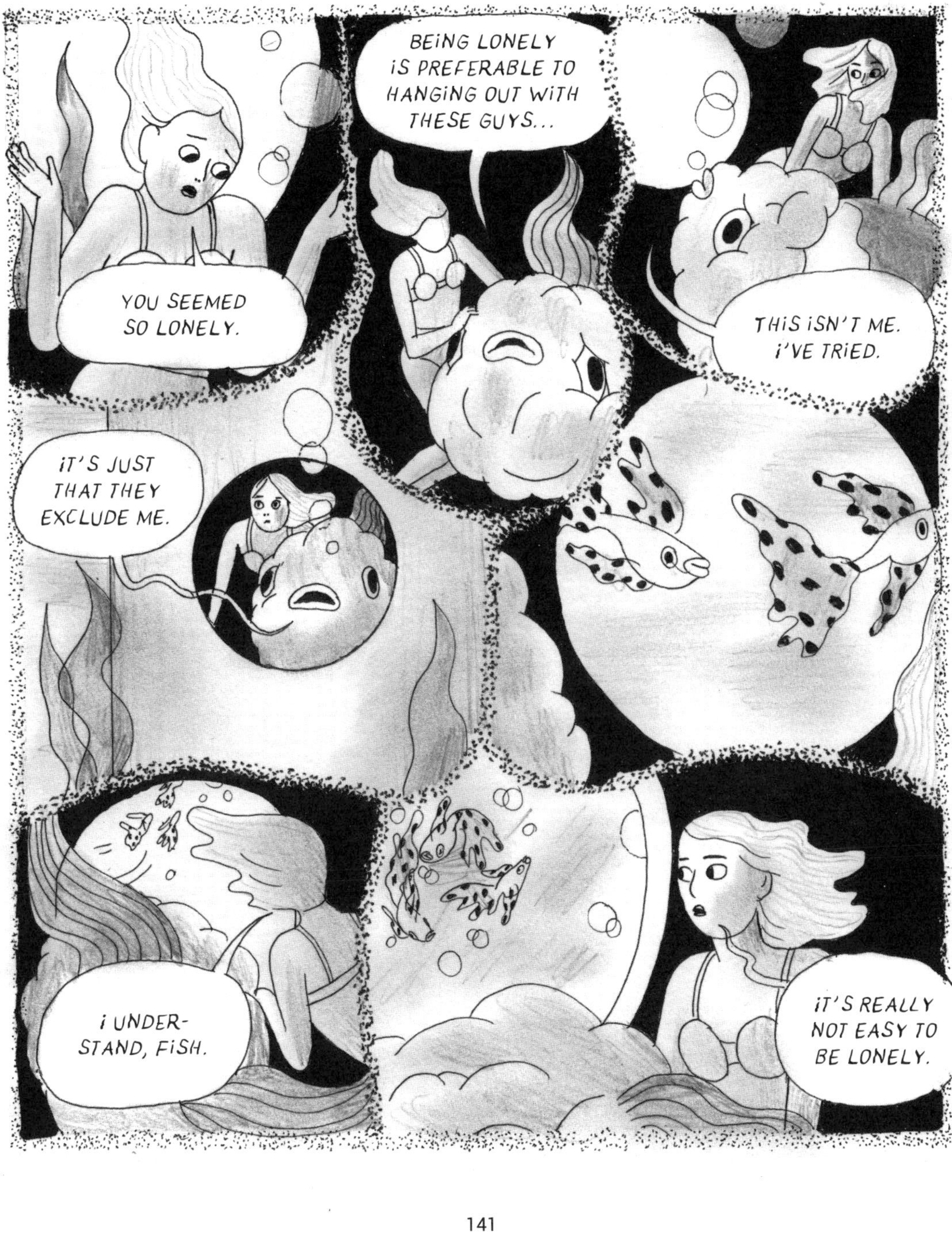
YOU SEEMED SO LONELY.
BEING LONELY IS PREFERABLE TO HANGING OUT WITH THESE GUYS...
THIS ISN'T ME. I'VE TRIED.
IT'S JUST THAT THEY EXCLUDE ME.
I UNDER-STAND, FISH.
IT'S REALLY NOT EASY TO BE LONELY.

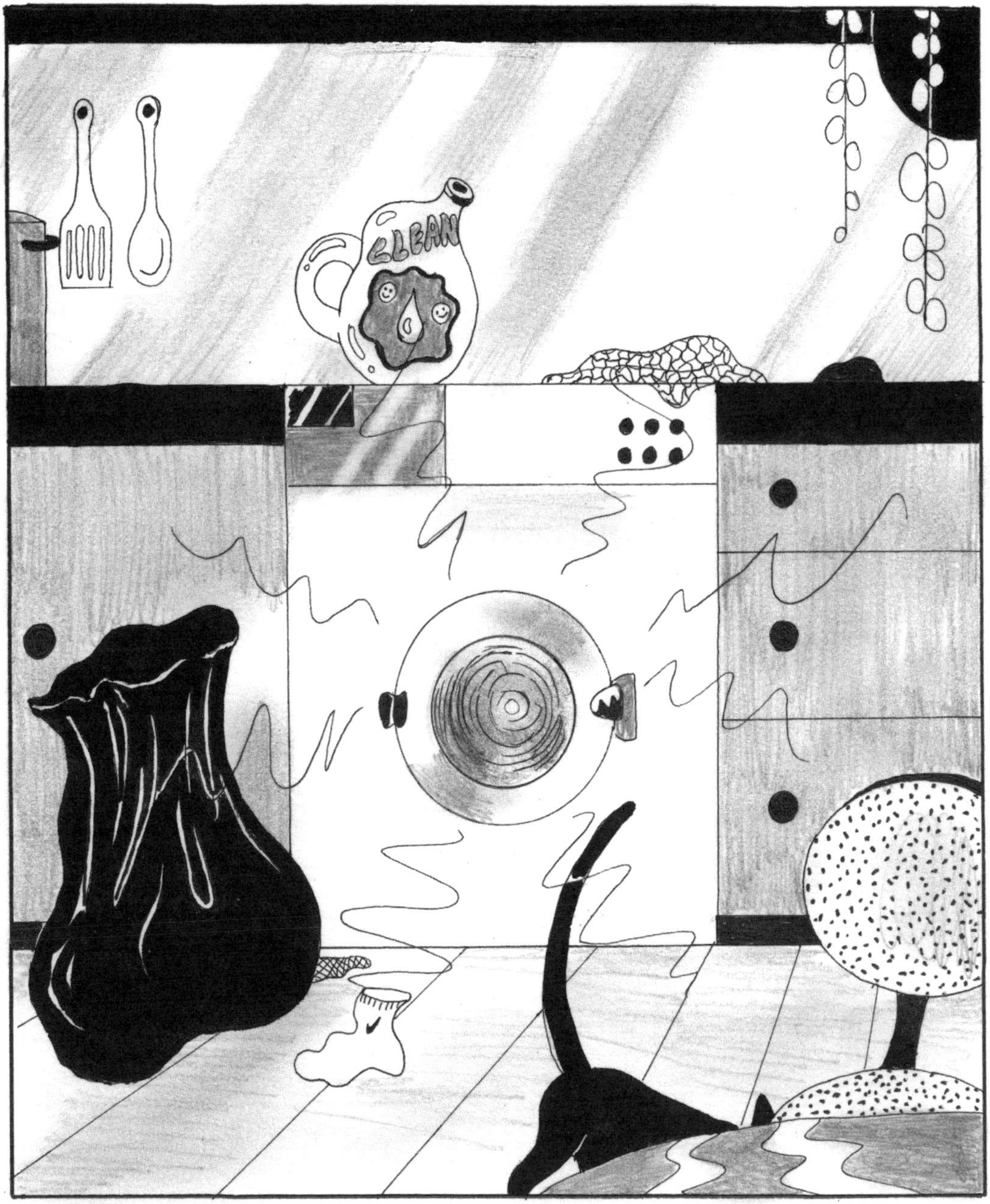
CLEAN

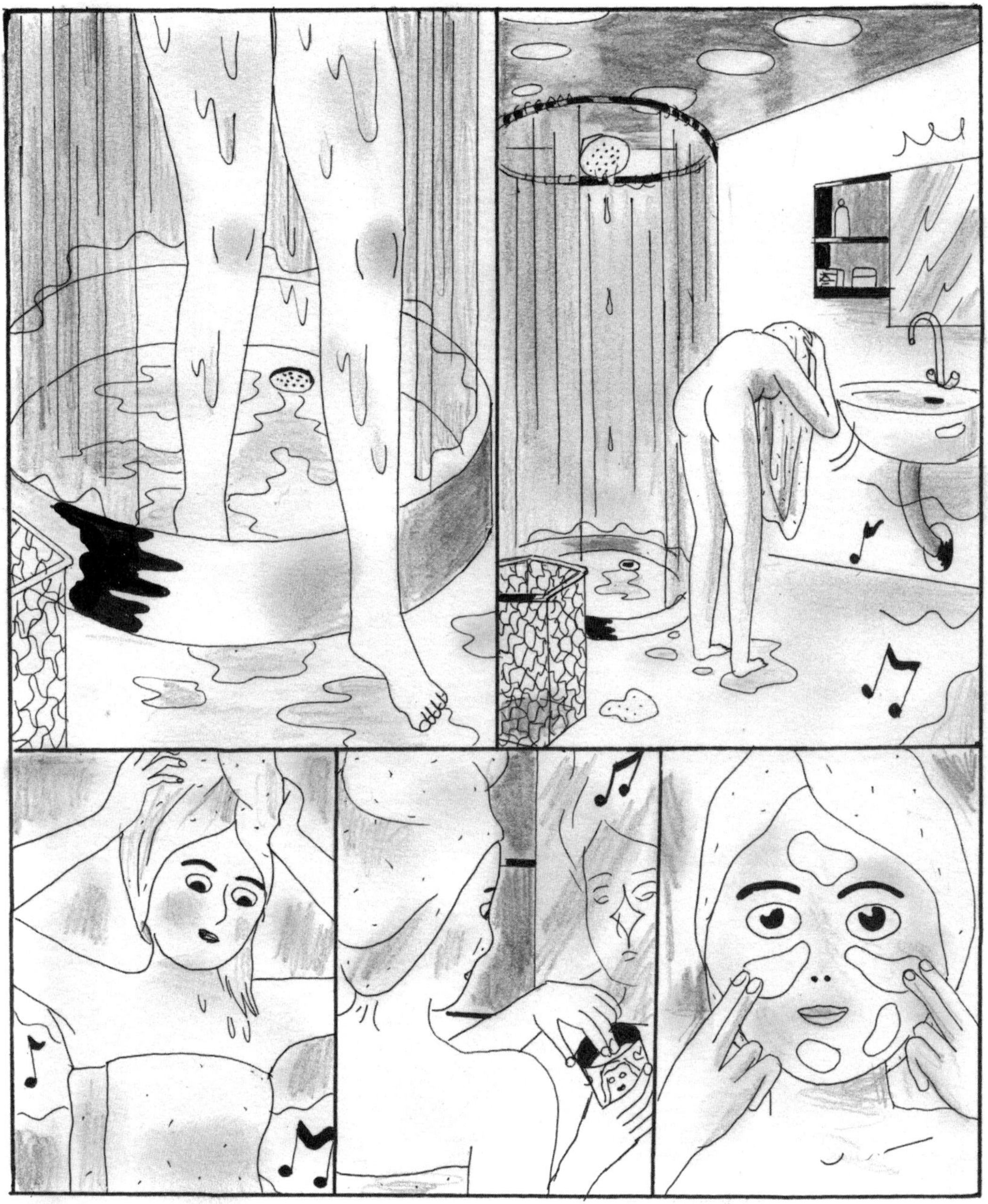

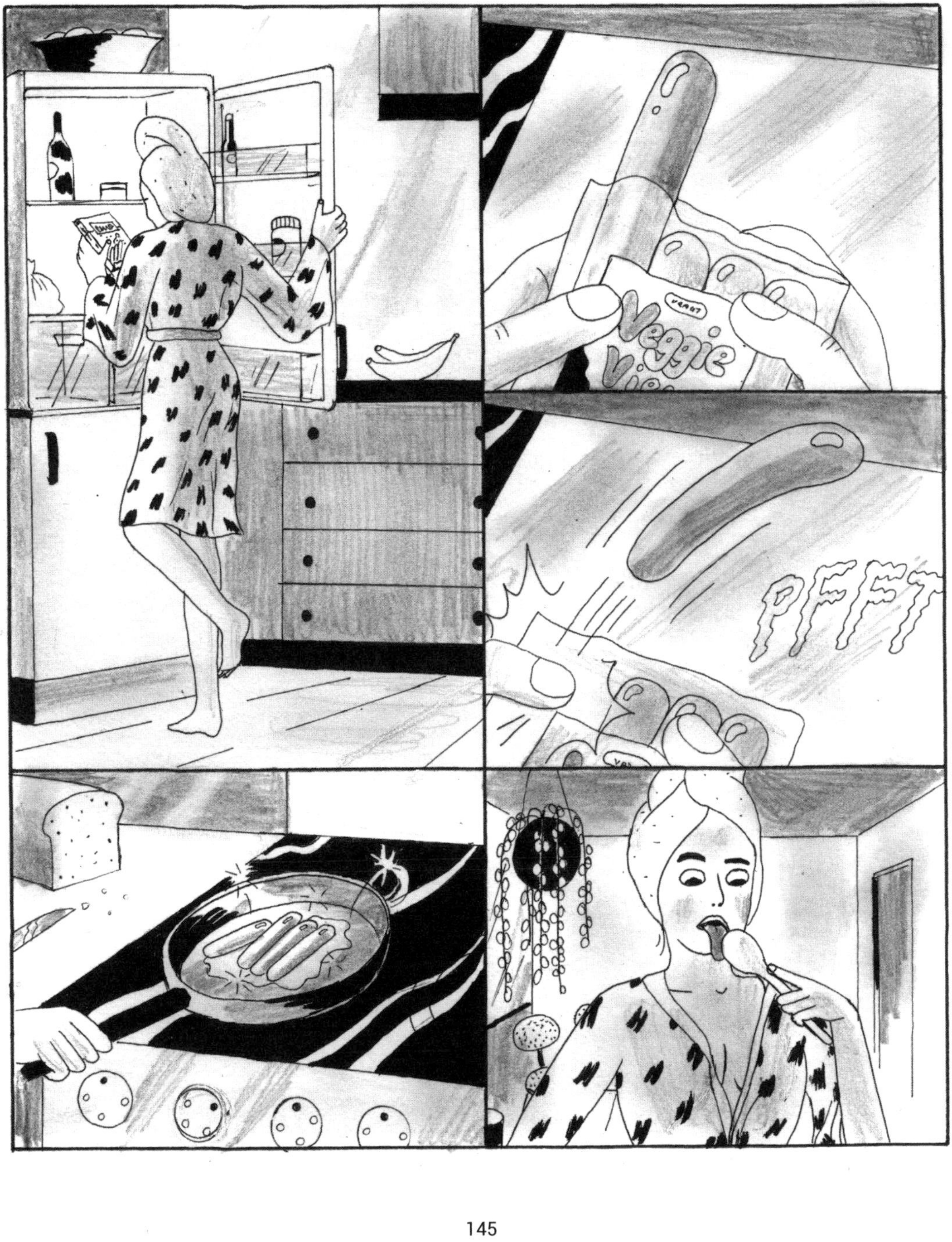
Veggie
PFFT

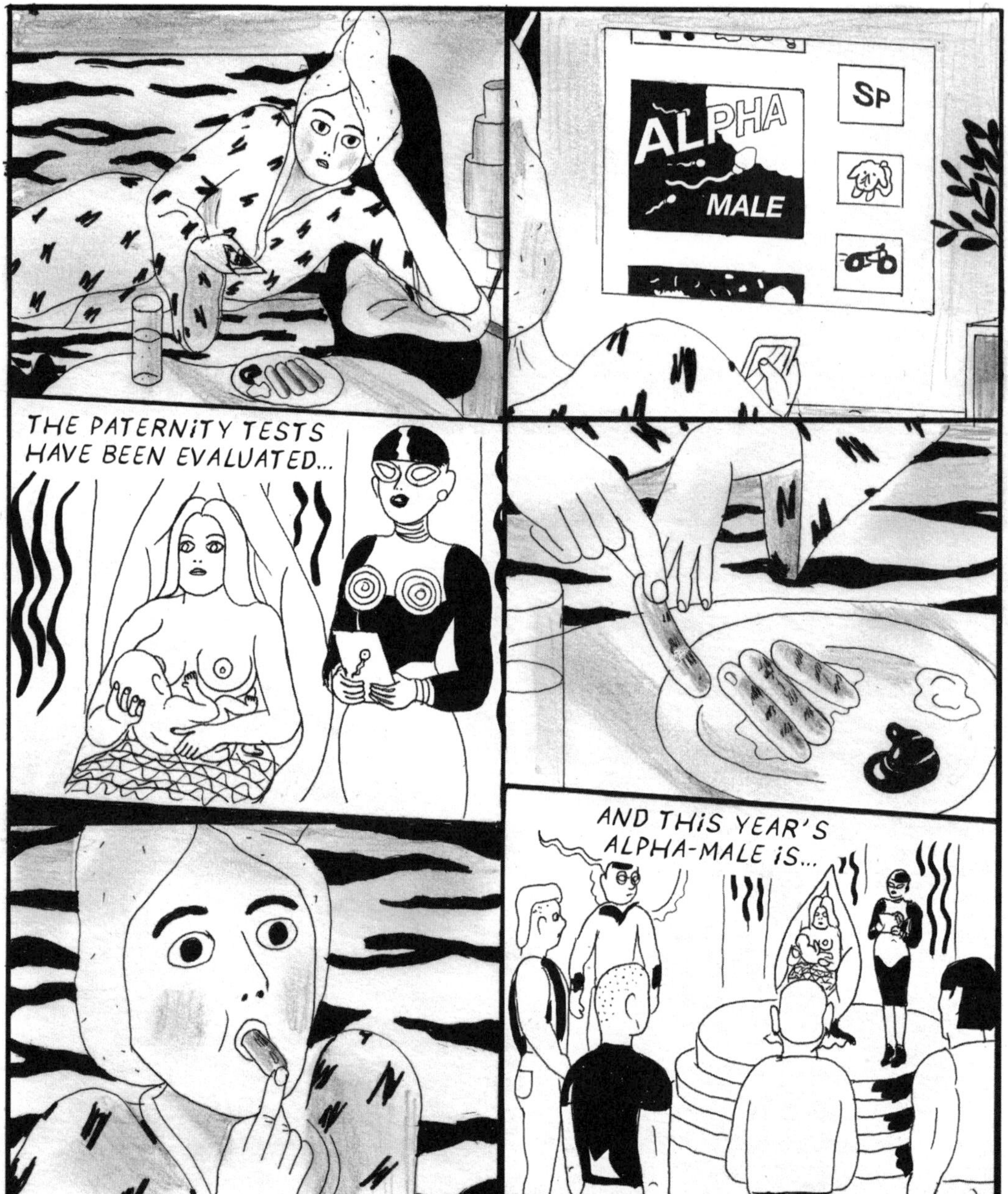
ALPHA
MALE
SP
THE PATERNITY TESTS HAVE BEEN EVALUATED...
AND THIS YEAR'S ALPHA-MALE IS...

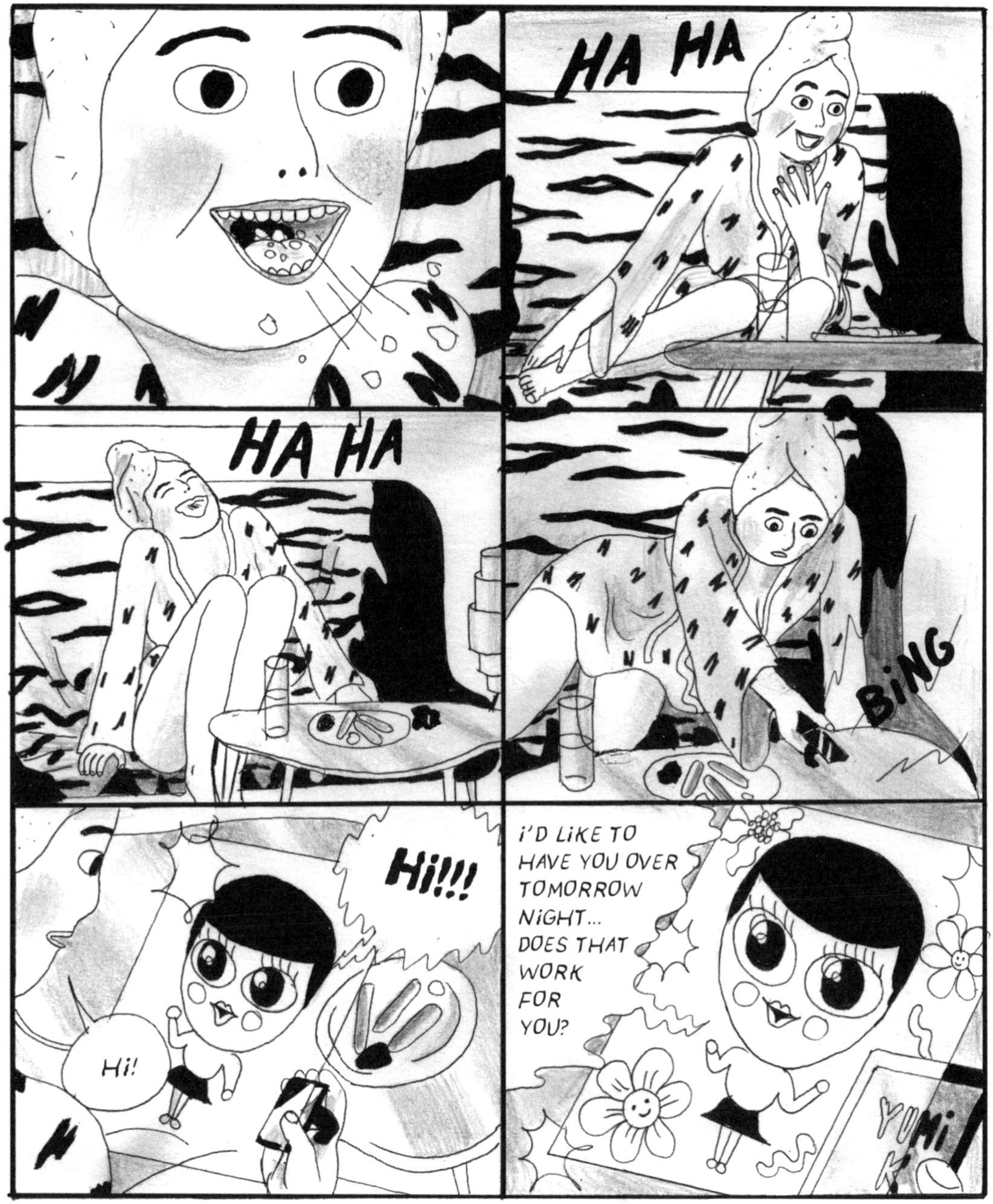
HA HA
HA HA
BiNG
Hi!!!
Hi!
i'D LiKE TO HAVE YOU OVER TOMORROW NiGHT... DOES THAT WORK FOR YOU?
YUMi

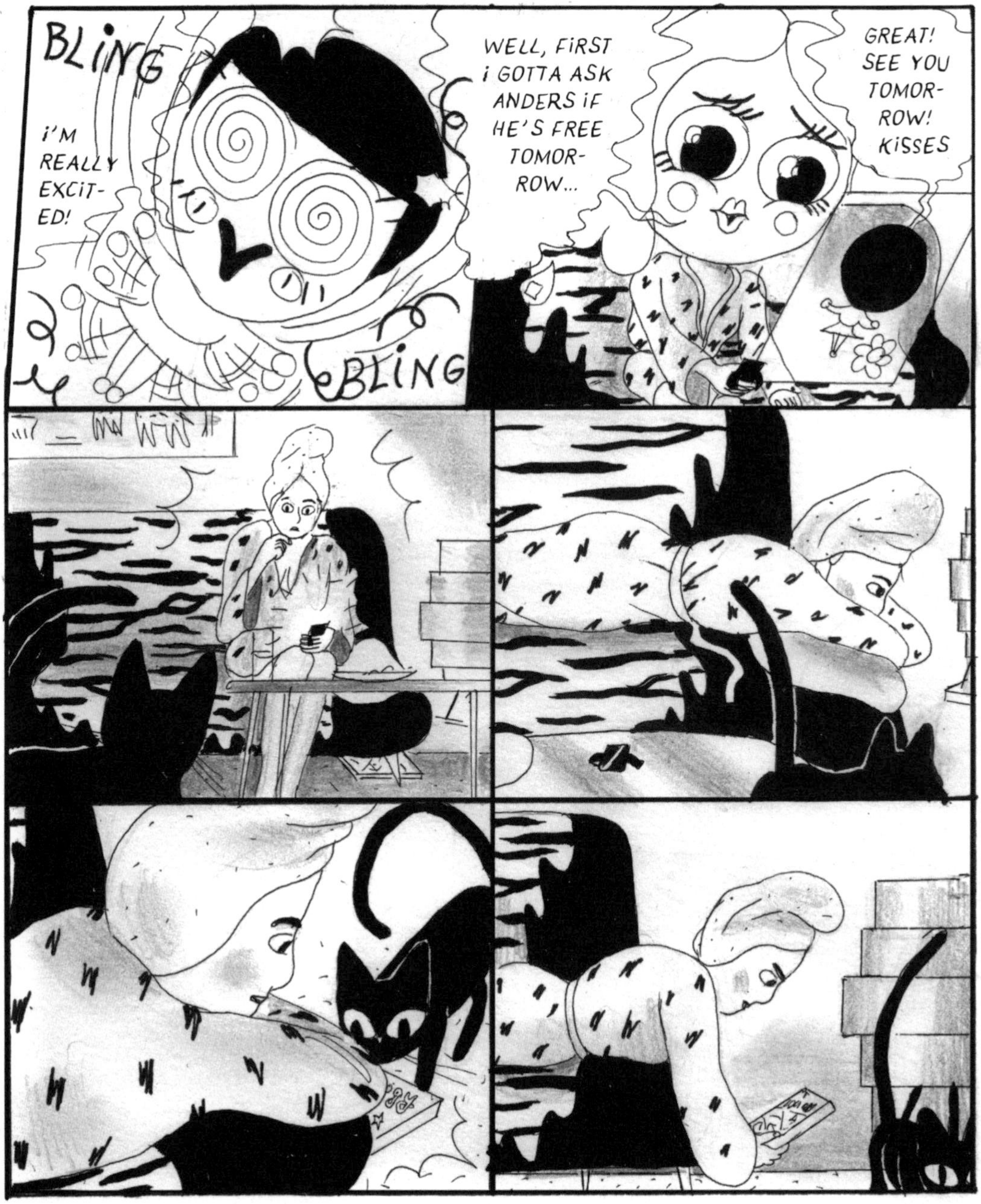
BLING
I'M REALLY EXCIT-ED!
BLING
WELL, FIRST I GOTTA ASK ANDERS IF HE'S FREE TOMOR-ROW...
GREAT! SEE YOU TOMOR-ROW! KISSES

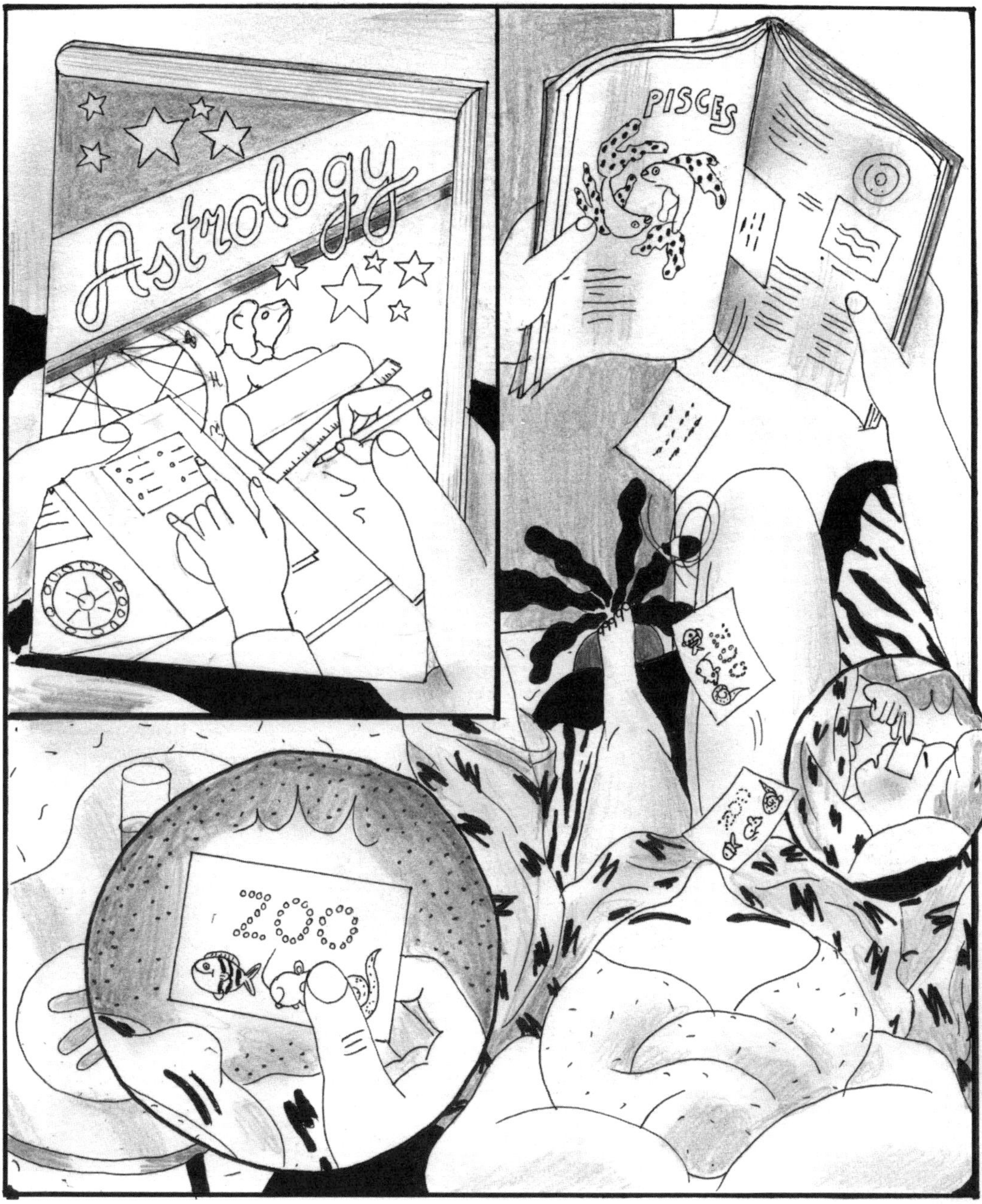
Astrology
PISCES
ZOO

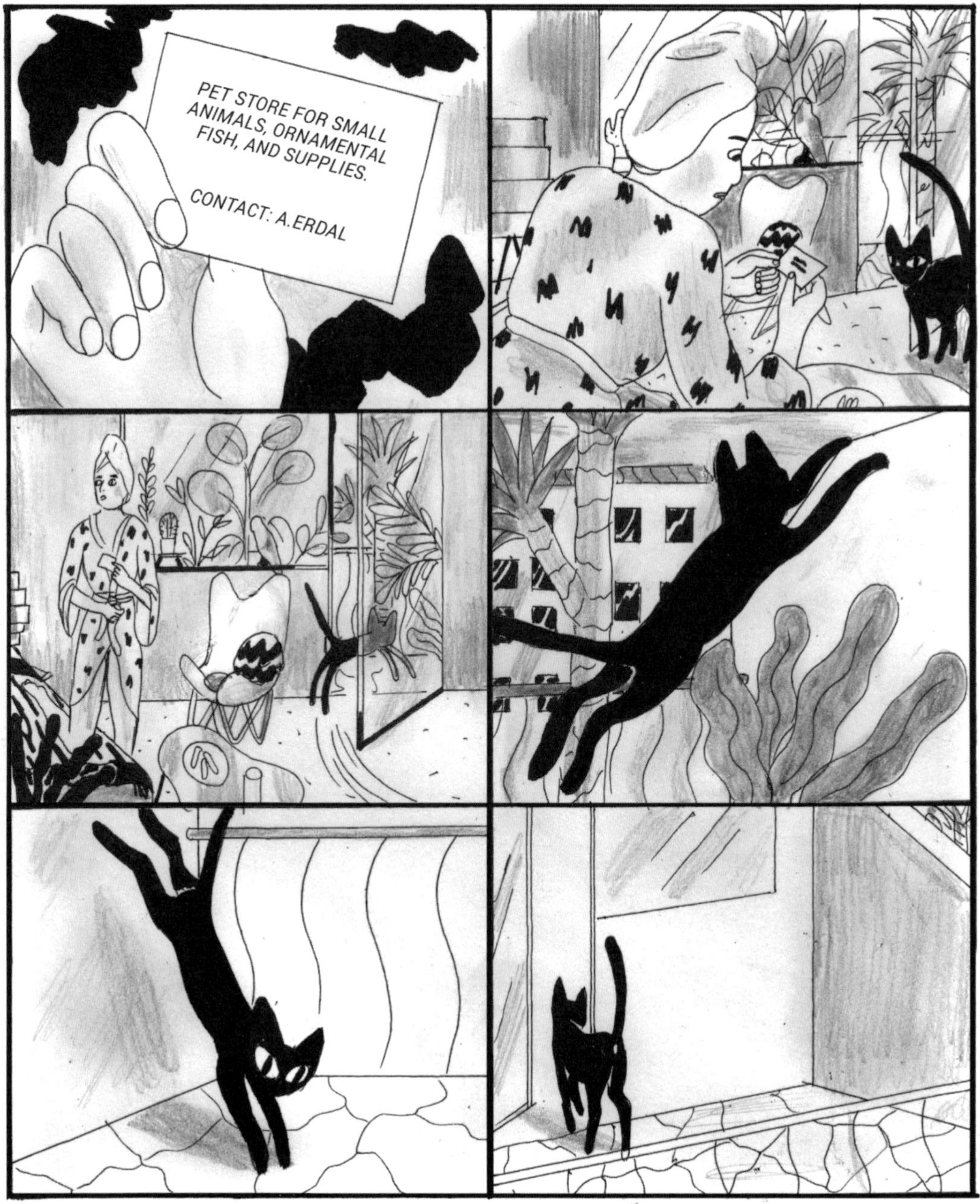
PET STORE FOR SMALL
ANIMALS, ORNAMENTAL
FISH, AND SUPPLIES.
CONTACT: A.ERDAL

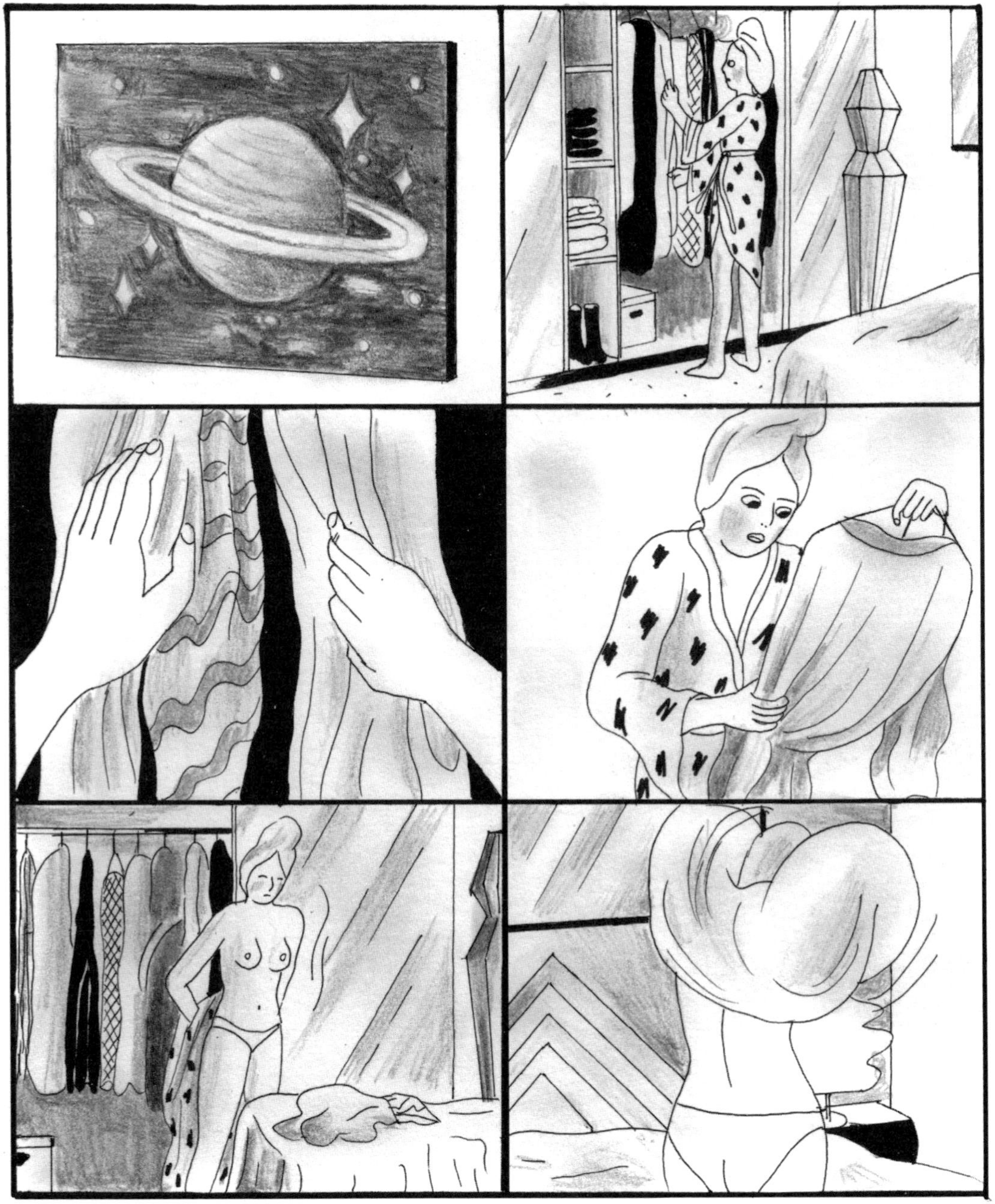

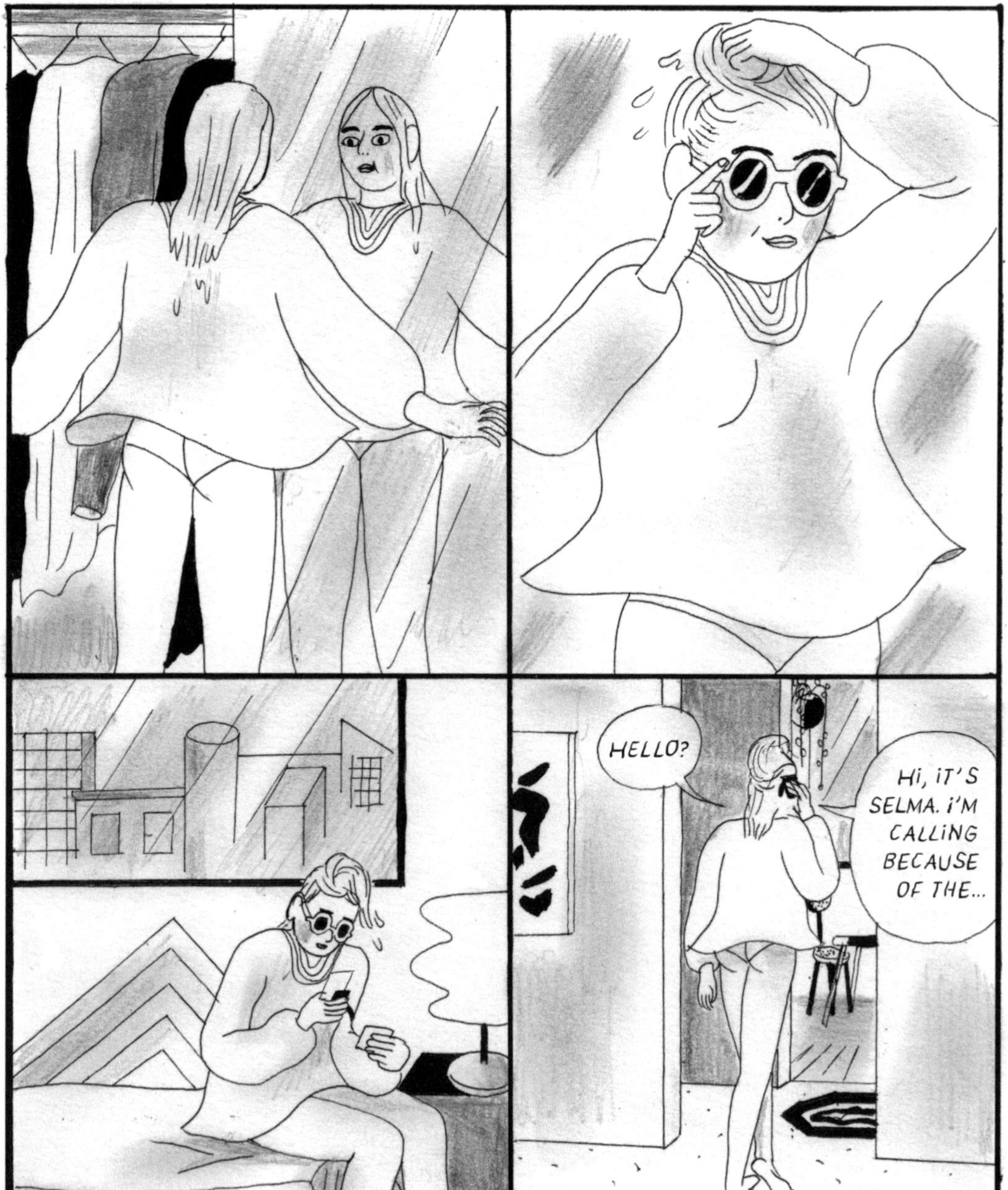
HELLO?
Hi, IT'S SELMA. I'M CALLING BECAUSE OF THE...

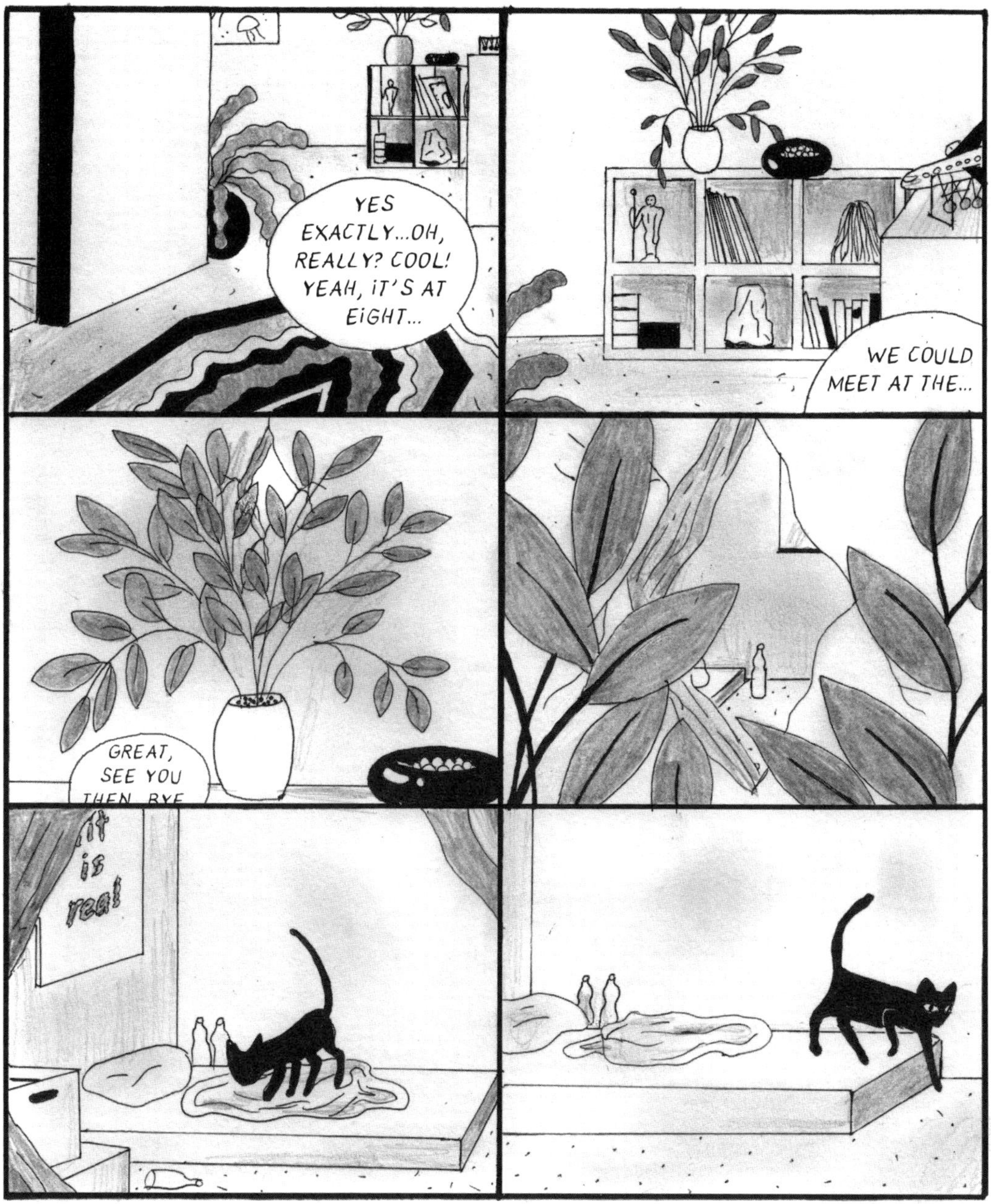
YES EXACTLY...OH, REALLY? COOL! YEAH, IT'S AT EIGHT...
WE COULD MEET AT THE...
GREAT, SEE YOU THEN. BYE
it is real

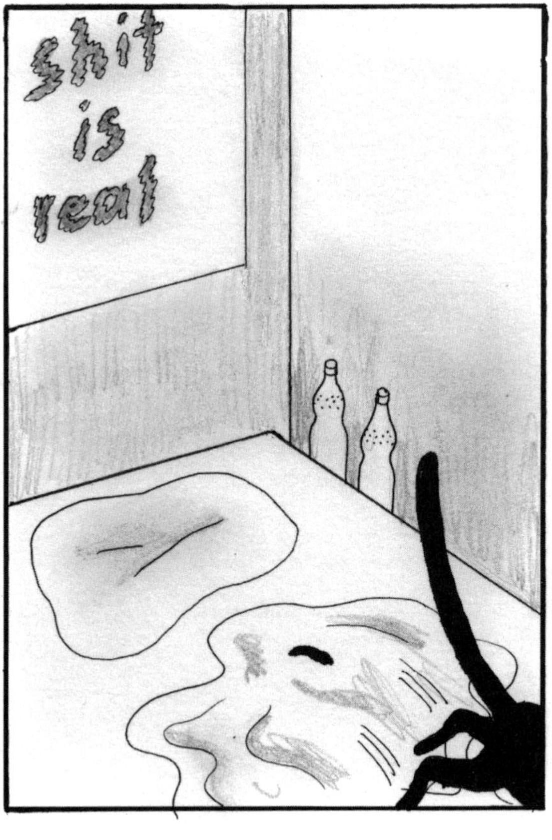
shit
is
real

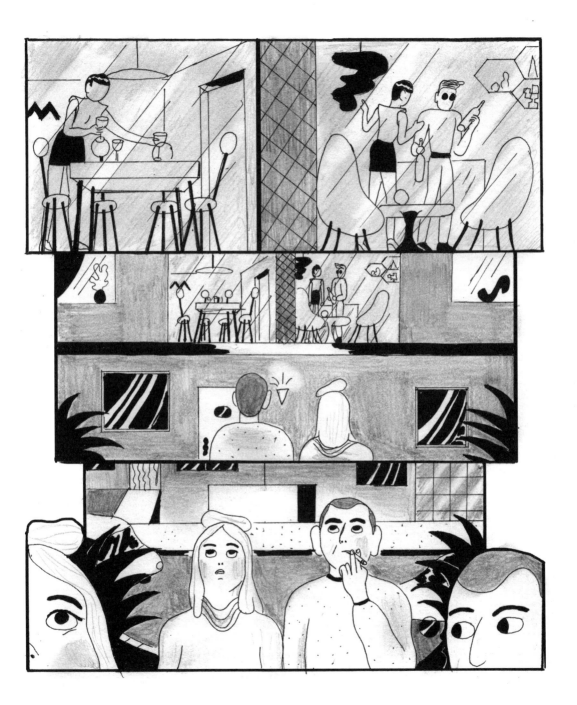

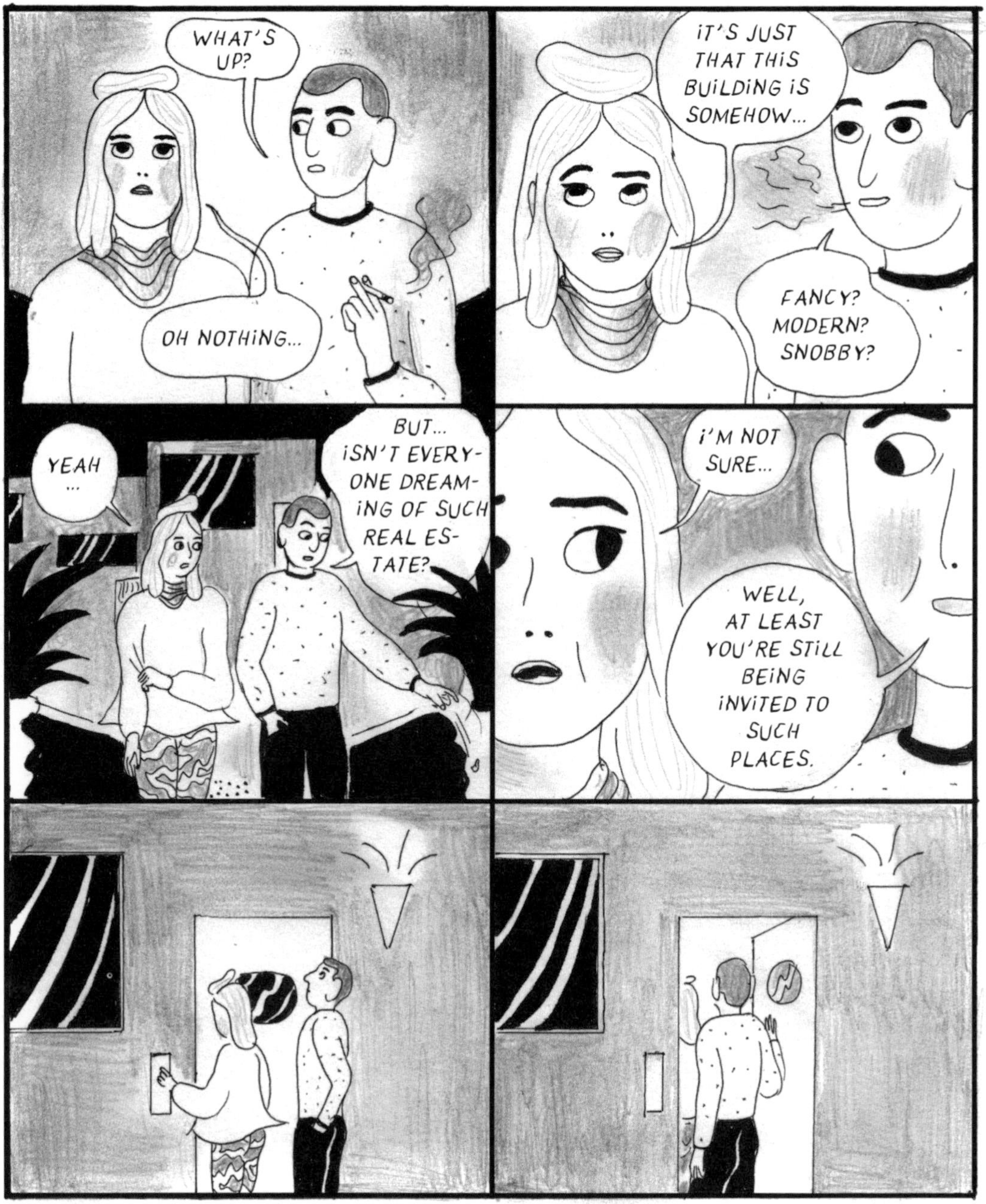
WHAT'S UP?
OH NOTHING...
IT'S JUST THAT THIS BUILDING IS SOMEHOW...
FANCY? MODERN? SNOBBY?
YEAH ...
BUT... ISN'T EVERY-ONE DREAM-ING OF SUCH REAL ES-TATE?
I'M NOT SURE...
WELL, AT LEAST YOU'RE STILL BEING INVITED TO SUCH PLACES.

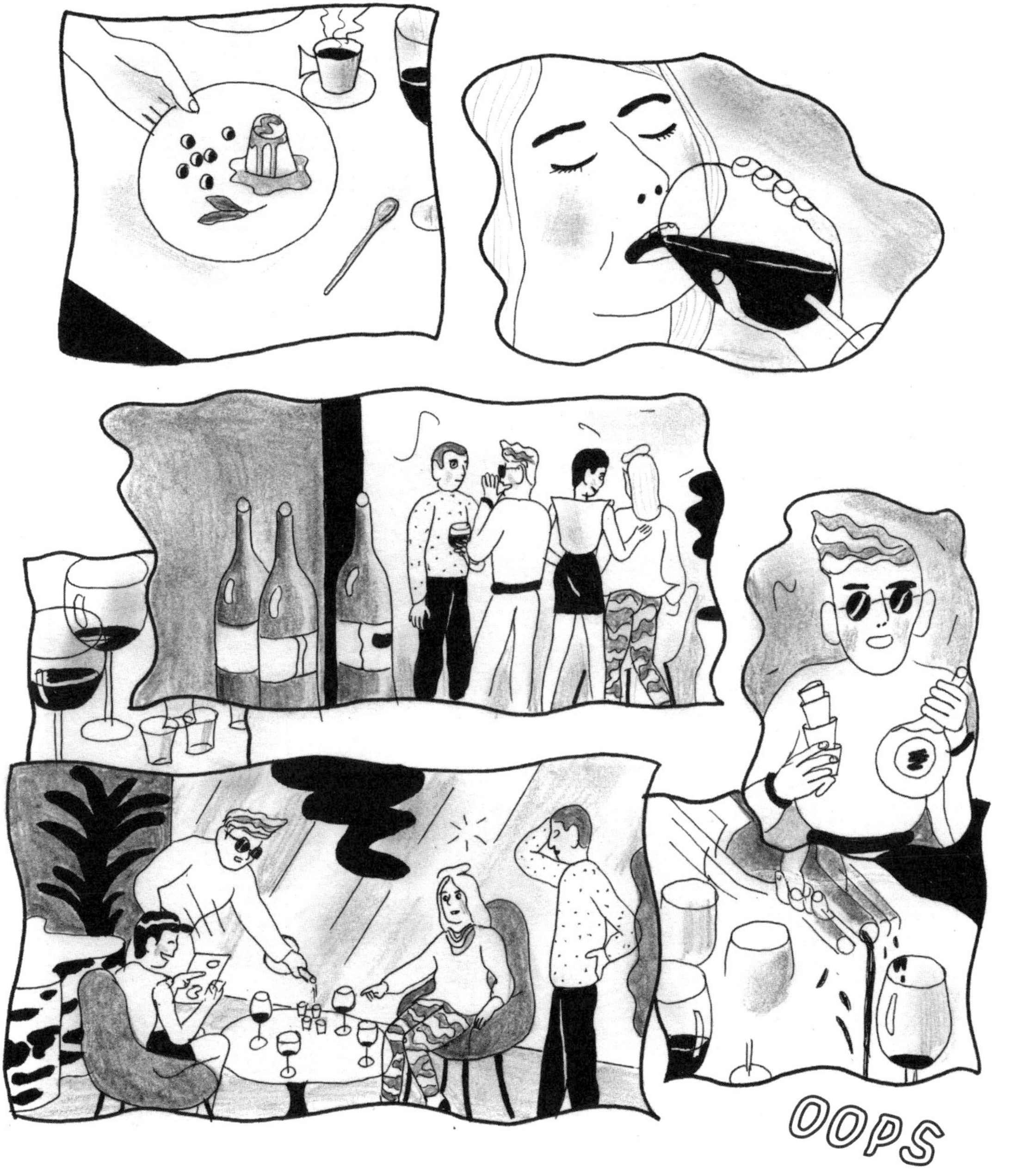
OOPS

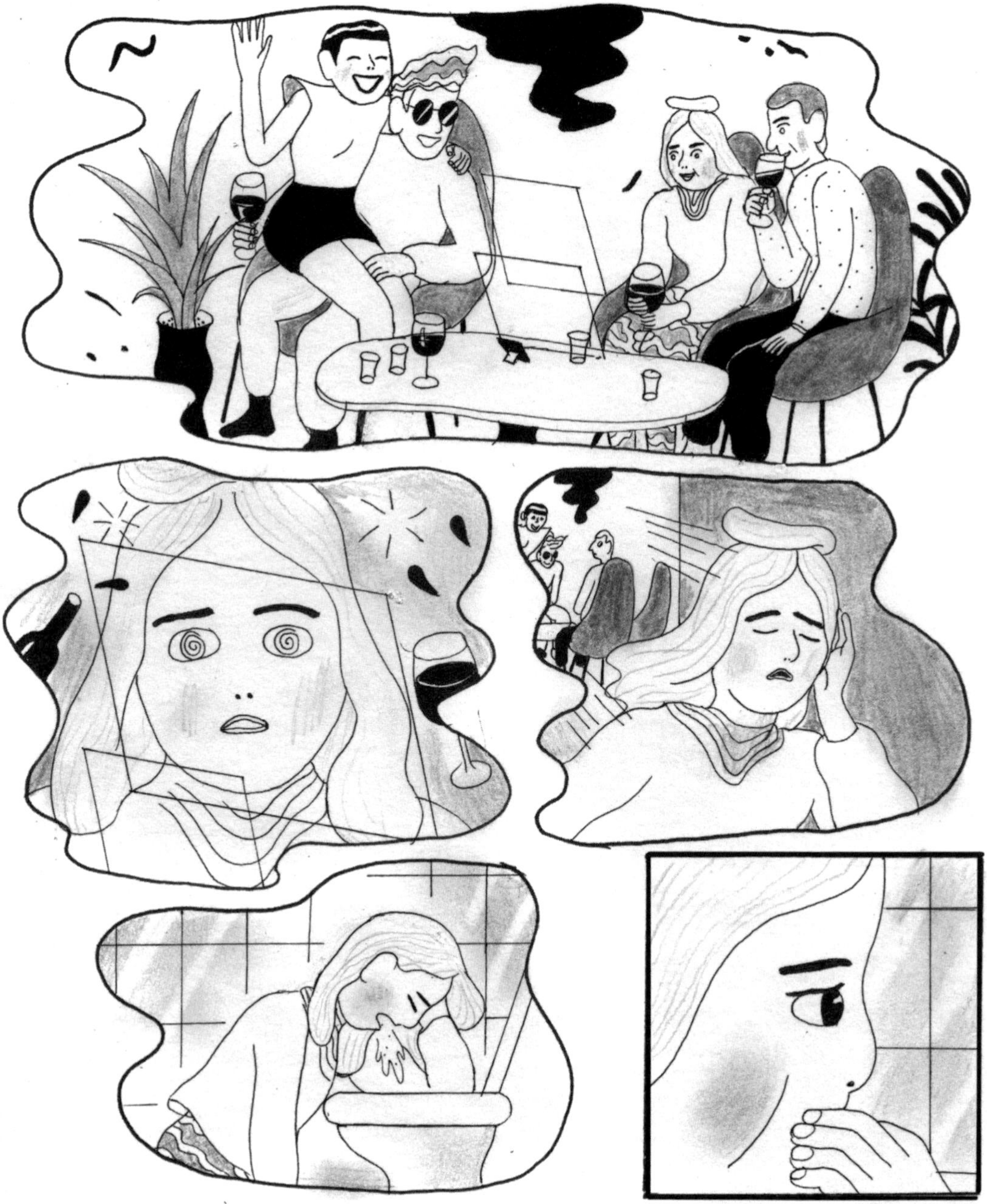

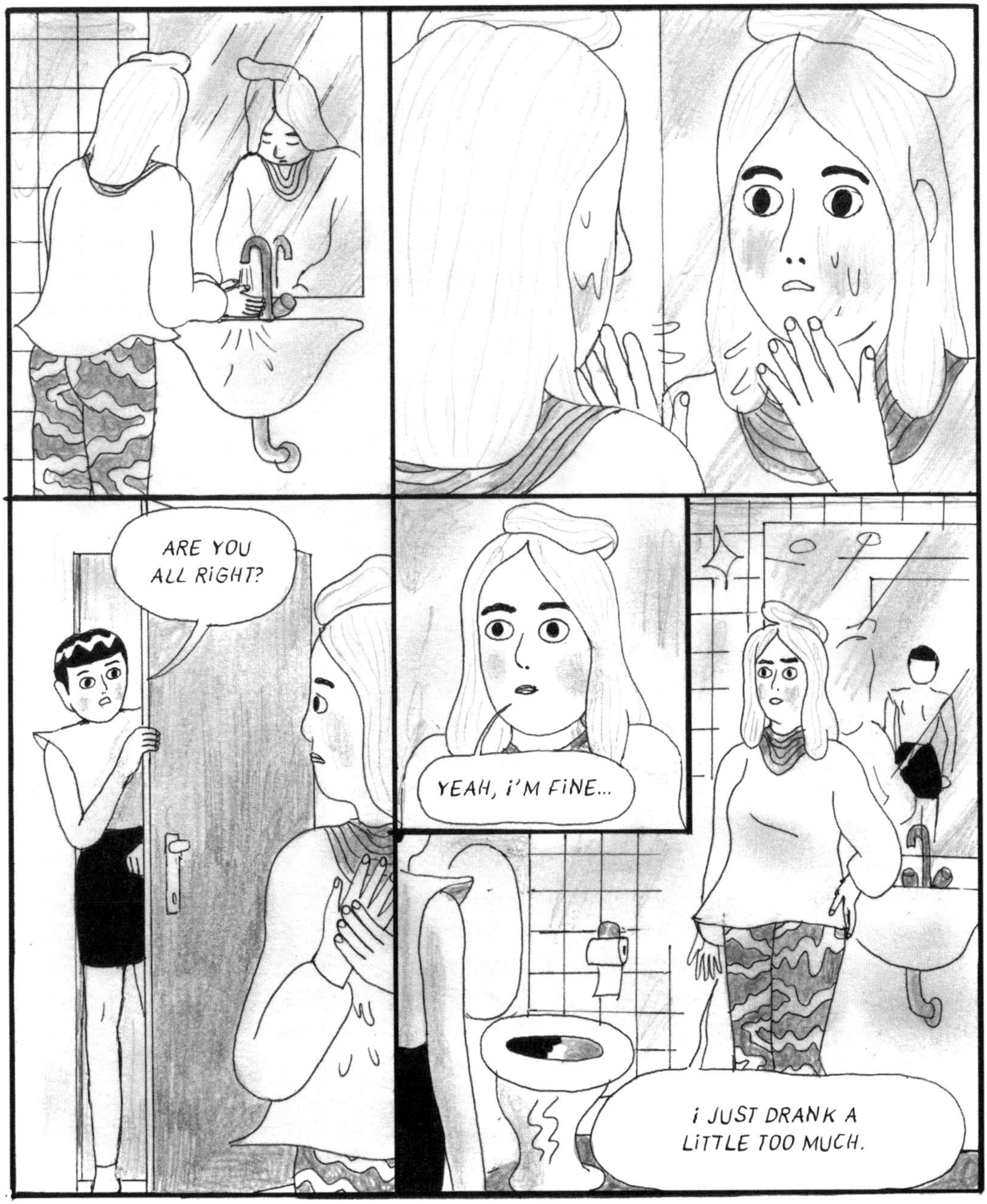
ARE YOU ALL RIGHT?
YEAH, I'M FINE...
I JUST DRANK A LITTLE TOO MUCH.

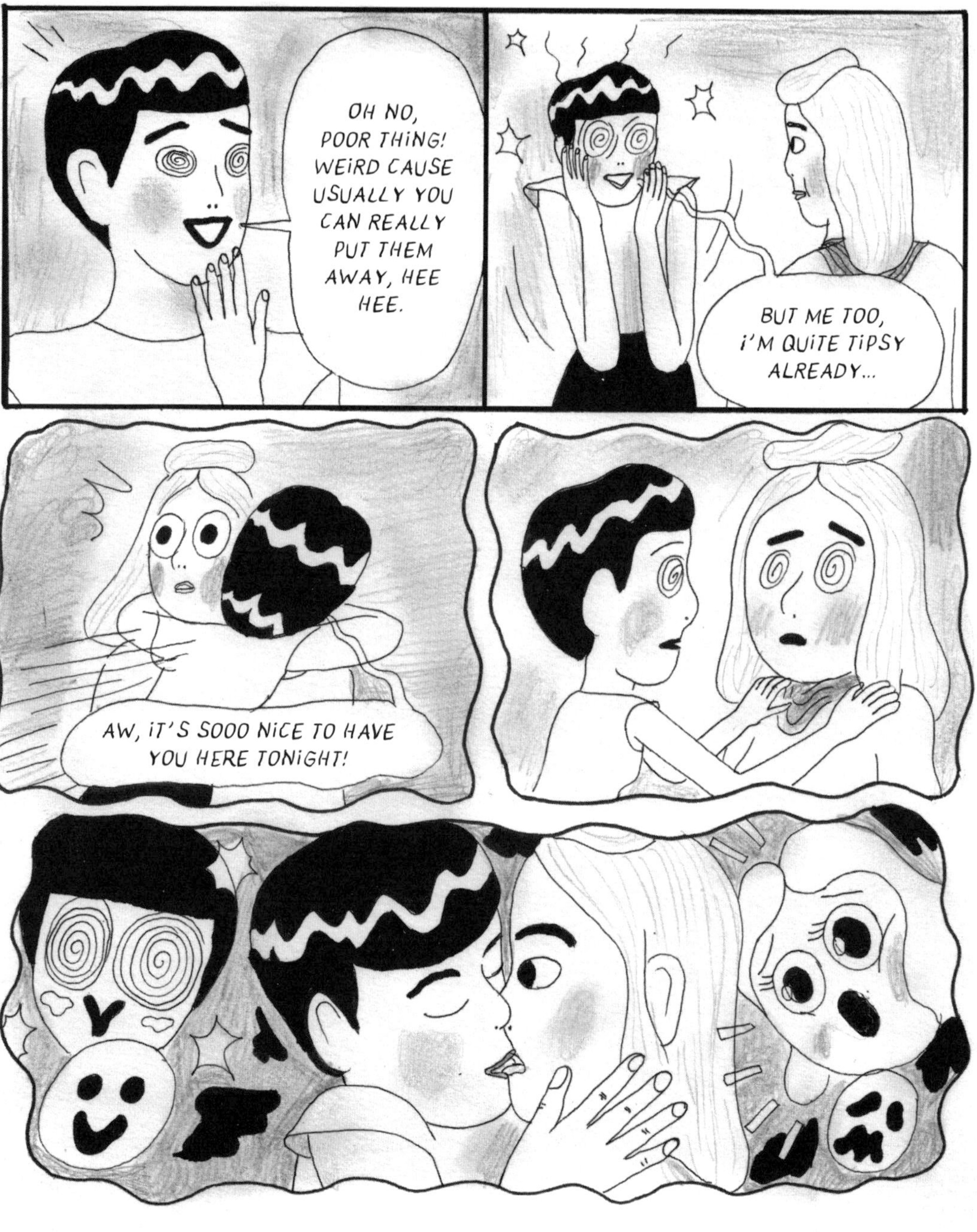
OH NO, POOR THING! WEIRD CAUSE USUALLY YOU CAN REALLY PUT THEM AWAY, HEE HEE.
BUT ME TOO, I'M QUITE TIPSY ALREADY...
AW, IT'S SOOO NICE TO HAVE YOU HERE TONIGHT!

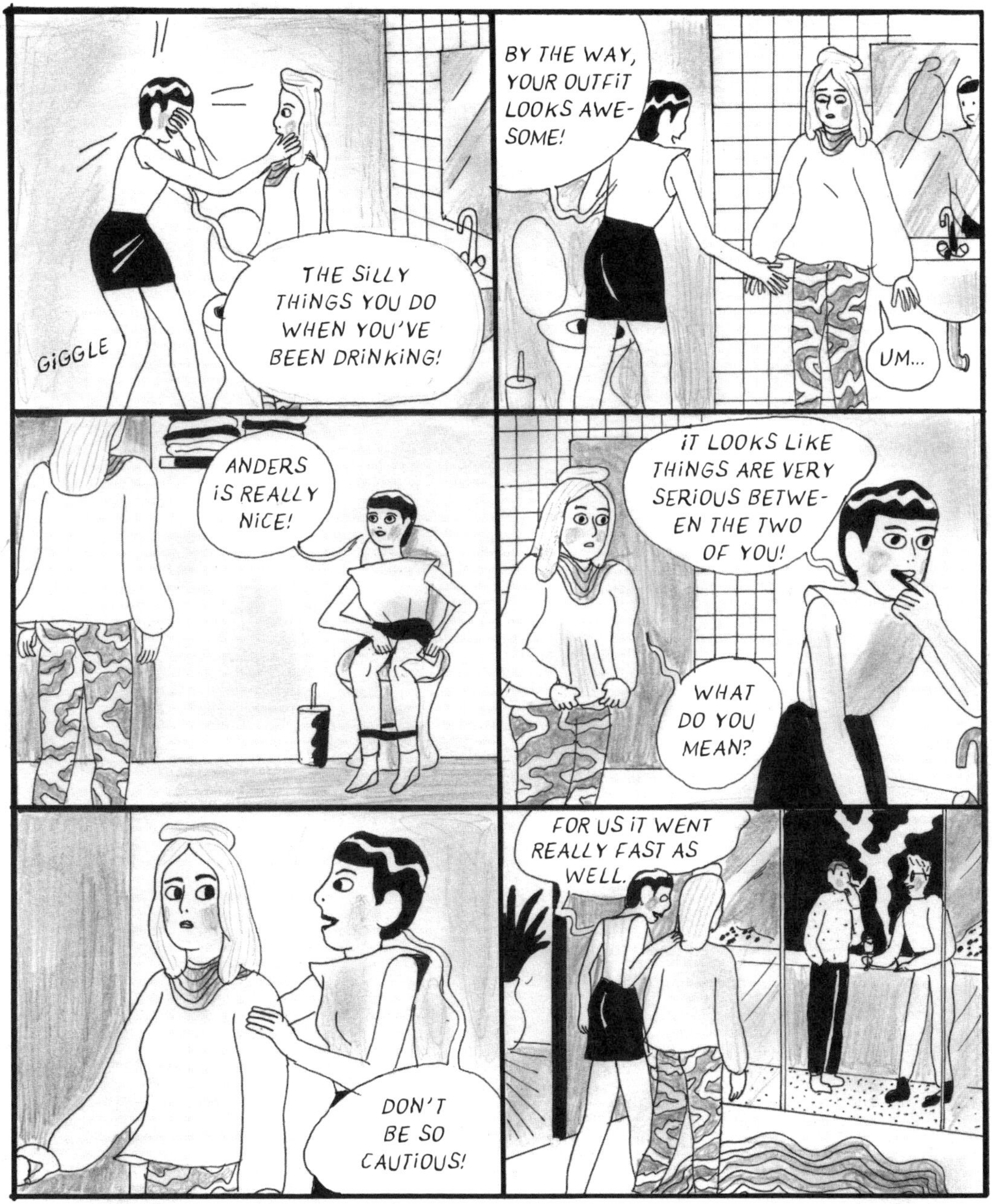
GIGGLE
THE SILLY THINGS YOU DO WHEN YOU'VE BEEN DRINKING!
BY THE WAY, YOUR OUTFIT LOOKS AWE-SOME!
UM...
ANDERS IS REALLY NICE!
IT LOOKS LIKE THINGS ARE VERY SERIOUS BETWE-EN THE TWO OF YOU!
WHAT DO YOU MEAN?
DON'T BE SO CAUTIOUS!
FOR US IT WENT REALLY FAST AS WELL.

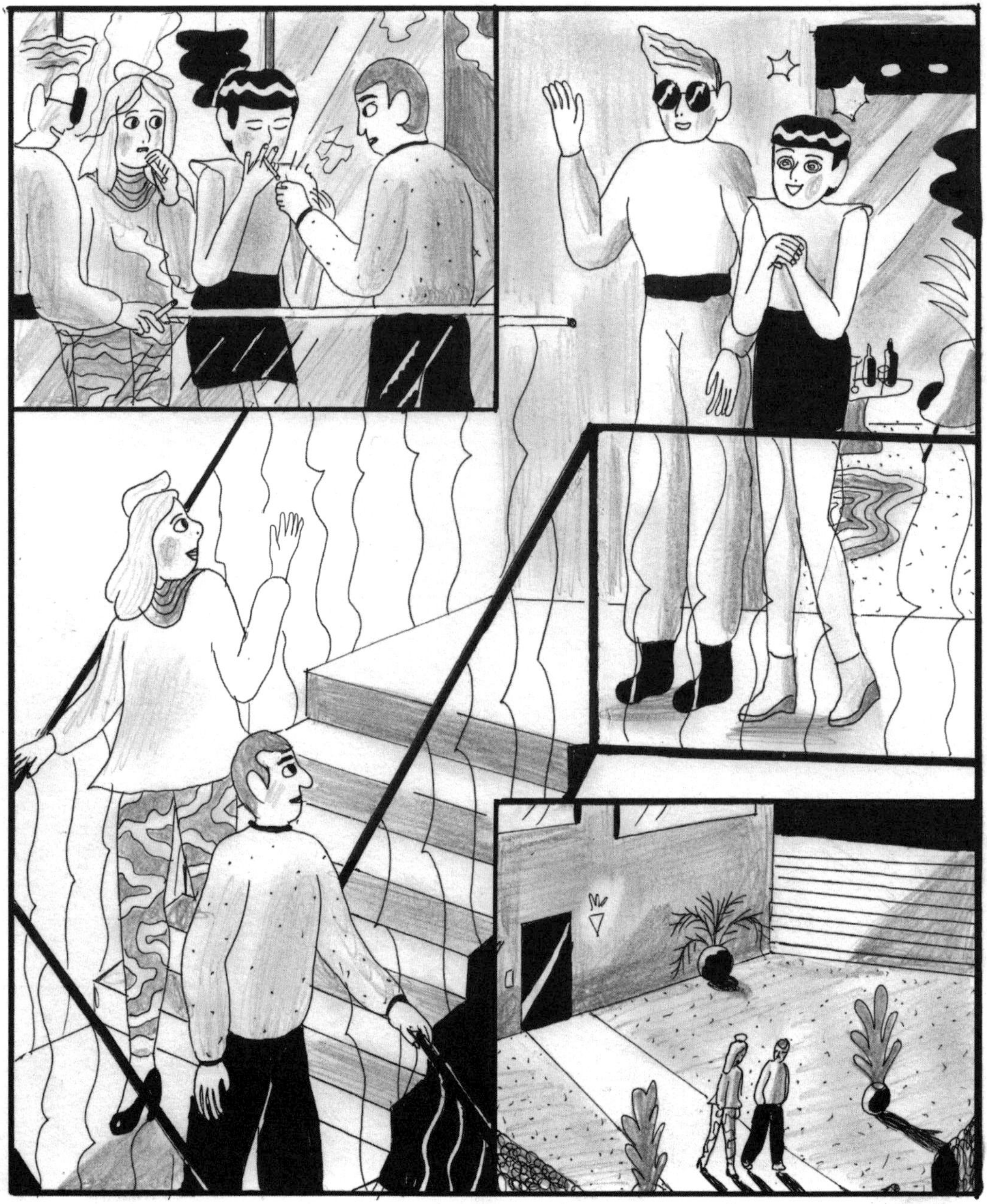

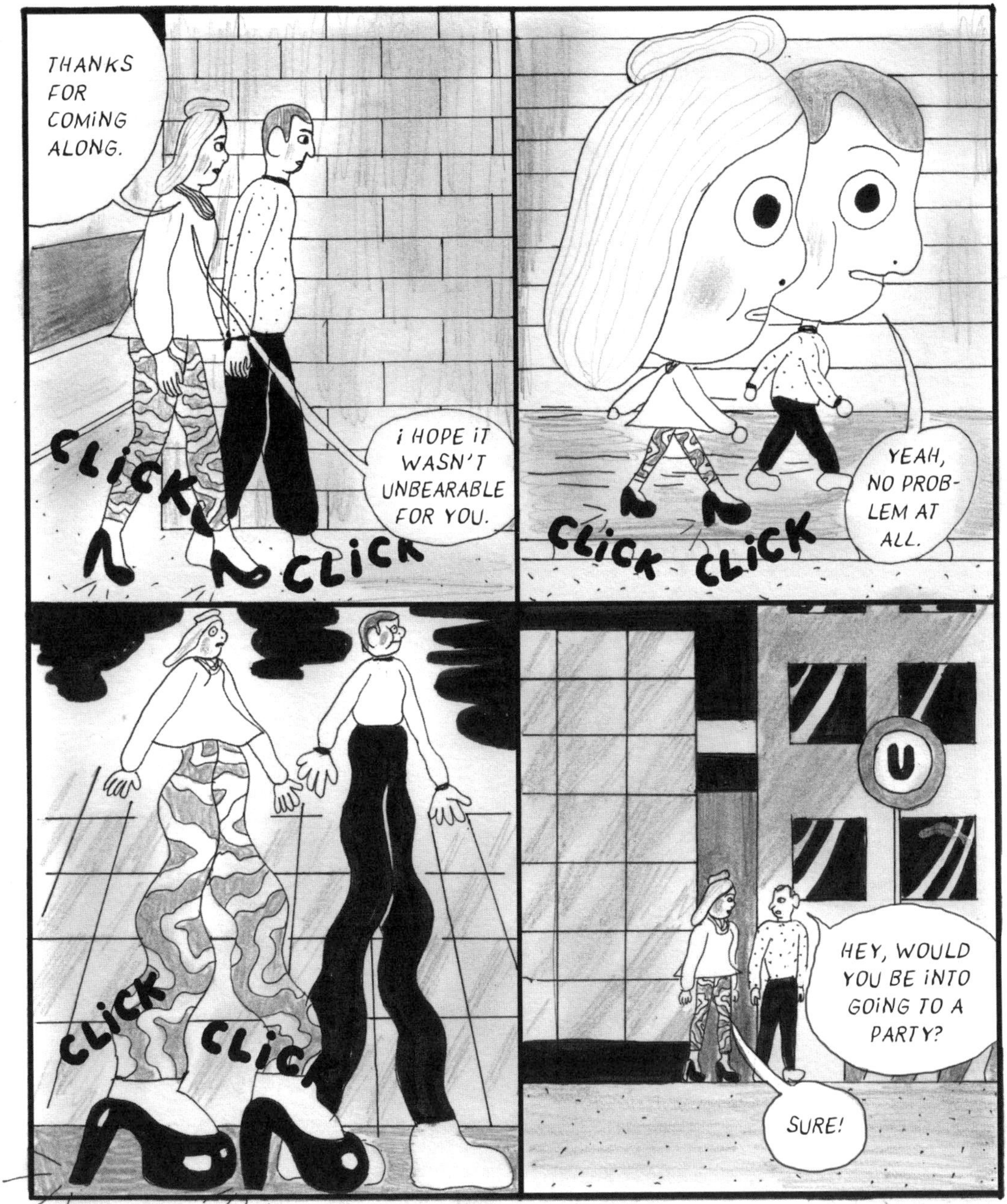
THANKS FOR COMING ALONG.
CLICK
CLICK
I HOPE IT WASN'T UNBEARABLE FOR YOU.
CLICK
CLICK
YEAH, NO PROB-LEM AT ALL.
CLICK
CLICK
U
HEY, WOULD YOU BE INTO GOING TO A PARTY?
SURE!

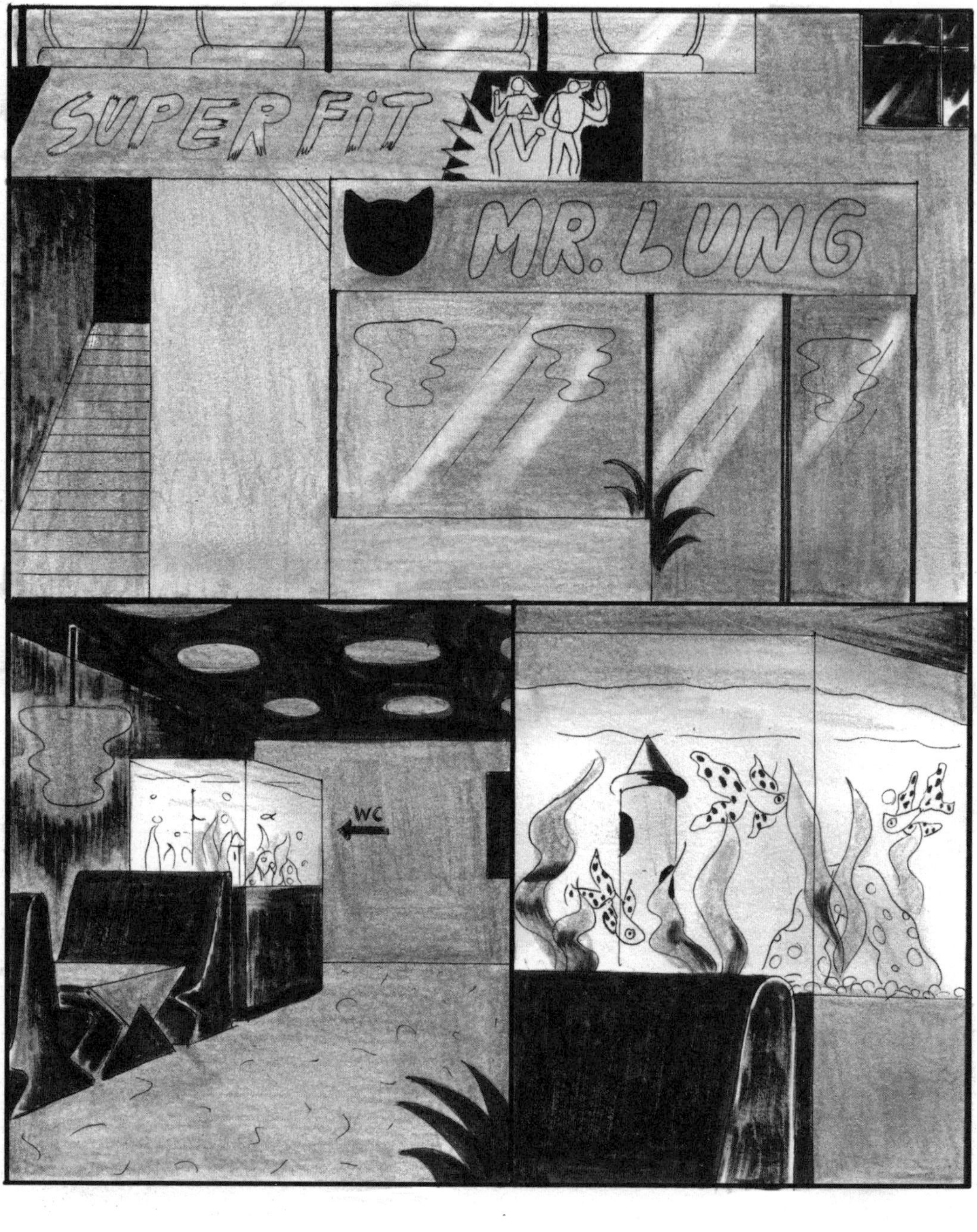
SUPER FIT
MR. LUNG
WC

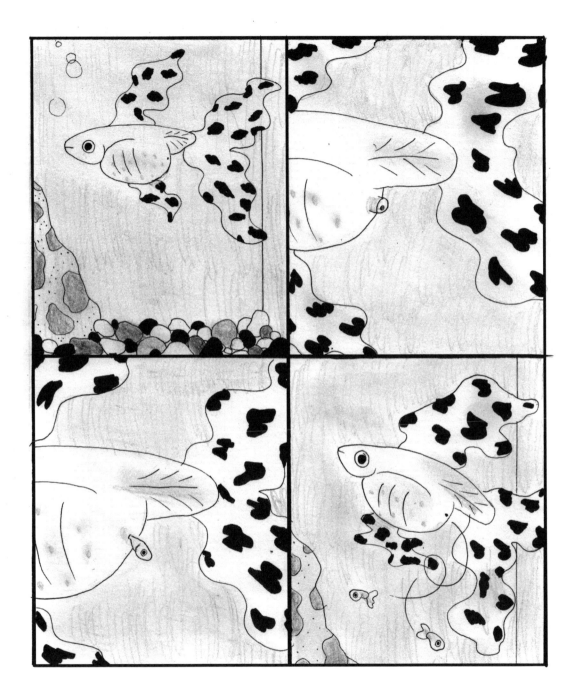

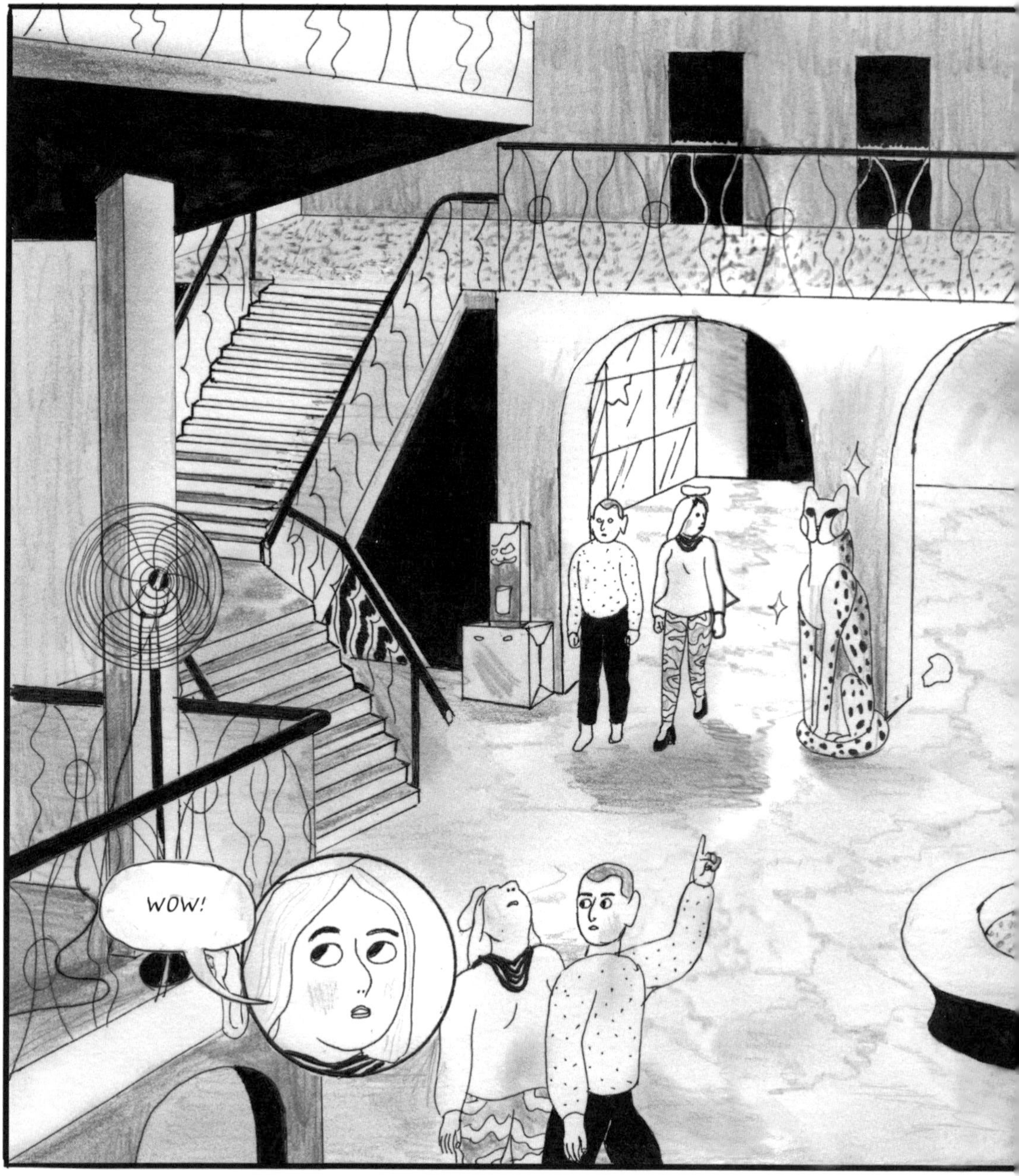
WOW!

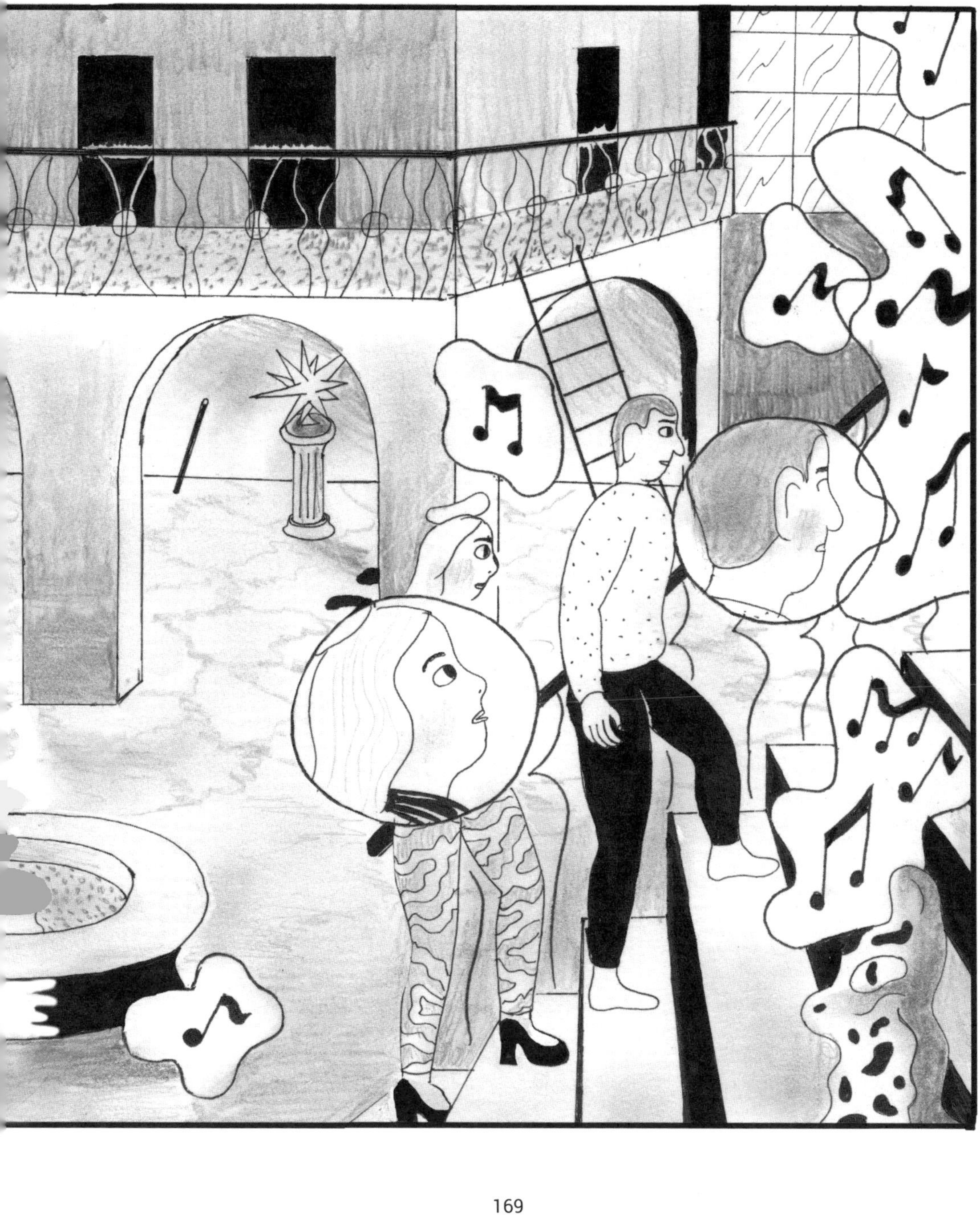

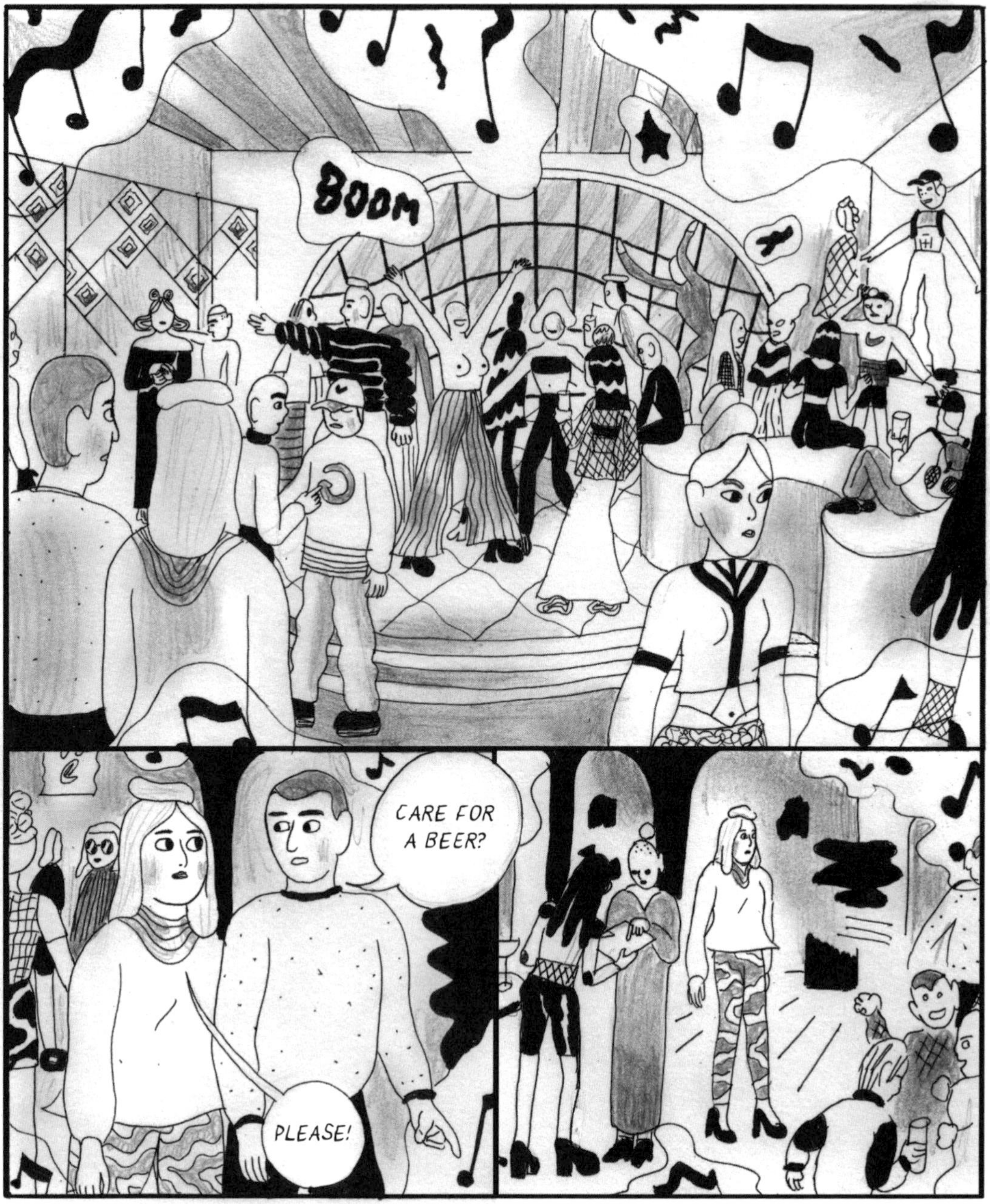
BOOM
CARE FOR A BEER?
PLEASE!

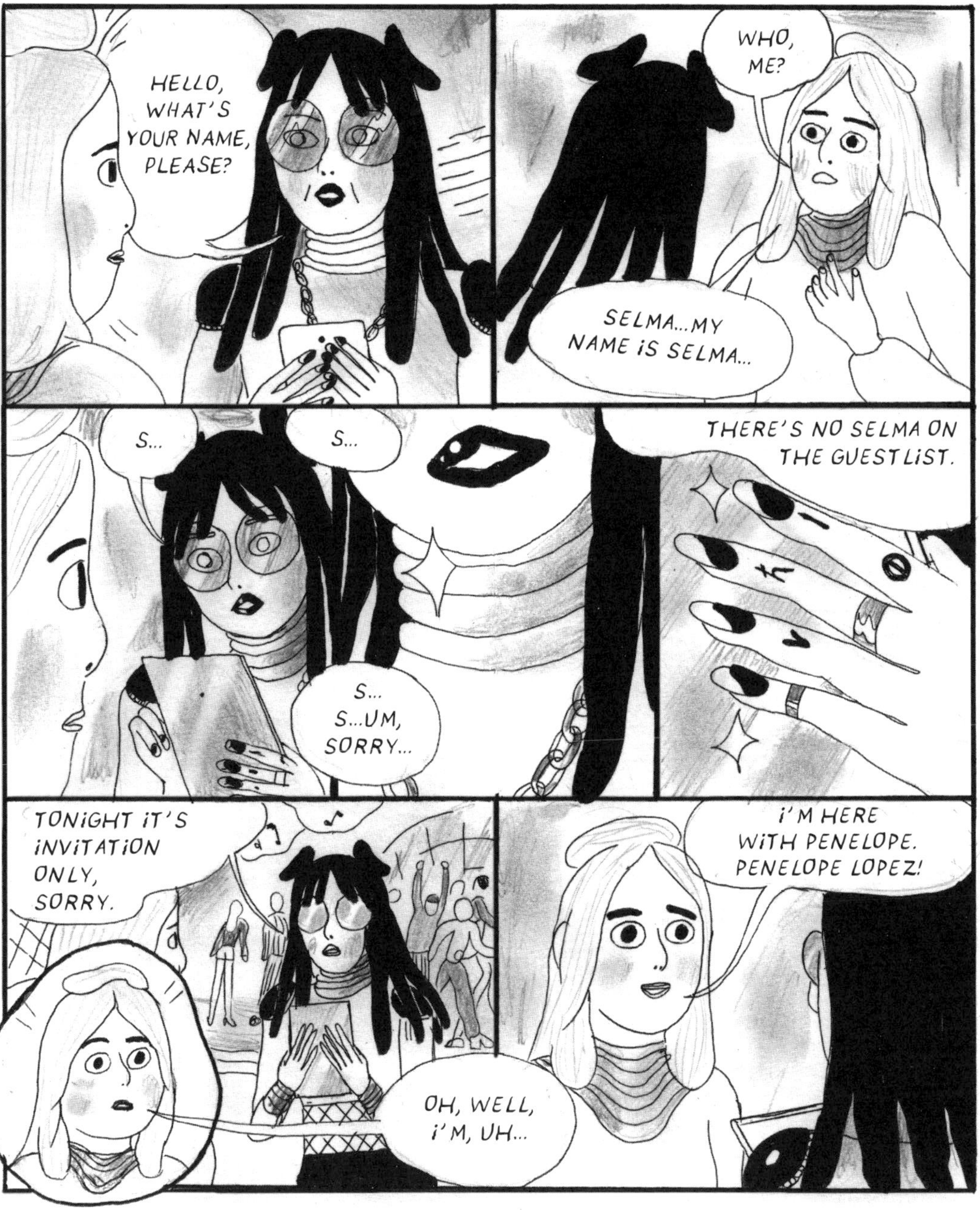
HELLO, WHAT'S YOUR NAME, PLEASE?
WHO, ME?
SELMA...MY NAME iS SELMA...
S...
S...
S... S...UM, SORRY...
THERE'S NO SELMA ON THE GUESTLiST.
TONIGHT iT'S iNVITATiON ONLY, SORRY.
OH, WELL, i'M, UH...
i'M HERE WiTH PENELOPE. PENELOPE LOPEZ!

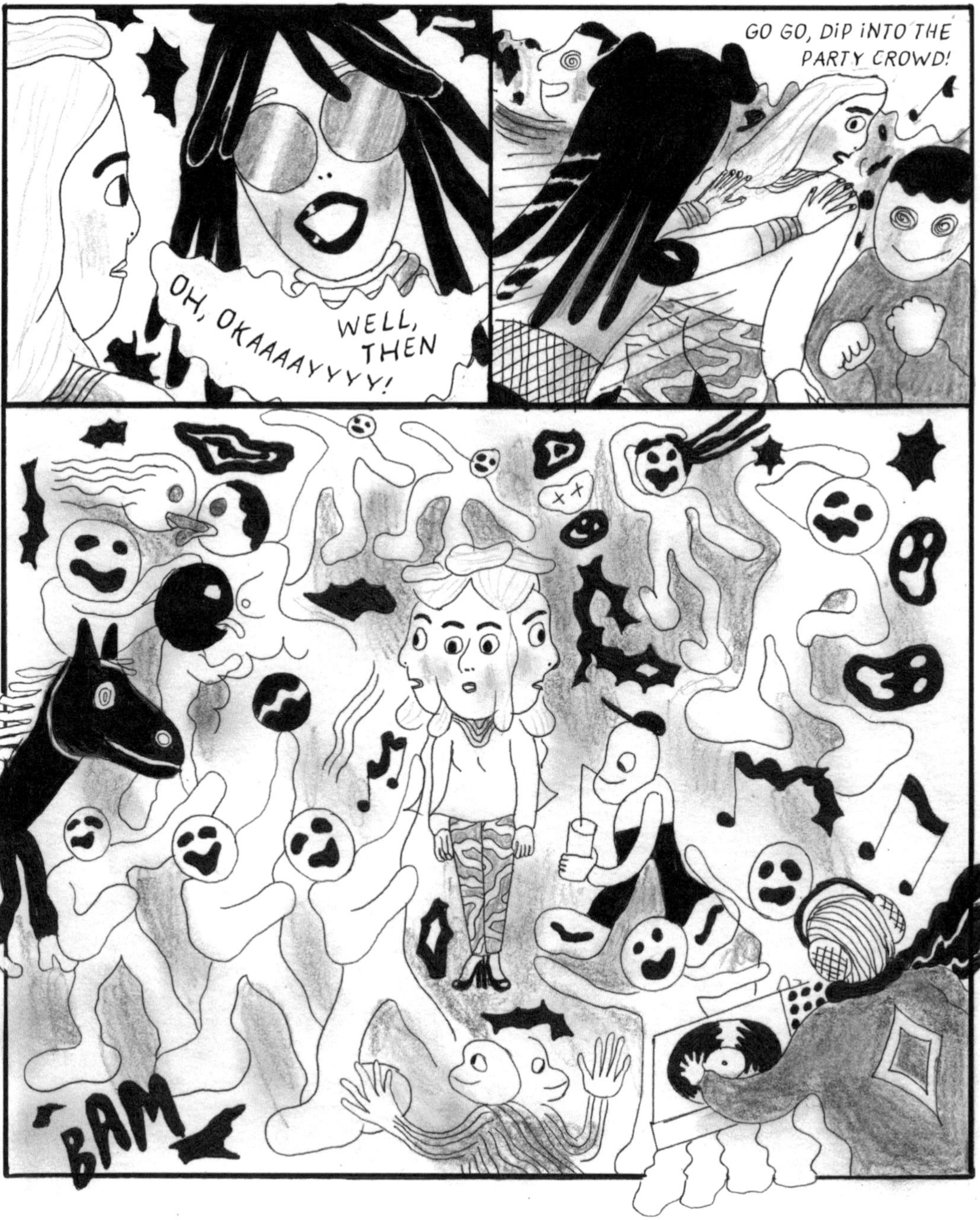
OH, OKAAAAYYYY!
WELL, THEN
GO GO, DIP INTO THE PARTY CROWD!
BAM

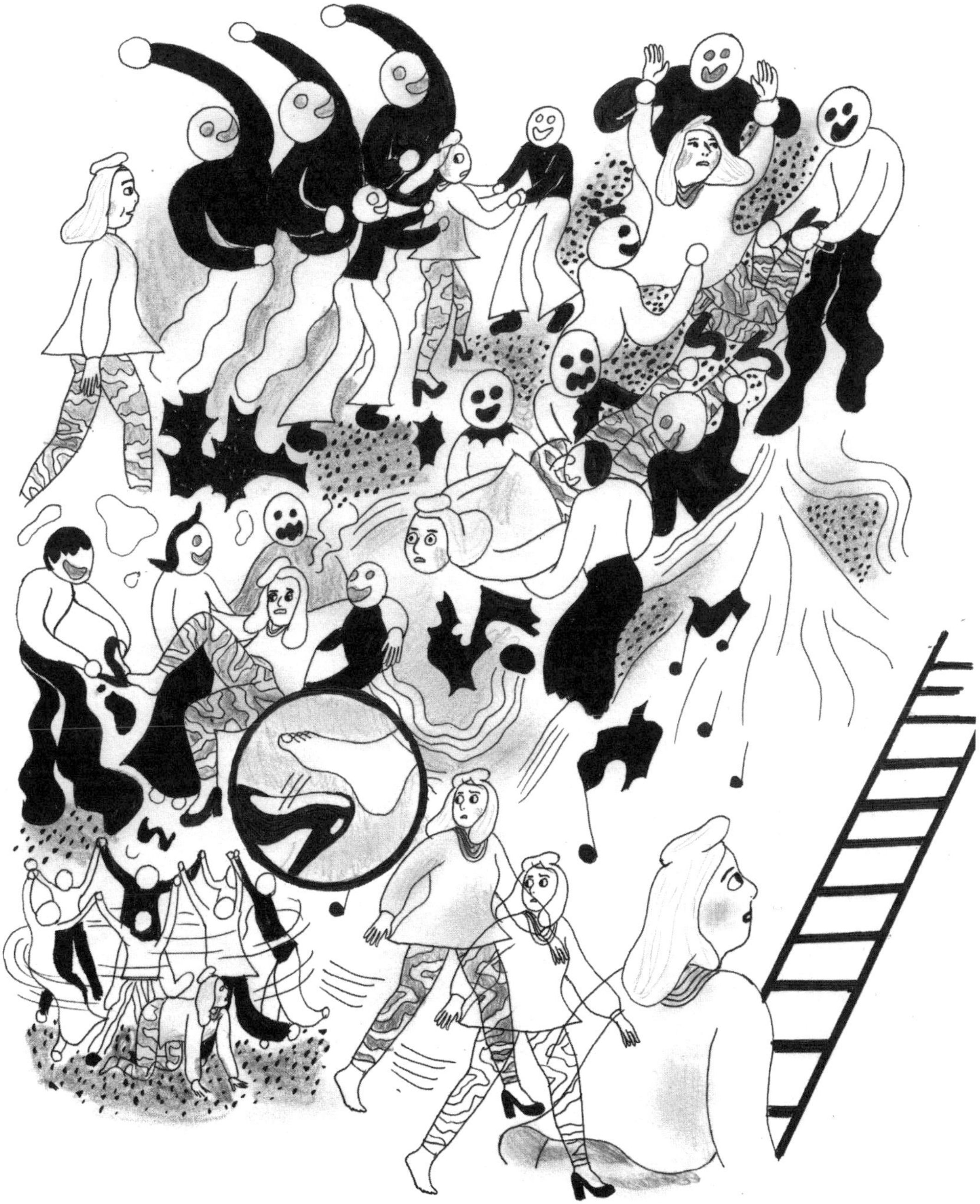

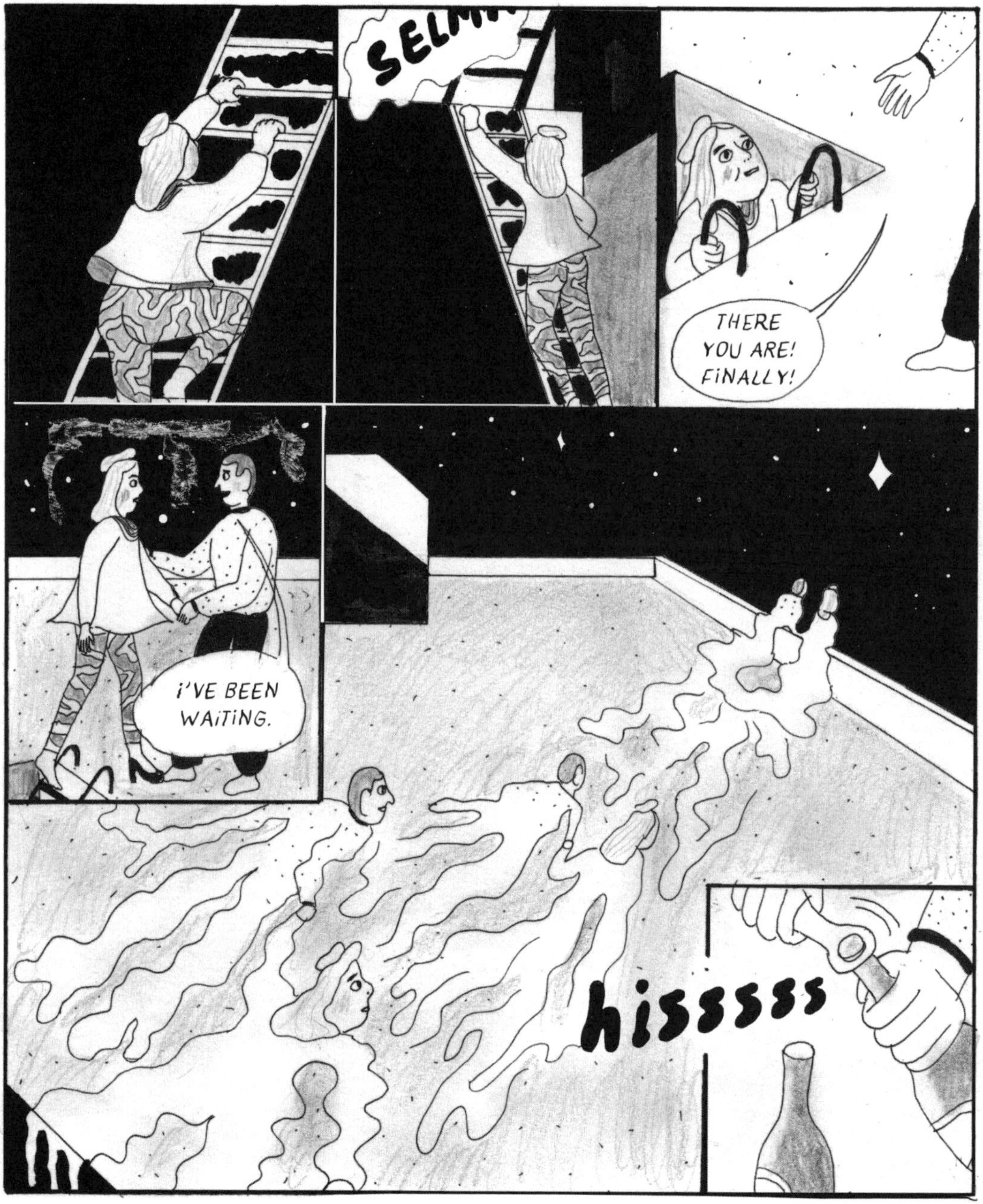
SELM
THERE YOU ARE! FINALLY!
I'VE BEEN WAITING.
hissssss

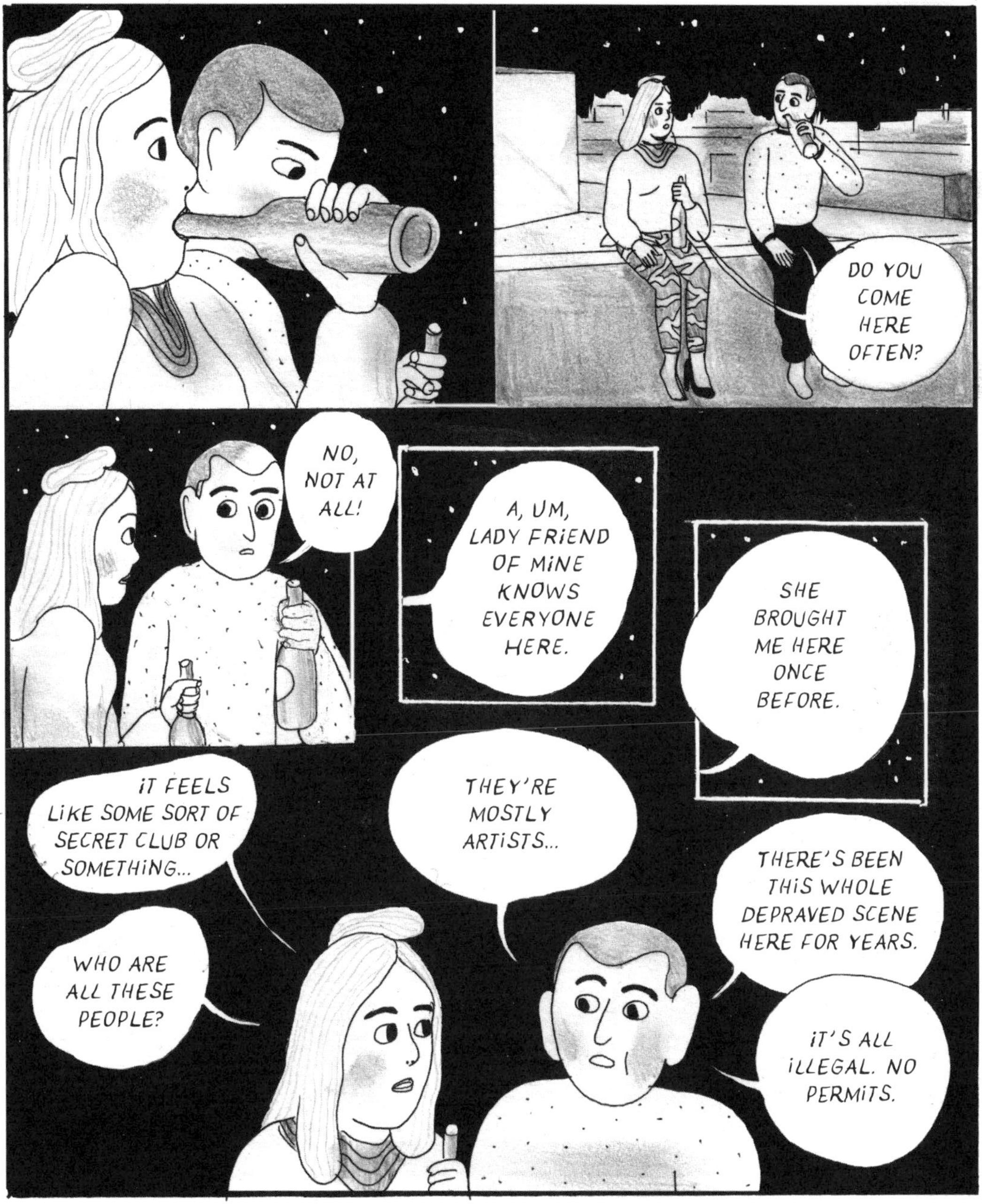
DO YOU COME HERE OFTEN?
NO, NOT AT ALL!
A, UM, LADY FRIEND OF MINE KNOWS EVERYONE HERE.
SHE BROUGHT ME HERE ONCE BEFORE.
IT FEELS LIKE SOME SORT OF SECRET CLUB OR SOMETHING...
WHO ARE ALL THESE PEOPLE?
THEY'RE MOSTLY ARTISTS...
THERE'S BEEN THIS WHOLE DEPRAVED SCENE HERE FOR YEARS.
IT'S ALL ILLEGAL. NO PERMITS.

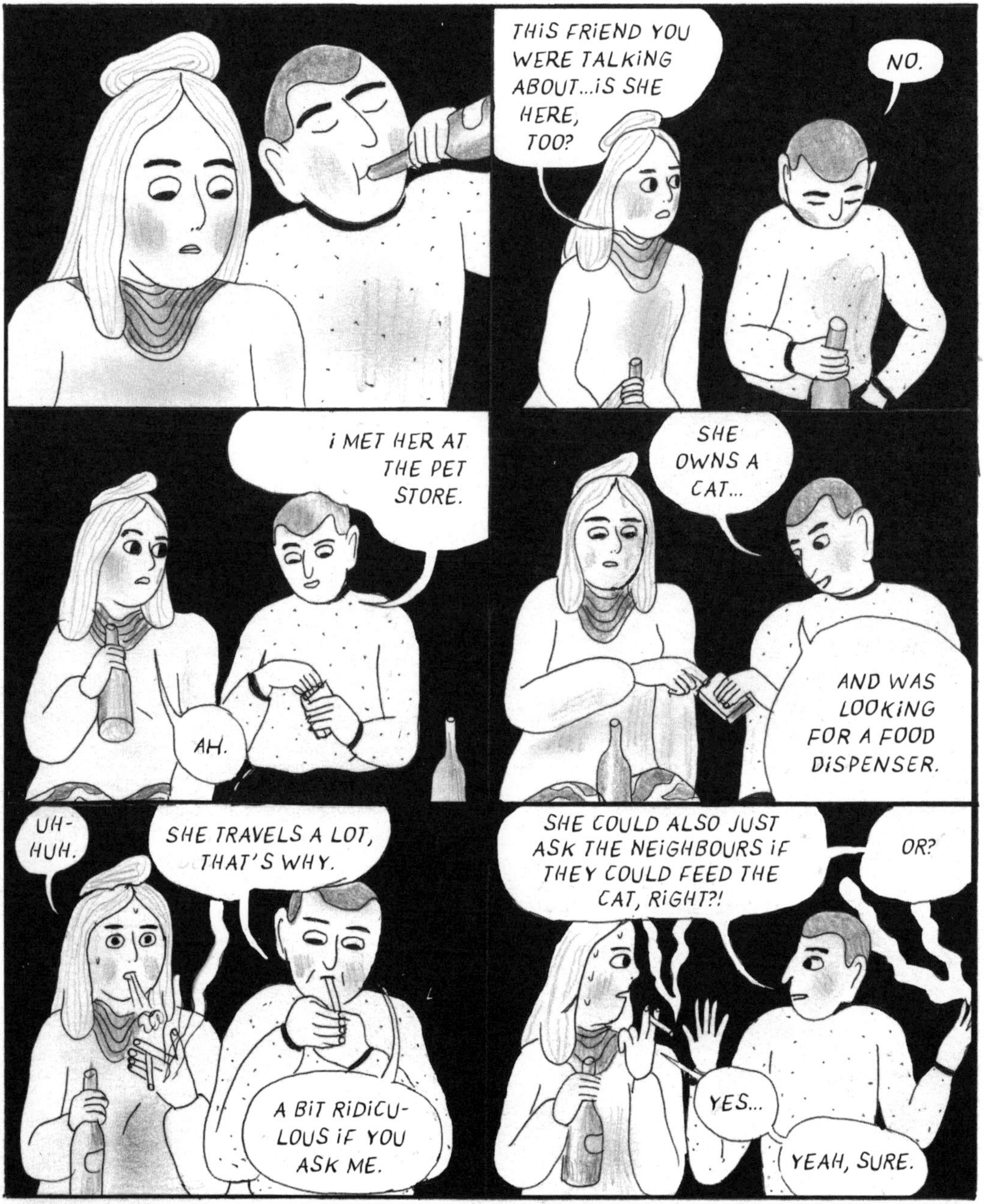
THIS FRIEND YOU WERE TALKING ABOUT...IS SHE HERE, TOO?
NO.
I MET HER AT THE PET STORE.
AH.
SHE OWNS A CAT...
AND WAS LOOKING FOR A FOOD DISPENSER.
UH-HUH.
SHE TRAVELS A LOT, THAT'S WHY.
A BIT RIDICU-LOUS IF YOU ASK ME.
SHE COULD ALSO JUST ASK THE NEIGHBOURS IF THEY COULD FEED THE CAT, RIGHT?!
OR?
YES...
YEAH, SURE.

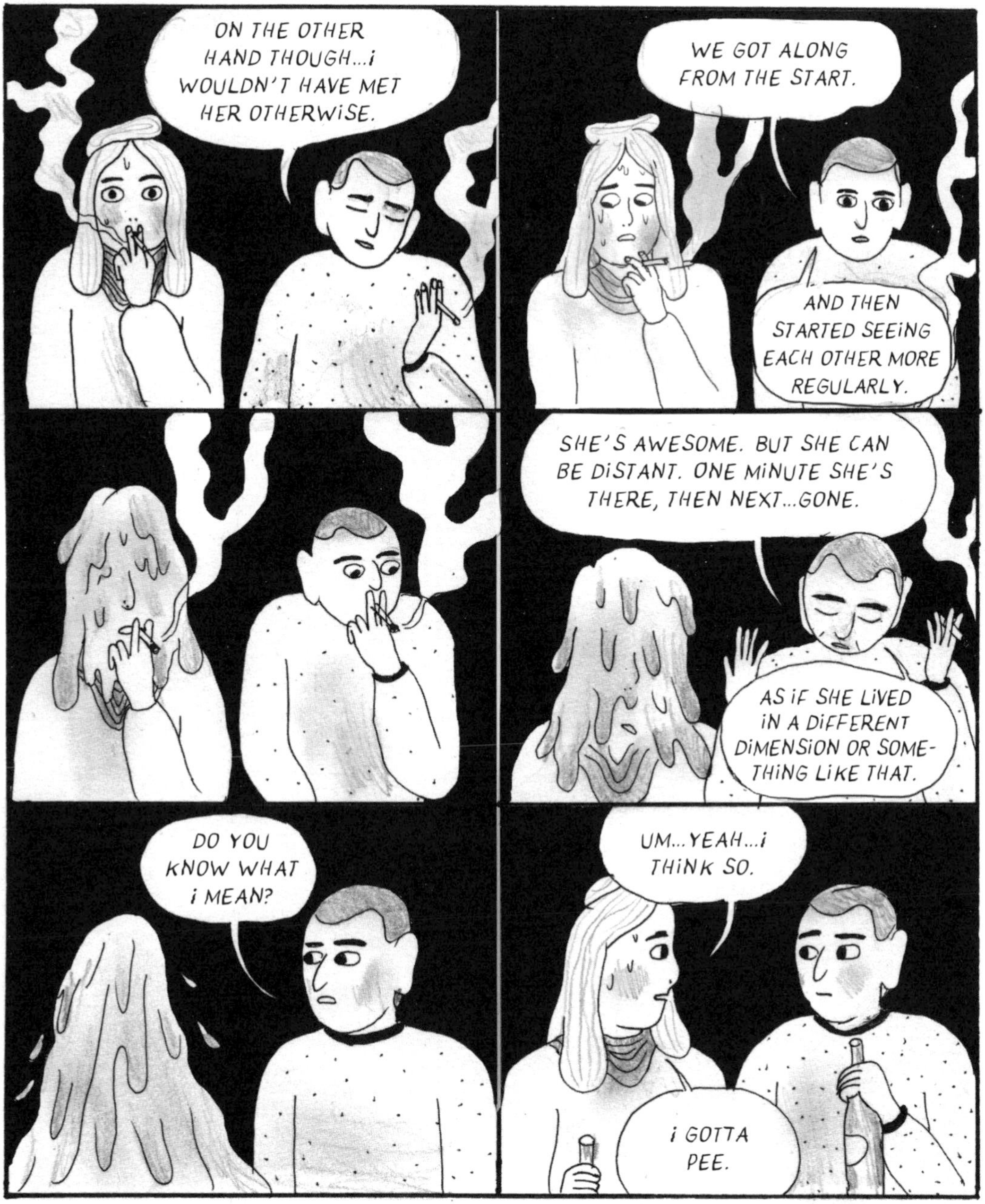
ON THE OTHER HAND THOUGH...i WOULDN'T HAVE MET HER OTHERWiSE.
WE GOT ALONG FROM THE START.
AND THEN STARTED SEEiNG EACH OTHER MORE REGULARLY.
SHE'S AWESOME. BUT SHE CAN BE DiSTANT. ONE MiNUTE SHE'S THERE, THEN NEXT...GONE.
AS iF SHE LiVED iN A DiFFERENT DiMENSiON OR SOME-THiNG LiKE THAT.
DO YOU KNOW WHAT i MEAN?
UM...YEAH...i THiNK SO.
i GOTTA PEE.

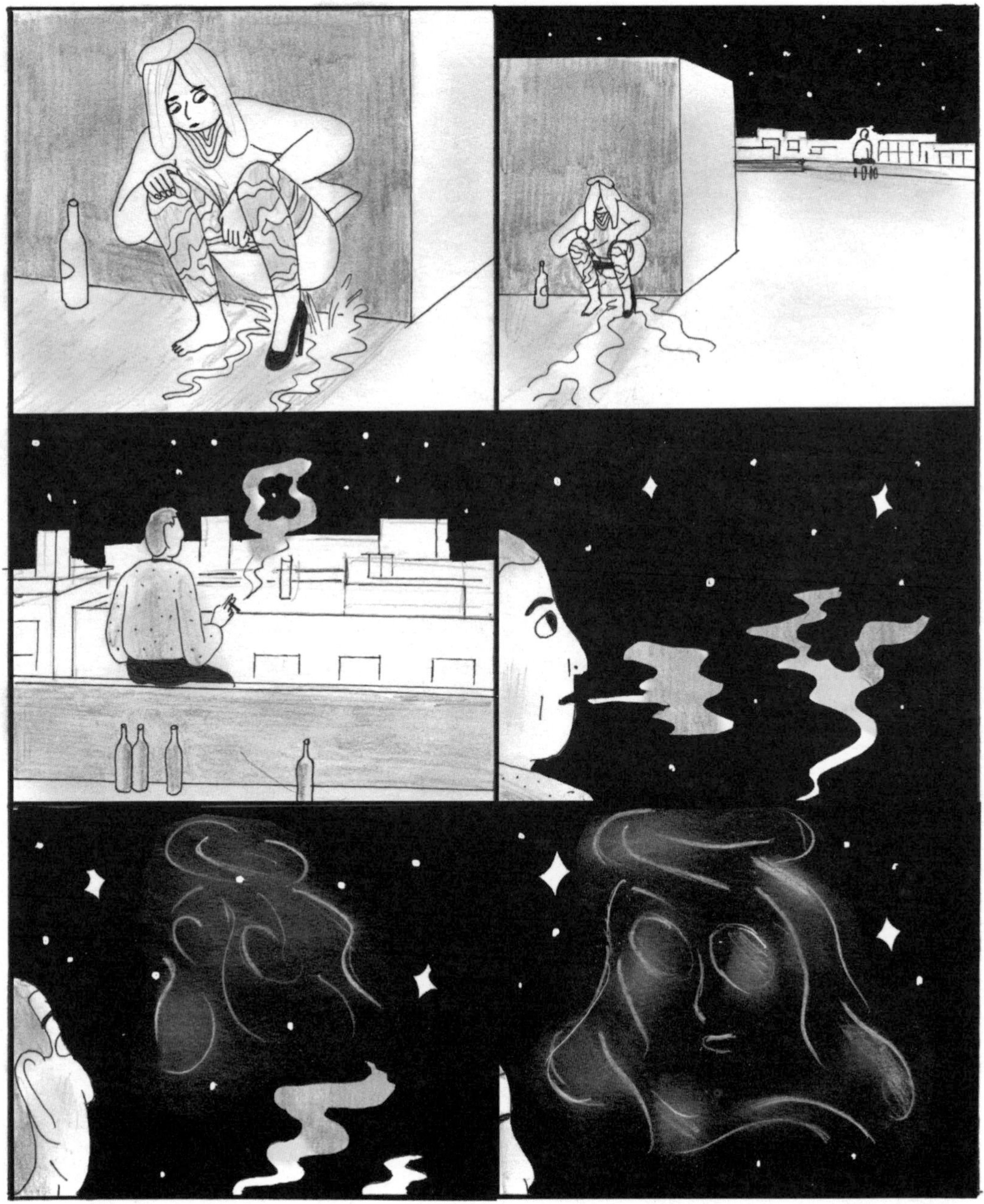

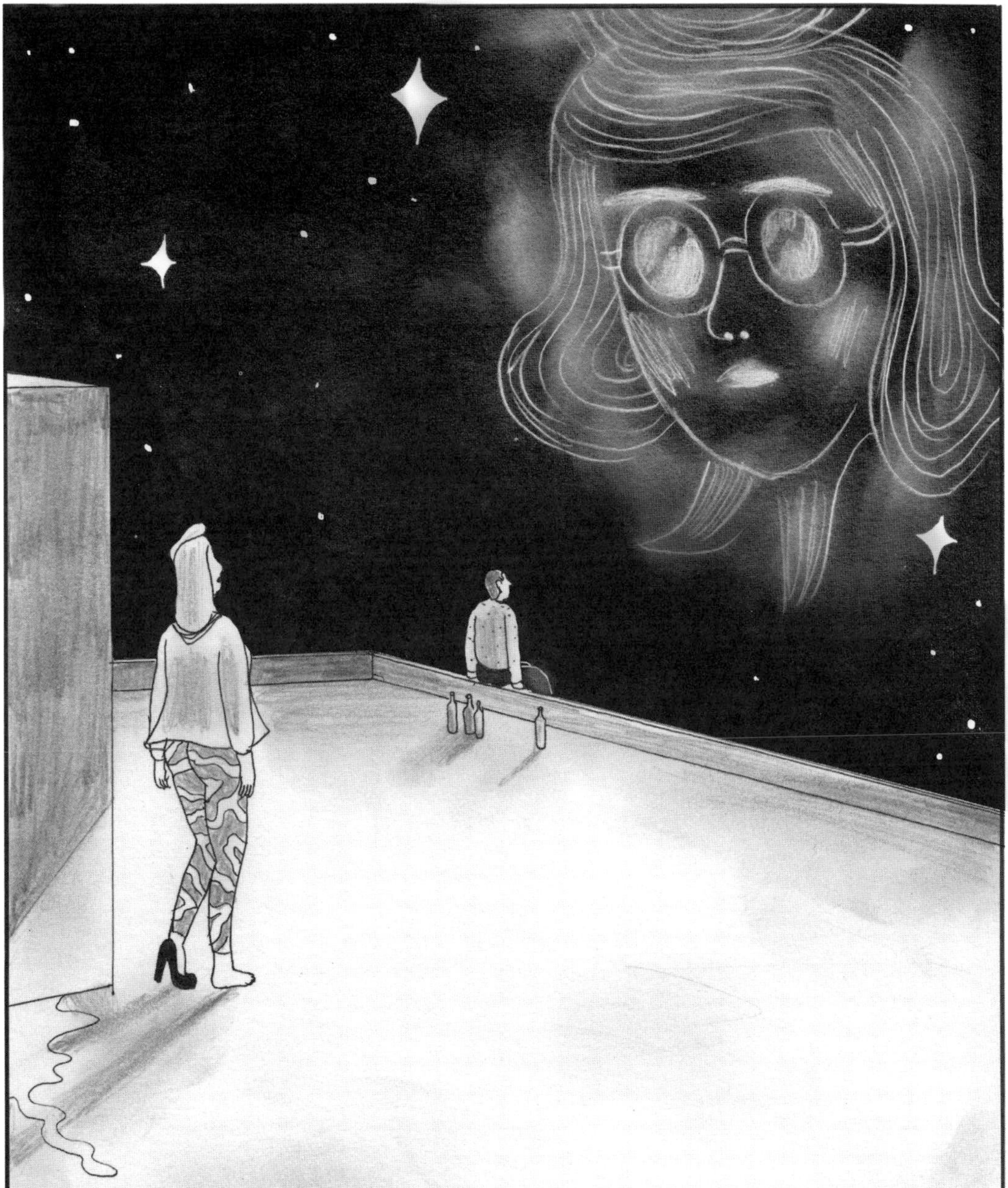

DONK

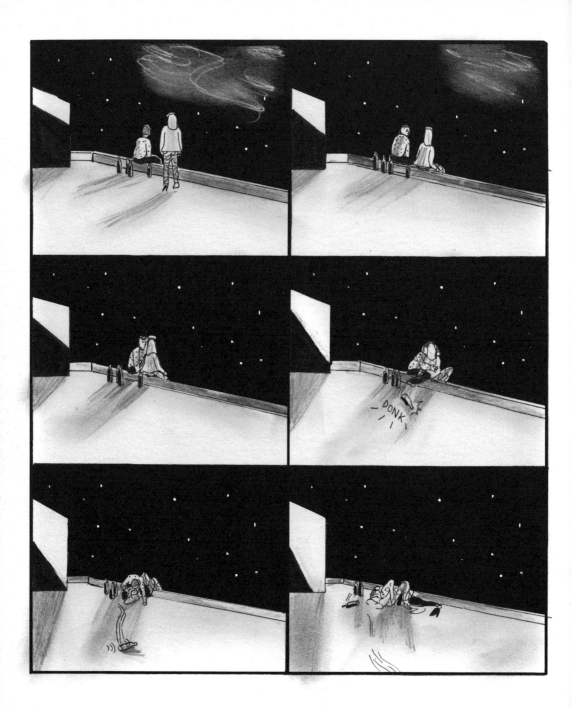

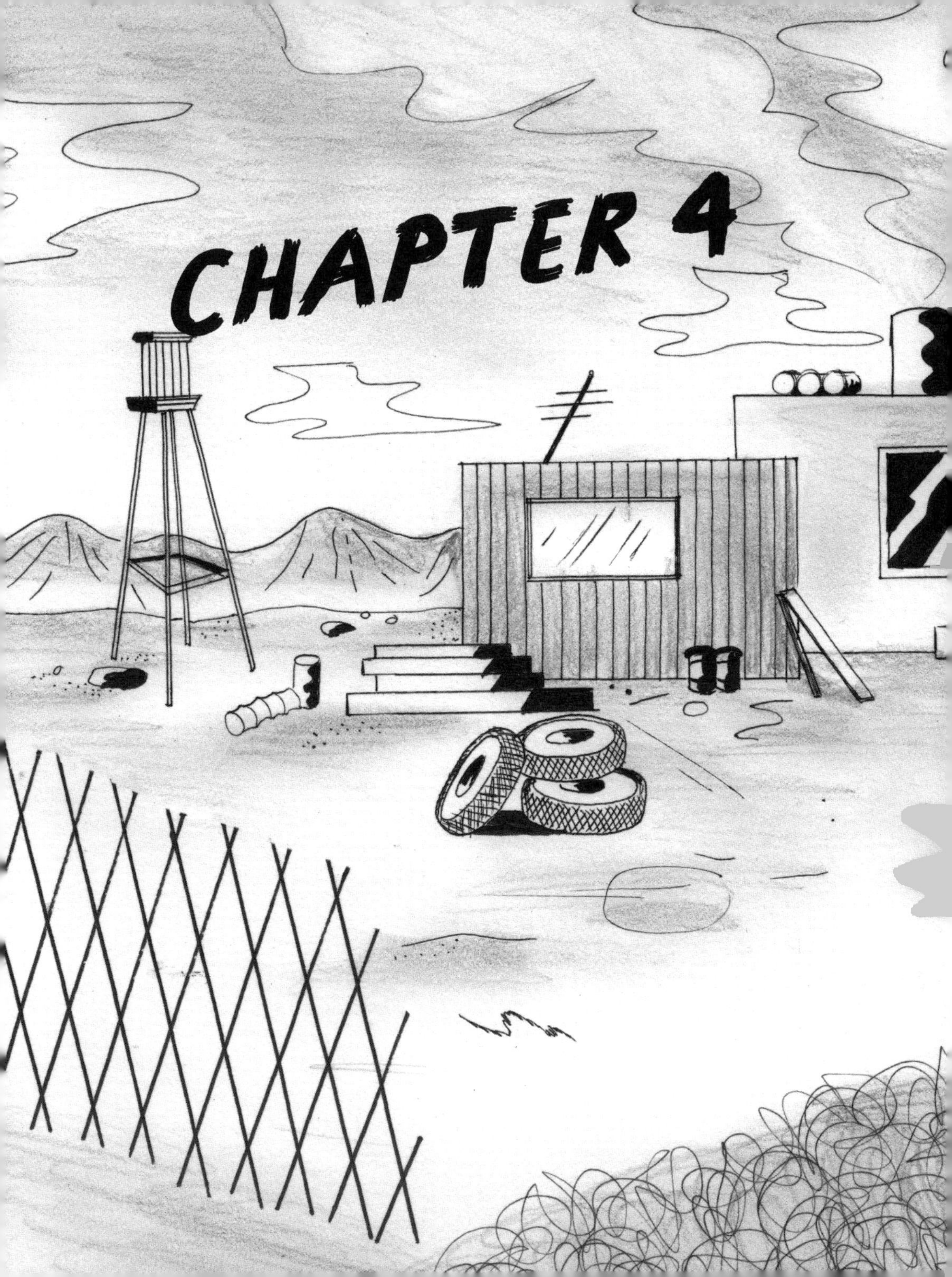
CHAPTER 4

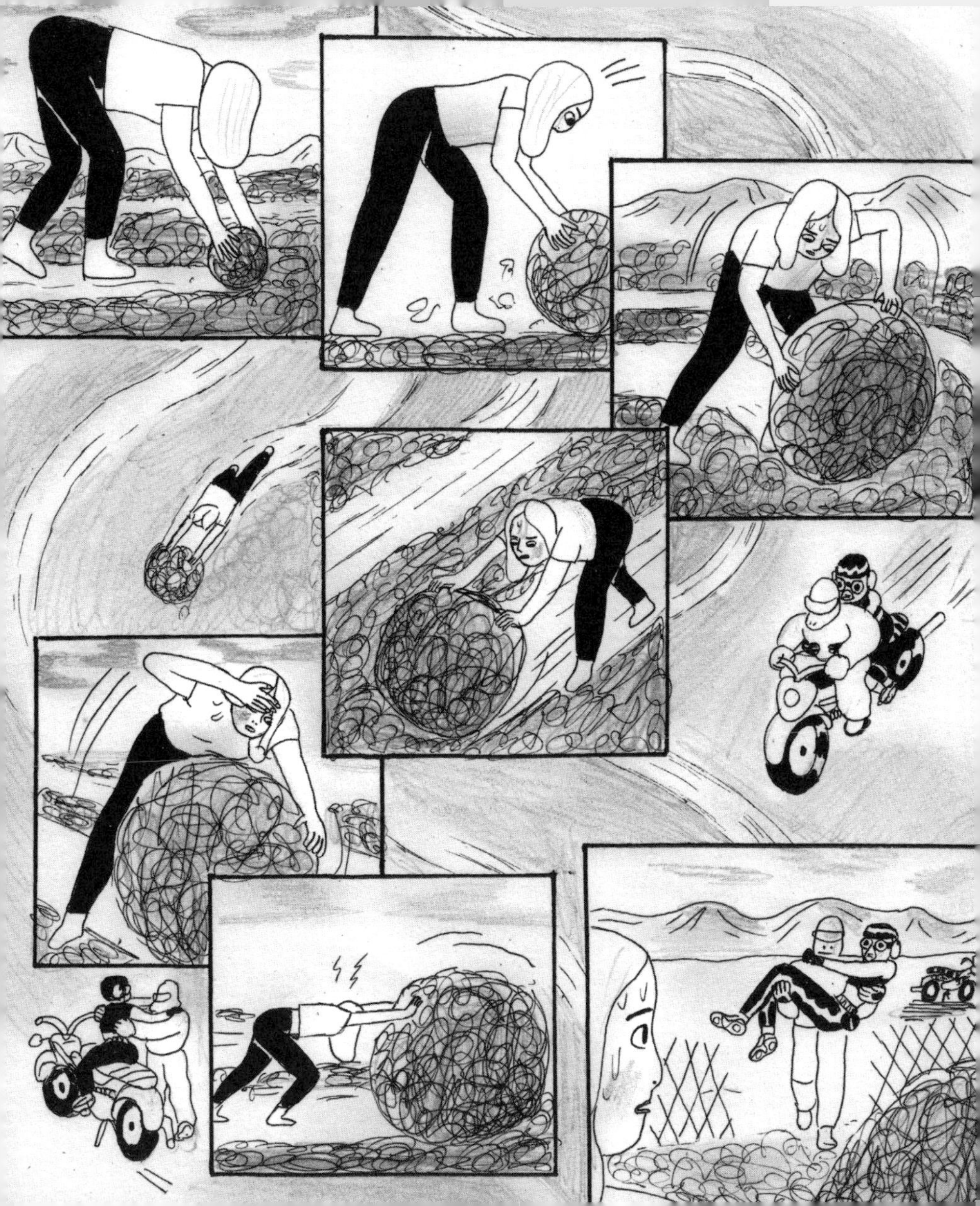

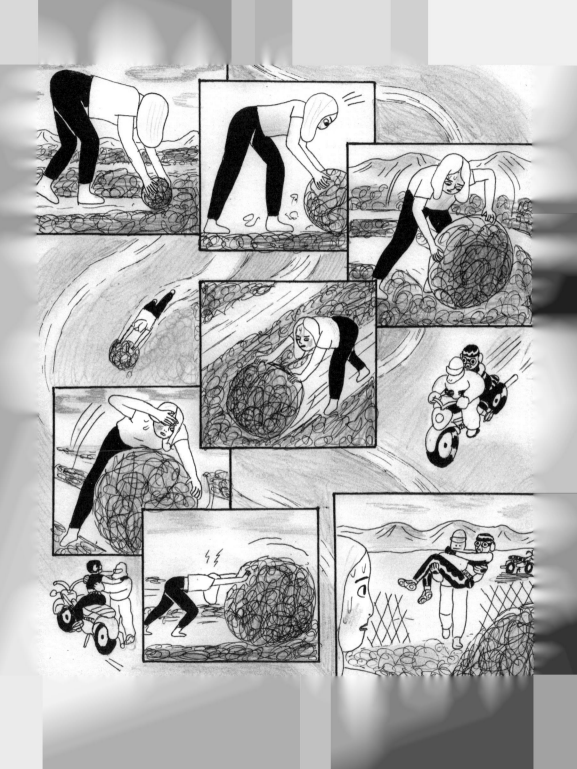

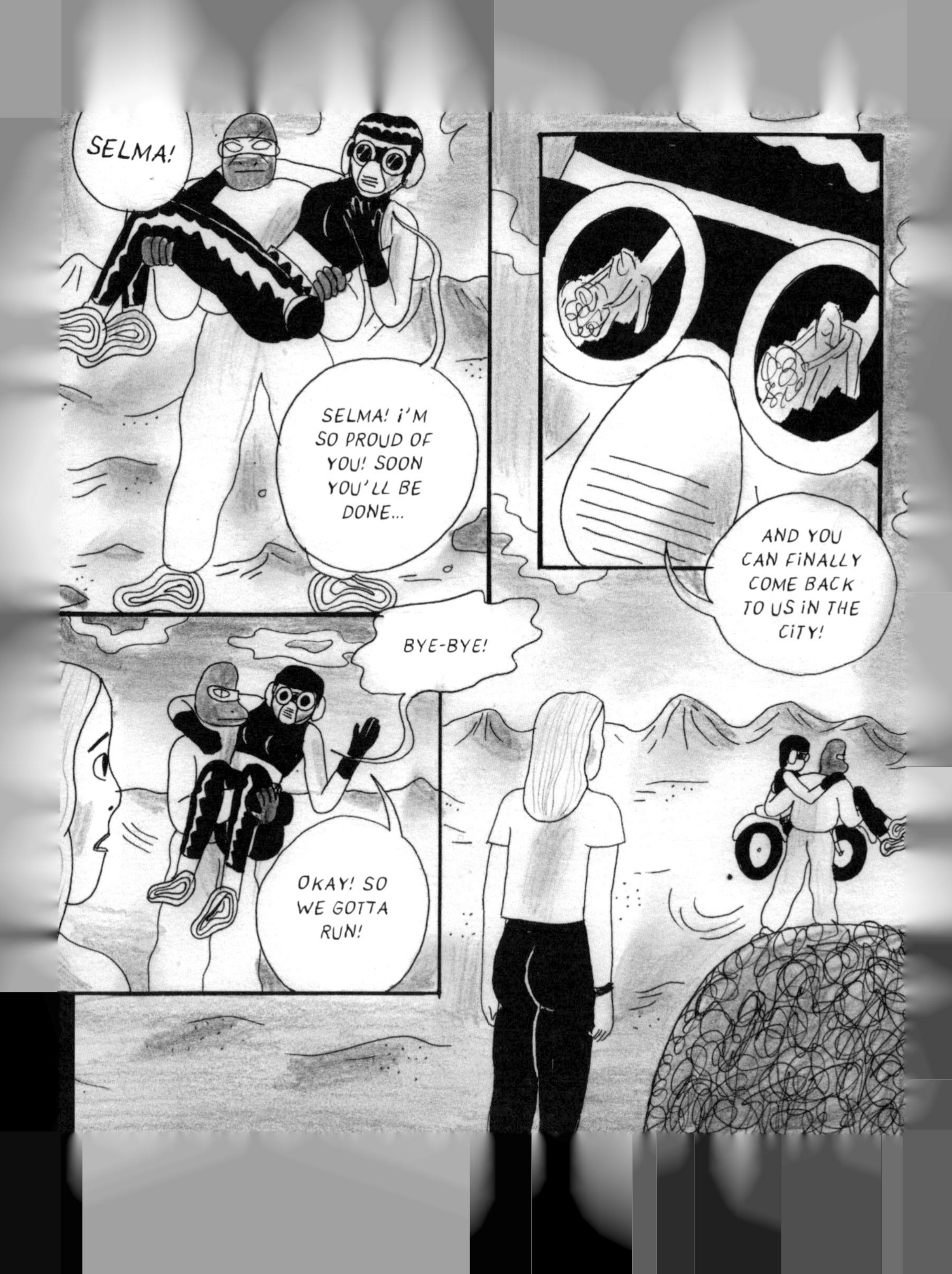
SELMA!
SELMA! I'M SO PROUD OF YOU! SOON YOU'LL BE DONE...
AND YOU CAN FINALLY COME BACK TO US IN THE CITY!
BYE-BYE!
OKAY! SO WE GOTTA RUN!

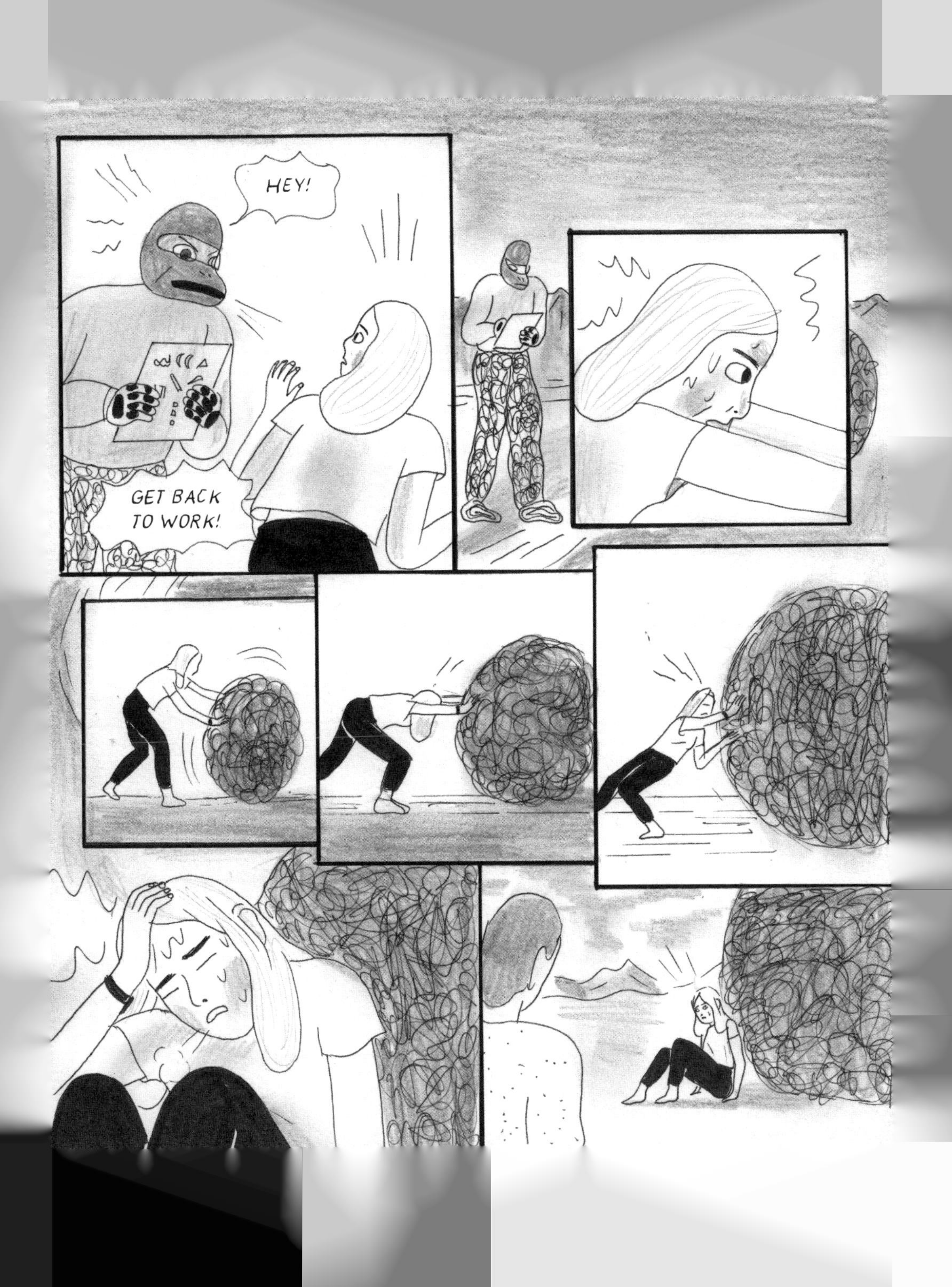
HEY!
GET BACK TO WORK!

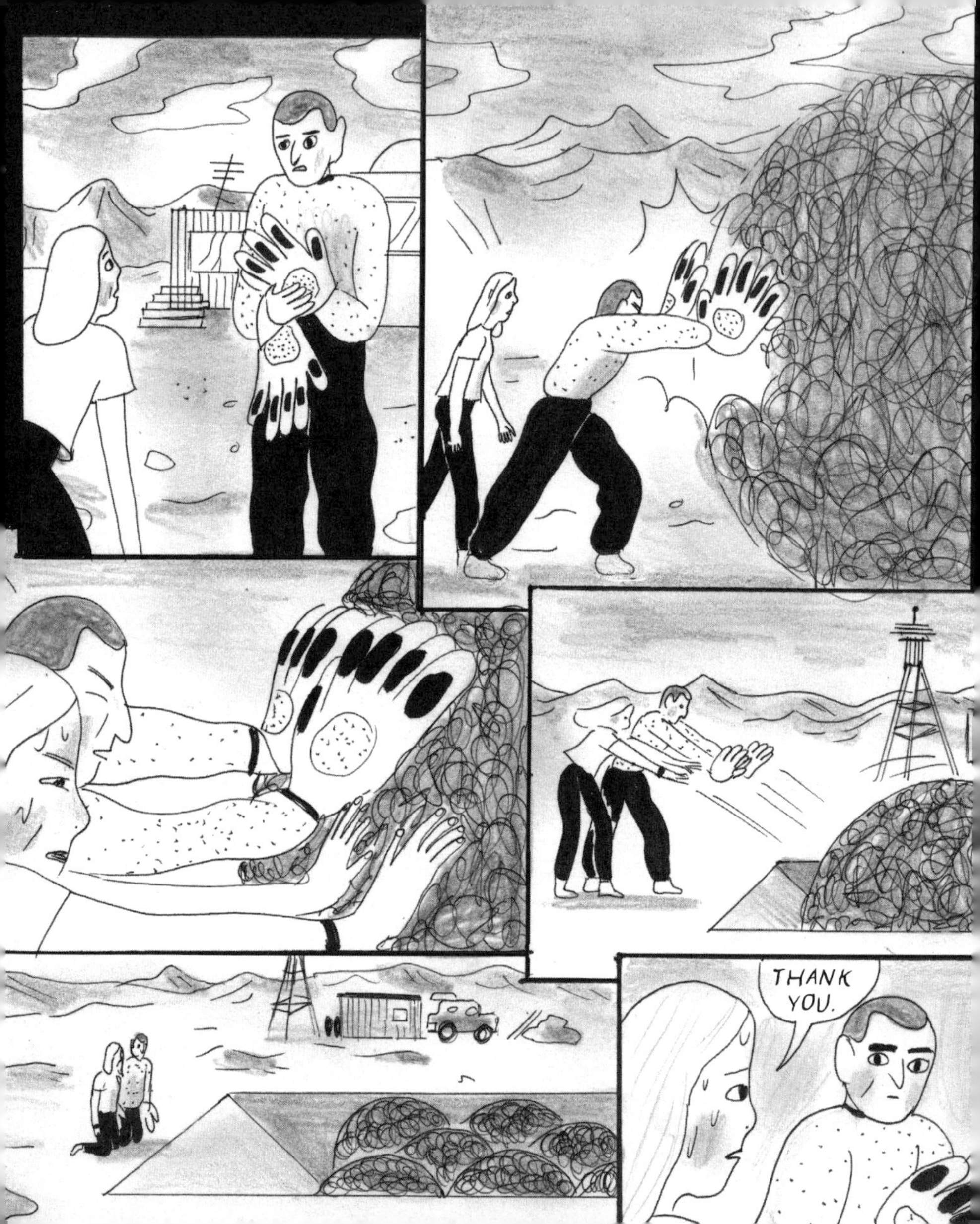
THANK YOU.

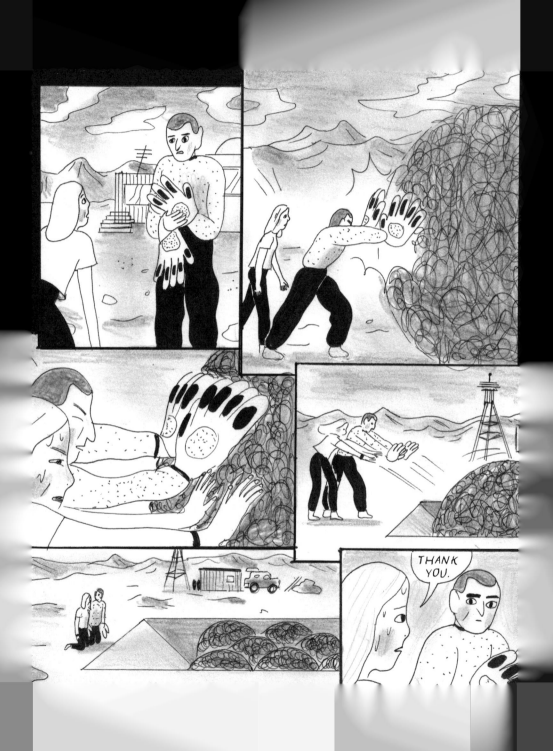

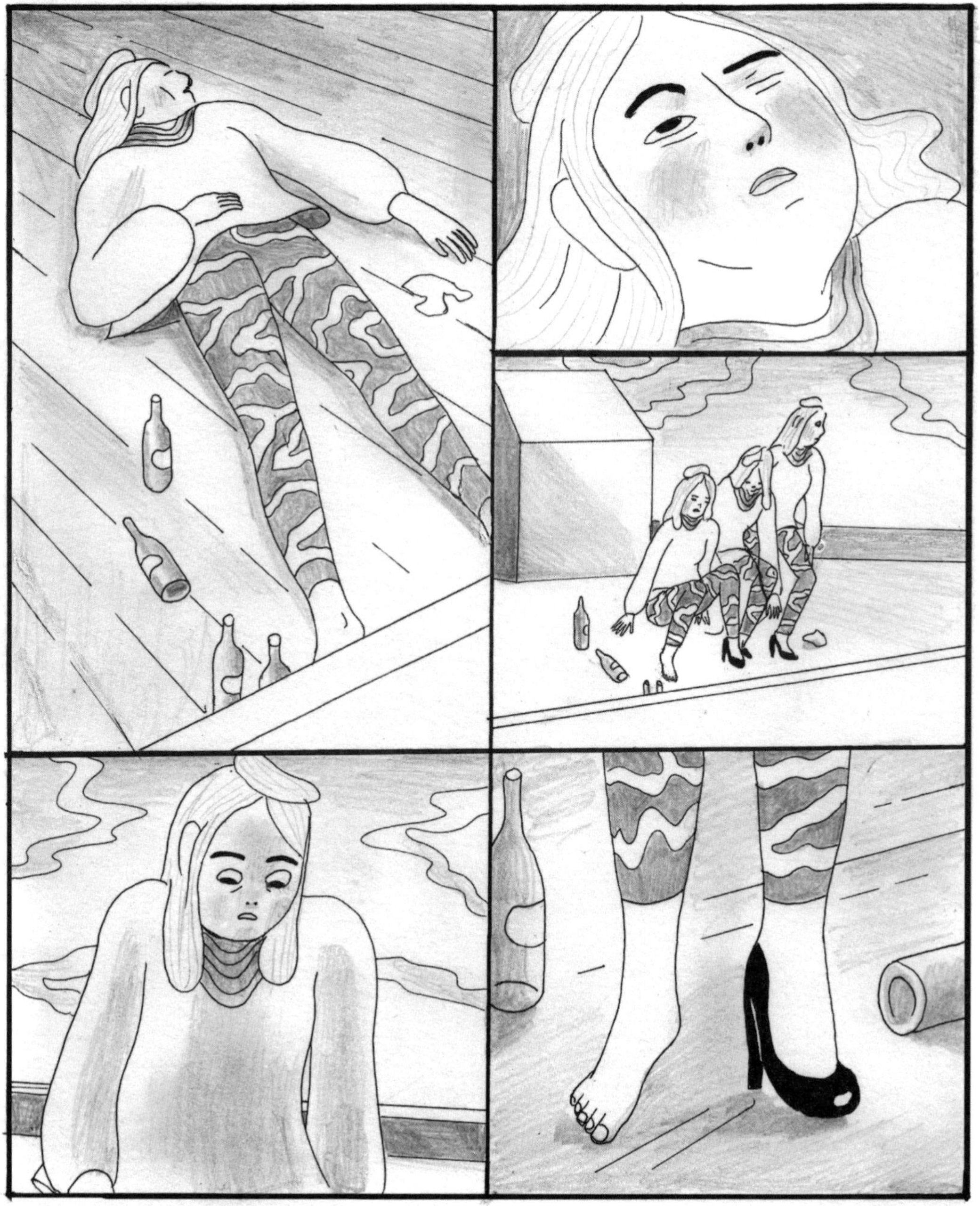

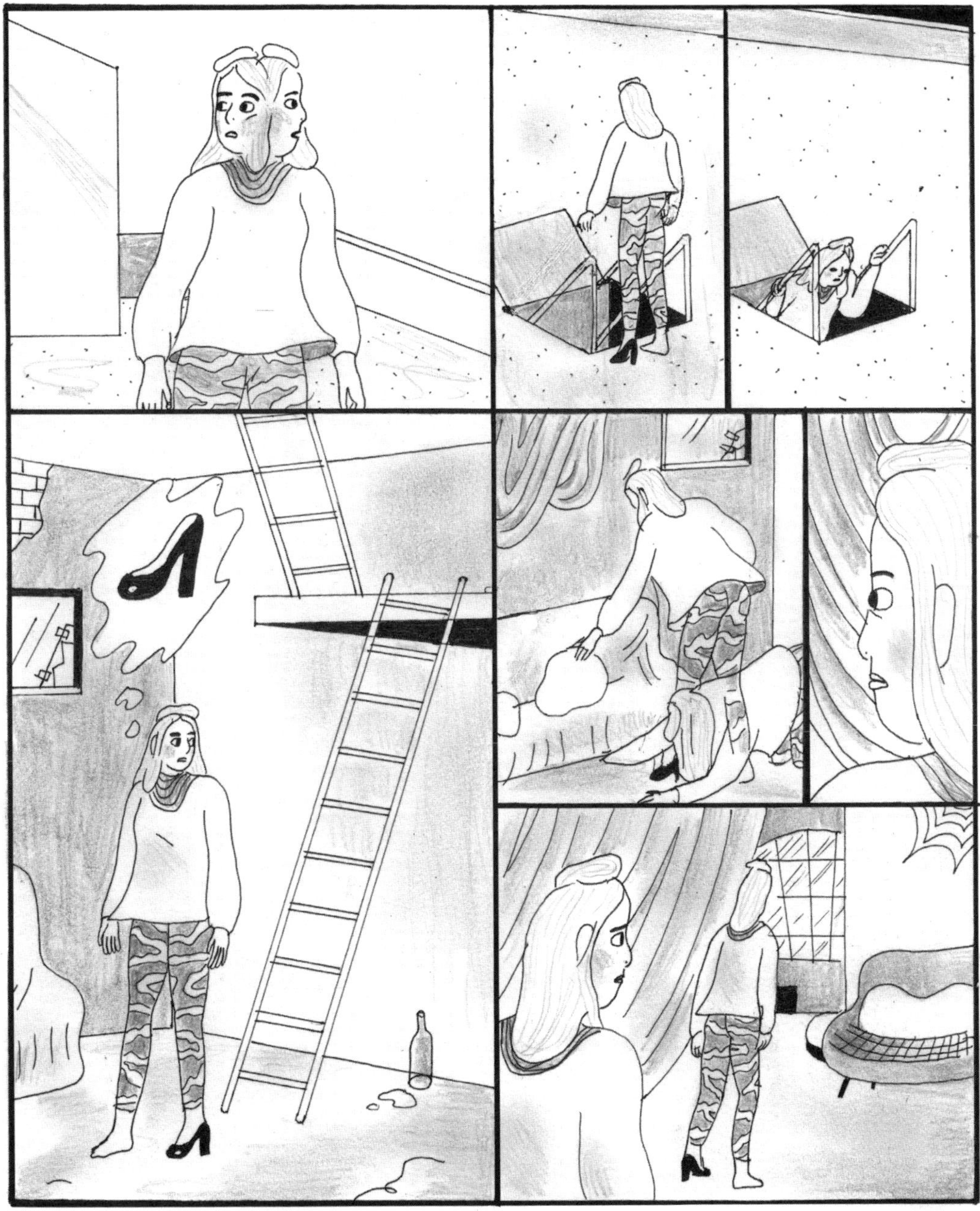

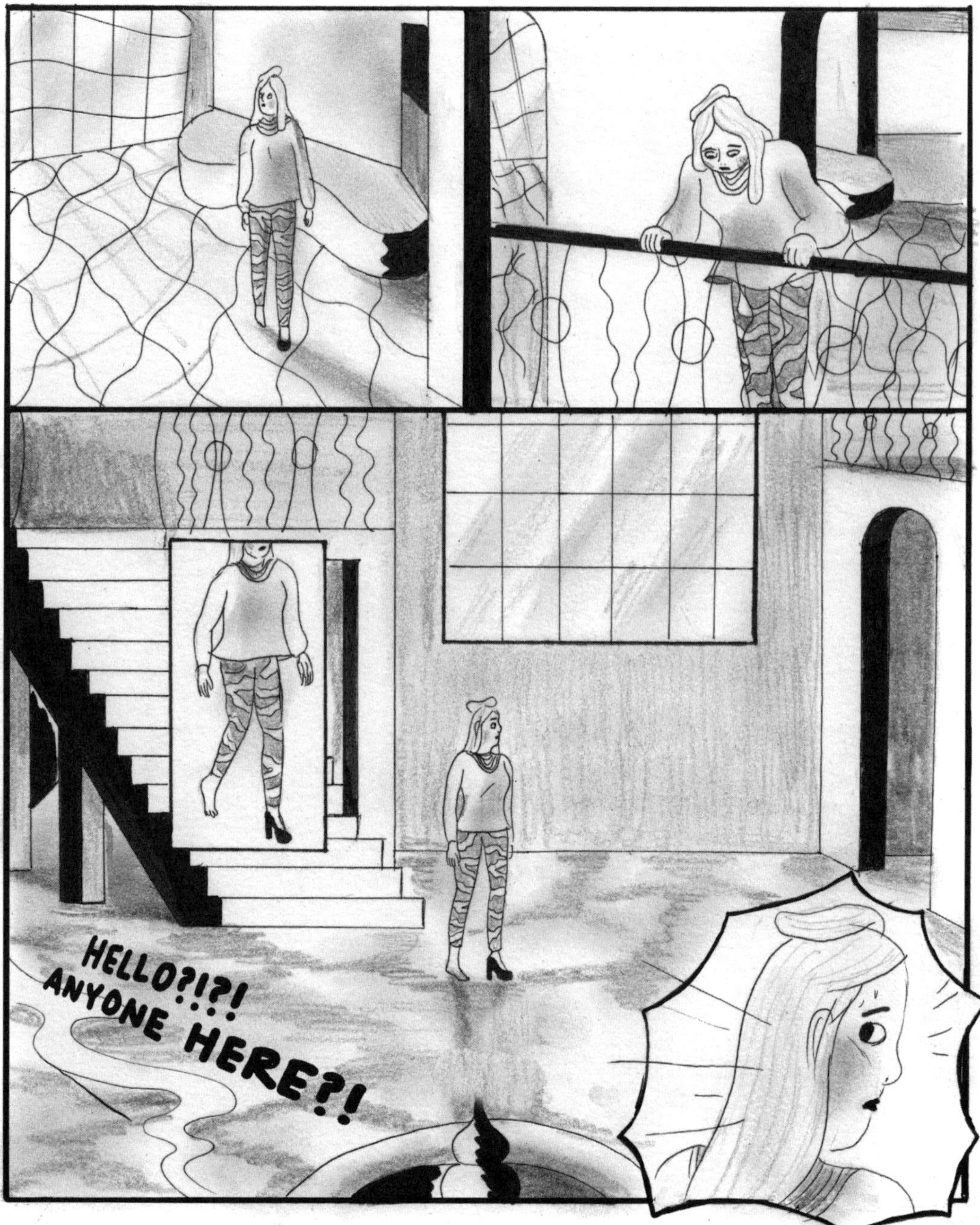
HELLO?!?!
ANYONE HERE?!

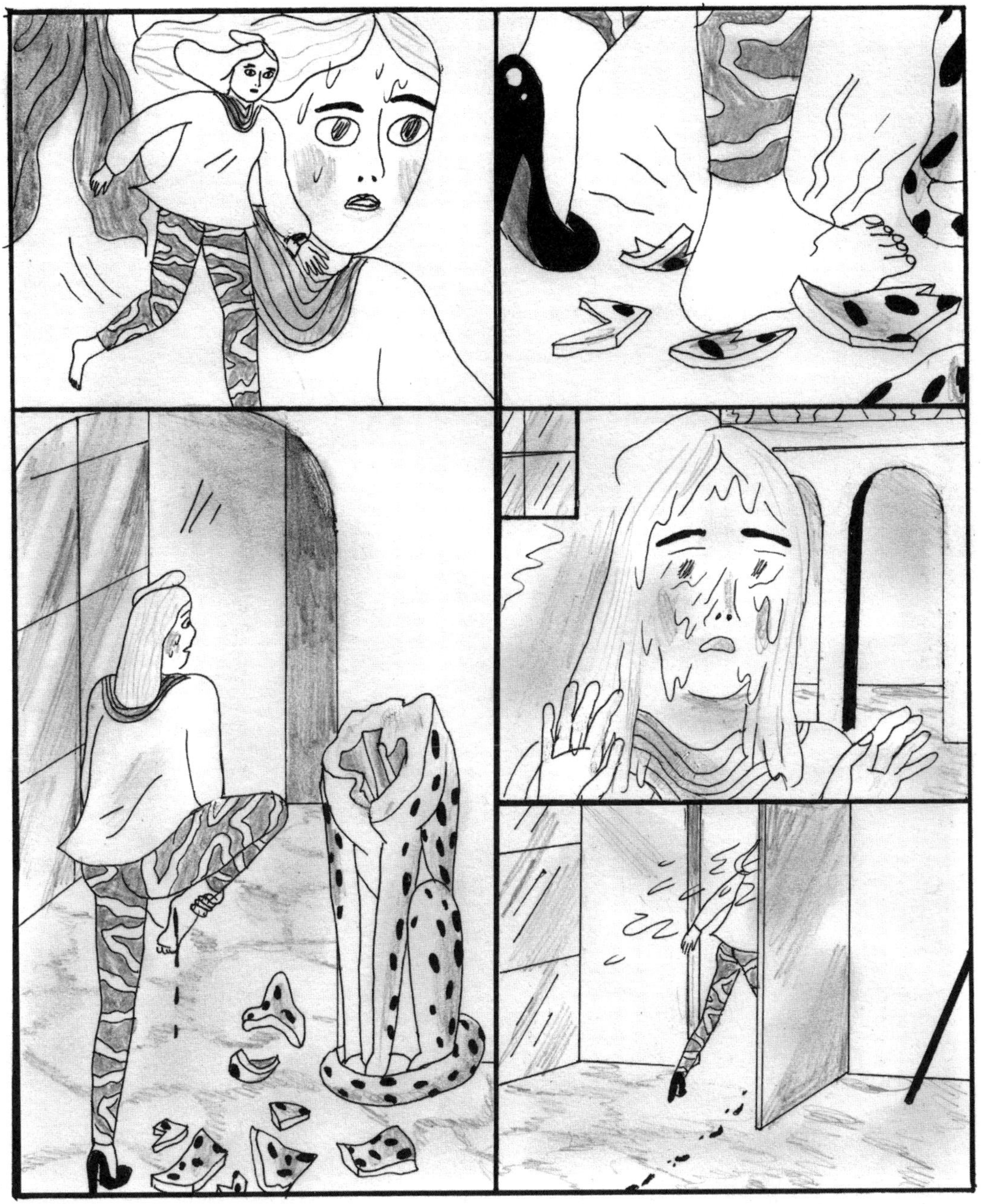

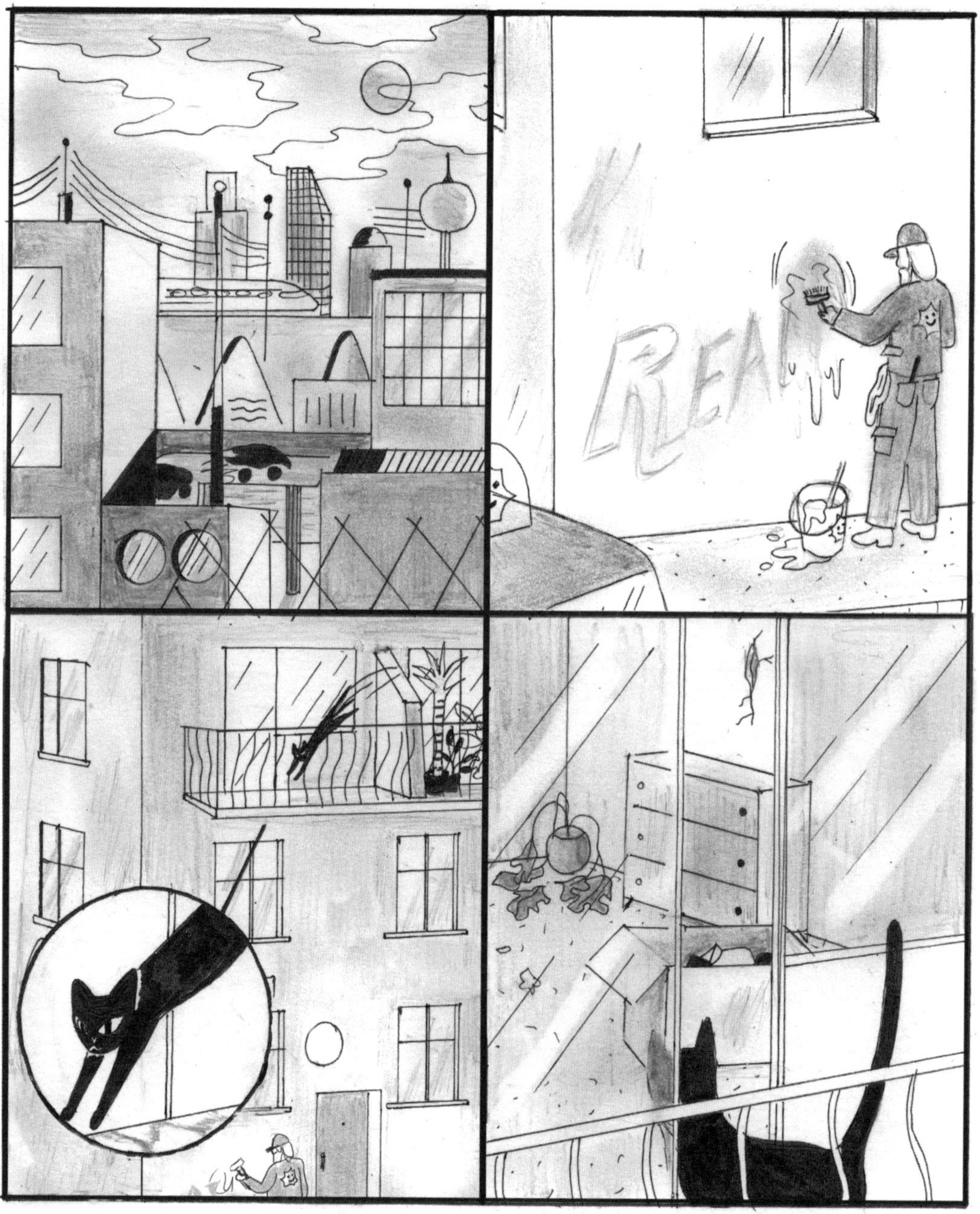
REAL

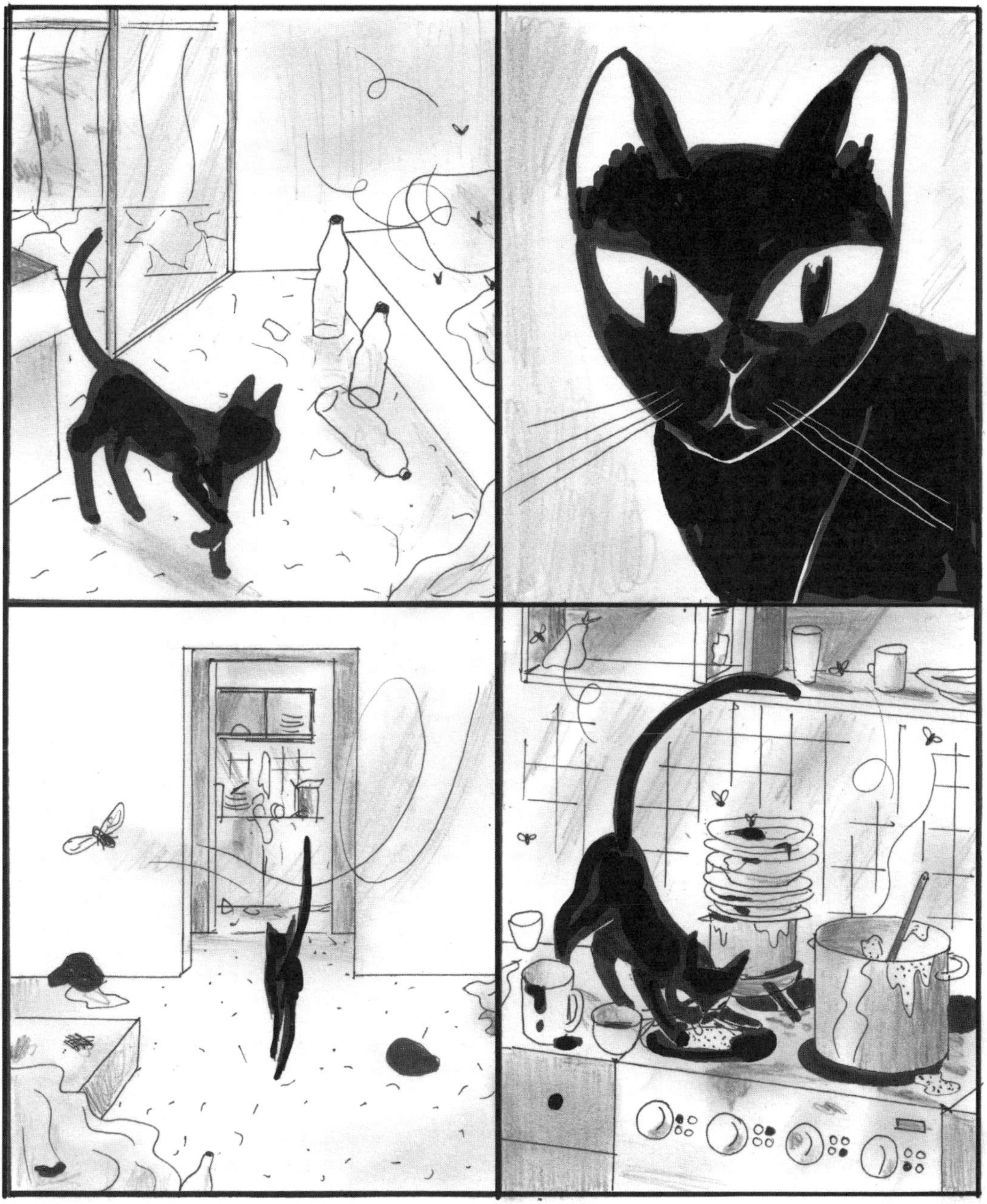

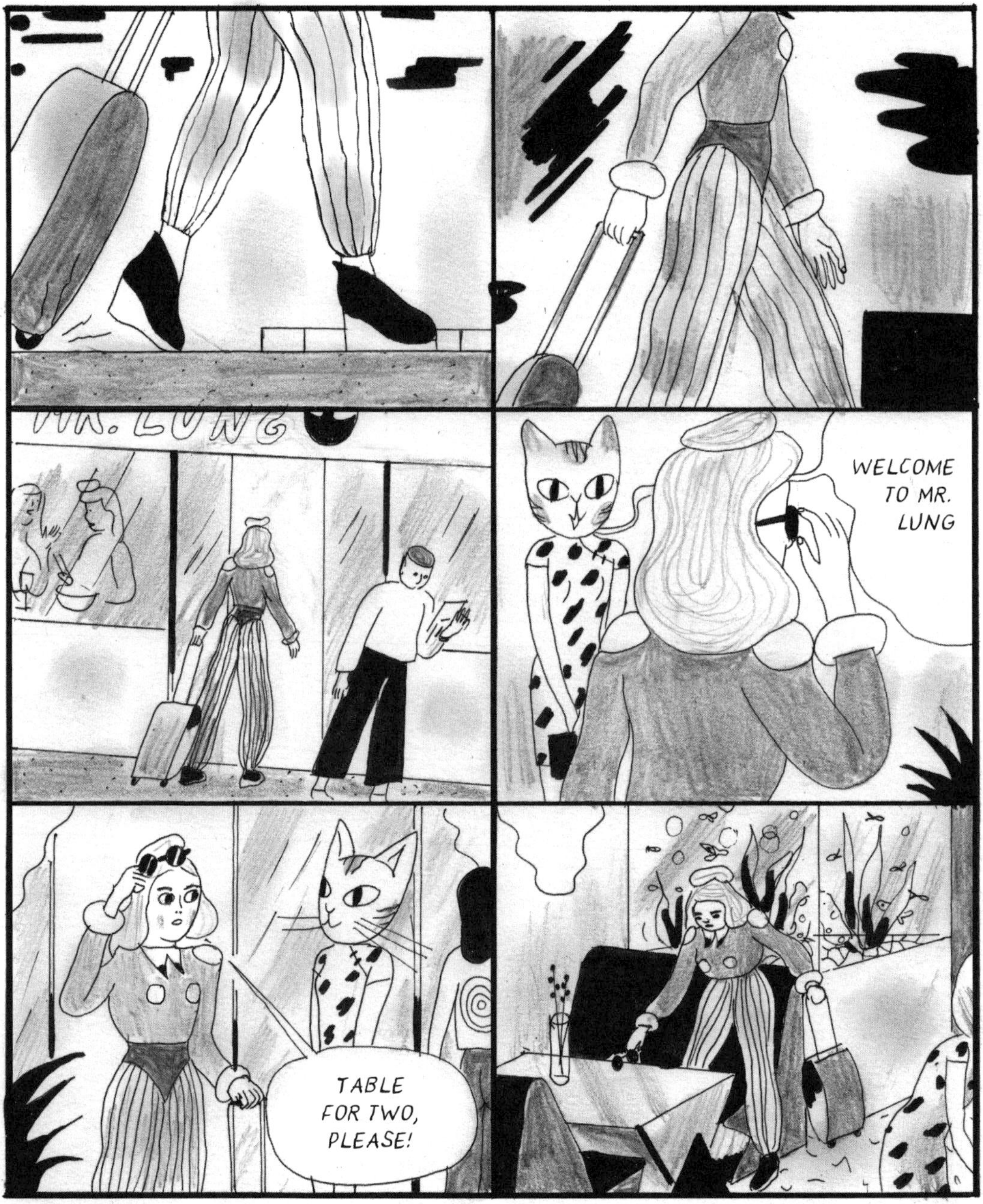
MR. LUNG
WELCOME TO MR. LUNG
TABLE FOR TWO, PLEASE!

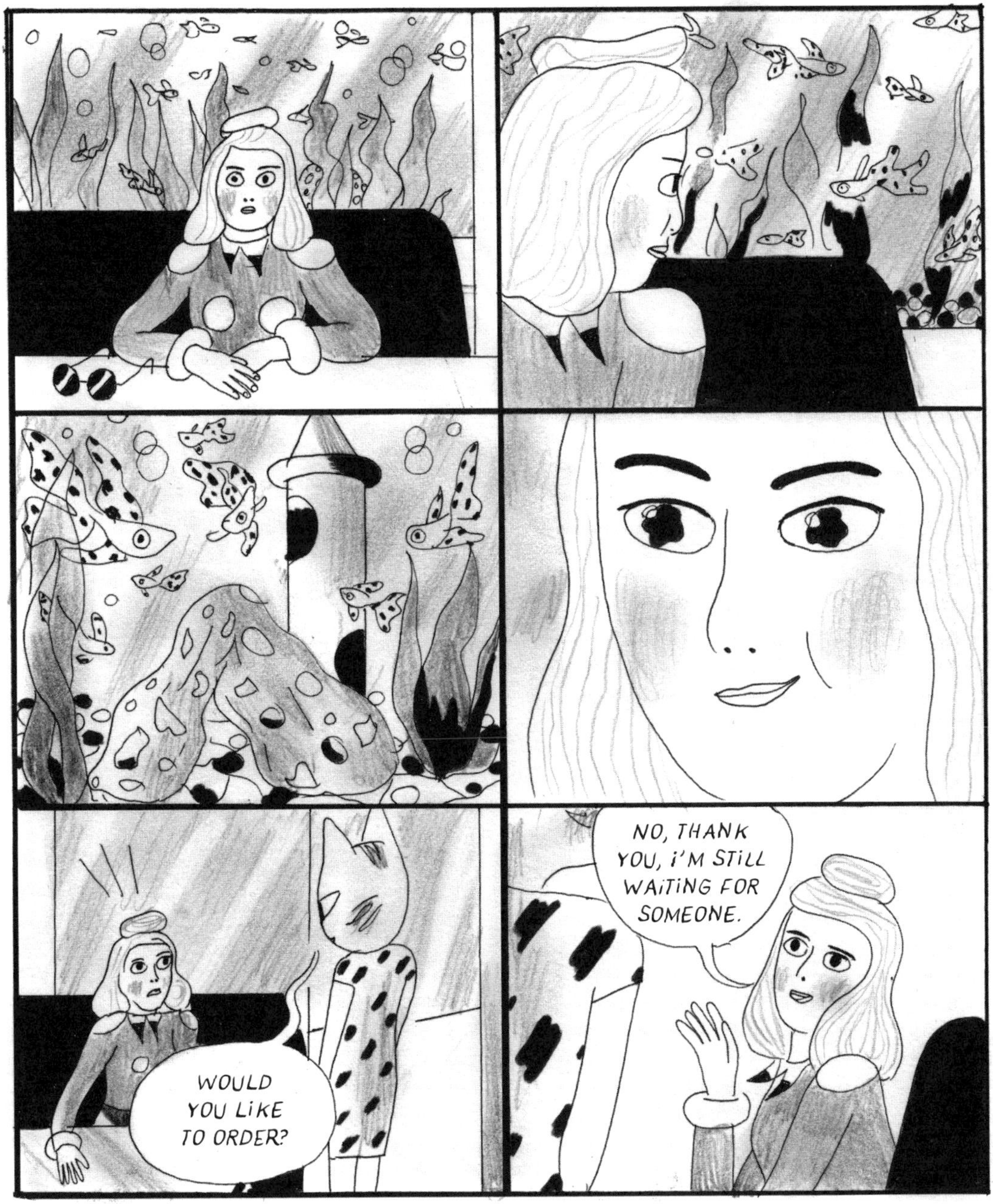
WOULD YOU LIKE TO ORDER?
NO, THANK YOU, I'M STILL WAITING FOR SOMEONE.

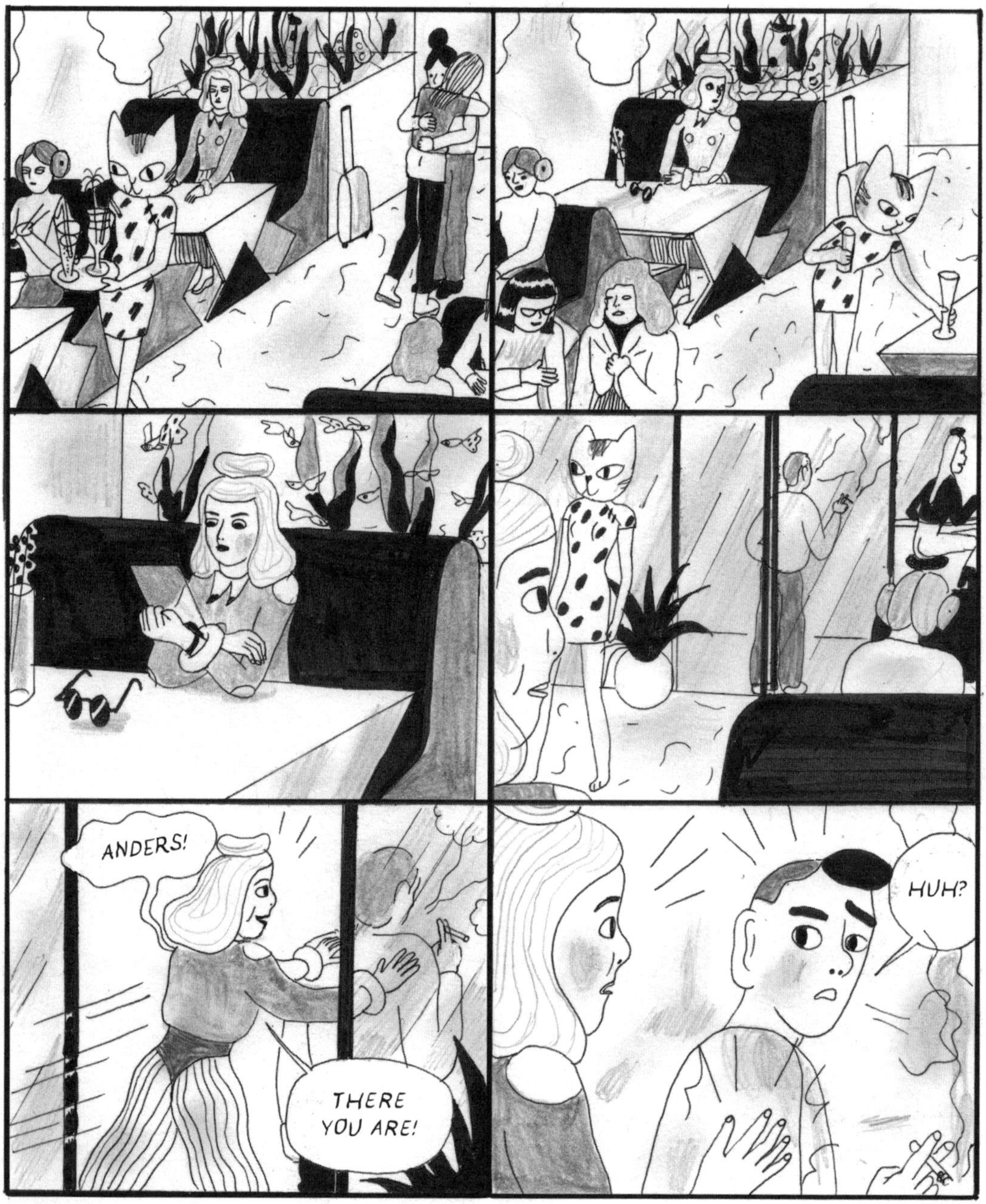
ANDERS!
THERE YOU ARE!
HUH?

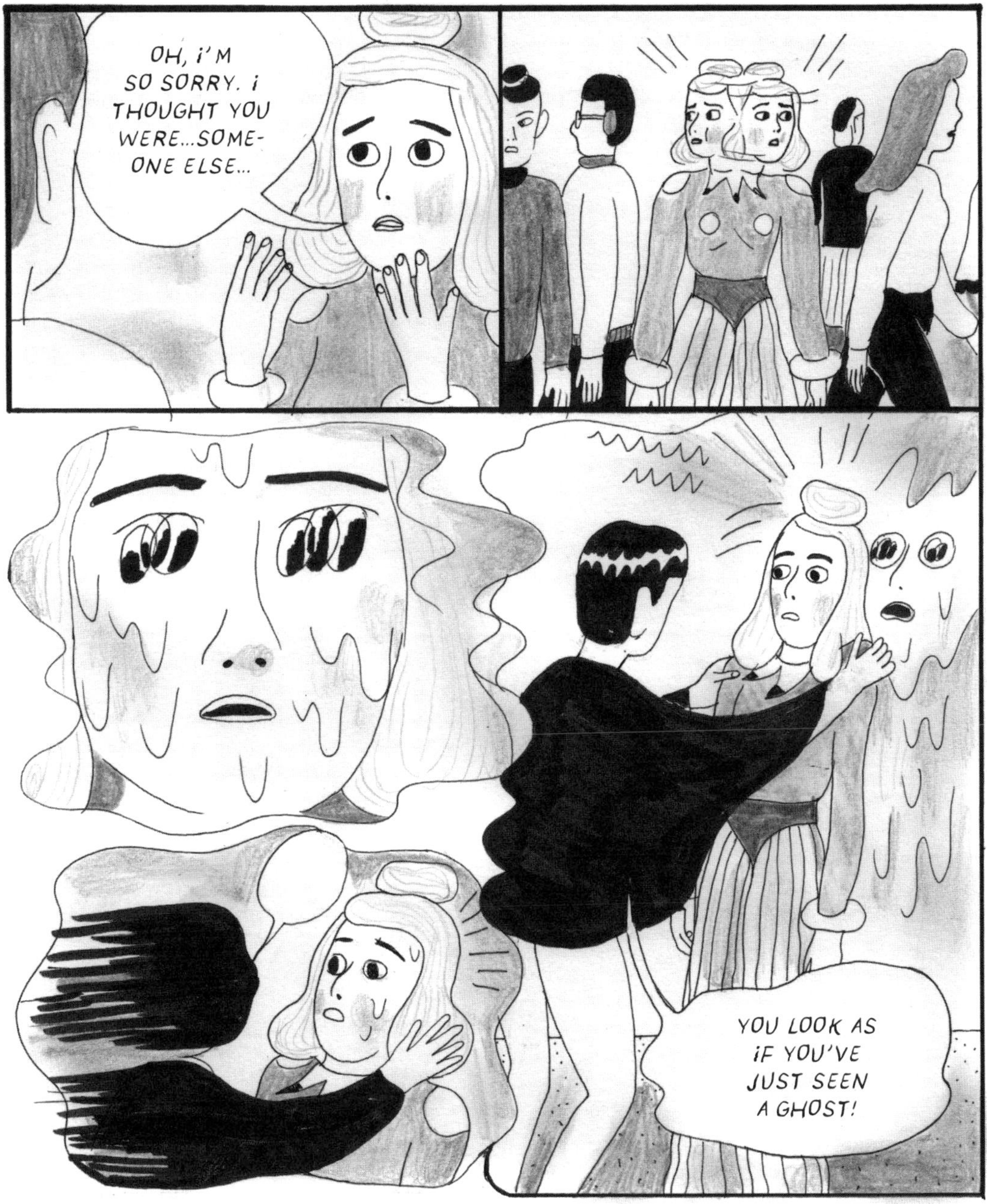
OH, I'M SO SORRY. I THOUGHT YOU WERE...SOME-ONE ELSE...
YOU LOOK AS IF YOU'VE JUST SEEN A GHOST!

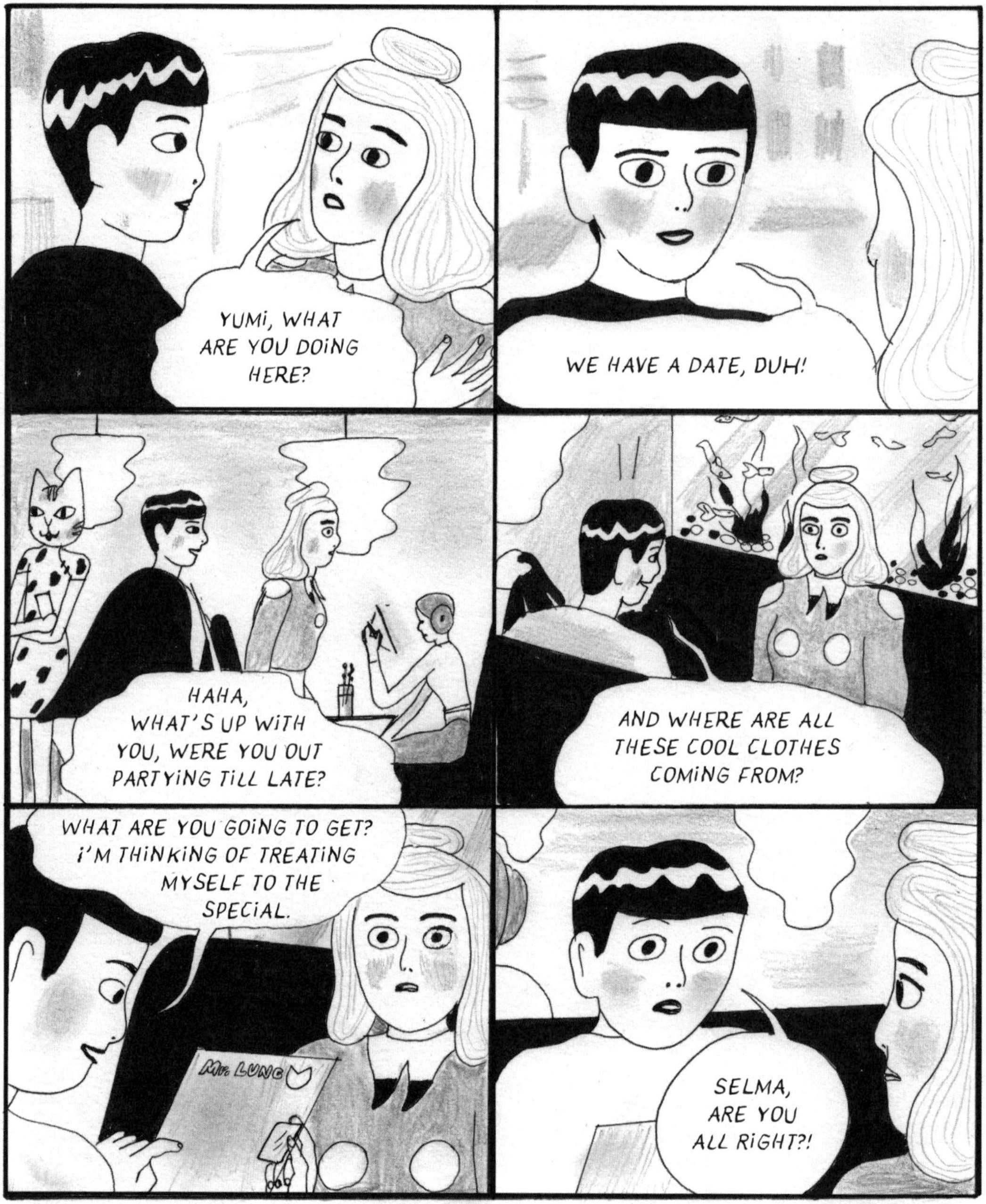
YUMi, WHAT ARE YOU DOiNG HERE?
WE HAVE A DATE, DUH!
HAHA, WHAT'S UP WiTH YOU, WERE YOU OUT PARTYiNG TiLL LATE?
AND WHERE ARE ALL THESE COOL CLOTHES COMiNG FROM?
WHAT ARE YOU GOING TO GET? i'M THiNKiNG OF TREATiNG MYSELF TO THE SPECiAL.
Mr. LUNG
SELMA, ARE YOU ALL RiGHT?!

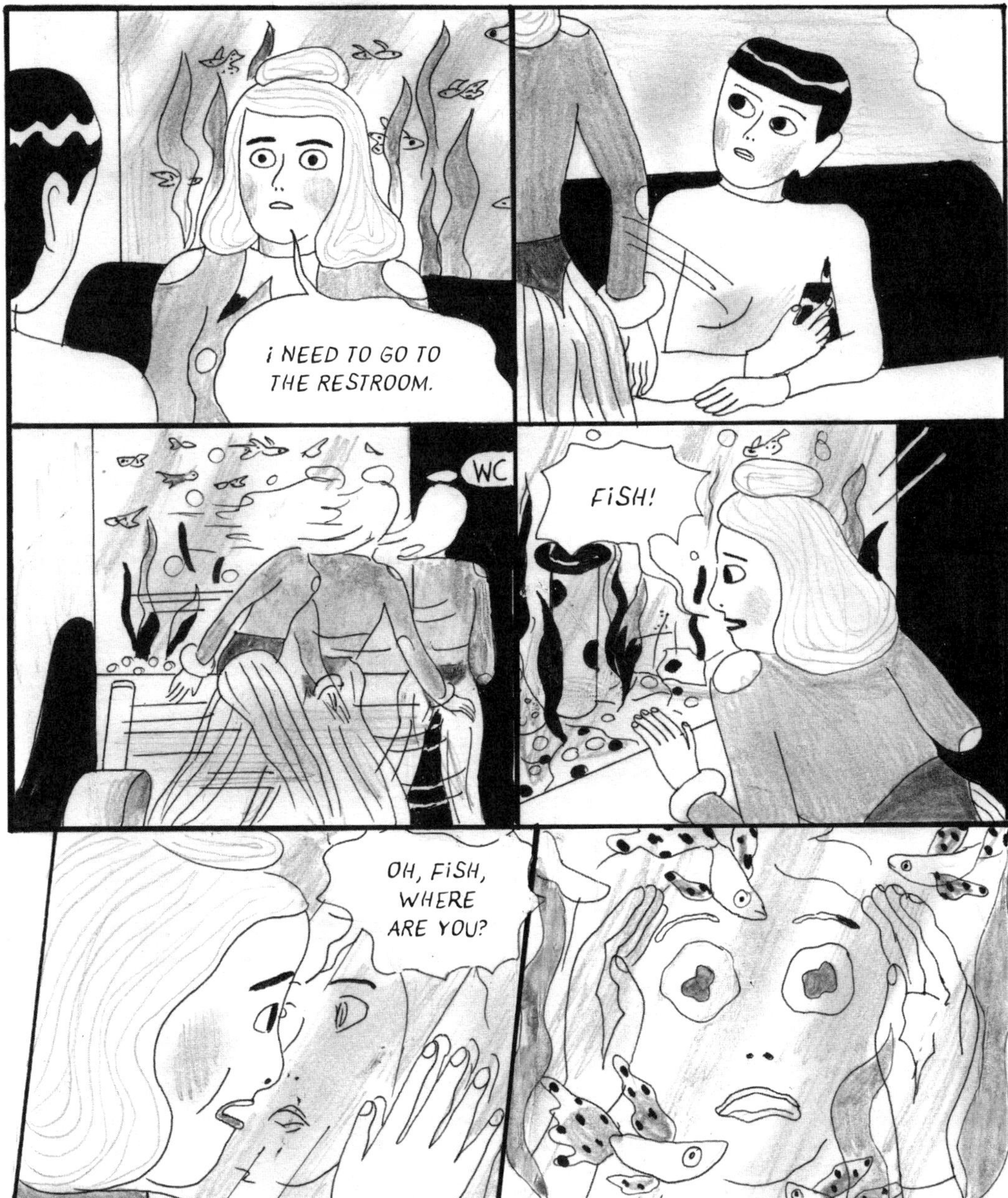
I NEED TO GO TO THE RESTROOM.
WC
FISH!
OH, FISH, WHERE ARE YOU?

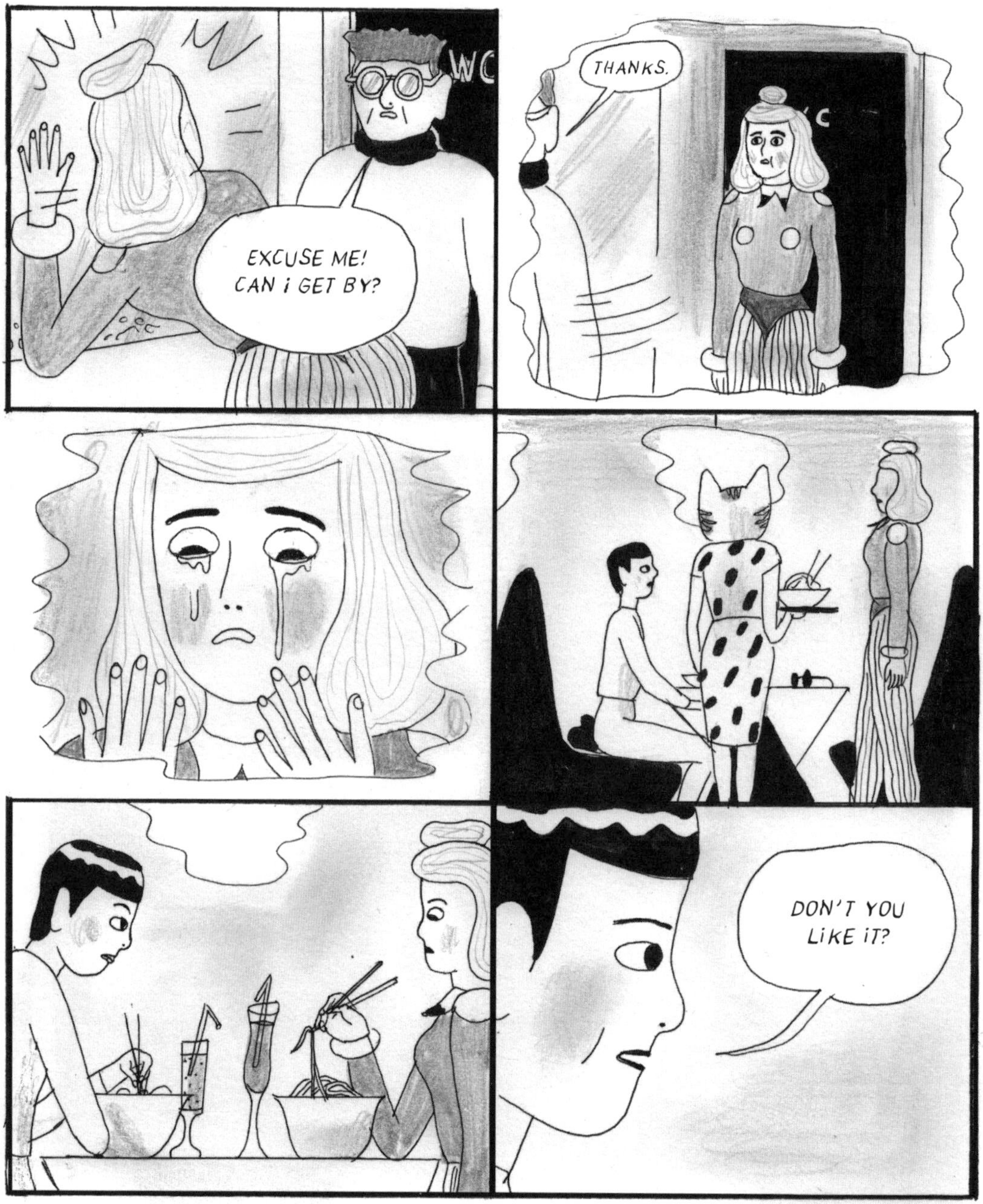
EXCUSE ME! CAN i GET BY?
THANKS.
DON'T YOU LiKE iT?

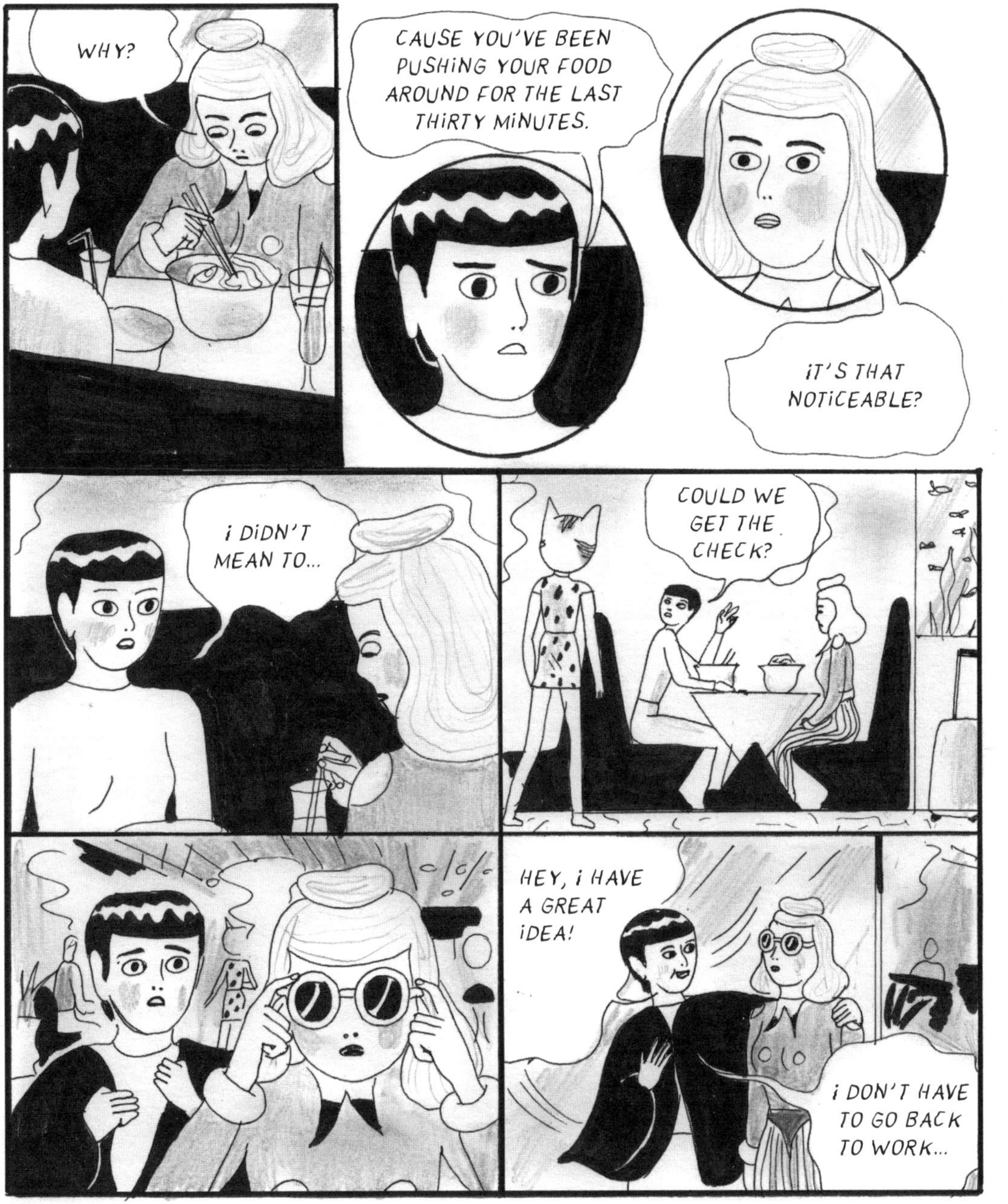
WHY?
CAUSE YOU'VE BEEN PUSHING YOUR FOOD AROUND FOR THE LAST THIRTY MINUTES.
IT'S THAT NOTICEABLE?
I DIDN'T MEAN TO...
COULD WE GET THE CHECK?
HEY, I HAVE A GREAT IDEA!
I DON'T HAVE TO GO BACK TO WORK...

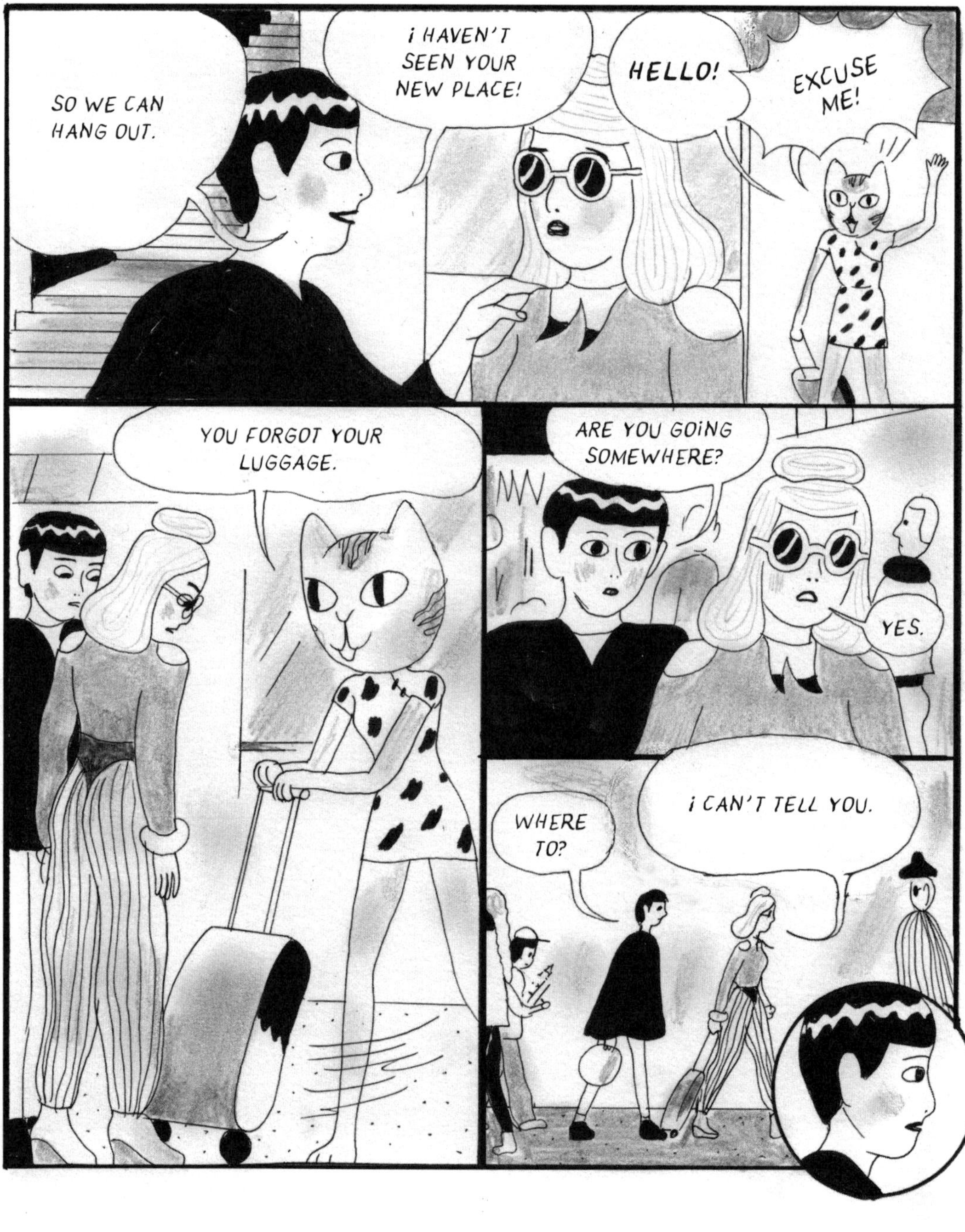
SO WE CAN HANG OUT.
i HAVEN'T SEEN YOUR NEW PLACE!
HELLO!
EXCUSE ME!
YOU FORGOT YOUR LUGGAGE.
ARE YOU GOiNG SOMEWHERE?
YES.
WHERE TO?
i CAN'T TELL YOU.

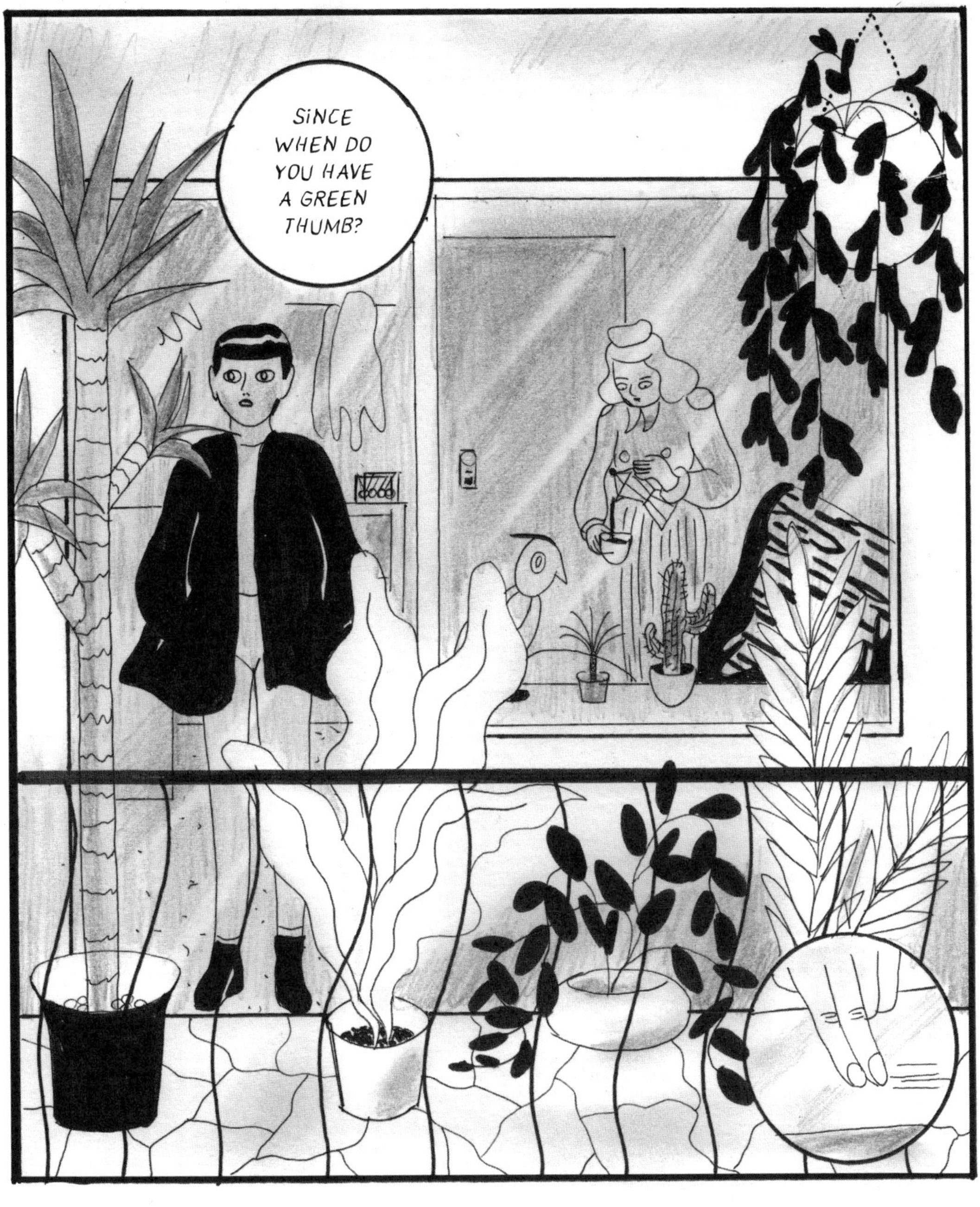
SiNCE WHEN DO YOU HAVE A GREEN THUMB?

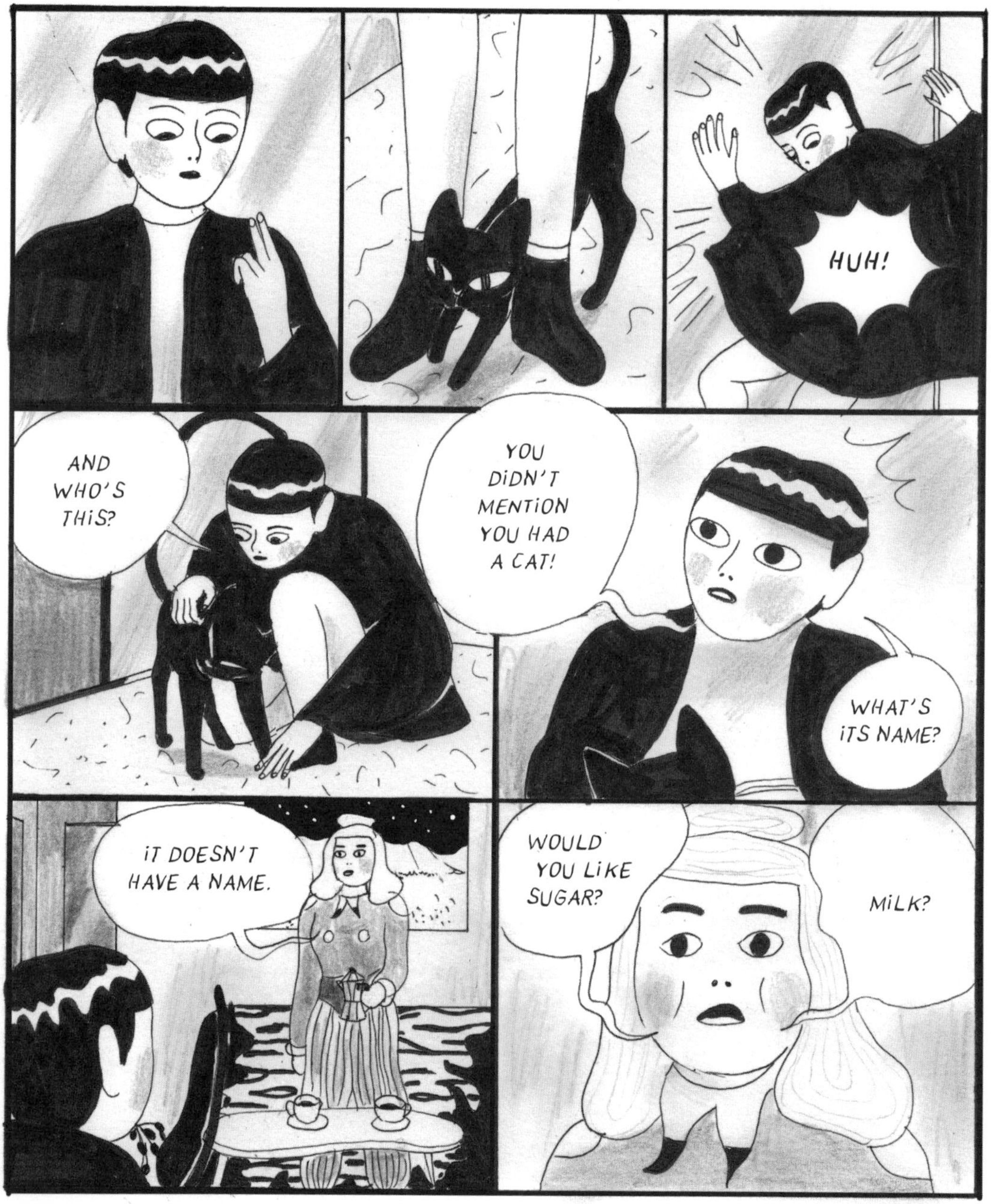
HUH!
AND WHO'S THIS?
YOU DIDN'T MENTION YOU HAD A CAT!
WHAT'S ITS NAME?
IT DOESN'T HAVE A NAME.
WOULD YOU LIKE SUGAR?
MILK?

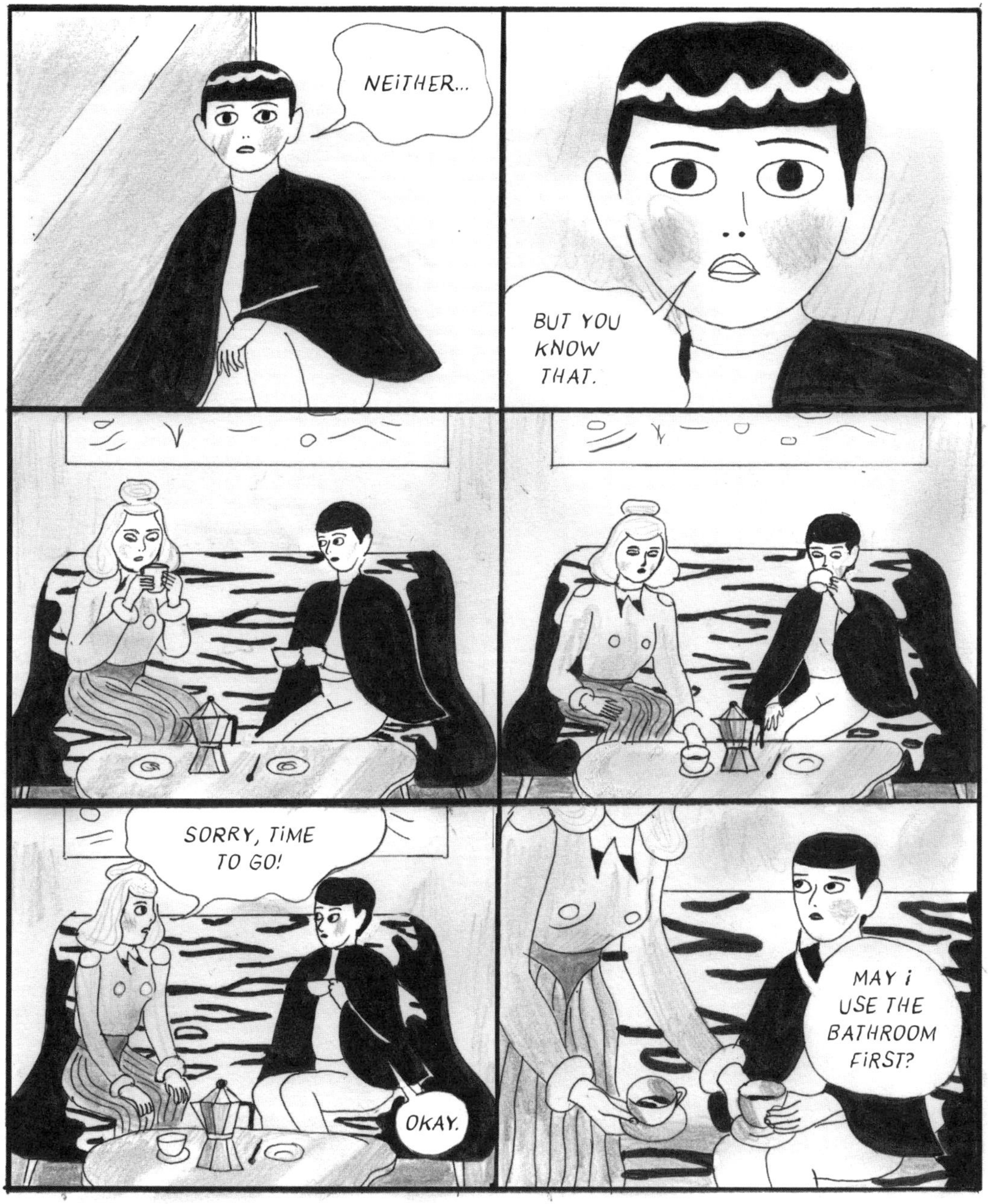
NEiTHER...
BUT YOU KNOW THAT.
SORRY, TiME TO GO!
OKAY.
MAY i USE THE BATHROOM FiRST?

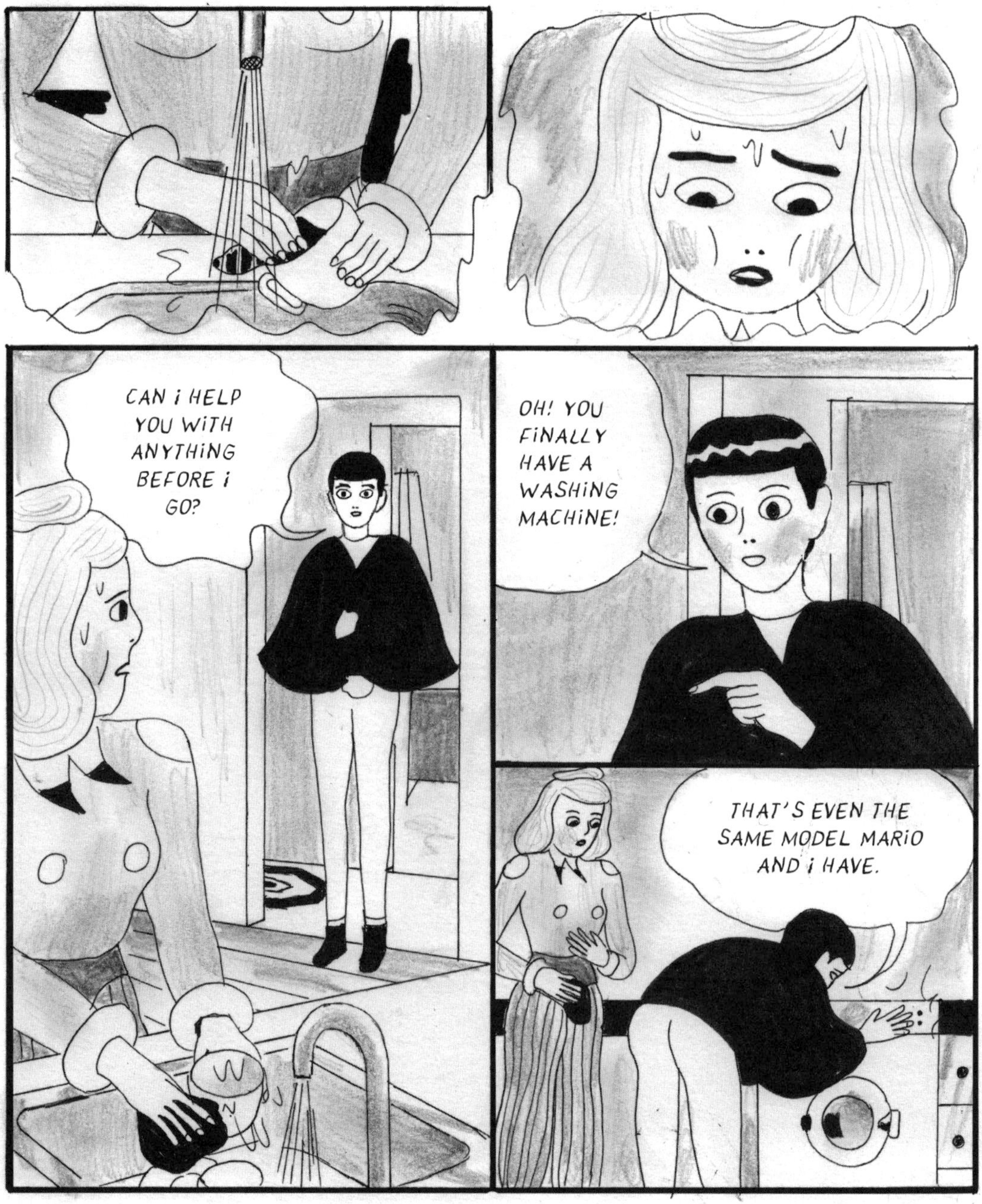
CAN I HELP YOU WITH ANYTHING BEFORE I GO?
OH! YOU FINALLY HAVE A WASHING MACHINE!
THAT'S EVEN THE SAME MODEL MARIO AND I HAVE.

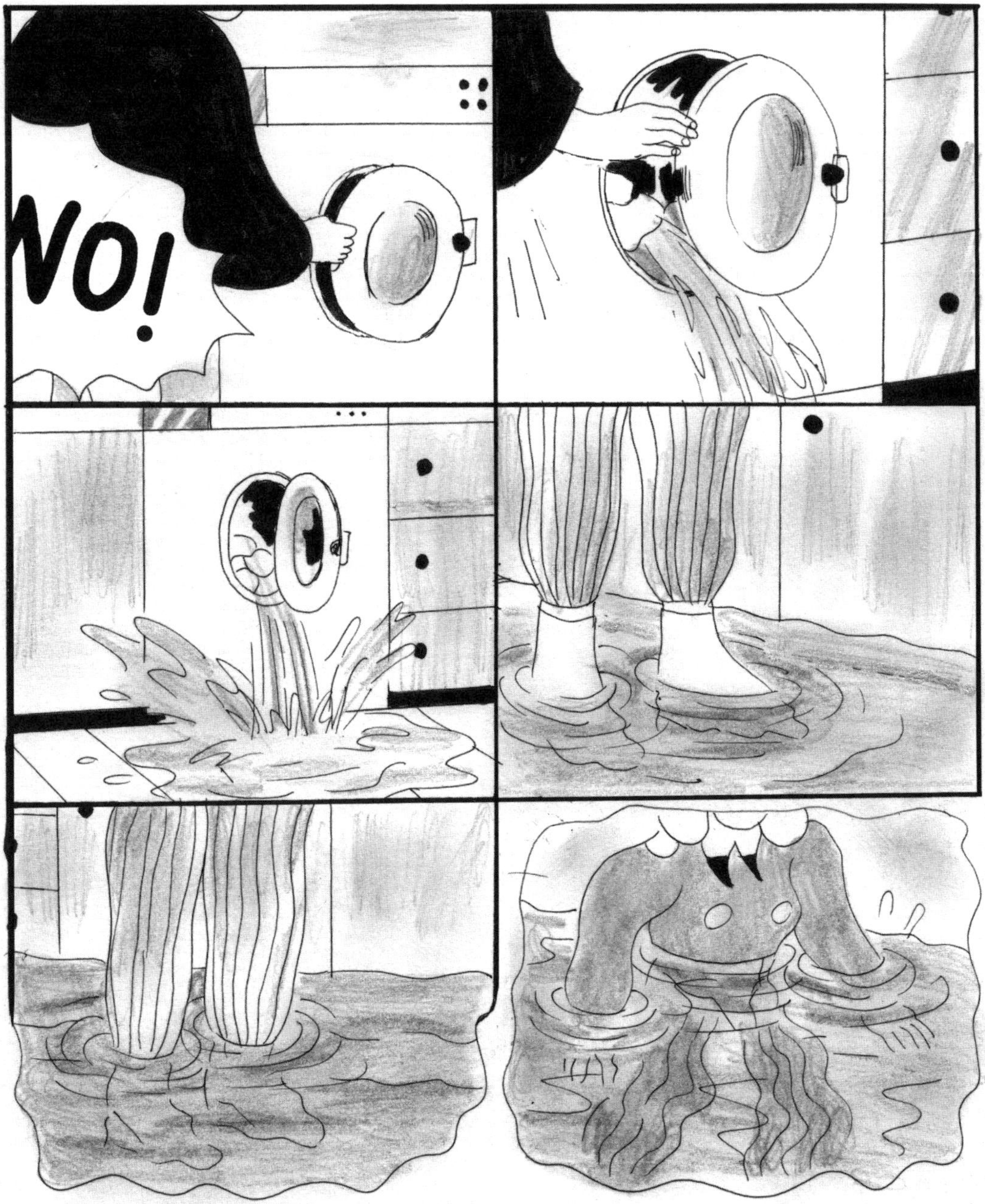
NO!

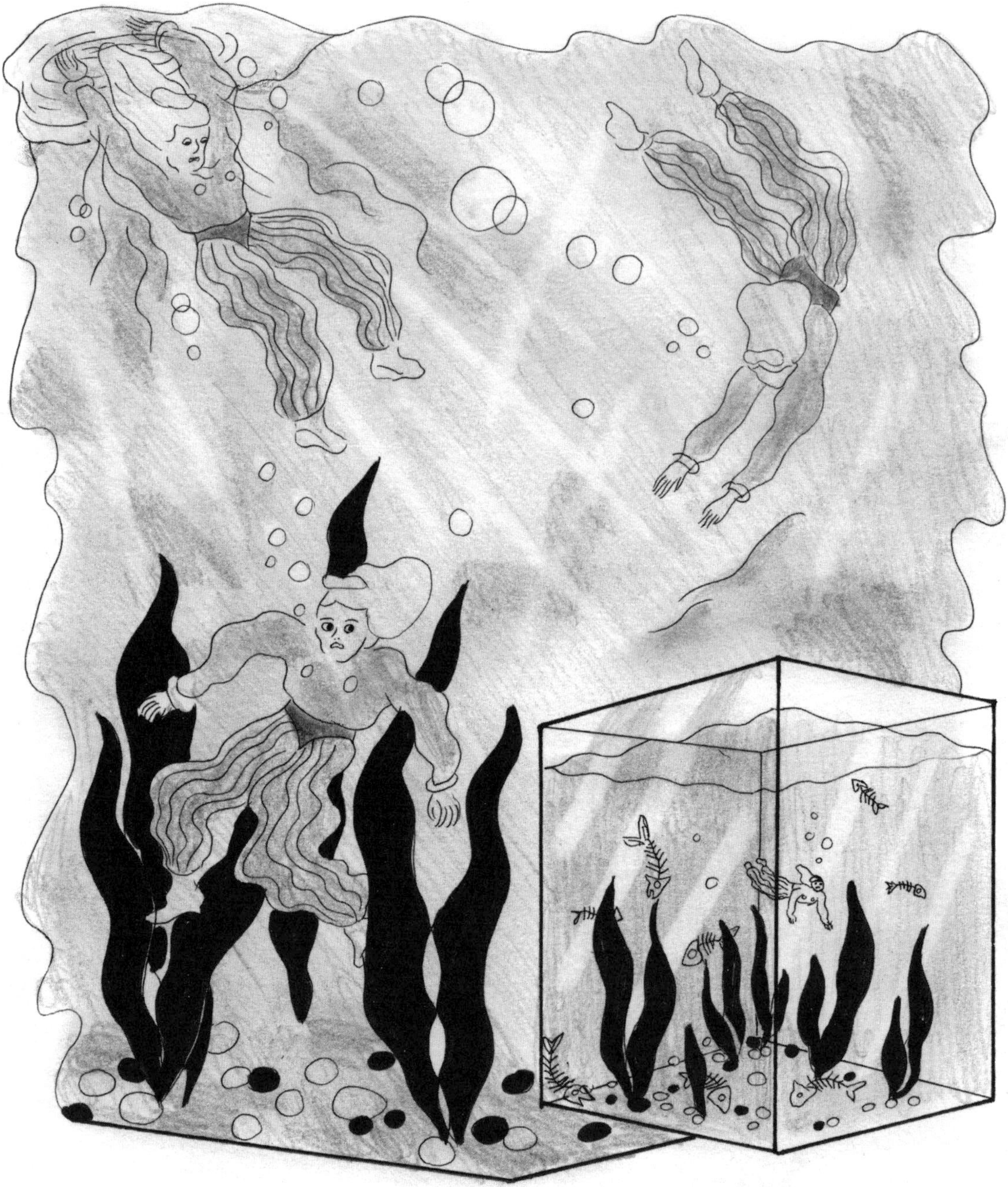

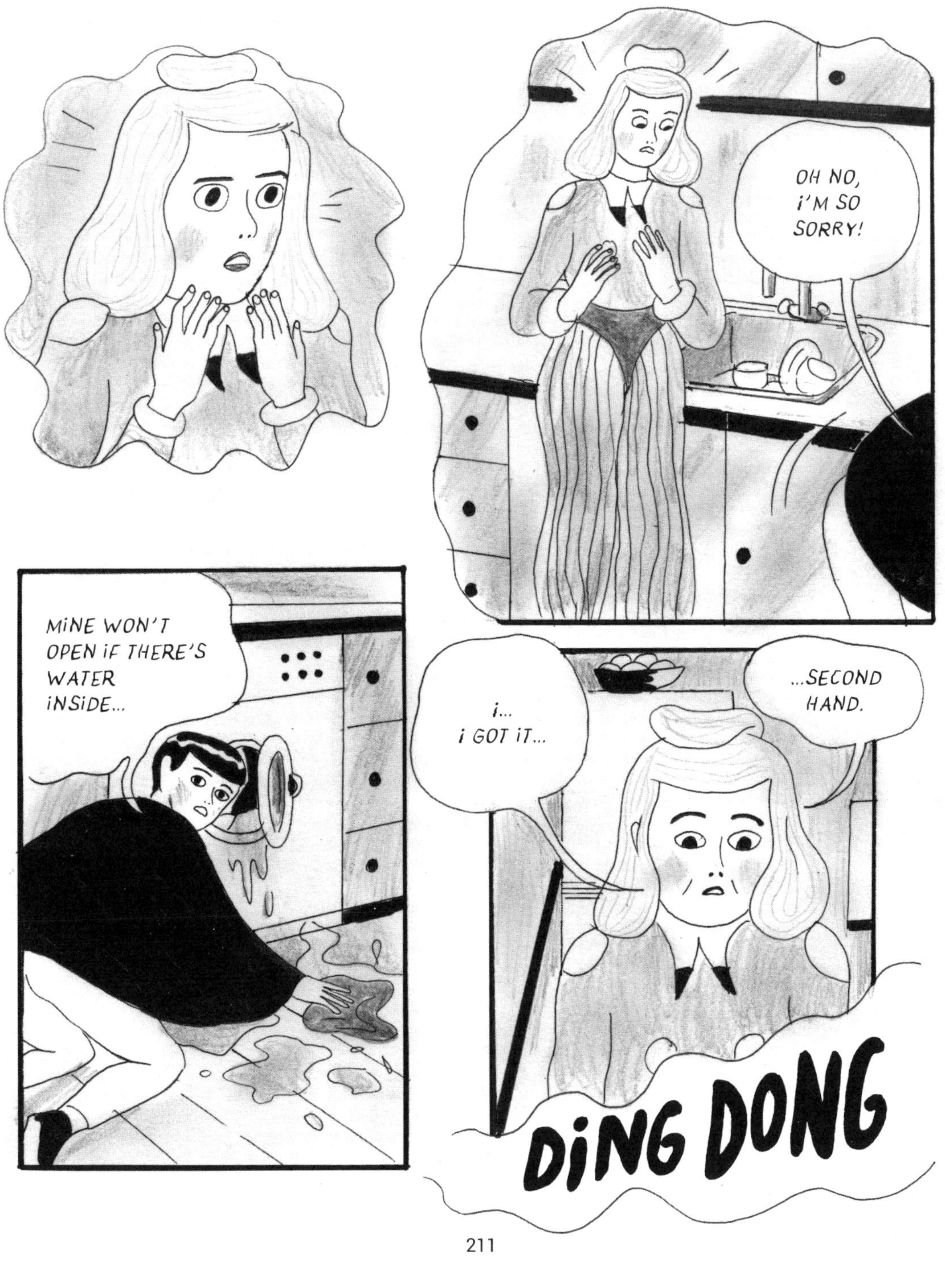
OH NO, I'M SO SORRY!
MINE WON'T OPEN IF THERE'S WATER INSIDE...
I... I GOT IT...
...SECOND HAND.
DING DONG

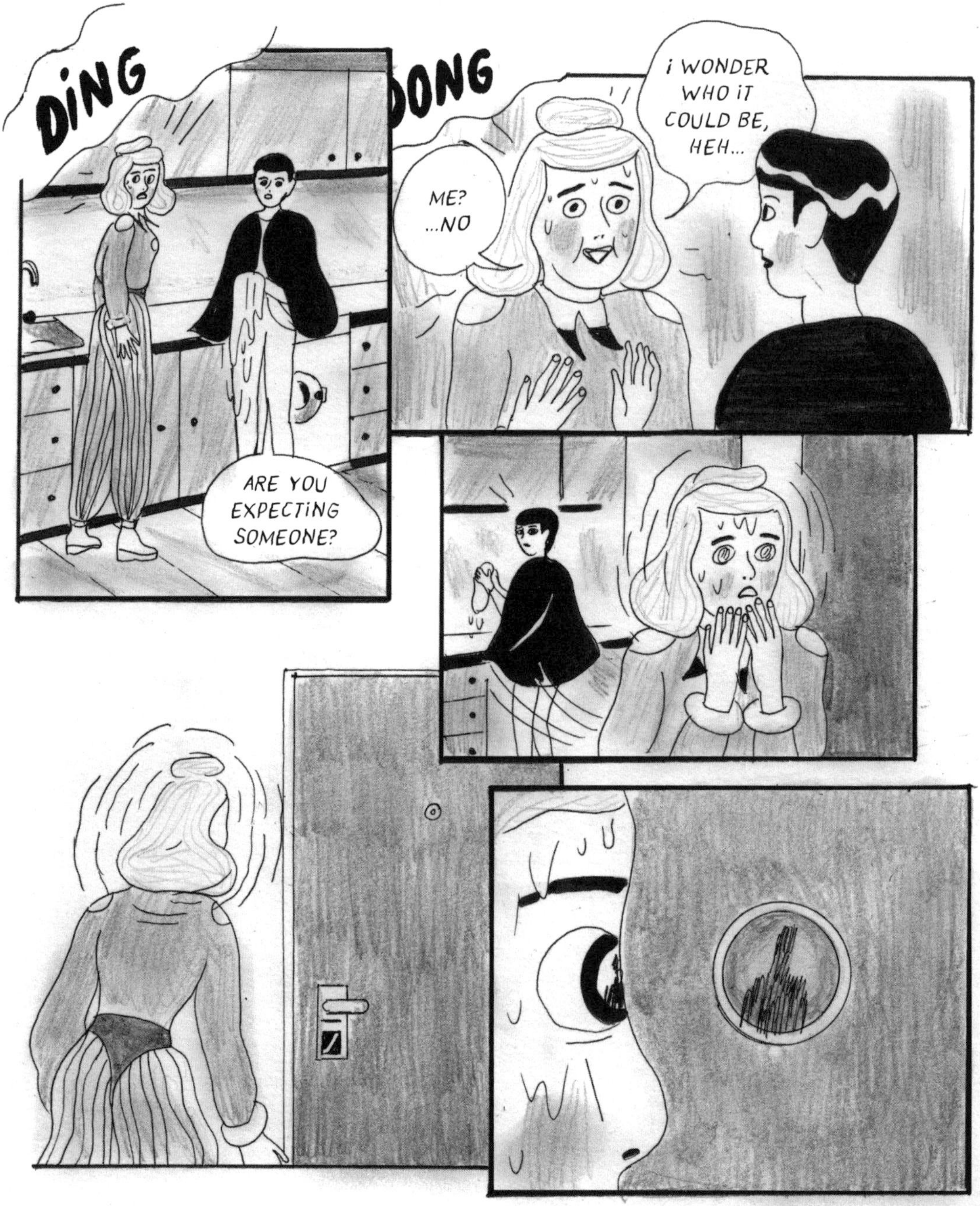
DING
DONG
ARE YOU EXPECTING SOMEONE?
ME? ...NO
I WONDER WHO IT COULD BE, HEH...

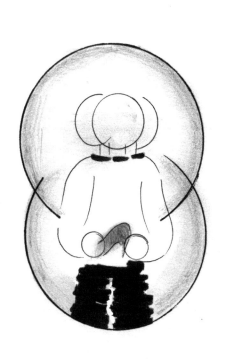

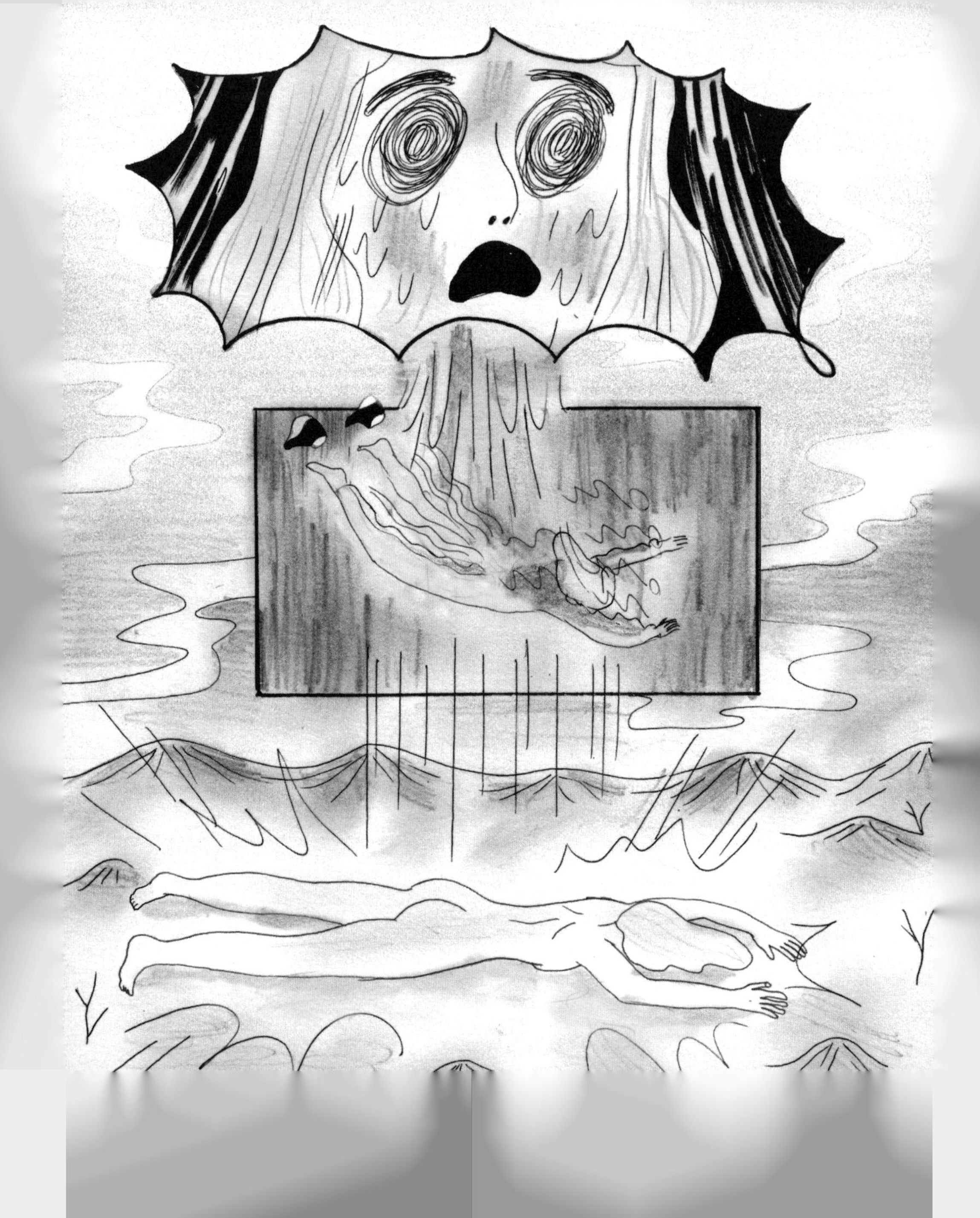

SELMA
SELMA!
OMiGOD! ARE YOU OKAY?
UHM...
i GUESS.
WELL, iN THAT CASE, GET UP AND GET BACK TO WORK!

COME ON!
HA
HA
HA
HA
HA
HA
HA
HA
HA
HA
HA
HA
HA
HA
HA
HA

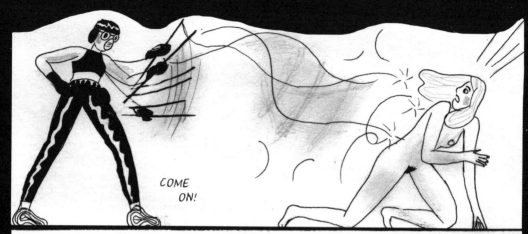

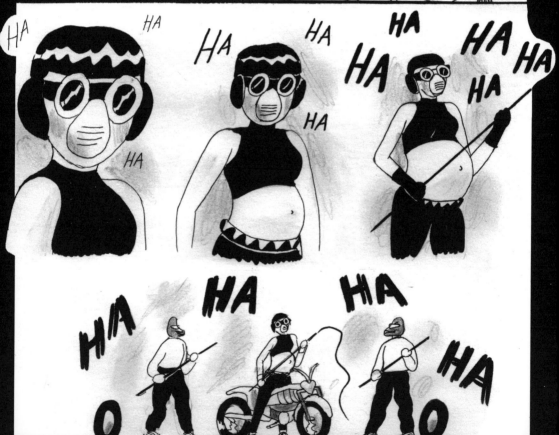

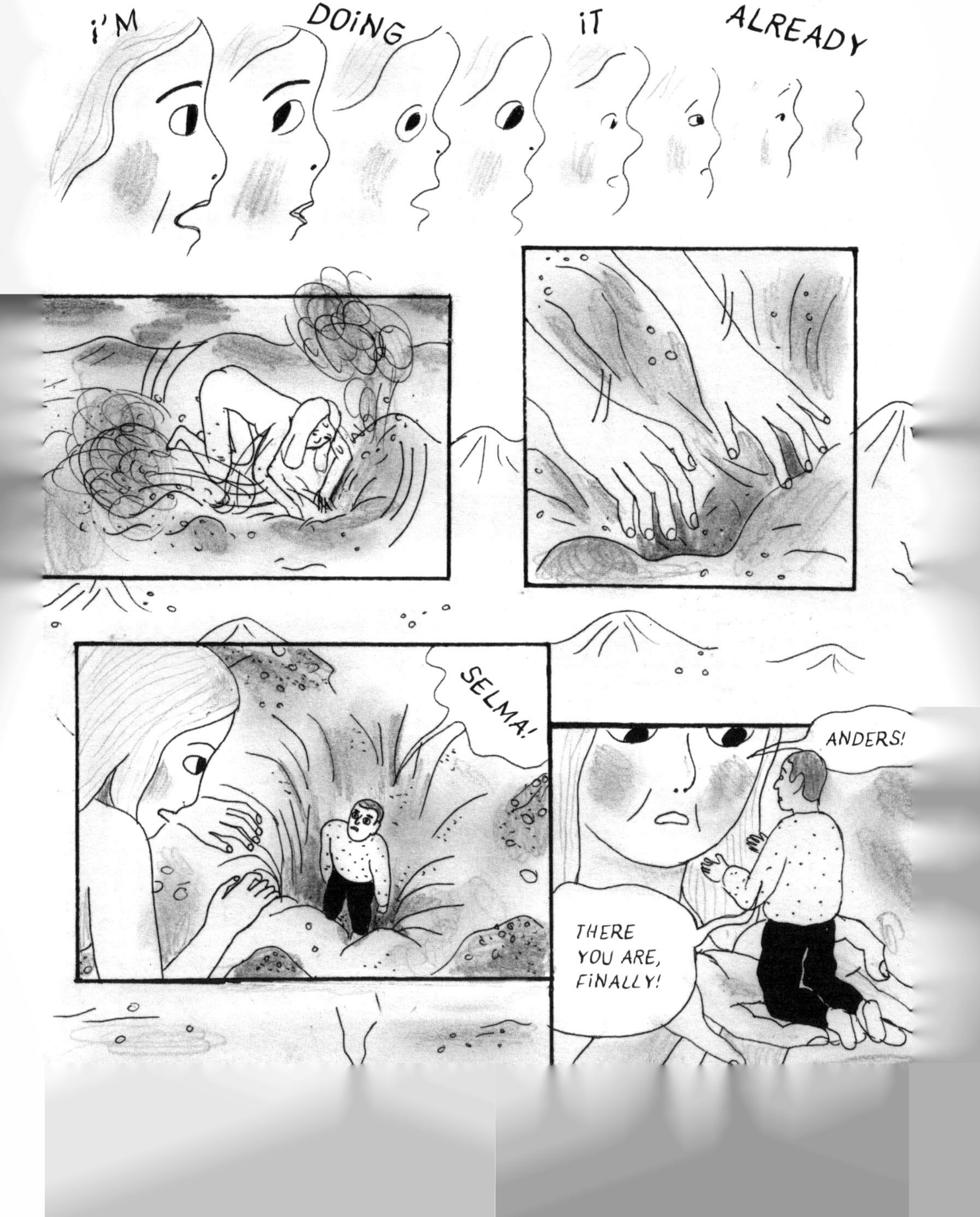
I'M DOING IT ALREADY
SELMA!
ANDERS!
THERE YOU ARE, FINALLY!

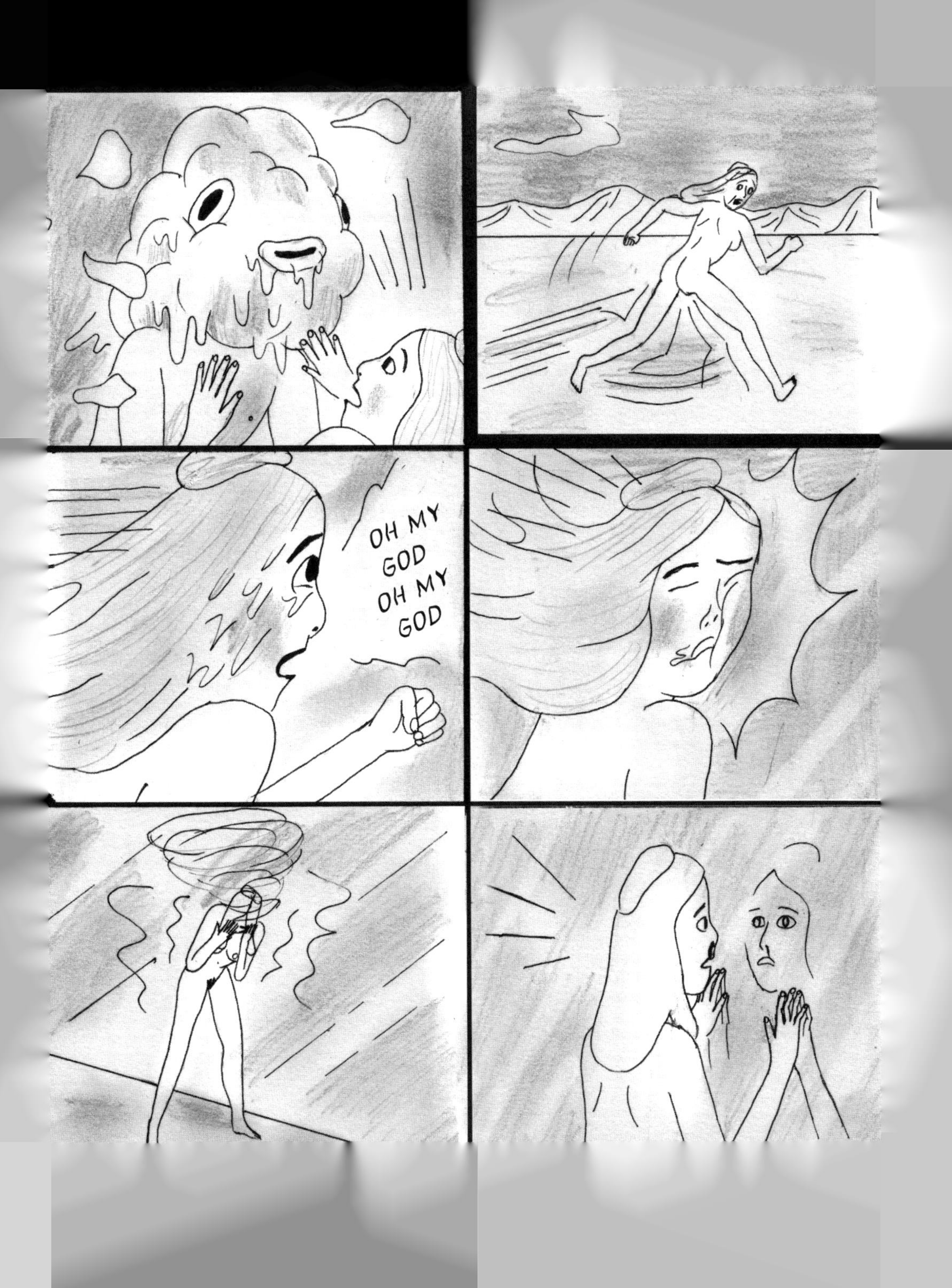
OH MY
GOD
OH MY
GOD

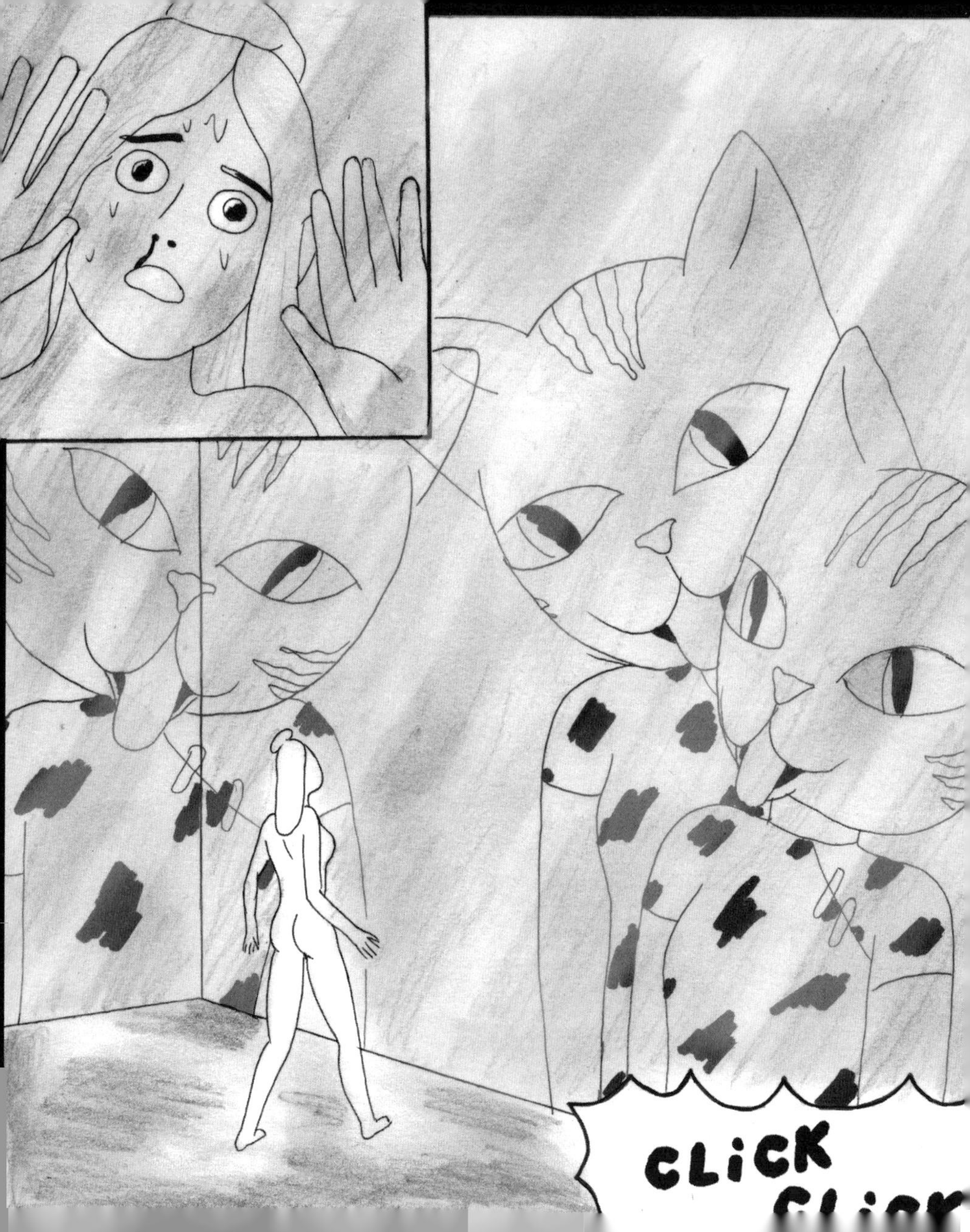
CLICK

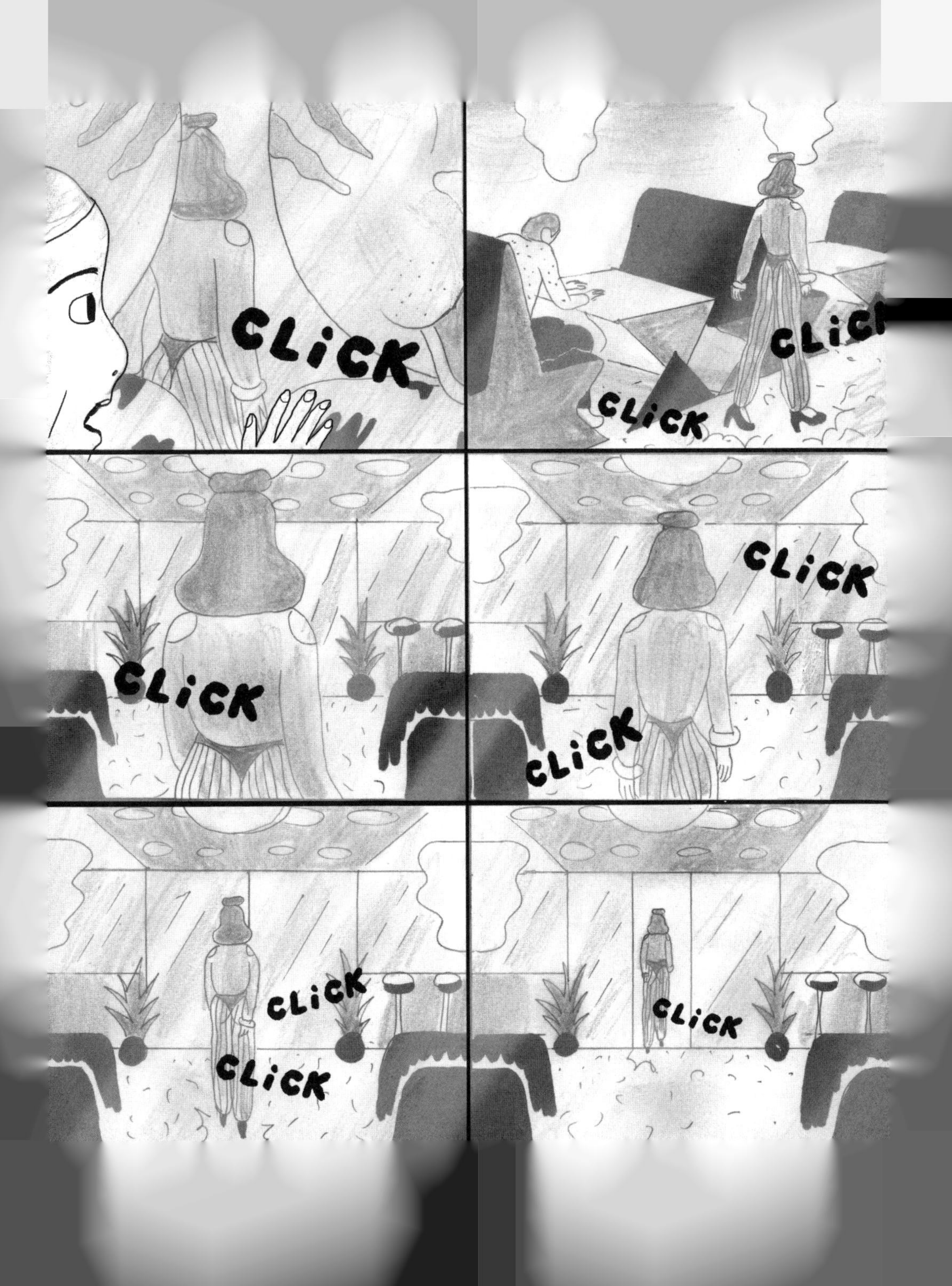
CLICK
CLICK
CLICK
CLICK
CLICK
CLICK
CLICK
CLICK
CLICK

PENELOPE...
NO...
NO.

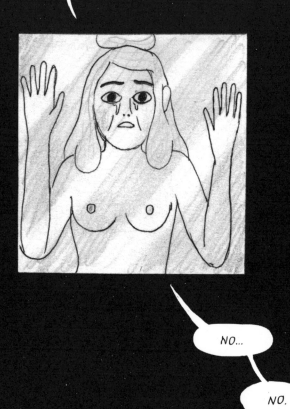

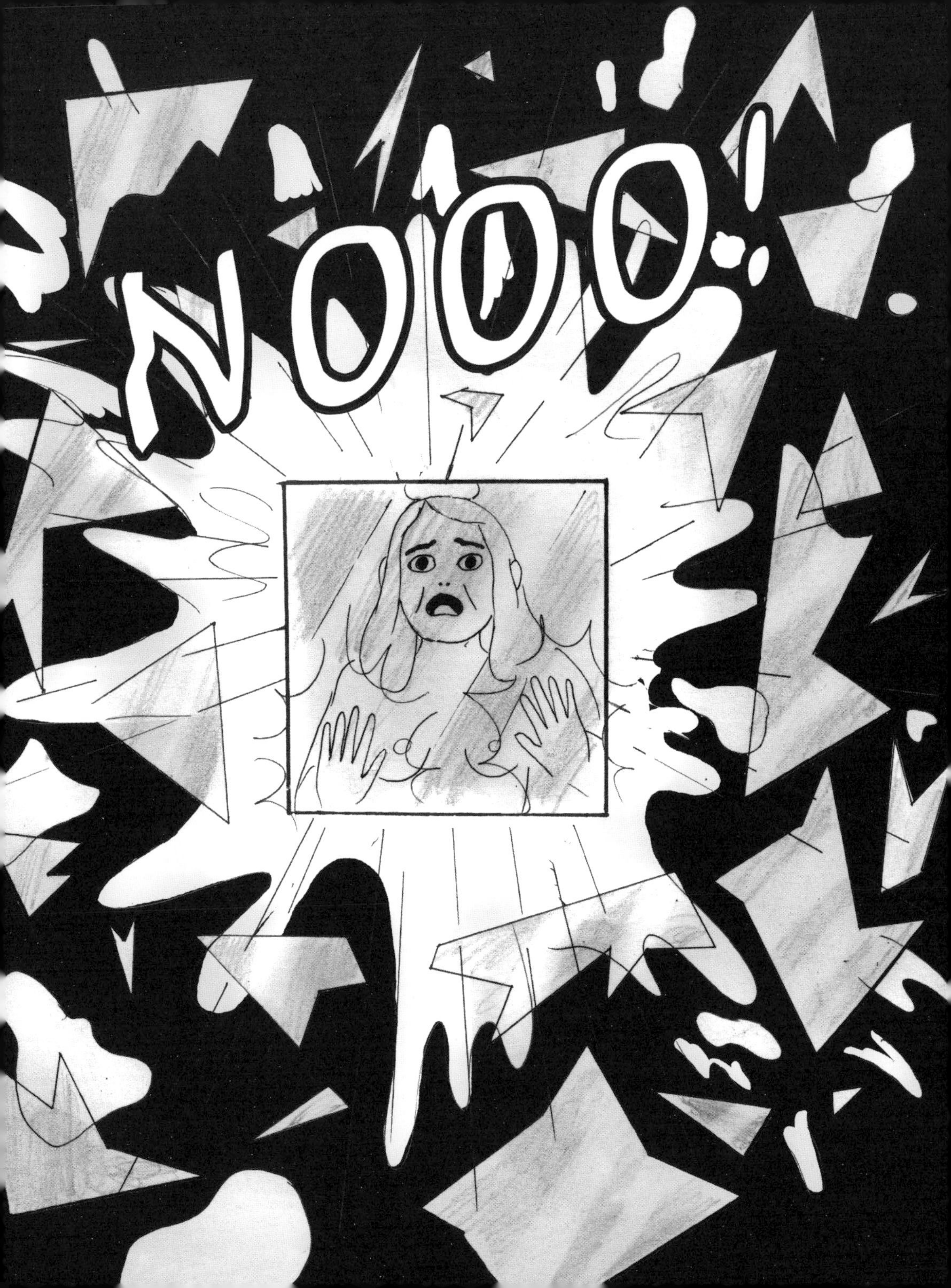
NOOO!

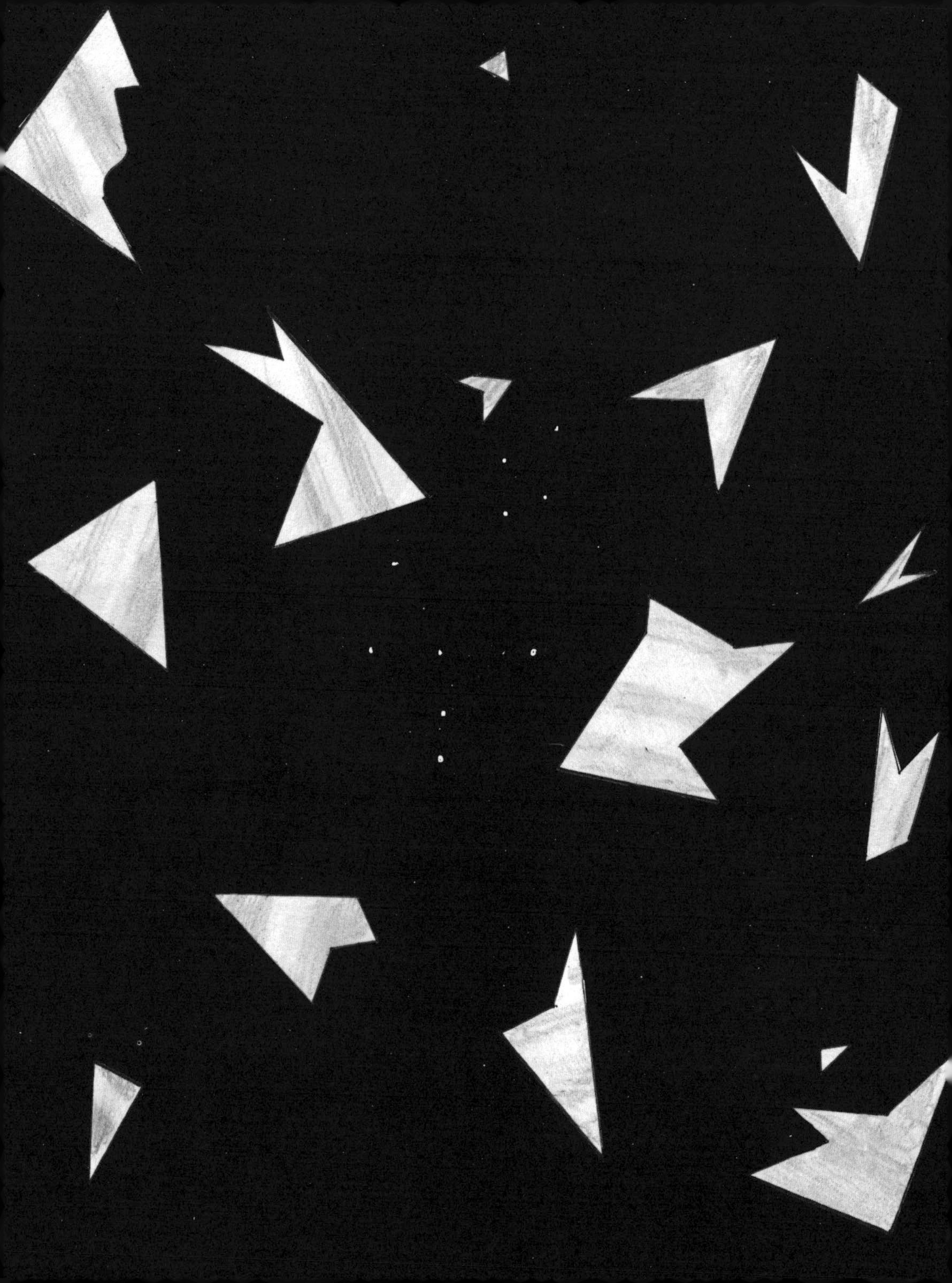

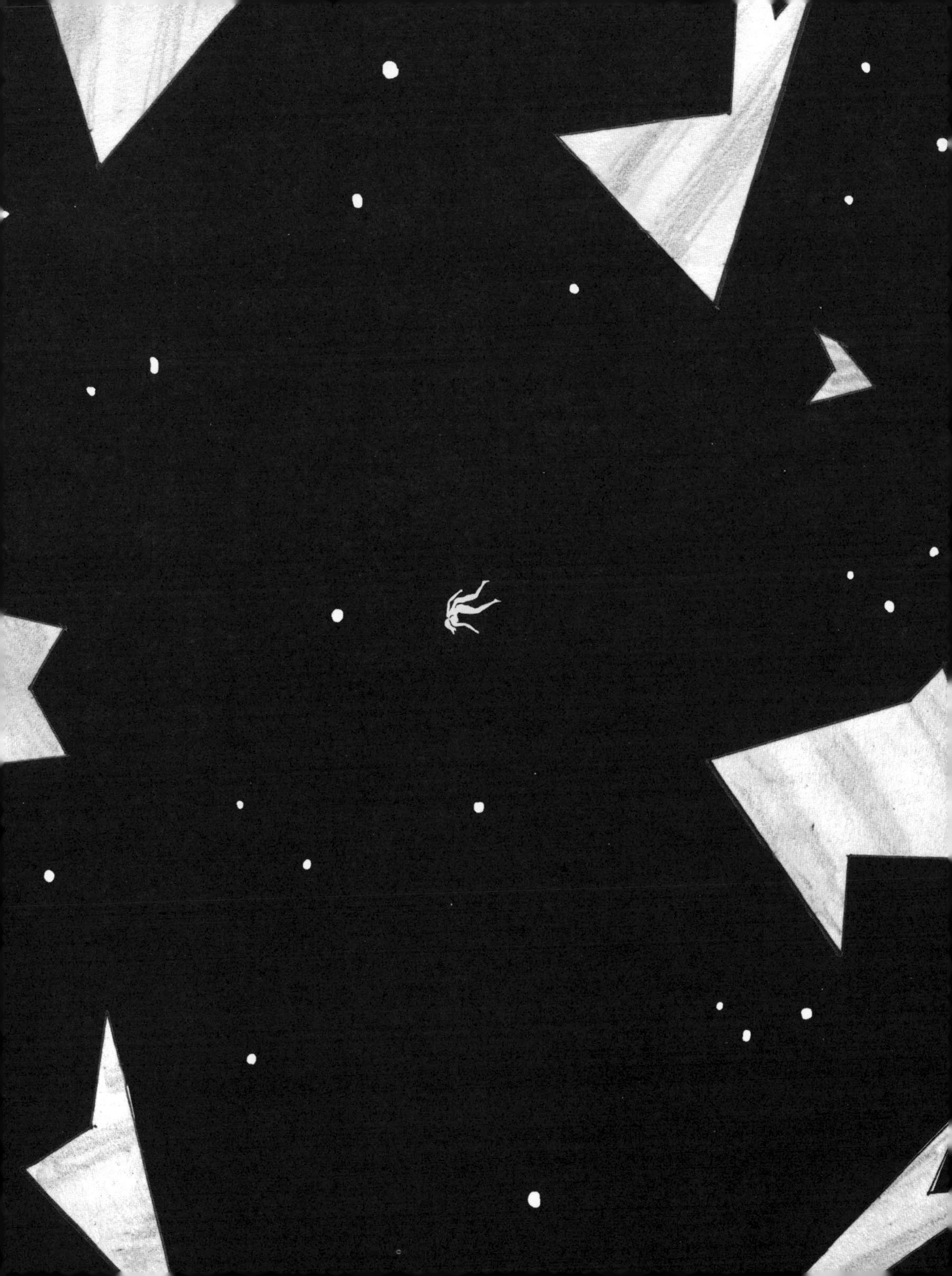

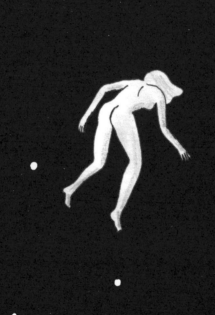

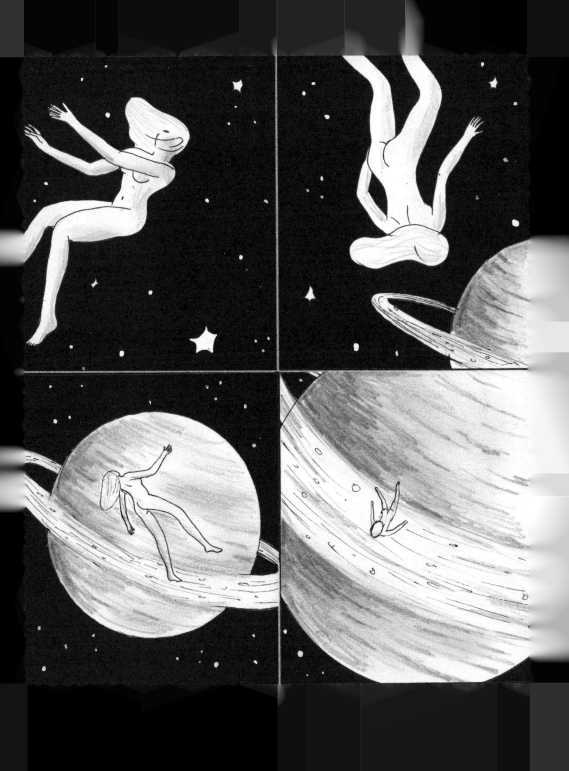

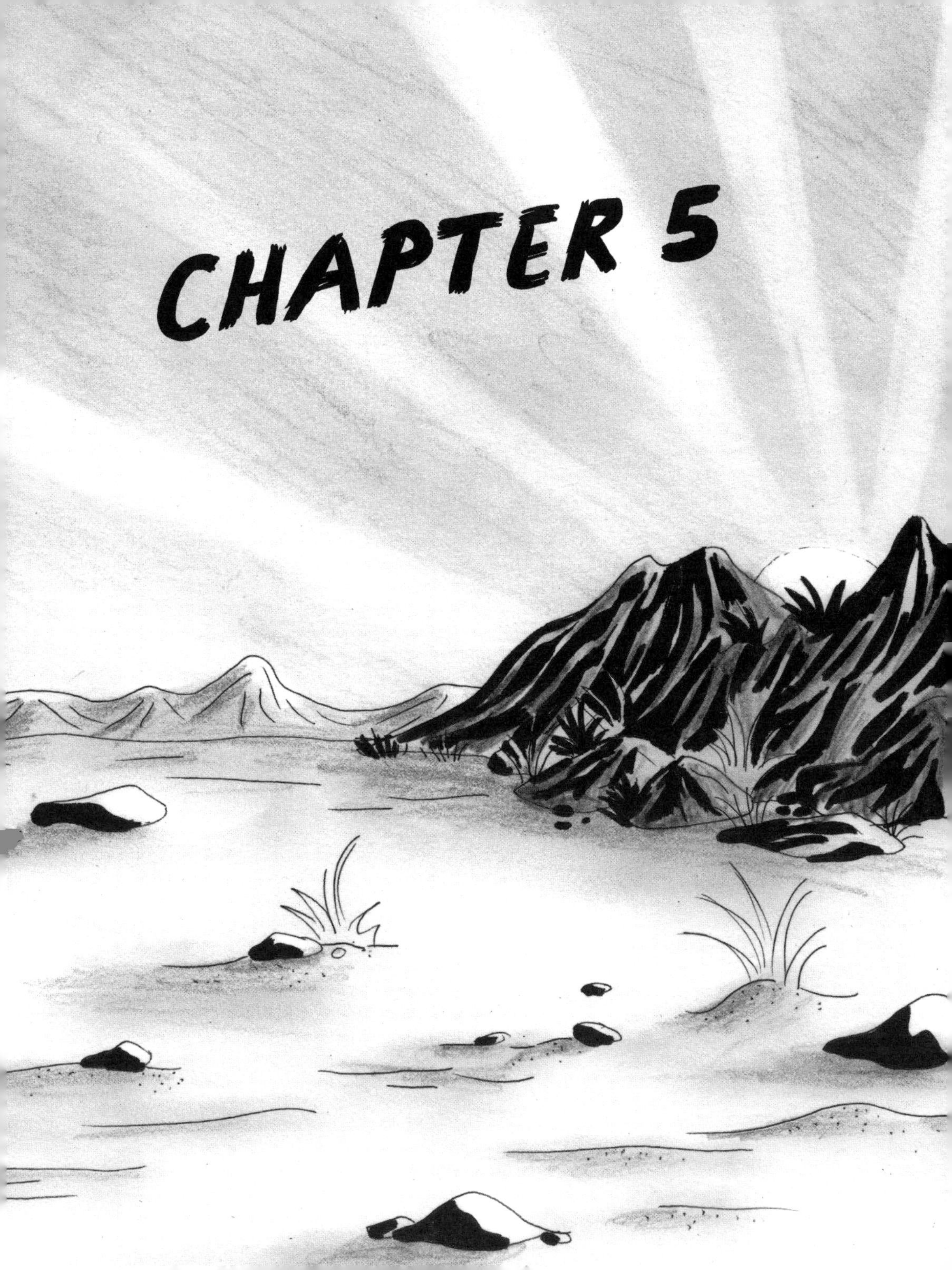
CHAPTER 5

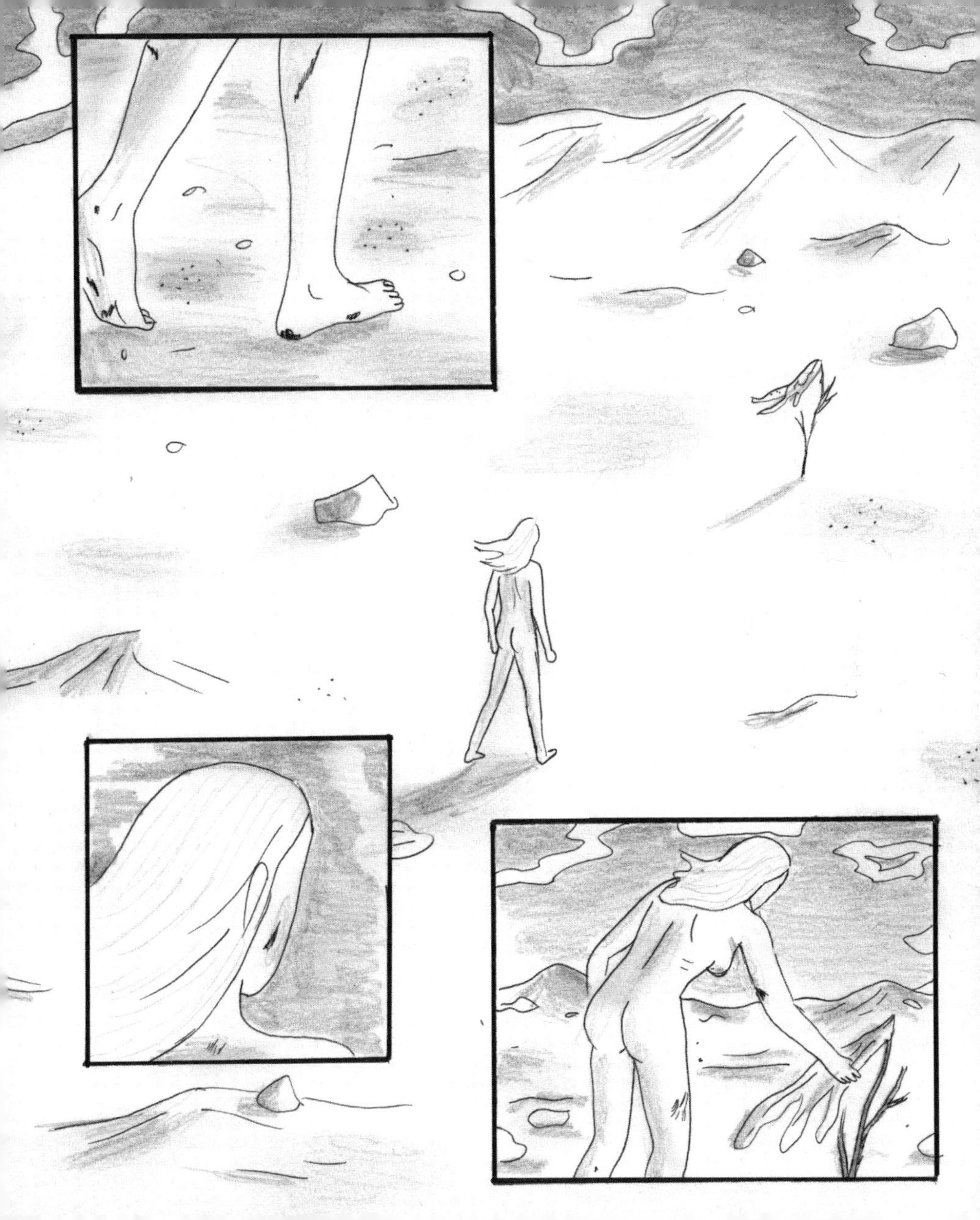

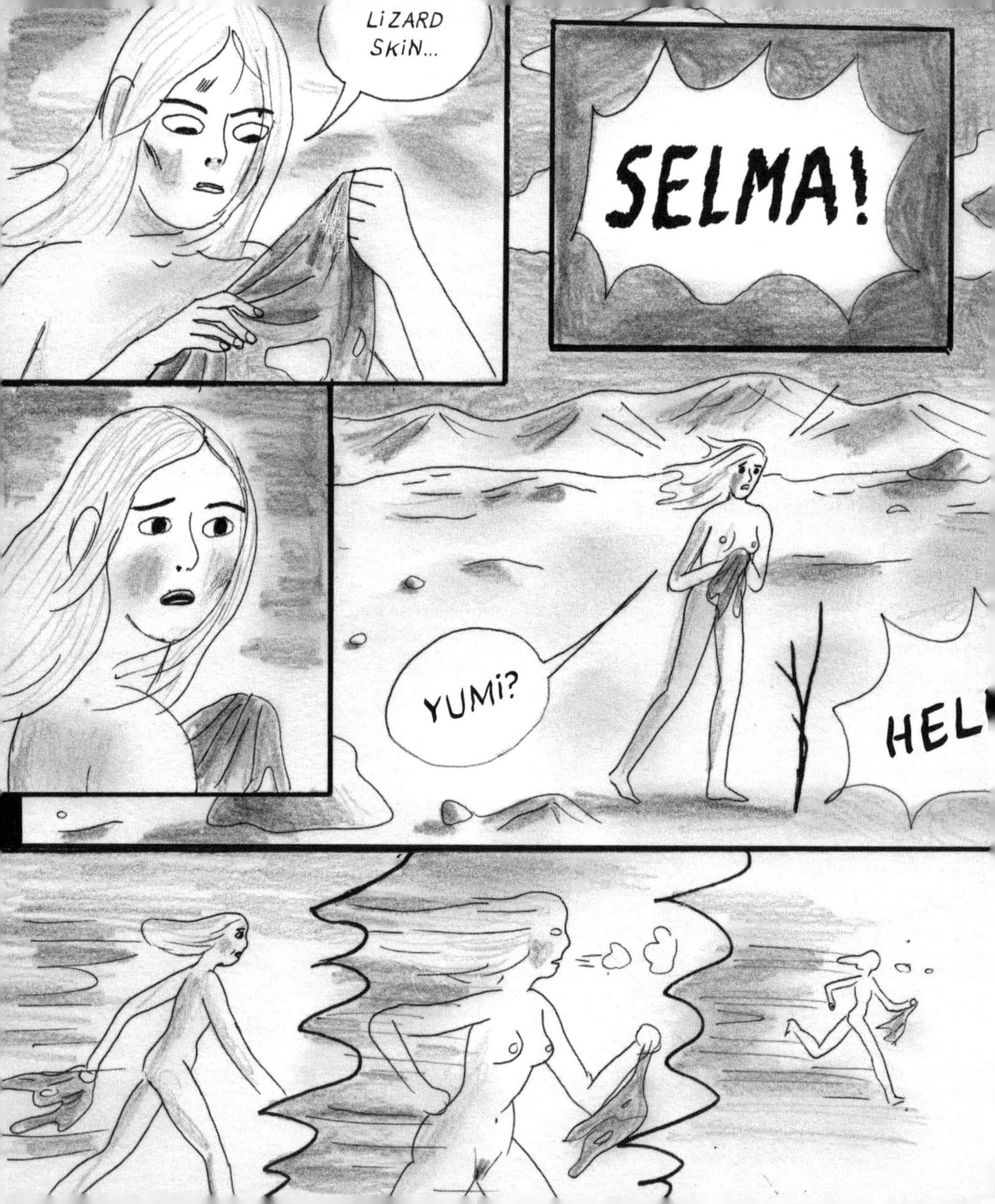
LIZARD SKIN...
SELMA!
YUMI?
HEL

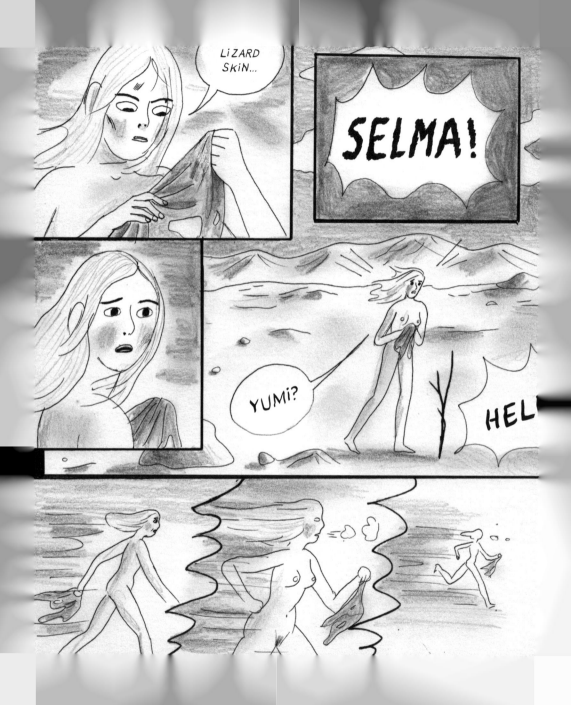

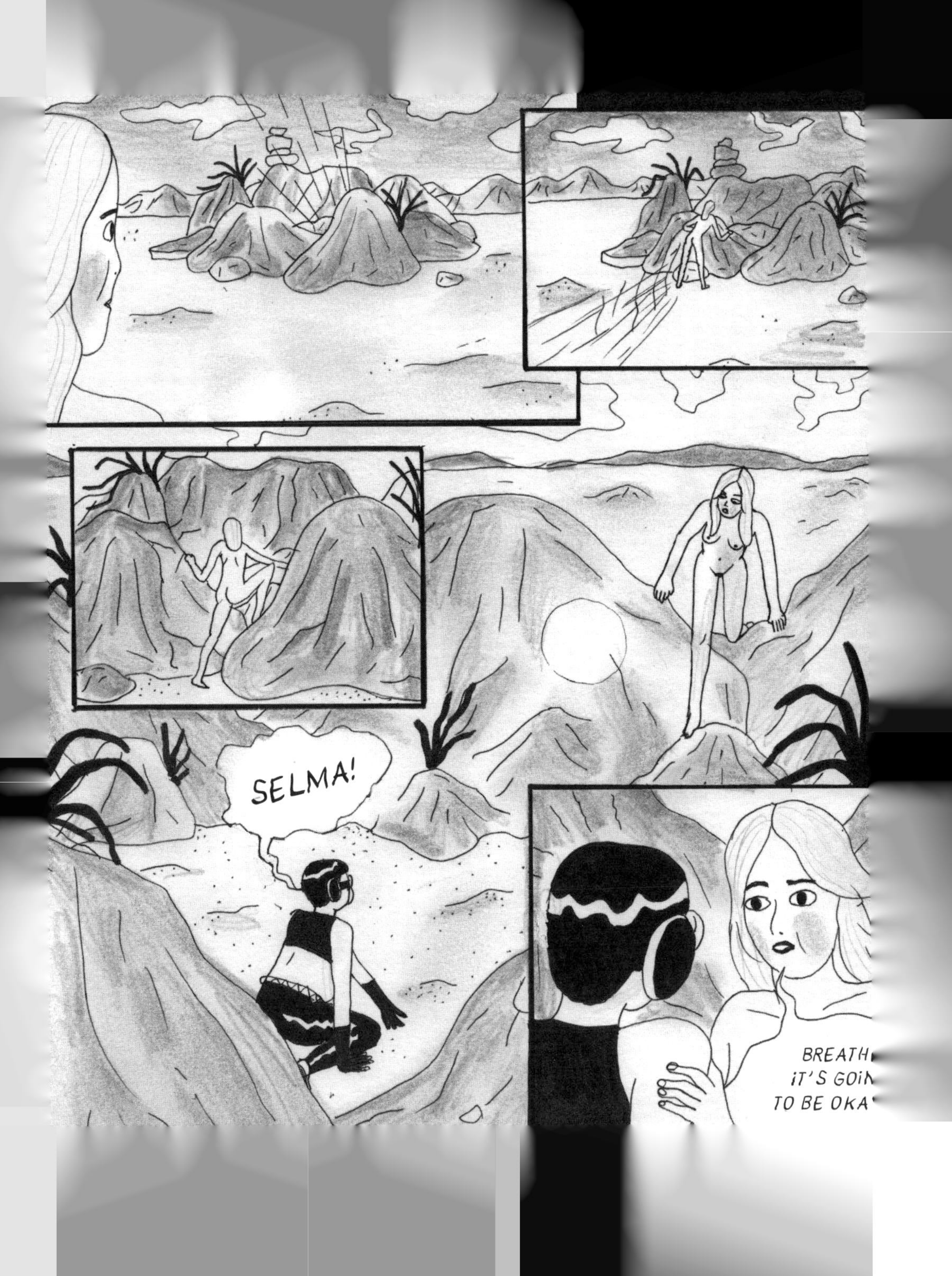
SELMA!
BREATH
IT'S GOIN
TO BE OKA

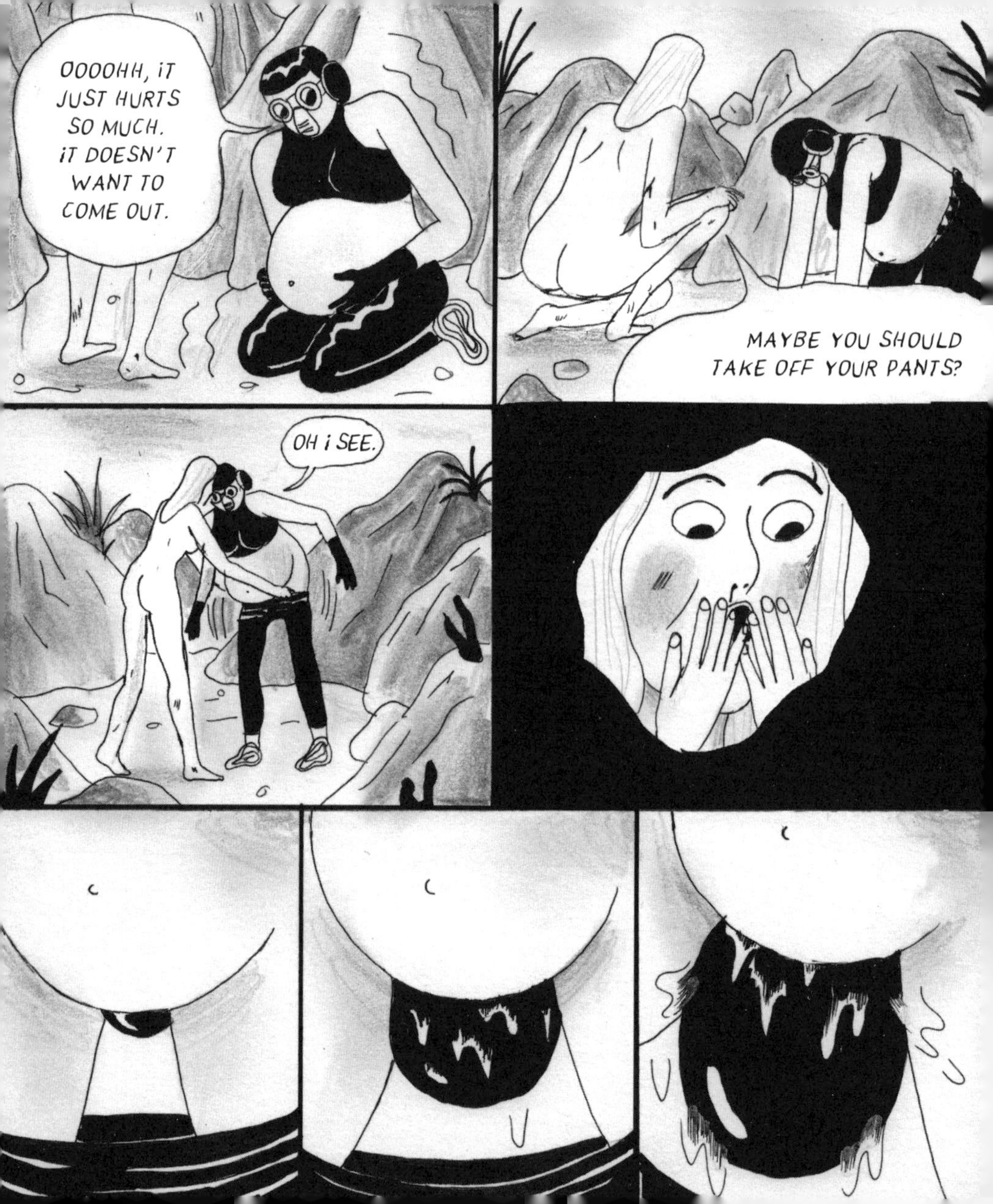
OOOOHH, iT JUST HURTS SO MUCH. iT DOESN'T WANT TO COME OUT.
MAYBE YOU SHOULD TAKE OFF YOUR PANTS?
OH i SEE.

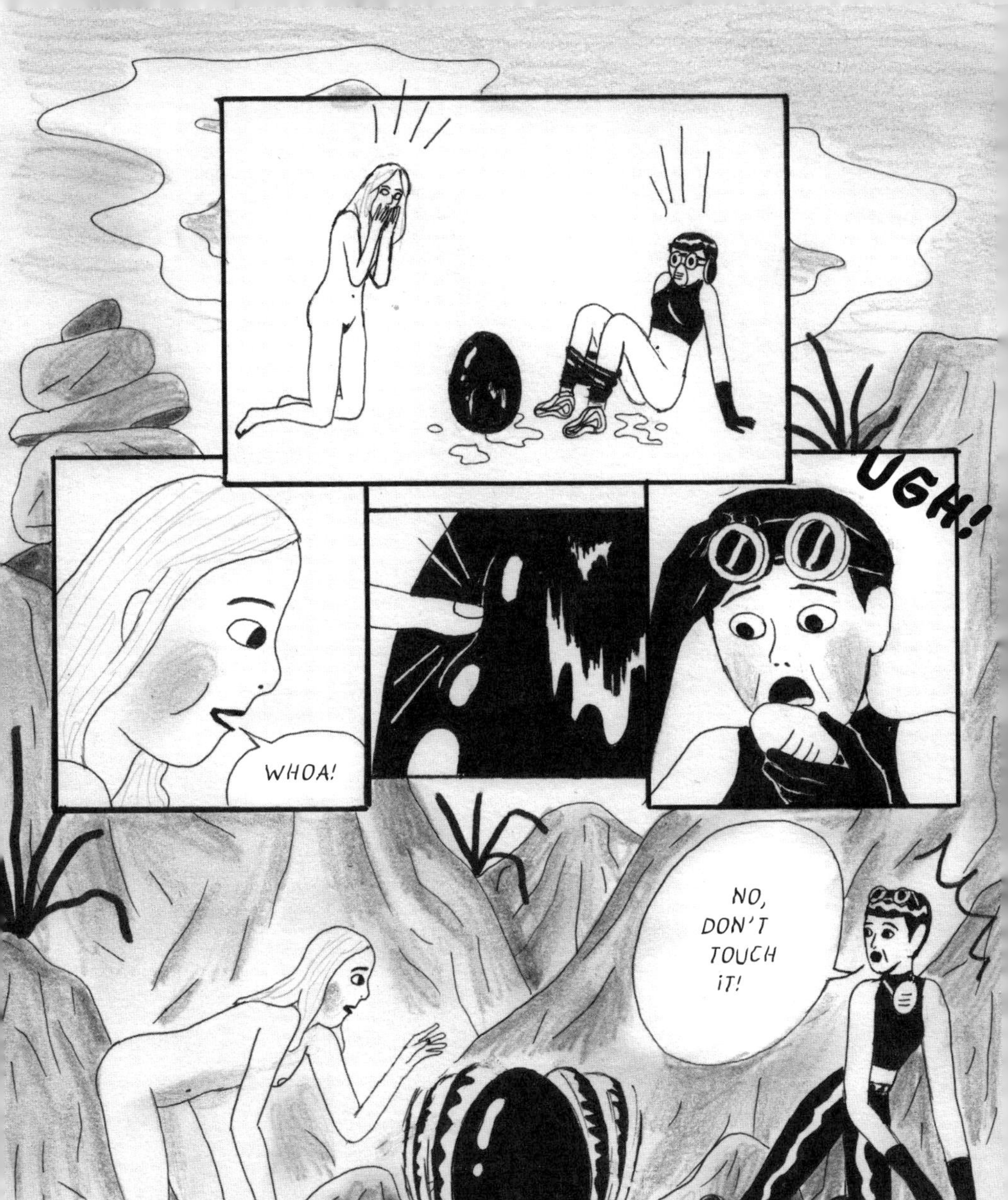
WHOA!
UGH!
NO, DON'T TOUCH IT!

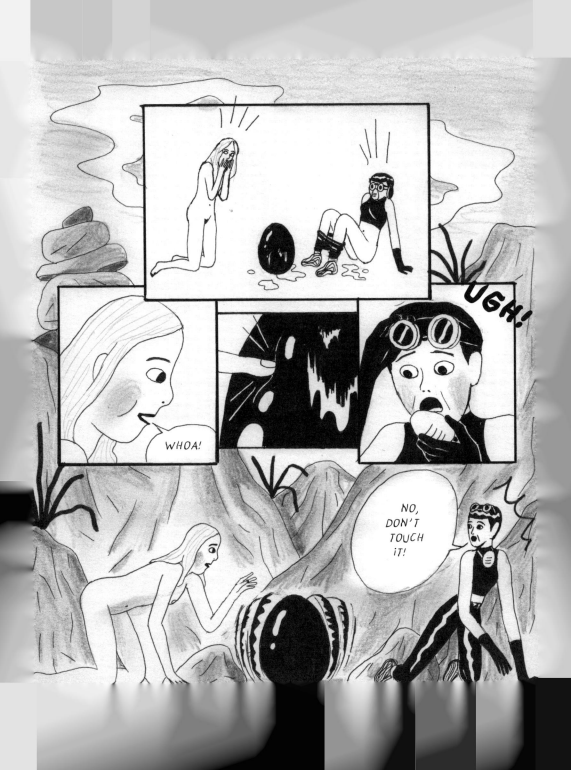

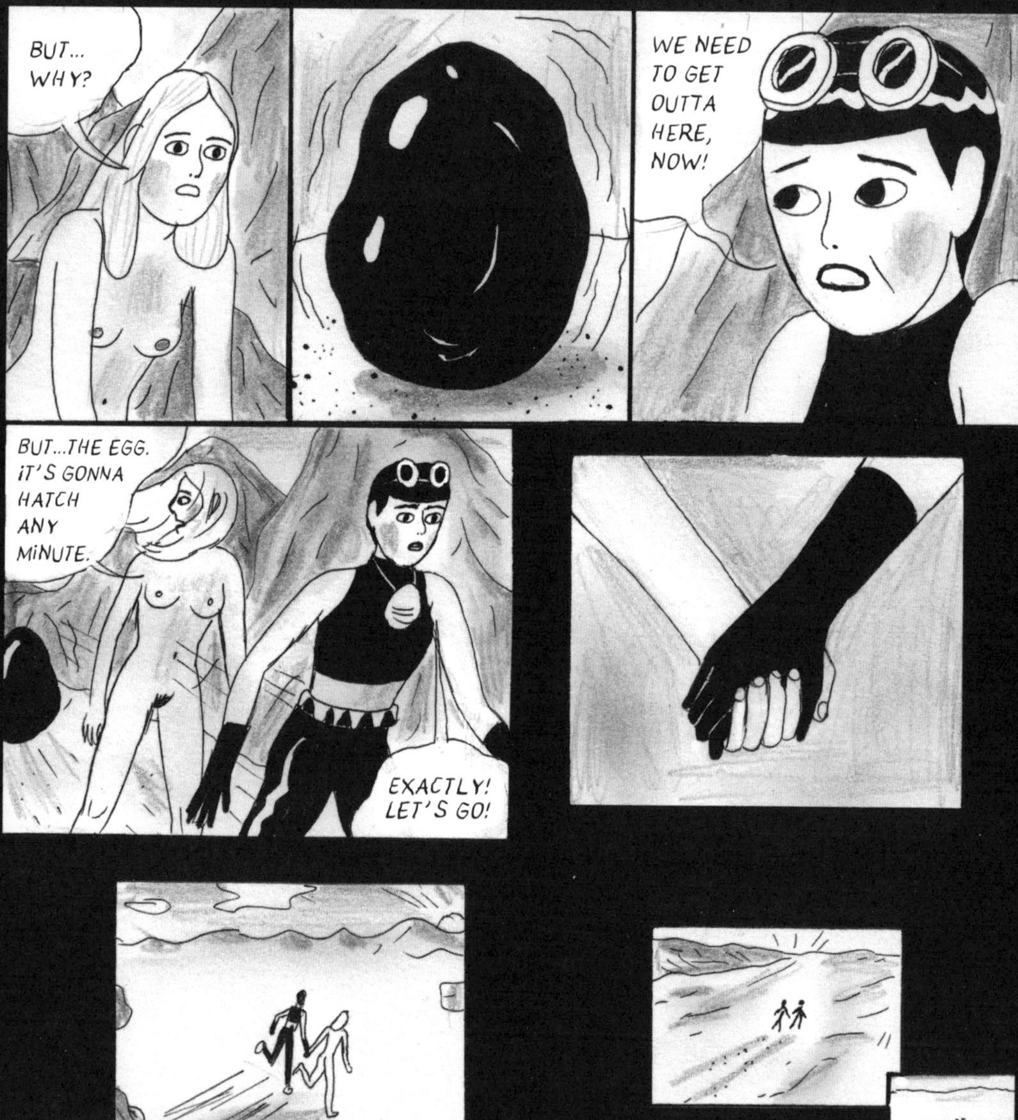
BUT... WHY?
WE NEED TO GET OUTTA HERE, NOW!
BUT...THE EGG. IT'S GONNA HATCH ANY MINUTE.
EXACTLY! LET'S GO!

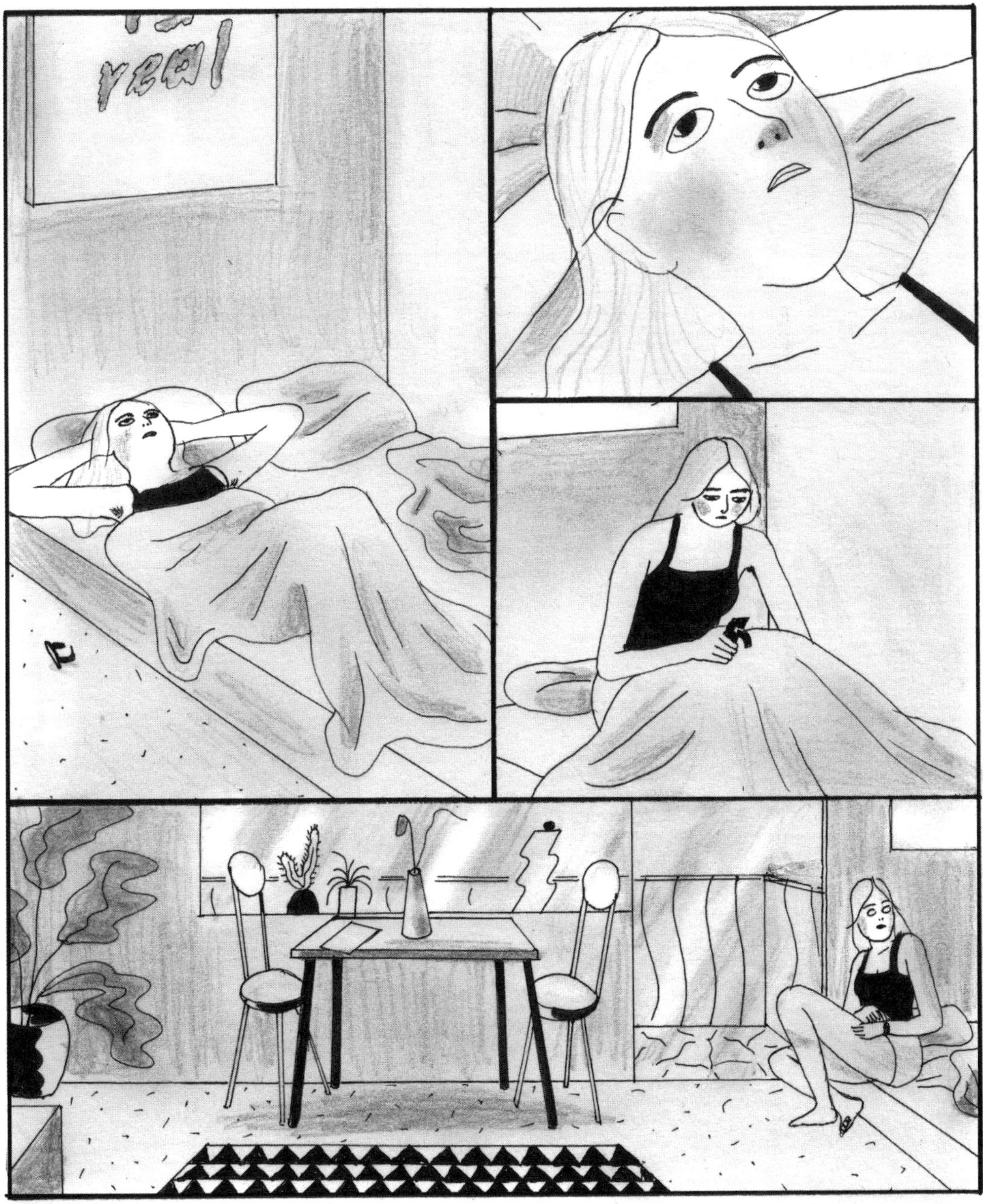

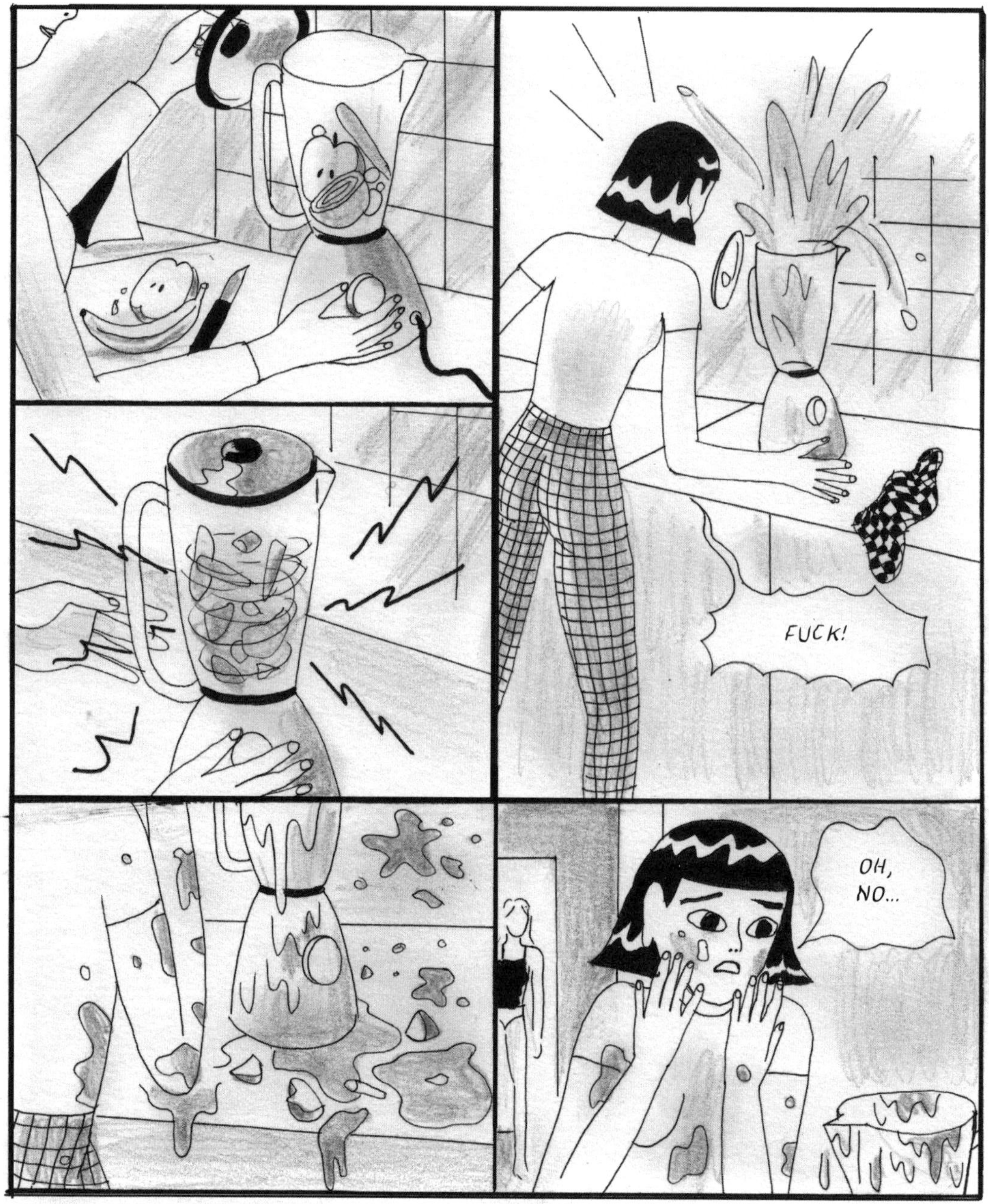
FUCK!
OH, NO...

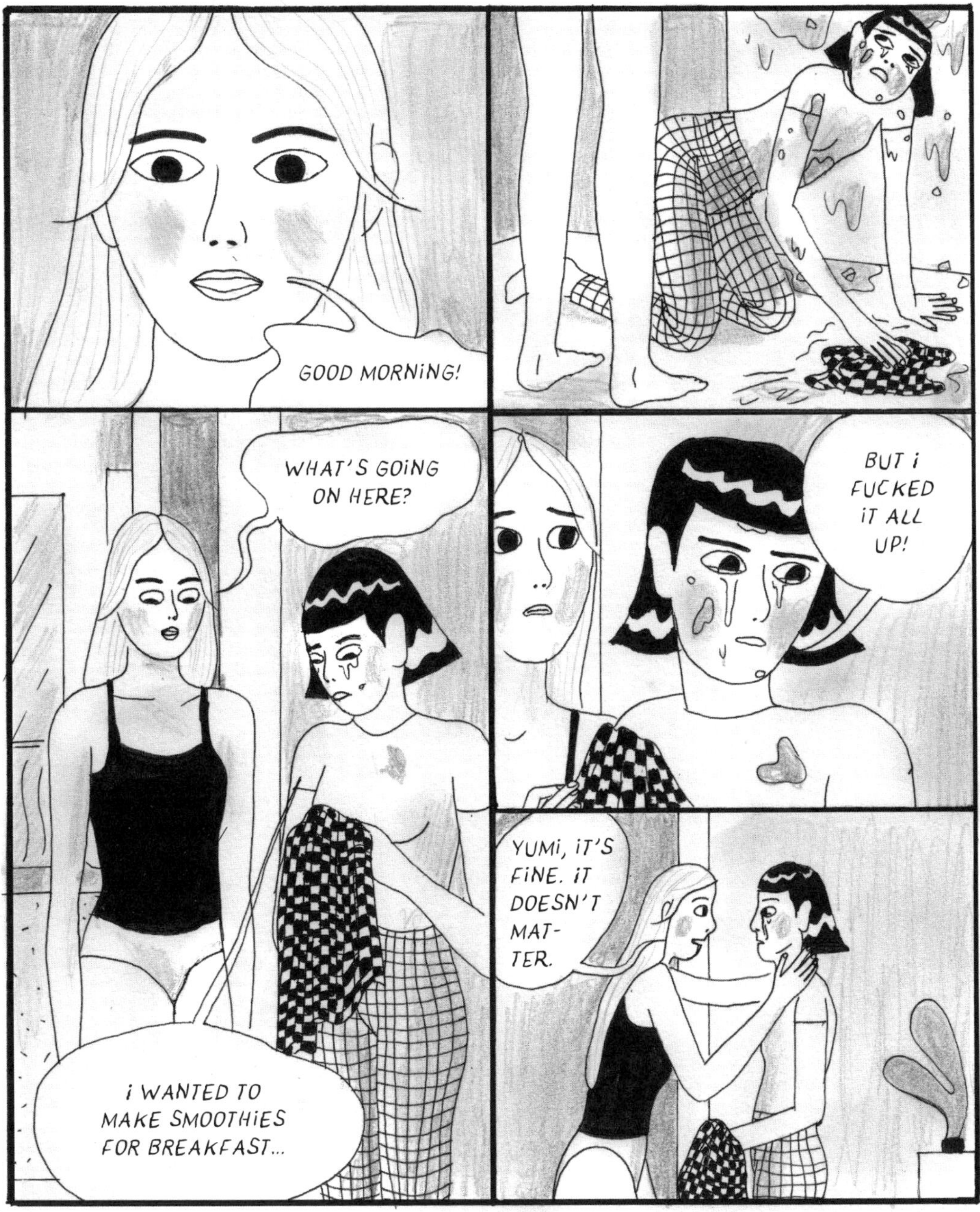
GOOD MORNiNG!
WHAT'S GOiNG ON HERE?
i WANTED TO MAKE SMOOTHiES FOR BREAKFAST...
BUT i FUCKED iT ALL UP!
YUMi, iT'S FiNE. iT DOESN'T MAT-TER.

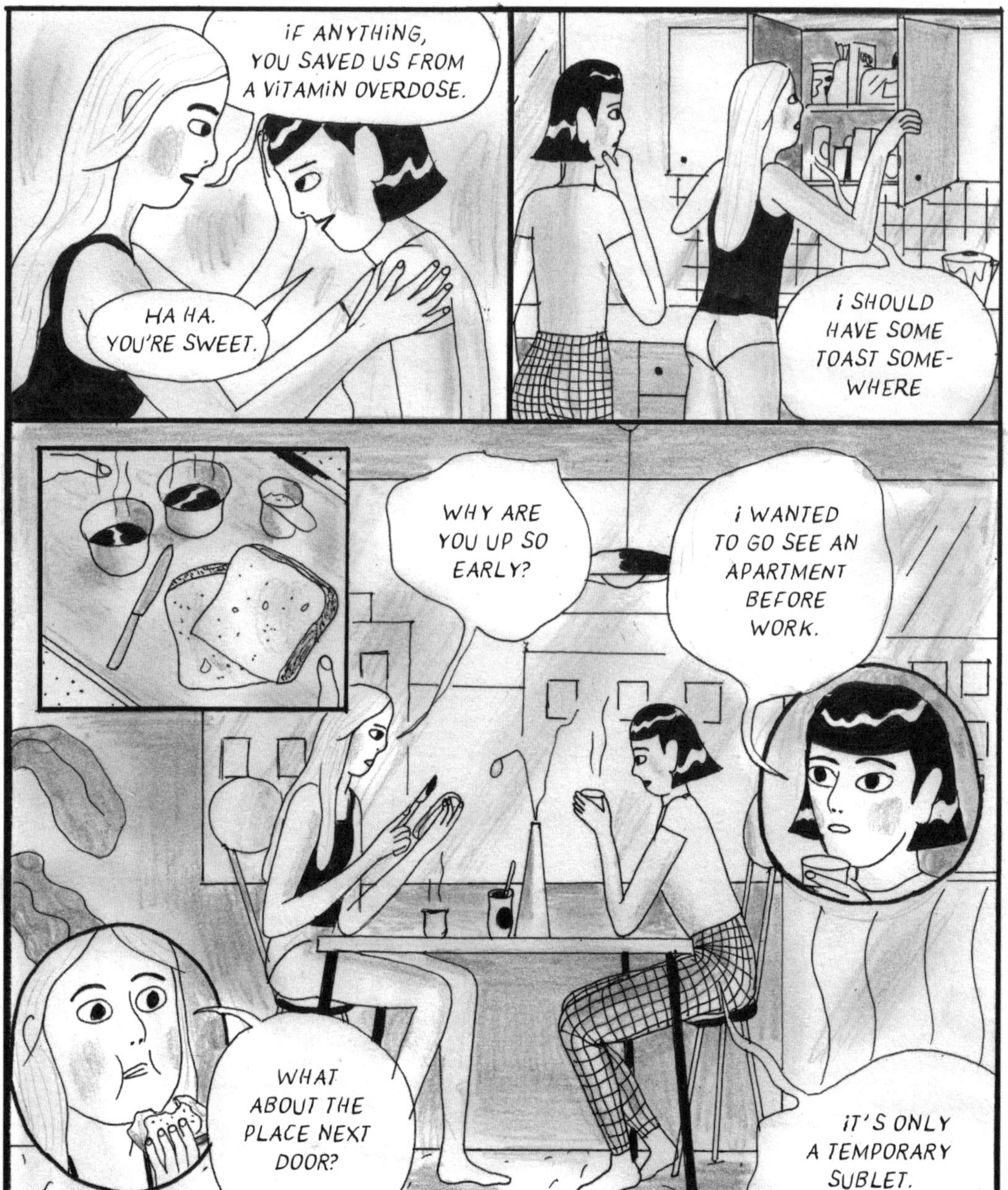
IF ANYTHING, YOU SAVED US FROM A VITAMIN OVERDOSE.
HA HA. YOU'RE SWEET.
I SHOULD HAVE SOME TOAST SOME-WHERE
WHY ARE YOU UP SO EARLY?
I WANTED TO GO SEE AN APARTMENT BEFORE WORK.
WHAT ABOUT THE PLACE NEXT DOOR?
IT'S ONLY A TEMPORARY SUBLET.

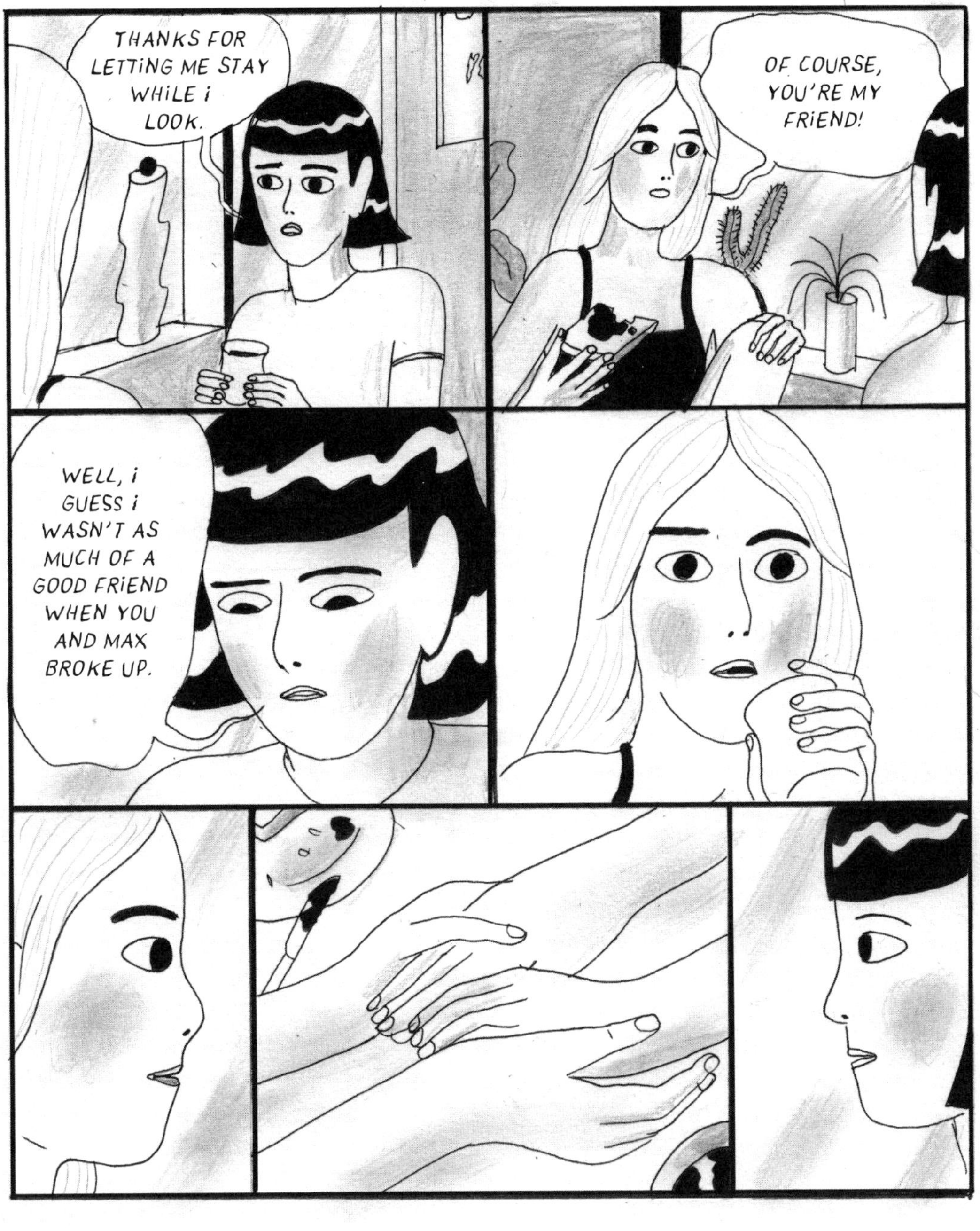
THANKS FOR LETTING ME STAY WHILE i LOOK.
OF COURSE, YOU'RE MY FRiEND!
WELL, i GUESS i WASN'T AS MUCH OF A GOOD FRiEND WHEN YOU AND MAX BROKE UP.

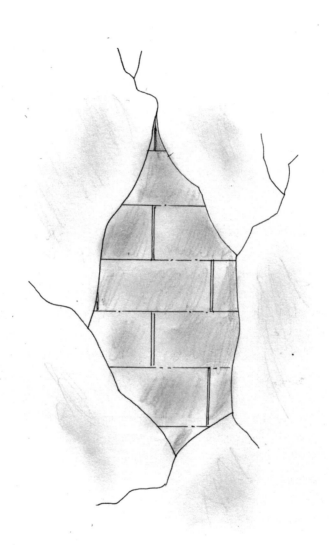

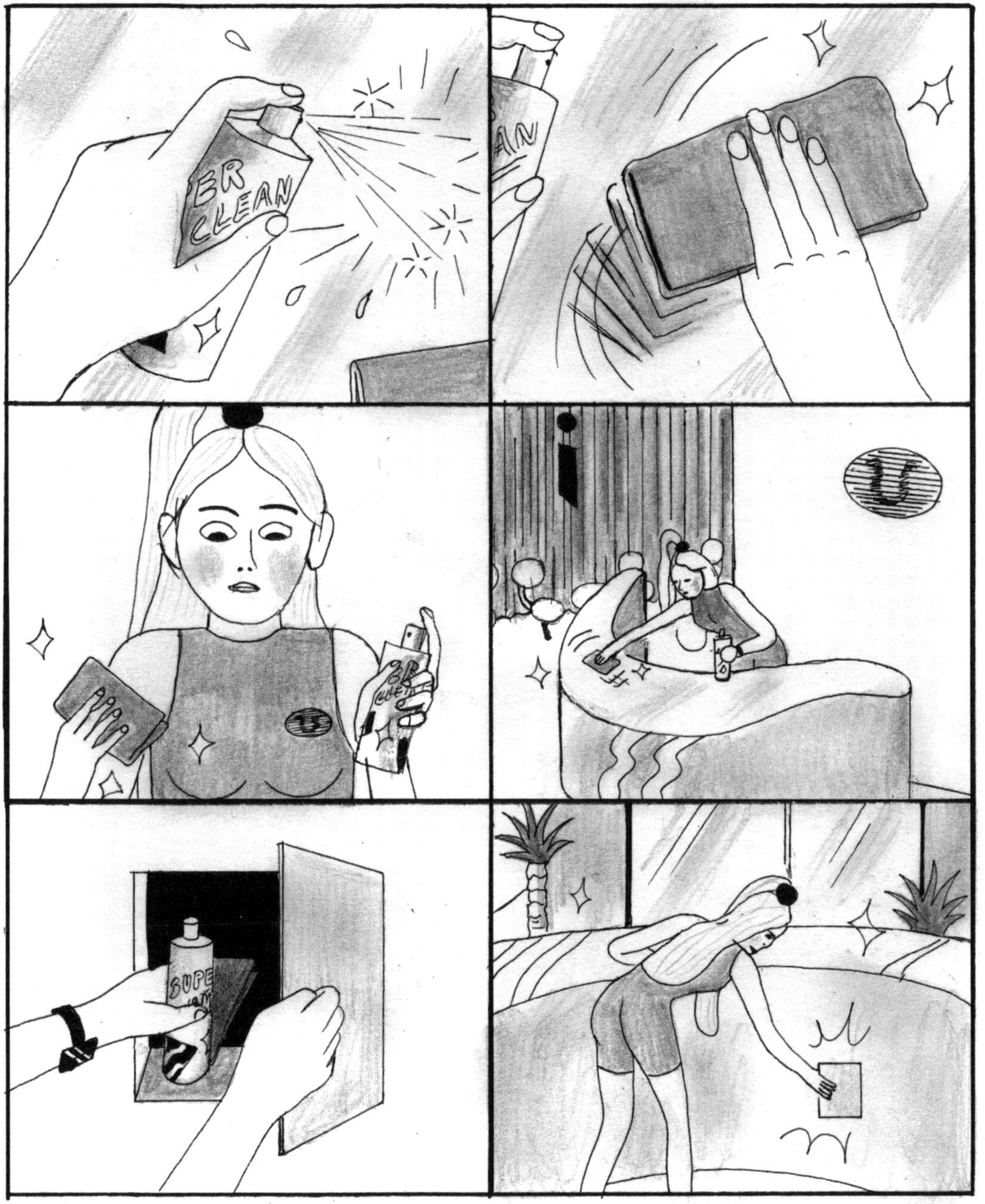
BR
CLEAN

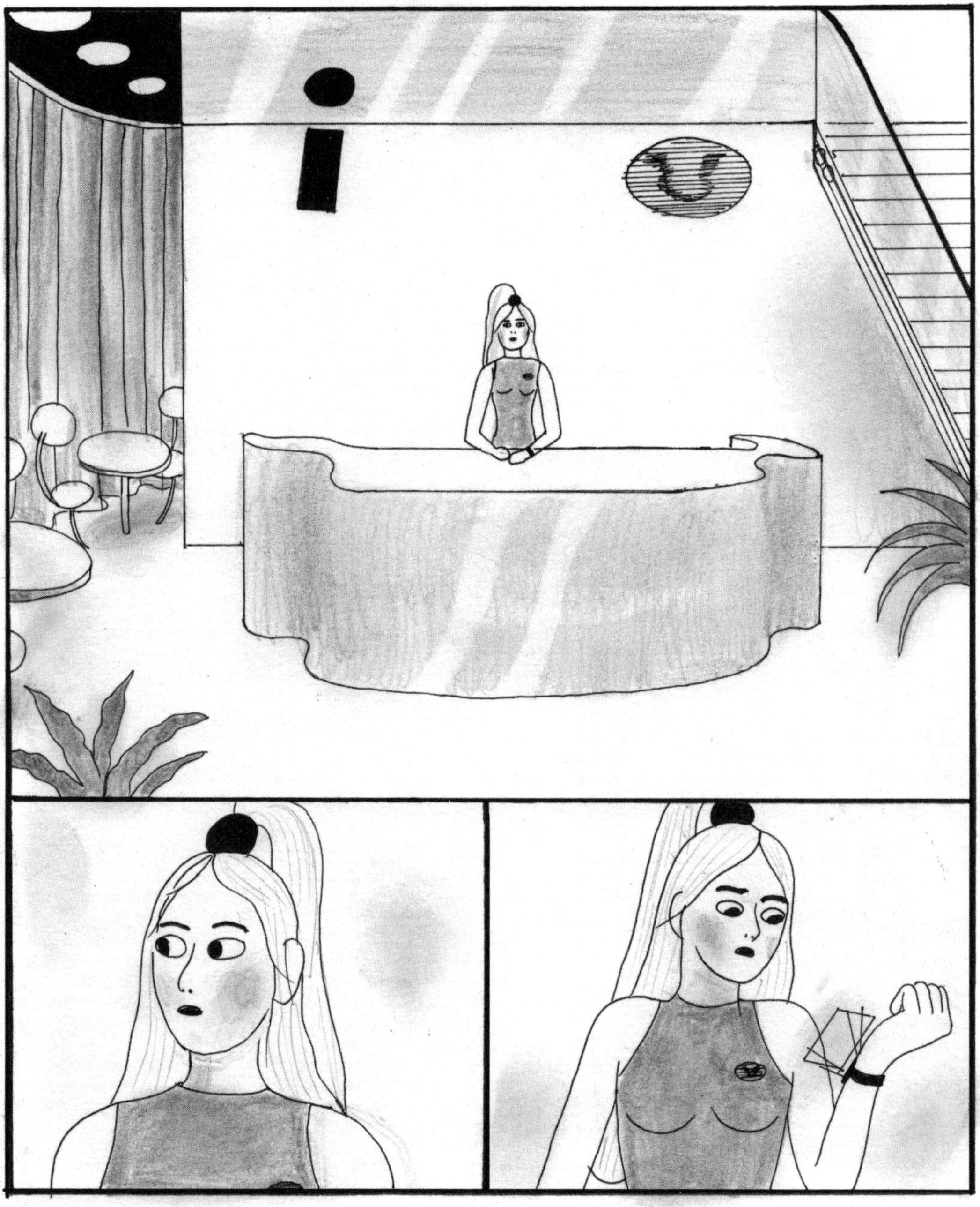

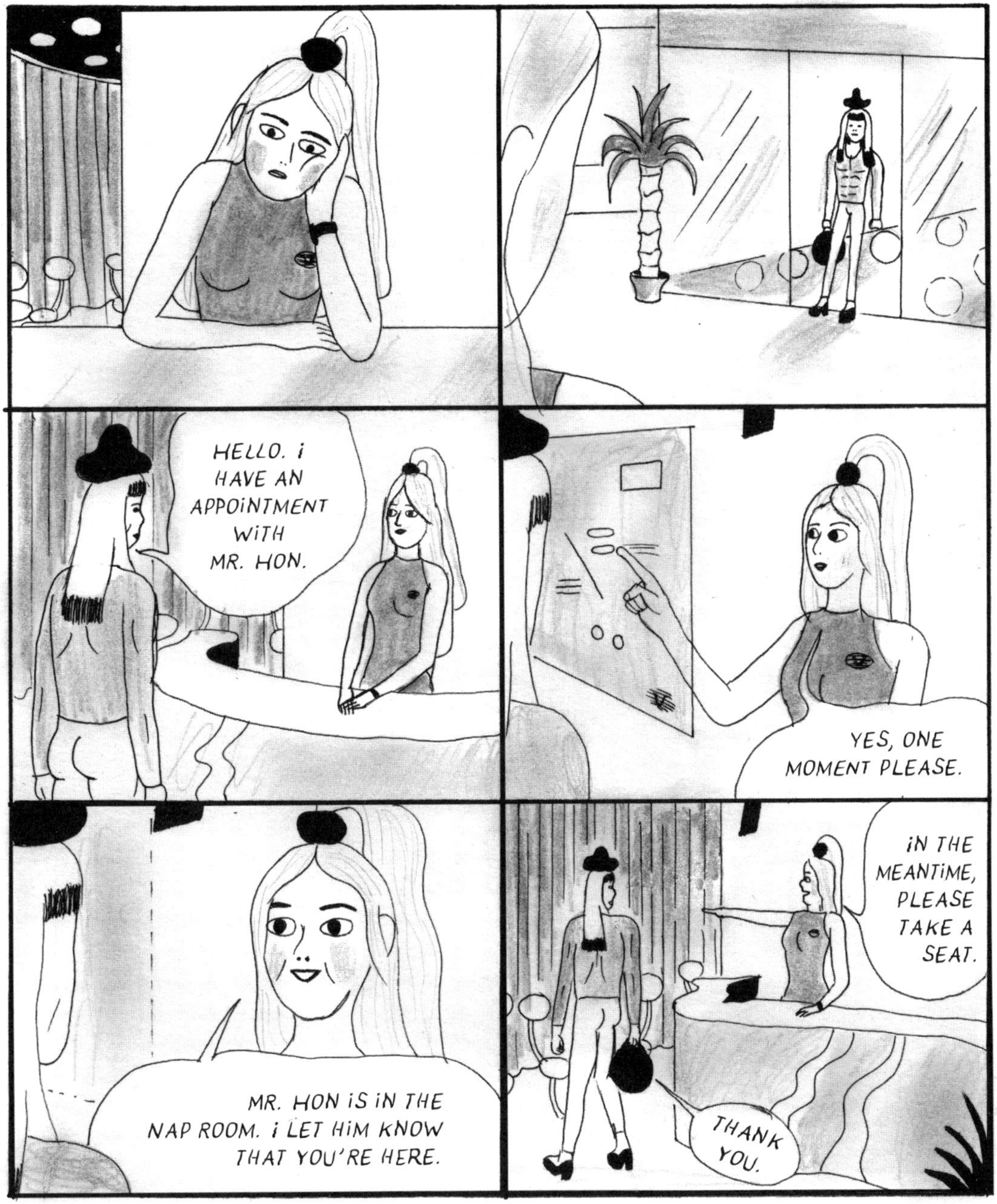
HELLO. I HAVE AN APPOINTMENT WITH MR. HON.
YES, ONE MOMENT PLEASE.
MR. HON IS IN THE NAP ROOM. I LET HIM KNOW THAT YOU'RE HERE.
IN THE MEANTIME, PLEASE TAKE A SEAT.
THANK YOU.

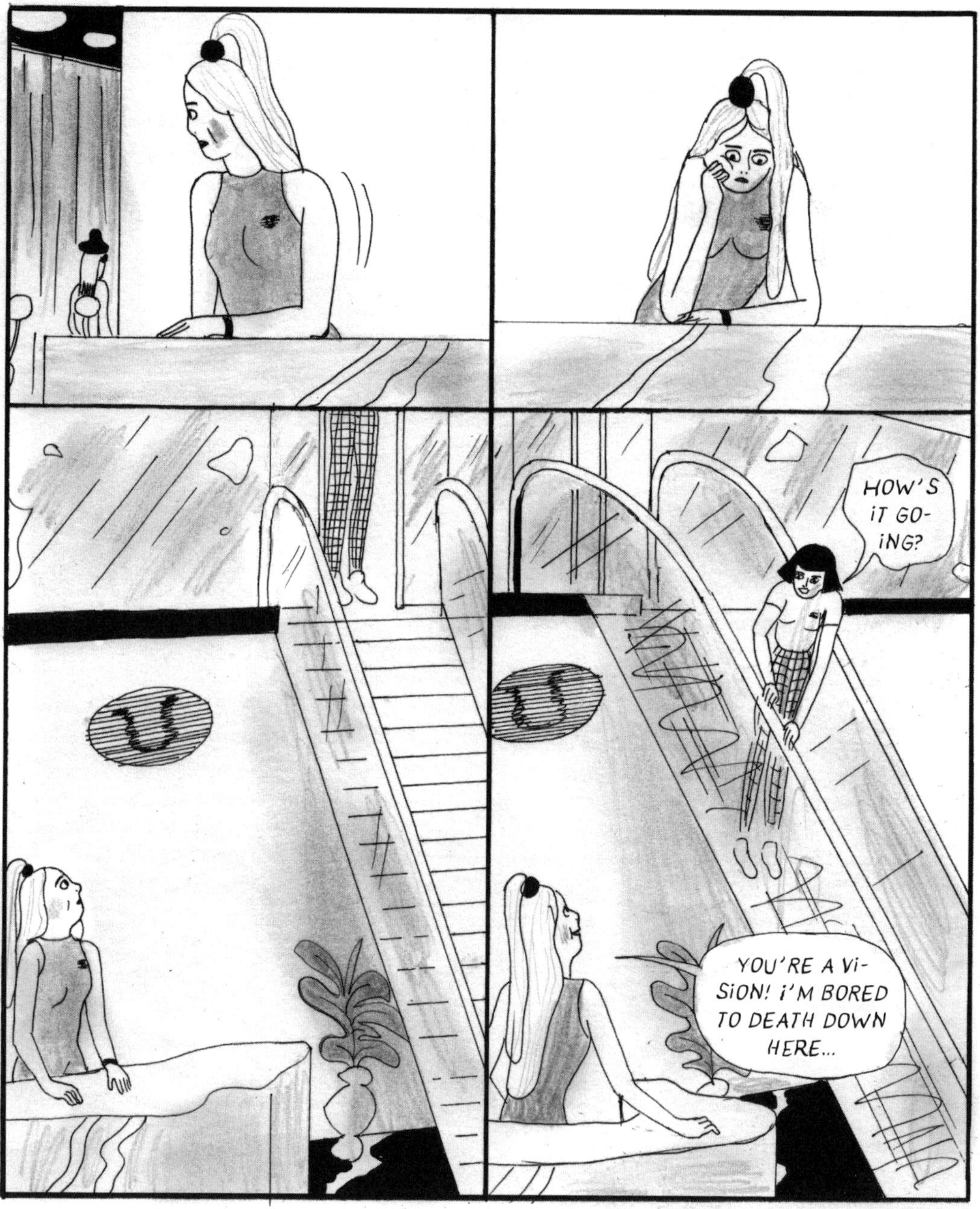
HOW'S iT GO-iNG?
YOU'RE A Vi-SiON! i'M BORED TO DEATH DOWN HERE...

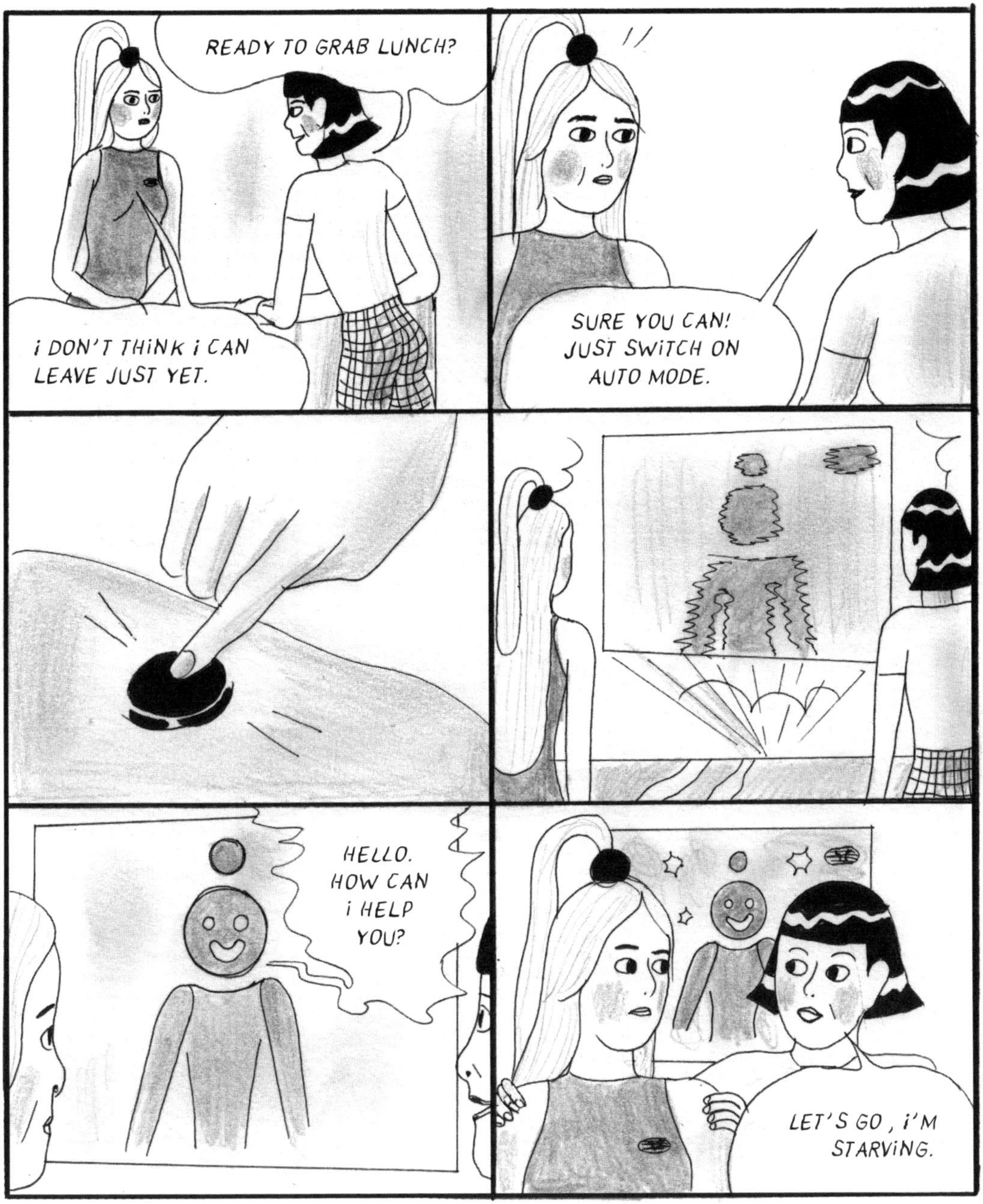
READY TO GRAB LUNCH?
i DON'T THiNK i CAN LEAVE JUST YET.
SURE YOU CAN! JUST SWITCH ON AUTO MODE.
HELLO. HOW CAN i HELP YOU?
LET'S GO, i'M STARViNG.

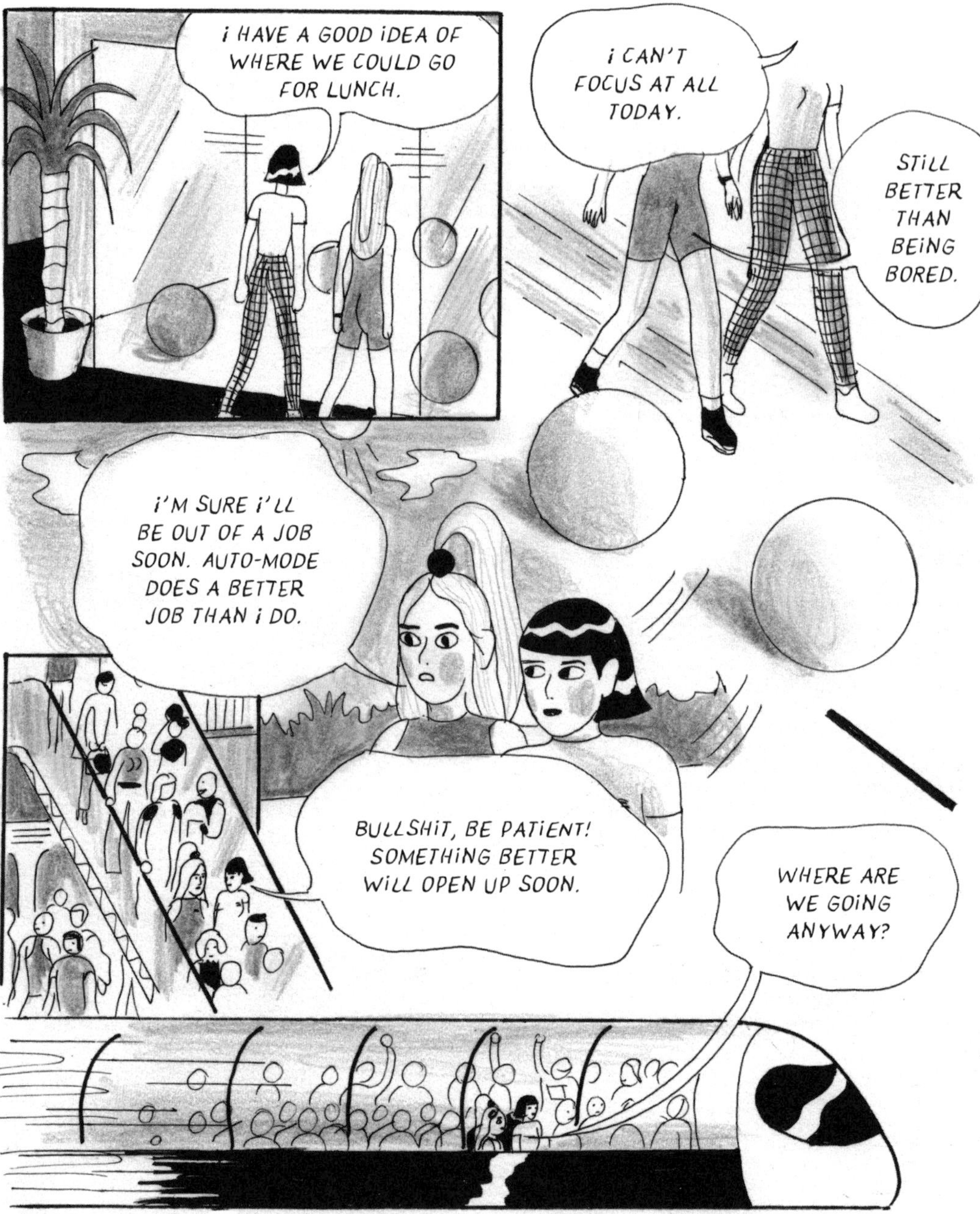

i HAVE A GOOD iDEA OF WHERE WE COULD GO FOR LUNCH.
i CAN'T FOCUS AT ALL TODAY.
STiLL BETTER THAN BEiNG BORED.
i'M SURE i'LL BE OUT OF A JOB SOON. AUTO-MODE DOES A BETTER JOB THAN i DO.
BULLSHiT, BE PATiENT! SOMETHiNG BETTER WiLL OPEN UP SOON.
WHERE ARE WE GOiNG ANYWAY?

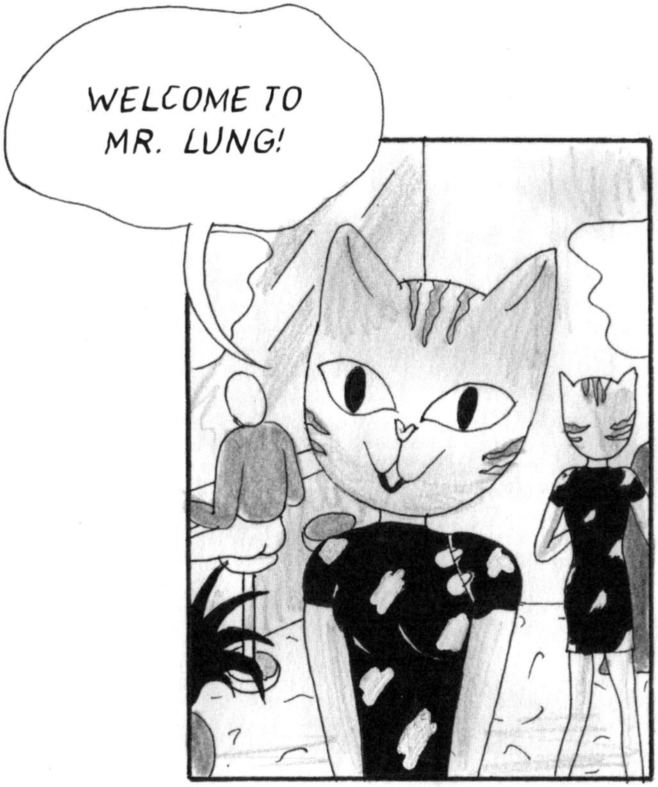
WELCOME TO MR. LUNG!

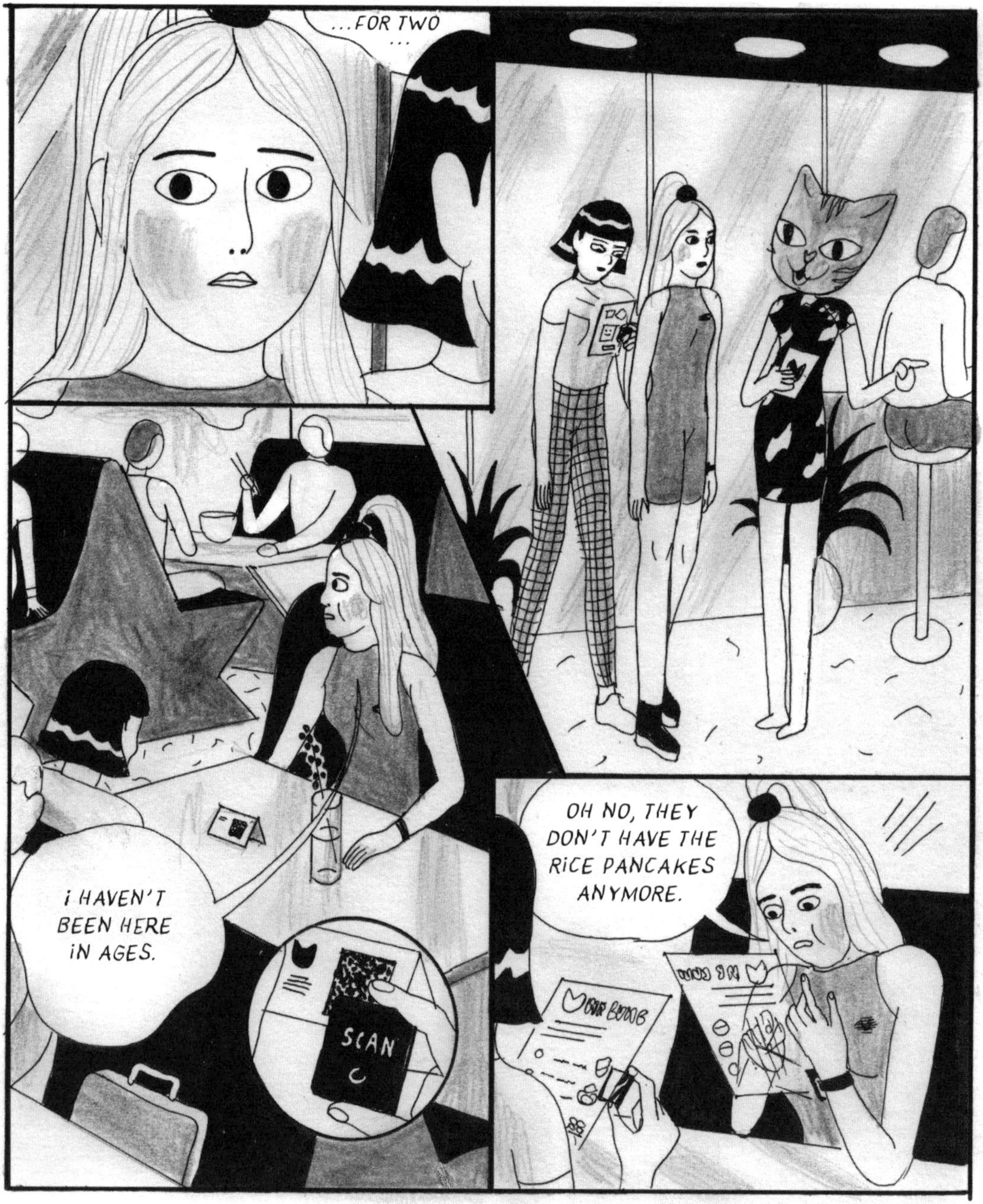
...FOR TWO
...
I HAVEN'T BEEN HERE IN AGES.
SCAN
OH NO, THEY DON'T HAVE THE RICE PANCAKES ANYMORE.

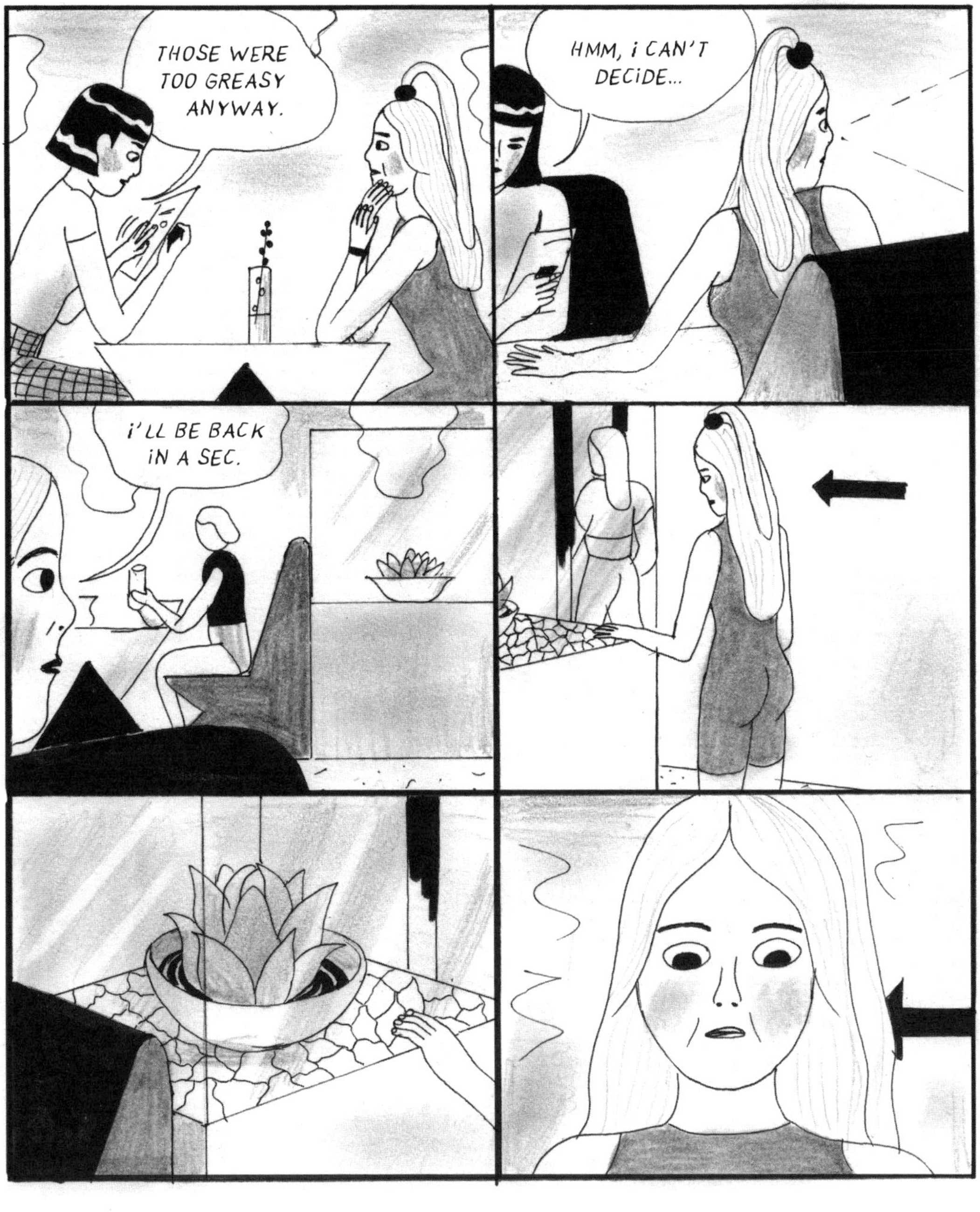
THOSE WERE TOO GREASY ANYWAY.
HMM, i CAN'T DECiDE...
i'LL BE BACK iN A SEC.

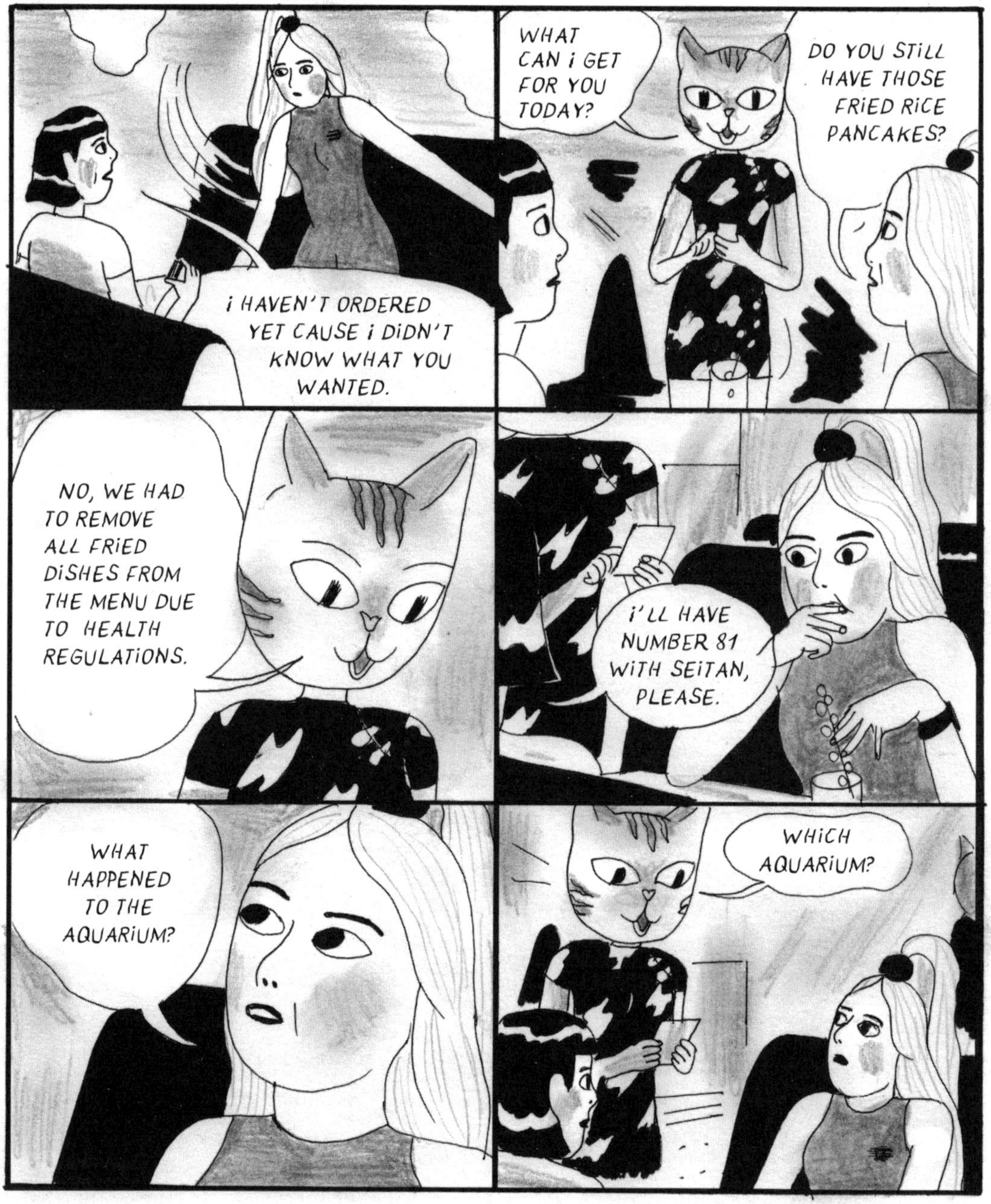
i HAVEN'T ORDERED YET CAUSE i DiDN'T KNOW WHAT YOU WANTED.
WHAT CAN i GET FOR YOU TODAY?
DO YOU STiLL HAVE THOSE FRiED RiCE PANCAKES?
NO, WE HAD TO REMOVE ALL FRiED DiSHES FROM THE MENU DUE TO HEALTH REGULATiONS.
i'LL HAVE NUMBER 81 WiTH SEiTAN, PLEASE.
WHAT HAPPENED TO THE AQUARiUM?
WHiCH AQUARiUM?

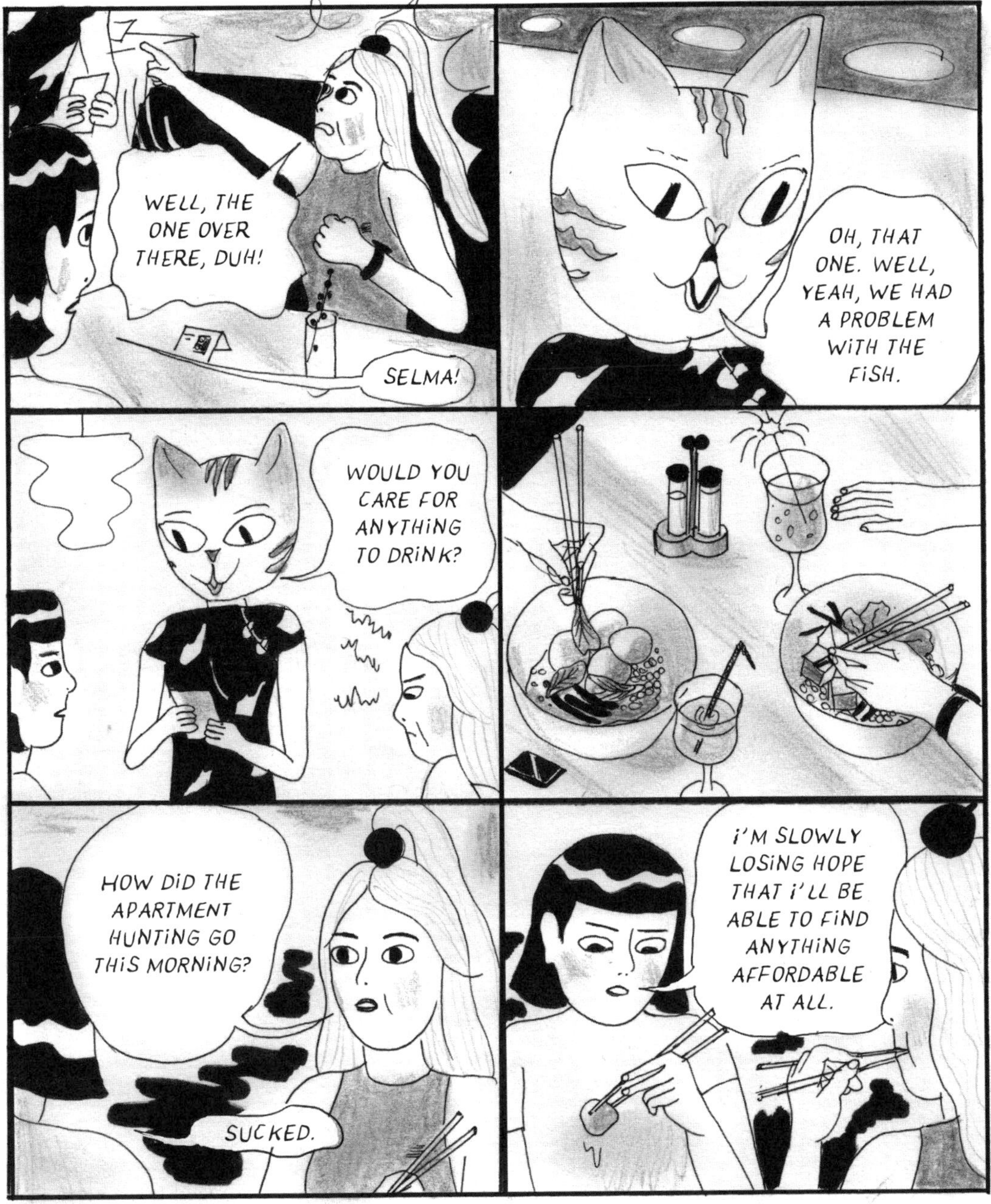
WELL, THE ONE OVER THERE, DUH!
SELMA!
OH, THAT ONE. WELL, YEAH, WE HAD A PROBLEM WITH THE FISH.
WOULD YOU CARE FOR ANYTHING TO DRINK?
HOW DID THE APARTMENT HUNTING GO THIS MORNING?
SUCKED.
I'M SLOWLY LOSING HOPE THAT I'LL BE ABLE TO FIND ANYTHING AFFORDABLE AT ALL.

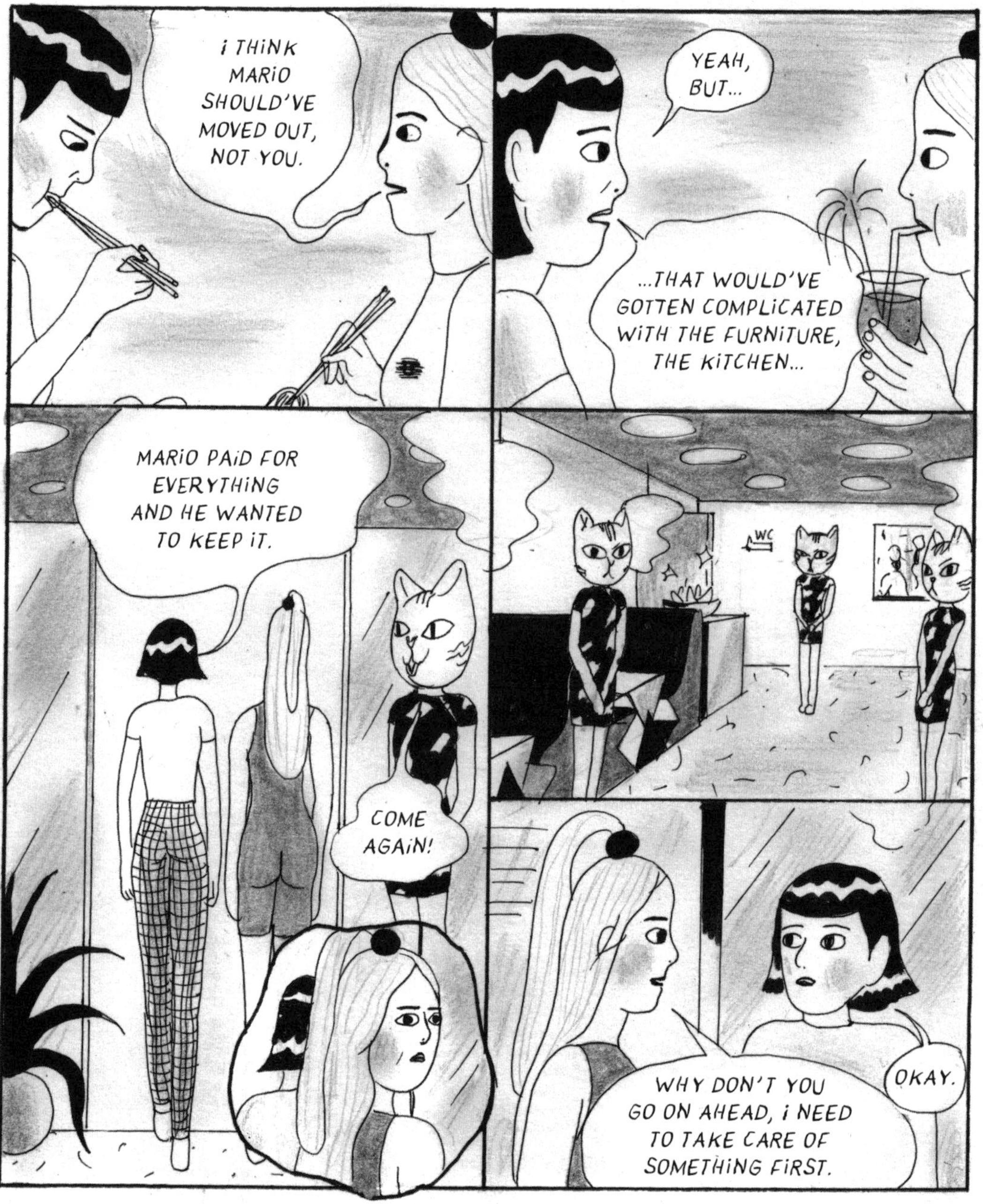
I THINK MARIO SHOULD'VE MOVED OUT, NOT YOU.
YEAH, BUT...
...THAT WOULD'VE GOTTEN COMPLICATED WITH THE FURNITURE, THE KITCHEN...
MARIO PAID FOR EVERYTHING AND HE WANTED TO KEEP IT.
COME AGAIN!
WC
WHY DON'T YOU GO ON AHEAD, I NEED TO TAKE CARE OF SOMETHING FIRST.
OKAY.

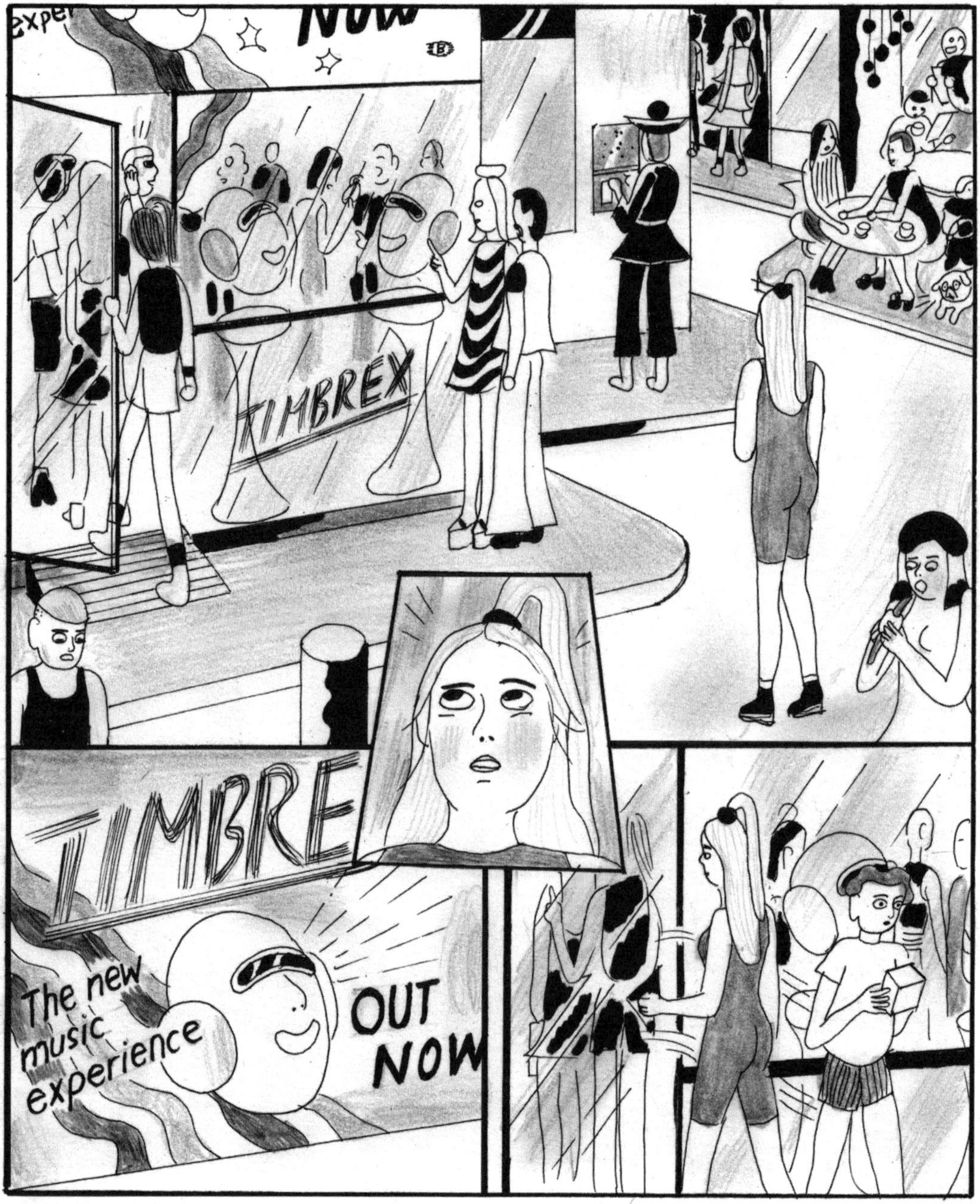

exper
NOW
TIMBREX
TIMBRE
The new music experience
OUT NOW

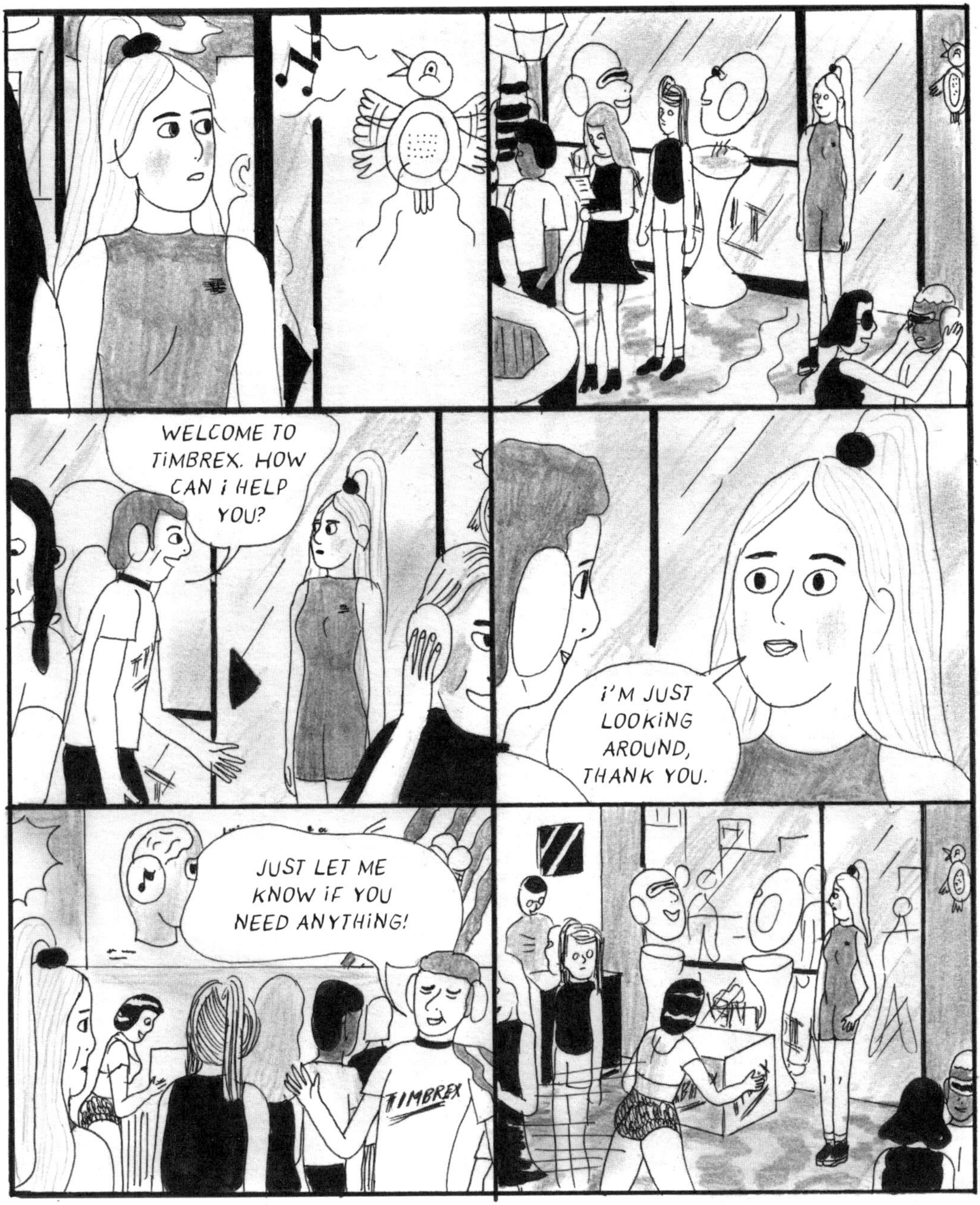
WELCOME TO TIMBREX. HOW CAN I HELP YOU?
I'M JUST LOOKING AROUND, THANK YOU.
JUST LET ME KNOW IF YOU NEED ANYTHING!
TIMBREX

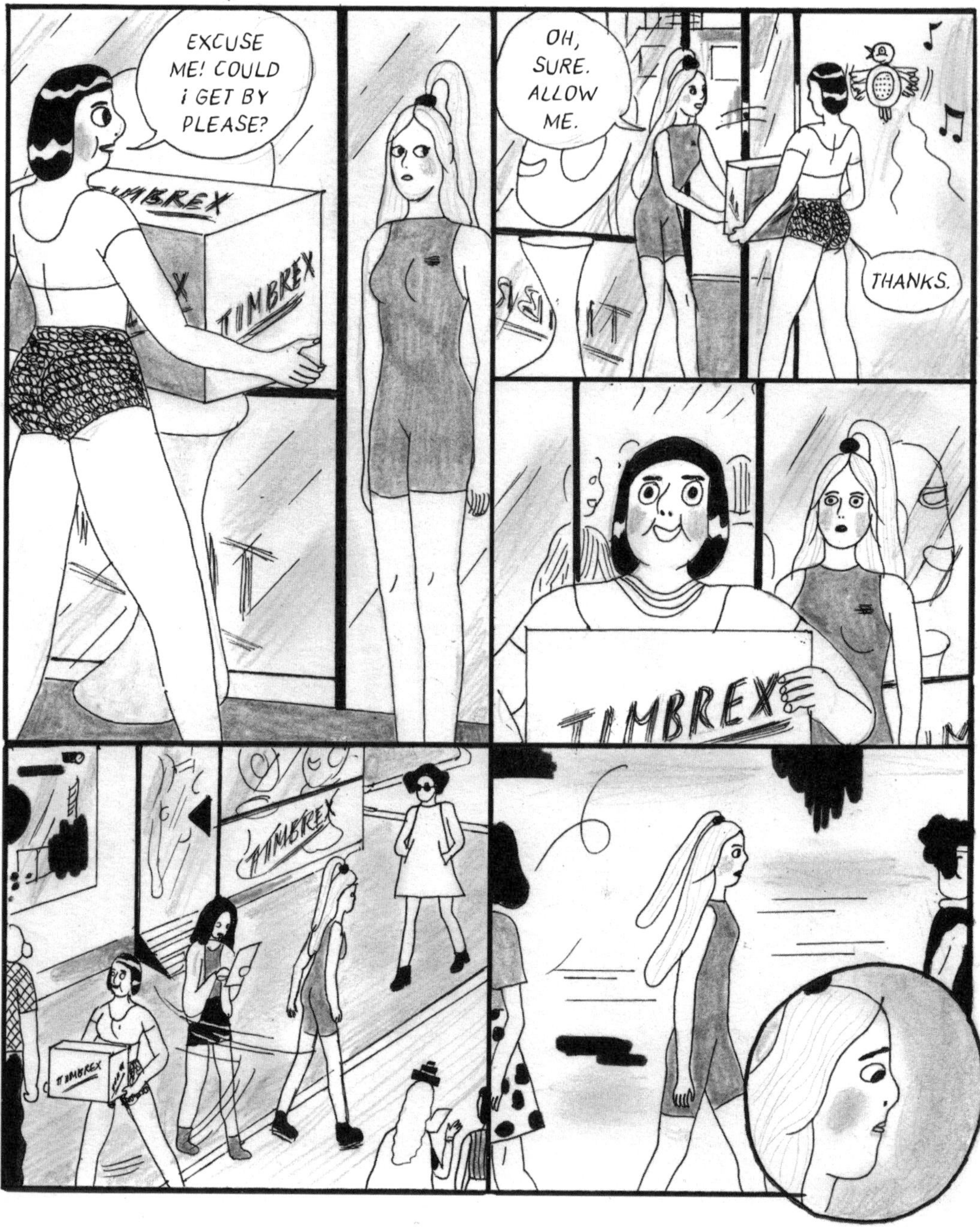
EXCUSE ME! COULD i GET BY PLEASE?
TIMBREX
OH, SURE. ALLOW ME.
THANKS.
TIMBREX
TIMBREX
TIMBREX

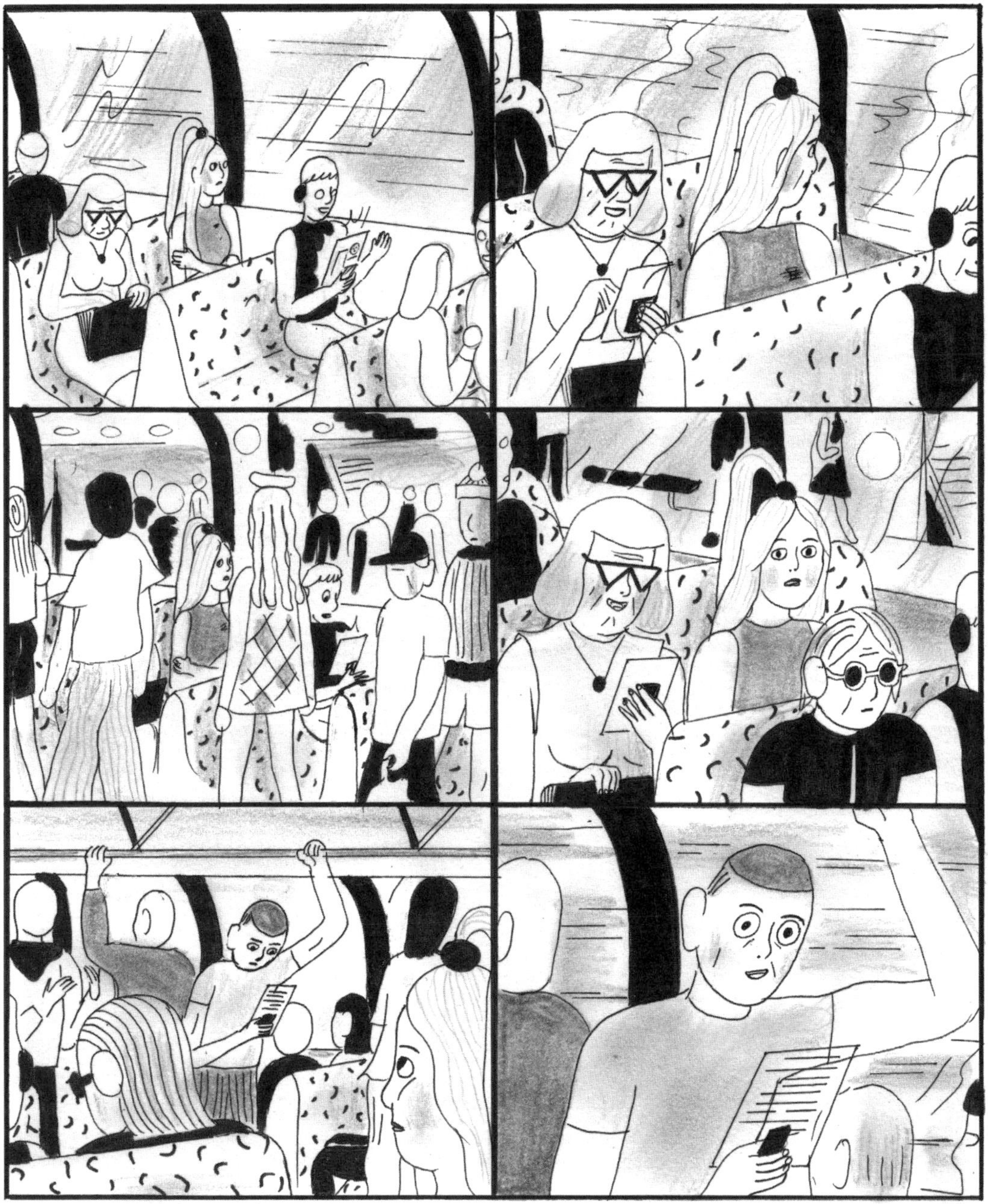

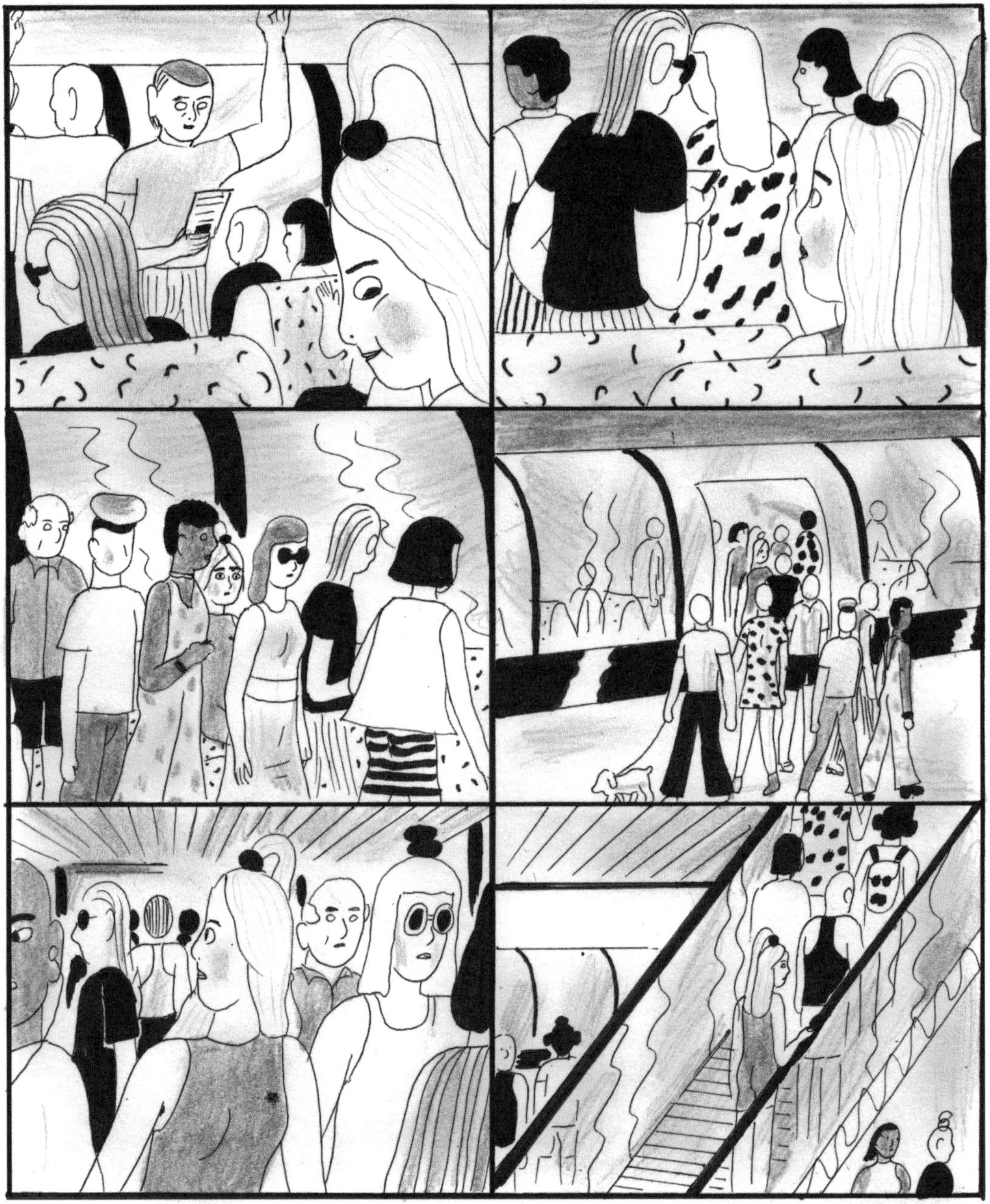

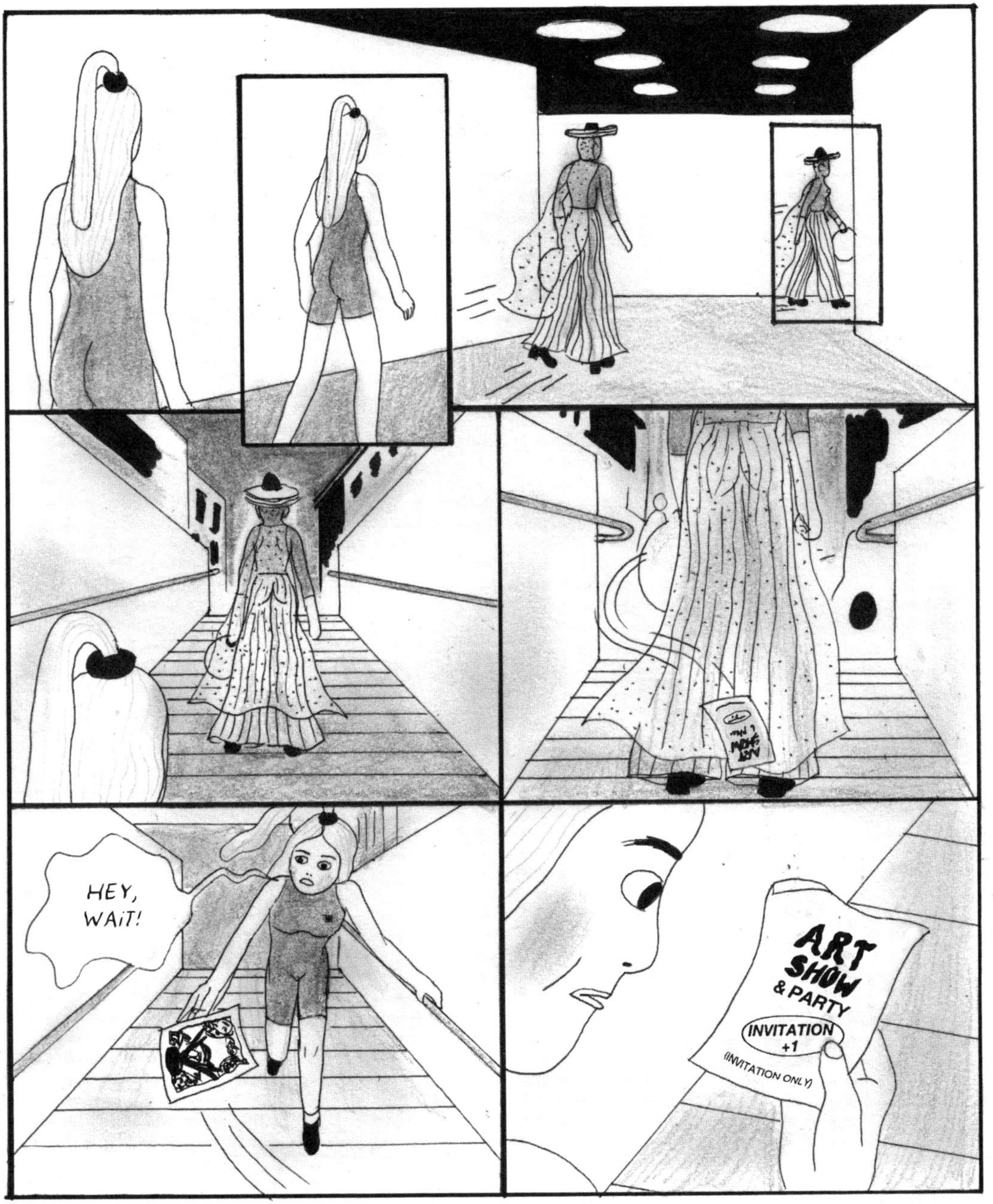
HEY, WAIT!
ART SHOW & PARTY
INVITATION +1
(INVITATION ONLY)

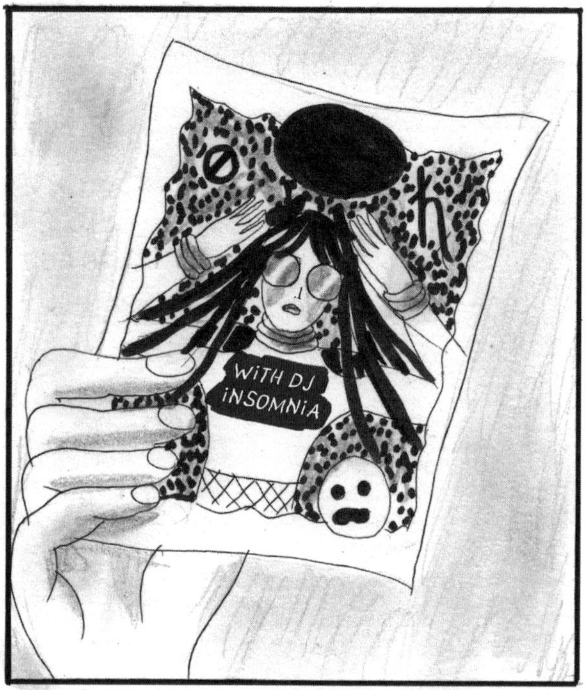
WITH DJ
INSOMNIA

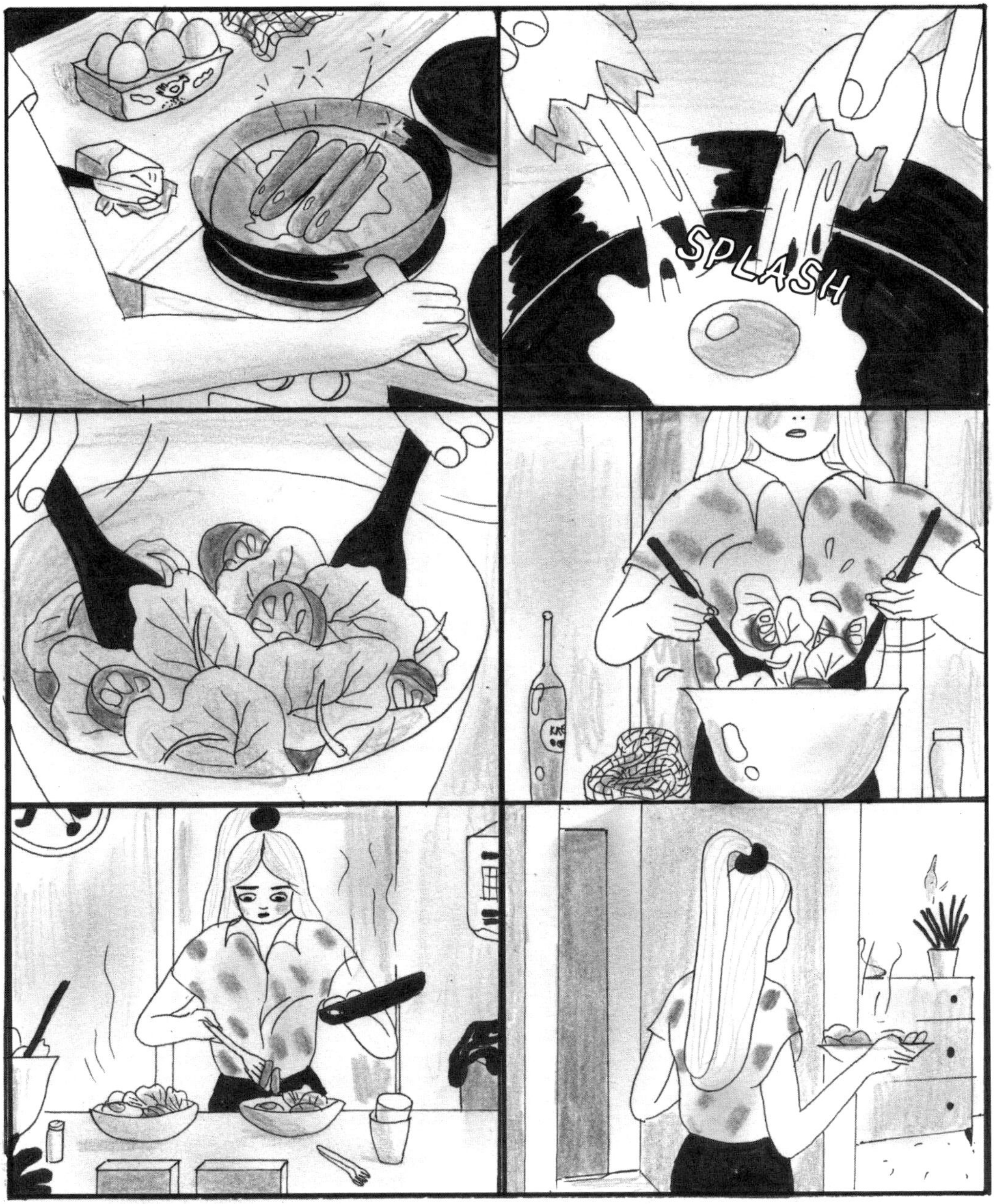
SPLASH

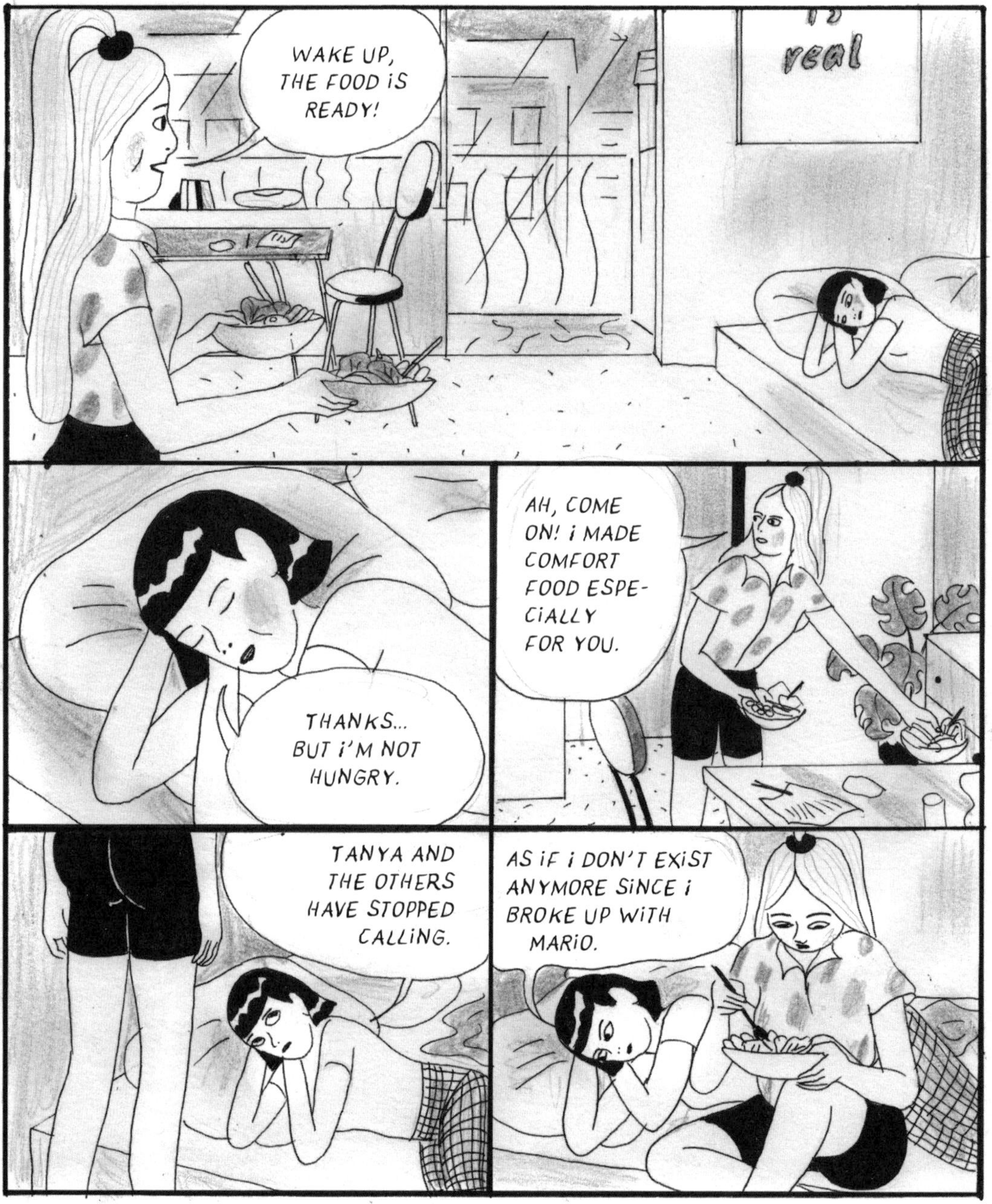
WAKE UP, THE FOOD iS READY!
real
AH, COME ON! i MADE COMFORT FOOD ESPE-CiALLY FOR YOU.
THANKS... BUT i'M NOT HUNGRY.
TANYA AND THE OTHERS HAVE STOPPED CALLiNG.
AS iF i DON'T EXiST ANYMORE SiNCE i BROKE UP WiTH MARiO.

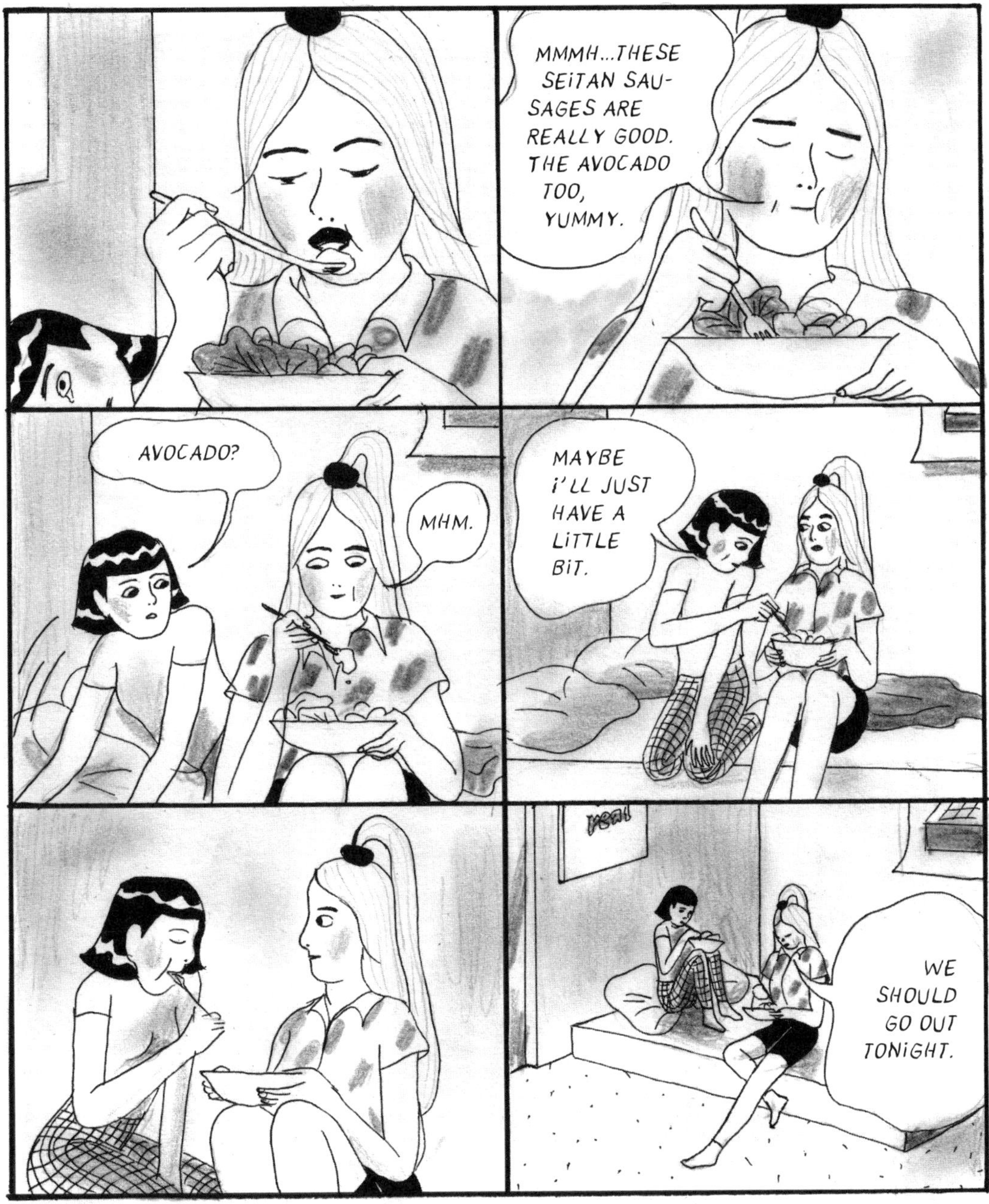
MMMH...THESE SEiTAN SAU-SAGES ARE REALLY GOOD. THE AVOCADO TOO, YUMMY.
AVOCADO?
MHM.
MAYBE i'LL JUST HAVE A LiTTLE BiT.
WE SHOULD GO OUT TONiGHT.

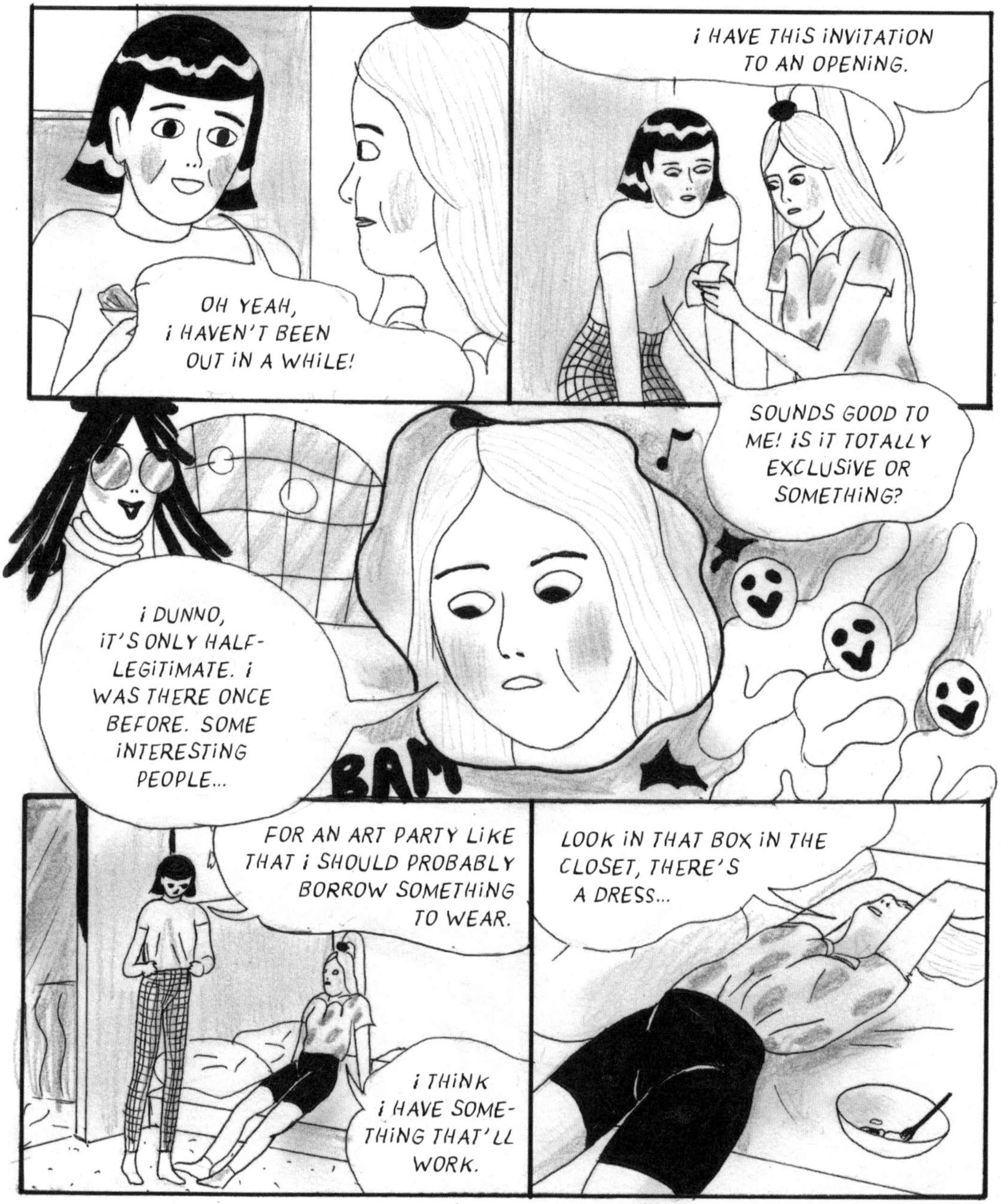
OH YEAH, i HAVEN'T BEEN OUT iN A WHiLE!
i HAVE THiS iNViTATiON TO AN OPENiNG.
SOUNDS GOOD TO ME! iS iT TOTALLY EXCLUSiVE OR SOMETHiNG?
i DUNNO, iT'S ONLY HALF-LEGiTiMATE. i WAS THERE ONCE BEFORE. SOME iNTERESTiNG PEOPLE...
BAM
FOR AN ART PARTY LiKE THAT i SHOULD PROBABLY BORROW SOMETHiNG TO WEAR.
i THiNK i HAVE SOME-THiNG THAT'LL WORK.
LOOK iN THAT BOX iN THE CLOSET, THERE'S A DRESS...

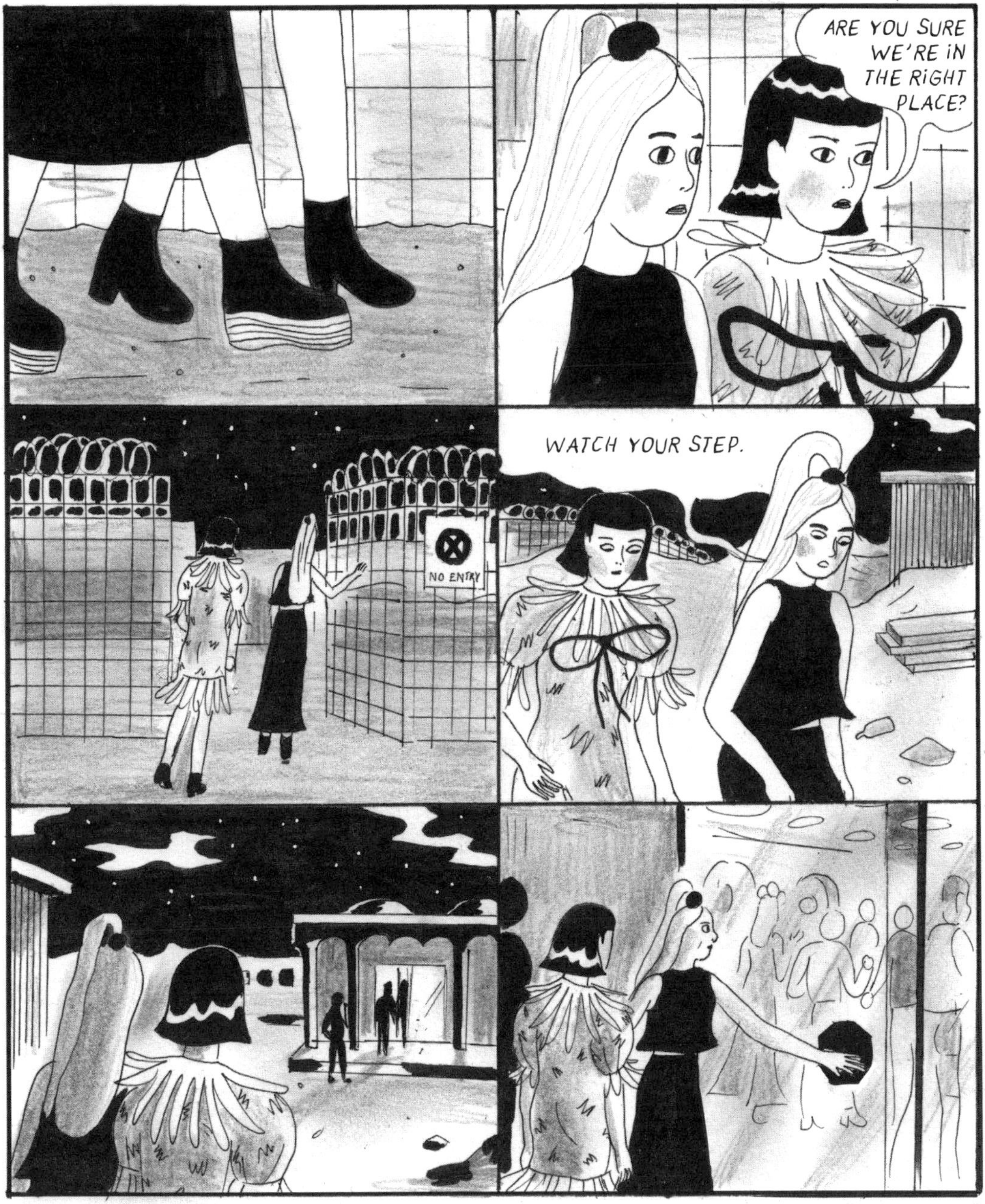
ARE YOU SURE WE'RE IN THE RIGHT PLACE?
NO ENTRY
WATCH YOUR STEP.

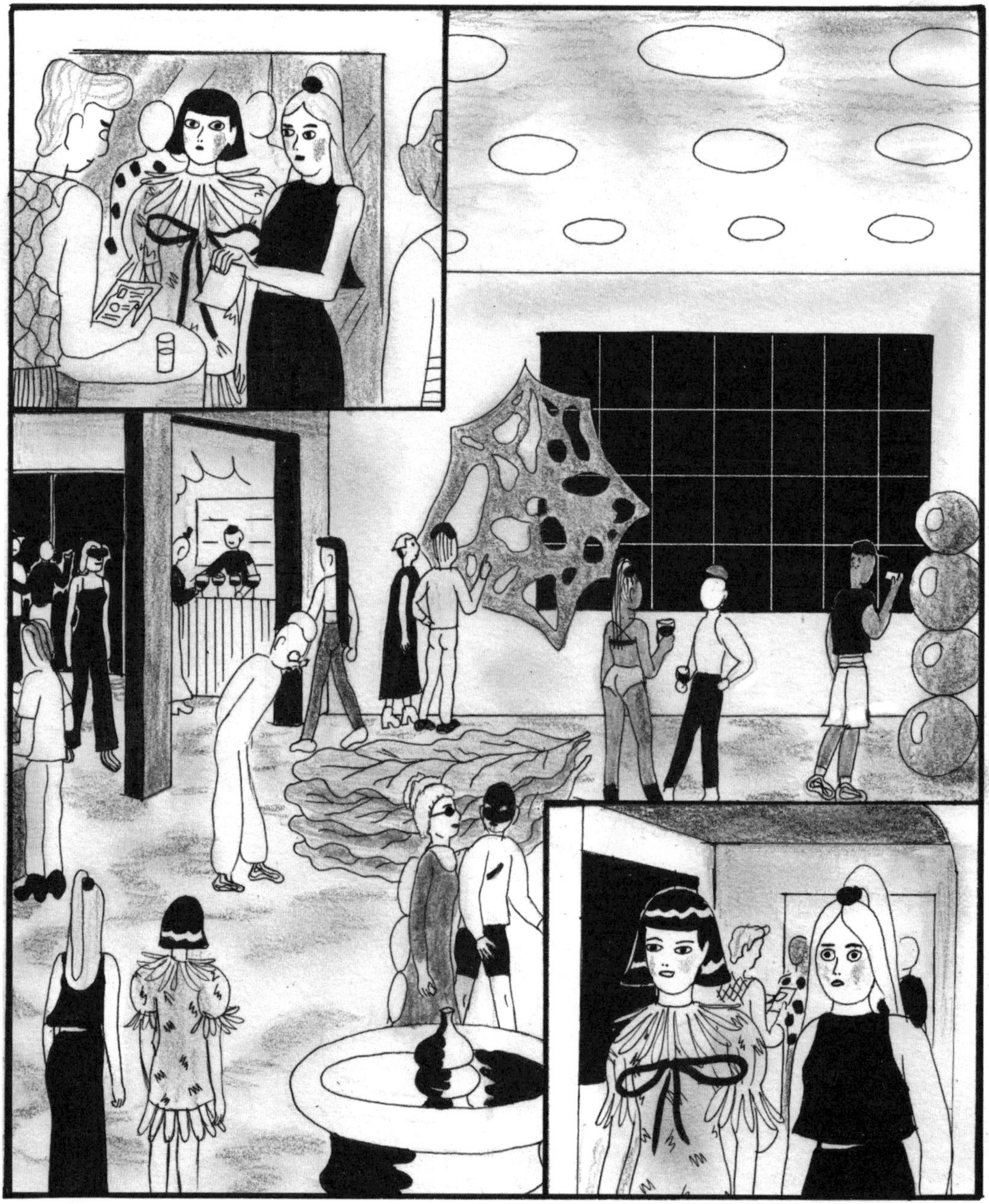

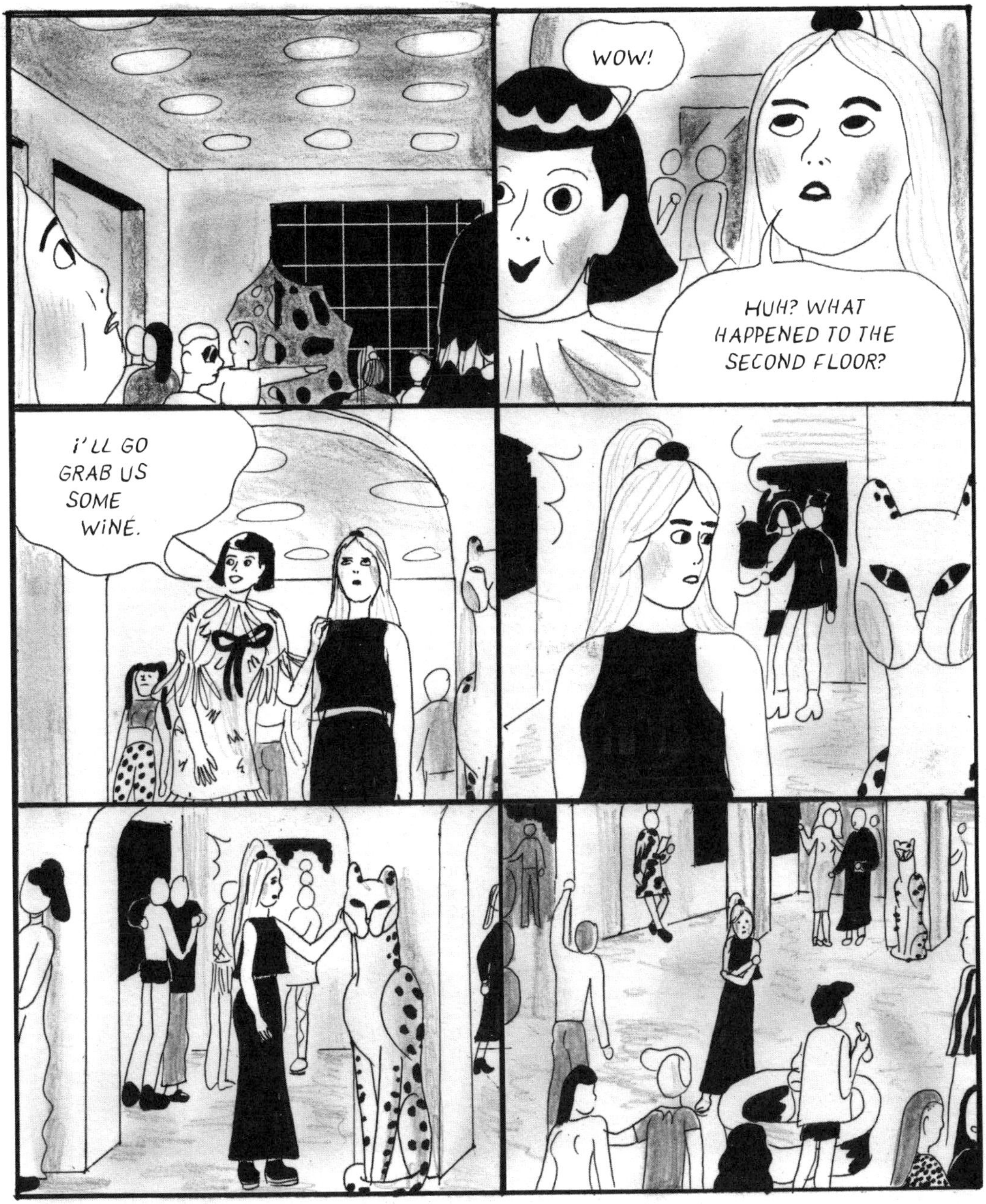
WOW!
HUH? WHAT HAPPENED TO THE SECOND FLOOR?
I'LL GO GRAB US SOME WINE.

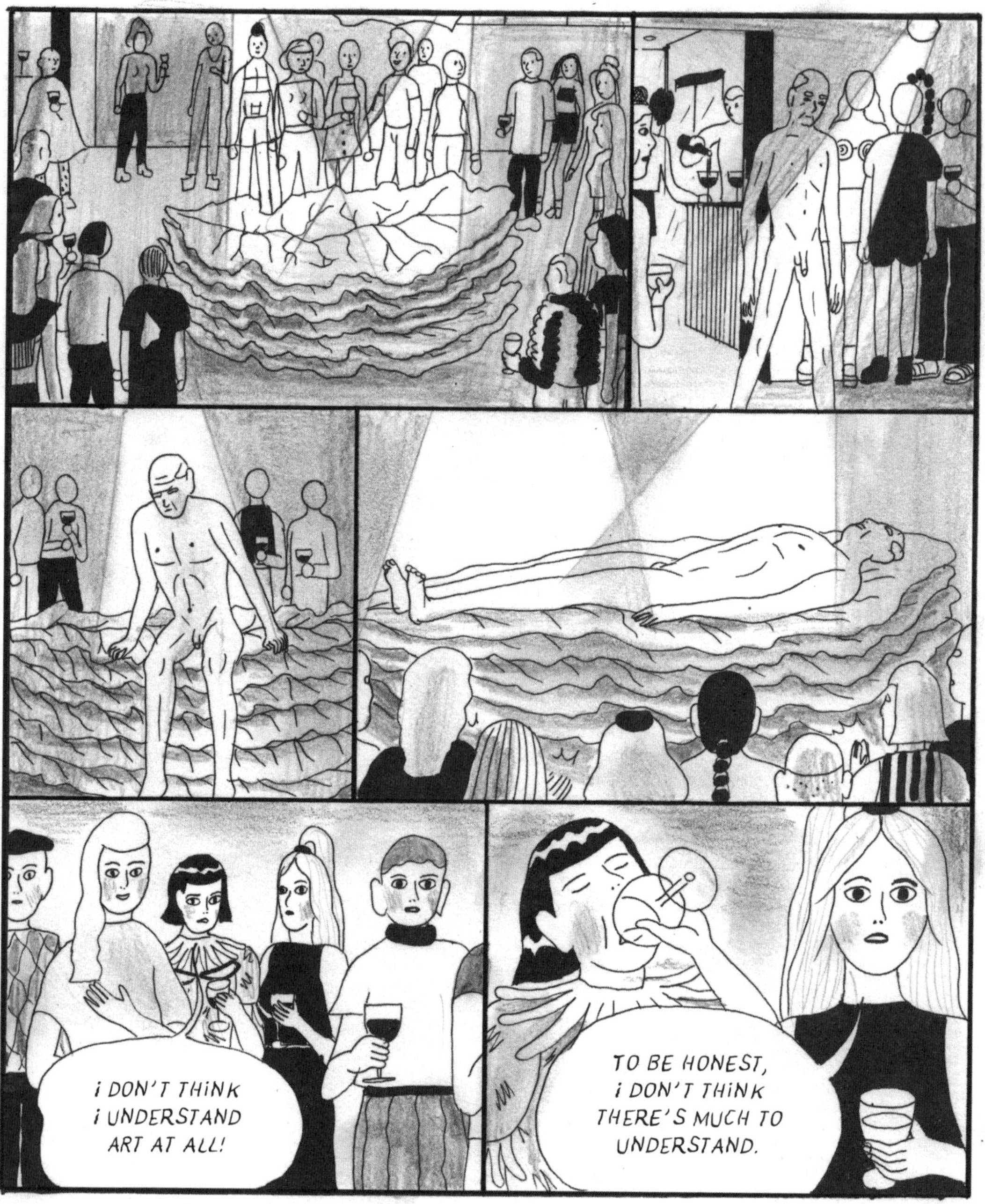
i DON'T THiNK
i UNDERSTAND
ART AT ALL!
TO BE HONEST,
i DON'T THiNK
THERE'S MUCH TO
UNDERSTAND.

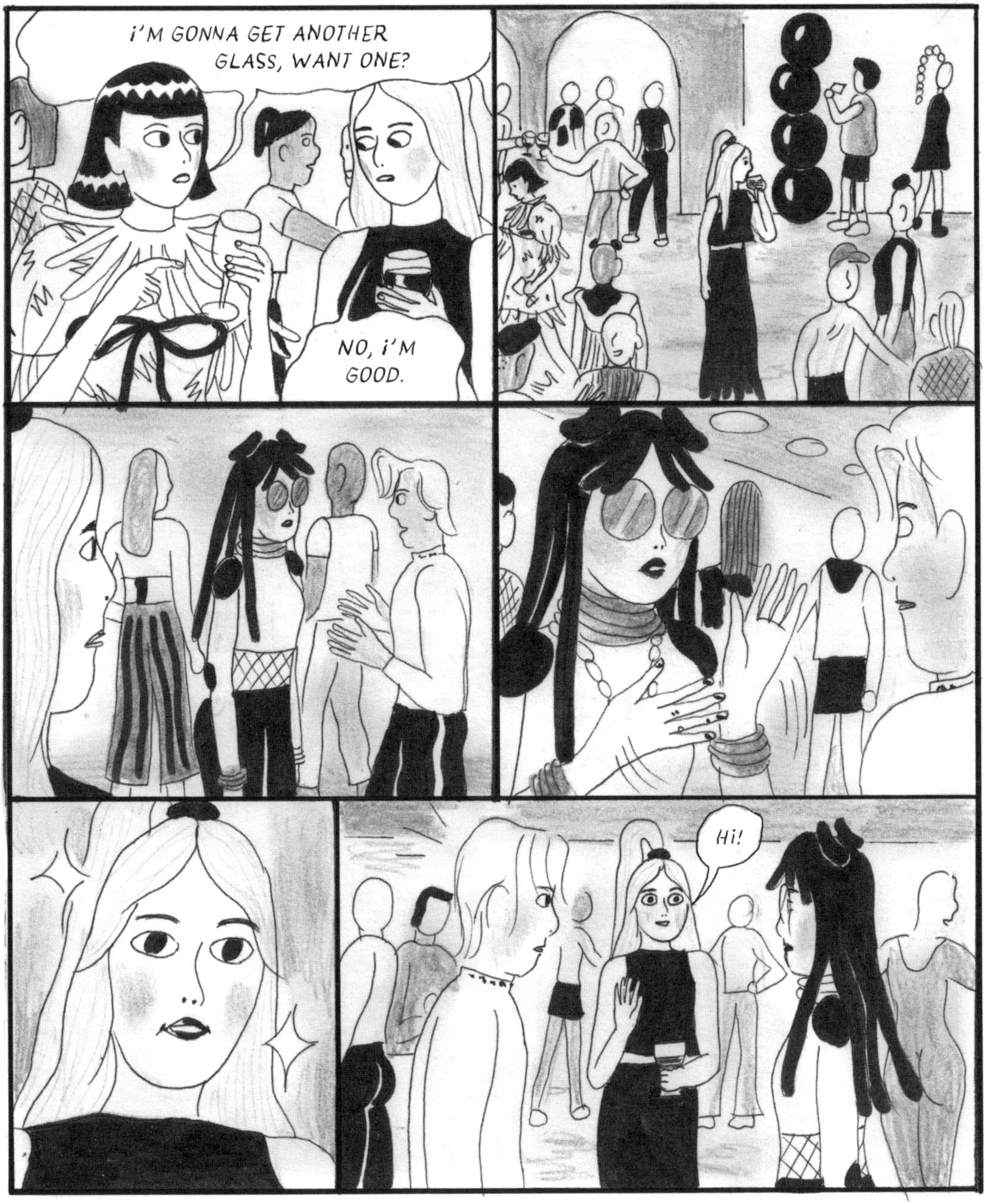
I'M GONNA GET ANOTHER GLASS, WANT ONE?
NO, I'M GOOD.
Hi!

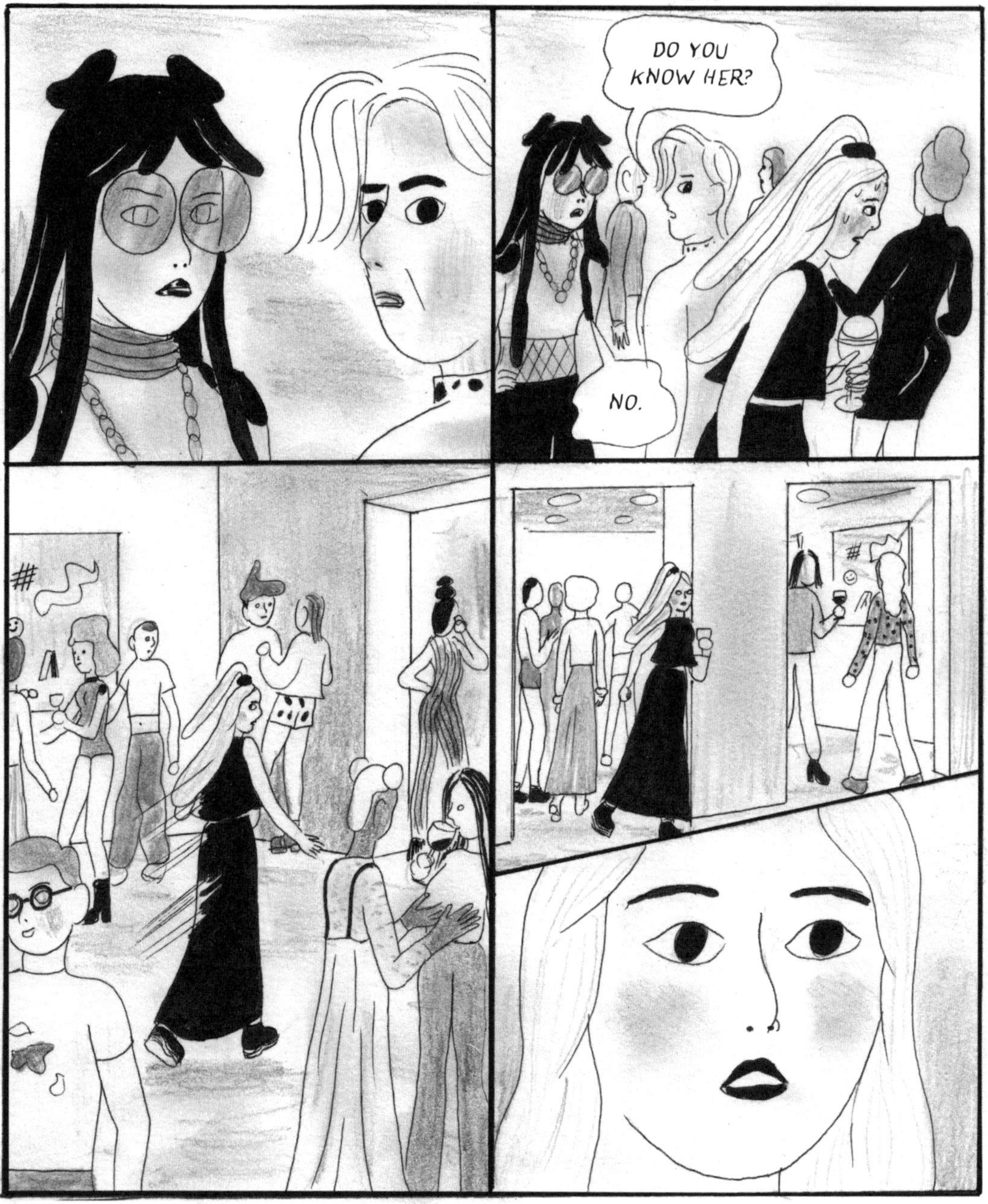
DO YOU KNOW HER?
NO.

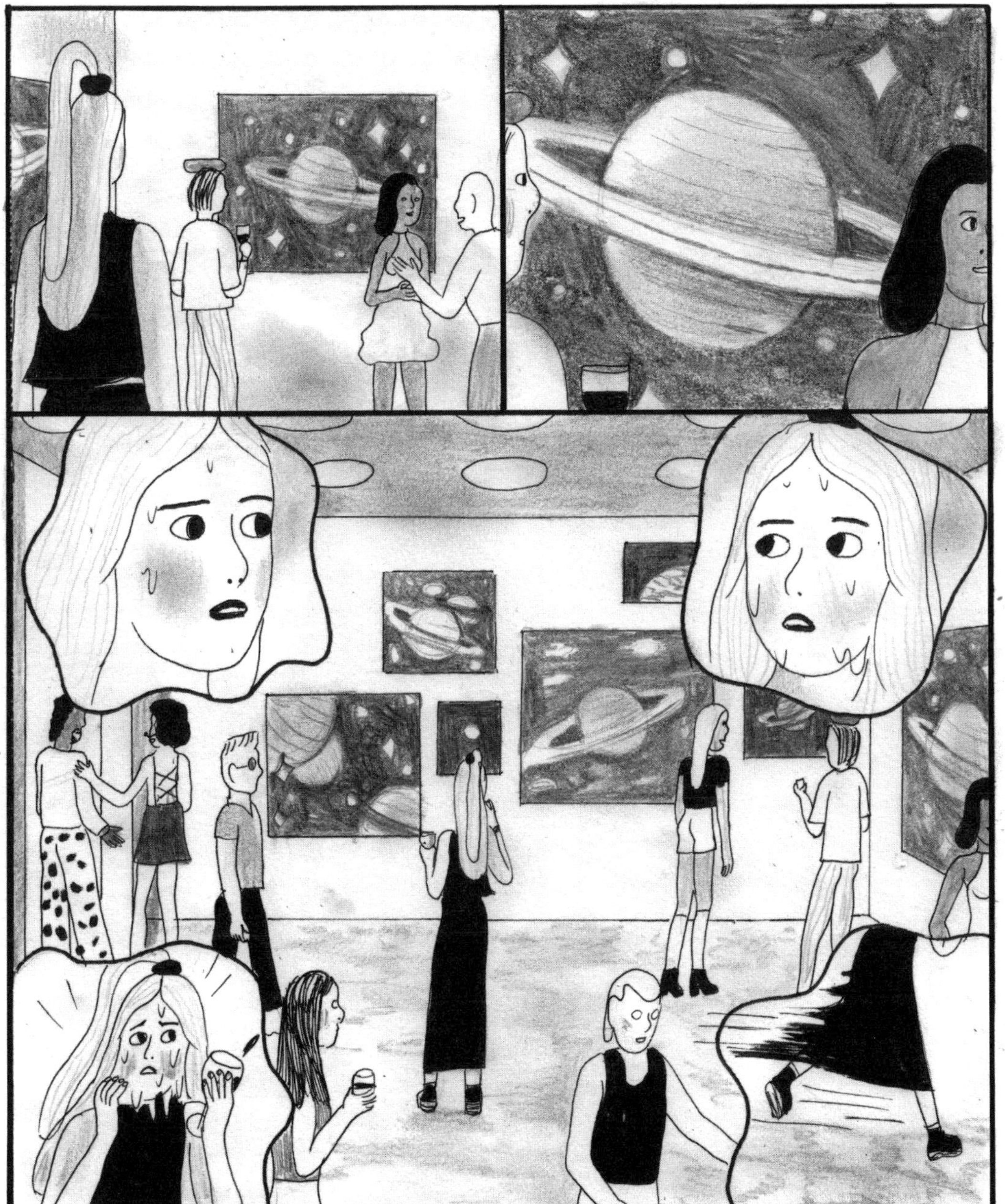

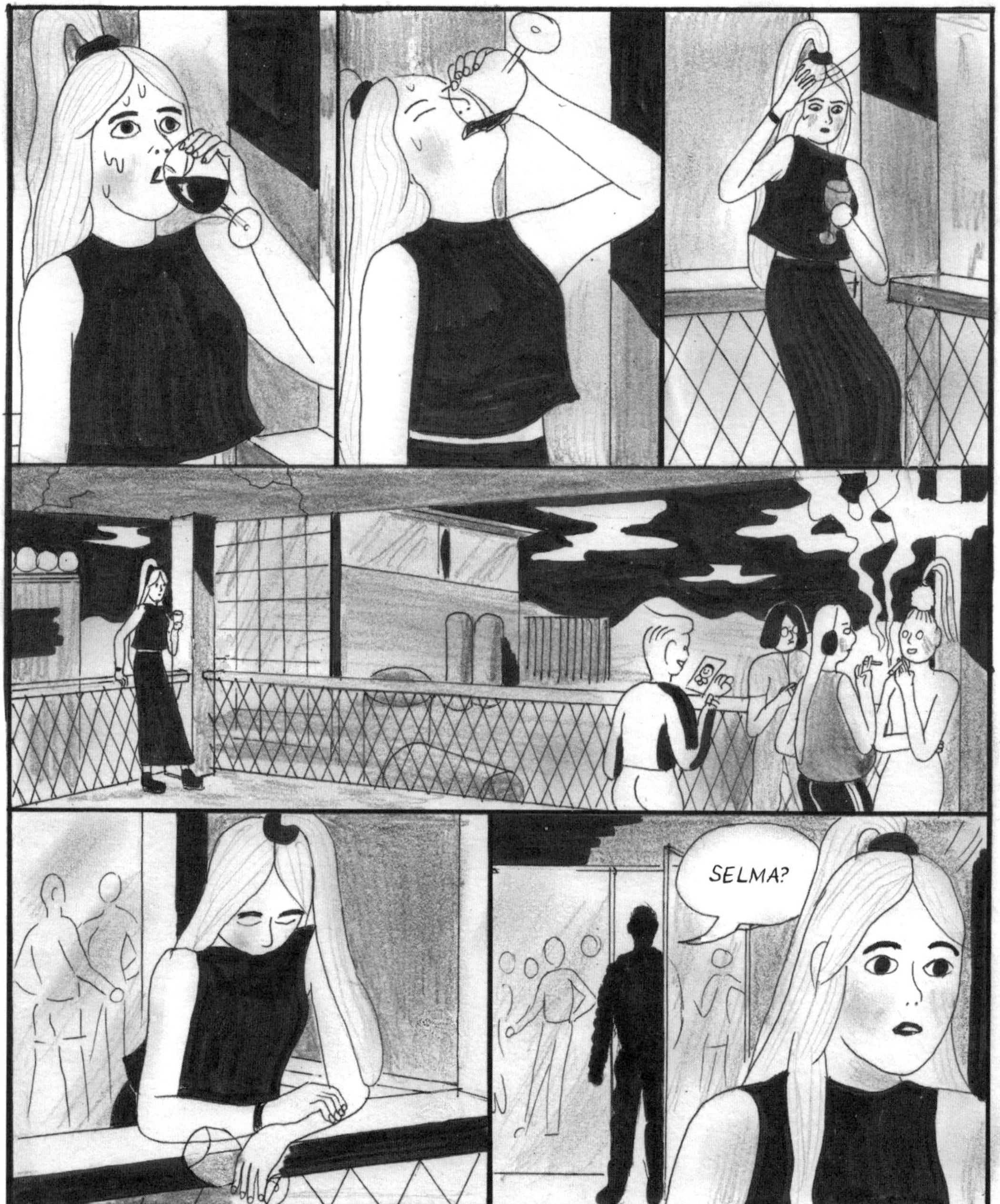
SELMA?

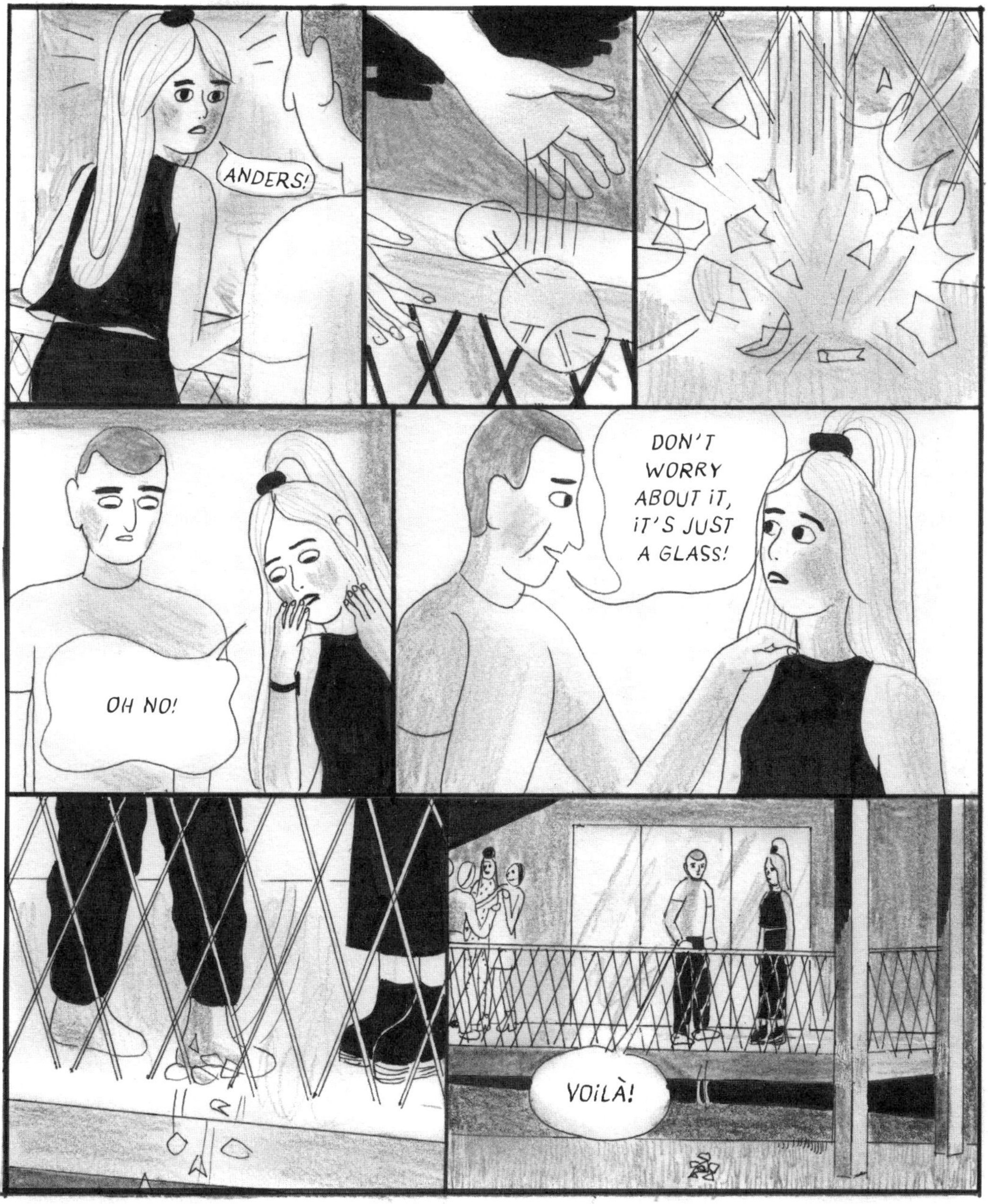
ANDERS!
OH NO!
DON'T WORRY ABOUT IT, IT'S JUST A GLASS!
VOILÀ!

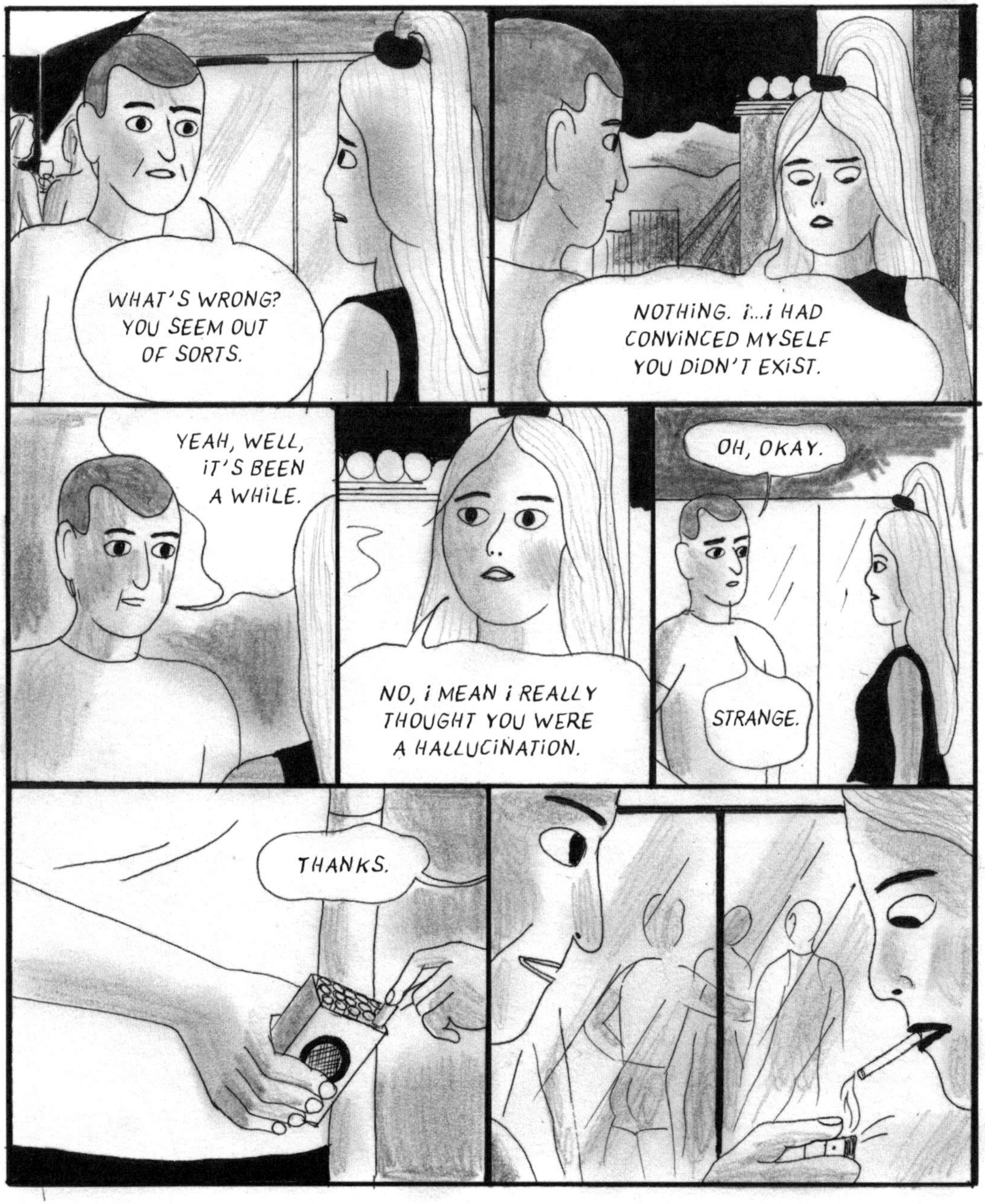
WHAT'S WRONG? YOU SEEM OUT OF SORTS.
NOTHING. I...I HAD CONVINCED MYSELF YOU DIDN'T EXIST.
YEAH, WELL, IT'S BEEN A WHILE.
NO, I MEAN I REALLY THOUGHT YOU WERE A HALLUCINATION.
OH, OKAY.
STRANGE.
THANKS.

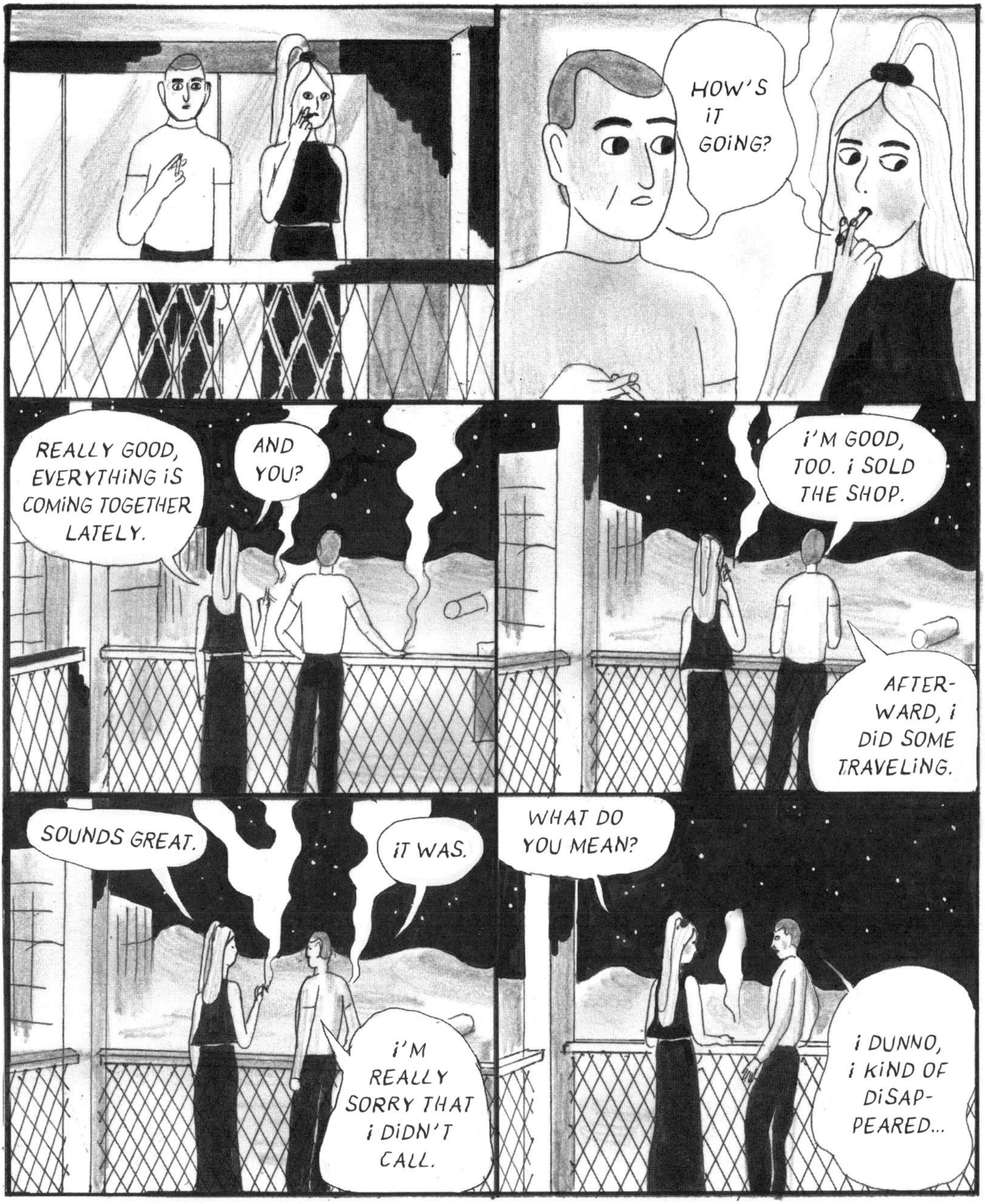
HOW'S iT GOiNG?
REALLY GOOD, EVERYTHiNG iS COMiNG TOGETHER LATELY.
AND YOU?
i'M GOOD, TOO. i SOLD THE SHOP.
AFTER-WARD, i DiD SOME TRAVELiNG.
SOUNDS GREAT.
iT WAS.
i'M REALLY SORRY THAT i DiDN'T CALL.
WHAT DO YOU MEAN?
i DUNNO, i KiND OF DiSAP-PEARED...

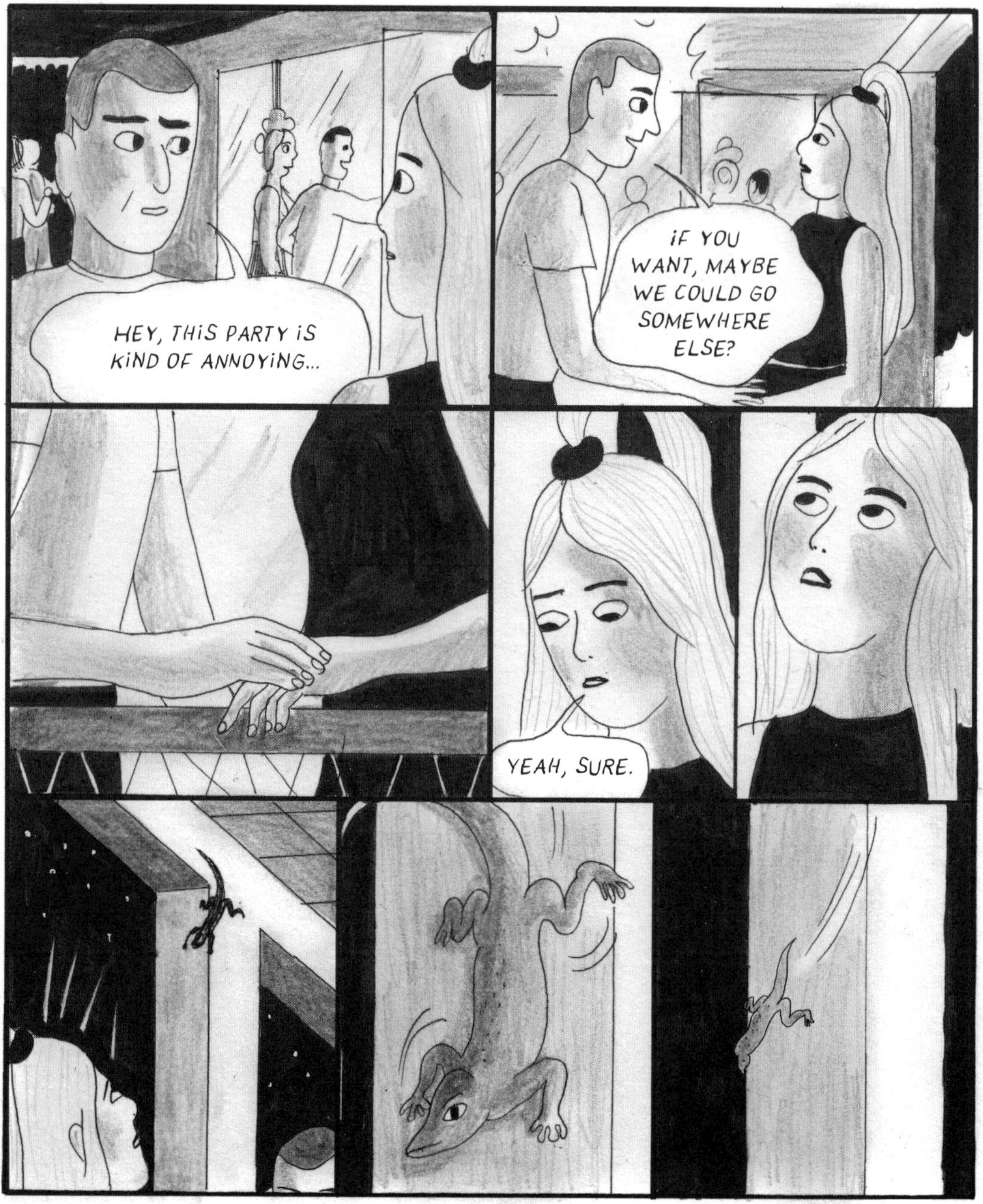
HEY, THIS PARTY IS KIND OF ANNOYING...
IF YOU WANT, MAYBE WE COULD GO SOMEWHERE ELSE?
YEAH, SURE.

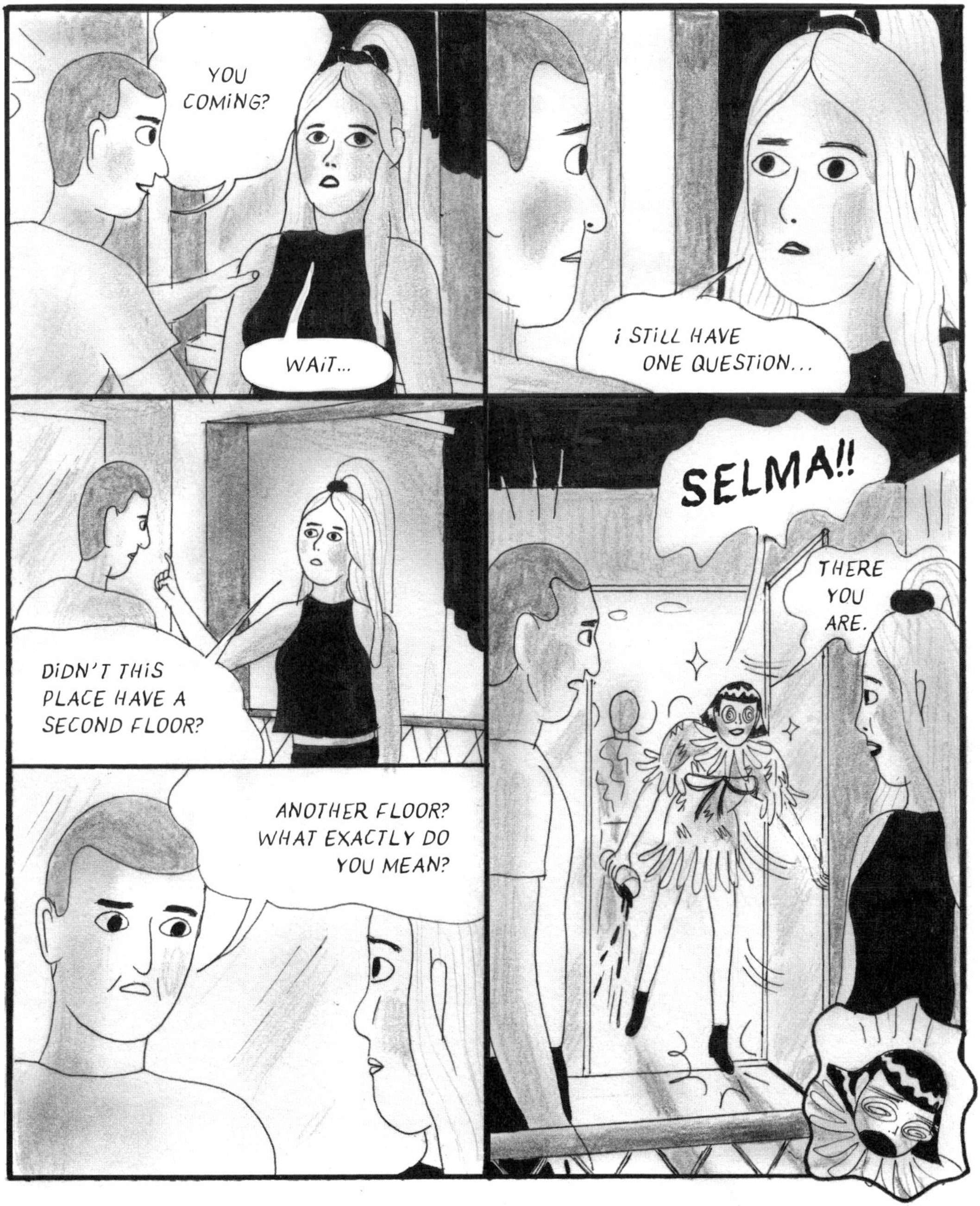
YOU COMING?
WAIT...
i STILL HAVE ONE QUESTION...
DIDN'T THIS PLACE HAVE A SECOND FLOOR?
ANOTHER FLOOR? WHAT EXACTLY DO YOU MEAN?
SELMA!!
THERE YOU ARE.

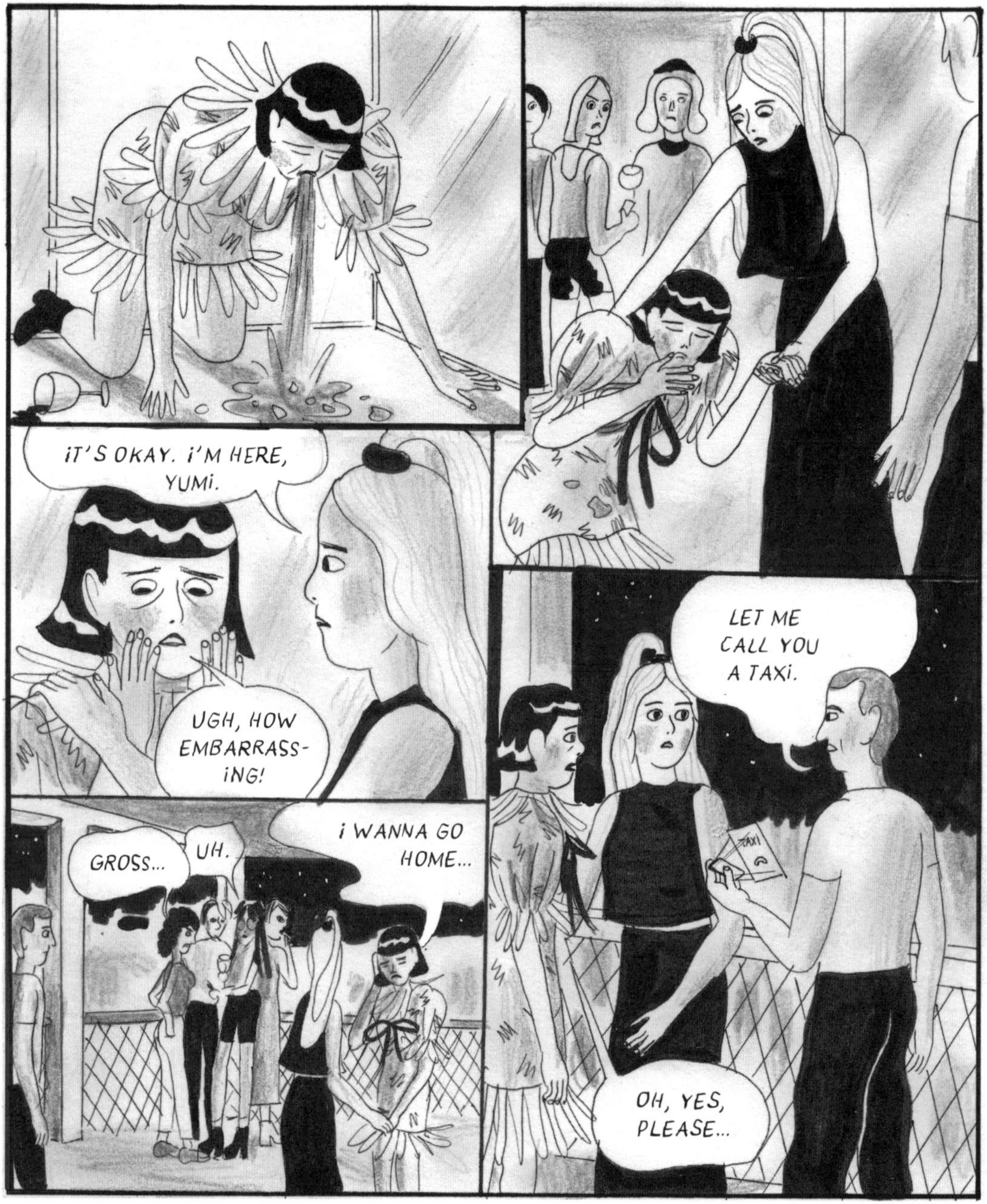
IT'S OKAY. I'M HERE, YUMI.
UGH, HOW EMBARRASS-ING!
LET ME CALL YOU A TAXI.
OH, YES, PLEASE...
GROSS...
UH.
I WANNA GO HOME...

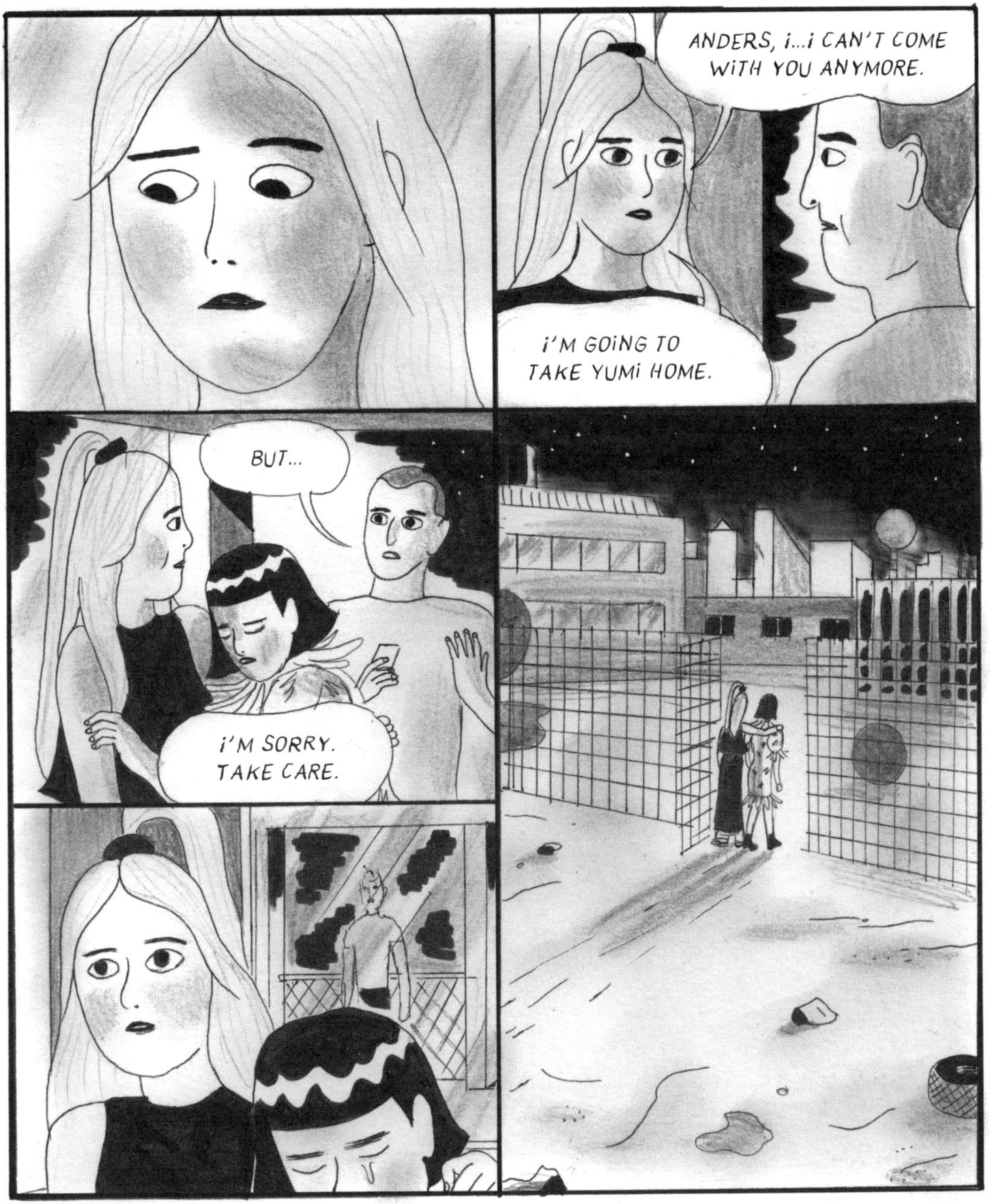
ANDERS, i...i CAN'T COME WITH YOU ANYMORE.
i'M GOING TO TAKE YUMi HOME.
BUT...
i'M SORRY. TAKE CARE.

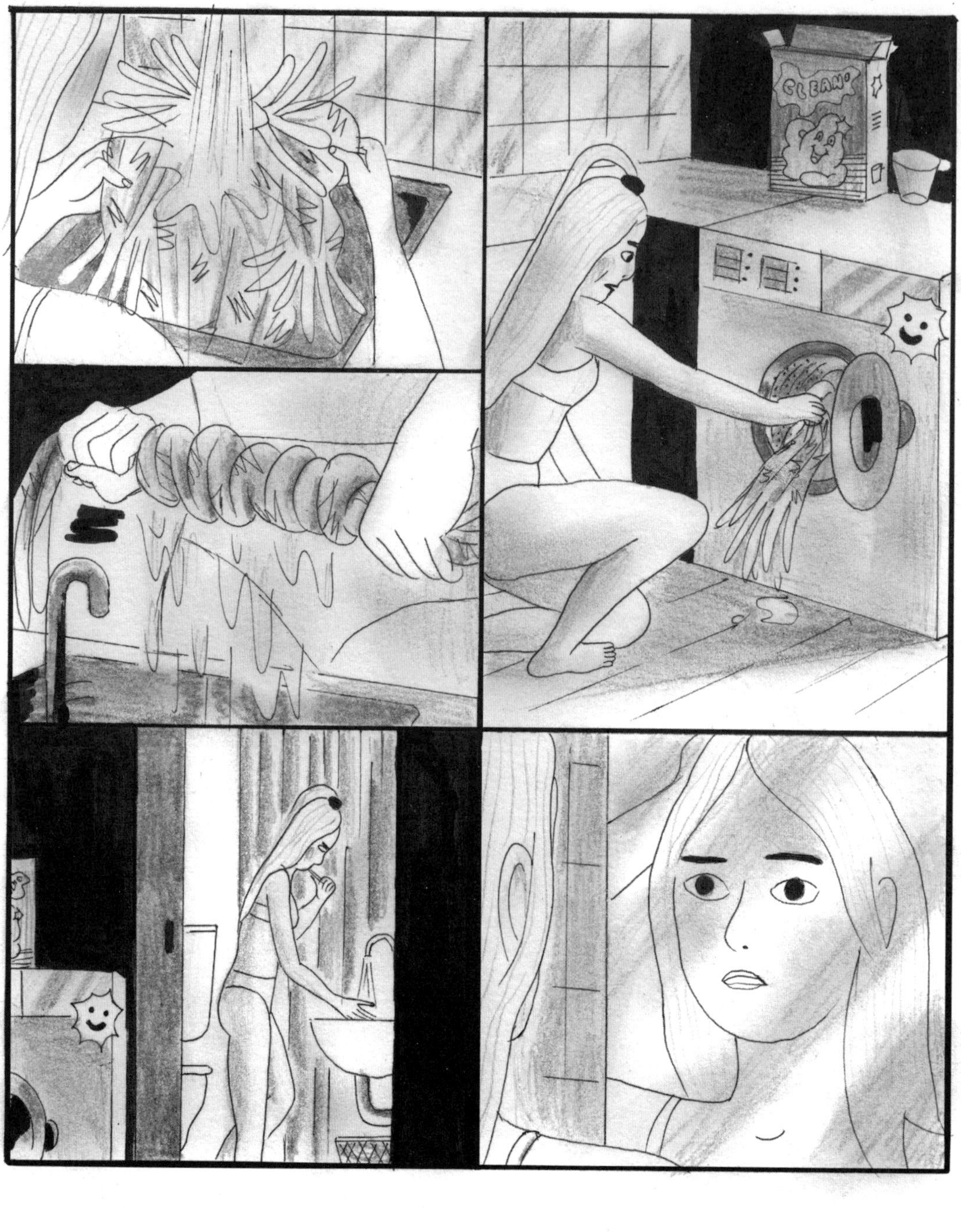
CLEAN

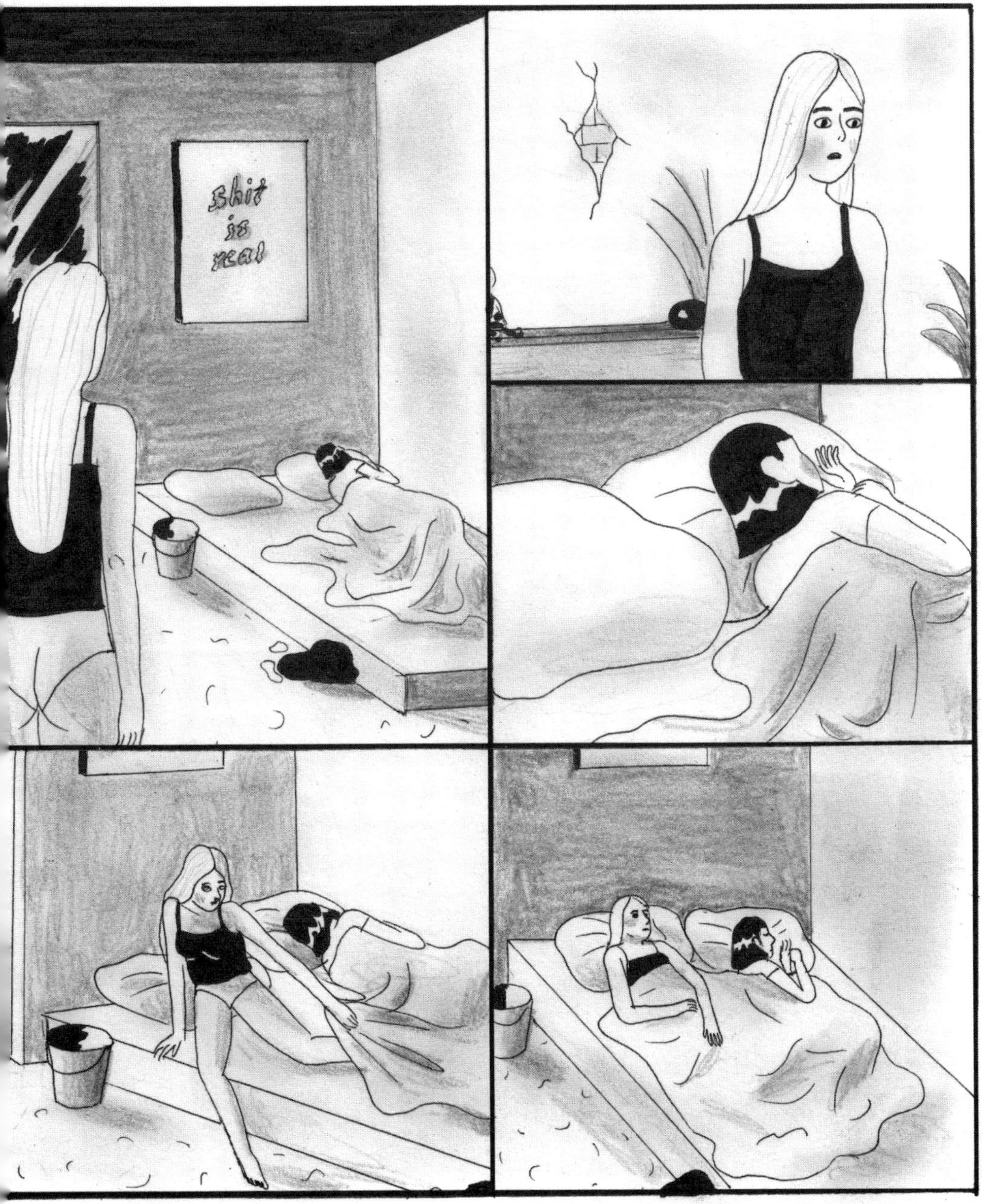
Shit
is
real

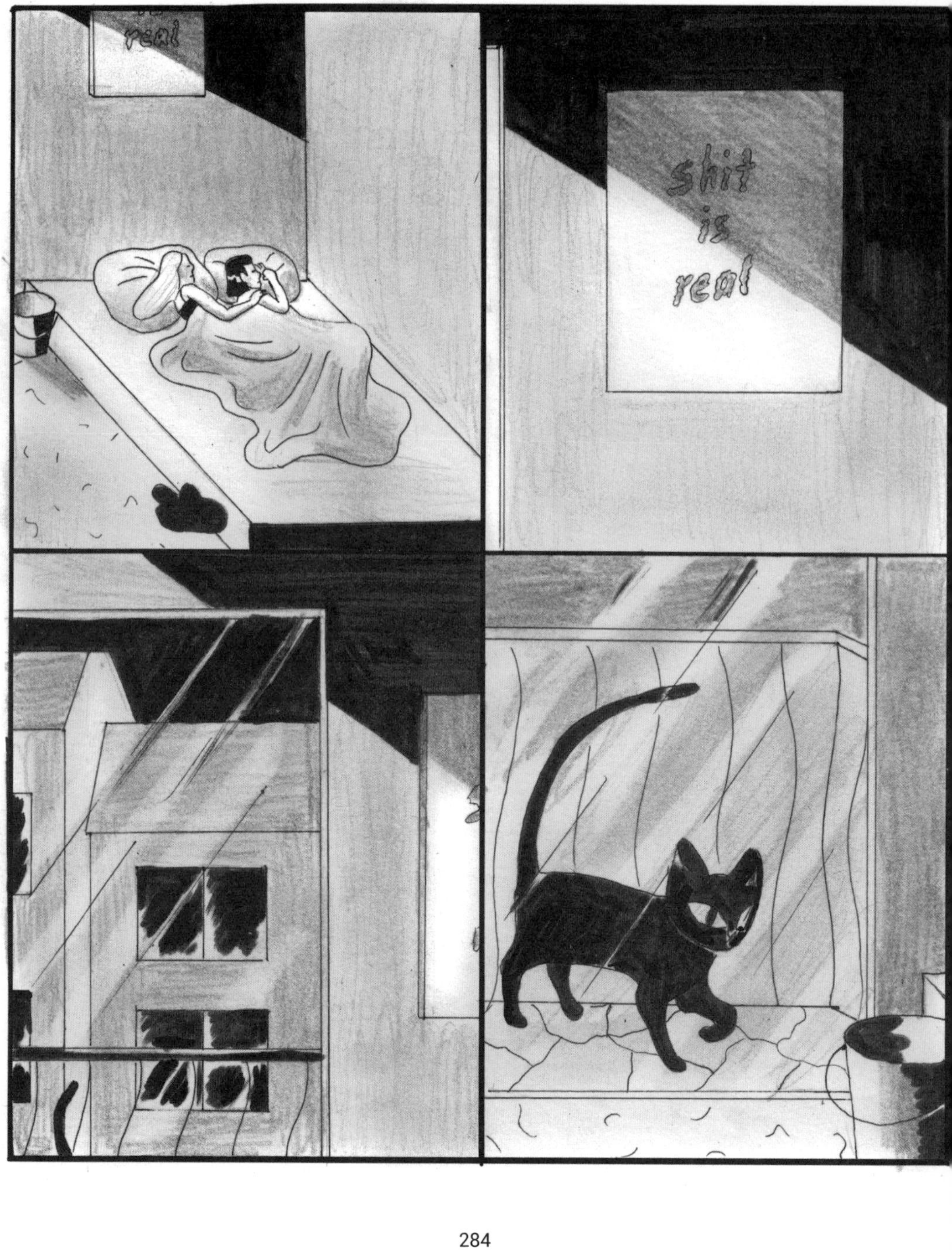
real
shit is real

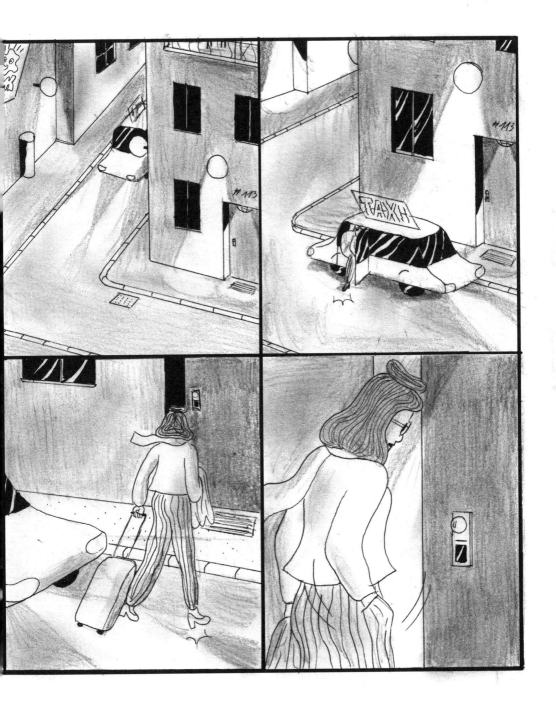

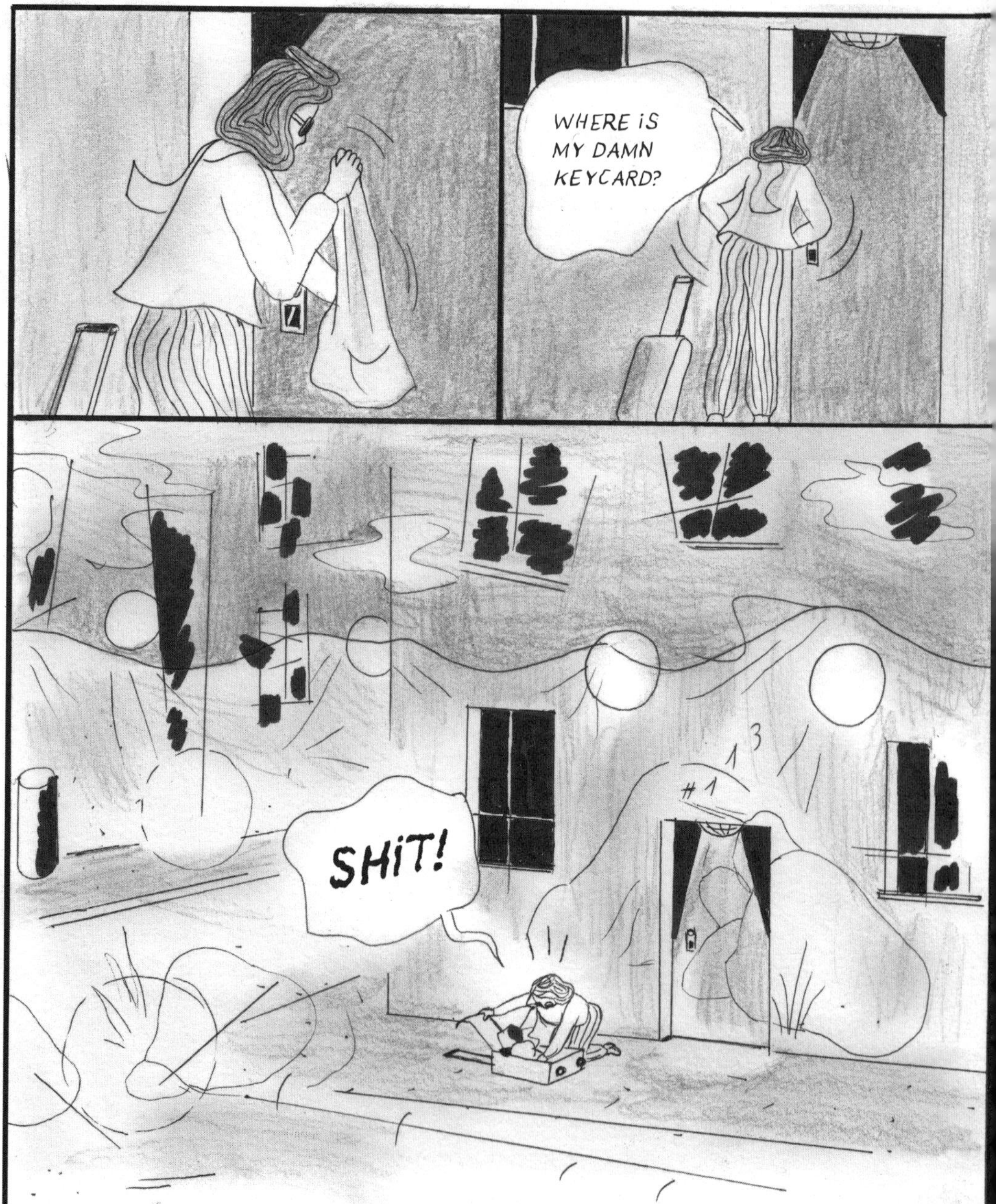
WHERE iS MY DAMN KEYCARD?
#113
SHiT!

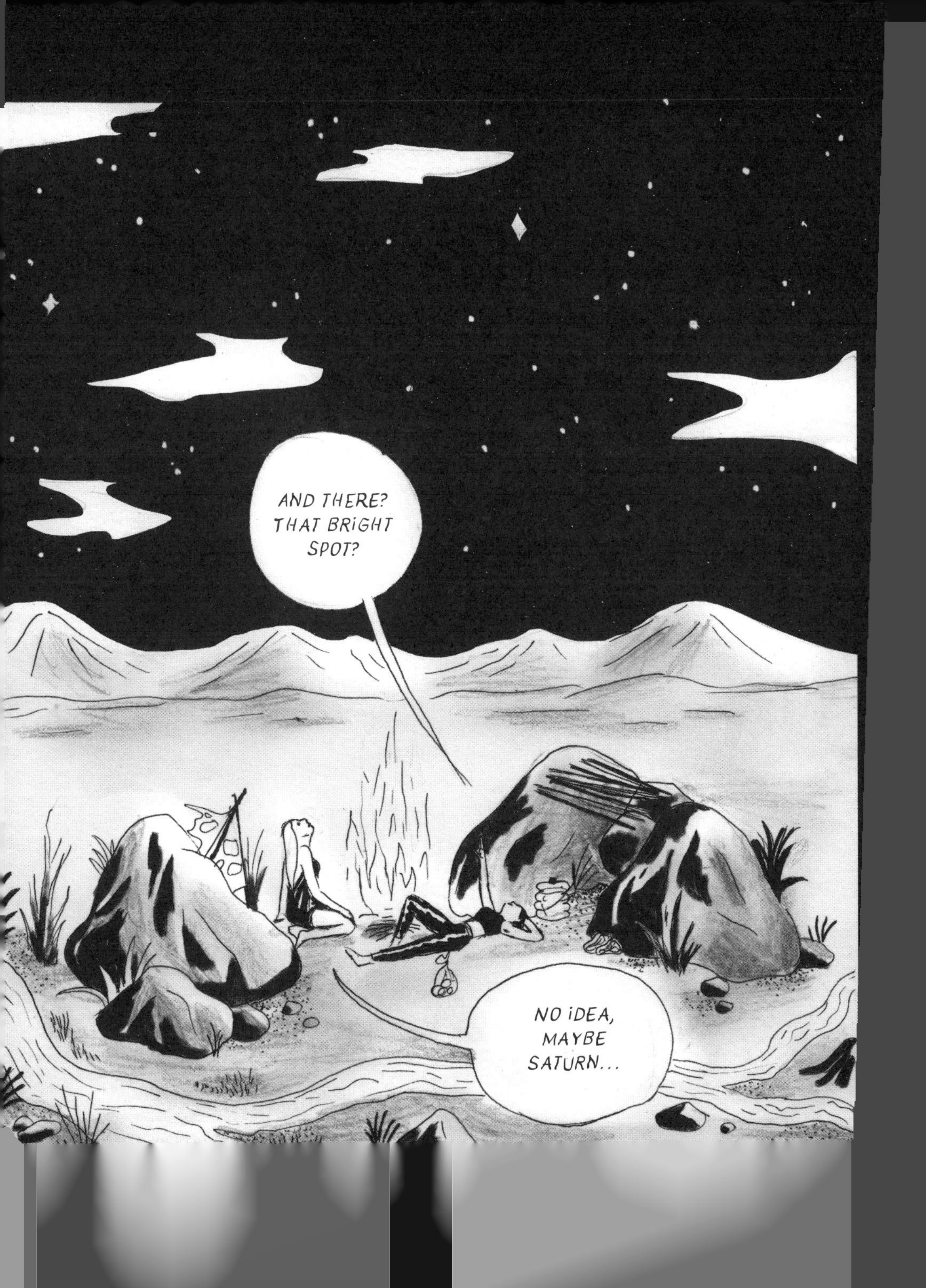
AND THERE? THAT BRIGHT SPOT?
NO IDEA, MAYBE SATURN...

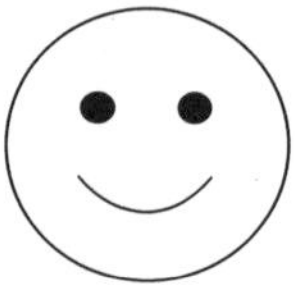

Aisha Franz was born in Fürth, Germany, and was named after an elephant from TV. She studied illustration at the School of Art and Design in Kassel and has worked as a freelance illustrator and cartoonist since graduating. Franz has published three graphic novels in German; her books have been translated into English, Italian, Spanish, and French. Her work has been exhibited in Germany, Belgium, Mexico, and Italy, and she currently lives in Berlin, where she's part of the comics collective The Treasure Fleet.

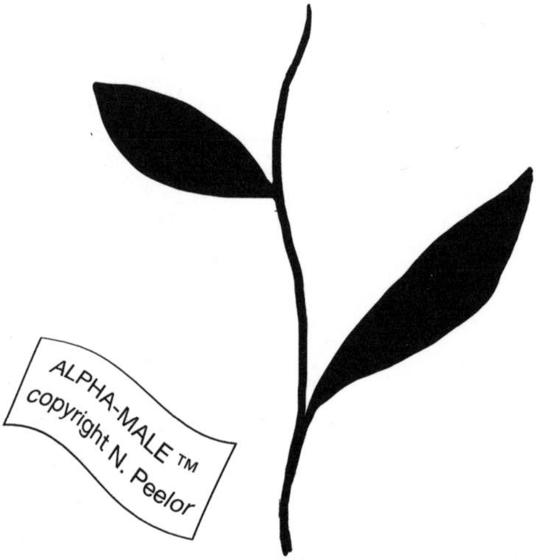
ALPHA-MALE ™
copyright N. Peelor